New Mexico Baptisms

San Felipe de Neri Church

in Albuquerque, NM

1829-1850

Extracted & Transcribed

By

Members of the

New Mexico Genealogical Society

Published by

New Mexico Genealogical Society

Library of Congress Control Number
2018932796

ISBN: 978-1-942626-65-7

Copyright © 2018

New Mexico Genealogical Society
P. O. Box 27559
Albuquerque, NM 87125

And
Archdiocese of Santa Fe
4000 St. Joseph's Place NW
Albuquerque, NM 87120

Table of Contents

Introduction

The year was 1706, the founding of New Mexico's fourth Spanish villa (after Santa Fe, Guadalupe del Paso, and Santa Cruz de la Cañada) to be called la Villa de Alburquerque de San Francisco Xavier del Bosque.

The New Mexico Genealogical Society (NMGS) undertook the extraction of records from the registers in the collection under the direction of Fray Angelico Chavez in 1974 and begun publishing extractions several years ago, beginning with Albuquerque Baptisms (1706-1850).

This first book was published as a surname book. As the rest of the books were published in date order over the years, we wanted to change this book also to reflect date order versus surname order. The methodology used for this book was to extract and validate the records using a format that was easy to understand and yet maintain as much of the integrity of the record as possible. We did not use abbreviated names such as Ant° but spelled it out as Antonio.

Some years have missing months and are not as plentiful as one would think, but we don't know what is missing by month, but we do know the years. When the original book was done they used materials at the Archives of the Archdiocese in Santa Fe. The original books were limp coarse bison-hide, sometimes torn and incomplete. The current extractions were done with the microfilm of these pages. With new technology, we were able to expand the screens and see the records clearer than was done 40+ years ago. Mistakes have been corrected and yet we know there may still be additional corrections within these pages. All researchers should consult the film for further verification.

AASF Film used was Reel #1 and 2. These records can also be found on Family History Library Film #16635 and 16636.

This publication of baptism records will be of great assistance to historians and social anthropologists and those wishing to learn more about their family history. This area known as San Felipe de Neri de Alburquerque was an important center in the time of colonial expansion and settlement during the Spanish period.

Reference: Chavez, Fray Angelico, *Archive of the Archdiocese of Santa Fe*, 1957

Acknowledgements

The New Mexico Genealogical Society is pleased to publish this book of baptisms found in registers from the Mission Church at San Felipe de Neri de Alburquerque, later spelled Albuquerque. One of the purposes of our organization is to publish various New Mexico records for the benefit of those studying history and family genealogy. The extractions are made as near to the original document as possible so that the researcher may make his or her own interpretations of the record. Errors brought to our attention will be corrected in the New Mexico Genealogist.

The Alburquerque records were first done in 1980. In 2017, the first book was retyped, proofed and edited by many volunteers: Henrietta M. Christmas, Angela Lewis, Terri Carlson, Mary Peterson, Daria Landress, Bonita Rasmussen, MaryAnn Cole, Patricia Sanchez Rau, Bernadette Langbein, Gaye Funk, and Nancy Lopez. The publications team decided, due to the volume of the book, to separate into two books – this being Volume II.

We appreciate the use of the records from the Archives of the Archdiocese of Santa Fe and are grateful for their gracious support of NMGS. Photo: New Mexico State Records Center and Archives #13766.

Pueblo de Santa Ana •

Rio Grande

• Bernalillo   • Las Huertas
                      • Placitas

• Sandia Pueblo

Corrales •

Poblazion

• Alameda
• Los Garcias
• Los Ranchos de Albuquerque
• Los Poblanos
• Los Griegos   • Los Gallegos
• Los Candelarias
• Los Duranes

Rio Grande

Albuquerque   • San Antonio

Atrisco •   • Carnué

Upper Pajarito •

Armijo •

Los Arenales •

Pajarito •

Los Padillas •

Isleta Pueblo •

Albuquerque Area Map

Abbreviations

NS – means no surname; yet in the original book they used the surname of the godparent.

s/ - son of

d/ - daughter of

ch/ - children of

am/ - maternal parents

legit - legitimate

ap/ - paternal parents

b. – born

gp/ godparents

Items underlined = typed as shown.

B-6 (Box 6) 1828—1835, AASF, Reel #1
Continued from Book I, *Baptisms – Albuquerque, New Mexico*

GUTIERRES, Maria de los Reyes (parvula)
bap 6 Jan 1829; legit d/ Pedro Antonio Gutierres & Maria Guadalupe Garcia; ap/ Miguel Gutierres & Juana Griego; am/ not stated; gp/ Baltasar Romero & Paula Lucero.

CANDELARIA, Maria de los Reyes
bap 6 Jan 1829; d/ Enrique Candelaria & Ysabel Garcia; ap/ Antonio Candelaria & Maria Manuela Rael; am/ Juan de Jesus Garcia & Rosa Sabedra; gp/ Juan Barela & Maria Josefa Chaves.

Frame 1255
MARTIN, Jose de los Reyes (parvulo)
bap 6 Jan 1829; legit s/ Pablo Martin & Francisca Moya; gp/ Antonio Martin & Teodora Garcia.

SANCHEZ, Maria Marcelina (parvula)
bap 6 Jan 1829; legit d/ Mariano Sanchez & Lorensa Lopes; ap/ Felipe Sanchez & Maria Ynes Garcia; am/ Jose Maria Lopes & Barbara Baca; gp/ Rafael Duran & Catarina Pacheco.

MARTIN, Antonio Jose (parvulo)
bap 8 Jan 1829; legit s/ Jesus de la Crus Martin & Victoria Gutierrez; gp/ Manuel Anaya & Maria Felipa Martin.

Frame 1256, #23
GRIEGO, Maria Teofila de los Dolores (parvula)
bap 9 Jan 1829; legit d/ Rafael Griego & Barbara Apodaca; ap/ Rafael Griego & Ana Maria Lopes; am/ Jose Apodaca & Gertrudis Lucero; gp/ Bentura Apodaca & Dolores Lucero.

NUANES, Antonio de los Reyes (parvulo)
bap 9 Jan 1829; legit s/ Santiago Nuanes & Maria Ynes Garcia; ap/ Geronimo Nuanes & Barbara Maes; am/ Martin Garcia & Ana Maria Apodaca; gp/ Jose Gregorio Garcia & Maria Candelaria Luna.

HERRERA, Maria Antonia (parvula)
bap 11 Jan 1829; legit d/ Jesus Herrera & Catarina Santillan; ap/ Jesus Andres Herrera & Dolores Garcia; am/ Miguel Santillanes & Ana Maria Lobato; gp/ Jesus Maria Sandoval & Maria Teresa Luna.

Frame 1256-1257
LOPES, Jesus Antonio de Jesus (parvulo)
bap 14 Jan 1829; legit s/ Antonio Lopes & Faviana Garcia; ap/ not stated; gp/ Hermenejildo Candelaria & Maria Ramona Candelaria.

GONSALES, Jose de Jesus (parvulo)
bap 15 Jan 1829; legit s/ Jose Gonsales & Francisca Garcia; ap & am/ not stated; gp/ Pablo Garcia & Maria Antonia Martines.

ROMERO, Maria Josefa Ygnacia (parvula)
bap 28 Jan 1829; legit d/ Diego Antonio Romero & Encarnacion Valencia; ap/ Miguel Antonio Romero & Victoria Garcia; am/ Juan Domingo Valencia & Maria Antonia Salasar; gp/ Francisco Ortega & Ygnacia Basan.

Frame 1258, #24
RODARTE, Juan Antonio Fabian (parvulo)
bap 28 Jan 1829; legit s/ Juan Rodarte & Maria Francisca Candelaria; ap & am/ not stated; gp/ Juan
Cristobal Gonzales.

GRIEGO, Maria Petra de los Dolores (parvula)
bap 30 Jan 1829; legit d/ Francisco Griego & Rosa Lopes; ap/ Pedro Griego & Guadalupe Perea; am/
Francisco Perea & Feliciana Barbero; gp/ Venturo Apodaca & Dolores Torres.

NS, Juan Francisco Alfonzo (parvulo)
bap 30 Jan 1829; s/ unknown parents; gp/ Juan Gutierres & Dolores Mora.

SANTILLAÑES, Jose Francisco (parvulo)
bap 1 Feb 1829; legit s/ Miguel Santillañes & Josefa Martin; ap & am/ not stated; gp/ Julian Padilla &
Maria Petra Padilla.

Frame 1258-1259
ROMERO, Jose Anastacio (parvulo)
bap 1 Feb 1829; legit s/ Diego Antonio Romero & Maria Juliana Montaño; ap/ Miguel Antonio Romero
& Juana Garcia; am/ Andres Montaño & Dolores Apodaca; gp/ Jose Dolores Cordova & Ygnacia
Valencia.

NS, Maria de los Dolores (parvula)
bap 2 Feb 1829, 3 days old; d/ unknown parents; gp/ Ambrocio Armijo & Marta Ansures.

NS, Jose Francisco (parvulo)
bap 2 Feb 1829, 7 days old; s/ unknown parents; gp/ Jose Vicente Gurule & Eugenia Gurule.

GARCIA, Jose Blas Candelaria (parvulo)
bap 3 Feb 1829, b. previous day; legit s/ Jose Vicente Garcia & Paula Chaves, ap/ Ysidro Garcia & Maria
Simona Ballejos; am/ Juan Chaves & Maria Barbara Armijo; gp/ Antonio Jose Chaves & Maria Manuela
Esparsa.

Frame 1260, #25
NS, Jose Pablo (parvulo)
bap 4 Feb 1829, b. 15 Jan; s/ unknown parents; gp/ Marcos Sanches Vergara & Nicolasa Sanches
Vergara.

PEÑA, Maria Andrea Felipa (parvula)
bap 5 Feb 1829; legit d/ Lorenso Peña & Juana Maria Chaves; ap/ Mariano Chaves & Soledad Gutierres;
am/ Miguel Antonio Chaves & Juana Lorensa Baca; gp/ Jose Chaves & Barbara Chaves.

ALIRI, Maria Candelaria (parvula)
bap 5 Feb 1829; legit d/ Jose Benito Aliri & Juana Garcia; ap & am/ not stated; gp/ Jose Cordova & Maria
Micaela Cordova.

Frame 1261

BACA, Salbador Antonio (parvulo)
bap 7 Feb 1829; legit s/ Juan Domingo Baca & Maria Dolores Lucero; ap & am/ not stated; gp/ Rafael Lucero & Maria Juana Baca.

GUTIERRES, Maria Gertrudis (parvula)
bap 15 Feb 1829; legit d/ Miguel Loreto Gutierres & Maria Manuela Rael; ap & am/ not stated; gp/ Gabriel Gurule & Maria Gertrudis Rael.

GARCIA, Maria Apolonia (parvula)
bap 15 Feb 1829; legit d/ Jose Manuel Garcia & Maria Dolores Lopes; ap/ Jose Garcia & Maria Coronado; am/ unknown; gp/ Jose Gregorio Apodaca & Maria Manuela Torres.

Frame 1262, #26

LUJAN, Maria Petra (parvula)
bap 15 Feb 1829; legit d/ Pablo Lujan & Juana Anaya; ap/ Juan Antonio Lujan & Candelaria Lucero; am/ Pablo Anaya & Lorensa Pacheco; gp/ Cristoval Pacheco & Maria Petra Maldonado.

SALASAR, Manuel Antonio (parvulo)
bap 16 Feb 1829; legit s/ Ramon Salasar & Rufina Chaves; ap & am/ not stated; gp/ Ysidro Jaramillo & Catarina Mestas.

GARCIA, Francisco Antonio (parvulo)
bap 18 Feb 1829; legit s/ Jose Garcia & Marta Duran; ap/ Dionicio Garcia & Juana Lucero; am/ Teodoro Duran & Maria Lucero; gp/ Francisco Duran & Maria Dolores Duran.

Frame 1263

SANDOVAL, Francisco Romulo (parvulo)
bap 19 Feb 1829; legit s/ Domingo Sandoval & Concepcion Montoya; ap/ Miguel Sandoval & Maria Ygnacia Armenta; am/ Pedro Montoya & Maria Luna; gp/ Francisco Sandoval & Manuela Carillo.

MONTAÑO, Pedro Jose (parvulo)
bap 24 Feb 1829; legit s/ Manuel Montaño & Guadalupe Garcia; ap/ Jose Montaño & Micaela Santillanes; am/ Julian Garcia & Barbara Serna.

GRIEGO, Maria Rafaela (parvula)
bap 24 Feb 1829; legit d/ Luis Griego & Maria Antonia Lopes; ap & am/ not stated; gp/ Jose Mireles & Guadalupe Garcia.

Frame 1264, #27

SANCHES, Maria Antonia (parvula)
bap 1 Mar 1829; natural d/ Maria Sanches; gp/ Anastacio Hernandez & Maria Antonia Esparza.

GRIEGO, Maria del Carmen Serafina (parvula)
bap 1 Mar 1829; legit d/ Geronimo Griego & Balvina Lucero; ap & am/ not stated; gp/ Don Jose Mateo Esparza & Maria del Carmen Esparza.

SANDOVAL, Antonio Lorenzo (parvulo)
bap 2 Mar 1829, 8 days old; legit s/ Juan Sandoval & Maria de la Lus Garcia; ap & am/ not stated; gp/ Lorenso Barela & Maria Antonia Baca.

Frame 1265
GARCIA, Jose Roman (parvulo)
bap 4 Mar 1829; legit s/ Francisco Garcia & Encarnacion Apodaca; ap/ Juan Cristoval Garcia & Rafaela Gonzales; am/ Jose Manuel Apodaca & Lus Garcia; gp/ Antonio Garcia & Margarita Rael.

RUIS, Romualdo (parvulo)
bap 4 Mar 1829, legit s/ Ygnacio Ruis & Ysidora Lopes; ap/ Antonio Ruis & Ysabel Armijo; am/ Diego Lopes & Juliana Chaves; gp/ Francisco Armijo & Barbara Ortis.

MONTOYA, Maria Rosalia (parvula)
bap 4 Mar 1829; legit d/ Juan Cristoval Montoya & Monica Gonsales; ap/ Felipe Montoya & Maria de la Lus Lopes; am/ Juan Gonsales & Maria Antonia Armijo; gp/ Julian Tenorio & Benigna Chaves.

Frame 1266, #28
LUCERO, Maria Rafaela (parvula)
bap 5 Mar 1829; legit d/ Hermenegildo Lucero & Francisca Sanches; ap & am/ not stated; gp/ Antonio Rael & Maria Soledad Miera.

MARTINES, Eucebio de Jesus (parvulo)
bap 5 Mar 1829; legit s/ Juan Martines & Alfonsa Candelaria; ap & am/ not stated; gp/ Jesus Gregorio Griego & Maria Guadalupe Mora.

MARTIN, Barbara Antonia (parvula)
bap 6 Mar 1829; legit d/ Francisco Martin & Encarnacion Garcia; ap/ Pedro Martin & Dolores Abeitia; am/ Juan Pablo Garcia & Barbara Bernal; gp/ Jose Antonio Pineda & Dolores Montoya.

GARVISO, Juan Manuel
bap 8 Mar 1829, at Ysleta; legit s/ Felix Garviso & Viviana Ribera; ap & am/ not stated; gp/ Manuel Benabides.

Frame 1267
SANCHES, Jose Victorino (parvulo)
bap 8 Mar 1829; legit Rafael Sanches & Maria Ysabel Candelaria; ap/ Pedro Sanches & Maria de la Lus Baca; am/ Tomas Candelaria & Juana Chaves; gp/ Juan Jose Sanches & Rita Luna.

APODACA, Maria de los Dolores (parvula)
bap 8 Mar 1829, of Pajarito of Ysleta jurisdiction; legit d/ Gregorio Apodaca & Manuela Torres; ap & am/ not stated; gp/ Rafael Martin & Maria Dolores Sedillo.

VALENCIA, Jose Ramon (parvulo)
bap 13 Mar 1829; legit s/ Julian Valencia & Refugio Rael; ap/ Juan Domingo Valencia & Maria Ygnacia Salasar; am/ Eusebio Rael & Rosa Montoya; gp/ Ygnacio Miera & Quiteria Rael.

Frame 1268, #29
NS, Maria Benigna (parvula)
bap 13 Mar 1829; d/ unknown parents; gp/ Juan Nepomuceno Griego & Maria Josefa Duran.

MONTOYA, Ambrocio de Jesus (parvulo)
bap 14 Mar 1829, b. same day; legit s/ Francisco Montoya & Jesusa Armijo; ap/ Pablo Montoya & Maria Reyes Garcia; am/ Lucas Armijo & Barbara Ortiz; gp/ Ambrocio Armijo & Maria Antonia Ortis.

CHAVEZ, Juana Maria (parvula)
bap 17 Mar 1829; legit d/ Blas Chavez & Gertrudis Sandoval; ap/ Juan Miguel Chaves & Guadalupe Gutierrez; am/ Lorenso Sandoval & Juana Senteno; gp/ Domingo Sanches & Quiteria Gonsales.

Frame 1269
GURULE, Jose Vicente (parvulo)
bap 19 Mar 1829, b. 15 Mar; legit s/ Jose Pablo Gurule & Juana Mora; ap/ Juan Cristoval Gurule & Josefa Valencia; am/ Pablo Mora & Maria Gurule; gp/ Jose Montaño & Juliana Montaño.

MARTIN, Maria Gertrudis (parvula)
bap 19 Mar 1829, b. same day; legit d/ Juan Martin & Antonia Lucero; ap/ Marcos Martin & Francisca Jaramillo; am/ Juan Lucero & Francisca Lucero; gp/ Pedro Carabajal & Maria Gertrudis Gonsales.

JARAMILLO, Antonia Abad (parvulo)
bap 19 Mar 1829, b. 15 Mar; legit d/ Juan Jose Jaramillo & Trinidad Otero; ap & am/ not stated; gp/ Mateo Archuleta & Maria Reyes Sedillo.

Frame 1270, #30
SANCHES, Jesus Maria (parvulo)
bap 21 Mar 1829; legit s/ Juan Sanches & Maria Manuela Lobato; ap & am/ not stated; gp/ Jesus Maria Sedillo & Maria Marta Sedillo.

GARCIA, Maria Josefa (parvula)
bap 21 Mar 1829; legit d/ Antonio Garcia & Juana Saes; ap/ Francisco Garcia & Manuela Gonzales; am/ Juan Saes & Maria Gertrudis Torres; gp/ Felipe Montoya & Maria de la Lus Lopez,

MONTOYA, Juana (parvula)
bap 22 Mar 1829, of los Padillas, jurisdiction of Ysleta; legit d/ Mariano Montoya & Maria Ysabel Chavez; ap/ Juan Cristoval (Montoya) & Maria Luisa Padilla; am/ Juan Jose Chaves & Maria Josefa Trujillo; gp/ Jose Antonio Montoya & Maria Josefa Montoya.

Frame 1271
TELLES, Encarnacion de los Dolores (parvula)
bap 29 Mar 1829; b. 25 Mar; legit d/ Jose Santos Telles & Barbara Sedillo, ap/ Julio Telles & Cacilda Barela; am/ Pablo Sedillo & Magdalena Candelaria; gp/ Salvador Sedillo & Juana Maria Sanches.

GRIEGO, Maria Encarnacion (parvula)
bap 29 Mar 1829, b. 25 Mar; legit d/ Pedro Griego & Ana Maria Salasar; ap/ Jose Maria Griego & Candelaria Armijo; am/ Toribio Salazar & Maria Dolores Gutierres; gp/ Jose Manuel Montaño & Maria Guadalupe Garcia.

GONSALES, Juana (parvula)
bap 29 Mar 1829; legit d/ Hilario Gonsales & Maria Rita Rael; ap/ Jose Antonio Gonsales & Maria Chaves; am/ Antonio Rael & Francisca Padilla; gp/ Sabino Gonsales & Maria de Jesus Luna.

Frame 1272, #31
HERRERA, Jose Marcos (parvulo)
bap 30 Mar 1829, from Ysleta jurisdiction; legit s/ Jose Roque Herrera & Rafaela Baca; ap & am/ not stated; gp/ Ygnacio Mariño & Maria Concepcion Sanches.

GUTIERRES, Ana Maria (parvula)
bap 31 Mar 1829; legit d/ Ysidor Gutierres & Dolores Martin; ap & am/ not stated; gp/ Marcos Ruis & Ana Maria Ruis.

SALASAR, Juana Maria (parvula)
bap 31 Mar 1829; legit d/ Juan Nasareno Salasar & Maria Rita Tafoya; ap & am/ not stated; Vicente Montoya & Lugarda Montoya.

NS, Maria Josefa (parvula)
bap 31 Mar, b. 22 Mar; d/ unknown parents; gp/ Jose Lucero & Marcelina Valencia.

Frame 1273
LOPES, Jose Tomas (parvulo)
bap 2 Apr 1829; legit s/ Antonio Lopes & Gertrudis Trujillo; ap/ Jose Lopes & Gertrudis Lopes; am/ Juan Trujillo & Manuela Apodaca; gp/ Encarnacion Sandoval & Francisca Lopes.

NS, Juan Nepomuceno (parvulo)
bap 2 Apr 1829, b. 28 Mar; s/ unknown parents; gp/ Salbador Antonio Salasar & Maria Luisa Trujillo.

TORRES, Maria de Altagracia (parvula)
bap 2 Apr 1829, b. 28 Mar; legit d/ Salbador Torres & Maria Josefa Salazar; ap/ Santiago Torres & Josefa Herrera; am/ Bernardo Salazar & Maria Tapia; gp/ Juan Luis Garcia.

LUCERO, Juan Cristoval (parvulo)
bap 4 Apr 1829, b. 2 Apr; legit s/ Pablo Lucero & Maria Antonia Luna; ap & am/ not stated; gp/ Cristobal Montoya & Maria de la Lus Lopes.

Frame 1274, #32
CHAVES, Jose Vicente (parvulo)
bap 5 Apr 1829, b. 2 Apr; s/ Jose Chaves & Francisca Montoya; ap/ Juan Chaves & Barbara Armijo; am/ Pedro Montoya & Maria Luna; gp/ Juan Domingo Sandoval & Concepcion Montoya.

GRIEGO, Jose Vicente (parvulo)
bap 5 Apr 1829, b. 2 Apr; legit s/ Juan Domingo Griego & Juana Romero; ap & am/ not stated; gp/ Jose Manuel Nuanes & Maria Paula Candelaria.

ARANDA, Jose Antonio (parvulo)
bap 9 Apr 1829; legit s/ Juan Cristoval Aranda & Soledad Armijo; ap/ Antonio Aranda & Antonia Garcia; am/ Manuel Santiago Armijo & Petra Perea; gp/ Manuel Jaramillo & Rosalia Jaramillo.

NS, Maria Cleofas (parvula)
bap 9 Apr 1829; d/ unknown parents; gp/ Jose Maria Chaves & Antonia Trebol.

Frame 1275
SANCHES, Jose Antonio (parvulo)
bap 10 Apr 1829, 5 days old; legit s/ Antonio Sanches & Magdalena Griego; ap & am/ not stated; gp/ Domingo Valencia & Paula Martinez.

Baptisms – Albuquerque, New Mexico
1829–1850

CANDELARIA, Jose Dolores (parvulo)
bap 10 Apr 1829, 3 days old; legit s/ Julian Candelaria & Francisca Nuanes; ap & am/ not stated; gp/ Juan Gallego & Francisca Montaño.

Frames 1275-1276, #33
GALLEGO, Jose Onofre de los Dolores
bap 12 Apr 1829, b. 10 Apr; legit s/ Cristoval Gallego & Carmen Gutierres; ap & am/ not stated; gp/ Francisco Ortega & Ygnacia Basan.

GURULE, Maria Apolonia
bap 12 Apr 1829, b. 10 Apr; legit d/ Domingo Gurule & Ysidora Nuanes; ap & am/ not stated; gp/ Juan Cristobal Garcia & Ana Maria Apodaca.

CHAVES, Juana Maria (parvula)
bap 19 Apr 1829, b. previous day; legit d/ Pedro Chaves & Margarita Montoya; ap/ Santiago Chaves & Maria Luisa Jaramillo; am/ Felipe Montoya & Maria de la Lus Lopes; gp/ Juan Cristobal Montoya & Monica Gonzales.

Frames 1276-1277
GONSALES, Maria Guadalupe Aniceta (parvula)
bap 19 Apr 1829, b. 17 Apr; legit d/ Lorenso Gonsales & Maria Teodora Salazar; ap & am/ not stated; gp/ Miguel Antonio Gutierres & Maria Micaela Santillanes.

ANAYA, Francisco Antonio (parvulo)
bap 20 Apr 1829, b. 16 Apr; s/ Ramon Anaya & Ana Maria Lopes; ap/ Manuel Anaya & Maria Antonia Apodaca; am/ Miguel Lopes & Lucia Duran; gp/ Francisco Sandoval & Paula Sandoval.

NS, Jose Santos (parvulo)
bap 21 Apr 1829, b. 16 Apr, in jurisdiction of Ysleta; s/ unknown parents; gp/ Estevan Padilla & Maria Gertrudes Otero.

Frames 1277-1278, #34
GARCIA, Maria Toribia
bap 23 Apr 1829; 17 Apr; legit d/ Andres Garcia & Juana Torres; ap/ Antonio Garcia & Maria de la Lus Romero; am/ Jose Torres & Trinidad Cordova; gp/ Jose Sanches & Gregoria Rael.

YTURRIETA, Jose Sotero (parvulo of los Padillas)
bap 25 Apr 1829, in the jurisdiction of Ysleta, b. 22 Apr; legit s/ Pedro Yturrieta & Juana Chaves; ap/ Manuel Yturrieta & Barbara Ballejos; am/ Jose Antonio Chaves & Teodora Duran; gp/ Juan Montoya & Manuela Padilla.

LUCERO, Jose Miguel (parvulo)
bap 8 May 1829, b. previous day; legit s/ Francisco Lucero & Manuela Aragon; ap/ Juan de Jesus Lucero & Justa Pino; am/ Tadeo Aragon & Maria Luisa Valencia; gp/ Jose Miguel Lucero & Andrea Pacheco.

Frame 1279
MONTOYA, Maria Monica de los Dolores (parvula)
bap 8 May 1829, b. previous day; legit d/ Jose Maria Montoya & Clara Armijo; ap/ Pablo Montoya & Maria Reyes Gutierres; am/ Lucas Armijo & Barbara Ortis; gp/ Pedro Armijo & Monica Duran.

NS, Felipe (parvulo)
bap 8 May 1829, 5 days old; s/ unknown parents; gp/ Vicente Sanches Vergara & Maria Josefa Mestas.

CHAVES, Juan Pedro (parvulo)
bap 9 May 1829, 11 days old, from the jurisdiction of Ysleta; legit s/ Juan Antonio Chaves & Gertrudis Torres; ap & am/ not stated; gp/ Mariano Montoya & Ysabel Chaves.

Frame 1280, #35
APODACA, Dolores de la Crus (parvula)
bap 10 May 1829, b. 3 May; legit d/ Francisco Apodaca & Tomasa Barela; ap/ Jose Apodaca & Gertrudis Lucero; am/ Juan Barela & Josefa Chaves; gp/ Manuel Vigil & Catarina Ortis.

PEREA, Miguel Antonio (parvulo)
bap 10 May 1829, b. 29 Apr; legit s/ Manuel Perea & Gregoria Duran; ap & am/ not stated; gp/ Luciano Santillanes & Gertrudis Duran.

MARTINEZ, Juan Nepomoceno de la Cruz (parvulo)
bap 13 May 1829; legit s/ Jose Martinez & Estefana Jaramillo; ap & am/ not stated; gp/ Jose Antonio Aragon & Ana Maria Aragon.

Frame 1281
CHAVES, Maria Catarina (parvula)
bap 18 May 1829; legit d/ Antonio Chaves & Ynes Gonzales; ap & am/ not stated; gp/ Diego Martin & Maria Manuela Esparsa.

SAVEDRA, Manuel Antonio (parvulo)
bap 13 May 1829, b. previous day; legit s/ Jose Savedra & Paula Montoya; ap/ Francisco Savedra & Maria de la Luz Chaves; am/ Felipe Montoya & Maria Juana Garcia; gp/ Luis Garcia & Gracia Montolla.

NS, Juana Maria (parvula)
bap 22 May 1829, b. 14 May; d/ unknown parents; gp/ Ynes Lopes.

NS, Jose Pablo (parvulo)
bap 22 May 1829, about 15 days old, of Sebolleta; s/ unknown parents; gp/ Lorenso Ortis & Tomasa Garcia.

Frame 1282, #36
CANDELARIA, Maria Antonia (parvula)
bap 22 May 1829, 8 days old; legit d/ Juan Pablo Candelaria & Guadalupe Herrera; ap/ not stated; am/ Vicente Herrera & Maria Antonia Montaño; gp/ Salbador Sanches & Maria Ollalla Tafoya.

GONSALES, Juana Maria de los Dolores (parvula)
bap 24 May 1829, b. 18 May; legit d/ Francisco Gonsales & Maria Antonia Garviso; ap/ Felipe Gonsales & Maria de la Lus Gurule; am/ Francisco Garviso & Maria de la Luz Samora; gp/ Manuel Antonio Gonsales & Maria Manuela Gonsales.

CORDOVA, Jose Maria (parvulo)
bap 24 May 1829, b. 26 of same; legit s/ Bautista Cordova & Maria Manuela Serna; ap/ Nicolas Cordova & Maria Ignacia Duran; am/ Juan Serna & Barbara Gallego; gp/ Juan Jose Sanches & Rita Luna.

Frame 1283
NS, Jose Manuel (parvulo)
bap 24 May 1829, b. 18 May; s/ unknown parents; gp/ Salvador Sedillo & Juana Maria Sanches.

ROMERO, Maria Ysidora (parvula)
bap 27 May 1829, b. 15 May; d/ Don Luis Romero & Maria Gertrudis Pino; ap/ Andres Romero & Manuela Gutierres; am/ Felis Pino & Balbanera Rael; gp/ Don Fernando Aragon & Doña Encarnacion Baldes.

NS, Maria Josefa Asencion (parvula)
bap 28 May 1829, of the Pueblo Santa Ana; d/ Juana Maria NS; ap & am/ not stated; gp/ Francisco Ortega & Ygnacia Basan.

Frame 1284, #37
GARCIA, Maria Marcelina (parvula)
bap 6 Jun 1829, b. 1 Jun; legit d/ Jose Antonio Garcia & Dolores Mora; ap/ Juan Garcia & Juliana Montaño; am/ Ysidro Mora & Juana Marques; gp/ Juan Gutierres & Juana Marques.

GRIEGO, Jose Pablo de Jesus (parvulo)
bap 9 Jun 1829, b. 7 Jun; legit s/ Jose Miguel Griego & Dolores Garcia; ap/ Antonio Griego & Rosalia Montaño; am/ Santiago Garcia & Matiana Perea; gp/ Marcos Ruis & Dolores Torres.

SAMORA, Maria Antonia Bernardina (parvula)
bap 13 Jun 1829, b. 9 Jun; legit d/ Jose Samora & Rafaela Martin; ap & am/ not stated; gp/ Juan de Jesus Carabajal & Maria Luisa Archuleta.

Frame 1285
ESPINOSA, Cristoval (parvulo)
bap 14 Jun 1829, b. 10 Jun; legit s/ Pomuceno Espinosa & Juana Catarina Ansures; ap & am/ not stated; gp/ Casimiro Duran & Petra Vara Sedillo.

CANDELARIA, Antonio Jose (parvulo)
bap 16 Jun 1829, b. 13 Jun; legit s/ Jose Candelaria & Francisca Gonsales; ap/ Florencio Candelaria & Maria Vicenta Duran; am/ Jose Antonio Gonsales & Maria Barbara Candelaria; gp/ Pablo Cisneros & Mariana Cisneros.

MONTAÑO, Antonio Jose (parvulo)
bap 18 Jun 1829, b. 13 Jun; legit s/ Salbador Montaño & Manuela Ortis; ap/ Joaquin Montaño & Barbara Olguin; am/ Miguel Ortis & Rosalia Garcia; gp/ Juan Domingo Valencia & Paula Martines.

Frame 1286, #38
SANCHES, Maria de los Dolores Paulina (parvula)
bap 25 Jun 1829, b. 22 Jun; legit d/ Domingo Sanches & Quiteria Gonsales; ap/ Jose Sanches & Gregoria Rael; am/ Juan Gonsales & Barbara Castillo; gp/ Manuel Sanches & Petra Sanches.

CANDELARIA, Maria Juana (parvula)
bap 28 Jun 1829, b. 24 Jun; legit d/ Ramon Candelaria & Manuela Martines; ap/ Francisco Candelaria & Lus Armijo; am/ Baltasar Martin & Maria Antonia Griego; gp/ Juan Domingo Valencia & Paula Martin.

Frame 1287
ROMERO, Jose Estanislao (parvulo)
bap 29 Jun 1829, b. 27 Jun; legit s/ Baltasar Romero & Paula Lucero; ap/ Miguel Antonio Romero &
Juana Garcia; am/ Diego Lucero & Maria Juliana Gurule; gp/ Rafael Apodaca & Juana Maria Romero.

NS, Juana de los Dolores
bap 12 Jul 1829; d/ unknown parents; gp/ Rafael Armijo & Maria Antonia Mestas.

SERNA, Maria Gertrudis Nabor (parvula)
bap 12 Jul 1829; legit d/ Jose Patricio Serna & Jacinta Nepomucena Anaya; ap & am/ not stated; gp/
Manuel Armijo & Maria Gertrudis Mestas.

Frame 1288, #39
DURAN, Jose Marcelino Nepomuceno (parvulo)
bap 12 Jul 1829; legit s/ Juan Rafael Duran & Josefa Apodaca; ap/ Teodora Duran & Ana Maria Lucero;
am/ Jose Apodaca & Gertrudis Lucero; gp/ Bentura Apodaca & Dolores Torres.

SABEDRA, Jose Nabor (parvulo)
bap 12 Jul 1829; legit s/ Pablo Sabedra & Gertrudis Apodaca; ap/ Jose Sabedra & Maria de la Lus
Sedillo; am/ Nicolas Apodaca & Lus Garcia; gp/ Cristoval Savedra.

GONSALES, Maria Ysabel (parvula)
bap 12 Jul 1829, legit d/ Juan Crisostomo Gonsales & Victoria Garcia; ap & am/ not stated; gp/ Manuel
Candelaria & Maria Decideria Candelaria.

Frame 1289
BARELA, Ana Maria Magdalena (parvula)
bap 26 Jul 1829; legit d/ Santiago Barela & Juana Aranda; ap & am/ not stated; gp/ Juan Cristoval Armijo
& Maria Manuela Armijo.

SABEDRA, Ana Maria (parvula)
bap 26 Jul 1829; legit d/ Juan Sabedra & Maria Dolores Baca; ap & am/ not stated; gp/ Jesus Francisco
Sabedra & Maria Paula Montoya.

GONSALES, Juana Lorensa (parvula)
bap 13 Aug 1829, b. 10 Aug; legit d/ Juan Gonsales & Ana Maria Sandoval; ap/ Jose Gonsales &
Gertrudis Rael; am/ Lorenso Sandoval & Juana Senteno; gp/ Salvador Sanches & Maria Olaya Tafolla.

Frame 1290, #40
SANDOVAL, Pedro Atancio
bap 18 Aug 1829; s/ Deonicio Sandoval & Juana Martina; ap/ Lorensio Sandoval & Juana Lente; am/
Pedro Martin & Dolores Abeyta; gp/ Esteban Candelaria & Maria de Jesus Luna.

ANALLA, Jose Anastacio (parvulo)
bap 19 Aug 1829, b. 17 Aug; s/ Jose Miguel Analla & Maria Antonia Garcia; ap/ Felipe Analla & Dolores
Torres; am/ Juan Rafael Garcia & Manuela Muñis; gp/ Juan Ysidoro Candelaria & Maria Gertrudis
Jaramillo.

Frames 1290-1291
NS, Maria Francisca (parvula)
bap 26 Aug 1829, b. 16 Aug; d/ unknown parents; gp/ Salvador Romero & Maria Antonia Romero.

SANCHES, Maria Francisca (parvula)
bap 26 Aug 1829, b. 21 Aug; d/ Lorenso Sanches & Isabel Armijo; ap & am/ not stated; gp/ Diego Baca & Maria Francisca Samora.

Note: Priest's visit 28 Aug 1829.

Frame 1292, #41
NS, Maria Rosalia
bap 29 Aug 1829, about 5 years old; Navajo Indian, d/ unknown parents; gp/ Maria Josefa Griego.

NS, Maria Dolores
bap 30 Aug 1829, 8 days old; d/ unknown parents; gp/ Marcelina Marques & Juan Torres.

MONTOYA, Juan Jose (parvulo)
bap 1 Sep 1829, b. 29 Aug; s/ Juan Montoya & Leocadia Chaves; ap/ Pedro Montoya & Ana Maria Luna; am/ Juan Chaves & Barbara Armijo; gp/ Juan Antonio Rael & Soledad Miera.

Frame 1293
RAEL, Juan Esteban
bap 2 Sep 1829, 3 days old; legit s/ Antonio Rael & Francisca Padilla; ap/ Julian Rael & Maria Sanches; am/ Francisco Padilla & Bernarda Garcia; gp/ Ygnacio Candelaria & Maria Lucia Garcia.

CANDELARIA, Maria Clara (parvula)
bap 10 Sep 1829, b. 6 Sep; legit d/ Victorio Candelaria & Ana Maria Chaves; ap/ Francisco Candelaria & Maria de la Lus Armijo; am/ Geronimo Chaves & Ysidra Gonzales; gp/ Francisco Paulin Chaves & Serafina Chaves.

GARCIA, Jose de Jesus (parvulo)
bap 11 Sep 1829, b. 9 Sep; s/ Juan Garcia & Maria Antonia Martin; ap/ Juan Luis Garcia & Maria Gertrudis Griego; am/ Francisco Martin & Ventura Mora; gp/ Diego Antonio Garcia & Maria Ramona Candelaria.

Frame 1294, #42
JARAMILLO, Maria de Jesus (parvula)
bap 12 Sep 1829, b. 10 Sep; d/ Roman Jaramillo & Gertrudis Martin; ap/ Segundo Jaramillo & Juliana Chaves; am/ Luis Martino & Barbara Sanches; gp/ Antonio Martin & Barbara Sanches.

MARTIN, Jose Santos (parvulo)
bap 27 Sep 1829, 16 days old; s/ Antonio Jose Martin & Maria Luciana Lucero; ap/ Vicente Martin & Maria Ysabel Maldonado; am/ Juan de Jesus Lucero & Justa Pino; gp/ Antonio Jose Sanches & Rosalia Martin.

SANTILLANES, Miguel Antonio (parvulo)
bap 29 Sep 1829, b. 26 Sep; legit s/ Antonio Santillanes & Geralda Garcia; ap/ Juan Jose Santillanes & Juliana Gonsales; am/ Cristobal Garcia & Rafaela Duran; gp/ Juan Pablo Martines & Maria Antonia Griego.

Frame 1295
NS, Juana Maria (parvula)
bap 29 Sep 1829, b. 24 Sep 1829; d/ unknown parents; gp/ Antonio Jose Montaño & Maria Micaela Santillanes.

NS, Maria de los Angeles (parvula)
bap 5 Oct 1829, b. 2 Oct; d/ unknown parents; gp/ Dolores Sandoval & Maria Josefa Baca.

NS, Maria Brigida (parvula)
bap 7 Oct 1829, b. same day; d/ unknown parents; gp/ Juan Apodaca & Maria Ysabel Sanches.

Frame 1296, #43
GARCIA, Manuel Antonio (parvulo)
bap 7 Oct 1829, b. same day; legit s/ Guadalupe Garcia & Dolores Candelaria; ap & am/ not stated; gp/ Juan Lucero & Maria Manuela Sabedra.

ARAGON, Maria Teresa de Jesus (parvula)
bap 24 Oct 1829; legit d/ Juan Andres Aragon; ap & am/ not stated; gp/ Juan Domingo Gonsales & Maria Nasarena Archuleta.

SERNA, Lucas (parvulo)
bap 26 Oct 1829; s/ Cacildo Serna & Silberia Archuleta; ap & am/ not stated; gp/ Andres Ortega.

Frame 1297
MARTIN, Maria de los Angeles (parvula)
bap 26 Oct 1829; legit d/ Jose Martin & Rosalia Lucero; ap & am/ not stated; gp/ Francisco Montaño & Marcelina Montaño.

GARCIA, Ana Maria (parvula)
bap 26 Oct 1829; legit d/ Juan Garcia & Juana Montaño; ap & am/ not stated; gp/ Andres Noanes & Ana Maria Noanes.

BACA, Maria Teresa de Jesus (parvula)
bap 1 Nov 1829, b. 16 Oct; legit d/ Jose Baca & Maria Antonia Garcia; ap/ Domingo Baca & Ana Maria Ortis; am/ Salvador Garcia & Toribia Chaves; gp/ Geronimo Jaramillo & Gertrudis Lucero.

Frame 1298, #44
MARTINES, Jose Maria de los Santos (parvulo)
bap 1 Nov 1829, b. 14 Oct; legit s/ Jose Maria Martines & Barbara Garcia; ap & am/ not stated; gp/ Jose Cleto Garcia & Maria Ynes Gurule.

ARAGON, Maria Barbara de los Dolores (parvula)
bap 4 Nov 1829, b. 31 Oct; legit d/ Jose Miguel Aragon & Maria Manuela Esparza; ap/ Jose Manuel Aragon & Maria Barbara Chaves; am/ Teodoro Esparsa & Maria Josefa Angulo; gp/ Ramon Aragon & Maria Encarnacion Baldes.

Frame 1299
AVILA, Juan de Jesus (parvulo)
bap 27 Nov 1829, b. 24 Nov 1829; s/ Miguel Avila & Maria Lugarda Montoya; ap & am/ not stated; gp/ Ramon Chaves & Dolores Sanches.

MONTOYA, Manuel Antonio (parvulo)
bap 27 Nov 1829, b. 22 Nov; legit s/ Jose Montoya & Dolores Garcia; ap/ Jose Alexandro Montoya & Barbara Chacon; am/ Pedro Garcia & Ana Maria Analla; gp/ Francisco Sandoval & Paula Sandoval.

Frame 1300, #45
NS, Jose Basilio
bap 27 Nov 1829, b. 20 Nov; s/ unknown parents; gp/ Juan Antonio Griego & Candelaria Luna.

BARELA, Manuel Gregorio (parvulo)
bap 28 Nov 1829, b. 25 Nov; legit s/ Antonio Barela & Catalina Ortis; ap/ Juan Barela & Josefa Chaves; am/ Lorenso Ortis & Rafaela Ruis; gp/ Gregorio Ortis & Maria Clara Sarracino.

Frame 1301
RAEL, Sabino Antonio (parvulo)
bap 29 Nov 1829, b. 27 Nov 1829; natural s/ Estefana Rael; gp/ Sabino Gonzales & Maria de Jesus Luna.

NS, Juana Andrea (parvula)
bap 29 Nov 1829, b. 25 Nov 1829; d/ unknown parents; gp/ Jose Chaves & Maria Antonia Candelaria.

Note: 2 Dec 1829, delivered and received Albuquerque. Jose Francisco Leyva.

Frame 1302, #46
NS, Jose Antonio (parvulo)
bap 4 Dec 1829, b. 2 Dec 1829; s/ unknown parents; gp/ Jose Onofre Duran & Maria Dolores Duran.

PEREA, Jose Maria (parvulo)
bap 4 Dec 1829, b. 8 Nov 1829; s/ Jose Miguel Perea & Maria Manuela Sanches; ap/ Jose Perea & Maria Antonia Candelaria; am/ not stated; gp/ Jose Montoya & Maria Dolores Garcia.

Frames 1302-1303
MONTAÑO, Juana Andrea (parvula)
bap 6 Dec 1829, b. 1 Dec; d/ Joaquin Montaño & Maria Duran; ap/ Joaquin Montaño & Maria Barbara Olguin; am/ Manuel Duran & Matilda NS; gp/ Bernardo Valencia & Paula Martin.

CANDELARIA, Maria Rosa (parvula)
bap 6 Dec 1829, b. 1 Dec 1829; d/ Antonio Candelaria & Maria Antonia Garcia; ap/ Jose Candelaria & Maria Garcia; am/ Juan de Jesus Garcia & Rosa Sebedra; gp/ Jose Alejo Garcia & Maria Asencion Garcia.

NUANES, Maria Trinidad – from Los Candelarias
bap 14 Dec 1829, 2 days old; d/ Santiago Nuanes & Maria Ines Garcia; ap/ Geronimo Nuanes & Barbara Ballejos; am/ Martin Garcia & Ana Maria Apodaca; gp/ Jose Ygnacio Gallego & Juana Armijo.

Frame 1304, #47
GARCIA, Manuela Antonia
bap 15 Dec 1829, 7 days old; d/ Jose Antonio Garcia & Rosa Gallego; ap/ Luis Garcia & Tomasa Olguin; am/ Antonio Jose Gallego & Magdalena Garcia; gp/ Andres Ortega.

ANAYA, Guadalupe (parvula)
bap 15 Dec 1829, b. 12 Dec; legit d/ Miguel Anaya & Micaela Rios; ap/ Dionicio Anaya & Juana Griego; am/ not stated; gp/ Alfonso Jaramillo & Micaela Garcia.

Frame 1304-1305
LOPES, Maria Asencion
bap 15 Dec 1829, 3 days old; legit d/ Miguel Lopes & Juana Carabajal; ap & am/ not stated; gp/ Lorenso Lucero & Rosalia Lucero.

ANAYA, Juana Evangelita
bap 27 Dec 1829; legit d/ Ysidro Anaya & Dolores Chaves, residents of this jurisdiction; ap & am/ not stated; gp/ Manuel Anaya & Isidora Madrid.

SAES, Lazaro
bap 27 Dec 1829, 11 days old; legit s/ Juan Saes & Gertrudis Torres; ap/ Paulin Saes & Ana Maria Gurule; am/ Jose Torres & Trinidad Truxillo; gp/ Francisco Sandoval & Manuela Carrillo.

Frame 1306, #48
ARAGON, Jose Dario
bap 28 Dec 1829, 11 days old; s/ Juan Rafael Aragon & Catalina Savedra; ap & am/ not stated; gp/ Luciano (Serna) & Barbara Serna.

SANCHES, Jose Tomas (of los Ranchos)
bap 30 Dec 1829, 2 days old; s/ Gabriel Sanches & Maria Gallego; ap & am/ not stated; gp/ Don Andres Ortega & Doña Juana Garcia, residents of this jurisdiction.

CASTILLO, Maria Barbara de los Dolores (of Alameda)
bap 30 Dec 1829, 3 days old; legit d/ Juan Miguel Castillo & Rosalia Martinez, residents of Alameda; ap/ Antonio Jose Castillo & Quiteria Chaves; am/ Ysidro Martin & Dorotea Montaño; gp/ Juan Gonsales & Barbara Castillo.

Frame 1307
ROMERO, Maria Rosalia (of los Ranchos)
bap 29 Dec 1829, 3 days old; legit d/ Jose Miguel Romero & Francisca Montaño; ap/ Miguel Antonio Romero & Juana Garcia; am/ Salvador Montaño & Gregoria Chaves; gp/ Jose Antonio Garcia & Tomasa Griego.

GARCIA, Maria Tomasa de los Dolores (of Albuquerque)
bap 30 Dec 1829, 1 day old; d/ Jose Garcia & Bibiana Candelaria, residents of this plaza; ap & am/ not stated; gp/ Jose Armijo & Dolores Ortiz.

ROMERO, Juan Antonio (of los Ranchos)
bap 31 Dec 1829, 1 day old; s/ Diego Antonio Romero & Encarnacion Valencia; ap & am/ not stated; gp/ Diego Antonio Romero & Juliana Montana.

3 Jan 1830 – incomplete entry and not on next page.

Frame 1308, #49
GURULE, Jose Tomas (of los Ranchos)
bap 3 Jan 1830, 7 days old; legit s/ Antonio Gurule & Guadalupe Padilla; ap/ Vicente Gurule & Maria Antonia Garcia; am/ not stated; gp/ Pedro Aranda & Juana Aranda.

NS, Jose de Jesus
bap 3 Jan 1830, 11 days old; s/ unknown parents, born in the house of Juan Nepomuceno Gabaldon of Albuquerque; gp/ Alfonso Lucero & Juana Lucero.

NS, Maria Tomasa de los Reyes (of los Candelarias)
bap 5 Jan 1830, 12 days old; d/ unknown parents, left at door of house of Maria Barbara Candelaria; gp/ Pablo Roman Sisneros & Mariana de Jesus Sisneros, residents of Los Candelarias.

Frames 1308-1309
GARCIA, Manuel Antonio (of los Ranchos)
bap 5 Jan 1830, 6 days old; legit s/ Juan Antonio Garcia & Gregoria Candelaria; ap/ Juan Garcia & Ysabel Romero; am/ Ygnacio Candelaria & Concepcion Chaves; gp/ Juan Tomas Aragon & Gertrudis Garcia.

MONTOYA, Maria Ysidora (of Alameda)
bap 6 Jan 1830, 5 days old; legit d/ Rafael Montoya & Ana Maria Duran; ap/ Pedro Montoya & Maria Luna; am/ Salvador Duran & Ana Maria Candelaria; gp/ Manuel Padilla & Maria Antonia Otero, residents of Alameda.

NS, Ana Maria (of Albuquerque)
bap 23 Jan 1830, 6 days old; d/ unknown parents, left at the door of the house of Don Ambrosio Armijo; gp/ Manuela Arbizu.

Frames 1309-1310, #50
GALLEGO, Juan Antonio Abad (of Albuquerque)
bap 23 Jan 1830, 6 days old; s/ Juan Antonio Gallego & Petra Lopes; ap & am/ were ignored; gp/ Juan Apodaca & Teodora Ansures.

GARCIA, Juan Anastacio
bap 23 Jan 1830, 2 days old; s/ Jose Antonio Garcia & Ygnacia Candelaria; ap/ Felix Garcia & Ysabel Lopes; am/ Antonio Candelaria & Manuela Rael; gp/ Miguel Antonio Jaramillo & Lorenza Lucero.

NS, Jose Domingo (of Albuquerque)
bap 24 Jan 1830, 8 days old; s/ unknown parents, left at door of the house of Antonia Mestes; gp/ Miguel Sandoval & Francisca Lopes.

Frames 1310-1311
GALLEGO, Pedro Jose (of Albuquerque)
bap 24 Jan 1830, 11 days old; legit s/ Basilio Gallego & Clara Peña; ap/ Antonio Jose Gallego & Magdalena Garcia; am/ Agustin Peña & Dolores Chaves, gp/ Pedro (Aranda) & Juana Aranda.

GUTIERREZ, Antonio Maria (of Albuquerque)
bap 24 Jan 1830, 10 days old; s/ Juan Gutierrez & Manuela Garcia; ap/ Santiago Gutierrez & Pasquala Alexo; am/ not stated; gp/ Antonio Sandoval & Maria Candelaria Sandoval.

JARAMILLO, Jose Ygnacio (of Albuquerque)
bap 24 Jan 1830, 14 days old; s/ Lorenzo Jaramillo & Yldefonsa Gutierres; ap & am/ not stated; gp/ Manuel Antonio Candelaria & Ana Maria Candelaria.

Frame 1312, #51
SANCHES, Jose (of Albuquerque)
bap 24 Jan 1830, 4 days old; s/ Agustin Sanches & Dolores Lopes; gp/ Miguel Lopes & Nicanora Garcia.

NS, Paula
bap 24 Jan 1830, 2 days old; d/ unknown parents, left at door in house of Romualdo Chavez & Barbara Truxillo, cousins, & were the godparents.

CHAVEZ, Visente Perfecto (of Albuquerque)
bap 24 Jan 1830, 3 days old; s/ Nicolas Chavez & Barbara Sanchez; ap/ Jose Maria Chavez & Ygnacia Armijo; am/ Mariano Sanchez & Carmen Ybarri; gp/ Visente Sanchez & Ana Maria Mestas.

Frames 1312-1313
GUTIERRES, Juana de los Reyes
bap 24 Jan 1830, 5 days old; legit d/ Miguel Gutierres & Gregoria Armijo; ap/ Jose Francisco Gutierres & Dolores Aranda; am/ Pablo Armijo & Josefa Chaves; gp/ Nicolas Garcia & Reyes Apodaca.

NS, Juana Maria
bap 25 Jan 1830, 14 days old; d/ unknown parents, left at the door of the house of Juan Cristobal Gonzales; gp/ Juan Cristobal Gonzalez & Manuela Gonzalez.

GARCIA, Juan Antonio
bap 24 Jan 1830, 3 days old; legit s/ Diego Garcia & Barbara Cordova; gp/ Juan Antonio Truxillo & Juana Montoya.

Frame 1314, #52
MARTIN, Maria Juana de los Dolores (of Albuquerque)
bap 25 Jan 1830, 5 days old; legit d/ Pablo Martin & Francisca Moya; ap & am/ not stated; gp/ Jose Moya & Jesus Martin.

CHAVES, Maria Trinidad (of Atrisco)
bap 27 Jan 1830, 4 days old; legit d/ Juan Chaves & Micaela Sanches; ap & am/ not stated; gp/ Jose Dolores Chaves & Nicanora Garcia.

PADILLA, Juan Pablo (of Valencia)
bap 30 Jan 1830, 8 days old; legit s/ Bartolo Padilla & Gertrudis Garcia, residents of Valencia; ap/ not stated; am/ Francisco Garcia & Ana Maria Molina; gp/ Lorenso Montoya & Dolores Garcia.

Frame 1315
MARTIN, Francisco
bap 30 Jan 1830, 3 days old; legit s/ Felipe Martin & Victoria Saez, residents of Los Ranchos; ap/ Felipe Martin & Maria Truxillo; am/ Manuel Saez & Greg Martines; gp/ Miguel Saez & Ygnacia Salazar.

Baptisms – Albuquerque, New Mexico
1829–1850

BUTIERRES, Josef Antonio
bap 5 Feb 1830, 3 days old; legit s/ Josef Butierres & Gertrudis Gomes, from the plaza de los Gallegos; ap/ Bernardo Butierres & Juana Lopes; am/ Francisco Gomes & Mariana NS; gp/ Jose Antonio Aragon & Rosalia Montaño.

ANAYA, Maria Josefa
bap 7 Feb 1830, 1 day old; legit d/ Antonio Anaya & Tomasa Tafolla; gp/ Don Jose Tenorio & Doña Josefa Mestas.

Frame 1316, #53
LUSERO, Maria Eleuteria Margarita (of Albuquerque)
bap 23 Feb 1830, 2 days old; legit d/ Gregorio Lusero & Marta Lopez; ap/ Juan Jose Lusero & Ascencion Alexa; am/ Manuel Lopez & Encarnacion Duran; gp/ Jose Antonio Garcia & Ygnacia Candelaria.

DURAN, Maria Teodora de Jesus (of Albuquerque)
bap 24 Feb 1830, 22 days old; legit d/ Manuel Duran & Manuela Muñis; ap/ Antonio Duran & Maria Garcia; am/ Miguel Muñis & Ysabel Aleja; gp/ Carlos Lopes & Barbara Contreras.

NS, Maria Rosa
bap 24 Feb 1830, 15 days old; d/ unknown parents, placed in the house of Pasquala Candelaria; gp/ Jose Joaquin Ballejos & Francisca Candelaria.

Frame 1317
MONTAÑO, Juan Jose (of los Ranchos)
bap 24 Feb 1830, 16 days old; legit s/ Toribio Montaño & Ana Maria Candelaria; ap/ Jose Montaño & Micaela Santillanes; am/ Juan Candelaria & Juana Armijo; gp/ Jose (Montaño) & Juliana Montaño.

SANCHES, Maria Marcelina de Jesus
bap 25 Feb 1830, 4 days old; legit d/ Domingo Sanches & Luz Perea; ap/ Jose Sanches & Maria Griego; am/ Francisco Perea & Manuela Candelaria; gp/ Miguel Saez & Maria Ygnacia Salazar.

PADILLA, Juan Felipe de Jesus
bap 25 Feb 1830, 17 days old; legit s/ Julian Padilla & Juana Padilla; ap/ Francisco Padilla & Bernarda Garcia; am/ not stated; gp/ Visenta Gonsales.

Frame 1318, #54
LUZERO, Maria Desideria (of los Ranchos)
bap 25 Feb 1830, 16 days old; legit d/ Jose Anastacio Luzero & Juana Duran; ap/ Juan Luzero & Antonia Martinez; am/ Francisco Duran & Barbara Apodaca; gp/ Miguel Romero & Maria Ygnacia Montaño.

GURULE, Juana Josefa (los Ranchos)
bap 28 Feb 1830, 20 days old; legit d/ Felipe Gurule & Juana Candelaria; ap/ Visente Gurule & Maria Antonia Garcia; am/ Juan Miguel Gutierres & Maria de los Nieves Chaves; gp/ Francisco Ortega & Maria Ygnacia Basan.

LOBATO, Maria Librada
bap 28 Feb 1830, 15 days old; legit d/ Diego Lobato & Matilde Duran; ap/ not stated; am/ Miguel Duran & Ynes Griego; gp/ Jose Maria Griego & Guadalupe Mora.

Frame 1319
GARCIA, Maria Concepcion (of Los Candelarias)
bap 28 Feb 1830, 3 days old; d/ Desiderio Garcia & Nepomusena Candelaria; ap & am/ not stated; gp/ Felipe Griego & Margarita Gonzales.

ARIAS, Jose Simon
bap 28 Feb 1830, 12 days old; legit s/ Juan Arias & Andrea Griego; ap/ Miguel Arias & Andrea Griego; am/ Francisco Gomes & Juana Garcia; gp/ Antonio Sandoval & Desideria Candelaria.

MARTINEZ, Maria Paula de Jesus
bap 28 Feb 1830, 6 days old; legit d/ Jose Martinez & Dolores Serrano; ap & am/ not stated; gp/ Manuel Marquez & Guadalupe Lusero.

GRIEGO, Nestor Roman
bap 1 Mar 1830, 4 days old; legit s/ Roque Griego & Romana Torres; ap/ Francisco Griego & Antonia Montoya; am/ Jose Torres & Trinidad Truxillo; gp/ Jose Ygnacio Gallego & Juana Armijo.

Frame 1320, #55
ARMIJO, Juan Ylario
bap 7 Mar 1830, 8 days old; legit s/ Jose Miguel Armijo & Basilia Gonsalez; ap & am/ not stated; gp/ Salvador Sedillo & Juana Maria Sanches.

NS, Pedro
bap 7 Mar 1830, 1 day old; s/ unknown parents, left at house of Dolores Lopes; gp/ Jose Lusero & Teodora Ansures.

GARCIA, Manuel Antonio
bap 7 Mar 1830, 6 days old; legit s/ Diego Garcia & Ramona Candelaria; gp/ Antonio Ballejos & Dolores Baca.

APODACA, Juan Eusebio
bap 8 Mar 1830, 4 days old; legit s/ Rafael Apodaca & Estefana Salazar; ap/ not stated; am/ Juan Salazar & Manuela Truxillo; gp/ Bernabe Hernandes & Juana Gonsalez.

Frame 1321
ANAYA, Maria Juana
bap 8 Mar 1830, 7 days old; legit d/ Miguel Anaya & Maria Lopes; ap/ Antonio Anaya & Tomasa Tafolla; am/ Manuel Lopez & Josefa Apodaca; gp/ Antonio Anaya & Tomasa Tafolla.

LOPES, Jose Maria
bap 9 Mar 1830, 4 days old; legit s/ Bernabe Lopes & Cipriana Perea; ap/ Pedro Lopes & Maria Jaramillo; am/ Andres Perea & Diega Candelaria; gp/ Jose Lobato & Ascencion Sanches.

GARCIA, Jose Albino
bap 10 Mar 1830, 10 days old; legit s/ Miguel Garcia & Rosalia Barela; ap/ Luis Garcia & Tomasa Olguin; am/ Santiago Barela & Juana Aranda; gp/ Don Julian Tenorio & Doña Benigna Chaves.

GRIEGO, Juana Maria (of Los Gallegos)
bap 11 Mar 1830, 4 days old; legit d/ Manuel Griego & Catalina Samora; ap/ Blas Griego & Rosa Chaves; am/ Juan Francisco Samora & Ygnacia Balencia; gp/ Julian Belencia & Refugio Rael.

Frame 1322, #56
SERNA, Francisca Ramona (of los Gallegos)
bap 11 Mar 1830, 4 days old; legit d/ Matias Serna & Juana Baros, residents of Los Gallegos; gp/ Marcelino Garcia & Paula Montaño.

NS, Maria Luisa (of los Ranchos)
bap 12 Mar 1830, 3 days old; d/ unknown parents, left at house of Andres Ortega, resident of los Ranchos; gp/ Vicente Romero & Antonia Ortega.

CANDELARIA, Francisco Antonio (of los Duranes)
bap 13 Mar 1830, 4 days old; legit s/ Ermeregildo Candelaria & Dolores Jaramillo; ap/ Tomas Candelaria & Ursula Perea; am/ Cristobal Jaramillo & Elena Chaves; gp/ Pablo Martinez & Lorensa Lucero.

CHAVES, Francisco Eulogio
bap 14 Mar 1830, 2 days old; legit s/ Blas Chaves & Gertrudis Sandoval, residents of Alameda; gp/ Juan Carrillo & Ygnacia Armenta.

Frame 1323
GUTIERREZ, Jose Francisco
bap 31 Mar 1830, 5 days old; legit s/ Antonio Gutierrez & Rosalia Anaya; gp/ Gaspar Atencio & Ysabel Chaves.

MARTIN, Jose Gregorio (of los Gallegos)
bap 31 Mar 1830, 12 days old; legit s/ Jose Antonio Martin & Vitoria Griego; ap/ Jose Martin & Maria Antonia Griego; am/ Miguel Griego & Gertrudis Olguin; gp/ Diego Antonio Romero & Juliana Montaño.

SANDOVAL, Jose Antonio (of Alameda)
bap 1 Apr 1830, 14 days old; legit s/ Jose Maria Sandoval & Teresa Luna, residents of Alameda; gp/ Juan Carrillo & Ygnacia Armenta.

ARIAS, Maria Trinidad (of los Ranchos)
bap 1 Apr 1830, 13 days old; legit d/ Juan Domingo Arias & Juliana Lucero, residents of los Ranchos; gp/ Jose Lucero & Maria Dolores Valencia.

Frames 1323-1324, #57
GALLEGO, Francisco (of los Ranchos)
bap 1 Apr 1830, 16 days old; legit s/ Juan Gallego & Manuela Gurule; ap/ Salvador Gallego & Barbara Aragon; am/Vicente Gurule & Antonia Garcia, residents of los Poblanos; gp/ Manuel Jaramillo & Rosalia Jaramillo.

GARCIA, Maria Teodora (of Corrales)
bap 1 Apr 1830, 12 days old; legit d/ Juan Garcia & Juana Maria Chaves, residents of los Corrales; gp/ Domingo Cordova & Dolores Cordova.

GRIEGO, Antonio Teodoro (of los Duranes)
bap 3 Apr 1830, 12 days old; legit s/ Francisco Griego & Guadalupe Perea, residents of los Duranes; gp/ Teodoro Duran & Paula Duran.

NOANES, Maria Dolores (of Alameda)
bap 4 Apr 1830, 16 days old; legit d/ Anastacio Noanes & Barbara Gurule, residents of Alameda; gp/ Juan Bautista Lucero & Maria de los Dolores Aragon.

SERNA, Maria Soledad (of los Ranchos)
bap 7 Apr 1830, 4 days old; legit d/ Blas Serna & Josefa Ballejos, residents of los Ranchos; ap/ Juan Serna & Barbara Medina; am/ Luis Ballejos & Ana Maria Chaves; gp/ Jose Manuel Montaño & Guadalupe Garcia.

Frame 1325
GARCIA, Maria Antonia (of Alameda)
bap 7 Apr 1830, 5 days old; legit d/ Manuel Garcia & Barbara Apodaca, of Alameda; gp/ Jose Angel & Rosalia Chaves.

MARES, Juan Nepomuceno (of los Candelarias)
bap 12 Apr 1830, 2 days old; legit s/ Nicolas Mares & Manuela Garcia; ap/ not stated; am/ Antonio Garcia & Dolores Chaves; gp/ Francisco Sisneros & Ana Maria Candelaria, all of Candelaria.

APODACA, Maria Gertrudis
bap 13 Apr 1830, 2 days old; legit d/ Juan Apodaca & Ana Maria Sanchez, residents; gp/ Jose Lusero & Marcelina Valencia.

LOPEZ, Basilio de Jesus (of los Corrales)
bap 3 May 1830, 19 days old; legit s/ Lazaro Lopez & Gertrudis Santillanes, residents of Corrales; gp/ Salvador Garcia & Marcelena Montaño.

Frame 1326, #58
MOYA, Jose Vicente (of Alameda)
bap 3 May 1830, 10 days old; legit s/ Jose Gabriel Moya & Antonia Hurtado, residents of Alameda; gp/ Mariano Montoya & Barbara Montoya.

GUTIERRES, Felipe Santiago (of los Griegos)
bap 3 May 1830, 3 days old; legit s/ Juan Gutierres & Manuela Lopes, residents of los Griegos; gp/ Francisco Perea & Dionisia Perea.

NS, Jose Gregorio (of los Poblanos)
bap 3 May 1830, 10 days old; s/ unknown parents, left at the house of Bernardo Gutierres; gp/ Jose Gregorio Garcia & Candelaria Serna.

NS, Marcelino (of Poblanos)
bap 3 May 1830, 10 days old; s/ unknown parents, left at the house of Bernardo Gutierres; gp/ Marcelino Garcia & Paula Montaño.

Frame 1327
ANAYA, Dimas
bap 3 May 1830, 8 days old; legit s/ Tomas Anaya & Rafaela Garcia; gp/ Alfonso Saes & Juana Lobato.

GONSALES, Juana Maria (of Alameda)
bap 3 May 1830, 5 days old; d/ Jose Gonsales & Gertrudis Garcia, residents of Alameda; gp/ Antonio Gonsales & Juana Maria Garcia.

SEVERINO, Maria de la Crus
bap 3 May 1830, 2 days old; legit d/ Miguel Severino & Jacinta Lopes, residents of this villa; gp/ Mateo Suarez & Maria Ana Belasques.

NS, Lorenzo
bap 3 May 1830, 5 days old; s/ unknown parents, left at house of Jose Miguel Lopes; gp/ Jose Sisneros & Juliana Chaves.

Frame 1328, #59
LOPEZ, Maria Crus Lugarda
bap 3 May 1830, 4 days old; legit d/ Jose Cleto Lopez & Dolores Candelaria, residents of this villa; gp/ Juan Domingo Baca & Dolores Lusero.

ATENSIO, Mariana de Jesus (of los Candelarias)
bap 6 May 1830, 12 days old; d/ Gaspar Atensio & Francisca Candelaria; gp/ Jose Manuel (Sisneros) & Mariana Sisneros.

NS, Maria Catarina (of Carnue)
bap 6 May 1830, 7 days old; d/ unknown parents; gp/ Jose Ygnacio Truxillo & Marta Martines.

LOPES, Diego Antonio (of Duranes)
bap 11 May 1830, 7 days old; legit s/ Carlos Lopes & Barbara Contreras; ap/ Manuel Lopes & Encarnacion Duran; am/ Florencio Contreras & Ana Santillanes; gp/ Diego Antonio Lopes & Juliana Chaves.

Frame 1329
CANDELARIA, Maria de la Cruz (of los Griegos)
bap 11 May 1830, 8 days old; legit d/ Juan Visente Candelaria & Candelaria Lobato, residents of los Griegos; gp/ Salvador Perea & Gabriela Candelaria.

GOMES, Maria Micaela (of los Candelarias)
bap 11 May 1830, 4 days old; d/ Jose Gomes & Gregoria Griego, residents of los Candelarias; gp/ Jose Dolores Samora & Maria Ygnacia Valencia.

GARCIA, Maria Ysidora (of Carnue)
bap 22 May 1830, 11 days old; legit d/ Mateo Garcia & Reyes Sedillo, residents of Carnue; gp/ Salvador Apodaca & Dolores Apodaca.

BARRIO, Visente Perfecto (of Albuquerque)
bap 22 May 1830, 6 days old; legit s/ Jose Barrio & Rafaela Lopes, residents of the villa; gp/ Visente Sanches & Carmen Sanches.

Frame 1330, #60
LUSERO, Maria Micaela Facunda (of Alameda)
bap 23 May 1830, 9 days old; legit d/ Antonio Lusero & Maria Natividad Cordova, residents of Alameda; gp/ Miguel Santillanes & Juana Lusero.

GARCIA, Maria Rita
bap 23 May 1830, 2 days old; d/ Valentin Garcia & Francisca Brito, residents of los Ranchos; gp/ Felipe Brito & Juana Lucero.

LUNA, Maria Soledad (of los Ranchos)
bap 23 May 1830, 8 days old; legit d/ Diego Luna & Paula Perea, residents of los Ranchos; gp/ Manuel Garcia & Soledad Miera.

MARTINES, Juan Domingo
bap 23 May 1830, 8 days old; legit s/ Jose de la Cruz Martines & Victoria Anaya, residents of los Griegos; ap/ Pedro Martines & Juana Garcia; am/ not stated; gp/ Mariano Gutierres & Gregoria Gutierres.

Frame 1331
APODACA, Ysidro Antonio (of los Griegos)
bap 23 May 1830, 8 days old; legit s/ Julian Apodaca & Antonia Griego, residents of los Griegos; gp/ Julian Candelaria & Francisca Noanes, residents of the same plaza.

MONTOYA, Maria Desideria (of Alameda)
bap 23 May 1830, 4 days old; legit d/ Juan Montoya & Ana Maria Martinez, residents of Alameda; gp/ Juan Antonio Garcia & Francisca Gonsalez.

SANDOVAL, Maria Claudia (of los Corrales)
bap 24 May 1830, 2 days old; legit d/ Pedro Sandoval & Juana Chavez, residents of los Corrales; ap/ Miguel Sandoval & Ygnacia Armenta; am/ Geronimo Chavez & Encarnacion Gonsalez; gp/ Diego Martines & Marcelina Montaño.

VELASQUES, Manuel Antonio (of Atrisco)
bap 24 May 1830, 3 days old; legit s/ Antonio Velasques & Maria Manuela Chaves, residents of Atrisco; ap/ Pablo Velasques & Barbara Lopez; am/ Xavier Chaves & Maria de Jesus Armijo; gp/ Juan Chaves & Dolores Chaves.

Frame 1332, #61
APODACA, Felipe Santiago
bap 27 May 1830, 2 days old; legit s/ Ramon Apodaca & Juana Lusero, residents; gp/ Dolores Garcia & Monica Garcia.

TORRES, Maria Dolores
bap 8 Jun 1830, 8 days old; legit d/ Juan Maria Torres & Dolores Gutierrez, residents of los Griegos; gp/ Jose Sisneros & Juliana Chavez.

JARAMILLO, Maria Marta
bap 8 Jun 1830, 1 day old; legit d/ Juan Cruz Jaramillo & Manuela Mestas, residents; gp/ Ysidro Jaramillo & Catalina Mestas.

GABALDON, Jose Manuel
bap 12 Jun 1830, 3 days old; legit s/ Nepomuceno Gabaldon & Barbara Mestas, residents; ap/ Miguel Gabaldon & Gertrudis Chaves; am/ Ygnacio Mestas & Guadalupe Duran; gp/ Jose Lobato & Manuela Mestas.

Frame 1333
GURULE, Maria Marcelina Antonia
bap 12 Jun 1830, 11 days old; legit d/ Antonio Gurule & Maria Paula Serna, residents of los Poblanos; gp/ Salvador Serna & Barbara Gutierres.

LOBATO, Barbara Antonia
bap 13 Jun 1830, 4 days old; d/ Marcelino Lobato & Paula Montaño, residents of los Gallegos; ap/ Julian Lobato & Barbara Serna; am/ Andres Montaño & Paula Apodaca; gp/ Juan Lusero & Juana Lusero.

PACHECO, Jose Manuel
bap 13 Jun 1830, 15 days old; legit s/ Jose Pacheco & Juana Sedillo, residents of Carnue; gp/ Jose Manuel Truxillo & Juliana Martin.

FERNANDEZ, Jose Trinidad (of Alameda)
bap 13 Jun 1830, 10 days old; s/ Juan Crus Fernandez & Maria de Jesus Moya, residents of Alameda; gp/ Jose Cordova & Micaela Cordova.

Frames 1333-1334, #62
NS, Ana Maria
bap 13 Jun 1830, 8 days old; d/ unknown parents, left at house of Jose Miguel Romero; gp/ Domingo Romero & Ygnacia Montaño.

MONTOYA, Maria Trinidad
bap 13 Jun 1830, 3 days old; legit d/ Jose Maria Montoya & Gertrudis Garcia, residents of Corrales; gp/ Juan Antonio Lusero & Andrea Martines.

MOYA, Maria Manuela
bap 13 Jun 1830, 10 days old; legit d/ Ascencion Moya & Juana Sandoval, residents of Albuquerque; gp/ Manuel Antonio Samora & Tomasa Lopez.

MARTIN, Maria Antonia (of this jurisdiction)
bap 14 Jun 1830, 2 days old; legit d/ Rafael Martin & Manuela Samora, residents; gp/ Salvador Sanchez & Maria Eulalia Tafoya.

NS, Juan Jose de Jesus (of los Placeres)
bap 27 Jun 1830, 3 days old; s/ unknown parents, left at house of Rosa Perea, resident of los Placeres; gp/ Jose Visente Olguin & Dolores Garcia.

Frame 1335
GRIEGO, Maria Juana Petra (of los Gallegos)
bap 28 Jun 1830, 5 days old; d/ Vicente Griego & Guadalupe Rubi; ap/ Blas Griego & Rosa Chaves; am/ not stated; gp/ Pedro Montaño & Nepomucena Muñiz.

ANAYA, Juan (of Atrisco)
bap 29 Jun 1830, 2 days old; legit s/ Manuel Anaya & Ysidora Gonzales, residents of Atrisco; gp/ Manuel Herrera & Benigna Chaves.

PADILLA, Antonio Jose
bap 14 Jul 1830, 6 days old; legit s/ Jose Manuel Padilla & Maria Antonia Otero, residents; ap/ Bernardo Padilla & Manuela Sanches; am/ Santiago Otero & Manuela Padilla; gp/ Antonio Jose Sanches & Rosalia Martin.

CARABAJAL, Rosalia Quirina
bap 14 Jul 1830, 4 days old; legit d/ Juan Pedro Carabajal & Gertrudes Gonzales, residents; gp/ Don Visente Armijo & Doña Rosalia Mestas.

Frame 1336, #63
PEREA, Pedro Jose Juan Nepomuceno
bap 14 Jul 1830, 16 days old; s/ Ramona Perea & unknown father, vecina; gp/ Manuel Antonio Torres & Juana Nepomucena Ruiz.

CANDELARIA, Maria Barbara Gerarda
bap 15 Jul 1830, 2 days old; legit d/ Cristobal Candelaria & Ysidora Garcia; gp/ Jose Antonio Montaño & Juliana Montaño, all residents of this jurisdiction of Albuquerque.

LOPEZ, Maria Trinidad (of los Ranchos)
bap 15 Jul 1830, 5 days old; legit d/ Gaspar Lopez & Rosalia Duran; gp/ Jose Antonio Garcia & Rosa Gallego, all residents of los Poblanos.

TORRES, Ana Maria Nabor (of los Ranchos)
bap 15 Jul 1830, 4 days old; legit d/ Juan Torres & Ysabel Gutierrez, residents of los Ranchos; gp/ Jose Ygnacio Sanchez & Maria Ynes Martinez.

Frame 1337
NS, Rafaela Tranquilina (of this villa)
bap 15 Jul 1830, 8 days old; d/ unknown parents, left in house of Soledad Mestas, vecina; gp/ Rafael Armijo & Antonia Mestas.

NS, Juan Jose Mateo de los Dolores
bap 15 Jul 1830, 10 days old; s/ unknown parents, left at the house of Ysabel Jinza, vecina; gp/ Jose Lusero & Maria Gonzales.

PEREA, Maria del Refugio (of Alameda)
bap 16 Jul 1830, 12 days old; legit d/ Bartolo Perea & Josefa Candelaria, residents of Alameda; ap/ Miguel Perea & Antonia Duran; am/ Jose Tomas Candelaria & Ana Maria Gallegos; gp/ Jose Ramon Rael & Refugia Rael.

SEDILLO, Francisco Antonio (of Atrisco)
bap 19 Jul 1830, 3 days old; legit s/ Julian Sedillo & Cipriana Garcia, residents of los Ranchos de Atrisco; gp/ Jose Visente Olguin & Maria Dolores Garcia.

Frame 1338, #64
ANAYA, Juana Maria
bap 6 Aug 1830, 3 days old; legit d/ Juan Anaya & Maria Francisca Baca, of Los Ranchos de Atrisco; ap/ unknown; am/ Antonio Maria Baca & Barbara Ballejos; gp/ Luis Garcia & Altagracia Montoya.

CANDELARIA, Ana Maria de los Dolores (of Los Griegos)
bap 6 Aug 1830, 12 days old; legit d/ Julian Candelaria & Francisca Noanes, residents of los Griegos; ap/ Jose Tomas Candelaria & Ana Maria Gallego; am/ Geronimo Noanes & Barbara Maes; gp/ Diego Antonio Romero & Juliana Montaño.

LUCERO, Juan Jose Mateo de los Dolores (of Los Ranchos)
bap 6 Aug 1830, 6 days old; s/ Tomas Lucero & Dolores Valencia, residents of los Ranchos; ap/ Juan Lusero & Antonia Martin; am/ Juan Domingo Balencia & Ygnacia Salazar; gp/ Jose Lusero & Marcelina Valencia.

LUSERO, Maria de la Luz de los Dolores
bap 7 Aug 1830, 10 days old; legit d/ Ygnacio Lusero & Maria Casaos; ap/ Mariano Lusero & Antonia Atencio; am/ not stated; gp/ Jose Dolores (Lucero) & Maria Petra Lucero.

Frame 1339
CANDELARIA, Santiago (of Atrisco)
bap 7 Aug 1830, 14 days old; legit s/ Jose Candelaria & Dolores Gutierres, residents of Atrisco; gp/ Marcos Ruiz & Maria Antonia Sanches.

DURAN, Magdelena (of los Ranchos)
bap 8 Aug 1830, 15 days old; legit d/ Salvador Duran & Maria Garcia, residents of los Ranchos; gp/ Manuel Antonio (Barela) & Manuela Barela.

SAEZ, Maria Angela de Jesus (of Alameda)
bap 8 Aug 1830, 7 days old; legit d/ Ramon Saez & Manuela Pacheco, residents of Alameda; gp/ Juan Andres Aragon & Manuela Brito.

TENORIO, Maria Antonia (of los Ranchos)
bap 8 Aug 1830, about 5 years old, of the Ute Nation; adopted d/ Don Julian Tenorio & Doña Benigna Chavez; gp/ Don Pedro Aranda & Doña Juana Aranda.

Frame 1340, #65
SANDOVAL, Maria Monica de los Dolores (of los Corrales)
bap 8 Aug 1830, 20 days old; legit s/ Nicolas Sandoval & Maria Concepcion Armijo; gp/ Francisco Sandoval & Petra Gonzalez, all residents of Corrales.

TRUXILLO, Jose Rafael Cayetano (of Alameda)
Bap 12 Aug 1830, 10 days old; legit s/ Manuel Truxillo & Juana Garcia, residents of Alameda; ap/ Marcos Truxillo & Juana Castela; am/ Andres Garcia & Francisca Tafolla; gp/ Juan Antonio Rael & Soledad Miera.

GUTIERRES, Salvador Antonio (of los Poblanos)
bap 15 Aug 1830, 4 days old; legit s/ Pasqual Gutierres & Manuela Gallego, residents of los Poblanos; gp/ (missing) & Magdalena Griego.

GRIEGO, Luis Jose (of los Ranchos)
bap 27 Aug 1830, 9 days old; legit s/ Geronimo Griego & Albina Lusero; ap/ Miguel Griego & Gertrudis Olguin; am/ Juan Lusero & Antonia Martines, all residents of los Ranchos; gp/ Felipe Griego & Margarita Gonsales; residents of Corrales.

Frame 1341
BACA, Jose Maria
bap 17 Sep 1830, 13 days old; legit s/ Diego Baca & Francisca Samora, residents; gp/ Mariano Sanches & Juana Lorenza Lopes.

GURULE, Maria Rufina (of San Antonio)
bap 19 Sep 1830, 4 days old; d/ Diego Gurule & Teresa Gutierres; ap/ Juan Cristobal Gurule & Maria Ygnacia Martin; am/ Rafael Gutierres & Josefa Mares; gp/ Miguel Peralta & Monica Baca.

SANCHES, Maria Regina
bap 19 Sep 1830, 6 days old; legit d/ Salvador Sanches & Encarnacion Gurule, residents; gp/ Manuel Garcia & Rafaela Rael.

GARCIA, Jose Dolores
bap 19 Sep 1830, 3 days old; legit s/ Manuel Garcia & Juana Carrillo, residents of los Griegos; gp/ Francisco Ortega & Maria Ygnacia Basan.

Frame 1342, #66
RAEL, Maria Salome
bap 19 Sep 1830, 6 days old; legit d/ Juan Rael & Maria Gurule, residents of San Antonio; gp/ Jose Manuel Truxillo & Juliana Martin.

NS, Felipe Gorga
bap 20 Sep 1830, 8 days old; s/ unknown parents, left at the home of Antonia Maria Ruiz, resident; gp/ Marcos Ruiz & Balbina Candelaria.

GURULE, Maria Merced (of Alameda)
bap 28 Sep 1830, 5 days old; legit d/ Gabriel Gurule & Nicolasa Luna, residents of Alameda; gp/ Jose Maria Sandoval & Teresa Luna.

SANDOVAL, Francisco Antonio Victoriano (of Alameda)
bap 28 Sep 1830, 16 days old; legit s/ Jose Sandoval & Gertrudis Gonzales, residents of Alameda; gp/ Nicolas Sandoval & Concepcion Armijo.

Frame 1343
GARCIA, Jose Lino de Jesus (of los Candelarias)
bap 29 Sep 1830, 7 days old; legit s/ Pablo Garcia & Gregoria Garcia; ap/ Juan Garcia & Juana Barbara NS; am/ Juan Jose Garcia & Francisca Gonzales; gp/ Juan Gutierrez & Rita Salazar, all residents of los Candelarias.

NS, Maria Merced (of los Ranchos)
bap 29 Sep 1830, 4 days old; d/ unknown parents, left at the house of Maria Antonia Griego, resident of los Ranchos; gp/ Pablo Griego & Rosalia Gallego.

NS, Jose Maria Justo (of Sandia)
bap 8 Oct 1830, 3 days old; s/ unknown parents, left at the house of the Reverend Padre Fr. Manuel Garcia del Valle; gp/ Don Julian Tenorio & Doña Benigna Chaves, residents of los Ranchos.

Frames 1343-1344, #67
GONSALES, Jose Antonio (of Alameda)
bap 8 Oct 1830, 1 day old; legit s/ Sabino Gonsales & Maria Jesus Luna; ap/ Juan Domingo Gonsales & Maria Jesus Archuleta; am/ Joaquin Luna & Ana Maria Romero; gp/ Juan Domingo Gonsales & Maria de Jesus Archuleta.

SANCHES, Luz (of Atrisco)
bap 15 Oct 1830, 6 days old; legit s/ Ygnacio Sanches & Manuela Anaya, residents of Atrisco; gp/ Manuel Anaya & Ysidora Gonzales.

Baptisms – Albuquerque, New Mexico
1829–1850

GARCIA, Ambrosio
bap 16 Oct 1830, 4 days old; legit s/ Ysidro Garcia & Maria Martinez, residents; ap/ Tomas Garcia & Bernarda Garcia; am/ Marcos Martinez & Francisca Jaramillo; gp/ Mariano Armijo & Placida Armijo.

NS, Maria Quiteria (of San Antonio)
bap 17 Oct 1830, 13 days old; d/ unknown parents, left at the house of Josefa Padilla, resident of San Antonio; gp/ Ramon Samora & Marcelina Gallego.

Frame 1345
LOBATO, Antonio Jose
bap 26 Oct 1830, 3 days old; s/ Juan Felipe Lobato & Manuela Mestas; ap/ Juan Lobato & Maria Casaos; am/ Ygnacio Mestas & Guadalupe Garvisu; gp/ Don Ambrosio Armijo & Doña Maria Antonio Ortiz.

GUTIERRES, Pedro Jose
bap 27 Oct 1830, 8 days old; s/ Juan Gutierres & Rita Salazar; ap/ Juan Francisco Gutierres & Dolores Aranda; am/ Bentura Salasar & Barbara Nieto; gp/ Juan Pablo Gutierres & Maria Salome Gutierres.

GONSALES, Jose Florentino (of los Ranchos)
bap 28 Oct 1830, 12 days old; s/ Jose Gonsales & Francisca Garcia; ap/ Juan Gonsales & Maria de la Luz Montoya; am/ Juan Garcia & Maria de las Nieves Olana; gp/ Antonio Garcia & Maria Gregoria Candelaria.

Frame 1346, #68
ARMIJO, Ana Maria de los Santos
bap 7 Nov 1830, 8 days old; legit d/ Pedro Armijo & Lus Garcia; ap/ Pablo Armijo & Josefa Chaves; am/ Jose Lopes & Gertrudis Garcia; gp/ Visente Sanches & Ana Maria Mestas.

LOPEZ, Maria Monica de Jesus
bap 7 Nov 1830, 9 days old; legit d/ Miguel Lopez & Nicanor(a) Carabajal; ap/ Bernardo Lopez & Victoria Candelaria; am/ Jose Lopez & Maria Carabajal; gp/ Don Damaso Lopez & Doña Monica Chavez.

NS, Manuela de Jesus
bap 7 Nov 1830; adult Indian of Navajo nation; gp/ Don Damaso Lopez & Doña Francisca Chaves.

CHAVEZ, Jose Rafael (of Atrisco)
bap 7 Nov 1830, 7 days old; legit s/ Jose Dolores Chavez & Nicanor(a) Garcia; gp/ Jose Rafael Luzero & Juana Baca.

Frame 1347
LUSERO, Ylario
bap 7 Nov 1830, 3 days old; s/ Juan Lusero & Manuela Gurule; gp/ Juan Domingo Griego & Gertrudis Candelaria.

CHAVEZ, Juan Crisanto (of los Ranchos)
bap 7 Nov 1830, 10 days old; legit s/ Romualdo Chavez & Maria Barbara Valencia, residents of los Ranchos; gp/ Don Lucas Armijo & Doña Barbara Ortiz.

GALLEGO, Maria Soledad (of Candelarias)
bap 7 Nov 1830, 3 days old; legit d/ Ygnacio Gallego & Juana Armijo, residents of los Candelarias; gp/ Rafael Armijo & Soledad Peña.

LUNA, Maria Simona
bap 7 Nov 1830, 9 days old; legit d/ Francisco Luna & Concepcion Sena, residents; gp/ Joaquin Luna & Concepsion Luna.

Frame 1348, #69
DURAN, Juan Antonio (of los Candelarias)
bap 7 Nov 1830, 12 days old; legit s/ Salvador Duran & Josefa Candelaria, residents of los Candelarias; gp/ Rafael Montoya & Ana Maria Duran.

LUSERO, Maria Micaela (of Alameda)
bap 8 Nov 1830, 1 month old; legit d/ Juan Antonio Lusero & Juana Montaño, residents of Alameda; gp/ Juan Antonio Truxillo & Juana Montoya.

CANDELARIA, Jose Teodoro (of los Griegos)
bap 9 Nov 1830, 1 month old; legit s/ Ylario Candelaria & Valentina Duran, residents of los Griegos; gp/ Pedro Candelaria & Dolores Duran.

NS, Maria Tomasa
bap 30 Nov 1830, 6 days old; d/ unknown parents, left at the house of Miguel Antonio Garcia; gp/ Lorenso Ortiz & Tomasa Garcia.

Frame 1349
ANDERSON, Pablo
bap 30 Nov 1830; adult of the United States of North America; gp/ Don Santiago Abreu & Doña Trinidad Gabaldon.

NS, Maria Dolores
bap 30 Nov 1830, 15 days old; d/ unknown parents, left at house of Don Juan Armijo; gp/ Jose Rafael Sisneros & Juliana Chavez.

GONSALES, Ana Maria de Altagracia (of los Candelarias)
bap 30 Nov 1830, 15 days old; legit d/ Antonio Gonsales & Maria Garcia, residents of los Candelarias; gp/ Cayetano Garcia & Maria Luisa Chaves.

Frame 1350, #70
GUTIERRES, Damasio
bap 12 Dec 1830, 2 days old; legit s/ Juan Gutierres & Francisca Anaya, residents; ap/ Juan Miguel Gutierrez & Maria de las Nieves Chaves; am/ Manuel Anaya & Antonia Apodaca; gp/ Antonio Gutierres & Rosalia Anaya.

CONTRERAS, Maria Guadalupe (of Alameda)
bap 12 Dec 1830, 6 days old; legit d/ Tomas Contreras & Paula Chaves, residents of Alameda; gp/ Jose Chaves & Francisca Montoya.

GARCIA, Maria Guadalupe
bap 12 Dec 1830, days old; legit d/ Juan Garcia & Dolores Candelaria, residents; gp/ Cayetano Suares & Antonia Velasquez.

GRIEGO, Francisco Xavier
bap 12 Dec 1830, 9 days old; legit s/ Pablo Griego & Maria Ysidora Apodaca, residents; gp/ Jose Apodaca & Dolores Torres.

Frame 1351
MONTOYA, Maria Guadalupe Leocadia (of Angostura)
bap 13 Dec 1830, 4 days old; legit d/ Francisco Montoya & Jesus Armijo; gp/ Don Gregorio Ortiz & Doña Clara Sarracino.

RUIS, Leocardo Melquiades Nepomuceno
RUIS, Loecadio (in margin)
bap 13 Dec 1830, 4 days old; legit s/ Marcos Ruis & Balbina Candelaria, residents; gp/ Don Gregorio Ortiz & Doña Clara Sarracino.

GARCIA, Maria de los Dolores (of Alameda)
bap 21 Dec 1830, 12 days old; legit d/ Jose Antonio Garcia & Soledad Sandoval, residents of Alameda; gp/ Felix Garcia & Ysabel Lopes.

Frame 1352, #71
SANCHES, Maria Manuela de Jesus (of Atrisco)
bap 28 Dec 1830, 4 days old; legit d/ Gabriel Sanches & Juana Sedillo, residents of Atrisco; ap/ Felipe Sanches & Ynes Garcia; am/ Toribio Cedillo & Victoria Maldonado; gp/ Don Jose Baca & Gertrudes Baca.

GARCIA, Jose Francisco (of Alameda)
bap 27 Dec 1830, 14 days old; legit s/ Manuel Garcia & Rafaela Rael, residents of Alameda; ap/ Miguel Garcia & Ana Maria Ballejos; am/ Juan Antonio Rael & Soledad Miera; gp/ Francisco Silva & Josefa Gutierrez.

SANDOVAL, Maria Clara (of Alameda)
bap 27 Dec 1830, 10 days old; legit d/ Antonio Sandoval & Decideria Candelaria, residents of Alameda; gp/ Esteban Candelaria & Jesus Luna.

Frame 1353
CANDELARIA, Maria de Altagracia
bap 28 Dec 1830, 4 days old; d/ Enrriques Candelaria & Ysabel Garcia, residents; ap/ Antonio Candelaria & Antonia Garcia; am/ Juan de Jesus Garcia & Rosa Savedra; gp/ Luis Garcia & Alta Gracia Montoya.

GONZALES, Jose Tomas (of Alameda)
bap 28 Dec 1830, 7 days old; legit s/ Juan Gonzales & Ana Maria Sandoval, residents of Alameda; gp/ Santiago Padilla & Francisca Padilla.

GUTIERRES, Maria Victoria (of los Poblanos)
bap 28 Dec 1830, 4 days old; legit d/ Agustin Gutierres & Maria Gurule, residents of los Poblanos; gp/ Christoval Jaramillo & Marta Jaramillo.

DURAN, Juan de Jesus
bap 29 Dec 1830, 2 days old; legit s/ Rafael Duran & Rosa Barbera, residents; gp/ Luciano Santillanes & Gertrudis Duran.

Frame 1354, #72
NS, Maria Gertrudis de los Dolores (of Alameda)
bap 29 Dec 1830, 2 months old; d/ unknown parents, left at the house of Micaela Cordova, resident of Alameda; gp/ Diego Antonio Garcia & Barbara Cordova.

DEDO, Marta (of the villa)
bap 29 Dec 1830, 10 days old; legit d/ Luis Dedo & Guadalupe Martin, residents; gp/ Bartolo Peña & Soledad Pacheco.

TORRES, Juana Maria (of Manzano)
bap 30 Dec 1830, 1 month old; legit d Mariano Torres & Guadalupe Chaves, residents of Manzano; gp/ Jose Sisneros & Maria Josefa Juachina Chavez.

GARCIA, Juana Maria (of los Ranchos)
bap 30 Dec 1830, 3 days old; legit d/ Pablo Garcia & Antonia Martin, residents of los Ranchos; gp/ Jose Martin & Josefa Montoya.

Frame 1355
APODACA, Maria Manuela Antonia (of Duranes)
bap 1 Jan 1831, 2 days old; legit d/ Juan Antonio Apodaca & Petra Duran; gp/ Jose Maria Torres & Josefa Garcia.

GUTIERRES, Diego Antonio (of San Antonio)
bap 1 Jan 1831, 1 month old; legit s/ Juan Gutierres & Juana Mora, residents of San Antonio; ap/ Jose Gutierres & Josefa Mares; am/ Ysidro Mora & Juana Marques; gp/ Jose Ygnacio Truxillo & Manuela Antonia Truxillo.

LUZERO, Maria Juana Andrea (of San Antonio)
bap 2 Jan 1831, 1 month old; d/ Antonio Luzero & Petra Truxillo; ap/ Juan Luzero & Francisca Luzero; am/ Juan Truxillo & Manuela Apodaca; gp/ Salvador Sanches & Maria Olaya Tafoya.

NS, Francisco Antonio (of San Antonio)
bap 2 Jan 1831, 1 month old; s/ unknown parents, left at the house of Francisca Gurule, resident of San Antonio; gp/ Francisco Rael & Eugenia Gurule.

NS, Juan Jose (of los Ranchos)
bap 2 Jan 1831, 40 days old; s/ unknown parents, left at house of Juana Perea; gp/ Silverio Lopez & Juana Perea.

Frame 1356, #73
BACA, Francisco Antonio de los Reyes (of San Antonio)
bap 6 Jan 1831, 6 days old; s/ Reyes Baca & Manuela Archuleta, residents of San Antonio; gp/ Jose Sisneros & Juliana Chavez.

TRUXILLO, Maria Reyes (of los Ranchos)
bap 7 Jan 1831, some days old; legit d/ Jose Truxillo & Soledad Valencia, residents of los Ranchos; gp/ Esteban Candelaria & Jesus Luna.

SANDOVAL, Maria Perfecta
bap 24 Jan 1831, 11 days old; legit d/ Mariano Sandoval & Rafaela Ansures; gp/ Jose Dolores Marquez & Perfecta Sedillo.

GONSALES, Manuel de los Reyes (of Alameda)
bap 25 Jan 1831, 6 days old; legit s/ Rafael Gonsales & Maria de Jesus Aragon; ap/ Manuel Gonsales & Maria Truxillo; am/ Tadeo Aragon & Maria Luisa Valencia, all residents of Alameda; gp/ Jose Manuel Padilla & Catalina Padilla.

Frame 1357
MONTOYA, Maria Paula
bap 27 Jan 1831, 3 days old; legit d/ Jose Montoya & Maria de los Lus Candelaria; ap/ Pedro Montoya & Encarnacion Luna; am/ Juan de Jesus Candelaria & Gertrudis Tafolla, all residents of Alameda; gp/ Visente Montoya & Dolores Montoya.

MARTIN, Juan de Jesus (of this villa)
bap 27 Jan 1831, 6 days old; legit s/ Juan Martin & Antonia Lusero, residents; gp/ Lorenso Lusero & Rosalia Lusero.

LUJAN, Manuel Antonio (of Carnue)
bap 27 Jan 1831, 27 days old; legit s/ Miguel Lujan & Rita Sandoval; gp/ Juan Antonio Lujan & Candelaria Luzero.

JARAMILLO, Jose Pablo (of Ranchos de Atrisco)
bap 27 Jan 1831, 3 days old; legit s/ Agustin Jaramillo & Francisca Garcia, residents of Ranchos de Atrisco; gp/ Manuel Anaya & Ysidora Gonzales.

Frame 1357-1358, #74
NS, Juan Nepomuceno Melquizades
bap 27 Jan 1831, 8 days old; s/ unknown parents, left at the house of Jose Garcia, resident; gp/ Jose Luzero & Petra Lopes.

LOPES, Julian
bap 30 Jan 1831, 5 days old; legit s/ Manuel Lopes & Lus Romero, residents; gp/ Francisco Apodaca & Ysabel Apodaca.

ARIAS, Pedro Jose (of los Ranchos)
bap 2 Feb 1831, 3 days old; legit s/ Juan Cristobal Arias & Tomasa Martin, residents of los Ranchos; gp/ Ramon Candelaria & Manuela Martin.

PEÑA, Jose Dolores (of Atrisco)
bap 2 Feb 1831, 3 days old; leg s/ Bartolo Peña & Acencion Candelaria, residents of Atrisco; gp/ Jose Dolores Chaves & Nicanor(a) Garcia.

Frame 1358-1359
NS, Maria Micaela (of Carnue)
bap 3 Feb 1831, 8 days old; d/ unknown parents, left at the house of Nicanora Anaya, resident of Carnue; gp/ Patricio Gutierres & Monica Pacheco.

SERNA, Maria Candelaria (twin)
SERNA, Maria Altagracia (twin)
bap 4 Feb 1831, 3 days old; legit d/ Salvador Serna & Barbara Gutierres, residents; first gp/ Jose Montaño & Guadalupe Garcia; second gp/ Jose Antonio Martines & Quiteria Griego.

NS, Juana Maria (of los Ranchos)
bap 4 Feb 1831, 1 month old; d/ unknown parents, left at the house of Gertrudis Gurule, resident of los Ranchos; gp/ Jose Montaño & Juliana Montaño.

Frame 1360, #75
SANCHES, Jose Pablo (of Atrisco)
bap 4 Feb 1831, 2 days old; legit s/ Nicolas Sanches & Luisa Gallego, residents of Atrisco; gp/ Pablo Candelaria & Teresa Candelaria.

NS, Maria Dolores Romalda
bap 18 Feb 1831, 6 days old; d/ unknown parents, left at the house of Don Manuel Armijo; gp/ Don Juan Armijo & Doña Ana Maria Gabaldon.

ARMIJO, Maria Monica del Rosaria
bap 18 Feb 1831, 12 days old; legit d/ Don Ambrosio Armijo & Doña Maria Antonia Ortiz; ap/ Don Vicente Armijo & Doña Barbara Chavez; am/ Don Jose Ortiz & Doña Monica Duran; gp/ Don Cristobal Armijo & Doña Monica Duran.

Frames 1360-1361
GARCIA, Maria Gregoria
bap 19 Feb 1831, 6 days old; legit d/ Jose Garcia & Manuela Baca, residents; gp/ Jesus Lucero & Gregoria Candelaria.

CANDELARIA, Felipe
bap 19 Feb 1831, 6 days old; legit s/ Ramon Candelaria & Manuela Martin, residents; gp/ Miguel Antonio Jaramillo & Lorensa Lusero.

APODACA, Juan Francisco
bap 19 Feb 1831, 6 days old; legit s/ Rafael Apodaca & Barbara Molina, residents; gp/ Francisco Garcia & Polonia Ballejos.

HERRERA, Maria Polonia de
bap 19 Feb 1831, 6 days old; legit d/ Jose Manuel Herrera & Barbara Santillanes, residents of Atrisco; gp/ Baltazar Montaño & Juana Maria Garcia.

Frames 1361-1362, #76
SANCHES, Juan Felipe
bap 19 Feb 1831, 6 days old; legit s/ Antonio Sanches & Guadalupe Garbiso; gp/ Juan Felipe Lobato & Manuela Mestas.

Baptisms – Albuquerque, New Mexico
1829–1850

SAMORA, Maria Dolores
bap 20 Feb 1831, 15 days old; legit d/ Francisco Samora & Ygnacia Valencia, residents of los Ranchos; gp/ Antonio Truxillo & Dolores Truxillo.

LUJAN, Juan (of San Antonio)
bap 20 Feb 1831, 1 month old; legit s/ Pablo Lujan & Ana Maria Anaya, residents of San Antonio; gp/ Jose Rafael Sisneros & Juliana Chavez.

SAEZ, Juan Andres (of Los Ranchos)
bap 21 Feb 1831, 14 days old; legit s/ Yldefonso Saez & Juana Gutierres, residents of los Ranchos; gp/ Juan Domingo Gonsales & Maria Archuleta.

JINSO, Jesus Maria (of San Antonio)
bap 22 Feb 1831, 26 days old; legit s/ Santiago Jinso & Manuela Joyanca, residents of San Antonio; gp/ Jesus Maria Marquez & Manuela Anaya.

Frame 1363
BACA, Maria Dolores (of San Antonio)
bap 22 Feb 1831, 3 days old; d/ Pablo Baca & Benigna Gutierres; gp/ Juan Nepomuceno Carabajal & Dolores Torres.

APODACA, Jose Maria de Jesus
bap 23 Feb 1831, 10 days old; s/ Francisco Apodaca & Maria Tomasa Barela; ap/ Jose Apodaca & Petra Garcia; am/ Juan Barela & Josefa Chavez; gp/ Jose Tenorio & Barbara Apodaca.

NS, Juan Francisco Nepomuceno
bap 5 Mar 1831, 2 days old; s/ unknown parents, left at the house of Maria Petra Lopes; gp/ same as above in company with her son, Jose Lusero.

Frames 1363-1364, #77
GARCIA, Jose Nestor
bap 6 Mar 1831, 10 days old; s/ Jose Garcia & Marta Duran; gp/ Cristobal (Garcia) & Monica Garcia.

CHAVEZ, Jose Eleuterio (of Alameda)
bap 6 Mar 1831, 15 days old; legit s/ Jose Chavez & Francisca Montoya, residents of Alameda; ap/ Juan Chaves & Barbara Armijo; am/ Pedro Montoya & Ana Maria Luna; gp/ Felipe Chaves & Candelaria Chaves.

LUSERO, Maria Manuela
bap 6 Mar 1831, 7 days old; legit d/ Rafael Lusero & Juana Baca, residents of Atrisco; gp/ Juan Montoya & Manuela Garcia.

LOPEZ, Maria Balbina
bap 6 Mar 1831, 6 days old; legit d/ Miguel Lopez & Juana Carabajal, residents; gp/ Marcos Ruiz & Balbino Candelaria.

Frame 1365
JARAMILLO, Nicanora
bap 6 Mar 1831, 6 days old; legit d/ Miguel Jaramillo & Estefana Herrera, residents of Atrisco; gp/ Jose Dolores Chaves & Nicanora Garcia.

LUZERO, Juana Maria (of Alameda)
bap 6 Mar 1831, 7 days old; legit d/ Jose Miguel Luzero & Andrea Pacheco, residents of Alameda; gp/ Salvador Tafolla & Juana Lusero.

BACA, Juana Maria
bap 6 Mar 1831, 11 days old; legit d/ Simon Baca & Lorensa Candelaria, residents; gp/ Antonio Gonzales & Juana Maria Garcia.

Frames 1365-1366, #78
JARAMILLO, Jose Abran (of Albuquerque)
bap 27 Mar 1831, 10 days old; legit s/ Miguel Antonio Jaramillo & Lorensa Luzero; gp/ Blas Luzero & Gertrudis Luzero.

ARANDA, Maria Josefa (of Ranchos)
bap 27 Mar 1831, 10 days old; legit d/ Juan Cristobal Aranda & Soledad Armijo, residents of los Ranchos; gp/ Pedro Armijo & Petra Perea.

CORDOVA, Simon (of Alameda)
bap 27 Mar 1831, 3 days old; legit s/ Bautista Cordova & Manuela Serna, residents of Alameda; gp/ Blas Serna & Josefa Ballejos.

NS, Maria Dolores (of Alameda)
bap 27 Mar 1831, 3 days old; d/ unknown parents, left at the house of Esteban Candelaria, resident of Alameda; gp/ Tomas Sanches & Rita Luna.

Frame 1367
TRUXILLO, Juan Jose (of Alameda)
bap 27 Mar 1831, 11 days old; legit s/ Juan Antonio Truxillo & Juana Montoya, residents of Alameda; gp/ Jose Antonio Garcia & Soledad Sandoval.

SANDOVAL, Juana Maria (of Alameda)
bap 27 Mar 1831, 20 days old; legit d/ Dolores Sandoval & Juana Truxillo, residents of Alameda; gp/ Santiago Truxillo & Francisca Gonzalez.

SANTILLANES, Maria Polonia (of Alameda)
bap 27 Mar 1831, 8 days old; legit d/ Jose Miguel Santillanes & Josefa Martin, residents of Alameda; gp/ Jose Manuel Martin & Bibiana Truxillo.

APODACA, Jose Eulogio (of Alameda)
bap 27 Mar 1831, 8 days old; legit s/ Rafael Apodaca & Estefana Salazar, residents of Alameda; gp/ Miguel Santillanes & Juana Garcia.

Frame 1368, #79
NS, Tomas
bap 27 Mar 1831, 6 days old; s/ unknown parents, left at the house of Antonio Jose Sanches, resident of San Mateo; gp/ Jose Sisneros & Juliana Chaves.

ROMERO, Maria Valvina
bap 2 Apr 1831, 2 days old; d/ Diego Romero & Juliana Montaño; ap/ Santiago Romero & Maria Ygnacia Valencia; am/ Damian Apodaca & Victoria Gutierres; gp/ Jose Trujillo & Soledad Valencia.

LOPES, Francisca Paula Ricarda
bap 3 Apr 1831, 2 days old; d/ Ramon Lopes & Reyes Jaramillo, residents; gp/ Mariano Ruis & Ysidora Lopes. [Note: The child had not been named, and a note was added: "For reference, they named her Francisca Paula Ricarda."]

Frame 1369
LOPES, Antonio Jose
bap 3 Apr 1831, 2 days old; s/ Francisco Lopes & Francisca Candelaria, residents of the villa; gp/ Domingo Sanches & Luz Perea.

CHAVES, Juan Cristobal (of Alameda)
bap 3 Apr 1831, 2 days old; s/ Pedro Chaves & Margareta Montoya, residents of Alameda; gp/ Don Felipe Montoya & Doña Luz Lopez.

ROMERO, Francisco de Paula
bap 3 Apr 1831, 2 days old; legit s/ Diego Antonio Romero & Encarnacion Valencia, residents; gp/Juan Domingo Valencia & Paula Martin. [Note: See also entry below.]

Frames 1369-1370, #80
ROMERO, Francisca
bap 3 Apr 1831, 2 days old; d/ Diego Antonio Romero & Encarnacion Valencia, residents; gp/ Juan de Dios Chaves & Monica Luzero. [Note: See also entry above.]

SALAZAR, Francisco (of Alameda)
bap 3 Apr 1831, 2 days old; s/ Yldefonso Salazar & Catalina Luzero, residents of Alameda; gp/ Vicente Montoya & Dolores Montoya.

LUSERO, Maria Trinidad (of los Ranchos)
bap 17 Apr 1831, 4 days old; legit d/ Jose Maria Lusero & Dolores Griego, residents of los Ranchos; gp/ Jose Antonio Gutierres & Ysabel Griego.

Frames 1370-1371
MUÑIZ, Ygnacio (of los Duranes)
bap 23 Apr 1831, 3 days old; legit s/ Pablo Muñiz & Leonarda Perea, residents of los Duranes; ap/ Miguel Muñiz & Ysabel Duran; am/ Ygnacio Perea & Maria de la Lus Garcia; gp/ Jose Manuel Aragon & Antonia Teresa Candelaria.

NS, Anselmo (of los Candelarias)
bap 24 Apr 1831, 6 days old; s/ unknown parents, left at the house of Ysabel Sisneros, resident of los Candelarias; gp/ Jose Manuel Noanes & Maria Paula Candelaria.

NS, Maria Dolores
bap 24 Apr 1831, 2 days old; legit d/ unknown parents, left at the house of Francisco Savedra, resident; gp/ Sabino Baca & Tomasa Lopez.

Frame 1372, #81
MONTOYA, Maria Antonia de la Cruz (of Atrisco)
bap 4 May 1831, 4 days old; legit d/ Juan Montoya & Manuela Garcia, residents of Atrisco; ap/ Felipe Montoya & Juana Garcia; am/ Juan Ascensio Garcia & Barbara Chaves; gp/ Don Ambrosio Armijo & Doña Antonia Ortiz.

NS, Maria Juana Felipa
bap 6 May 1831, 6 days old; d/ unknown parents, left at the house of Manuel Sanchez, resident; gp/ Juan Armijo & Juana Armijo.

LOPEZ, Maria Marta (of San Antonio)
bap 7 May 1831, 8 days old; d/ Antonio Lopez & Gertrudis Truxillo, residents of San Antonio; gp/ Pedro Truxillo & Maria Antonia Truxillo.

Frame 1373
GRIEGO, Manuel Antonio
bap 7 May 1831, 2 days old; legit s/ Rafael Griego & Barbara Apodaca, residents; gp/ Manuel Antonio Apodaca & Maria Gertrudis Apodaca.

GARCIA, Antonio Jose Estanislado
bap 7 May 1831, 8 days old; legit s/ Ramon Garcia & Laureana Pacheco, residents; gp/ Juan Ysidro Gonzales & Maria del Rosario Duran.

APODACA, Francisco Esteban (of Alameda)
bap 8 May 1831, 5 days old; legit s/ Juan Jose Apodaca & Antonia Garcia, residents of Alameda; gp/ Jose Sanchez & Rafaela Ruiz.

Frame 1374, #82
SANCHES, Juana Josefa Ygnacia (of los Ranchos)
bap 8 May 1831, 6 days old; legit d/ Antonio Sanches & Magdalena Griego, residents of los Ranchos; gp/ Francisco Ortega & Maria Ygnacia Bazan.

NS, Maria Micaela
bap 8 May 1831, 6 days old; d/ unknown parents, left at the house of Juan Rafael Garcia; gp/ Juan Duran & Mariana Garcia.

GUTIERREZ, Manuel Gregorio (of los Griegos)
bap 9 May 1831, 6 days old; legit s/ Juan Gutierrez & Manuela Lopez, residents of los Griegos; gp/ Francisco Antonio Lobato & Maria Paula Perea.

Frame 1375
TAFOLLA, Pedro Antonio (of Alameda)
bap 25 May 1831, 5 days old; s/ Rafael Tafolla & Concepcion Gonzalez, residents of Alameda; gp/ Antonio Jose Maldonado & Maria Rosa Gonzales.

BACA, Jose (of Atrisco)
bap 25 May 1831, 6 days old; s/ Miguel Baca & Ysabel Gallego, residents of Atrisco; gp/ Jose Rafael Garcia & Ysidora Garcia.

PEREA, Ysidro (of los Candelarias)
bap 25 May 1831, 10 days old; s/ Bernardo Perea & Antonia Garcia, residents of los Candelarias; gp/ Santiago Noanes & Ynes Garcia.

Baptisms – Albuquerque, New Mexico
1829–1850

Frame 1376, #83
GUTIERREZ, Jose Prudencio
bap 26 May 1831, 7 days old; legit s/ Miguel Gutierrez & Gregoria Armijo, residents of los Candelarias; ap/ Jose Gutierrez & Dolores Garcia; am/ Pablo Armijo & Josefa Candelaria; gp/ Pedro Armijo & Petra Perea.

JARAMILLO, Jose Miguel (of San Antonio)
bap 26 May 1831, 14 days old; s/ Juan Jose Jaramillo & Trinidad Otero, residents of San Antonio; gp/ Santiago Otero & Ana Maria Otero.

GARCIA, Luciano
bap 26 May 1831, 2 days old; s/ Mariano Garcia & Andrea Carvajal, residents; gp/ Gregorio Garcia & Jetrudis Sanches.

Frame 1377
GALLEGO, Juana
bap 26 May 1831, 3 days old; d/ Cristobal Gallego & Carmen Gutieres, residents; gp/ Domingo Balencia & Paula Martines.

CANDELARIA, Maria Felipa
bap 26 May 1831, 15 days old; legit d/ Pedro Candelaria & Dolores Duran, residents; gp/ Juan Gutierrez & Rita Salazar.

GARCIA, Maria Rita
bap 26 May 1831, 3 days old; d/ Francisco Garcia & Reyes Candelaria, residents; gp/ Anastacio Lucero & Juana Duran.

Frame 1378, #84
CARABAJAL, Jose Dolores
bap 26 May 1831, 2 days old; legit s/ Domingo Carabajal & Toribia Sanchez, residents; gp/ Jose Dolores Chaves & Nicanora Garcia.

SANCHES, Felipe
bap 26 May 1831, 2 days old; legit s/ Mariano Sanches & Juana Lopes, residents; gp/ Juan Andres Moya & Simona Sanches.

NS, Antonio Jose
bap 26 May 1831, 3 days old; s/ unknown parents, left at the house of Francisco Perea; gp/ Antonio Jose Pacheco & Josefa Pacheco.

Frame 1379
ANALLA, Maria Ysabel
bap 27 May 1831, 6 days old; legit d/ Antonio Analla & Tomasa Duran; gp/ Relles Jaramillo & Ysabel Candelaria.

GARCIA, Maria Felipa
bap 27 May 1831, 2 days old; legit d/ Manuel Garcia & Josefa Molina, residents; gp/ Pedro Gutieres & Guadalupe Garcia.

Baptisms – Albuquerque, New Mexico
1829–1850

TRUJILLO, Maria Rita
bap 27 May 1831, 3 days old; legit d/ Antonio Trujillo & Marta Ricarda Crespin; gp/ Bicente Sanches & Carmen Sanches.

Frame 1380, #85
GARCIA, Maria Altagracia
bap 18 Jun 1831, 15 days old; legit d/ Antonio Maria Garcia & Juana Montaño, residents; ap/ Felix Garcia & Ysabel Lopez; am/ Salvador Montaño & Gregoria Chaves; gp/ Don Jose Tenorio & Doña Andrea Martin.

DURAN, Jose Gervasio (of los Duranes)
bap 21 Jun 1831, 2 days old; legit s/ Francisco Duran & Bernarda Gurule, residents; gp/ Juan Rafael Garcia & Petra Garcia.

LUJAN, Jose Domingo (of San Antonio)
bap 29 Jun 1831, 7 days old; s/ Juan Antonio Lujan & Candelaria Luzero, residents of San Antonio; gp/ Juan Gutierrez & Ana Maria Mora.

Frames 1380-1381
NS, Felipe Santiago (of Atrisco)
bap 31 Jul 1831, 7 days old; s/ unknown parents, left at the house of Toribio Chavez, resident of Atrisco; gp/ Jose Antonio (Garcia) & Maria Ysidora Garcia.

GONZALES, Maria Ygnacia
bap 3 Aug 1831, 4 days old; legit d/ Francisco Gonzales & Antonia Garvisu, residents; gp/ Ylario Gonzales & Rita Rael.

GUTIERRES, Lorenzo Jacinto
bap 16 Aug 1831, 8 days old; s/ Jose Gutierres & Rosalia Jaramillo, residents of los Barelas; gp/ Miguel Lopez & Nicanora Garcia.

Frame 1382, #86
SAVEDRA, Jose Tomas
bap 17 Aug 1831, 10 days old; s/ Manuel Savedra & Juliana Duran, residents; gp/ Francisco Sandoval & Maria Gertrudis Garcia.

ANAYA, Francisco
bap 17 Sep 1831, 3 days old; s/ Miguel Anaya & Maria Lopez, residents; gp/ Juan Barela & Tomasa Barela.

GARCIA, Juan Jose
bap 18 Sep 1831, 4 days old; s/ Blas Garcia & Francisca Aragon, residents; gp/ Pedro Sanches & Gregoria Rael.

LOPEZ, Juana Maria
bap 18 Sep 1831, 2 days old; d/ Felipe Lopez & Juana Torres, residents; gp/ Ventura Olguin & Juana Gutierrez.

Frame 1383
MORALES, Jose Rafael
bap 18 Sep 1831, 8 days old; s/ Jose Antonio Morales & Juana Romero, residents; gp/ Jose Rafael
Apodaca & Barbara Molina.

GRIEGO, Maria Balveneda de los Dolores
bap 18 Sep 1831, 4 days old; legit d/ Manuel Griego & Catalina Samora, residents; gp/ Diego Antonio
Romero & Juliana Montaño.

NS, Maria Barbara
bap 18 Sep 1831, 5 days old; d/ unknown parents, left at the home of Salvador Duran, resident; gp/ Juan
Garcia & Juana Mirabal.

Frame 1384, #87
ROMERO, Cipriano
bap 2 Oct 1831, 6 days old; s/ Manuel Romero & Petra Apodaca, residents; gp/ Julian Sedillo & Cipriana
Garcia.

GRIEGO, Maria Gerarda
bap 3 Oct 1831, 2 days old; s/ Jose Miguel Griego & Dolores Garcia, residents; gp/ Jose Antonio Martin
& Teodora Garcia.

SANTILLANES, Ana Maria
bap 4 Oct 1831, 7 days old; d/ Jose Santillanes & Juana Diego, residents of los Griegos; gp/ Visente
Candelaria & Reyes Griego.

GARCIA, Miguel Antonio
bap 5 Oct 1831, 7 days old; s/ Juan Garcia & Rita Lopez, residents; gp/ Dionisio Lopez & Gertrudis
Perea.

Frame 1385
SAVEDRA, Jose Dolores
bap 19 Oct 1831, 8 days old; legit s/ Juan Cristoval Savedra & Monica Garcia, residents; gp/ Cayetano
Suarez & Maria Antonia Velasques.

SAVEDRA, Maria Gertrudis
bap 19 Oct 1831, 11 days old; legit d/ Pablo Savedra & Gertrudis Apodaca, residents; gp/ Cayetano
Suares & Maria Antonia Velasques.

NS, Juan Jose
bap 20 Oct 1831, 9 days old; s/ unknown parents, left at the home of Antonio Elzida, resident; gp/ Juan
Apodaca & Ysabel Sanchez.

Frame 1386, #88
MUÑIS, Diego Antonio (of San Antonio)
bap 18 Nov 1831, 7 days old; s/ Jose Maria Muñis & Justa Romero, residents; gp/ Santiago Gallego &
Micaela Gutierres.

DURAN, Maria Josefa
bap 18 Nov 1831, 2 days old; legit d/ Juan Rafael Duran & Josefa Apodaca, residents; gp/ Jose Lucero & Petrona Lopes.

CHAVEZ, Jesus Maria Jose
bap 22 Nov 1831, 4 days old; legit s/ Juan de Dios Chavez & Monica Lucero; ap/ Estanislado Chaves & Soledad Ortega; am/ Mariano Lucero & Marcelina Valencia; gp/ Don Julian Tenorio & Doña Benigna Chavez.

Frame 1387
NS, Maria Francisca
bap 10 Dec 1831, 2 days old; d/ unknown parents, left at the home of Francisco Apodaca, resident; gp/ Juan Apodaca & Francisca Apodaca.

CANDELARIA, Juan Nepomuceno
bap 11 Dec 1831, 8 days old; s/ Pablo Candelaria & Mariana Garcia, residents of los Candelarias; gp/ Bentura Olguin & Juana Gutierres.

LUJAN, Jose Federico de Jesus
bap 11 Dec 1831, 5 days old; s/ Jose Maria Lujan & Dolores Duran, residents; gp/ Jose Lucero & Maria de la Luz Lopez.

Frame 1388, #89
GRIEGO, Jose Victoriano
bap 1 Jan 1832, 9 days old; s/ Jose Maria Griego & Guadalupe Mora, residents of los Griegos; gp/ Francisco Antonio Martines & Ventura Mora.

GONZALES, Juan Reyes
bap 6 Jan 1832, 2 days old; s/ Mariano Gonzales & Petra Griego, residents of los Ranchos; gp/ Geronimo Griego & Albina Luzero.

MARTINES, Maria Josefa de los Reyes
bap 7 Jan 1832, 2 days old; d/ Jose Antonio Martines & Quiteria Griego, residents of los Gallegos; gp/ Francisco Ortega & Ygnacia Basan.

Frame 1389
JARAMILLO, Maria Guadalupe Crispina
bap 8 Jan 1832, 2 days old; d/ Gregorio Jaramillo & Antonia Sanches, residents; gp/ Roque Jaramillo & Balbina Jaramillo.

CANDELARIA, Maria Nicanora
bap 27 Jan 1832, 12 days old; legit d/ Antonio Candelaria & Antonia Garcia, residents; gp/ Antonio Garcia & Ygnacia Candelaria.

PEREA, Juana
bap 29 Jan 1832 at 3 days old; d/ Juan Perea & Cruz Duran, residents of los Duranes; gp/ Antonio Aragon & Juana Lorenca Aragon.

GRIEGO, Jose Domingo
bap 29 Jan 1832, 4 days old; s/ Bernabe Griego & Cipriana Perea, residents; gp/ Agustin Lobato & Manuela Mestas.

Frame 1390, #90
APODACA, Maria Ygnacia
bap 31 Jan 1832, 9 days old; d/ Salvador Apodaca & Maria de la Luz Martines, residents of San Antonio; ap/ Nicolas Apodaca & Juana Perea; am/ Pedro Martin & Cruz Rios; gp/ Francisco Gurule & Josefa Martines.

NS, Pedro
bap 1 Feb 1832, 2 days old; s/ unknown parents, left at the house of Cristobal Garcia, resident; gp/ Jose Ygnacio Olguin & Ysabel Jaramillo.

OLGUIN, Juan Martin
bap 19 Feb 1832, 5 days old; s/ Juan Olguin & Yldefonsa Sedillo, residents; gp/ Jose Miguel Griego & Dolores Garcia.

NS, Maria Josefa
bap 19 Feb 1832, 2 days old; d/ unknown parents, left at the house of Juan Gabaldon; gp/ Jose Tenorio & Josefa Mestas.

Frame 1391
ROMAN, Nestor
bap 1 Mar 1832, 4 days old; s/ Pablo Roman & Francisca Ruiz, residents; gp/ Francisco Sisneros & Juana Maria Candelaria.

ANAYA, Maria Francisca
bap 1 Mar 1832, 15 days old; d/ Juan Anaya & Dolores Montaño, residents; gp/ Agustin Jaramillo & Francisca Garcia.

NS, Maria Ysabel
bap 1 Mar 1832, 6 days old; d/ unknown parents, left at the home of Francisco Savedra; gp/ Antonio Anaya & Josefa Tafolla.

GURULE, Maria del Refugio
bap 2 Mar 1832, 2 days old; d/ Juan de Dios Gurule & Maria de la Luz Lujan, residents; gp/ Rafael (Sisneros) & Ana Maria Sisneros.

Frame 1292, #91
CARABAJAL, Juan Pedro Gabriel
bap 24 Mar 1832, 5 days old; s/ Juan Carabajal & Gertrudis Gonzales, residents; gp/ Jesus (Lopes) & Maria de la Luz Lopes.

CHAVEZ, Eulogio
bap 24 Mar 1832, 2 days old; s/ Nicolas Chavez & Barbara Garcia, residents; gp/ Jesus (Lopez) & Maria de la Luz Lopez.

MONTOYA, Maria Francisca Octaviana
bap 25 Mar 1832, 4 days old; d/ Don Juan Montoya & Doña Clara Jaramillo, residents; gp/ Don Julian Tenorio & Doña Benigna Chaves.

Frames 1392-1393
NS, Jose Ventura Velario
bap 25 Mar 1832, 3 days old; s/ unknown parents, placed in the house of Jose Miguel Lopez, resident; gp/ Ventura Apodaca & Dolores Torres.

SAMORA, Jose Agapito
bap 25 Mar 1832, 6 days old; s/ Jose Samora & Rafaela Martin, residents; gp/ Juan Noanes & Juana Maria Martin.

NS, Jose Manuel
bap 25 Mar 1832, 2 days old; s/ unknown parents, left at the house of Rafael Luzero, resident; gp/ Jesus Maria Marquez & Manuela Anaya.

GARCIA, Maria de Jesus Simona
bap 25 Mar 1832, 2 days old; d/ Antonio Garcia & Maria del Carmen Sanchez, residents; gp/ Don Vicente Armijo & Doña Maria Jesus Otero.

Frame 1394, #92
LOPEZ, Juana Maria
bap 28 Mar 1832, 2 days old; d/ Juan Lopez & Antonia Sanchez, residents; gp/ Antonio Garcia & Ana Maria Mestes.

MARTINEZ, Domingo
bap 29 Mar 1832, 4 days old; s/ Jose Maria Martinez & Barbara Garcia, residents of los Griegos; gp/ Jose Manuel Montaño & Guadalupe Garcia.

ARMIJO, Maria Monica
bap 25 Apr 1832, 8 days old; d/ Don Ambrosio Armijo & Doña Antonia Ortiz, residents; ap/ Don Viscente Armijo & Barbara Chaves; am/ Marcos Ortiz & Monica Duran; gp/ Cristobal Armijo & Doña Monica Duran.

Frame 1395
NS, Maria de la Ascencion
bap 25 Apr 1832, 6 days old; d/ unknown parents, left at the house of Don Ambrosio Armijo, resident; gp/ Salvador Armijo & Cesaria Carabajal.

GARCIA, Jose Toribio de la Trinidad
bap 25 Apr 1832, 6 days old; s/ Juan Garcia & Juana Maria Sanchez, residents; gp/ Don Julian Armijo & Doña Mariana Sarracino.

Frames 1395-1396, #93
ARCHIVIQUE, Ana Maria
bap 25 Apr 1832, 1 day old; d/ Matias Archivique & Maria Manuela Sanches, residents; gp/ Mariano Lucero & Marcelina Valencia.

GARCIA, Agustin Maria
bap 26 Apr 1832, 18 days old; s/ Maria Antonia Garcia, vecina of Sandia; gp/ Manuel Garcia & Soledad Miera.

NS, Jose Esmerigildo
bap 26 Apr 1832, 13 days old; s/ unknown parents, left at the home of Don Francisco Ortega, resident; gp/ the same Don Francisco Ortega & Doña Ygnacia Basan.

GARCIA, Maria Polonia de los Dolores
bap 26 Apr 1832, 17 days old; d/ Julian Garcia & Euduvige Gomez, residents of los Ranchos; gp/ Ygnacio Gutierrez & Maria del Carmen Gomes.

Frame 1397
MONTOYA, Maria Petra
bap 1 May 1832, 3 days old; d/ Jose Maria Montoya & Gertrudis Garcia, residents of Corrales; gp/ Antonio Garcia & Josefa Garcia.

ARAGON, Maria Felipe Valeria
bap 1 May 1832, 4 days old; d/ Antonio Aragon & Ana Maria Montaño, residents of los Ranchos; gp/ Pablo Yrisarri & Reyes Jaramillo.

JARAMILLO, Bernardino
bap 20 May 1832, 5 days old; s/ Geronimo Jaramillo & Gertrudis Lusero, residents; gp/ Jose Torribio Chaves & Dolores Montoya.

Frame 1398, #94
NS, Jose Francisco
bap 20 May 1832, 10 days old; s/ unknown parents, left at the home of Cristobal Gallego, resident; gp/ Antonio Maria Sanchez & Micaela Lucero.

SANCHES, Juan Nepomuceno Francisco Trinidad
bap 20 May 1832, 8 days old; legit s/ Gabriel Sanches & Rafaela Ortiz, residents; gp/ Julian Armijo & Doña Mariana Sarracino.

GURULE, Juana Maria
bap 20 May 1832, 6 days old; d/ Diego Gurule & Teresa Gutierrez, residents; gp/ Salvador (Apodaca) & Dolores Apodaca.

NS, Juana Maria
bap 20 May 1832, 10 days old; d/ unknown parents, left at the home of Don Juan Armijo; gp/ Pablo Candelaria & Juana Candelaria.

Frame 1399
APODACA, Maria Trinida Crus
bap 20 May 1832, 19 days old; d/ Juan Apodaca & Maria Sanches, residents; gp/ Jose Apodaca & Dolores Torres.

CRESPIN, Miguel Antonio
bap 20 May 1832, 3 days old; s/ Juan Andres Crespin & Manuela Jaramillo, residents; gp/ Manuel Antonio Peña & Soledad Lopes.

ARCHULETA, Maria Monica
bap 23 May 1832, 6 days old; d/ Mateo Archuleta & Reyes Sedillo, residents of San Antonio; gp/ Juan Sanches & Maria Antonia Rosa Lobato.

SAMORA, Luis Jose
bap 27 May 1832, 3 days old; s/ Juan Francisco Samora & Ygnacia Valencia, residents; gp/ Julian Valencia & Refugio Rael.

Frame 1400, #95
ARMIJO, Maria Lucrecia
bap 17 Jun 1832, 3 days old; d/ Ygnacio Armijo & Francisca Sisneros, residents of los Candelarias; gp/ Torribio Noanes & Ana Maria Candelaria.

TRUXILLO, Maria Manuela Roberta (of Alameda)
bap 17 Jun 1832, 11 days old; d/ Jose Truxillo & Soledad Valencia; ap/ Antonio Truxillo & Maria Duran; am/ Juan Domingo Valencia & Ygnacia Salazar; gp/ Miguel Saez & Ygnacia Salazar.

MONTOYA, Maria Antonia
bap 17 Jun 1832, 5 days old; d/ Rafael Montoya & Ana Maria Duran, residents; gp/ Ygnacio Ruiz & Ysidora Lopez.

GARCIA, Maria Manuela
bap 17 Jun 1832, 6 days old; d/ Miguel Garcia & Rosalia Rael, residents; gp/ Francisco Barela & Juana Aranda.

Frame 1401
GARCIA, Pasquala
bap 17 Jun 1832, 5 days old; d/ Antonio Garcia & Guadalupe Barreras, residents; gp/ Francisco (Perea) & Antonia Perea.

ANAYA, Maria Gertrudes
bap 17 Jun 1832, 3 days old; d/ Manuel Anaya & Felipa Garcia, residents; gp/ Jose (Lusero) & Gertrudis Lusero.

SERNA, Maria Manuela Silveria
bap 20 Jun 1832, 1 day old; d/ Antonio Serna & Guadalupe Gutierrez, residents; ap/ not stated; am/ Miguel Gutierrez & Simona Griego; gp/ Pedro Antonio Gutierrez & Guadalupe Garcia.

LUSERO, Jose Julian
bap 20 Jun 1832, 3 days old; legit s/ Merejildo Lusero & Francisca Sanches, residents; ap/ not stated; am/ Felipe Sanches & Maria Trujillo; gp/ Julian Balencia & Refugio Rael.

Frame 1402, #96
GONSALES, Maria Luisa
bap 21 Jul 1832, 3 days old; d/ Juan Maria Gonsales & Luz Marquez, residents; gp/ Esteban Mora & Antonia Mora.

NS, Maria Victoria
bap 22 Jun 1832, 5 days old; d/ unknown parents, left at the house of Eufemia Gurule, vecina; gp/ Francisco Garcia & Encarnacion Apodaca.

Baptisms – Albuquerque, New Mexico
1829–1850

SEDILLO, Maria de la Luz
bap 12 Jul 1832, 6 days old; s/ Don Toribio Sedillo & Ysabel Sanchez, residents; gp/ Jose Ramon Sanchez & Maria Paula Montoya.

Frame 1403
DURAN, Maria Guadalupe
bap 12 Jul 1832, 20 days old; d/ Manuel Duran & Manuela Muñiz, residents; gp/ Don Diego Lopez & Doña Maria de la Luz Lopez.

GARCIA, Filomeno Lorenzo
bap 13 Jul 1832, 20 days old; legit s/ Jose Antonio Garcia & Ygnacia Candelaria; ap/ Felix Garcia & Ysabela Lopez; am/ Antonio Candelaria & Manuela Rael; gp/ Pedro Sedillo & Francisca Chavez.

GARCIA, Pablo
bap 15 Jul 1832, 6 days old; legit s/ Antonio Garcia & Tomasa Griego; ap/ Tomas Garcia & Encarnacion Garcia; am/ Jose Griego & Josefa Olguin, residents; gp/ Pablo Yrisarri & Ana Maria Ortega.

Frame 1404, #97
CORDOVA, Jose Maria Nabonor
bap 15 Jul 1832, 5 days old; s/ Marcos Cordova & Juana Duran, residents of Alameda; gp/ Jose de Jesus Angel & Rosalia Chavez.

NS, Antonio Jose
bap 28 Aug 1832, 2 days old; s/ unknown parents; gp/ Don Ambrosio Armijo & Doña Antonia Ortiz.

ARANDA, Soledad Bartola
bap 29 Aug 1832, 3 days old; d/ Pedro Aranda & Rosalia Jaramillo, residents; gp/ Andres Ortega & Juana Andrea Garcia.

GRIEGO, Maria Rosa
bap 30 Aug 1832, 4 days old; d/ Jose Vitoriano Griego & Jesus Chaves, residents; gp/ Pablo Garcia & Ana Gregoria Garcia.

Frame 1405
GARCIA, Rosalia
bap 30 Aug 1832, 4 days old; d/ Juan Antonio Garcia & Gregoria Candelaria, residents; ap/ Juan Garcia & Ysabel Romero; am/ Ygnacio Candelaria & Ygnacia Chaves; gp/ Miguel Garcia & Rosalia Barela.

APODACA, Juana Maria
bap 30 Aug 1832, 8 days old; Cristobal Apodaca & Yldefonsa Candelaria, residents; ap & am/ not stated; gp/ Bentura Olguin & Juana Gutierrez.

Frame 1406, #98
CHAVEZ, Maria Gertrudis
bap 11 Sep 1832, 2 days old, at San Diego de Jemez; legit d/ Juan Chavez & Maria Micaela Sanchez, residents of the Rancho de Atrisco; ap/ Jose Maria Chavez & Maria Ygnacia Armijo; am/ Feliz Sanchez & Anna Maria Aguirre; gp/ Manuel Antonio Sanchez & Maria Josefa Apodaca, residents of Sebolleta.

ARCHULETA, Maria Ramona de los Dolores
bap 12 Sep 1832, 7 days old; d/ Agustin Archuleta & Dolores Sanchez, residents; ap & am/ not stated; gp/
Juan Varela & Josefa Chaves.

Frame 1407
RAEL, Maria Rosa Agustina
bap 31 Aug 1832, 4 days old; d/ unknown parents, left at the house of Estefana Rael, vecina; gp/ Felipe
(Gurule) & Gertrudis Gurule.

CANDELARIA, Jose Visente de Jesus
bap 20 Sep 1832, 6 days old; legit s/ Juan Vicente Candelaria & Candelaria Carrillo, residents; gp/
Domingo Gonzales & Maria Nazarena NS.

MONTOYA, Barbara Cornelia
bap 23 Sep 1832, 8 days old; legit d/ Jose Maria Montoya & Clara Armijo, residents; gp/ Jose Armijo &
Barbara Ortiz.

Frame 1408, #99
CHAVES, Amado
bap 24 Sep 1832, 12 days old; s/ Romualdo Chaves & Barbara Trujillo, residents; gp/ Don Julian Tenorio
& Doña Benigna Chavez.

CORDOVA, Jose Ygnacio
bap 24 Sep 1832, 20 days old; legit s/ Juan Bautista Cordova & Manuela Serna, residents of Alameda; gp/
Juan de los Reyes Montoya & Gertrudis Moya.

NS, Maria Manuela de los Dolores
bap 24 Sep 1832, 4 days old; d/ unknown parents, left at the home of Juana Pacheco, resident; gp/ Juan
Felipe Lobato & Manuela Mestas.

Frame 1409
LUCERO, Maria de la Luz Cruz
bap 6 Oct 1832, 8 days old; d/ Ygnacio Lucero & Ana Maria Ramirez, residents; gp/ Miguel (Perea) &
Dionisia Perea.

GALLEGO, Jose Miguel
bap 6 Oct 1832, 8 days old; s/ Ygnacio Gallego & Juana Armijo, residents; ap/ Felipe Gallego & Luisa
Griego; am/ Cristobal Armijo & Matilde Duran; gp/ Jose Ramon Marez & Ana Maria Noanes.

GARCIA, Maria de Jesus
bap 7 Oct 1832, 3 days old; d/ Jose Garcia & Manuel(a) Montoya; ap/ Cristobal Garcia & Manuela Otero;
am/ Felipe Montoya & Maria de la Luz Lopez, all residents; gp/ Salvador Luzero & Antonia Luzero.

Frame 1410, #100
GARCIA, Maria Micaela
bap 7 Oct 1832, 9 days old; d/ Romualdo Garcia & Ana Maria Arias, residents; gp/ Juan Arias & Maria
Euduvige Gomes.

NS, Maria Francisca
bap 7 Oct 1832, 4 days old; d/ unknown parents, left at the home of Maria Paula Ortega, vecina; gp/ Bernardo Gutierrez & Dolores Ortega.

NS, Francisco
bap 10 Oct 1832, 3 days old; s/ unknown parents, left at the home of Bernardo Gutierrez, resident; gp/ Cristobal Gallego & Carmen Gutierrez.

Frames 1410-1411
GUTIERRES, Maria Clara del Pilar
bap 21 Oct 1832, 9 days old; d/ Miguel Gutierres & Gregoria Armijo, residents; ap/ Juan Francisco Gutierres & Dolores Aranda; am/ Pablo Armijo & Josefa Chavez; gp/ Juan Montoya & Clara Jaramillo.

LOPEZ, Jose Rafael
bap 21 Oct 1832, 8 days old; s/ Angelo Lopez & Ana Maria Marquez; ap/ Manuel Lopez & Encarnacion Duran; am/ Diego Marquez & Maria Sanches, all residents; gp/ Jose Rafael Apodaca & Barbara Molina.

MONTOYA, Maria Rosalia
bap 23 Oct 1832, 2 days old; d/ Jose Montoya & Dolores Garcia, residents; ap & am/ not stated; gp/ Antonio Gutierrez & Rosalia Anaya.

GUTIERREZ, Maria Francisca
bap 23 Oct 1832, 19 days old; d/ Bernardo Gutierrez & Dolores Ortega, residents; gp/ Juan Gallego & Gertrudis Gallego.

Frame 1412, #101
GRIEGO, Ana Maria
bap 24 Oct 1832, 15 days old; d/ Jose Griego & Tomasa Lopez, residents of los Griegos; ap/ Antonio Griego & Rosalia Duran; am/ Paulin Lopez & Rafaela Muñis; gp/ Jose Dolores Samora & Ana Maria Perea.

MONTAÑO, Maria Benigna
bap 24 Nov 1832, 20 days old; d/ Jose Manuel Montaño & Guadalupe Garcia, residents; ap/ Jose Montaño & Micaela Santillanes; am/ Salvador Garcia & Andrea Tafolla; gp/ Juan Domingo Gonzales & Maria Nazarena NS.

Frames 1412-1413
CANDELARIA, Jose Felix de Jesus
bap 24 Nov 1832, 4 days old; s/ Ermeregildo Candelaria & Dolores Jaramillo, residents; gp/ Luis Jaramillo & Saturnina Jaramillo.

TORRES, Jose Marcelino
bap 24 Nov 1832, 15 days old; s/ Juan Torres & Dolores Gutierrez, residents; gp/ Felipe Gallego & Luisa Griego.

JARAMILLO, Jose Leonardo
bap 25 Nov 1832, 3 days old; s/ Marcos Jaramillo & Ana Maria Garcia, residents; ap/ Cristobal Jaramillo & Elena Chavez; am/ Diego Garcia & Ramona Candelaria; gp/ maternal grandparents.

Frame 1414, #102
BACA, Jose Felix
bap 25 Nov 1832, 3 days old; legit s/ Jose Baca & Antonia Garcia, residents; ap/ Juan Domingo Baca & Maria Gertrudis Ortiz; am/ Salvador Garcia & Toribia Chaves; gp/ Antonio Jose (Luzero) & Maria Gutierres Luzero.

NS, Maria Francisca
bap 25 Nov 1832, 6 days old; d/ unknown parents, left at the home of Francisco Martinez; gp/ the same, Francisco Martinez & Bentura Mora.

TORRES, Maria Polonia
bap 25 Nov 1832, 8 days old; legit d/ Francisco Torres & Juliana Montoya, residents; gp/ Antonio Griego & Candelaria Luna.

Frame 1415
PINEDA, Jose de la Cruz Desiderio
bap 25 Nov 1832, 11 days old; legit s/ Antonio Pineda & Ana Maria Griego, residents; gp/ Lorenzo Garcia & Matilde Ortiz.

LUZERO, Juan Jose de la Cruz Melquiado
bap 25 Nov 1832, 2 days old; legit s/ Jose Luzero & Maria Gertrudis Gutierrez, residents; gp/ Don Gregorio Ortiz & Doña Clara Sarracino.

SAEZ, Maria Leonarda
bap 26 Nov 1832, 5 days old; d/ Francisco Saez & Juliana Rael, residents of Alameda; gp/ Jose Saez & Martina Truxillo.

Frame 1416, #103
XARAMILLO, Jesus Maria
bap 30 Nov 1832, 2 days old; s/ Francisco Xaramillo & Guadalupe Duran, residents; gp/ Jesus Lopez & Maria de la Luz Lopez.

LUSERO, Maria Andrea
bap 2 Dec 1832, 3 days old; d/ Tomas Lusero & Dolores Valencia, residents; gp/ Juan Lusero & Antonia Martin.

ARIAS, Juan Andres
bap 2 Dec 1832, 3 days old; s/ Juan Cristobal Arias & Tomasa Martin, residents; gp/ Jose Maria Sandoval & Teresa Luna.

Frame 1417
CANDELARIA, Maria Bibiana de la Trinidad
bap 4 Dec 1832, 3 days old; legit d/ Jose Candelaria & Francisca Candelaria, residents; gp/ Blas Garcia & Maria Reyes Apodaca.

GARCIA, Ana Maria
bap 6 Dec 1832, 3 days old; legit d/ Francisco Garcia & Barbara Gabaldon, residents; gp/ Jose de Jesus Otero & Ana Maria Gabaldon.

PEREA, Maria Guadalupe
bap 6 Dec 1832, 2 days old; legit d/ Manuel Perea & Gregoria Duran, residents; gp/ Francisco Antonio Duran & Bernarda Gurule.

Frame 1418, #108
ARIAS, Juan Antonio
bap 20 Feb 1833, 12 days old; legit s/ Juan Domingo Arias & Juliana Lucero, residents; gp/ Diego Luna & Manuela Garcia.

MARTINEZ, Jose Romualdo
bap 20 Feb 1833, 20 days old; legit s/ Gregorio Martinez & Gregoria Candelaria, residents; gp/ Juan Gallego & Francisca Candelaria.

MARTINEZ, Maria Anastacia
bap 20 Feb 1833, 15 days old; legit d/ Diego Martinez & Marcelina Montaño, residents; gp/ Juan Jose Lusero & Gertrudis Chavez.

Frames 1418-1419
NS, Faustina
bap 20 Feb 1833, 6 days old; d/ unknown parents, left at the house of Vitalia Apodaca, vecina; gp/ Agustin Leal & Guadalupe Garcia.

BARRIOS, Maria Antonia
Bap 20 Feb 1833, 6 days old; legit d/ Jose Barrios & Juana Carabajal, residents; Antonio Jose (Armijo) & Placida Armijo.

TORRES, Maria Polonia
bap 20 Feb 1833, 6 days old; legit d/ Juan Torres & Ysabel Gutierrez, residents; gp/ Anastacio Lusero & Juana Duran.

FLORES, Blas
bap 20 Feb 1833, 15 days old; s/ Miguel Flores & Marcelina Savedra, residents; gp/ Ramon Gallego & Gertrudis Gallego.

Frame 1420, #109
SALAZAR, Jose Deciderio
bap 20 Feb 1833, 9 days old; s/ Juan Salazar & Ramona Sanchez, residents; ap/ Torribio Salazar & Apolonaria Gutierres; am/ Jose Sanchez & Gregoria Rael; gp/ Mariano (Salazar) & Maria de Jesus Salazar.

NS, Maria Ramona
bap 20 Feb 1833, 11 days old; d/ unknown parents, left at the house of Guadalupe Otero, vecina; gp/ Guadalupe Otero & Miguel Lopez.

GARCIA, Maria Eleuteria
bap 20 Feb 1833, 3 days old; d/ Antonio Garcia & Juana Saez; gp/ Bernabe Hernandez & Juana Gonsales.

Frame 1421
GONSALES, Jose Miguel
bap 20 Feb 1833, 6 days old; s/ Juan Gonsales & Maria de Jesus Moya, residents; gp/ Juan Miguel (Garcia) & Juana Garcia.

APODACA, Pedro Antonio
bap 20 Feb 1833, 5 days old; s/ Juan Antonio Apodaca & Petra Duran, residents; gp/ Alexandro Duran & Quiteria Garcia.

GUTIERREZ, Maria Gertrudis
bap 20 Feb 1833, 5 days old; d/ Esteban Gutierrez & Quiteria Montoya, residents; gp/ Antonio Jose Lusero & Gertrudis Lucero.

Frames 1421-1422, #110
ARMIJO, Maria de Jesus del Refugio
bap 20 Feb 1833, b. 7 Jan 1833; d/ Pablo Armijo & Sofia Sandoval, residents; ap/ Francisco Armijo & Francisca Gonzales; am/ Manuel Sandoval & Maria Antonia Valencia; gp/ Don Visente Armijo & Doña Maria de Jesus Otero.

GARCIA, Ramon Antonio
bap 215 Feb 1833, 11 days old; s/ Pablo Garcia & Antonia Martines, residents; gp/ Juan Miguel Castillo & Rosalia Martinez.

SANCHEZ, Jose Nestor
bap 3 Mar 1833, 3 days old; legit s/ Mariano Sanchez & Juana Lopez, residents; ap/ Felipe Sanchez & Ynez Garcia; am/ Jose Maria Lopez & Barbara Baca; gp/ Don Cristobal Pacheco & Doña Petra Maldonado.

MARES, Juan Cristobal
bap 4 Mar 1833, 6 days old; s/ Juan Mares & Gertrudis Griego, residents; ap/ Jose Maria Mares & Rita Perea; am/ Lorenso Griego & Guadalupe Candelaria; gp/ Jose Antonio Martin & Teodora Garcia.

Frame 1423
CHAVEZ, Jose Gabriel Eleuterio
bap 4 Mar 1833, 12 days old; s/ Blas Chavez & Gertrudis Sandoval, residents; ap/ Juan Miguel Chaves & Guadalupe Rael; am/ Lorenso Sandoval & Juana Garcia; gp/ Diego Antonio Chaves & Maria Ygnacia Montoya.

GARCIA, Antonio Jose Casimiro
bap 4 Mar 1833, 2 days old; s/ Francisco Garcia & Manuela Carrillo; ap/ Francisco Garcia & Manuela Gonzales; am/ Juan Carrillo & Ygnacia Armenta, all residents; gp/ Juan Bautista Castillo & Juana Catarina Garcia de Noriega.

NOANES, Antonio Toribio
bap 4 Mar 1833, 3 days old; s/ Felipe Noanes & Manuela Montaño; ap/ Geronimo Noanes & Barbara Maese; am/ Toribio Montaño & Josefa Apodaca; gp/ Visente Gonzales & Bibiana Chaves.

Frames 1423-1424, #111
CANDELARIA, Francisca Antonia
bap 5 Mar 1833, 3 days old; d/ Julian Candelaria & Francisca Antonia Noanes, residents; gp/ Atanacio Gallego & Guadalupe Garcia.

SANCHES, Maria Rufina
bap 5 Mar 1833, 9 days old; d/ Diego Sanches & Juana Maria Gallego, residents; gp/ Juan Domingo Valencia & Maria Paula Martines.

CANDELARIA, Jose Francisco
bap 6 Mar 1833, 9 days old; s/ Francisco Candelaria & Lorenza Padilla, residents; gp/ Juan Eusebio Griego & Ysidora Garcia.

GARCIA, Juana Maria
bap 8 Mar 1833, 2 days old; d/ Juan Pablo Garcia & Gregoria Garcia; ap/ Juan Garcia & Juana Barbara NS; am/ Juan Jose Garcia & Francisca Gonsales; gp/ Jose Ygnacio Gallegos & Juana Armijo.

Frame 1425
CHAVEZ, Maria Francisca
bap 9 Mar 1833, 4 days old; d/ Rafael Chavez & Juana Nepomucena Apodaca; ap & am/ not stated; gp/ Jose Antonio Montoya & Juana Maria Chavez.

CHAVEZ, Maria Benigna
bap 11 Mar 1833, 4 days old; d/ Juan Chavez & Ysidora Chavez; ap/ Domingo Chavez & Manuela Aguirre; am/ Antonio Chavez & Manuela Garcia, all residents; gp/ Juan Chavez & Dolores Chavez.

LUNA, Maria Rafaela (of Alameda)
bap 12 Mar 1833, 3 days old; d/ Diego Luna & Paula Perea, residents of Alameda; ap/ Bernardo Luna & Catalina Garcia; am/ Francisco Perea & Manuela Candelaria; gp/ Juan Antonio Rael & Rafaela Rael.

Frame 1426, #112
GONZALES, Jose Gregorio
bap 17 Mar 1833, 7 days old; s/ Juan Miguel Gonzales & Juana Mora, residents; gp/ Jose Martin & Soledad Martin.

LOPEZ, Jose Gregorio
bap 17 Mar 1833, 5 days old; s/ Lasaro Lopez & Gertrudis Santillanes, residents; ap/ Jesus Lopez & Barbara Jaramillo; am/ Guadalupe Santillanes & Micaela Carrillo; gp/ Jose Maria Sandoval & Teresa Luna.

Frames 1426-1427
MONTOYA, Maria Antonia Altagracia
bap 17 Mar 1833, 8 days old; d/ Luis Montoya & Guadalupe Martines; gp/ Ygnacio Mondragon & Maria Antonia Martines.

GARCIA, Antonio Jose
bap 18 Mar 1833, 15 days old; legit s/ Francisco Antonio Garcia & Maria Bernardina Apodaca, residents of Tome; ap/ Jose Garcia & Margarita Aragon; am/ Juan Gregorio Apodaca & Barbara Noanes; gp/ Antonio Jose Garcia & Maria Asencion Lopez.

CARRIYO, Antonio Jose
bap 19 Mar 1833, 3 days old; s/ Santiago Carriyo & Lugarda Gutierres, residents; ap/ Miguel Carriyo & Bernarda Brito; am/ Juan Manuel Burtierres & Trinidad Gonsales; gp/ Juan Bautista Carriyo & Juana Casarina Garcia.

Frame 1428, #113
ROMERO, Jose Mateo
bap 20 Mar 1833, 8 days old; legit s/ Lino Romero & Josefa Garcia, residents; ap/ Luis Jose Romero & Juana Aragon; am/ Antonio Jose Silva & Ana Maria Garcia; gp/ Pablo Chaves & Dolores Lial.

NS, Juana Lorenza
bap 23 Mar 1833, 2 days old; d/ unknown parents; gp/ Manuel Romero & Maria Petra Apodaca.

Frames 1428-1429
MARES, Maria Faviana de la Encarnacion
bap 25 Apr 1833, 3 days old; d/ Luis Mares & Teresa Garcia; ap/ Francisco Mares & Juana Garcia; am/ NN Garcia & Tomasa Olguin; gp/ Juan Tomas Aragon & Maria Gertudis Garcia.

CANDELARIA, Maria Encarnacion
bap 29 Mar 1833, 4 days old; legit d/ Visente Candelaria & Ana Maria Chaves, residents; ap/ Francisco Candelaria & Maria de la Lus Armijo; am/ Geronimo Chaves & Encarnacion Gonzales; gp/ Ygnacio Candelaria & Luiza Garcia.

NS, Maria Josefa Altagracia
bap 29 Mar 1833, 2 days old; d/ unknown parents; gp/ Antonio Jose Candelaria & Maria Josefa Pacheco.

Frames 1429-1430, #114
ROMERO, Jose Anastacio
bap 4 Apr 1833, 7 days old; legit s/ Antonio Romero & Guadalupe Garcia, residents; ap/ Miguel Antonio Romero & Juana Garcia; am/ Jose Candelaria & Francisca Garcia; gp/ Baltazar Montaño & Maria Juana Garcia.

GRIEGO, Maria Veneranda
bap 7 Apr 1833, 7 days old; d/ Jose Eusevio Griego & Maria Ysidora Garcia; ap/ Juan Braulio Griego & Maria Ysavel Garcia; am/ Francisco Garcia & Guadalupe Otero; gp/ Antonio Garcia & Maria Ysavel Gayego.

GARCIA, Maria Graviela de Jesus
bap 7 Apr 1833; legit d/ Simon Garcia & Josefa Otero, residents; ap/ Santiago Otero & Maria Padiya; am/ Julian Otero & Maria Antonia Griego; gp/ Juan Jose Jaramiyo & Trinidad Otero.

Frame 1431
NS, Francisco Antonio
bap 8 Apr 1833, 6 days old; s/ unknown parents; gp/ Dolores Garcia & Manuela Sanches.

ANZURES, Jose Dionicio
bap 8 Apr 1833, 2 days old; legit s/ Rafael Anzures & Mariana Lopez, residents; ap/ Juan Anzures & Barbara Garcia; am/ Pascual Lopes & Rosa Garcia; gp/ Jose Armijo & Barbara Ortiz.

SANCHES, Jesus Ysidoro
bap 10 Apr 1833, 6 days old; legit s/ Gabriel Sanches & Maria Juana Sediyo, residents; ap/ Felipe Sanches & Maria Ynes Garcia; am/ Torivio Sediyo & Vitoria Maldonado; gp/ Juan Andres Moya & Simona Sanchez.

Frame 1432, #115
PEREA, Juan Ygnacio de Jesus
bap 10 Apr 1833, 2 days old; legit s/ Manuel Perea & Gertrudis Gurule, residents; ap/ Jose Manuel Perea & Rosalia Duran; am/ Antonio Gurule & Antonia Montoya; gp/ Bernardo Perea & Francisca Perea.

NS, Maria Luiza
bap 10 Apr 1833, 3 days old; d/ unknown parents; gp/ Christobal Jaramiyo & Maria Antonia Jaramiyo.

LUJAN, Maria Lorenza
bap 11 Apr 1833, 5 days old; legit d/ Miguel Lujan & Rita Sandobal, parishioners; ap/ Juan Antonio Lujan & Candelaria Lucero; am/ Miguel Sandobal & Martina Lucero; gp/ Juan Christobal Gurule & Maria Lorensa Rela.

Frame 1433
GURULE, Jose Agapito
bap 11 Apr 1833, 22 days old; legit s/ Juan Christobal Gurule & Maria Ygnacia Martines, parishioners; ap/ Jose Gurule & Maria Catarina Medina; am/ Jose Antonio Martines & Josefa Montolla; gp/ Jose Maria Lucero & Rosalia Lucero.

SERNA, Maria Petra de Jesus
bap 12 Apr 1833, 6 days old; legit s/ Salbador Serna & Barbara Gutierres, parishioners; ap/ Jose Antonio Serna & Maria Francisca Gutierres; am/ not stated; gp/ Matheo Lopez & Maria Petra Gutierres.

CANDELARIA, Maria Ysabel
bap 14 Apr 1833, 3 days old; legit d/ Enrrique Candelaria & Ysabel Garcia, parishioners; ap/ Antonio Candelario & Manuela Herrera; am/ Juan Jesus Garcia & Rose Sabedra; gp/ Felis Garcia & Maria Ygnacia Candelaria.

Frame 1434, #116
CANDELARIO, Maria de los Dolores
bap 16 Apr 1833, 12 days old; legit d/ Jose Candelario & Dolores Gutierres, parishioners; ap/ Salbador Candelario & Maria Chabes; am/ Antonio Gutierres & Ysidora Garcia; gp/ Juan Eusebio Griego & Ysidora Garcia.

MONTOLLA, Manuel Antonio
bap 17 Apr 1833, 7 days old; legit s/ Juan Montolla & Manuela Garcia, parishioners; ap/ Felipe Montolla & Juana Garcia; am/ Juan Acensio Garcia & Barbara Chabes; gp/ Felipe Herrera & Juana Garcia.

APODACA, Jose Antonio
bap 18 Apr 1833, 3 days old; legit s/ Pablo Apodaca & Ysabel Sarracino, parishioners; ap/ Jose Antonio Apodaca & Ysabel Martines; am/ Jose Guadalupe Sarracino & Dolores Torres; gp/ Jose Antonio Sandobal & Dolores Tapia.

Frame 1435
LOBATO, Anna Maria Meregilda
bap 18 Apr 1833, 6 days old; legit d/ Juan Lobato & Manuela Mestas, parishioners; ap/ Juan Lobato & Maria Casias; am/ Ygnacio Mestas & Maria Guadalupe Ortis; gp/ Don Juan Armijo & Doña Anna Maria Gabaldon.

LUCERO, David Aniceto
bap 18 Apr 1833, 2 days old; s/ Andres Lucero & Tomasa Garcia, parishioners; ap/ Manuel Lucero & Barbara Montolla; am/ Tomas Garcia & Juana Chabes; gp/ Nicola Lucero & Maria Gertrudis Lucero.

GONZALES, Juan Antonio
bap 21 Apr 1833, 8 days old; legit s/ Juan Gonzales & Anna Maria Sandobal, parishioners; ap/ Gaspar Gonsales & Anna Maria Rael; am/ Lorenzo Sandobal & Maria Sentena; gp/ Juan Antonio Truxillo & Juana Montolla.

Frame 1436, #117
PADILLA, Juan Jose Ramon
bap 23 Apr 1833, 4 days old; legit s/ Jose Manuel Padilla & Maria Antonia Otero, parishioners; ap & am/ not stated; gp/ Ramon Pino & Petra Pino.

BURTIERRES, Cayetano Prudencio
bap 28 Apr 1833, 2 days old; legit s/ Juan Burtierres & Francisca Anaya, parishioners; ap/ Miguel Gutierres & Maria Niebes Chaves; am/ Manuel Anaya & Maria Antonia Apodaca; gp/ Cayetano Suares & Maria Antonia Belasques.

Frames 1436-1437
GAYEGO, Maria Loreta de la Trinidad
bap 28 Apr 1833, 16 days old; legit d/ Christoval Gayego & Maria del Carmen Gutieres, parishioners; ap/ Jose Gallego & Josefa Baca; am/ Juan Miguel Gutierres & Maria Niebes Salazar, gp/ Don Tomas Geneds & Maria de la Luz Bazan,

GUTIERRES, Maria Francisca de la Trinidad
bap 5 May 1833, 8 days old; legit d/ Leonardo Gutierres & Soledad Garcia, parishioners; ap & am/ not stated; gp/ Juan Jose Sanches & Rafaela Ruiz.

NS, Juana Maria de la Cruz
bap 5 May 1833, 4 days old; d/ unknown parents; gp/ Pablo Lujan & Juana Jaramiyo.

Frames 1437-1438, #118
APODACA, Maria Monica
bap 7 May 1833, 3 days old; legit d/ Julian Apodaca & Antonia Griego, parishioners; ap/ Jose Apodaca & Madelena Perea; am/ Miguel Griego & Petrona Candelaria; gp/ Ygnacio Gayego & Juana Armijo.

GONZALES, Maria Josefa
bap 7 May 1833, 4 days old; legit d/ Francisco Gonzales & Maria Antonia Garvizo, parishioners; ap/ Felipe Gonzales & Maria de la Luz Gurule; am/ Francisco Garvizo & Maria de la Luz Garcia; gp/ Antonio Brito Gonzales & Maria de Jesus Nieto.

JARAMIYO, Jesus de la Cruz
bap 7 May 1833, 5 days old; legit s/ Agustin Jaramiyo & Francisca Garcia, parishioners; ap/ Juan Jaramiyo & Rosa Butierres; am/ Juan de Jesus Garcia & Rosa Savedra; gp/ Clemente Sarracino & Dolores Sarracino.

Frame 1439
GRIEGO, Jose Estanislao
bap 7 May 1833, 4 days old; legit s/ Manuel Griego & Catarina Samora, parishioners; ap/ Blas Griego & Maria Roza Chaves; am/ Juan Francisco Samora & Ygnasia Balencia; gp/ Andres Montaño & Maria Ygnasia Balencia.

NS, Jose Gregorio
bap 11 May 1833, 10 days old; s/ unknown parents; gp/ Jose Tomas Griego & Maria Monica Santiyanes.

CANDELARIA, Jose de los Dolores
bap 11 May 1833, 2 days old; legit s/ Ygnacio Candelaria & Maria Manuela Anaya, parishioners; ap/ Juan Candelaria & Tresa Chaves; am/ Pedro Anaya & Dolores Lopes; gp/ Juan Nepomuceno Sanchez & Maria Antonia Sanches.

Frame 1440, #119
GONZALES, Maria Antonia
bap 12 May 1833, 3 days old; legit d/ Jose Maria Gonzales & Gertrudis Garcia, parishioners; ap/ Leonicio Gonzales & Dolores Garcia; am/ Antonio Garzia & Margarita Rael; gp/ Pablo Trigiyo & Maria Micaela Trigiyo.

LUSERO, Maria Gregoria
bap 12 May 1833, 3 days old; d/ Jose Ygnacio Lusero & Maria Dolores Romero; ap/ Miguel Luzero & Maria Dimas Aragon; am/ Jose Romero & Rafaela Montoya; gp/ Jasinto Sanches & Maria Gregoria Rael.

SAIS, Juan Domingo
bap 4 May 1833, 3 days old; legit s/ Alfonso Sais & Juana Garzia, parishioners; ap/ Jose Sais & Juana Chaves; am/ Julian Garcia & Gertrudis Gayego; gp/ Jose Antonio Garcia & Tomasa Olguin.

Frame 1441
BACA, Maria Eluteria
bap 14 May 1833, 9 days old; legit d/ Pablo Baca & Begnina Burtierres, parishioners; ap/ Reyes Baca & Manuela Archuleta; am/ Rafael Burtierres & Josefa Mares; gp/ Jose Lusero & Maria Encarnacion Gurule.

CARAVAJAL, Jose Ysidro de Jesus
bap 17 May 1833, 3 days old; legit s/ Domingo Caravajal & Torivia Sanchez, parishioners; ap/ Faustino Caravajal & Barbara Lopes; am/ Jose Sanches & Tomasa Lopes; gp/ Rafael Garcia & Dolores Chaves.

Frame 1442, #120
SANCHES, Ysidro de la Trinidad
bap 18 May 1833, 4 days old; legit s/ Domingo Sanches & Perfecta Montoya, parishioners; ap/ Diego Antonio Sanches & Maria Ygnacia Anaya; gp/ Miguel Avila & Maria Lugarda Montoya.

NS, Maria Ysidra
bap 19 May 1833, 4 days old; d/ unknown parents; gp/ Andres Montaño & Maria Ygnacia Balencia.

SABEDRA, Maria Rosa
bap 19 May 1833, 8 days old; legit s/ Juan Christobal Sabedra & Monica Garcia, parishioners; ap/ Jose Sabedra & Mariquita Sediyo; am/ Ysidro Garcia & Gertrudis Sanches; gp/ Francisco Perea & Paula Sandoval.

Frame 1443
SARRACINO, Juliana Trinidad
bap 20 May 1833, 6 days old; legit d/ Don Francisco Sarracino & Doña Gertrudis Teyes, parishioners of Ysleta; ap/ Jose Rafael Sarracino & Doña Luiza Burtierres; am/ Julio Teyes & Casilda Baca; gp/ Don Julian Armijo & Doña Mariana Sarracino.

CONTRERAS, Maria Ysidora
bap 23 May 1833, 6 days old; legit d/ Jose Tomas Contreras & Paula Chaves, parishioners; ap/ Florencio Contreras & Anita Garcia; am/ Juan Bautista Chaves & Maria Barbara Armijo; gp/ Juan Bautista & Maria Candelaria Chaves.

Frame 1444, #121
APODACA, Maria Bisenta
bap 23 May 1833, 1 day old; legit d/ Christoval Apodaca & Maria Ysavel Sisnero, parishioners; ap/ Jose Apodaca & Madelena Perea; am/ Francisco Sisnero & Juana Candelaria; gp/ Juan Burtierres & Francisca Anaya.

SERNA, Ana Maria
bap 27 May 1833, 3 days old; legit d/ Tomas Serna & Rafaela Garcia, parishioners; ap/ Ysidro Garcia & Antonia Serna; am/ Juan Garcia & Maria Niebes Solana; gp/ Antonio Martin & Ana Maria Martin.

Frame 1445
ANSURES, Maria de la Asencion
bap 27 May 1833, 2 days old; legit d/ Luciano Ansures & Manuela Otero, parishioners; ap/ Pablo Rafael Ansures & Maria Lorenza Anaya; am/ Juan Jose Otero & Maria Manuela Garcia; gp/ Miguel Antonio Lujan & Rita Sandoval.

TRUGIYO, Maria Polinaria
bap 27 May 1833, 15 days old; legit d/ Juan Trugiyo & Manuela Apodaca, parishioners; ap/ Miguel Trugiyo & Antonia Dolores Garzia; am/ Jose Apodaca & Maria Gertrudes Lopes; gp/ Ygnacio Trugiyo & Maria Rita Lujan.

Frames 1445-1446, #122
VAYEJOS, Maria Felipa
bap 27 May 1833, 3 days old; legit d/ Juaquin Vayejos & Francisca Candelaria, parishioners; ap/ Patricio Mariano Bayejos & Teresa Cordova; am/ Tomas Candelaria & Ursula Hernandes; gp/ Marcos Jaramiyo & Ana Maria de Jesus Garcia.

SANCHES, Maria Teodoria Marcelina
bap 2 Jun 1833, 8 days old; legit d/ Salvador Sanches & Olaya Tafoya, parishioners; ap/ Bartolo Sanches & Rafaela Lopes; am/ Juan Ygnacio Tafoya & Maria Antonia Baca; gp/ Marcos Ruiz & Balbina Jaramiyo.

Frames 1446-1447
BARELA, Maria Petronila de los Dolores
bap 2 Jun 1833, 3 days old; legit s/ Antonio Abad Barela & Catarina Ortiz; ap/ Juan Barela & Josefa Chaves; am/ Lorenso Ortiz & Rafaela Ortiz; gp/ Rafael Garcia & Dolores Savedra.

LOVATO, Jesus Marcelino (twin)
bap 2 Jun 1833, 8 days old; legit s/ Francisco Lovato & Paula Perea; ap/ Christoval Lovato & Maria Roza Garcia; am/ Rafael Perea & Carmen Romero; gp/ Tomas Candelaria & Gertrudis Gavaldon. [Note: See also LOVATO, Jose de Jesus.]

Frames 1447-1448, #123
LOVATO, Jose de Jesus (twin)
bap 2 Jun 1833, 8 days old; legit / Francisco Lovato & Paula Perea, parishioners; ap/ Christoval Lovato & Maria Roza Garcia; am/ Rafael Perea & Carmen Romero; gp/ Don Visente Domingues & Doña Sesaria Cazares. [Note: See also LOVATO, Jesus Marcelino.]

GARCIA, Maria Josefa
bap 3 Jun 1833, 7 days old; legit d/ Juan Poseño Garcia & Victoria Garcia, parishioners; ap/ Juan Antonio Garcia & Josefa Valdonado; am/ Juan Garcia & Maria de los Niebes Zolano; gp/ Julian Sanches & Juana Catarina Candelaria.

CASTIYO, Antonio Jose
bap 6 Jun 1833, 15 days old; legit s/ Juan Miguel Castiyo & Rozalia Martin, parishioners; ap/ Antonio Jose Castiyo & Quiteria Chaves; am/ Ysidro Martin & Dorotea Griego; gp/ Juan Castiyo & Catarina Garcia.

Frame 1449
SANDOBAL, Antonio Maria Panfilo
bap 9 Jun 1833, 6 days old; s/ Antonio Sandobal & Maria Decideria Candelaria; ap/ Patricio Miguel Sandoval & Maria Manuela Gurule; am/ Esteban Candelaria & Maria de Jesus Luna; gp/ Miguel Luna & Maria Anastacia Lucero.

GARCIA, Noberto de Jesus Feliciano
bap 9 Jun 1833, 3 days old; legit s/ Juan Garcia & Yzabel Gurule, parishioners; ap/ Miguel Griego & Josefa Arias; gp/ Francisco Aranda & Manuela Barela.

Frames 1449-1450, #124
APODACA, Maria Antonia de Jesus
bap 9 Jun 1833, 3 days old; legit d/ Jose Antonio Apodaca & Barbara Benabides, parishioners; am/ Manuel Benabides & Pasquala Gallego; gp/ Antonio Carriyo & Juana Jaramiyo.

JARAMIYO, Manuel Antonio
bap 11 Jun 1833, 1 day old; legit s/ Miguel Jaramiyo & Estefana Herrera, parishioners; ap/ Miguel Jaramiyo & Gertrudis Candelaria; am/ Bisente Herrera & Maria Antonia Montaño; gp/ Juan Chabes & Micaela Sanches.

Frames 1450-1451
LUSERO, Margarita de Jesus
bap 11 Jun 1833, 1 day old; legit d/ Francisco Lusero & Ynes Montoya, parishioners; ap/ Juan Lusero & Maria Antonia Martin; am/ Juan Montoya (only); gp/ Jose Gonzales & Maria Juana Lucero.

ARANDA, Antonio Jose Bernabe
bap 11 Jun 1833, 3 days old; legit s/ Juan Christobal Aranda & Soledad Armijo, parishioners; ap/ Antonio Aranda & Antonia Tereza Garcia; am/ Santiago Armijo & Petra Perea; gp/ Francisco Ortega & Ygnacia Basan.

JARAMIYO, Juan Christobal Bernabe
bap 14 Jun 1833, 4 days old; legit s/ Manuel Jaramiyo & Gertrudis Mestas, parishioners; ap/ Jose Miguel Jaramillo & Ana Maria Ortega; am/ Mariano Mestas & Guadalupe Valencia; gp/ Juan Armijo & Juana Maria Chabes.

Frames 1451-1452, #125
LOPES, Maria del Refugio
bap 22 Jun 1833, 7 days old; d/ Francisco Lopes & Francisca Luna; ap/ Paulin Lopes & Anita Montaño; am/ Manuela Candelaria & Ysidro Luna; gp/ Juan Rafael Garcia & Manuela Muñiz.

GARCIA, Maria Getrudis
bap 23 Jun 1833, 4 days old; legit d/ Manuel Garcia & Ysabel Apodaca; ap/ Juan Christobal Garcia & Rafaela Gonzales; am/ Juan Nicolas Apodaca & Maria de la Luz Garcia; gp/ Antonio Jose Sanches & Rosalia Martin.

Frames 1452-1453
MONTOYA, Juana Candida de los Dolores
bap 25 Jun 1833, 2 days old; legit d/ Francisco Montoya & Jesusa Armijo, parishioners; ap/ Pablo Montoya & Maria de los Reyes Garcia; am/ Lucas Armijo & Barbara Ortis; gp/ Jose Armijo & Ana Maria Ruiz.

MONTOYA, Maria Marcelina Maxicima
bap 28 June 1833, 4 days old; legit d/ Rafael Montoya & Gertrudis Chabes, parishioners; ap/ Blas Montoya & Maria Luiza Padilla; am/ Agustin Chaves & Juana Sanches; gp/ Luciano Sediyo & Monica Lobera.

Frames 1453-1454, #126
APODACA, Maria Petra de los Dolores
bap 28 Jun 1833, 2 days old; legit d/ Francisco Apodaca & Tomaza Barrela, parishioners; ap/ Jose Apodaca & Gertrudis Lusero; am/ Juan Barrela & Maria Josefa Chabes; gp/ Rafael Apodaca & Barbara Molina.

LUSERO, Maria Marcelina
bap 30 Jun 1833, 3 days old; legit d/ Miguel Lusero & Andrea Pacheco, parishioners; ap/ Juan de Jesus Lusero & Juzta Pino; am/ Francisco Pacheco & Marta Sandobal; gp/ Juan Antonio Trugiyo & Juana Maria Montoya.

GARCIA, Maria Marciala de los Dolores
bap 30 Jun 1833, 1 day old; legit d/ Salbador Garcia & Guadalupe Armijo, parishioners; ap/ Pedro Garcia & Ana Maria Lopes; am/ Santiago Armijo & Rosalia Chabes; gp/ Tomas Candelaria & Gertrudis Gabaldon.

Frame 1455
SAIS, Maria Soledad
bap 19 Jul 1833, 6 days old; legit d/ Jose Sais & Maria Martina Trugillo, parishioners; ap/ Salbador Sais & Juana Aragon; am/ Mariano Trugillo & Maria Luiza Cordoba; gp/ Jesus Maria Trujillo & Rosalia Mariño.

GALLEGO, Juzto Rufino
bap 25 Jul 1833, 2 days old; legit s/ Juan Antonio Gallego & Petra Lopez, parishioners; ap/ Juan Tafolla & Soledad Gallego; am/ Bernardo Lopez & Relles Lujan; gp/ Manuela Antonia Sandobal.

SANCHES, Santiago
bap 28 Jul 1833, 4 days old; legit s/ Domingo Sanches & Maria de la Luz Perea, parishioners; ap/ Jose Sanches & Mariquita Griego; am/ Francisco Perea & Manuela Candelaria; gp/ Jose Maria Sandobal & Tereza Luna.

Frame 1456, #127
CHABES, Manuel Antonio
bap 31 Jul 1833, 3 days old; legit s/ Jose Dolores Chabes & Nicanora Garcia, parishioners; ap/ Xavier Gabriel Chabes & Maria de Jesus Armijo; am/ Jose de Jesus Garcia & Rosa Sabedra; gp/ Manuel Herrera & Begnina Chabes.

BACA Ana Maria de Jesus
bap 3 Jul 1833, 7 days old; legit d/ Ramon Baca & Maria Gertrudis Garcia, parishioners; ap/ Diego Baca & Dolores Leyba; am/ Francisco Garcia & Maria Jesus Sais; gp/ Diego Garcia & Ramona Candelario.

GONSALES, Juan Ygnacio
bap 4 Aug 1833, 5 days old; legit s/ Antonio Gonsales & Juana Sandobal, parishioners; ap/ Nerio Gonsales & Maria Griego; am/ Miguel Sandobal & Ygnacia Armenta; gp/ Domingo Griego & Margarita Gonsales.

Frame 1457
NS, Jose Francisco
bap 5 Aug 1833, 1 day old; s/ unknown parents, left at the home of Jose Garcia; gp/ Juan Cristobal Sabedra & Doña Monica Garcia.

Frames 1458-1459 – Priest Notation

Frame 1460, #129
SANDOBAL, Maria Juana Tiburcia del Rallo
bap 11 Aug 1833, 1 day old; legit d/ Francisco Sandobal & Maria Getrudis Garcia, parishioners; ap/ Jose Sandobal & Petrona Sabedra; am/ Braulia Garcia; gp/ Ygnacio Ruiz & Maria Ysidora Lopes.

Frames 1460-1461
GONSALES, Maria Rita
bap 11 Aug 1833, 1 month old; legit d/ Christobal Gonsales & Manuela Garcia, parishioners; ap/ Fernando Gonsales & Dorotea Griego; am/ Francisco Garcia & Manuela Gonsales; gp/ Antonio Garcia & Juana Sais.

GARCIA, Juan Christobal Nicolas
bap 12 Aug 1833, 2 days old; legit s/ Juan Guadalupe Garcia & Dolores Candelaria, parishioners; ap/ Manuel Garcia & Maria Ygnacia Analla; am/ Jose Tomas Candelaria & Ana Maria Griego; gp/ Christobal Pacheco & Petra Baldonado.

BURTIERRES; Antonio Jose
bap 12 Aug 1833, 4 days old; legit s/ Antonio Burtierres & Luperta Lopes, parishioners; ap/ Antonio Burtierres & Francisca Sanches; am/ Mateo Lopes & Maria Manuela Chabes; gp/ Juan Padilla & Rozala Chabes.

Frame 1462, #130
DURAN, Antonio Jose
bap 18 Aug 1833, 1 day old; legit s/ Salbador Duran & Soledad Perea, parishioners; ap/ Miguel Duran & Ynes Griego; am/ Francisco Perea & Feliciana Martines; gp/ Pedro Candelaria & Dolores Duran.

LOPES, Ysidra Anastacia
bap 18 Aug 1833, 1 day old; legit d/ Carlos Lopes & Barbara Contreras, parishioners; ap/ Manuel Lopes & Encarnacion Duran; am/ Florencio Contreras & Anita Estrada; gp/ Juan Chabes & Ysidera Chabes.

Frames 1462-1463
BALENCIA, Juan Esteban
bap 18 Aug 1833, 3 days old; s/ Juan Balencia & Guadalupe Candelaria, parishioners; ap/ not stated; am/ Grabiel Candelaria & Francisca Jaramillo; gp/ Jose Maria Mares & Maria Rita Perea.

BACA, Maria Rafaela
bap 18 Aug 1833, 1 day old; legit d/ Simon Baca & Lorenza Candelaria, parishioners; ap/ not stated; am/ Andres Griego & Barbara Candelaria; gp/ Rafael Lopes & Maria Luiza Chabes.

CANDELARIA, Maria del Rallo Gregoria
bap 24 Aug 1833, 2 days old; legit d/ Pablo Candelaria & Madalegna Garcia, parishioners; ap & am/ not stated; gp/ Juan Pablo Candelaria & Ana Gregoria Garcia.

Frame 1464, #131
GONZALES, Jose Antonio
bap 25 Aug 1833, 5 days old; legit s/ Antonio Gonzales & Maria Garcia, parishioners; ap/ Jose Antonio Gonzales & Maria Barbara Candelaria; am/ Francisco Garcia & Soledad Lopes; gp/ Jose Ramon Mares & Ana Maria Noanes.

LOURIANO, Jesus Maria y Jose
bap 27 Aug 1833, 7 days old; legit s/ Manuel Louriano & Cruz Romero, parishioners; ap/ Jose Louriano & Maria Antonia Caravajal; am/ Francisco Romero & Dolores Garcia; gp/ Bentura Apodaca & Dolores Torres.

ROMERO, Jesus Maria y Jose
bap 2 Sep 1833, 3 days old; legit s/ Baltazar Romero & Paula Lusero, parishioners; ap/ Miguel Antonio Romero & Juana Garcia; am/ Diego Lusero & Julian Sandobal; gp/ Juan Pablo Garcia & Ana Gregoria Garcia.

Frame 1465
NS, Maria Ramona
bap 2 Sep 1833, 1 day old; d/ unknown parents, left at the home of Don Manuel Armijo; gp/ Don Juan Armijo & Doña Ana Maria Gabaldon.

CANDELARIA, Maria del Rallo de los Dolores
bap 2 Sep 1833, 2 days old; legit d/ Rafael Candelaria & Maria Antonia Garcia, parishioners; ap/ Antonio Candelaria & Antonia Garcia; am/ Felis Garcia & Maria Ysabel Lopes; gp/ Jose Rafael Garcia & Dolores Sabedra.

SEDILLO, Maria Regina
bap 7 Sep 1833, 2 days old; legit d/ Julian Sedillo & Maria Sipriana Garcia, parishioners; ap/ Antonio Sedillo & Antonia Baca; am/ Francisco Garcia & Guadalupe Otero; gp/ Felipe Herrera & Juana Garcia.

GARCIA, Maria de Jesus
bap 24 Sep 1833, 6 days old; legit d/ Jose Bisente Garcia & Maria Paula Chabes, parishioners; ap/ unknown; am/ Juan Chabes & Barbara Armijo; gp/ Don Jesus Lucero & Doña Maria de Jesus Lucero.

Frame 1466, #132
BURTIERRES, Felipe
bap 20 Sep 1833, 3 days old; legit s/ Jose Antonio Burtierres & Yzabel Griego, parishioners; ap/ not stated; am/ Jose Griego & Gertrudis Balencia; gp/ Felipe Duran & Juana Gonzales.

NS, Atanasio Mateo
bap 25 Sep 1833, 4 days old; s/ unknown parents, left at the home of Esteban Candelaria; gp/ Julian Sanches & Catarina Candelaria.

BURTIERRES, Maria del Rayo
bap 27 Sep 1833, 5 days old; legit d/ Francisco Burtierres & Manuela Cordoba, parishioners; ap/ Francisco Burtierres & Maria Antonia Zalasar; am/ Marcos Cordoba & Rafaela Salazar; gp/ Don Roque Chabes & Doña Bibiana Chabes.

Frame 1467
MORALES, Jose Miguel
bap 29 Sep 1833, 3 days old; legit s/ Jose Antonio Morales & Juana Garcia, parishioners; ap & am/ not stated; gp/ Bibian Sabedra & Doña Eulogia Sabedra.

GABALDON, Jose Consausion
bap 29 Sep 1833, 1 day old; legit s/ Pomuceno Gabaldon & Barbara Mestas, parishioners; ap/ Jose Miguel Gabaldon & Maria Guadalupe Chabes; am/ Ygnacio Mestas & Guadalupe Ortiz; gp/ Don Jose Maria Montoya & Doña Clara Armijo.

NS, Jesus Maria
bap 3 Oct 1833, 1 day old; d/ unknown parents, left at the home of Ynes Lopes; gp/ Don Mariano Armijo & Doña Antonia Ortiz.

SALAZAR, Maria Francisca
bap 6 Oct 1833, 3 days old; legit d/ Lucas Salazar & Maria Rosalia Ginzo, parishioners; ap/ Julian Salazar & Gertrudes Aragon; am/ Jose Pablo Ginzo & Gertrudes Gonsales; gp/ Ramon Ginzo & Gertrudis Gonzales.

Frames 1467-1468, #133
NS, Jose Telesfor
bap 7 Oct 1833, 15 days old; s/ unknown parents, left at the house of Bisente Ferrar Castoreno; gp/ Bisente Ferrar Castoreno & Micaela Chabes.

ARMIJO, Francisco Antonio
bap 8 Oct 1833, 4 days old; legit s/ Manuel Armijo & Soledad Garcia, parishioners; ap/ not stated; am/ Antonio Garcia & Margarita Rael; gp/ Leonicio Apodaca & Maria Eluteria Garcia.

GRIEGO, Jose Ygnacio
bap 11 Oct 1833, 3 days old; legit s/ Juan Ysidro Griego & Bentura Lusero, parishioners; ap/ Francisco Griego & Maria Antonia Serna; am/ Juan Lusero & Maria Antonia Martin; gp/ Jose Gonzales & Ygnacia Montaño.

SANDOBAL, Maria Encarnacion
bap 15 Oct 1833, 15 days old; legit d/ Jose Angel Sandobal & Gertrudis Gonzalez, parishioners; ap/ Miguel Sandobal & Maria Ygnacia Armenta; am/ Antonio Gonzales & Ana Maria Rael; gp/ Antonio Sandobal & Maria Petra Gonzales.

Frames 1468-1469
MUÑIZ, Salbador Antonio
bap 15 Oct 1833, 4 days old; legit s/ Francisco Muñiz & Maria Teodora Sais, parishioners; ap/ Jose Maria Muñiz & Barbara Garcia; am/ not stated; gp/ Antonio Garcia & Rozalia Barrela.

BACA, Maria Francisca
bap 16 Oct 1833, 5 days old; legit d/ Juan Baca & Rafaela Cordoba, parishioners; ap/ Simon Baca & Lorenza Garcia; am/ Nicolas Cordoba & Ygnacia Duran; gp/ Salbador Garcia & Estefana Cordoba.

NS, Maria Dolores
bap 19 Oct 1833; d/ unknown parents, left at the house of Miguel Seberino; gp/ Dolores Lopes.

CORDOBA, Ana Maria de Jesus
bap 19 Oct 1833, 5 days old; legit d/ Diego Cordoba & Juliana Santillanes, parishioners; ap/ Salbador Cordoba & Ana Maria Gonsales; am/ Juan Jose Santillanes & Gertrudis Tafolla; gp/ Pablo Griego.

Frame 1470, #134
MONTOYA, Rumaldo de Jesus
bap 21 Oct 1833, 3 days old; legit s/ Julian Montoya & Dolores Lopes, parishioners; ap/ Luis Montoya & Gregoria Ginzo; am/ not stated; gp/ Ygnacio Ruiz & Maria Ysidora Lopes.

GRIEGO, Pedro Antonio
bap 22 Oct 1833, 2 days old; legit s/ Jose Griego & Monica Santiyanes, parishioners; ap/ Miguel Griego & Petra Candelaria; am/ Antonio Santiyanes & Geralda Garcia; gp/ Diego Garcia & Ramona Candelaria.

CANDELARIA, Maria Edubije
bap 23 Oct 1833, 8 days old; legit d/ Ramon Candelaria & Manuela Martin, parishioners; ap/ Francisco Candelaria & Maria de la Luz Armijo; am/ Baltazar Martin & Maria Antonia Griego; gp/ Ysidro Luna & Maria Teodora Peña.

Frames 1470-1471
HERERA, Maria Juana
bap 23 Oct 1833, 3 days old; legit d/ Jose Herera & Maria Barbara Santillanes, parishioners; ap/ Jose Andres Herera & Dolores Garcia; am/ Miguel Santillanes & Ana Maria Fernandes; gp/ Juan Bautista Lusero & Maria Lorenza Lusero.

TRUGILLO, Maria Petra
bap 23 Oct 1833, 4 days old; legit d/ Antonio Trugillo & Juana Montoya, parishioners; ap/ Juan Jose Trugillo & Maria Luiza Cordoba; am/ Pedro Montoya & Maria Encarnacion Luna; gp/ Jose Sandobal & Maria Terza Luna.

BURTIERRES, Maria de Jesus
bap 24 Oct 1833, 4 days old; legit d/ Juan Burtierres & Juana Mora, parishioners; ap/ Rafael Burtierres & Josefa Mares; am/ Ysidro Mora & Juana Marques; gp/ Juan Christobal Rael & Lorenza Rael.

NS, Maria del Rayo
bap 29 Oct 1833, 8 days old; d/ unknown parents, left at the house of Asencion Montoya; gp/ Jose Analla & Tomaza Tafoya.

Frame 1472, #135
GARCIA, Antonio Nemecio
bap 31 Oct 1833, 5 days old; legit s/ Juan Garcia & Rita Lopez, parishioners; ap/ not stated; am/ Luis Lopez & Antonia Lopez; gp/ Don Marcos Ruiz & Doña Balbina Candelaria.

DURAN, Maria Guadalupe Santos
bap 2 Nov 1833, 3 days old; legit d/ Rafael Duran & Rosa Muñis, parishioners; ap & am/ not stated; gp/ Juan Burtierres & Maria Rita Salasar.

GARCIA, Jose Narcisco
bap 2 Nov 1833, 4 days old; legit s/ Blas Garcia & Francisca Aragon, parishioners; ap/ Andres Garcia & Francisca Tafoya; am/ Tadeo Aragon & Maria Luiza Balencia; gp/ Tadeo Aragon & Maria Luiza Balencia.

Frame 1473
NS, Diego Hilario
bap 3 Nov 1833, 1 day old; s/ unknown parents, left at the house of Don Diego Lopes; gp/ Ysidora Lopes.

GARCIA, Maria Ygnacia
bap 5 Nov 1833, 3 days old; legit d/ Juan Rafael Garcia & Encarnacion Lucero, parishioners; ap/ Juan Rafael Garcia & Manuela Muñiz; am/ Gregorio Lucero & Marta Lopes; gp/ Jose Manuel Aragon & Tereza Candelaria.

BACA, Juan Bautista
bap 5 Nov 1833, 4 days old; legit s/ Diego Baca & Maria Francisca Samora, parishioners; ap/ not stated; am/ Mariano Samora & Rafaela Muñiz; gp/ Baltazar Sabedra & Guadalupe Sabedra.

Frames 1473-1474, #136
BURTIERRES, Maria Antonia
bap 12 Nov 1833, 2 days old; legit d/ Agustin Burtierres & Josefa Gurule, parishioners; ap/ Antonio Burtierres & Antonia Herrera; am/ Bernardo Gurule & Maria Sarafina NS; gp/ Jose Torres & Josefa Lusero.

ABILA, Jesus Maria
bap 15 Nov 1833, 2 days old; legit s/ Miguel Abila & Lugarda Montoya, parishioners; ap/ not stated; am/ Pedro Montoya & Maria Encarnacion Luna; gp/ Don Juan Montoya & Maria de la Luz Lopes.

TORRES, Barbara Antonia
bap 16 Nov 1833, 3 days old; legit d/ Luciano Torres & Maria Gregoria Candelaria, parishioners; ap/ unknown; am/ Christobal Candelaria & Rosalia Garcia; gp/ Tadeo Garcia & Barbara Antonia Griego.

Frame 1475
NS, Maria Teodora
bap 19 Nov 1833, 3 days old; d/ unknown parents, left at the house of Maria Perea; gp/ Mariano Martin & Maria Ledubina Martin.

APODACA, Maria Beneranda de la Trinidad
bap 24 Nov 1833, 4 days old; legit d/ Jose Francisco Apodaca & Maria Garcia, parishioners; am/ Juan Christobal Garcia & Rafaela Aragon; gp/ Don Grabiel Sanches & Doña Clara Sarracino.

GRIEGO, Maria Placida
bap 24 Nov 1833, 2 days old; legit d/ Juan Griego & Estefana Garcia, parishioners; ap & am/ not stated; gp/ Gabriel Sanches & Rafaela Ruiz.

Frame 1476, #137
JARAMILLO, Maria Sicilia
bap 24 Nov 1833, 13 days old; legit d/ Juan Jose Jaramillo & Trinidad Otero, parishioners; ap/ Pablo Jaramillo & Consancion Burtierres; am/ Julian Otero & Manuela Antonia Otero; gp/ Diego Gurule & Tereza Burtierres.

MORA, Bisente Sicilio
bap 24 Nov 1833, 4 days old; legit d/ Luisano Mora & Manuela Antonia Trugillo, parishioners; ap/ Ysidro Mora & Juana Garcia; am/ Juan Trugillo & Manuela Apodaca; gp/ Bisente Gonzales & Juana Garcia.

PACHECO, Juan de Jesus
bap 27 Nov 1833, 5 days old; legit s/ Francisco Pacheco & Juana Gonzales, parishioners; ap/ Francisco Pacheco & Mata Sandobal; am/ Jose Gonzales & Ana Maria Rael; gp/ Jose Bisente Garcia & Paula Chabes.

Frame 1477
GRIEGO, Maria Esozequia de la Trinidad
bap 28 Nov 1833, 3 days old; legit d/ Jose Griego & Maria Manuela Barela, parishioners; ap/ Miguel Griego & Gertrudis Olguin; am/ Santiago Barela & Juana Aranda; gp/ Don Julian Armijo & Doña Mariana Sarracino.

LUNA, Juan de Jesus
bap 29 Nov 1833, 8 days old; legit s/ Francisco de Jesus Luna & Consaupcion Sena, parishioners; ap/ Joaquin Luna & Ana Maria Romero; am/ Francisco Sena & Manuela Martines; gp/ Juan Gonzales & Maria de Jesus Luna.

Frames 1477-1478, #138
CANDELARIA, Pedro Manuel
bap 3 Dec 1833, 2 days old; legit s/ Pedro Candelaria & Dolores Duran, parishioners; ap/ Bernardo Candelaria & Marta Martin; am/ Francisco Duran & Lorenza Ramires; gp/ Jose Torres & Josefa Lucero.

PEREA, Manuel Antonio
bap 4 Dec 1833, 9 days old; legit s/ Salbador Perea & Grabriela Candelaria, parishioners; ap/ Jose Perea & Bictoria Garcia; am/ Ygnacio Candelaria & Consaupcion Chabes; gp/ Diego Antonio Romero & Encarnacion Balencia.

ANALLA, Juan Nicolas
bap 11 Dec 1833, 8 days old; legit s/ Teodoro Analla & Agustina Zamora, parishioners; ap/ Mariano Analla & Felipa Lopes; am/ Antonio Samora & Dolores Apodaca; gp/ Jose Maria Lusero & Maria Gurule.

Frame 1479
MONTAÑO, Jose Concepucion
bap 11 Dec 1833, 3 days old; legit s/ Anisento Montaño & Maria Manuela Gonzales, parishioners; ap/ Jose Montaño & Micaela Santillanes; am/ Juan Christobal Gonzales; gp/ Jose Candelaria & Micaela Candelaria.

NS, Maria de la Luz
bap 12 Dec 1833; d/ unknown parents, Indian of Tinipana nation; gp/ Juan Christobal Ortega & Doña Ygnacia Bazan.

LUJAN, Jesus Rafael
bap 15 Dec 1833, 5 days old; legit s/ Pablo Lujan & Juana Analla, parishioners; ap/ Juan Antonio Lujan & Candelaria Lusero; am/ Pablo Analla & Lorenza Pacheco; gp/ Pablo Armijo & Mariana Lopes.

Frame 1480, #139
ARMIJO, Maria Josefa
bap 16 Dec 1833, 1 day old; legit d/ Don Juan Christobal Armijo & Doña Juana Maria Chabes, parishioners; ap/ Don Juan Armijo & Doña Rosalia Ortega; am/ Don Francisco Chabes & Doña Ana Maria Castillo; gp/ Don Juan Perea & Doña Josefa Chabes.

SANCHES, Maria Ysabel
bap 17 Dec 1833, 2 days old; legit d/ Dolores Sanches & Juana Candelaria, parishioners; ap/ Manuel Sanches & Ana Maria Jaramillo; am/ Pablo Candelaria & Andrea Jaramillo; gp/ Juan Apodaca & Maria Sanches.

GONZALES, Maria Altagracia
bap 17 Dec 1833, 3 days old; legit d/ Don Santiago Gonzales & Doña Maria Angela Aragon, parishioners; ap/ Don Juan Gonsales & Doña Maria Antonia Armijo; am/ Don Manuel Aragon & Doña Mariana Sanchez; gp/ Don Juan Aragon & Doña NN Serrano.

Frame 1481
NS, Bisente Albino de Jesus
bap 18 Dec 1833, 3 days old; s/ unknown parents, placed in house of Doña Antonia Mestas; gp/ Bisente Armijo & Doña Jesus Otero.

BURTIERRES, Jesus Maria
bap 19 Dec 1833, 5 days old; legit s/ Jose Burtierres & Gertrudis Gomes, parishioners; ap/ Juan Lopes & Bernarda Burtierres; am/ Francisco Gomes & Mariana Gomes; gp/ Francisco Candelaria & Manuela Gallego.

JARAMILLO, Juana de los Dolores
bap 19 Dec 1833, 1 day old; legit d/ Sidro Jaramillo & Catarina Mestas, parishioners; ap/ not stated; am/ Francisco Mestas & Gertrudis Pacheco; gp/ Ambrosio Lopes & Juana Lopes.

Frame 1482, #140
DURAN, Maria del Rallo
bap 26 Dec 1833, 2 days old; legit d/ Juan Rafael Duran & Josefa Apodaca, parishioners; ap/ Teodoro Duran & Maria Jaramillo; am/ Jose Apodaca & Gertrudis Lusero; gp/ Jose Francisco Apodaca & Maria Ygnacia Lopes.

GARCIA, Manuel Antonio
bap 2 Jan 1834, 1 day old; legit s/ Antonio Garcia & Carmen Sanches, parishioners; ap/ Don Felis Garcia & Doña Yzabel Lopes; am/ Bisente Sanches & Maria Mª Martinez; gp/ Salbador Garcia & Yzabel Lopes.

CHABES, Jose Rafael
bap 7 Jan 1834, 8 days old; legit s/ Blas Chabes & Paula Chabes, parishioners; ap/ Juan Jose Chabes & Maria Josefa Trugillo; am/ Antonio Chaves & Manuela Garcia; gp/ Rafael Montolla & Maria Gertrudis Chabes.

Frame 1483
GALLEGO, Maria Rafaela
bap 8 Jan 1834, 8 days old; legit d/ Vacilio Gallego & Clara Peña, parishioners; ap/ Antonio Jose Gallego & Magdalena Garcia; am/Agustin de Peña & Dolores Chabes; gp/ Rafael Armijo & Catarina Armijo.

NS, Maria Josefa
bap 8 Jan 1834, 7 days old; d/ unknown parents, left at the home of Don Luisano Sedillo; gp/ Don Pedro Sedillo & Doña Monica Chabes.

Frames 1483-1484, #141
ARAGON, Jose de los Relles
bap 9 Jan 1834, 4 days old; legit s/ Juan de Jesus Aragon & Rosalia Aragon, parishioners; ap/ Tadeo Aragon & Maria Luiza Balencio; am/ Manuel Gonzales & Toribia Armijo; gp/ Miguel Sanches & Barbara Sanches.

BUSTAMANTE, Jose de los Relles
bap 11 Jan 1834, 8 days old; legit s/ Policarpio Bustamante & Guadalupe Larrañaga, parishioners; ap/ Bernado Bustamante & Anastacia Griego; am/ Mariano Larrañaga & Jesus Ortiz; gp/ Miguel Antonio Griego & Maria Rosalia Barrela.

SISNERO, Maria del Rallo Agapita
bap 12 Jan 1834, 3 days old; legit s/ Pablo Sisnero & Francisca Ruiz, parishioners; ap/ Francisco Sisnero & Maria Juana Duran; am/ Antonio Ruiz & Maria Ysabel Armijo; gp/ Jose Ruiz & Ana Maria Ruiz.

Frames 1484-1485
GONZALES, Maria del Rallo
bap 13 Jan 1834, 7 days old; legit d/ Bisente Gonzales & Juana Garcia, parishioners; ap/ Salbador Gonzales & Gregoria Lopez; am/ Francisco Garcia & Encarnacion Apodaca; gp/ Miguel Savedra & Maria Gertrudis Burtierres.

DURAN, Antonio Jose
bap 18 Jan 1834, 1 day old; legit s/ Salbador Duran & Josefa Candelaria, parishioners; ap/ Miguel Duran & Ynes Garcia; am/ Berrando Candelaria & Marta Martin; gp/ Juan Duran & Gregoria Duran.

Baptisms – Albuquerque, New Mexico
1829–1850

Frames 1485-1486, #142
BURTIERRES, Maria Antonia
bap 18 Jan 1834, 7 days old; legit d/ Francisco Burtierres & Manuela Montoya, parishioners; ap/ Santiago Burtierres & Josefa Martin; am/ Juan Montoya & Ynes Garcia; gp/ Jose Antonio Martin & Quiteria Griego.

MARTIN, Antonio Jose
bap 23 Jan 1834, 3 days old; legit s/ Juan Martin & Antonia Lusero, parishioners; ap/ Marcos Martin & Francisca Jaramillo; am/ Juan Lucero & Francisca Lusero; gp/ Juan Apodaca & Maria Yzabel Sanches.

ANALLA, Maria de Rallo
bap 23 Jan 1834, 3 days old; legit d/ Calletano Analla & Manuela Antonia Perea, parishioners; ap/ Antonio Analla & Tomasa Tafolla; am/ Bentura Perea & Juana Lopes; gp/ Rafael Lusero & Juana Baca.

Frame 1487
GURULE, Jose Domingo
bap 25 Jan 1834, 8 days old; legit s/ Grabiel Gurule & Micaela Luna, parishioners; ap/ Jose Gurule & Anamaria Gonzales; am/ Ysidro Luna & Maria Duran; gp/ Jose Francisco Padilla & Francisca Padilla.

NS, Maria Yldefonsa
bap 25 Jan 1834, 3 days old; d/ unknown parents, left at the house of Jose Maria Mares; gp/ Rafael Mares & Maria Rita Perea.

Frames 1487-1488, #143
MONTAÑO, Jose Francisco
bap 29 Jan 1834, 2 days old; legit s/ Pedro Montaño & Pomuzena Chama, parishioners; ap/ Jose Montaño & Micaela Santillanes; am/ Lucrecio Chama & Guadalupe Sanches; gp/ Jose Maria Griego & Guadalupe Mora.

CHABES, Jose Francisco
bap 2 Feb 1834, 5 days old; legit s/ Tomas Chabes & Monica Ortega, parishioners; ap/ not stated; am/ Juan Andres Ortega & Juana Maria Aragon; gp/ Don Francisco Ortega & Doña Ygnacia Basan.

ANALLA, Maria Francisca
bap 2 Feb 1834, 4 days old; legit d/ Juan Analla & Dolores Montaño, parishioners; ap/ Pablo Anaya & Juana Gongora; am/ not stated; gp/ Geronimo Apodaca & Polonia Apodaca.

Frame 1489
GARCIA, Maria Teodora
bap 7 Feb 1834, 1 day old; legit d/ Manuel Garcia & Juana Martines, parishioners; ap/ Juan Crus Gar Garcia & Maria de Lopes Chabes; am/ Melchor Martines & Anita Carillo; gp/ Julian Apodaca & Maria Antonia Griego.

BURTIERRES; Juan Nepomuceno
bap 8 Feb 1834, 2 days old; legit s/ Felipe Burtierres & Rosa Candelaria, parishioners; ap/ Miguel Burtierres & Maria Simona Griego; am/ not stated; gp/ Jose Samora & Josefa Griego.

NS, Jesus Maria
bap 8 Feb 1834, 8 days old; s/ unknown parents, left at the home of Maria Asencion Griego; gp/ Antonio Analla & Tomasa Tafolla.

67

Baptisms – Albuquerque, New Mexico
1829–1850

Frame 1490, #144
LUSERO, Maria Candelaria
bap 10 Feb 1834, 8 days old; legit d/ Antonio Lusero & Natibidad Cordoba, parishioners; ap/ Xabier Lusero & Gertrudis Gonsales; am/ Nicolas Cordoba & Maria Ygnacia Duran; gp/ Jose Montolla & Maria de la Luz Candelaria.

LOPES, Maria Bignina del Rallo
bap 15 Feb 1834, 4 days old; legit d/ Miguel Lopes & Nicanora Garcia, parishioners; ap/ Bernando Lopes & Relles Lujan; am/ Jose Garcia & Gertrudis Lopes; gp/ Jose Garcia & Gertrudis Lopes.

Frames 1490-1491
TELLES, Jose Ramon
bap 15 Feb 1834, 3 days old; legit s/ Jose Santos Telles & Barbara Sedillo, parishioners; ap/ Julio Telles & Casilda Barrela; am/ Pablo Sedillo & Madalena Candelaria; gp/ Julio Telles & Josefa Telles.

HERRERA, Maria Rosalia
bap 15 Feb 1834, 2 days old; legit d/ Manuel Herrera & Begnina Chabes, parishioners; ap/ Bisente Herrera & Maria Antonia Montaño; am/Antonio Chabes & Manuela Garcia; gp/ Nepomosena Sanches & Dolores Chabes.

SANTILLANES, Maria Polonia
bap 15 Feb 1834, 3 days old; legit d/ Jose Miguel Santillanes & Maria Ynes Martines, parishioners; ap/ Miguel Santillanes & Maria Duran; am/ Antonio Martin & Maria Manuela Trugillo; gp/ Roque Chabes & Maria Bibiana Chabes.

Frames 1491-1492, #145
CANDELARIA, Maria Rosalia
bap 16 Feb 1834, 1 day old; legit d/ Hilario Candelaria & Balentina Duran, parishioners; ap/ Jose Tomas Candelaria y Mirabal; am/ Francisco Duran & Lorenza Ramires; gp/ Francisco Antonio Candelaria & Consansion Candelaria.

LOPES, Jose Rafael
bap 16 Feb 1834, 3 days old; legit s/ Bisente Lopes & Ana Maria Burtierres, parishioners; ap/ not stated; am/ Simon Burtierres & Maria Candelaria; gp/ Rafael Burtierres & Maria Salome Burtierres.

GINSO, Maria Antonia
bap 22 Feb 1834, 8 days old; legit d/ Santiago Ginso & Manuela Anaya; ap & am/ not stated; gp/ Antonio Garcia & Ana Maria Mestas.

Frame 1493
LUJAN, Maria de Rallo
bap 22 Feb 1834, 1 day old; legit d/ Jose Maria Lujan & Dolores Duran, parishioners; ap/ Antonio Lujan & Juana Mirabal; am/ Teodoro Duran & Maria Lusero; gp/ Bentura Apodaca & Dolores Torres.

ANALLA, Maria de la Trinidad
bap 23 Feb 1834, 3 days old; legit d/ Martin Analla & Viatris Garcia, parishioners; ap/ Felipe Analla & Dolores Griego; am/ Francisco Garcia & Francisca Candelaria; gp/ Juan Armijo & Paula Jaramillo.

Frame 1494, #146
NS, Maria Petra
bap 25 Feb 1834, 8 days old; d/ unknown parents, left at the home of Balbina Anzures; gp/ Francisco
Montoya & Maria Ysabel Montoya.

LOPES, Maria Matilde
bap 25 Feb 1834, 2 days old; legit d/ Jose Bernabe Lopes & Sipriana Perea, parishioners; ap/ Juan Lopes
& Roza Jaramillo; am/ Jose Antonio Perea & Lucia Chabes; gp/ Ygnacio Tapia & Juana Montaño.

GRIEGO, Jose de Jesus
bap 26 Feb 1834, 2 days old; legit s/ Jose Ramos Griego & Maria de Jesus Candelaria, parishioners; ap/
Ramon Griego & Rosa Jaramillo; am/ not stated; gp/ Luis Garcia & Luiza Chabes.

Frame 1495
GRIEGO, Maria de la Trinidad Nestora
bap 27 Feb 1834, 2 days old; legit d/ Rafael Griego & Barbara Apodaca, parishioners; ap/ Rafael Griego
& Ana Maria Lopes; am/ Jose Apodaca & Gertrudis Lusero; gp/ Juan Antonio Sarracino & Luiza
Burtierres.

GURULE, Jesus Maria
GUTIERRES, Jesus Maria (in margin)
bap 2 Mar 1834, 3 days old; s/ Felipe Gurule & Ana Maria Lopes; ap & am/ not stated; gp/ Pedro
Butierres & Barbara Gutierres.

GURULE, Maria Ladubina
bap 2 Mar 1834, 3 days old; legit d/ Santiago Gurule & Rita Ginso, parishioners; ap/ Juan Jose Gurule &
Maria Valencia; am/ not stated; gp/ Juan Apodaca & Yzabel Sanches.

Frame 1496, #147
SANCHES, Jose Francisco Antonio
bap 2 Mar 1834, 8 days old; legit s/ Salbador Sanches & Encarnacion Gurule, parishioners; ap/ Diego
Antonio Sanches & Maria Ygnacia Analla; am/ Lagos Gurule & Maria Juana Padilla; gp/ Antonio Rael &
Andrea Rael.

GARCIA, Maria Manuela
bap 9 Mar 1834, 4 days old; legit d/ Antonio Garcia & Guadalupe Barreras, parishioners; ap/ Bisente
Garcia & Maria Manuela Romero; am/ not stated; gp/ Juan Manuel Garcia & Paula Garcia.

Frame 1497
BURTIERRES, Maria Serafina
bap 9 Mar 1834, 4 days old; legit d/ Juan Burtierres & Manuela Garcia, parishioners; ap/ Santiago
Burtierres & Josefa Martines; am/ Biscente Garcia & Manuela Romero; gp/ Ygnacio Gurule & Maria
Bentura Aragon.

SAMORA, Francisco Antonio
bap 9 Mar 1834, 8 days old; legit s/ Dolores Samora & Ana Maria Perea, parishioners; ap/ Mariano
Samora & Rafaela Muñiz; am/ Ygnacio Perea & Lus Garcia; gp/ Luciano Santillanes & Francisca
Santillanes.

APODACA, Jose Victor
bap 10 Mar 1834, 5 days old; legit s/ Rafael Apodaca & Estefana Zalazar, parishioners; ap/ Juan
Francisco Apodaca & Soledad Bª NS; am/ Juan Salazar & Manuela Trugillo; gp/ Agustin Sandobal &
Francisca Romero.

Frame 1498, #148
LOPES, Maria Manuela
bap 11 Mar 1834, 3 days old; d/ Gaspar Lopes & Rozalia Duran; ap/ Gaspar Lopes & Matilde Lusero;
am/ Manuel Duran & Manuela Analla; gp/ Don Mariano Elizarre & Doña Manuela Barrela.

BURTIERRES, Maria Clara
bap 11 Mar 1834, 3 days old; legit d/ Juan Burtierres & Maria Manuela Lopes, parishioners; ap/ Miguel
Burtierres & Simona Griego; am/ Tomas Lopes & Ygnacia Apodaca; gp/ Antonio Serna & Guadalupe
Burtierres.

Frames 1498-1499
LOPES, Josefa Antonia
bap 12 Mar 1834, 1 day old; legit d/ Felipe Lopes & Juliana Torres, parishioners; ap/ Juan Lopes & Rosa
Jaramillo; am/ Pedro Antonio Torres & Guadalupe Garcia; gp/ Jose Maria Torres & Josefa Antonia
Garcia.

CHABES, Jose Rafael
bap 13 Mar 1834, 5 days old; legit s/ Juan Antonio Chabes & Gertrudis Torres; ap/ not stated; am/
Santiago Torres & Josefa Jollanca; gp/ Blas Chabes & Maria Balbaneda Garcia.

APODACA, Maria Monica
bap 15 Mar 1834, 3 days old; legit d/ Jose Miguel Apodaca & Catarina Padilla; ap/ NN Apodaca &
Rozalia Gonzales; am/ Jose Manuel Padilla & Mari(a) Antonia Otero; gp/ Christobal Montoya & Monica
Gonzales.

Frame 1500, #149
LUSERO, Antonio Maria de Jesus
bap 10 Mar 1834, 3 days old; legit s/ Antonio Lusero & Juana Lusero, parishioners; ap/ not stated; am/
Alfonso Lusero & Manuela Chrispin; gp/ Antonio Maria Garcia & Juana Montaño.

GURULE, Jose Antonio
bap 17 Mar 1834, 1 day old; legit s/ Lorenso Gurule & Maria Ysidora Noanes, parishioners; ap/ Manuel
Gurule & Maria Petra Garcia; am/ Geronimo Noanes & Barbara Maese; gp/ Jose Garcia & Maria
Candelaria.

SANCHES, Maria Jacoba
bap 23 Mar 1834, 3 days old; legit d/ Jose Gabriel Sanches & Rafaela Ruis, parishioners; ap/ Antonio
Jose Sanches & Rosalia Martines; am/ Lorenso Ruiz & Barbara Ydalgo; gp/ Don Gregorio Ortiz & Doña
Clara Saracino.

Frame 1501
RUIZ, Manuel Melquides
bap 25 Mar 1834, 3 days old; legit s/ Marcos Ruiz & Balbina Candelaria, parishioners; ap/ Antonio Ruiz
& Maria Ysabel Armijo; am/ Juan Ysidro Candelaria & Gertrudis Jaramillo; gp/ Jose Apodaca & Dolores
Torres.

APODACA, Maria Encarnacion
bap 26 Mar 1834, 2 days old; legit d/ Leonicio Apodaca & Maria Eluteria Garcia, parishioners; ap/ Jose Manuel Apodaca & Rozalia Gonsales; am/ Antonio Garcia & Margarita Rael; gp/ Pedro Antonio Chabes & Ana Maria Chabes.

APODACA, Francisco Antonio
bap 26 Mar 1834, 2 days old; legit s/ Juan Apodaca & Maria Manuela Gurule, parishioners; ap/ Gregorio Apodaca & Maria Yzabel Lusero; am/ not stated; gp/ Casimiro Candelaria & Maria Griego.

Frame 1502, #150
ROMERO, Maria Encarnacion
bap 30 Mar 1834, 3 days old; legit d/ Diego Romero & Juliana Montaño, parishioners; ap/ Santiago Romero & Dolores Apodaca; am/ Andres Montaño & Andrea Chabes; gp/ Don Juan Christobal Armijo & Doña Juana Chabes.

OLGUIN, Maria Juana
bap 30 Mar 1834, 1 day old; legit s/ Jose Olguin & Juana Perea, parishioners; ap & am/ not stated; gp/ Jose Joaquin Olguin & Micaela Belasques.

TRUGILLO, Maria del Rallo de la Luz
bap 30 Mar 1834, 3 days old; legit d/ Antonio Trugillo & Marta Chrespin, parishioners; ap/ Juan Trugillo & Manuela Apodaca; am/ Juan Chrespin & Madalena Martines; gp/ Jesus Lopes & Maria de la Lus Lopes.

Frame 1503
SANDOBAL, Juan Bautista
bap 7 Apr 1834, 3 days old; legit s/ Dolores Sandobal & Juana Trugillo, parishioners; ap/ Juan Sandobal & Josefa Apodaca; am/ Baltazar Trugillo & Teresa Gallego; gp/ Don Lorenso Ortis & Doña Refugia Rael.

MUÑIS, Jose Antonio
bap 8 Apr 1834, 8 days old; legit s/ Blas Muñis & Ygnacia Martines, parishioners; ap/ Jose Maria Muñis & Barbara Samora; am/ Jose Maria Martines & Antonia Lusero; gp/ Jose Antonio Sedillo & Petra Carabajal.

Frame 1504, #151
NS, Juan Ysidro
bap 9 Apr 1834, 6 days old; s/ unknown parents, placed in the house of Barbara Ballejos; gp/ Antonio Martines & Gregoria Gurule.

NS, Jose Maria de Jesus
bap 10 Apr 1834, 3 days old; s/ unknown parents, left at the home of Juan Sais; gp/ Miguel Santillanes & Maria Albina Santillanes.

NS, Maria del Rallo
bap 13 Apr 1834, 3 days old; d/ unknown parents, left at the home of Maria Edubije Gomes; gp/ Jose Gomes & Ynes Gomes.

Frame 1505
GARCIA, Manuela Antonia
bap 13 Apr 1834, 4 days old; legit d/ Rumualdo Garcia & Ana Maria Arias, parishioners; ap/ Juan Garcia & Josefa Martines; am/ Juan Arias & Merced Gomes; gp/ Lasaro Torres & Manuela Arias.

CARABAJAL, Maria del Rallo Esmeregilda
bap 13 Apr 1834, 1 day old; legit d/ Juan Pedro Carabajal & Gertrudis Gonsales; ap/ Lorenso Carabajal & Quiterna Sandoval; am/ Manuel Gonzales & Toribia Armijo; gp/ Nicanor Quezada & Dolores Torres.

MARTIN, Maria Polonia
bap 14 Apr 1834, 3 days old; legit d/ Rafael Martin & Manuela Analla, parishioners; ap/ Marcos Martin & Francisca Jaramillo; am/ Ysidro Analla & Guadalupe Garcia; gp/ Jose Ygnacio Olguin & Maria Brigida Burtierres.

Frame 1506, #152
ZALASAR, Jose Gregorio
bap 15 Apr 1834, 1 day old; legit s/ Juan Alonso Zalazar & Catarina Lusero, parishioners; ap/ Luis Salasar & Maria Ysabel Rael; am/ Domingo Lucero & Maria Juliana Gurule; gp/ Domingo Sanches & Juana Sanches.

SAIS, Maria Paula
bap 15 Apr 1834, 7 days old; legit d/ Ramon Sais & Margarita Pacheco, parishioners; ap/ Salvador Sais & Juana Maria Aragon; am/ Francisco Pacheco & Marta Duran; gp/ Lagos Gurule & Albina Gurule.

Frames 1506-1507
GARCIA, Jose Tiburcio
bap 15 Apr 1834, 2 days old; legit s/ Antonio Garcia & Barbara Antonia Cordoba; ap/ Manuel Garcia & Maria Matilda Lucero; am/ Nicolas Cordoba & Maria Ygnacia Duran; gp/ Juan Andres Molla & Maria Simona Sanches.

DURAN, Aniceto de Jesus
bap 16 Apr 1834, 1 day old; legit s/ Juan Duran & Juliana Garcia, parishioners; ap/ Manuel Duran & Matilde Lusero; am/ Rafael Garcia & Manuela Barbero; gp/ Francisco Apodaca & Tomasa Barrela.

GARCIA, Jose Crecencio
bap 20 Apr 1834, 2 days old; legit s/ Deciderio Garcia & Nepomusena Candelaria, parishioners; ap/ Juan Jose Garcia & Maria Yzabel Romero, am/ Ygnacio Candelario & Maria Conzacion Chabes; gp/ Tadio Garcia & Barbara Antonia Griego.

Frame 1508, #153
MONTOLLA, Pedro Antonio
bap 24 Apr 1834, 8 days old; legit s/ Juan Montolla & Maria Martin, parishioners; ap/ not stated; am/ Antonio Martin & Maria Ygnacia Griego; gp/ Rafael Tafolla & Constancion Gonzales.

SAMORA, Maria del Rallo
bap 25 Apr 1834, 3 days old; legit d/ Nepomoseno Samora & Guadalupe Ballejos, parishioners; ap & am/ not stated; gp/ Jesus Lopes & Maria Rita Burtierres.

Frames 1508-1509
NS, Maria Secilia
bap 27 Apr 1834, 3 days old; d/ unknown parents, left at the house of Jose Miguel Lopes; gp/ Desiderio
Duran & Manuela Duran.

BURTIERRES, Juan Jose
bap 28 Apr 1834, 1 day old; legit s/ Simon Burtierres & Dolores Candelaria, parishioners; ap/ not stated;
am/ Florencio Candelaria & Maria Duran; gp/ Jose Candelaria & Francisca Gonsales.

HERRERA, Maria Prudencia
bap 28 Apr 1834, 11 days old; legit d/ Juan Herrera & Barbara Jaramillo, parishioners; ap/ Bisente
Herrera & Maria Antonia Montaño; am/ Miguel Jaramillo & Gertrudis Griego; gp/ Bartolo Garcia &
Juana Maria Padilla.

Frame 1510, #154
OTERO, Jose Marcos
bap 29 Apr 1834, 3 days old; s/ Julian Otero & Manuela Antonia Padilla, parishioners; ap/ Santiago Otero
& Manuela Padilla; am/ Marcos Padilla & Madalela Garcia; gp/ Juan Gonzales & Ana Maria Otero.

MARTINES, Felipe de Jesus
bap 2 May 1834, 10 days old; legit s/ Antonio Jose Martines & Luciana Lusero, parishioners; ap & am/
not stated; gp/ Bisente Montolla & Soledad Miera.

Frame 1511
CANDELARIA, Maria Catarina
bap 3 May 1834, 4 days old; legit d/ Jesus Candelaria & Tomasa Chaves, parishioners; ap/ not stated; am/
Antonio Chabes & Gertrudis Torres; gp/ Maria Gertrudis Chabes.

PEREA, Jose Ramon Nepomuceno
bap 4 May 1834, 4 days old; legit s/ Jose Maria Perea & Polonia Chabes, parishioners; ap/ Pedro Chabes
& Maria Dolores Aranda; am/ Geronimo Chabes & Encarnacion Chabes; gp/ Nepomoceno Montolla &
Maria de Jesus Lusero.

NS, Jesus del Cruz
bap 4 May 1834, 2 days old; s/ unknown parents, left at the home of Manuela Rael; gp/ Acencion Griego
& Maria Toribia Garcia.

Frame 1512, #155
CORDOBA, Maria Micaela
bap 8 May 1834, 3 days old; legit d/ Juan Bautista Cordoba & Maria Manuela Serna, parishioners; ap/
Nicolas Cordoba & Maria Ygnacia Duran; am/ not stated; gp/ Juan Antonio Griego & Candelaria Luna.

GARCIA, Jose Antonio
bap 7 May 1834, 5 days old; legit s/ Manuel Garcia & Maria Rael, parishioners; gp/ Jose Martin & Maria
de la Lus Lopes.

Frames 1512-1513
MARTIN, Jose Estanislado
bap 9 May 1834, 5 days old; legit s/ Pablo Martin & Francisca Molla, parishioners; ap & am/ not stated;
gp/ Jose Samora & Josefa Griego.

NS, Jose Marcos
bap 9 May 1834, 3 days old; s/ unknown parents, left at the home of Barbara Garcia; gp/ Marcos Analla & Maria Ynes Gurule.

BURTIERRES, Jose Gregorio
bap 11 May 1834, 3 days old; legit s/ Pascual Burtierres & Manuela Gallego, parishioners; ap & am/ not stated; gp/ Ygnacio Burtierres & Carmen Gomes.

Frame 1514, #156
HERRERA, Ygnacio Nepomoceno
bap 14 May 1834, 4 days old; s/ Felipe Herrera & Juana Garcia, parishioners; ap/ Bicente Herrera & Maria Antonia Montaño; am/ Francisco Garcia & Guadalupe Otero; gp/ Don Ygnacio Trugillo & Doña Ysidora La(page cut off) pe.

GARCIA, Jose Gregorio
bap 16 May 1834, 3 days old; legit s/ Francisco Garcia & Encarnacion Apodaca, parishioners; ap/ not stated; am/ Nicolas Apodaca & Maria de la Lus Garcia; gp/ Jose Lusero & Dolores Torres.

NS, Maria Antonia
bap 19 May 1834, 4 years old; d/ unknown Navajo Indian parents; gp/ Don Manuel Jaramillo.

Frame 1515
NS, Maria Paula
bap 19 May 1834, 4 years old; d/ unknown Navajo Indian parents; gp/ Don Manuel Jaramillo.

MUÑIS, Manuel Antonio (twin)
bap 19 May 1834, 1 day old; legit s/ Pablo Muñis & Maria Leonarda Perea, parishioners; ap/ Miguel Muñis & Maria Ysabel Alejo; am/ Ynacio Perea & Lus Garcia; gp/ Leonicio Lopes & Maria Gertrudis Perea. [Note: See also MUÑIS, Maria Dolores.]

Frames 1515-1516, #157
ANALLA, Maria del Rallo Rozalia
bap 23 May 1834, 3 days old; legit d/ Miguel Analla & Maria Lopes; ap/ Antonio Analla & Tomasa Tafolla; am/ Manuel Lopes & Josefa Apodaca; gp/ Blas Chabes & Paula Chabes.

MUÑIS, Maria Dolores (twin)
bap 24 May 1834, 4 days old; d/ Pablo Muñis & Leonarda Perea; ap/ Miguel Muñis & Maria Ysabel Jaramillo; am/ Ygnacio Perea & Lus Garcia; gp/ Mateo Duran. [Note: See also MUÑIS, Manuel Antonio.]

GARCIA, Maria Rita Begnina
bap 25 May 1834, 4 days old; legit d/ Antonio Garcia & Tomasa Griego, parishioners; ap/ Juan Garcia & Josefa Gurule; am/ Manuel Griego & Gertrudis Olguin; gp/ Don Julian Tenorio & Doña Begnina Chaves.

Frame 1517
MONTOLLA, Jose Atanacio
bap 25 May 1834, 5 days old; legit s/ Jose Montolla & Loreta Arias, parishioners; ap & am/ not stated; gp/ Atanacio Montolla & Colasa Jaramillo.

GARCIA, Pedro Antonio
bap 26 May 1834, 3 days old; legit s/ Juan Garcia & Bicenta Garcia, parishioners; ap/ Juan Garcia & Juana Barbara Molina; am/ Juan Jose Garcia & Francisca Candelaria; gp/ Rafael Armijo & Soledad Peña.

Frames 1517-1518, #158
CHABES, Jose Fernando
bap 3 Jun 1834, 3 days old; legit s/ Xabier Chabes & Alfonsa Sena, parishioners; ap/ Geronimo Chabes & Encarnacion Gonsales; am/ Francisco Sena & Manuela Martin; gp/ Diego Chabes & Josefa Chabes.

NS, Maria Juana
bap 2 Jun 1834, 3 days old; d/ unknown parents, placed in the house of Pascual Montoia; gp/ Pascual Cruz.

CANDELARIA, Jose Melquiades
bap 9 Jun 1834, 2 days old; legit s/ Tomas Candelaria & Gertrudis Gabaldon, parishioners; ap/ Pablo Candelaria & Andrea Carabajal; am/ not stated; gp/ Mariano Armijo & Antonia Ortis.

GURULE, Maria Juana
bap 10 Jun 1834, 10 days old; d/ Marcelo Gurule & Maria Petra Burtierres, parishioners; ap/ Antonio Gurule & Maria Antonia Herrera; ap/ Francisco Burtierres & Maria Manuela Brito.

Frame 1519
NS, Jose Ambrocio
bap 10 Jun 1834, 4 days old; s/ unknown parents, left at the house of Juana Perea; gp/ Rafael Gallego & Rosalia Gallego.

NS, Jose Antonio
bap 15 Jun 1834, 3 days old; s/ unknown parents, left at the home of Catarina Candelaria; gp/ Rafael Lopes & Luiza Chabes.

Frames 1519-1520, #159
NS, Antonio Jose
bap 15 Jun 1834, 3 days old; s/ unknown parents, left at the house of Josefa Martines; gp/ Josefa Martines.

CHABES, Juan Maximiano
bap 16 Jun 1834, 4 days old; legit s/ Don Fernando Chabes & Doña Barbara Trugillo, parishioners; ap/ Don Estanilao Chabes & Doña Soledad Ortega; am/ Don Jose Trugillo & Doña Soledad Valencia; gp/ Don Jose Martines & Doña Maria Antonia Gonzales.

JARAMILLO, Juan Christobal
bap 19 Jun 1834, 1 day old; legit s/ Gregorio Jaramillo & Antonia Sanches; ap/ NN Jaramillo & Manuela Lusero; am/ Bisente Sanches & Gertrudis Rael; gp/ Jose Jaramillo & Grabiela Jaramillo.

Frame 1521
MONTOLLA, Jose Julian
bap 21 Jun 1834, 3 days old; legit s/ Jose Maria Montolla & Clara Armijo, parishioners; ap/ Pablo Montolla & Relles Burtierres; am/ Lucas Armijo & Barbara Ortis; gp/ Juan Armijo & Ana Maria Gabaldon.

SANCHES, Maria Juana
bap 24 Jun 1834, 5 days old; legit d/ Juan Jose Sanches & Maria Candelaria, parishioners; ap/ Nicolas Sanches & Maria Luiza Gallego; am/not stated; gp/ Nicolas Sanches & Mariana Sabedra.

Frame 1522, #160
GARCIA, Jose Mariano
bap 24 Jun 1834, 4 days old; legit s/ Manuel Garcia & Maria Barbara Carbajal, parishioners; ap/ Pedro Garcia & Barbara Chabes; am/ Faustin Carbajal & Suzana Lopes; gp/ Maximo Chabes & Rita Chabes.

CHABES, Maria Petra
bap 3 Jul 1834, 5 days old; legit d/ Antonio Chabes & Maria Ygnacia Montolla, parishioners; ap/ Geronimo Chabes & Encarnacion Gonzales; am/ Mariano Montolla & Maria Relles Mestas; gp/ Mariano Montolla & Maria Relles Mestas.

Frames 1522-1523
MONTAÑO, Jose Andres
bap 20 Jul 1834, 11 days old; legit s/ Toribio Montaño & Ana Maria Candelaria, parishioners; ap/ Jose Montaño & Micaela Santillanes; am/ Juan Candelaria & Juana Armijo; gp/ Don Andres Lucero & Doña Tomasa Garcia.

DURAN, Jose Martin
bap 20 Jul 1834, 6 days old; legit s/ Francisco Duran & Maria Burtierres, parishioners; ap/ Manuel Duran & Matilde Jaramillo; am/ Manuel Candelaria & Juana Barbero; gp/ Juan Candelaria & Ana Gregoria Candelaria.

Frames 1523-1524, #161
TRUGILLO, Juan Jose
bap 20 Jul 1834, 4 days old; legit s/ Mariano Trugillo & Luiza Cordoba, parishioners; ap/ Marcos Trugillo & Juana Castelo; am/ Marcos Cordoba & Rafaela Garcia; gp/ Rafael Trugillo & Maria Gurule.

MONTOLLA, Maria Polonia de Jesus
bap 4 Aug 1834, 3 days old; d/ Juan Montolla & Maria Gurule; ap/ Pedro Montolla & Maria Luna; am/ Ygnacio Gurule & Polonia Nieto; gp/ Diego Romero & Encarnacion Valencia.

Frames 1524-1525
ARMIJO, Jose Francisco de la Trinidad
bap 8 Sep 1834, 2 days old; legit s/ Don Julian Armijo & Doña Mariana Sarracino, parishioners; ap/ Don Bisente Armijo & Doña Barbara Chabes; am/ Don Rafael Sarracino & Doña Maria Luisa Burtierres; gp/ Don Gregorio Ortis & Doña Clara Sarracino.

CHABES, Maria Soledad
bap 9 Sep 1834, 3 days old; legit d/ Don Mariano Chabes & Doña Josefa Perea, parishioners; ap/ Don Francisco Xabier Chabes & Doña Ana Maria del Castillo; am/ Don Pedro Jose Perea & Doña Maria Soledad Torres; gp/ Don Pedro Perea & Doña Maria Soledad Torres.

Frames 1525-1526, #162
APODACA, Maria del Rallo Soledad
bap 10 Sep 1834, 3 days old; legit d/ Juan Apodaca & Maria Sanches, parishioners; ap/ Jose Apodaca & Maria Gertrudis Lusero; am/ Diego Antonio Sanches & Maria Ygnacia Analla; gp/ Bartolo Apodaca & Maria Soledad Telles.

MOLLA, Jesus Antonio
bap 15 Sep 1834, 3 days old; legit s/ Vitorino Molla & Maria de Jesus Martines, parishioners; ap/ not stated; am/ Pedro Martines & Juana Garcia; gp/ Manuel Analla & Felipa Martines.

ARANDA, Josefa Ygnacia de la Cruz
bap 17 Sep 1834, 8 days old; legit d/ Pedro Aranda & Rosalia Jaramillo, parishioners; ap/ Antonio Aranda & Maria Antonia Rosa Garcia; am/ Jose Miguel Jaramillo & Ana Maria Ortega; gp/ Don Francisco Ortega & Doña Ygnacia Basan.

Frame 1527
MONTOLLA, Jesus de Jose
bap 18 Sep 1834, 3 days old; legit s/ Jose Montolla & Dolores Garcia, parishioners; ap/ not stated; am/ Pedro Garcia & Maria Analla; gp/ Rafael Lusero & Maria Ysidora Garcia.

GARCIA, Maria del Rallo
bap 18 Sep 1834, 3 days old; legit d/ Julian Garcia & Brigida Gomes, parishioners; ap/ Carpio Garcia & Maria Griego; am/ not stated; gp/ Don Bicente Sanches & Doña Ana Maria Mestas.

Frame 1528, #163
NS, Maria Josefa
bap 21 Sep 1834, 8 days old; d/ unknown parents, left at the house of Julian Chabes; gp/ Bentura Apodaca & Maria Yzabel Apodaca.

LUSERO, Juan de Jesus Nepomuceno
bap 21 Sep 1834, 3 days old; legit s/ Juan Jose Lusero & Maria Gertrudis Chabes, parishioners; ap/ Diego Armijo (Lucero) & Maria Antonia Armijo; am/ Antonio Chabes & Maria Alfonsa Armijo; gp/ Jesus Lusero & Maria Luiza Martines.

GARCIA, Maria Soledad
bap 22 Sep 1834, 2 days old; legit d/ Salbador Garcia & Paula Sandobal, parishioners; ap/ Pedro Garcia & Maria Analla; am/ Miguel Sandobal & Francisca Lopes; gp/ Francisco Garcia & Maria Luiza Garcia.

Frame 1529
LOPES, Maria Grabiela
bap 22 Sep 1834, 3 days old; legit d/ Francisco Lopes & Guadalupe Perea, parishioners; ap/ Bernardo Lopes & Relles Lujan; am/ Jose Miguel Perea & Manuela Sanches; gp/ Don Mariano Armijo & Doña Grabiela Jaramillo.

GALLEGO, Jesus Maria
bap 26 Sep 1834, 3 days old; legit s/ Juan Antonio Gallego & Petra Lujan, parishioners; ap/ Francisco Gallego & Maria Soledad Candelaria; am/ Bernardo Lopes & Relles Lujan, gp/ Dolores Torres.

GURULE, Jesus Maria
bap 26 Sep 1834, 3 days old; legit s/ Juan de Jesus Gurule & Maria de la Lus Lujan, parishioners; ap/ Jose Maria Gurule & Maria Candelaria; am/ Antonio Lujan & Maria Candelaria; gp/ Dolores Torres.

Frame 1530, #164
NIETO, Antonio Maria
bap 9 Oct 1834, 3 days old; legit s/ Juan Rafael Nieto & Maria Gregoria Montaño, parishioners; ap/ Juan Nieto & Gertrudis Salazar; am/ Salbador Montaño & Gregoria Chabes; gp/ Antonio Maria Garcia & Juana Montaño.

PINO, Maria Brigida del Refugio
bap 10 Oct 1834, 2 days old; legit d/ Juan Antonio Pino & Maria Teodora Martines, parishioners; ap/ Felis Pino & Balbaneda Rael; am/ not stated; gp/ Antonio Jose Pino & Monica Mestas.

LUSERO, Jesus Maria
bap 12 Oct 1834, 7 days old; legit s/ Francisco Lusero & Maria Aragon, parishioners; ap/ not stated; am/ Tadeo Aragon & Maria Luiza Balencia; gp/ Manuel Garcia & Rafaela Rael.

Frame 1531
PEREA, Maria del Rallo Petra
bap 14 Oct 1834, 4 days old; s/ Juan Perea & Crus Duran; ap/ Francisco Perea & Feliciana Barbaro; am/ Pedro Duran & Josefa Antonia Jaramillo; gp/ Rafael Duran & Juana Pacheco.

GARCIA, Jose Claudio de Jesus
bap 18 Oct 1834, 3 days old; s/ Juan Cristobal Garcia & Maria Francisca Gurule; ap/ Jose Luis Garcia & Juana Candelaria; am/ Jose Gurule & Maria Gallego; gp/ Juan Tomas Aragon & Maria Gertrudis Garcia.

NS, Maria de Rallo
bap 18 Oct 1834, 1 day old; d/ unknown parents, left at the house of Doña Ursula Chabes; gp/ Miguel Antonio Candelaria & Dolores Candelaria.

Frame 1532, #165
GARCIA, Maria Teresa de Jesus
bap 18 Oct 1834, 3 days old; legit d/ Jose Antonio Garcia & Maria Ygnacia Candelaria, parishioners; ap/ Don Felis Garcia & Doña Yzabel Lopes; am/ Antonio Candelaria & Manuela Rael; gp/ Pedro Armijo & Maria de la Lus Garcia.

BURTIERRES, Maria Placida
bap 19 Oct 1834, 10 days old; legit d/ Crus Burtierres & Guadalupe Jaramillo, parishioners; ap/ Pedro Butierres & Francisca Silva; am/ Mariano Jaramillo & Juana Martines; gp/ Don Diego Montolla & Doña Maria Dolores Montolla.

CHABES, Pedro Jose
bap 19 Oct 1834, 7 days old; legit s/ Miguel Chabes & Decideria Gurule, parishioners; ap/ Juan Chabes & Maria Clara Sanches; am/ Ana Maria Gonsales (only); gp/ Maria Manuela Lusero.

Frame 1533
NS, Maria Teresa
bap 28 Oct 1834, 5 days old; d/ unknown parents, left at the home of Maria Luna; gp/ Jose Maria Sandobal & Maria Teresa Luna.

BACA, Maria del Rallo
bap 29 Oct 1834, 4 days old; legit d/ Sabino Baca & Maria Tomasa Lopes, parishioners; ap/ not stated; am/ Jose Lopes & Maria Antonia Carabajal; gp/ Teodoro Lopes & Crus Romero.

LOPES, Maria de Altagracia
bap 29 Oct 1834, 2 days old; legit d/ Jose Cleto Lopes & Maria Dolores Candelaria, parishioners; ap/ Manuel Lopes & Josefa Apodaca; am/ Pablo Candelaria & Andrea Montolla; gp/ Salbador Antonio Martines & Maria de Altagracia Martines.

Frame 1534, #166
GARCIA, Jose Rafael
Bap 30 Oct 1834, 7 days old; legit s/ Manuel Garcia & Maria Tomasa Sena, parishioners; ap/ Juan Garcia & Paula Candelaria; am/ Francisco Sena & Maria Manuela Martines; gp/ Francisco Luna & Consepcion Sena.

ARMIJO, Maria del Rallo
bap 31 Oct 1834, 2 days old; legit d/ Don Juan Armijo & Maria Paula Jaramillo, parishioners; ap/ Don Santiago Armijo & Doña Maria Petra Perea; am/ Miguel Antonio Jaramillo & Doña Lorensa Lusero; gp/ Doña Maria Elena del Rallo Domingues.

NS, Maria Luiza
bap 31 Oct 1834, 5 days old; d/ unknown parents, left at the home of Pablo Candelaria; gp/ Rafael Lopes & Maria Luiza Chabes.

Frame 1535
CARRILLO, Maria Francisca Salome
bap 5 Nov 1834, 7 days old; legit d/ Ramon Carrillo & Maria Lucia Trugillo, parishioners; ap/ not stated; am/ Antonio Trugillo & Micaela Santillanes; gp/ Manuel Garcia & Rafaela Rael.

SANCHES, Maria de los Dolores
bap 6 Nov 1834, 4 days old; legit d/ Ygnacio Sanches & Manuela Analla, parishioners; gp/ Salbador Candelaria & Maria de Jesus Padilla.

NS, Maria de Rallo Nestora
bap 8 Nov 1834, 8 days old; d/ unknown parents, left at the house of Juan Antonio Lujan; gp/ Pablo Lujan & Juana Analla.

Frame 1536, #167
CORDOBA, Jesus Maria
bap 8 Nov 1834, 1 day old; legit s/ Don Vicente Cordoba & Doña Maria Juana Romero, parishioners; ap/ Jose Antonio Cordoba & Maria Yzabel Jaques; am/ Felipe Romero & Maria Manuela Montolla; gp/ Doña Maria Elena del Rallo Domingues.

ORTIS, Maria Andrea
bap 15 Nov 1834, 5 days old; legit d/ Don Lorenso Ortis & Doña Andrea Rael, parishioners; ap/ Jesus Marcos Ortis & Monica Duran; am/ Antonio Rael & Francisca Padilla; gp/ Don Julian Valencia & Doña Refugia Rael. [Note: See also entry below.]

ORTIS, Maria Andrea
bap 15 Nov 1834, 5 days old; legit d/ Don Lorenso Ortis & Doña Andrea Rael, parishioners; ap/ Jesus Marcos Ortis & Monica Duran; am/ Antonio Rael & Maria Francisca Padilla; gp/ Don Lagos Gurule & Doña Juana Maria Padilla. [Note: See also entry above.]

Frame 1537
GALLEGO, Maria Gertrudes
bap 16 Nov 1834, 4 days old; legit d/ Jesus Gallego & Maria del Rosario Garcia, parishioners; ap/ Joaquin Gallego & Matiana Sabedra; am/ not stated; gp/ Juan Baca & Maria Antonia Garcia.

ROMERO, Julian de Jesus
bap 16 Nov 1834, 8 days old; legit s/ Antonio Romero & Guadalupe Montaño, parishioners; ap/ Miguel Antonio Romero & Juana Garcia; am/ Juan Jose Montaño & Francisca Gonzales; gp/ Juan Pablo Garcia & Gregoria Garcia.

NS, Jose Maria
bap 16 Nov 1834, 7 days old; s/ unknown parents, left at the home of Ana Maria Candelaria; gp/ Jose Gonsales & Maria Agnes Luna.

Frame 1538, #168
APODACA, Manuel Antonio
bap 19 Nov 1834, 4 days old; legit s/ Rafael Apodaca & Juana Romero, parishioners; ap/ Jose Apodaca & Madalena Perea; am/ Miguel Antonio Romero & Juana Garcia; gp/ Manuel Garcia & Rafaela Rael.

ARIAS, Maria Rufina
bap 19 Nov 1834, 4 days old; legit d/ Christobal Arias & Tomasa Martines, parishioners; ap/ Pablo Arias & Encarnacion Valencia; am/ Baltasar Martines & Maria Antonia Griego; gp/ Juan Domingo Valencia & Doña Paula Martines.

Frames 1538-1539
SANCHES, Jose Maria (twin)
bap 20 Nov 1834, 1 day old; legit s/ Diego Sanches & Juana Maria Gallegos, parishioners; ap/ Antonio Jesus Sanches & Rozalia Martines; am/ Juan Gallego & Manuela Antonia Gurule; gp/ Antonio Jesus Sanches & Rosalia Martines.

SANCHES, Ana Maria Rufina (twin)
bap 20 Nov 1834, 1 day old; legit d/ Diego Sanches & Ana Maria Gallego, parishioners; ap/ Antonio Jose Sanches & Rozalia Martines; am/ Juan Gallego & Manuela Antonia Gurule; gp/ Dolores Gallego & Ana Gregoria Gallego.

GONSALES, Maria Guterna
bap 21 Nov 1834, 9 days old; legit d/ Jose Gonsales & Maria de Jesus Salasar, parishioners of Sandia; ap/ not stated; am/ Toribio Salasar & Polonia Burtieres; gp/ Francisco Silba & Doña Josefa Burtieres.

Frame 1540, #169
PEREA, Jose Dolores
bap 21 Nov 1834, 9 days old; legit s/ Jose Eluterio Perea & Ana Maria Burtieres, parishioners of Sandia; ap/ Baltasar Perea & Petra Chabes; am/ Domingo Burtieres & Maria Acencion Baca; gp/ Don Juan Burtieres & Maria Rosa Burtieres.

NOANES, Maria de Rallo Feliciana
bap 21 Nov 1834, 1 day old; legit d/ Salbador Noanes & Maria Guadalupe Garcia, parishioners; ap/ Geronimo Nuanes & Barbara Maese; am/ Juan Garcia & Maria Ysabel Romero; gp/ Tadeo Garcia & Doña Barbara Antonia Griego.

Frames 1540-1541
ANALLA, Jose Atanacio
bap 22 Nov 1834, 3 days old; legit s/ Jose Rosalio Analla & Teresa Candelaria, parishioners; ap/ Manuel Analla & Maria Ysidora Lopes; am/ Juan Pablo Candelaria & Guadalupe Herrera; gp/ Salbador Herrera & Maria Ygnacia Chabes.

GARCIA, Juana Maria
bap 22 Nov 1834, 3 days old; legit d/ Alejo Garcia & Gracia Garcia, parishioners; ap/ Juan de Jesus Garcia & Rosa Sabedra; am/ Juan Garcia & Barbara Chabes; gp/ Bartolo Garcia & Juana Maria Padilla.

CHABES, Felipe de Jesus
bap 22 Nov 1834, 2 days old; legit s/ Don Jose Maria Chabes & Doña Manuela Armijo, parishioners from Ysleta; ap/ Don Francisco Xabier Chabes & Doña Ana Maria Castillo; am/ Don Juan Armijo & Doña Rosalia Ortega; gp/ Don Juan Armijo & Doña Josefa Chabes.

Frames 1541-1542, #170
CASTILLO, Maria del Rallo Paula
bap 23 Nov 1834, 3 days old; legit d/ Matias Castillo & Polonia Analla, parishioners; ap/ Juan de la Crus Castillo & Rosa Sabedra; am/ not stated; gp/ Paula Montolla & Juan Andres Molla.

ROMERO, Maria del Rallo (twin)
bap 24 Nov 1834, 2 days old; twin legit d/ Jose Miguel Romero & Maria Ygnacia Montaño, parishioners; ap/ Antonio Romero & Juana Garcia; am/ Salbador Montaño & Gregoria Chabes; gp/ Baltasar Romero & Paula Lusero. [Note: See also entry below.]

ROMERO, Jose Maria (twin)
bap 24 Nov 1834, 1 day old; twin legit s/ Jose Miguel Romero & Ygnacia Montaño, parishioners; ap/ Antonio Romero & Juana Garcia; am/ Salbador Montaño & Gregoria Chabes; gp/ Jose Apodaca & Ygnacia Apodaca. [Note: See also entry above.]

Frame 1543
RAEL, Maria del Carmen
bap 6 Dec 1834, 8 days old; d/ Julian Rael & Maria Ygnacia Silba, parishioners of Sandia; gp/ Bicente Montolla & Rosa Montolla.

SANDOBAL, Josefa
bap 6 Dec 1834, 6 days old; legit d/ Mariano Sandobal & Maria Edubije Garcia, parishioners; ap/ Miguel Sandobal & Maria Manuela Gonsales; am/ Blas Garcia & Francisca Aragon; gp/ Bisente Montolla & Maria Roza Montolla.

RODARTE, Jose Nicolas
bap 6 Dec 1834, 1 day old; legit s/ Pablo Rodarte & Maria Antonia Martin, parishioners; ap/ Antonio Rodarte & Maria Lusero; am/ not stated; gp/ Don Tadeo Garcia & Barbara Antonia Griego.

Frame 1544, #171
NS, Maria Nicolasa
bap 14 Dec 1834, 8 days old; d/ unknown parents, left at the home of Diego Cordoba; gp/ Domingo Cordoba.

CHABES, Maria Trinidad
bap 17 Dec 1834, 3 days old; legit d/ Nicolas Chabes & Barbara Garcia, parishioners; ap/ Diego Chabes
& Maria Ygnacia Jaramillo; am/ Jose Garcia & Juana Chabes; gp/ Don Salbador Jaramillo & Doña Maria
Gertrudis Baca.

Frame 1545
SAMORA, Maria Guadalupe
bap 17 Dec 1834, 6 days old; legit d/ Jose Samora & Dolores Mora, parishioners; ap/ Juan Samora &
Julian Montaño; am/ Ysidro Mora & Juana Marques; gp/ Don Miguel Garcia & Doña Rosalia Barela.

NS, Maria Lucia de los Dolores
bap 19 Dec 1834, 3 days old; d/ unknown parents, left at the house of Luarda Marques; gp/ Gregorio
Griego & Josefa Duran.

Frames 1545-1546, #172
SANCHES, Juana Maria
bap 22 Dec 1834, 3 days old; legit d/ Christobal Sanches & Concepcion Valencia, parishioners; ap/ Felipe
Sanches & Maria Trujillo; am/ Juan Domingo Valencia (only); gp/ Bisente Montolla & Rosa Montolla.

GRIEGO, Maria Tomasa
bap 24 Dec 1834, 3 days old; legit d/ Juan Antonio Griego & Candelaria Luna, parishioners; ap/ Felipe
Griego & Margarita Gonsales; am/ Ycidro Luna & Manuela Candelaria; gp/ Baltasa Romero & Paula
Lusero.

CARRILLO, Juan Acencio
bap 1 Jan 1835, 5 days old; legit s/ Santiago Carrillo & Lucarda Burtierres, parishioners; ap/ Miguel
Carrillo & Bernarda Brito; am/ Manuel Burtierres & Maria Trinidad Gonsales; gp/ Juan Burtierres &
Maria Cordoba.

Frames 1546-1547
GALLEGO, Manuel Antonio
bap 1 Jan 1835, 9 days old; legit s/ Jose Gallego & Gregoria Tafolla, parishioners of Sandia; ap/ Antonio
Gallego & Maria Antonia Chabes; am/ Juan Tafolla & Maria Francisca Fernandes; gp/ Jose Gallego &
Ysabel Jaramillo.

GARCIA, Jose Ramon
bap 5 Jan 1835, 1 day old; legit s/ Juan Rafael Garcia & Encarnacion Lusero, parishioners; ap/ Juan
Rafael Garcia & Manuela Muñis; am/ Gregorio Lusero & Marta Lopes; gp/ Juan Garcia & Petra Garcia.

LOBATO, Jose Ygnacio de Guadalupe
bap 5 Jan 1835, 1 day old; legit s/ Juan Felipe Lobato & Manuela Mestas, parishioners; ap/ Juan Lobato
& Maria Casados; am/ Ygnacio Mestas & Guadalupe Duran; gp/ Bautista Mestas & Guadalupe Duran.

Frame 1548, #173
SABEDRA, Maria Grabiela
bap 8 Jan 1835, 1 day old; legit d/ Manuel Sabedra & Elena Duran, parishioners; ap/ Jose Sabedra &
Maria Sedillo; am/ Salbador Duran & Balbaneda Garcia; gp/ Juan Ygnacio Garcia & Soledad Garcia.

LOPES, Antonio Ygnacio
bap 9 Jan 1835, 1 day old; legit s/ Jose Lopes & Maria Marques, parishioners; ap/ Manuel Lopes & Encarnacion Duran; am/ not stated; gp/ Ygnacio Lusero & Hilaria Lusero.

CANDELARIA, Maria Cipriana de los Dolores
bap 10 Jan 1835, 3 days old; legit d/ Salbador Candelaria & Maria de Jesus Padilla, parishioners; ap/ Juan Candelaria & Teresa Chabes; am/ Antonio Padilla & Manuela Aguirre; gp/ Don Julian Sedillo & Doña Cipriana Garcia.

Frame 1549
GARCIA, Maria Dolores
bap 12 Jan 1835, 3 days old; legit d/ Ysidro Garcia & Ana Maria Martines, parishioners; ap/ Tomas Garcia & Paula Garcia; am/ Marcos Martines & Francisca Jaramillo; gp/ Bentura Apodaca & Dolores Torres.

GONSALES, Maria Yzabel
bap 16 Jan 1835, 3 days old; legit d/ Juan Gonsales & Balbina Lopes, parishioners; ap/ Juan Domingo Gonsales & Maria Archuleta; am/ Gaspar Lopes & Maria Rosalia Duran; gp/ Juan Domingo Gonsales & Maria Archuleta.

Frames 1549-1550, #174
MONTOLLA, Maria Cecilia
bap 18 Jan 1835, 8 days old; d/ Juan Montolla & Rafaela Aragon, parishioners; ap/ Juan Montolla & Rita Valencia; am/ not stated; gp/ Pablo Barrela & Juana Aranda.

PEREA, Maria Paula
bap 18 Jan 1835, 8 days old; legit d/ Antonio Perea & Candelaria Guana, parishioners; ap/ Luis Perea & Guadalupe Garcia; am/ not stated; gp/ Francisco Griego & Josefa Sandoval.

GONSALES, Jose Anastacio
bap 19 Jan 1835, 8 days old; legit s/ Juan Gonsales & Ana Maria Otero, parishioners; ap/ Jose Manuel Gonsales & Antonia Rosa Ortega; am/ Julian Otero & Manuela Padilla; gp/ Juan Rael & Maria Lorenza Rael.

Frame 1551
ROMERO, Maria Polonia
bap 22 Jan 1835, 3 days old; legit d/ Antonio Romero & Maria Lugarda Gonsales, parishioners; ap/ Miguel Romero & Manuela Gonsales; am/ Miguel Gonsales & Polonia Burtierres; gp/ Juan Gonsales & Jacinta Martines.

GRIEGO, Maria Canuta
bap 22 Jan 1835, 3 days old; legit d/ Manuel Griego & Catarina Samora, parishioners; ap/ Blas Griego & Rosa Chabes; am/ Jose Francisco Samora & Maria Ygnacia Valencia; gp/ Juan Domingo Valencia & Paula Martines.

Frames 1551-1552, #175
GARCIA, Francisco Antonio
bap 22 Jan 1835, 1 day old; legit s/ Juan Felis Garcia & Juana Maria Archuleta, parishioners; ap/ Jose Felis Garcia & Maria Ysabel Lopes; am/ Antonio Archuleta & Josefa Lujan; gp/ Francisco Sandoval & Maria Garcia.

Baptisms – Albuquerque, New Mexico
1829–1850

NS, Pablo Antonio
bap 26 Jan 1835, 1 day old; s/ unknown parents, left at the home of Doña Ursula Chabes; gp/ Miguel Antonio Candelaria & Tomasa Padilla.

NS, Maria Paula
bap 26 Jan 1835, 5 days old; d/ unknown parents, left at the home of Bernardo Burtierres; gp/ Domingo Cerna & Juana Serna.

NS, Maria Paula
bap 26 Jan 1835, 2 days old; d/ unknown parents, left at the house of Miguel Garcia; gp/ Leonicio Garcia & Maria Marta Garcia.

Frame 1553
SANCHES, Salbador Antonio
bap 27 Jan 1835, 1 day old; legit s/ Nepomuceno Sanches & Dolores Chabes, parishioners; ap/ Felix Sanches & Maria Aguirre; am/ Antonio Chabes & Manuela Garcia; gp/ Salbador Herrera & Manuela Garcia.

BACA, Maria del Rallo de Jesus
bap 27 Jan 1835, 3 days old; legit d/ Antonio Baca & Manuela Lusero, parishioners; ap/ Rafael Baca & Juana Rita Candelaria; am/ Alfonso Lusero & Manuela Chrispin; gp/ Don Manuel Robles & Doña Elena Domingues.

Frame 1554, #176
APODACA, Maria del Rallo
bap 27 Jan 1835, 3 days old; legit d/ Rafael Apodaca & Barbara Molina, parishioners; ap/ Jose Apodaca & Gertrudis Lusero; am/ not listed; gp/ Agustin Chabes & Juana Sanches.

ARAGON, Juan de Jesus
bap 28 Jan 1835, 8 days old; s/ Don Eusebio Aragon & Maria Micaela Santillanes, parishioners; ap/ Don Jose Manuel Aragon & Doña Barbara Chabes; am/ Don Guadalupe Santillanes & Doña Micaela Carrillo; gp/ Don Jesus Lusero & Doña Maria Montolla.

NS, Juan Nepomoceno
bap 28 Jan 1835, 6 days old; s/ unknown parents, left at the house of Julian Padilla; gp/ Jose Molla & Maria Paula Urtado.

Frame 1555
GURULE, Pablo Antonio
bap 29 Jan 1835, 5 days old; legit s/ Grabiel Gurule & Nicolasa Luna, parishioners; ap/ Jose Domingo Gurule & Ana Maria Gonsales; am/ Ysidro Luna & Manuela Candelaria; gp/ Diego Luna & Paula Perea.

SANCHES, Maria de Altagracia
bap 30 Jan 1835, 8 days old; legit d/ Juan Sanches & Manuela Gonzales, parishioners; ap/ Felipe Sanches & Maria Ynes Garcia; am/ Jose Manuel Gonzales & Maria Rosa Carrillo; gp/ Manuel Sanches & Maria Lopes.

Frame 1556, #177
ARAGON, Miguel Antonio
bap 4 Feb 1835, 3 days old; s/ Juan Andres Aragon & Concepcion Salazar, parishioners; ap/ not stated:
am/ Diego Salazar & Josefa Baca; gp/ Antonio Jose Griego & Maria Lubina Burtierres.

SENA, Maria Placida
bap 5 Feb 1835, 2 days old; legit d/ Miguel Sena & Maria Ysidora Garcia, parishioners; ap/ Francisco
Cena & Maria Manuela Martines; am/ Juan Garcia & Maria Francisca Gallego; gp/ Dolores Samora.

BURTIERRES, Felipe de Jesus
bap 5 Feb 1835, 1 day old; legit s/ Juan Burtierres & Francisca Analla, parishioners; ap/ Miguel Burtierres
& Maria Chabes; am/ Manuel Analla & Maria Antonia Apodaca; gp/ Francisco Sisneros & Mariana
Cisneros.

Frame 1557
CHABES, Jose Antonio Melguides
bap 6 Feb 1835, 1 day old; legit s/ Juan de Dios Chabes & Monica Lusero, parishioners; ap/ Estanislado
Chabes & Soledad Ortega; am/ Mariano Lusero & Marcelina Valencia; gp/ Christobal Sanches &
Concepcion Valencia.

APODACA, Maria Felipa
bap 7 Feb 1835, 3 days old; legit d/ Antonio Apodaca & Petra Duran, parishioners; am/ Miguel Duran &
Barbara Cerna; gp/ Manuel Carabajal & Ramona Perea.

Frame 1558, #178
MONTAÑO, Felipe de Jesus
bap 7 Feb 1835, 2 days old; s/ Antonio Jose Montaño & Maria Rita Luna, parishioners; ap/ Juan Jose
Montaño & Micaela Santillanes; am/ Ysidro Luna & Manuela Candelaria; gp/ Ysidro Luna & Teodora
Peña.

ARZE, Maria del Rallo de la Luz
bap 11 Feb 1835, 26 days old; natural d/ Maria del Carmen Arze; gp/ Don Nicanor Quesada & Doña
Maria de la Luz Lopes.

NS, Pedro Antonio
bap 15 Feb 1835, 2 days old; s/ unknown parents, left at the home of Doña Petra Maldonado; gp/
Rumaldo Candelaria & Juana Candelaria.

Frame 1559
CORDOBA, Maria Polonia
bap 15 Feb 1835, 6 days old; d/ Felis Cordoba & Rosalia Mariño, parishioners; ap/ Marcos Cordoba &
Rafaela Garcia; am/ Juan Mariño & Maria Ysidora Sanches; gp/ Mariano Chabes & Maria Bibiana
Chabes.

BURTIERRES, Manuel Antonio
bap 15 Feb 1835, 3 days old; legit s/ Leonardo Burtierres & Soledad Garcia, parishioners; ap/ Santiago
Burtierres & Juana Martines; am/ not stated; gp/ Rafael Apodaca & Juana Maria Apodaca.

Frame 1560, #179
BUTIERES, Manuel Antonio
bap 15 Feb 1835, 4 days old; s/ Esteban Butieres & Quiteria Montolla, parishioners; ap & am/ not stated; gp/ Jose Dolores Apodaca & Ygnacia Garcia.

MONTOLLA, Maria del Rallo de Jesus
bap 17 Feb 1835, 3 days old; d/ Jose Rafael Montolla & Maria Gertrudis Chabes, parishioners; ap/ Juan Montolla & Maria Luisa Padilla; am/ Agustin Chabes & Juana Sanches; gp/ Miguel Padilla & Maria Sanches.

LOPES, Maria Petra
bap 19 Feb 1835, 2 days old; legit d/ Leonicio Lopes & Gertrudis Perea, parishioners; ap/ not stated; am/ Cimon Perea & Cacilda Apodaca; gp/ Jesus Gallego & Luiza Griego.

Frame 1561
NS, Jose Ygnacio
bap 22 Feb 1835, 2 days old; s/ unknown parents, left at the home of Acencio Molla; gp/ Salbador Lopes & Relles Lopes.

NS, Maria de Jesus
bap 22 Feb 1835, 2 days old; d/ unknown parents, left at the home of Bicente Candelaria; gp/ Mariano (Burtierres) & Maria Gregoria Burtierres.

TORRES, Maria del Rallo
bap 22 Feb 1835, 3 days old; legit d/ Juan Torres & Dolores Burtierres, parishioners; gp/ Salbador Torres & Maria Torres.

Frame 1562, #180
PEREA, Salbador Antonio
bap 22 Feb 1835, 3 days old; legit s/ Juan Jose Perea & Francisca Tafolla, parishioners; ap/ Bentura Perea & Juana Lopes; am/ Juan Ygnacio Tafolla & Maria Antonia Baca; gp/ Salbador Tafolla & Juana Lusero.

NS, Maria Josefa
bap 23 Feb 1835, 5 days old; d/ unknown parents, left at the home of Ysidora Garcia; gp/ Blas Lusero & Grabiela Jaramillo.

Frame 1563
GARCIA, Francisco Antonio
bap 24 Feb 1835, 3 days old; s/ Jose Rafael Garcia & Dolores Chabes, parishioners; ap/ Francisco Garcia & Guadalupe Otero; am/ Juan Chaves & Micaela Sanches; gp/ Julian Sedillo & Cipriana Garcia.

NS, Jose Antonio
bap 24 Feb 1835, 3 days old; s/ unknown parents, left at the home of Don Juan Armijo; gp/ Don Juan de los Dios Chabes & Doña Marcelina Valencia.

SANCHES, Pedro Antonio
bap 25 Feb 1835, 3 days old; legit s/ Christobal Sanches & Monica Gonzales; ap/ Felipe Montoya & Maria de la Lus Lopes; am/ Juan Gonsales & Maria Antonia Armijo; gp/ Pedro Antonio Montoya & Maria Rosa Montoya.

Frame 1564, #181
SANCHES, Maria Gertrudes de los Dolores
bap 1 Mar 1835, 3 days old; d/ Nasario Sanches & Candelaria Baca, parishioners; ap/ Antonio Jose Sanches & Rosalia Martines; am/ Antonio Jesus Baca & Maria Gertrudis Castillo; gp/ Antonio Jose Maldonado & Bibiana Gonsales.

CHRESPIN, Maria Paula
bap 3 Mar 1835, 2 days old; d/ Juan Andres Chrespin & Manuela Jaramillo, parishioners; ap/ Juan Chrespin & Madelina Martinez; am/ Alfonso Jaramillo & Luisa Lopes; gp/ Hilario Griego & Guadalupe Griego.

GRIEGO, Manuel Antonio
SANDOBAL, Manuel Antonio (in margin)
bap 3 Mar 1835, 3 days old; legit s/ Francisco Griego & Josefa Sandobal, parishioners; ap & am/ not stated; gp/ Salbador Sandobal & Maria Rita Griego.

Frames 1564-1565
GARCIA, Pablo Antonio Casimiro
bap 4 Mar 1835, 3 days old; s/ Juan Garcia & Juana Maria Chabes, parishioners; ap/ Francisco Garcia & Manuela Gonsales; am/ Juan Chabes & Barbara Armijo; gp/ Miguel Castillo & Maria de la Lus Montoya.

LUCERO, Pedro Antonio
bap 4 Mar 1835, 2 days old; s/ Jose de los Niebes Lusero & Eulogia Sabedra; ap/ Andres Lusero & Tomasa Garcia; am/ Francisco Sabedra & Maria de la Lus Chabes; gp/ Pedro Armijo & Maria Petra Perea.

NS, Jose de la Trinidad
bap 4 Mar 1835, 4 days old; s/ unknown parents, left at the home of Maria Gurule; gp/ Jose Antonio Martines & Maria Teodora Garcia.

Frame 1566, #182
MOLINA, Maria del Rallo Barbara
bap 5 Mar 1835, 2 days old; d/ Pedro Molina & Maria Manuela Analla, parishioners; ap/ Miguel Molina & Maria Gertrudis Burtierres; am/ Cimon Anaya & Maria Manuela Sanches; gp/ Juan Apodaca & Barbara Apodaca.

SANCHES, Maria Tomasa
bap 7 Mar 1835, 7 days old; legit d/ Francisco Sanches & Maria Burtierres, parishioners; ap/ not stated; am/ Ysidro Burtierres & Dolores Martines; gp/ Jose Samora & Juana Griego.

GONSALES, Maria Tomasa
MOLLA, Maria Tomasa (in margin)
bap 7 Mar 1835, 7 days old; legit d/ Cruz Gonsales & Maria Molla, parishioners; ap/ Antonio Gonsales & Barbara Basques; am/ Eusebio Molla & Maria Montolla; gp/ Juan Baca & Marzelina Baca.

Frame 1567
CARRILLO, Maria Tomasa
bap 8 Mar 1835, 1 day old; legit d/ Antonio Carrillo & Felipa Garcia; ap & am/ not stated; gp/ Manuel Garcia & Tomasa Cena.

ANALLA, Maria Nicolasa (twin)
bap 9 Mar 1835, 1 day old; legit d/ Salbador Analla & Barbara Sanches, parishioners; ap/ Pedro Analla & Dolores Lauriano; am/ Manuel Sanches & Dolores Chabes; gp/ Nicolas Mares & Maria Manuela Chabes.

ANALLA, Maria Trinidad (twin)
bap 9 Mar 1835, 1 day old; legit s/ Salbador Analla & Barbara Sanches, parishioners; ap/ Ycidro Analla & Dolores Lauriano; am/ Manuel Sanches & Dolores Chabes; gp/ Maria Luisa Chabes.

Frame 1568, #183
LUNA, Juan Bautista
bap 12 Mar 1835, 2 days old; legit s/ Francisco Luna & Concepcion Cena, parishioners; ap/ Joaquin Luna & Maria Romero; am/ Miguel Cena & Manuela Martines; gp/ Bicente Montolla & Josefa Martines.

NS, Francisco Roman
bap 12 Mar 1835, 1 day old; s/ unknown parents, left at the home of Jesus Gallegos; gp/ Pedro Antonio Sais & Dolores Candelaria.

Frames 1568-1569
PEREA, Maria Antonia
bap 13 Mar 1835, 6 days old; legit d/ Bartolo Perea & Josefa Candelaria; ap/ Miguel Perea & Antonia Martines; am/ Jose Tomas Candelaria & Ana Maria Mirabal; gp/ Don Julian Apodaca & Doña Maria Antonia Griego.

ARMIJO, Maria del Rallo Ysabel
bap 14 Mar 1835, 1 day old; legit d/ Jesus Armijo & Monica Pacheco, parishioners; ap/ not stated; am/ Jose Pacheco & Juana Sedillo; gp/ Don Juan Apodaca & Doña Maria Ysabel Sanches.

GALLEGO, Jose de Jesus Amador
bap 15 Mar 1835, 3 days old; legit s/ Christobal Gallego & Carmen Butierrez, parishioners; ap/ not stated; am/ Juan Miguel Gutierres & Maria de los Niebes Chaves; gp/ Don Mariano Lusero & Doña Martina Valencia.

Frame 1570, #184
GARCIA, Guadalupe Victoria
bap 18 Mar 1835, 1 day old; legit d/ Jose Garcia & Manuela Baca, parishioners; ap/ Tomas Garcia & Bernarda Carbajal; am/ not stated; gp/ Jesus Lopes & Maria de la Lus Lopez.

GARCIA, Maria Gertrudis
bap 18 Mar 1835, 3 days old; legit d/ Antonio Garcia & Yzabel Gallego, parishioners; ap/ Francisco Garcia & Guadalupe Otero; am/ Joaquin Gallego & Mariana Sanches; gp/ Manuel Chabes & Dolores Chabes.

LUJAN, Jose Casimiro
bap 19 Mar 1835, 8 days old; legit s/ Miguel Lujan & Rita Sandobal, parishioners; ap/ not stated; am/ Miguel Sandobal & Maria Martines; gp/ Bartolo Sanches & Francisca Sanches.

Frame 1571
NS, Maria Josefa
bap 19 Mar 1835, 3 days old; d/ unknown parents, left at the home of Eugenia Gurule; gp/ Pablo Armijo & Josefa Sandoval.

NS, Maria Gregoria
bap 22 Mar 1835, 9 days old; d/ unknown parents, left at the home of Julian Valencia; gp/ Manuel Garcia & Barbara Lopes.

CORDOBA, Francisco de la Encarnacion
bap 25 Mar 1835, 2 days old; legit s/ Marcos Cordoba & Juana Duran, parishioners; ap/ Antonio Cordoba & Alfonsa Cedillo; am/ not stated; gp/ Grabiel Gurule & Rafaela Rios.

Frame 1572, #185
NS, Francisco Antonio
bap 27 Mar 1835, 3 days, s/ unknown parents, left at the home of Juan Garcia; gp/ Francisco Duran & Bernarda Gurule.

NS, Teodocio
bap 29 Mar 1835, 3 days old; s/ unknown parents; gp/ Miguel Corrales & Maria Ynes Martines.

Frames 1572-1573
GONSALES, Maria Cista de los Dolores
bap 30 Mar 1835, 5 days old; d/ Don Santiago Gonsales & Doña Manuela Aragon; ap/ Don Juan Gonzales & Doña Maria Antonia Armijo; am/ Manuel Aragon & Doña Maria Montolla; gp/ Don Julian Perea & Doña Nepomucena Gallegos.

APODACA, Ysidora
bap 8 Apr 1835, 3 days old; legit d/ Antonio Apodaca & Juana Samora, parishioners; ap/ Nicolas Apodaca & Maria de la Lus Garcia; am/ Jose Samora & Rafaela Martines; gp/ Jose Garcia & Juana Cordoba.

SANDOBAL, Mariano
bap 8 Apr 1835, 3 days old; legit s/ Antonio Sandobal & Maria de Sideria Candelaria, parishioners; gp/ Christobal Montoya & Maria Bibiana Chabes.

Frame 1574, #186
SAMORA, Jesus Maria Florian
bap 9 Apr 1835, 3 days old; legit s/ Jose Samora & Rafaela Martines, parishioners; ap/ Juan Christobal Samora & Maria Ygnacia Garcia; am/ Ysidro Martines & Dolores Montaño; gp/ Salvador Apodaca & Maria Clara Burtierres.

PADILLA, Victoria de la Trinidad
bap 9 Apr 1835; legit d/ Manuel Padilla & Maria Antonia Otero, parishioners; ap/ Bernardo Padilla & Francisca Chabes; am/ not stated; gp/ Damacio Gurule & Maria Dolores Gurule.

CHABES, Maria Refugio
bap 12 Apr 1835, 7 days old; legit d/ Jose Chabes & Micaela Sanches, parishioners; ap/ Jose Maria Chabes & Maria Ygnacia Armijo; am/ Felis Sanchez & Maria Aguirre; gp/ Francisco Antonio Sanchez & Dolores Chabes.

Frame 1575
MARTINES, Maria Ygnacia
bap 12 Apr 1835, 3 days old; legit d/ Felipe Martines & Victoria Arias, parishioners; ap/ not stated; am/ Miguel Arias & Gregoria Martinez; gp/ Felipe Samora & Maria Ygnacia Valencia.

ROMERO, Jose Amador
bap 14 Apr 1835, 2 days old; legit s/ Diego Romero & Encarnacion Valencia, parishioners; ap/ not stated; am/ Dominguez Valencia & Ygnacia Garcia; gp/ Don Andres Ortega.

GURULE, Jose Damasio
bap 15 Apr 1835, 11 days old; legit s/ Felipe Gurule & Juana Bustamante, parishioners; ap & am/ not stated gp/ Domingo Valencia & Paula Martines.

Frame 1576, #187
NS, Maria del Rallo
bap 15 Apr 1835, 1 day old; d/ unknown parents, criada of Juan Sanches; gp/ Tomas Chabes & Rosalia Chabes.

ROMERO, Maria del Rallo
bap 15 Apr 1835; d/ Manuel Romero & Petra Apodaca, parishioners; ap/ not stated; am/ Jesus Apodaca & Gertrudis Lusero; gp/ Manuel Olguin & Dolores Garcia.

TORRES, Jose Vacilio
bap 19 Apr 1835, 5 days old; legit s/ Francisco Torres & Juliana Montolla, parishioners; ap/ Salbador Torres & Getrudis Baca; am/ Antonio Montolla & Maria Ana Sanches; gp/ Doña Ygnacia Bazan.

Frames 1576-1577
JARAMILLO, Maria Petra
bap 19 Apr 1835, 3 days old; legit d/ Ysidro Jaramillo & Catarina Mestas, parishioners; ap/ not stated; am/ Francisco Mestas & Gertrudis Pacheco; gp/ Carlos Lopes & Barbara Contreras.

LUSERO, Maria Manuela Tibursia
bap 20 Apr 1835, 4 days old; legit d/ Jose Ygnacio Lusero & Maria Dolores Tenorio, parishioners; ap/ Miguel Lusero & Maria Dimas Aragon; am/ Juan Romero & Rafaela Tenorio; gp/ Tomas Tafolla & Soledad Montolla.

SANCHES, Antonio Jose de los Dolores
bap 21 Apr 1835, 2 days old; legit s/ Antonio Sanches & Madalena Griego, parishioners; ap/ Antonio Jose Sanches & Sebastiana Ortega; am/ Miguel Griego & Gertrudes Olguin; gp/ Don Juan Montolla & Doña Clara Jaramillo.

Frame 1578, #188
LUSERO, Jesus Jose
bap 22 Apr 1835, 2 days old; legit s/ Jose Lusero & Maria Gertrudis Burtierres, parishioners; ap/ Juan Jose Lucero & Petra Lopes; am/ Antonio Burtierres & Francisca Sanches; gp/ Doña Elena Domingues.

BUTIERRES, Maria Ynes
bap 23 Apr 1835, 2 days old; legit d/ Salbador Butierres & Nicolasa B__ (unreadable); ap & am/ not stated; gp/ Rafaela Cordoba.

CARABAJAL, Juan Marselino
bap 27 Apr 1835, 3 days old; legit s/ Manuel Carabajal & Teresa Martines, parishioners; ap & am/ not stated gp/ Jose Benabides & Pascuala Gallego.

Frame 1579
GARCIA, Maria de los Dolores
bap 28 Apr 1835, 5 days old; legit d/ Juan Garcia & Yzabel Garcia, parishioners; ap/ Tomas Garcia & Bernarda Tafolla; am/ Ramon Garcia & Acencion Lopes; gp/ Salbador Sanches & Olalla Tafolla.

BRITO, Maria del Rallo Marcelina (twin)
bap 29 Apr 1835, 3 days old; twin legit d/ Antonio Brito & Maria Nieta, parishioners; ap & am/ not stated; gp/ Don Juan Domingo Balencia & Doña Paula Martines. [Note: See also BRITO, Maria Dolores.]

Frame 1580, #189
BRITO, Maria Dolores (twin)
bap 29 Apr 1835, 3 days old; twin legit d/ Antonio Brito & Maria Nieta; ap & am/ not stated; gp/ Don Pedro Aranda & Doña Rosalia Jaramillo. [Note: See also BRITO, Maria del Rallo Marcelina.]

GONSALES, Juan Bautista
bap 30 Apr 1835, 21 days old; legit s/ Christobal Gonsales & Manuela Garcia, parishioners; ap/ Fernando Gonsales & Dorotea Griego; am/ Francisco Garcia & Manuela Gonsales; gp/ Don Nicolas Sandobal & Doña Concepcion Armijo.

Frames 1580-1581
NS, Jose Anastacio de la Cruz
bap 3 May 1835, 3 days old; s/ unknown parents, left at the home of Juan Domingo Griego; gp/ Jose Anastacio Lucero & Juana Duran.

CASTILLO, Maria Josefa
bap 3 May 1835, 7 days old; legit d/ Miguel Castillo & Rosalia Martines, parishioners; ap/ Antonio Jose Castillo & Quiteria Chabes; am/ Ysidro Martines & Dorotea Montaño; gp/ Don Bicente Sanches & Doña Francisca Sanches.

Frame 1582, #190
NS, Jose de Jesus Amador
bap 8 May 1835, 2 days old; s/ unknown parents, left at the home of Jose Garcia; gp/ Rafael (Candelaria) & Maria Ysabel Candelaria.

CERNA, Maria Trinidad
bap 8 May 1835, 2 days old; d/ Antonio Cerna & Maria Guadalupe Burtierres, parishioners; ap & am/ not stated; gp/ Juan Christobal Garcia & Rita Lopes.

SAIS, Maria de la Crus
bap 9 May 1835, 7 days old; legit d/ Alfonsa Sais & Juana Mora, parishioners; ap/ not stated; am/ Juan Mora & Maria Luisa Burtierres; gp/ Don Miguel Sais & Doña Maria Ygnacia NS

Frame 1583
NS, Maria Biatriz
bap 9 May 1835, 3 days old; d/ unknown parents, left at the home of Ambrocio Mestas; gp/ Lorenzo Mestas & Ana Josefa Mestas.

JARAMILLO, Juan Antonio
bap 22 May 1835, 2 days old; legit s/ Salbador Jaramillo & Gertrudis Baca, parishioners; ap/ Geronimo Jaramillo & Gertrudis Lucero; am/ Jesus Baca & Antonia Garcia; gp/ Juan Rafael Garcia & Dolores Chabes.

Frame 1584, #191
SABEDRA, Maria Tomasa
bap 23 May 1835, 7 days old; legit d/ Juan Cristobal Sabedra & Monica Garcia, parishioners; ap/ Jose Sabedra & Maria Sedillo; am/ Ysidro Garcia & Gertrudis Sanches; gp/ Don Jose Jaramillo & Doña Lorensa Lusero.

SANCHES, Jose Felis
bap 24 May 1835, 7 days old; legit s/ Juan Sanches & Guadalupe Chabes, parishioners; ap/ Antonio Jose Sanches & Rosalia Martines; am/ Juan Chabes & Juliana Rael; gp/ Don Felis Sanches & Doña Sebastiana Cena.

NS, Maria Felipa
bap 26 May 1835, 3 days old; d/ unknown parents, left at the home of Francisca Martines; gp/ Juan Jose Martines & Tomasa Armenta.

Frame 1585
LOPES, Jose Federico de Jesus
bap 26 May 1835, 1 day old; legit s/ Ramon Lopes & Relles Jaramillo, parishioners; ap/ Bicente Lopes & Maria Antonia Chabes; am/ Miguel Jaramillo & Gertrudis Lusero; gp/ Marcos Ruis & Balbina Jaramillo.

JARAMILLO, Maria Acencion
bap 28 May 1835, 2 days old; legit d/ Manuel Jaramillo & Gertrudis Mestas, parishioners; ap/ Miguel Jaramillo & Ana Maria Ortega; am/ Mariano Mestas & Guadalupe Otero; gp/ Don Andres Ortega & Juana Garcia.

Frame 1586, #192
SANCHES, Maria Petra Francisca
bap 1 Jun 1835, 4 days old; d/ Gabriel Sanches & Doña Rafaela Ruis, parishioners; ap/ Don Antonio Jose Sanches & Doña Rosalia Martines; am/ Lorenso Ruis & Hurbana Ydalgo; gp/ Gregorio Ortiz & Clara Sarrazino.

GRIEGO, Pedro Asencio
bap 2 Jun 1835, 4 days old; legit s/ Pedro Griego & Anastacia Salazar, parishioners; ap/ Jose Maria Griego & Maria Candelaria Armijo; am/ Toribio Salazar & Polonia Burtierres; gp/ Juan Bicente Candelaria & Ynes Martines.

Frame 1587
BACA, Maria Juana
bap 2 Jun 1835, 8 days old; legit d/ Pablo Baca & Benigna Burtierres, parishioners; ap/ Relles Baca & Manuela Archuleta; am/ Rafael Burtierres & Josefa Mares; gp/ Juan Sandobal & Juana Baca.

GURULE, Maria Bicenta
bap 6 June 1835, 18 days old; legit d/ Diego Gurule & Teresa Burtierres, parishioners; ap/ Juan Cristobal Gurule & Maria Ygnacia Martines; am/ not stated; gp/ Bicente Gonsales & Juana Garcia.

MANSANARES, Jose Manuel
bap 7 Jun 1835, 6 days old; legit s/ Jose Mansanares & Estefana Jaramillo, parishioners; ap & am/ not stated; gp/ Bernardo Balencia & Paula Martines.

Frame 1588, #193
SANDOBAL, Jose Pedro
bap 7 Jun 1835, 4 days old; s/ Dolores Sandobal & Juana Trugillo; ap/ not stated; am/ Baltasar Trugillo & Teresa Gallego; gp/ Julian Valencia & Refugio Rael. [Note: See also entry below.]

SANDOBAL, Jose Pedro
bap 7 Jun 1835, 4 days old; legit s/ Dolores Sandobal & Juana Trugillo, parishioners; ap/ unknown; am/ Baltasar Trugillo & Teresa Gallego; gp/ Julian Valencia & Refugio Rael. [Note: See also entry above.]

TORRES, Maria Noberta
bap 8 Jun 1835, 3 days old; legit d/ Juan Torres & Zabel Burtierres, parishioners; ap & am/ not stated; gp/ Lasaro Torres & Micaela Arias.

Frame 1589
GARCIA, Maria Juana
bap 9 Jun 1835, 3 days old; d/ Juan Garcia & Barbara Herrera, parishioners; gp/ Jacinto Sanches & Gregoria Rael.

NS, Manuel Antonio
bap 18 Jun 1835, 4 days old; s/ unknown parents, left at the home of Maria Lopes; gp/ Juan Manuel Benavides & Juana Lopes.

Frames 1589-1590, #194
GURULE, Jose Roberto
bap 18 Jun 1835, 4 days old; s/ Nicolas Gurule & Donasiana Martines, parishioners; ap/ not stated; am/ Jose Martines & Rosalia Lusero; gp/ Pablo Martines & Maria Antonia Lusero.

NS, Maria Manuela
bap 19 Jun 1835, 1 day old; d/ unknown parents, left at the home of Don Juan Armijo; gp/ Don Mariano (Armijo) & Doña Juana Armijo.

MAES, Maria Manuela
bap 21 Jun 1835, 3 days old; legit d/ Juan Andres Maes & Maria Cimona Sanches, parishioners; ap/ not stated; am/ Mariano Sanches & Francisca Gabaldon; gp/ Jose de la Nieves Lusero & Maria Eulogia Sabedra.

Frame 1591
APODACA, Jose Amador de Jesus
bap 4 Jul 1835, 1 day old; legit s/ Don Bicente Apodaca & Doña Paula Mestas, parishioners; ap/ Miguel Apodaca & Catarina Chabes; am/ Pedro Mestas & Maria Antonia Duran; gp/ Don Juan Armijo & Doña Ana Maria Gabaldon.

SANDOBAL, Miguel Antonio
bap 5 Jul 1835, 1 day old; legit s/ Francisco Sandobal & Maria Garcia, parishioners; ap/ Jose Sandobal & Petra Sabedra; am/ not stated; gp/ Don Julian Sedillo & Doña Cipriano Garcia.

Frame 1592, #195
GONZALES, Maria Petra (of Bernalillo)
bap 8 Jul 1835, 10 days old; d/ Felipe Gonzales & Margarita Cena, parishioners of Sandia; ap/ Nerio Gonzales & Maria Griego; am/ not stated; gp/ Mariano Mares & Bicenta Garcia.

ARAGON, Maria del Rallo Gertrudis
bap 9 Jul 1835, 4 days old; d/ Rafael Aragon & Catarena Sabedra; ap/ stated; am/ Pablo Sabedra & Gertrudis Apodaca; gp/ maternal grandparents.

Frames 1592-1593
CANDELARIA, Maria Yzabel
bap 9 Jul 1835, 11 days old; legit d/ Ramon Candelaria & Manuela Martines, parishioners; ap/ Francisco Candelaria & Maria de la Lus Armijo; am/ Baltazar Martines & Maria Antonia Griego; gp/ Domingo Sanches & Maria de la Lus Perea.

NS, Jose Nicanor
bap 25 Jul 1835, 3 days old; s/ unknown parents, left at the home of Alfonsa Garcia; gp/ Juan Rafael Nieto & Juana Arias.

ROMERO, Ana Maria
bap 26 Jul 1835, 3 days old; legit d/ Bicente Romero & Maria Antonia Ortega, parishioners; ap & am/ not stated; gp/ Bicente Lopes & Maria Antonia Burtierres.

Frames 1593-1594, #196
GALLEGO, Juan Cristobal
bap 1 Aug 1835; 3 days old; legit s/ Antonio Gallego & Petra Padilla, parishioners; ap/ Rafael Gallego & Barbara Gonzales; am/ Manuel Padilla & Maria Antonia Otero; gp/ Francisco Padilla & Francisca Padilla.

GONSALES, Pedro Antonio
bap 3 Aug 1835, 3 days old; legit s/ Francisco Gonsales & Francisca Garcia, parishioners; ap & am/ not stated; gp/ Luis Mares & Teresa Garcia.

GARCIA, Juan Manuel
bap 3 Aug 1835, 3 days old; legit s/ Bartolo Garcia & Juana Maria Padilla, parishioners; ap/ Juan Garcia & Barbara Chabes; am/ Diego Antonio Padilla & Manuela Aguirre; gp/ Don Juan Montolla & Doña Manuela Garcia.

Frames 1594-1595
GRIEGO, Jose Lorenso
bap 10 Aug 1835, 2 days old; legit s/ Tomas Griego & Monica Santillanes, parishioners; ap/ Miguel Griego & Petra Garcia; am/ Antonio Santillanes & Geralda Garcia; gp/ Pablo Carrillo & Maria Petra Santillanes.

GONSALES, Maria Clara de Jesus (of Bernalillo)
bap 12 Aug 1835, 3 days old; d/ Juan Gonsales & Jacinta Martines, parishioners of Sandia; ap/ Miguel Gonsales & Polonia Chabes; am/ Pablo Martines & Maria Manuela Martines; gp/ Juan Nepomuceno Martines & Maria Manuela Martines.

BURTIERRES, Jose Ramon (of Bernalillo)
bap 12 Aug 1835, 4 days old; legit s/ Jose Antonio Burtierres & Tomasa Jaramillo, parishioners of Sandia; ap/ Salbador Martines & Rita Burtierres; am/ Mariano Jaramillo & Juana Martines; gp/ Jose Burtierres & Dolores Burtierres.

Frame 1596, #187
LOPES, Maria Romona
bap 16 Aug 1835, 2 days old; legit s/ Juan Christobal Lopes & Rita Sedillo, parishioners; ap/ Jose Maria Lopes & Barbara Baca; am/ Gregorio Sedillo & Juana Candelaria; gp/ Jesus Francisco Apodaca & Maria Ygnacio Lopes.

MARQUES, Francisco Esteban
bap 16 Aug 1835, 2 days old; legit s/ Jose Dolores Marques & Perfecto Sedillo, parishioners; ap/ not stated; am/ Esteban Sedillo & Andrea Sandobal; gp/ Salbador Apodaca.

Frame 1597
MUÑIS, Manuel Antonio
bap 17 Aug 1835, 2 days old; legit s/ Juan Christobal Muñis & Antonia Maria Pacheco, parishioners; ap/ Jose Maria Muñis & Barbara Samora; am/ Geronimo Pacheco & Pascuala Sanches; gp/ Felipe Martines & Victoria Sais.

NS, Maria Luisa
bap 23 Aug 1835, 6 days old; d/ unknown parents, left at the home of Paula Chabes; gp/ Jose (Chabes) & Paula Chabes.

ARMIJO, Jose de Jesus
bap 23 Aug 1835, 6 days old; legit s/ Rafael Armijo & Soledad Peña, parishioners; ap/ Pablo Armijo & Josefa Chabes; am/ unknown; gp/ Don Pablo Burtierres & Doña Juana Sena.

Frame 1598, #198
ORTEGA, Maria Ygnacia Bartola
bap 26 Aug 1835, 2 days old; legit d/ Don Francisco Ortega & Maria Ygnacia Basan, parishioners; ap/ Don Andres Ortega & Doña Juana Andrea Garcia; am/ not stated; gp/ Don Andres Ortega & Doña Juana Andrea Garcia.

CANDELARIA, Jesus Maria
bap 4 Sep 1835, 3 days old; s/ Julian Candelaria & Gregoria Candelaria; ap/ Jose Tomas Candelaria & Ana Maria Gallego; am/ Salbador Candelaria & Maria Gertrudis Lopes; gp/ Jose Chabes & Ana Maria Candelaria.

Frames 1598-1599
GRIEGO, Juan de Dios Ramon
bap 10 Sep 1835, 2 days old; legit s/ Pablo Griego & Juana Montolla, parishioners; ap/ Don Felipe Griego & Doña Margarita Gonzales; am/ Don Juan Nepomuceno Montolla & Doña Maria de Jesus Lusero; gp/ Don Tadeo Garcia & Doña Barbara Griego.

CANDELARIA, Jose Vitoriano
bap 11 Sep 1835, 5 days old; legit s/ Manuel Candelaria & Francisca Griego, parishioners; ap/ Bicente Candelaria & Candelaria Lobato; am/ not stated; gp/ Felipe Garcia & Maria Ynes Gurule.

LUSERO, Maria de la Lus
bap 12 Sep 1835, 3 days old; legit d/ Juan Lusero & Micaela Trugillo, parishioners; ap/ Miguel Lusero & Maria Dimas Aragon; am/ Antonio Trugillo & Juana Montolla; gp/ Pedro Trugillo & Maria de la Lus Perea.

Frames 1599-1600, #199
GONSALES, Jose Guillermo Amado
bap 16 Sep 1835, 3 days old; legit s/ Don Sabino Gonsales & Maria de Jesus Luna, parishioners; ap/ Juan Domingo Gonsales & Maria Archuleta; am/ Joaquin Luna & Maria Romero; gp/ Don Julian Tenorio & Doña Begnina Chabes.

SANCHES, Jose Cornelio
bap 18 Sep 1835, 2 days old; legit s/ Domingo Sanches & Perfecta Montoya, parishioners; ap/ Don Antonio Sanches & Doña Maria Ygnacia Analla; am/ Pedro Montolla & Maria de la Luna; gp/ Antonio Sandobal & Teresa de la Luna.

APODACA, Maria del Rallo Serafina
bap 23 Sep 1835, 2 days old; d/ Francisco Apodaca & Tomasa Barela, parishioners; ap/ Jose Apodaca & Gertrudis Lusero; am/ Juan Barela & Josefa Chabes; gp/ Francisco Apodaca & Maria Ygnacia Lopes.

Frames 1600-1601
NS, Maria del Rayo de Jesus
bap 26 Sep 1835, 3 days old; d/ unknown parents, left at the home of Bitorino Molla; gp/ Jose Antonio Martines & Quitoria Griego.

NS, Juan Manuel
bap 29 Sep 1835, 2 days old; s/ unknown parents, left at the home of Don Pablo Elisarri; gp/ Juan Gonsales & Balbina Lopes.

NS, Jose Tanislado
bap 2 Oct 1835, 5 days old; s/ unknown parents, placed in the home of Juan Butierres; gp/ Manuel Garcia & Josefa Molina.

Frame 1602, #200
CANDELARIA, Antonio Jose
bap 2 Oct 1835, 8 days old; legit s/ Francisco Antonio Candelaria & Maria Lorensa Padilla, parishioners; ap/ Juan Candelaria & Teresa Chabes; am/ Diego Antonio Padilla & Manuela Garcia; gp/ Don Julian Sedillo & Doña Cipriana Garcia.

PEREA, Maria del Rallo
bap 4 Oct 1835, 2 days old; s/ (torn) Perea & Juliana Chabes, parishioners; ap/ Pedro Perea & Josefa Garcia; am/ not stated; gp/ Francisco Armijo & Soledad Armijo.

CORDOBA, Maria Francisca
bap 6 Oct 1835, 2 days old; d/ Mariano Cordoba & Ysidora Analla, parishioners; ap/ Manuel Cordoba & Guadalupe Cerna; am/ Pedro Analla & Dolores Burtierres; gp/ Antonio Garcia & Maria Ysidora Garcia.

Frame 1603
SAMORA, Maria Placida
bap 6 Oct 1835, 5 days old; d/ Jose Samora & Josefa Griego, parishioners; ap/ Francisco Samora & Maria Ygnacia Valencia; am/ not stated; gp/ Christobal Sanches & Concepcion Valencia. [Note: See also Frame 1604, #1.]

NS, Maria Francisca
bap 7 Oct 1835, 4 days old; d/ unknown parents, left at the home of Lugarda Cordoba; gp/ Jose Antonio (Cordoba) & Estefana Cordoba.

NS, Maria del Rallo Carmen
bap 9 Oct 1835, 2 days old; d/ unknown parents; gp/ Juan Eusebio Sabedra & Maria Ysidora Garcia.

AASF, Reel #2
B-7 (Box 7) 1835–1838

Frame 1604, #1
SAMORA, Maria Placida
bap 6 Oct 1835, 5 days old; legit d/ Jose Samora & Josefa Griego, parishioners; ap/ Francisco Samora & Maria Ygnacia Valencia; am/ not stated; gp/ Christobal Sanches & Maria Concepcion Valencia. [Note: See also Frame 1603.]

ANALLA, Maria Rallo Placida
bap 7 Oct 1835, 3 days old; legit d/ Ramon Analla & Ana Maria Lopes, parishioners; ap/ Manuel Analla & Maria Antonia Apodaca; am/ Miguel Lopes & Lucia Duran; gp/ Manuel Burtieres & Rosalia Analla.

SEDILLO, Jose Francisco Bicente Eduardo
bap 13 Oct 1835, 4 days old; legit s/ Pedro Sedillo & Francisca Chabez, parishioners; ap/ Pablo Sedillo & Madelena Garcia; am/ Jose Chabes & Rafaela Gabaldon; gp/ Don Jose Armijo & Doña Clara Armijo.

Frame 1605
SANCHES, Juana Maria
bap 14 Oct 1835, 3 days old; legit d/ Antonio Sanches & Maria Lucero, parishioners; ap/ Antonio Jose Sanchez & Sebastiana Ortega; am/ Lorenso Lucero & Crus Sabedra; gp/ Jose Antonio Martines & Quiteria Griego.

BACA, Jose de Jesus
bap 15 Oct 1835, 1 day old; s/ Juan Domingo Baca & Dolores Lucero, parishioners; ap/ Lasaro Baca & Guadalupe Carabajal; am/ Juan Lucero & Francisca Lucero; gp/ Maria Lucero.

OTERO, Maria del Rollo
bap 18 Oct 1835, 2 days old; d/ Juan Otero & Rosalia Jaramillo, parishioners; ap & am/ not stated; gp/ Jose Francisco Apodaca & Maria Ygnacia Lopes.

Frame 1606, #2
GARCIA, Maria Juana Leocadia
bap 19 Oct 1835, 2 days old; legit d/ Francisco Garcia & Ana Maria Montolla, parishioners of Sandia; ap/ not stated; am/ Antonio Montolla & Maria Salome Burtierres; gp/ Jose Rafael C̲ilba & Maria Francisca Silba.

SAVEDRA, Miguel Antonio
bap 25 Oct 1835, 8 days old; legit s/ Cristobal Savedra & Ana Maria Martinez, parishioners; ap/ Juan Savedra & Juliana Montaño; am/ Felipe Martinez & Juana Mora; gp/ Felipe Martinez & Bibian Sais.

TRUGILLO, Maria Ursula
bap 25 Oct 1835, 5 days old; legit d/ Pedro Trugillo & Maria Sanches, parishioners; ap/ Juan Jose Trugillo & Maria del Carmen Tafolla; am/ Domingo Sanches & Maria de la Lus Perea; gp/ Manuel Garcia & Rafaela Rael.

Frame 1607
CANDELARIA, Jose Rafael
bap 25 Oct 1835, 1 day old; legit s/ Enriques Candelaria & Isabel Garcia, parishioners; ap & am/ not stated; gp/ Salbador Sedillo & Ana Maria Sanches.

BURTIERRES, Cimon de Jesus
bap 28 Oct 1835, 3 days old; legit s/ Miguel Antonio Burtierres & Maria Albina Santillanes, parishioners; ap/ Miguel Burtierres & Maria Manuela Rael; am/ Juan Miguel Santillanes & Micaela Gonsales; gp/ Doña Maria Elena Domingues.

Frames 1607-1608, #3
JARAMILLO, Maria de Jesus
bap 30 Oct 1835, 2 days old; d/ Manuel Jaramillo & Dolores Jaramillo, parishioners; ap/ Juan de Jesus Jaramillo & Rosa Sabedra; am/ not stated; gp/ Don Jose Dolores Chaves & Doña Nicanor Garcia.

NS, Maria Dolores
bap 1 Nov 1835, 9 days old; d/ unknown parents, left at the home of Pedro Martines; gp/ Francisco Xavier Martines & Maria Dolores Martines.

LUSERO, Maria del Rallo
bap 3 Nov 1835, 8 days old; d/ Jose Manuel Lusero & Francisca Garcia, parishioners; ap & am/ not stated; gp/ Luis Mares & Teresa Garcia.

Frames 1608-1609
RAEL, Jose Rafael
bap 10 Nov 1835, 6 days old; legit s/ Santiago Rael & Maria Serafina Chabes, parishioners; ap & am/ not stated; gp/ Manuel Garcia & Rafaela Rael.

BARELA, Jose Rafael
bap 10 Nov 1835, 7 days old; legit s/ Antonio Barela & Catarina Ortiz; ap/ Juan Barela & Josefa Chabes; am/ Lorenzo Ortiz & Rafaela Ruis; gp/ Rafael Apodaca & Barbara Molina.

JARAMILLO, Maria del Refugio
bap 11 Nov 1835, 4 days old; legit d/ Marcos Jaramillo & Ana Maria Garcia, parishioners; ap/ Christobal Jaramillo & Maria Elena Chabes; am/ Diego Garcia & Maria Ramona Candelaria; gp/ Pablo Cisneros & Francisca Ruis.

Frame 1610, #4
NS, Jose Florencio
bap 15 Nov 1835, 6 days old; s/ unknown parents, left at the home of Don Salbador Montaño; gp/ Juan Antonio Aragon & Maria Padilla.

OLGUIN, Antonio Jose
bap 15 Nov 1835, 7 days old; s/ Jose Olguin & Juana Perea, parishioners; ap & am/ not stated; gp/ Juan Gonsales & Maria de la Lus Gonsales.

Frames 1610-1611
GRIEGO, Prudencia Concepcion
bap 17 Nov 1835, 4 days old; d/ Juan Isidoro Griego & Bentura Lucero, parishioners; ap/ Francisco Griego & Maria Antonia Cerna; am/ Juan Lucero & Maria Antonia Martines; gp/ Don Joaquin Luna & Doña Concepcion Luna.

MUÑIS, Maria Rosalia de los Dolores
bap 18 Nov 1835, 4 days old; d/ Faustin Muñis & Antonia Lucero, parishioners; gp/ Jose Patricio Lucero & Maria Cecilia Lucero.

NS, Manuel Antonio
bap 19 Nov 1835, 8 days old; s/ unknown parents, placed in the home of Nazario Sanches; gp/ Salbador Sais & Maria Luiza Cordoba.

Frames 1611-1612, #5
MOYA, Maria Antonia de los Dolores
bap 20 Nov 1835, 3 days old; d/ Vitorino Molla & Maria de Jesus Martines, parishioners; ap/ Manuel Antonio Molla & Maria Juliana Sandobal; am/ Pedro Martines & Juana Maria Garcia; gp/ Maria Dolores Torres.

BACA, Maria Juliana
bap 20 Nov 1835, 2 days old; legit d/ Diego Baca & Francisca Samora, parishioners; ap & am/ not stated; gp/ Don Juan Gil & Doña Teodora Lopes.

Frames 1612-1613
NS, Maria Josefa Lauriana de Jesus
bap 21 Nov 1835, 3 days old; d/ unknown parents, placed in the home of Feliciana Gabaldon; gp/ Maria Josefa Torres.

NS, Jose Clemente
bap 29 Nov 1835, 3 days old; s/ unknown parents; gp/ Jose Lopes & Barbara Apodaca.

GARCIA, Maria Francisca
bap 3 Dec 1835, 2 days old; d/ Juan Rafael Garcia & Encarnacion Lucero, parishioners; ap/ Juan Rafael Garcia & Manuela Muñiz; am/ Gregorio Lucero & Martha Lopes; gp/ Luciano Santillanes & Maria Gertrudis Duran.

Frame 1614, #6
NS, Maria Andrea
bap 6 Dec 1835, 26 days old; d/ unknown parents; gp/ Don Juan Sandobal & Doña Juana Baca.

ARMIJO, Nicolas Ambrosio
bap 7 Dec 1835, 3 days old; legit s/ Don Juan Christobal Armijo & Doña Juana Chabes, parishioners; ap/ Don Juan Armijo & Doña Rosalia Ortega; am/ Don Francisco Chabes & Doña Ana Maria Castillo; gp/ Don Juan Armijo & Doña Barbara Armijo.

NS, Jose de Jesus
bap 7 Dec 1785, 3 days old; s/ unknown parents, placed in the home of Dolores Otero; gp/ Christobal Garcia & Maria Yzabel Jaramillo.

Frame 1615
ARMIJO, Maria Concepcion Antonia
bap 8 Dec 1835, 2 days old; legit d/ Don Mariano Armijo & Doña Grabiela Jaramillo, parishioners; ap/ Don Ambrocio Armijo & Doña Maria Antonia Ortiz; am/ Don Miguel Antonio Jaramillo & Doña Lorenza Lucero; gp/ Antonio Jose Armijo & Maria Antonia Ortis.

SABEDRA, Maria Barbara Candelaria
bap 11 Dec 1835, 2 days old; legit d/ Jose Sabedra & Barbara Peña, parishioners; ap & am/ not stated; gp/ Mateo Peña & Barbara Yturrieta.

NS, Jose Guadalupe
bap 12 Dec 1835, 4 days old; s/ unknown parents, placed in the home of Don Francisco Ortega; gp/ Juan Martines & Maria Matilde Martines.

NS, Maria Guadalupe
bap 14 Dec 1835, 5 days old; d/ unknown parents, left at the home of Don Felipe Montolla; gp/ Bisente Montolla & Maria Rosa Montolla.

Frame 1616, #7
MONTOLLA, Juan Nepomucena (of Bernalillo)
bap 14 Dec 1835, 4 days old; legit s/ Don Bicente Montolla & Doña Maria Filomena Santieseban, parishioners, of Sandia; ap/ Don Bicente Montolla & Doña Maria Barbara Gonsales; am/ Don Jose Alejandro Santisteban & Doña Candelaria Martinez; gp/ Don Jose Martinez & Doña Maria Antonia Gonsales.

ARCHIBEQUE, Jose Clemente (of Bernalillo)
bap 14 Dec 1835, 22 days old; legit s/ Marcelino Archibeque & Juana Salazar, parishioners of Sandia; ap/ Agustin Archibeque & Manuela Chabes; am/ Joaquin Chabes & Bicenta Gallego; gp/ Jose Alejandro Santisteban & Maria Manuela Martines.

Frames 1616-1617
MORALES, Salbador Antonio
bap 14 Dec 1835, 4 days old; legit s/ Jose Antonio Morales & Juana Gonsales, parishioners; ap & am/ not stated; gp/ Salbador Sanches & Olalla Tafolla.

CHABES, Francisco Candido
bap 17 Dec 1835, 3 days old; legit s/ Toribio Chabes & Lorensa Perea, parishioners; ap/ not stated; am/ Juan Perea & Gertrudis Jaramillo; gp/ Pablo Carrillo & Maria Petra Santillanes.

ESQUIBEL, Jose Francisco Guadalupe
bap 17 Dec 1835, 4 days old; legit s/ Mariano Esquibel & Josefa Garcia, parishioners; ap/ Juan de Dios Esquibel & Guadalupe Trugillo; am/ Jose Francisco Garcia & Maria Ortega; gp/ Jose Trinidad Garcia & Maria Jaramillo.

Frames 1617-1618
BUTIERREZ, Maria Monica
bap 18 Dec 1835, 5 days old; d/ Juan Butierrez & Juana Mora, parishioners; ap/ not stated; am/ Cidro Mora & Juana Marques; gp/ Juan Montolla & Maria Dolores Montolla.

NS, Maria Guadalupe
bap 21 Dec 1835; Moquino Indian, purchased by Don Bicente Armijo; gp/ Don Pedro Mestas & Doña Maria Antonia Mestas.

GARCIA, Maria del Rallo Concepsion
bap 22 Dec 1835, 3 days old; d/ Juan Garcia & Maria Manuela Salasar, parishioners; ap/ Manuel Garcia & Juana Gurule; am/ Toribio Salasar & Polinaria Gutierres; gp/ Baltasar Romero & Paula Lucero.

Frame 1619
CISNERO, Jose Tomas Anisteo
bap 24 Dec 1835, 3 days old; s/ Pablo Cisnero & Francisca Ruis, parishioners; ap/ Francisco Sisneros & Maria Juana Candelaria; am/ Don Antonio Ruis & Doña Maria Ysabel Armijo; gp/ Don Diego Garcia & Doña Ramona Candelaria.

GARCIA, Maria Juliana
bap 27 Dec 1835, 8 days old; legit d/ Manuel Garcia & Barbara Lopes, parishioners; ap & am/ not stated; gp/ Marcelino Aragon & Marcelina Aragon.

CHABES, Jose Tomas
bap 28 Dec 1835, 3 days old; legit s/ Antonio Chabes & Ynes Apodaca, parishioners; ap & am/ not stated; gp/ Jose Dario Lucero & Nicolasa Lucero.

Frames 1619-1620, #9
LUCERO, Estaban Sabino (of the Pueblo)
bap 30 Dec 1835, 3 days old; legit s/ Juan Pedro Lucero & Maria de Jesus Garcia, of Sandia Pueblo; gp/ Juan Nepomuceno Ortega & Maria Rosalia Ortega.

MONTOLLA, Jose Manuel
bap 3 Jan 1836, 3 days old; legit s/ Christobal Montolla & Monica Gonsales, parishioners; ap/ Felipe Montolla & Maria de la Luz Lopes; am/ Juan Gonsales & Maria Antonia Armijo; gp/ Roque Chabes & Briana Chabes.

TRUGILLO, Maria Manuela
bap 10 Jan 1836, 11 days old; d/ Ygnacio Trugillo & Rita Lujan, parishioners; ap/ Juan Trugillo & Manuela Apodaca; am/ Juan Antonio Lujan & Candelaria Lopes; gp/ Bicente Montolla & Maria Josefa Martines.

Frame 1621
CANDELARIA, Guadalupe de Jesus
bap 23 Jan 1836, 9 days old; natural d/ Ysabel Candelaria; gp/ Doña Ysidora Lopes.

HERRERA, Maria Gertrudis
bap 31 Jan 1836, 2 days old; d/ Manuel Herrera & Beginia Chabes, parishioners; ap/ Bicente Herrera & Maria Antonia Montaño; am/ Antonio Chabes & Manuela Garcia; gp/ Don Salbador Jaramillo & Doña Maria Gertrudis Baca.

Frames 1621-1622, #10
LUJAN, Juan Hilario
bap 31 Jan 1836, 15 days old; s/ Pablo Lujan & Juana Analla, parishioners; ap & am/ not stated; gp/ Don Juan Noanes & Ana Maria Noanes.

ANALLA, Jose Domingo
bap 1 Feb 1836, 9 days old; s/ Juan Analla & Maria Dolores Sanches, parishioners; ap & am/ not stated; gp/ Diego Antonio Garcia & Juana Maria Cordoba.

BUTIERRES, Jose Felipe de Jesus
bap 1 Feb 1836, 2 days old; s/ Juan Butierres & Francisca Analla, parishioners; ap/ not stated; am/ Manuel Analla & Maria Antonia Apodaca; gp/ Don Juan Apodaca & Doña Maria Sanches.

PADILLA, Jose Manuel Melqueades
bap 2 Feb 1836, 5 days old; s/ Roman Padilla & Manuela Candelaria, parishioners; ap/ not stated; am/ Pablo Candelaria & Andrea Carbajal; gp/ Don Juan Pablo Garcia & Ana Gregoria Garcia.

Frame 1623
GARCIA, Jose Bernardo
bap 9 Feb 1836, 8 days old; s/ Juan Garcia & Maria Juana Santillanes, parishioners; ap/ Juan Luis Garcia & Maria Griego; am/ Luisano Santillanes & Maria Gertrudis Duran; gp/ Luciano Santillanes & Maria Santillanes.

CARABAJAL, Blas Christobal
bap 9 Feb 1836, 4 days old; s/ Pedro Carabajal & Gertrudes Gonsales, parishioners; ap & am/ not stated; gp/ Bentura Apodaca & Dolores Torres.

Frame 1624, #11
GRIEGO, Maria Ildefonsa
bap 9 Feb 1836, 17 days old; d/ Jose Griego & Paula Garcia, parishioners; ap & am/ not stated; gp/ Guadalupe Chabes & Leonardo Padilla.

LUJAN, Maria Juana Dorotea
bap 10 Feb 1836, 6 days old; d/ Jose Maria Lujan & Dolores Duran, parishioners; ap/ not stated; am/ Teodoro Duran & Maria Lopes; gp/ Don Jose Armijo & Doña Barbara Ortis.

APODACA, Maria del Rallo
bap 10 Feb 1836, 4 days old; d/ Pablo Apodaca & Teodora Sarracino, parishioners; ap & am/ not stated; gp/ Geronimo Candelaria & Maria Candelaria.

Frame 1625
NS, Maria de la Candelaria
bap 11 Feb 1836, 10 days old; d/ unknown parents; gp/ Christobal Gallego & Carmen Burtierres.

SALAZAR, Maria Desideria
bap 13 Feb 1836, 8 days old; legit d/ Lucas Salazar & Rosalia Ginzo, parishioners; ap & am/ not stated; gp/ Bicente Luna & Teodora Peña.

YTURRIETA, Jose Mateo
bap 13 Feb 1836, 6 days old; legit s/ Antonio Yturrieta & Estefana Candelaria; ap & am/ not stated; gp/ Mateo Lopes & Lorensa Padilla.

Frame 1626, #12
GARCIA, Maria Beginia
bap 13 Feb 1836, 3 days old; d/ Jose Manuel Garcia & Ysabel Apodaca, parishioners; ap/ Christobal Garcia & Rafaela Armijo; am/ not stated; gp/ Antonio Garcia & Margarita Rael.

BURTIERRES, Jose Desiderio
bap 13 Feb 1836, 4 days old; legit s/ Antonio Burtierres & Guadalupe Garcia, parishioners; ap & am/ not stated; gp/ Felipe Noanes & Maria Manuela Montaño.

TRUGILLO, Maria del Refugio
bap 15 Feb 1836, 2 days old; legit d/ Santiago Trugillo & Ramona Trugillo, parishioners; ap & am/ not stated; gp/ Pedro Antonio Montolla & Rosa Montolla.

Frame 1627
CANDELARIA, Juan Nepomuceno Manuel Gregorio
bap 16 Feb 1836, 2 days old; legit s/ Jose Ygnacio Candelaria & Niebes Ortiz, parishioners; ap/ Juan Ysidro Candelaria & Gertrudis Jaramillo; am/ not stated; gp/ Don Gregorio Ortiz & Doña Clara Sarracino.

GARCIA, Maria Juana
bap 19 Feb 1836, 2 days old; legit d/ Juan Garcia & Juana Chabes, parishioners; ap/ Francisco Garcia & Manuela Gonzales; am/ Juan Chabes & Barbara Armijo; gp/ Don Lorenzo Sandobal & Doña Juana Sandobal.

Frames 1627-1628, #13
CHABES, Maria Dolores de Jesus
bap 19 Feb 1836, 1 day old; legit d/ Jose Dolores Chabes & Nicanora Garcia, parishioners; ap/ Xabier Chabes & Maria de Jesus Armijo; am/ Juan Garcia & Rosa Sabedra; gp/ Maria de Jesus Padilla.

NS, Maria Gertrudis
bap 20 Feb 1836, 3 days old; d/ unknown parents; gp/ Doña Ygnacio Lopez & Doña Gertrudis Lopez.

TRUGILLO, Jose Julian
bap 20 Feb 1836, 5 days old; legit s/ Juan Antonio Trugillo & Juana Montolla, parishioners; ap & am/ not stated; gp/ Don Christobal Montolla & Doña Monica Gonzales.

Frame 1629
SANDOBAL, Maria Juana
bap 21 Feb 1836, 5 days old; d/ Jose Miguel Sandobal & Antonia Lucero, parishioners; ap & am/ not stated; gp/ Ygnacio Gurule & Juana Garcia.

MONTOLLA, Maria Cimona
bap 22 Feb 1836, 4 days old; d/ Juan Maria Montolla & Maria Juana Garcia, parishioners of Sandia; ap/ Bicente Montolla & Barbara Gonsales; am/ Lorenzo Garcia & Ana Maria Jaramillo; gp/ Don Miguel Antonio Gonsales & Doña Maria Lugarda Garcia.

Frame 1630, #14
GARCIA, Juan Seberino
bap 23 Feb 1836, 3 days old; s/ Juan Garcia & Rita Lopes, parishioners; ap/ Martin Garcia & Ana Maria Apodaca; am/ Luis Lopes & Antonia Lopes; gp/ Don Jose Ramon Mares & Doña Ana Maria Noanes.

GRIEGO, Maria Petra
bap 24 Feb 1836, 4 days old; d/ Manuel Griego & Catarina Samora, parishioners; ap/ Blas Griego & Maria Rosa Chabes; am/ Francisco Samora & Maria Ygnacia Valencia; gp/ Don Pedro Armijo.

Frame 1631
GARCIA, Juana Maria
bap 24 Feb 1836, 5 days old; d/ Miguel Garcia & Rosalia Barrela; ap/ Antonio Garcia & Tomasa Olguin; am/ Santiago Barrela & Juana Aranda; gp/ Don Juan Christobal Armijo & Doña Juana Maria Chabes.

RAEL, Maria de Altagracia
bap 24 Feb 1836, 5 days old; d/ Juan Rael & Maria Gurule, parishioners; ap & am/ not stated; gp/ Francisco Gutierrez & Candelaria Martines.

Frames 1631-1632, #15
MONTOLLA, Maria del Rallo
bap 25 Feb 1836, 2 days old; d/ Juan Montolla & Manuela Garcia, parishioners; ap/ Felipe Montolla & Juana Garcia; am/ Acencio Garcia & Barbara Chabes; gp/ Don Jose Rafael Garcia & Doña Maria Dolores Chabes.

NS, Jesus Maria Antonio
bap 26 Feb 1836, 5 days old; s/ unknown parents, left at the home of Don Pedro Armijo; gp/ Doña Dolores Torres.

Frames 1632-1633
GARCIA, Jose Ramon
bap 28 Feb 1836, 3 days old; s/ Deciderio Garcia & Nepomucena Candelaria, parishioners; ap & am/ not stated; gp/ Antonio Garcia & Gregoria Candelaria.

MUÑIS, Maria Paula Eluteria
bap 2 Mar 1836, 3 days old; legit d/ Francisco Muñis & Teodora Arias, parishioners; ap/ Jose Maria Muñis & Barbara Savedra; am/ Miguel Arias & Gregoria Martines; gp/ Juan Noanes & Concepcion Martines.

NS, Ramon Albino
bap 3 Mar 1836, 3 days old; s/ unknown parents; gp/ Jose Maria Sandobal & Teresa Luna.

Frame 1634, #16
CHABES, Maria de la Merced
bap 3 Mar 1836, 5 days old; legit d/ Antonio Chabes & Maria Ygnacia Montolla, parishioners; ap/ Geronimo Chabes & Encarnacion Gonsales; am/ Mariano Montolla & Relles Mestas; gp/ Francisco Chabes & Alfonsa Cena.

ROMERO, Maria Albina
bap 6 Mar 1836, 4 days old; d/ Domingo Romero & Petra Padilla, parishioners; ap/ Miguel Antonio Romero & Juana Garcia; am/ Julian Padilla & Ana Maria Padilla; gp/ Jose Antonio Garcia & Tomasa Griego.

Frame 1634-1635
BURTIERRES, Maria del Rallo
bap 6 Mar 1836, 3 days old; d/ Francisco Burtierres & Manuela Montolla, parishioners; ap & am/ not stated; gp/ Ygnacio Romero & Maria Monica Romero.

GALLEGO, Maria Rosalia
bap 6 Mar 1836, 3 days old; legit d/ Vasilio Gallego & Clara Peña, parishioners; ap/ Antonio Jose Gallego & Madalena Garcia; am/ not stated; gp/ Don Ramon Gallego & Doña Rosalia Montaño.

ARIAS, Maria Rosalia
bap 6 Mar 1836, 3 days old; d/ Juan Domingo Arias & Juliana Lucero; ap/ Felipe Arias & Andrea Garcia; am/ unknown; gp/ Don Pedro Aranda & Doña Rosalia Jaramillo.

Frame 1636, #17
MARTINES, Jose Tomas
bap 7 Mar 1836, 3 days old; s/ Jose Antonio Martines & Quiteria Griego, parishioners; ap/ Jose Martines & Maria Antonia Sanches; am/ Miguel Griego & Gertrudis Olguin; gp/ Jose Antonio Garcia & Albina Lusero.

GRIEGO, Maria Tomasa
bap 7 Mar 1836, 3 days old; d/ Grabial Griego & Eulogia Romero, parishioners; ap & am/ not stated; gp/ Nicolas Valencia & Maria Paula Martinez.

Frame 1637
ARCHIBEQUE, Maria del Rallo
bap 7 Mar 1836, 8 days old; legit d/ Matias Archibeque & Maria Sanches, parishioners; ap/ not stated; am/ Felipe Sanches & Maria Ynez Garcia; gp/ Maria Gertrudis Buttierrez.

SANCHES, Jose Tomas
bap 7 Mar 1836, 4 days old; legit s/ Christobal Sanches & Maria Concepcion Valencia, parishioners; ap & am/ not stated; gp/ Don Jose Armijo & Doña Soledad Armijo.

ANSURES, Jose Casimiro
bap 8 Mar 1836, 5 days old; s/ Rafael Ansures & Mariana Lopes, parishioners; ap & am/ not stated; gp/ Jose Angel Lopes & Ana Maria Marques.

Frame 1638, #18
HERRERA, Francisco Antonio
bap 8 Mar 1836, 7 days old; legit s/ Jose Herrera & Barbara Santillanes, parishioners; ap/ Jose Andres Herrera & Maria Dolores Garcia; am/ Miguel Santillanes & Ana Maria Hernandes; gp/ Juan Jose Sanches & Antonia Rita Luna.

GARCIA, Manuel de Jesus
bap 12 Mar 1836, 3 days old; legit d/ Manuel Garcia & Concepcion Lopes, parishioners; ap/ Pedro Garcia & Maria Analla; am/ not stated; gp/ Manuela Antonia Perea.

Frames 1638-1639
CHABES, Jose Gregorio
bap 12 Mar 1836, 5 days old; s/ Don Rumaldo Chabes & Doña Barbara Trugillo, parishioners; ap/ Estanislado Chabes & Doña Soledad Ortega; am/ Don Jose Trugillo & Doña Soledad Valencia; gp/ Don Pedro Aranda & Doña Rosalia Jaramillo.

MARTINES, Maria Eulogia
bap 13 Mar 1836, 3 days old; d/ Antonio Jose Martines & Maria Luciana Lucero, parishioners; ap/ Bicente Martines & Maria Ysabel Maldonado; am/ Juan de Jesus Lucero & Maria Justa Pino; gp/ Don Juan Antonio Rael & Doña Maria de la Lus Rael.

BURTIERRES, Maria Tomasa
bap 14 Mar 1836, 8 days old; d/ Pascual Burtierres & Manuela Gallego, parishioners; ap/ Miguel Burtierres & Maria Niebes Chaves; am/ Salbador Gallego & Barbara Aragon; gp/ Dolores Gallego & Ana Gregoria Gallego.

Frame 1640, #19
NS, Maria Benigna
bap 15 Mar 1836, 1 day old; d/ unknown parents, left at the home of Doña Guadalupe Garbiso, gp/ Miguel Perea & Margarita Ortiz.

MORA, Maria Francisca
bap 23 Mar 1836, 12 days old; d/ Luciano Mora & Manuela Antonia Trugillo, parishioners; ap/ not stated; am/ Juan Trugillo & Manuela Apodaca; gp/ Manuel Burtierres & Rosalia Analla.

GARCIA, Maria Josefa
bap 23 Mar 1836, 5 days old; d/ Antonio Garcia & Guadalupe Barreras, parishioners; ap & am/ not stated; gp/ Pedro Sanches & Juana Sanches.

Frame 1641
NS, Maria Dolores
bap 25 Mar 1836, 4 days old; d/ unknown parents, left at the home of Juan Sandobal; gp/ Juan Domingo Marques & Dolores Tenorio.

NS, Maria de los Dolores
bap 25 Mar 1836, 2 days old; d/ unknown parents; gp/ Pablo Carrillo & Petra Santillanes.

NS, Maria del Rallo de Jesus (Ute Indian)
bap 26 Mar 1836; d/ unknown parents, at the home of Doña Petra Perea; gp/ Don Juan Armijo & Doña Paula Jaramillo.

Frame 1642, #20
LOPES, Maria Ygnacia de los Dolores
bap 28 Mar 1836, 3 days old; d/ Lasaro Lopes & Gertrudis Santillanes, parishioners; ap & am/ not stated; gp/ Antonio Sandobal & Ana Maria Duran.

CHABES, Jose Maria
bap 18 Mar 1836, 1 day old; legit s/ Jose Antonio Chabes & Dolores Padilla, parishioners; ap & am/ not stated; gp/ Juan Manuel Benabides & Juana Padilla.

ANALLA, Juana Maria
bap 30 Mar 1836, 2 days old; d/ Jose Rosalio Analla & Teresa Candelaria, parishioners; ap & am/ not stated; gp/ Felipe Herrera & Juana Garcia.

Frame 1643
ARMIJO, Francisco Antonio
bap 2 Apr 1836, 3 days old; legit s/ Pedro Armijo & Maria de la Luz Garcia, parishioners; ap/ Pablo Armijo & Josefa Chabes; am/ Felis Garcia & Maria Ysabel Lopes; gp/ Juan Pablo Burtierres & Juana Sena.

GARCIA, Francisco Antonio
bap 2 Apr 1836, 9 days old; s/ Antonio Garcia & Juana Sais, parishioners; ap & am/ not stated; gp/ Relles Montolla & Maria Gertrudis Molla.

Frames 1643-1644
ROMERO, Jose Teodoro (of Bernalillo)
bap 3 Apr 1836, 15 days old; legit s/ Andres Romero & Ysabel Jaramillo, parishioners of Sandia; ap & am/ not stated; gp/ Don Julian Perea & Nepomusena Gallego.

NS, Maria Juana
bap 3 Apr 1836, 3 days old; d/ unknown parents; gp/ Jose Griego & Maria Ysabel Griego.

NS, Maria del Rallo
bap 4 Apr 1836, 5 days old; d/ unknown parents; gp/ Don Ramon Gallego & Doña Rosalia Montaño.

Frame 1645
CANDELARIA, Jose Amador
bap 8 Apr 1836, 3 days old; legit s/ Pedro Candelaria & Dolores Duran, parishioners; ap & am/ not stated; gp/ Pablo Carrillo & Petra Santillanes.

LOPES, Maria del Rallo
bap 10 Apr 1836, 2 days old; d/ Leonicio Lopes & Gertrudis Perea, parishioners; ap & am/ not stated; gp/ Don Juan Garcia & Doña Petra Garcia.

NS, Jesus Maria
bap 14 Apr 1836, 1 day old; s/ unknown parents; gp/ Dolores Torres.

Frame 1646, #22
ABILA, Polonio de Jesus
bap 14 Apr 1836, 3 days old; s/ Don Miguel Abila & Doña Lugarda Montolla, parishioners; ap/ not stated; am/ Pedro Montolla & Encarnacion Luna; gp/ Don Jose Maria Ortiz & Doña Dolores Montolla.

NS, Jose de Jesus
bap 15 Apr 1836, 2 days old; s/ unknown parents; gp/ Don Juan Armijo & Doña Juana Armijo.

Frames 1646-1647
APODACA, Maria de Altagracia
bap 16 Apr 1836, 4 days old; d/ Salbador Apodaca & Clara Burtierres, parishioners; ap & am/ not stated; gp/ Don Marcos Ruis & Doña Balbina Jaramillo.

BACA, Maria Aniceta
bap 17 Apr 1836, 3 days old; d/ Juan Baca & Rafaela Cordoba, parishioners; ap & am/ not stated; gp/ Christobal Montolla & Monica Gonsales.

CANDELARIA, Maria Paula
bap 17 Apr 1836, 4 days old; legit d/ Bisente Candelaria & Ana Maria Chabes, parishioners; ap & am/ not stated; gp/ Diego Luna & Maria Paula Perea.

Frame 1648, #23
SANCHES, Jose Melquiades
bap 21 Apr 1836, 3 days old; legit s/ Domingo Sanches & Quiteria Gonsales, parishioners; ap & am/ not stated; gp/ Don Julian Tenorio & Doña Benina Chabes.

NS, Jesus Maria
bap 22 Apr 1836, 5 days old; s/ unknown parents; gp/ Doña Micaela Gonsales.

Frames 1648-1649
DURAN, Jose Aniseto
bap 23 Apr 1836, 3 days old; s/ Rafael Duran & Rosa Gurule, parishioners; ap/ Ysidro Duran & Andrea Apodaca; am/ not stated; gp/ Manuel Aragon & Teresa Candelaria.

SAMORA, Jose Amador
bap 22 Apr 1836, 6 days old; s/ Nepomoceno Samora & Guadalupe Ballejos, parishioners; ap & am/ not stated; gp/ Don Lorenso Lusero & Doña Ynes Ruis.

NS, Maria del Rallo Gertrudis
bap 26 Apr 1836; Indian, of the house of Don Antonio Sandobal; gp/ Mateo Lopes & Manuela Sanches.

Frame 1650, #24
SANCHES, Jose de Jesus
bap 26 Apr 1836, 2 days old; s/ Domingo Sanches & Maria de la Lus Perea, parishioners; ap & am/ not stated; gp/ Jose Gonsales & Ana Maria Candelaria.

LUCERO, Felipe Santiago
bap 2 May 1836, 3 days old; s/ Diego Lucero & Dolores Lobato, parishioners; ap & am/ not stated; gp/ Pablo Griego & Maria Micaela Montolla.

MONTAÑO, Maria Guadalupe
bap 2 May 1836, 7 days old; d/ Pedro Montaño & Maria Nepomucena Lobato, parishioners; ap & am/ not stated; gp/ Christobal Salasar & Maria Montolla.

Frame 1651
NS, Maria Francisca
bap 2 May 1836, 7 days old; d/ unknown parents; gp/ Domingo Casados & Francisca Jaramillo.

NS, Jose Martin
bap 2 May 1836, 3 days old; s/ unknown parents; gp/ Manuel Analla & Felipa Martines.

NS, Pedro Antonio
bap 2 May 1836, 3 days old; s/ unknown parents; gp/ Geronimo Olguin & Dolores Olguin.

Frame 1652, #25
NS, Jose Mauricio
bap 2 May 1836, 5 days old; s/ unknown parents; gp/ Bicente Gonsales & Bibiana Gonsales.

GARCIA, Maria Catarina
bap 2 May 1836, 2 days old; legit d/ Don Juan Felis Garcia & Doña Juana Maria Sanches, parishioners; ap/ Don Felis Garcia & Doña Maria Yzabel Lopes; am/ not listed; gp/ Jose Francisco Garcia & Maria Soledad Garcia.

Frames 1652-1653
PEREA, Maria Monica
bap 3 May 1836, 3 days old; legit d/ Manuel Perea & Gregoria Duran, parishioners; gp/ Don Toribio Noanes & Doña Ana Maria Candelaria.

PEREA, Juan Felipe
bap 3 May 1836, 3 days old; legit s/ Manuel Perea & Gertrudis Gurule, parishioners; ap/ Jose Manuel Perea & Rosalia Duran; am/ not stated; gp/ Jose Manuel Perea & Rosalia Duran.

NS, Maria Polinaria
bap 3 May 1836, 3 days old; d/ unknown parents; gp/ Jose Antonio Apodaca & Barbara Benabides.

Frame 1654, #26
NS, Manuel Antonio
bap 3 May 1836, 3 days old; s/ unknown parents, placed in the home of Maria de la Lus Garcia; gp/ Juan Jose Vallejos & Maria Petra Telles.

GARCIA, Maria Gabriela
bap 5 May 1836, 4 days old; d/ Juan Antonio Garcia & Maria Gregoria Candelaria, parishioners; ap/ not stated; am/ Ygnacio Candelaria & Concepcion Chabes; gp/ Salbador Perea & Grabiela Candelaria.

LUCERO, Jose Tomas
bap 5 May 1836, 5 days old; s/ Anastacio Lucero & Juana Duran, parishioners; ap/ Juan Lucero & Maria Antonia Martines; am/ Francisco Duran & Barbara Carabajal; gp/ Tomas Lucero & Dolores Valencia.

Frame 1655
ARMIJO, Maria Ramona de Jesus
bap 5 May 1836, 3 days old; natural d/ Jesusa Armijo; gp/ Jose Lucero & Maria Gertrudis Burtierrez.

VALENCIA, Maria de la Cruz
bap 6 May 1836, 4 days old; d/ Jose Antonio Valencia & Juliana Burtierres, parishioners; ap/ not stated; am/ Cidro Burtierres & Dolores Martines; gp/ Miguel Noanes & Paula Candelaria.

NS, Jose Andres
bap 6 May 1836, 10 days old; s/ unknown parents, placed in the home of Maria de Jesus Montolla; gp/ Jose Mestas & Manuela Lucero.

Frame 1656, #27
TRUGILLO, Jose Estanislado
bap 10 May 1836, 4 days old; legit s/ Hermenegildo Trugillo & Francisca Sanches, parishioners; ap/ Jose Antonio Trugillo & Francisca Gonzales; am/ Felipe Sanches & Ana Maria Trugillo; gp/ Santiago Trugillo & Maria Salome Burtierres.

Frames 1656-1657
LOBATO, Maria Begnina
bap 10 May 1836, 3 days old; d/ Don Juan Felipe Lobato & Doña Manuela Mestas; ap/ Juan Lobato & Maria Albares; am/ Ygnacio Mestas & Guadalupe Garbiso; gp/ Don Antonio Ruiz & Doña Petra Maldonado.

ROMERO, Maria Barbara (of Bernalillo)
bap 19 May 1836, 5 days old; d/ Antonio Romero & Manuela Lucero, parishioners of Sandia; ap & am/ not stated; gp/ Roman Estrada & Guadalupe Jaramillo.

GONSALES, Jose Rafael
bap 19 May 1836, 16 days old; s/ Rafael Gonsales & Jesus Aragon, parishioners; gp/ Agustin Padilla & Maria Dolores Gonsales.

Frame 1658, #28
CHABES, Juan Nepomuceno
bap 22 May 1836, 4 days old; s/ Jose Miguel Chabes & Decideria Gurule, parishioners; ap & am/ not stated; gp/ Francisco Antonio Santillanes & Maria Rosa Santillanes.

NS, Maria Ysidora
bap 22 May 1836, 7 days old; d/ unknown parents, placed in the home of Don Jose Rafael Candelaria; gp/ Don Jose Rafael Candelaria & Doña Dolores Sabedra.

Frame 1659
GARCIA, Jose Antonio
bap 23 May 1836, 3 days old; s/ Jesus Garcia & Rosalia Gonsales, parishioners; ap/ Tadeo Garcia & Maria Luisa Valencia; am/ not stated; gp/ Bernardo Valencia & Paula Martines.

GARCIA, Felis de Jesus
bap 23 May 1836, 5 days old; s/ Manuel Garcia & Soledad Sanches, parishioners of Sandia; ap/ Cristobal Garcia & Manuela Baldes; am/ Juan Jose Sanches & Candelaria Cisneros, gp/ Prudencio Tapia & Teresa Gutierres.

Frames 1659-1660, #29
HERRERA, Mariano Dabid Amador de Jesus
bap 23 May 1836, 1 day old; s/ Juan Herrera & Barbara Jaramillo, parishioners; ap/ Bicente Herrera & Maria Antonia Montaño; am/ not stated; gp/ Don Mariano Ruis & Doña Ysidora Lopes.

SANCHES, Maria Teresa de Jesus
bap 23 May 1836, 5 days old; legit d/ Salbador Sanches & Olalla Tafolla, parishioners; ap/ Bartolo Sanches & Rafaela Lopes; am/ Juan Ignacio Tafolla & Maria Antonia Carabajal; gp/ Don Jose Armijo & Maria Barbara Ortiz.

Frames 1660-1661
GARCIA, Maria Trinidad
bap 24 May 1836, 3 days old; d/ Juan Guadalupe Garcia & Dolores Candelaria, parishioners; ap & am/ not stated; gp/ Don Jose Antonio Garcia & Doña Ygnacia Candelaria.

SANCHES, Maria Catarina
bap 25 May 1836, 3 days old; legit d/ Nicolas Sanches & Luisa Gallego, parishioners; gp/ Antonio Garcia & Maria Ysabel Gallego.

JARAMILLO, Maria del Refugio
bap 25 May 1836, 7 days old; legit d/ Manuel Gregorio Jaramillo & Josefa Garcia, parishioners; ap & am/ not stated; gp/ Tomas Telles & Paula Montolla.

Frame 1662, #30
GRIEGO, Antonia Teresa
bap 26 May 1836, 8 days old; legit d/ Antonio Griego & Ledubina Burtierres, parishioners; gp/ Lasaro Torres & Micaela Arias.

MARQUES, Maria del Rallo
bap 29 May 1836, 8 days old; legit d/ Jose Marques & Maria Francisca Padilla, parishioners; ap & am/ not stated; gp/ Maria Josefa Chabes.

APODACA, Maria Juana
bap 29 May 1836, 3 days old; legit d/ Rafael Apodaca & Estefana Salasar, parishioners; ap & am/ not stated; gp/ Jose Dolores Apodaca & Ygnacia Garcia.

Frame 1663
MONTAÑO, Maria Trinidad
bap 29 May 1836, 6 days old; d/ Toribio Montaño & Ana Maria Candelaria, parishioners; ap & am/ not stated; gp/ Antonio Noanes & Ana Maria Candelaria.

GONSALES, Maria Trenidad
bap 31 May 1836, 3 days old; legit d/ Juan Miguel Gonsales & Maria de la Lus Marques, parishioners; gp/ Ycidro Mora & Esmeregilda Padilla.

Frame 1664, #31
BURTIERRES, Maria del Rallo
bap 5 Jun 1836, 5 days old; legit d/ Juan Burtierres & Maria Manuela Garcia, parishioners; gp/ Antonio Sandobal & Maria Luna.

GONSALES, Jose Nestor
bap 5 Jun 1836, 3 days old; legit s/ Hilario Gonsales & Rita Rael, parishioners; gp/ Don Lorenzo Ortiz & Doña Maria Nestora Montolla.

CARRILLO, Manuel Antonio
bap 20 Jun 1836, 8 days old; s/ Jose Carrillo & Ana Maria Ballejos, parishioners; gp/ Manuel Burtierres & Rosalia Analla.

Frame 1665
SAIS, Luis Jose
bap 24 Jun 1836, 4 days old; legit s/ Ramon Sais & Margarita Pacheco, parishioners; gp/ Jose Miguel Lucero & Andrea Pacheco.

PEREA, Maria Guadalupe
bap 7 Jul 1836, 6 days old; legit d/ Antonio Perea & Candelaria Garcia, parishioners; gp/ Francisco Martines & Encarnacion Lucero.

Frames 1665-1666, #32
DURAN, Manuel Gregorio
bap 8 Jul 1836, 9 days old; natural s/ Manuela Duran; gp/ Doña Clara Sarracino.

JARAMILLO, Maria Yzabel Eulogia
bap 9 Jul 1836, 9 days old; legit d/ Gregorio Jaramillo & Antonia Lopes, parishioners; ap/ Jose Jaramillo & Manuela Lopes; am/ Manuel Lopes & Gertrudes Rael; gp/ Ygnacio Ruis & Maria Ysidora Lopes.

MORA, Jesus Maria
bap 17 Jul 1836, 8 days old; s/ Esteban Mora & Juana Maria Griego, parishioners; ap/ Ysidro Mora & Juana Marques; am/ not stated; gp/ Juan Cerna & Juana Cerna.

Frame 1667
GINSO, Jose Camilo
bap 24 Jul 1836, 10 days old; legit s/ Santiago Ginso & Manuela Analla, parishioners; gp/ Juan Sandobal & Juana Baca.

ESTRADA, Ana Maria Placida (of Bernalillo)
bap 26 Jul 1836, 3 days old; legit d/ Domingo Estrada & Maria Manuela Salasar, parishioners of Sandia; gp/ Tomas Gonsales & Maria Lugarda Garcia.

MONTOLLA, Maria del Refugio
bap 26 Jul 1836, 8 days old; d/ Francisco Montolla & Maria Montolla, of the pueblo of Sandia; gp/ Rafael Lauriano & Maria Relles NS.

Frame 1668, #33
CANDELARIA, Maria Antonia
bap 28 Jul 1836, 2 days old; legit d/ Bicente Candelaria & Maria Relles Griego, parishioners; ap/ Florencio Candelario & Maria Duran; am/ Mariano Griego & Antonia Garcia; gp/ Don Julian Apodaca & Doña Maria Antonia Griego.

CHABES, Jose Camilo de Jesus (of Bernalillo)
bap 3 Aug 1836, 8 days old; s/ Felipe Chabes & Desideria Muñis, parishioners of Sandia; gp/ Pedro Montaño & Nepomucena Muñis.

Frame 1669
GARCIA, Antonio Jose Demetrio
bap 5 Aug 1836, 3 days old; s/ Antonio Garcia & Carmen Sanches; ap/ Don Feliz Garcia & Doña Ysabel Lopes; am/ Don Bicente Sanches & Doña Ana Maria Mestas, gp/ Don Manuel Armijo & Doña Rosalia Mestas.

MONTAÑO, Melquiades de Jesus
bap 6 Aug 1836, 3 days old; legit s/ Joaquin Montaño & Maria Duran, parishioners; ap & am/ not stated;
gp/ Don Juan Domingo Gonzales & Maria Duran.

Frames 1669-1670, #34
NS, Maria de los Angeles
bap 7 Aug 1836, 7 days old; d/ unknown parents, left at the home of Maria Antonia Ortega; gp/ Bicente
Lopes & Maria Antonia Burtierres.

MALDONADO, Juan Esteban
bap 9 Aug 1836, 7 days old; legit s/ Anselmo Maldonado & Bibiana Gonsales, parishioners; ap/ Juan
Domingo Maldonado & Maria Manuela Aragon; am/ Juan Gonsales & Barbara Castillo; gp/ Don Felipe
Montolla & Doña Maria la Luz Lopes.

LOPES, Maria del Rallo
bap 12 Aug 1836, 6 days old; legit d/ Carlos Lopes & Barbara Contreras, parishioners; ap/ Manuel Lopes
& Encarnacion Duran; am/ not stated; gp/ Juan Rafael Duran & Encarnacion Lucero.

Frame 1671
GRIEGO, Maria Dolores
bap 12 Aug 1836, 6 days old; d/ Juan Griego & Estefana Garcia, parishioners; ap/ Francisco Griego &
Josefa Sandoval; gp/ Alonso Rael & Maria Martina Cordoba.

NS, Lorenso de Jesus (of Bernalillo)
bap 14 Aug 1836, 4 days old; s/ unknown parents, placed in the home of Juan Sais; gp/ Juan Chabes &
Ana Maria Montolla.

ANALLA, Maria del Rallo de Jesus
bap 22 Aug 1836, 3 days old; d/ Martin Analla & Biatris Garcia, parishioners; ap & am/ not stated; gp/
Miguel (Barbero) & Juana Barbero.

Frame 1672, #35
MARES, Maria Desideria
bap 28 Aug 1836, 5 days old; d/ Jose Manuel Mares & Francisca Candelaria, parishioners; ap/ Nicolas
Mares & Maria Manuela Chabes; am/ not stated; gp/ Blas Garcia & Maria Relles Apodaca.

MARTINES, Agustin de Jesus
bap 30 Aug 1836, 3 days old; legit s/ Jose de la Cruz Martines & Victoria Garcia, parishioners; ap & am/
not stated; gp/ Juan Burtierres & Manuela Lopes.

Frames 1672-1673
CARABAJAL, Francisco Esteban
bap 9 Sep 1836, 10 days old; s/ Domingo Carabajal & Toribia Sanches, parishioners; ap & am/ not stated;
gp/ Juan Sabedra & Guadalupe Sabedra. [Note: See also entry below.]

CARABAJAL, Melquiades Antonio
bap 10 Sep 1836, 10 days old; s/ Domingo Carabajal & Toribia Sanches, parishioners; ap & am/ not
stated; gp/ Juan Acencio Garcia & Teodora Padilla. [Note: See also entry above.]

CORDOBA, Maria Nicolasa
bap 10 Sep 1836, 11 days old; d/ Jose Anastacio Cordoba & Maria Manuela Garcia, parishioners; ap/ Nicolas Cordoba & Maria Ygnacia Duran; am/ not stated; gp/ Jose Miguel Lucero & Maria Manuela Garcia.

Frames 1673-1674, #36
BARRERAS, Jose Antonio
bap 11 Sep 1836, 4 days old; s/ Ysidro Barreras & Dolores Lopes, parishioners; ap/ Jose Barreras & Ana Maria Garcia; am/ Manuel Lopes & Maria de la Crus Romero; gp/ Luis Gonsales & Josefa Lopes.

GRIEGO, Francisco Antonio
bap 11 Sep 1836, 5 days old; s/ Juan Griego & Yzabel Gurule, parishioners; ap & am/ not stated; gp/ Francisco Lucero & Maria Ynes Montolla.

NS, Jose Ramon de los Niebes
bap 18 Sep 1836, 7 days old; s/ unknown parents, placed in the house of Maria Asencion Garcia, gp/ Luis Garcia & Maria de Alta Gracia Montolla.

Frame 1675
CARRILLO, Maria Pascuala
bap 22 Sep 1836, 5 days old; d/ Antonio Carrillo & Juana Peña, parishioners; ap & am/ not stated; gp/ Jose Maria Burtierres & Maria Pascuala Gallego.

GARCIA, Juan Pablo
bap 26 Sep 1836, 3 days old; legit s/ Manuel Garcia & Rafaela Rael, parishioners; ap/ not stated; am/ Juan Antonio Rael & Soledad Miera; gp/ Don Jose Antonio Martines & Doña Monica Ruis.

JARAMILLO, Manuel Antonio
bap 26 Sep 1836, 4 days old; legit s/ Juan Christobal Jaramillo & Ana Maria Sandobal, parishioners; ap & am/ not stated; gp/ Salbador Sandobal & Rita Griego.

Frame 1676, #37
BALDES, Miguel Antonio
bap 2 Oct 1836, 2 days old; legit s/ Antonio Baldes & Quirina Chabes, parishioners of Sandia; gp/ Marcelino Archibeque & Juana Salazar.

BACA, Maria Geronima
bap 2 Oct 1836, 3 days old; legit d/ Cimon Baca & Maria Lorensa Griego, parishioners; ap & am/ not stated; gp/ Juan Jose Sanches & Maria Guadalupe Chabes.

ARMIJO, Ambrocio de Jesus
bap 3 Oct 1836, 1 day old; legit s/ Mariano Armijo & Grabiela Jaramillo, parishioners; ap/ Don Ambrocio Armijo & Doña Antonia Ortis; am/ Don Miguel Antonio Jaramillo & Doña Lorensa Lucero; gp/ Don Ambrocio Armijo & Doña Placida Armijo.

Frame 1677
TRUGILLO, Maria Petra
bap 4 Oct 1836, 5 days old; legit d/ Pablo Trugillo & Maria de la Lus Gallego, parishioners; gp/ Juan Gonsales & Maria Manuela Gonsales.

SANCHES, Jose Geronimo (of Bernalillo)
bap 5 Oct 1836, 2 days old; legit s/ Mariano Sanches & Dolores Burtierres, parishioners of Sandia; gp/
Prudencio Tapia & Teresa Burtierres.

BURTIERRES, Francisco Xabier (of Bernalillo)
bap 6 Oct 1836, 4 days old; legit s/ Don Joseph Antonio Burtierres & Doña Manuela Antonia Chabes,
parishioners of Sandia; ap/ Don Juan Jose Burtierres & Doña Dolores Montolla; am/ Don Francisco
Chabes & Doña Ana Maria Castillo; gp/ Don Jose Antonio Martines & Doña Monica Ruis.

Frame 1678, #38
NS, Juan Francisco de Jesus
bap 17 Oct 1836, 15 days old; s/ unknown parents, placed in the home of Antonio Sandobal; gp/ Antonio
Sandobal & Ana Maria Duran.

HERRERA, Antonio Jose
bap 17 Oct 1836, 12 days old; s/ Salbador Herrera & Maria Ygnacia Chaves, parishioners; ap/ Bicente
Herrera & Maria Antonia Montaño; am/ not stated; gp/ Jose Rafael Garcia & Dolores Chabes.

Frames 1678-1679
GARCIA, Maria Lugarda
bap 18 Oct 1836, 3 days old; d/ Julian Garcia & Juana Lorensa Aragon, parishioners; ap/ Juan Jose Garcia
& Francisca Gonsales; am/ Jose Manuel Aragon & Maria Teresa Candelaria; gp/ Juan Pablo Garcia &
Gregoria Garcia.

LOPES, Julian Antonio
bap 20 Oct 1836, 2 days old; s/ Felipe Lopes & Juliana Torres, parishioners; ap/ Juan Lopes & Rosa
Jaramillo; am/ not stated; gp/ Florentino Griego & Juan Griego.

ROMERO, Julian Antonio
bap 21 Oct 1836, 4 days old; s/ Antonio Romero & Guadalupe Candelaria, parishioners; ap/ Miguel
Antonio Romero & Juana Garcia; am/ Jose Candelaria & Francisca Gonsales; gp/ Don Grabiel Sanches &
Doña Rafaela Ruis.

Frame 1680, #39
NS, Maria de los Angeles
bap 4 Oct 1836, 3 days old; d/ unknown parents, placed in the home of Doña Ursula Chabes; gp/ Antonio
Marques & Maria Dolores Toledo.

PADILLA, Maria Micaela
bap 5 Nov 1836, 3 days old; natural d/ Catarina Padilla; gp/ Jose Miguel Chaves & Maria Descideria
Gurule.

GARCIA, Jose Carlos
bap 8 Nov 1836, 8 days old; s/ Antonio Garcia & Tomasa Griego, parishioners; ap/ Juan Garcia &
Encarnacion Romero, am/ Miguel Griego & Gertrudes Olguin; gp/ Miguel Griego & Gertrudis Olguin.

Frame 1681
ARCHULETA, Salbador Manuel
bap 11 Nov 1836, 10 days old; s/ Mateo Archuleta & Relles Sedillo, parishioners; gp/ Pablo Baca & Begnina Burtierres.

LUCERO, Maria Teodora de Jesus
bap 11 Nov 1836, 3 days old; d/ Lorenso Lucero & Ynes Ruis, parishioners; ap & am/ not stated; gp/ Don Bentura Apodaca & Doña Dolores Torres.

LOPES, Maria del Rallo Gabriela
bap 13 Nov 1836, 8 days old; d/ Francisco Lopes & Francisca Luna, parishioners; gp/ Don Rafael Apodaca & Doña Barbara Molina.

Frame 1682, #40
BENABIDES, Maria del Rallo Clara
bap 29 Nov 1836, 4 days old; d/ Juan Manuel Benabides & Juana Lopes, parishioners; ap & am/ not stated; gp/ Antonio Burtierres & Luperta Lopes.

GARCIA, Maria Andrea Guadalupe
bap 30 Nov 1836, 3 days old; d/ Francisco Garcia & Manuela Carrillo, parishioners; gp/ Don Guadalupe Santillanes & Doña Guadalupe Ruis.

Frame 1683
GARCIA, Maria Andrea
bap 2 Dec 1836, 3 days old; natural d/ Gertrudis Garcia; gp/ Pedro Lopes & Petra Lopes.

MARTINES, Maria del Rallo
bap 2 Dec 1836, 3 days old; legit d/ Juan Martines & Antonia Lucero, parishioners; ap/ not stated; am/ Juan Lucero & Francisca Lucero; gp/ Maria Gertrudis Burtierres.

NS, Juan Ambrosio
bap 9 Dec 1836, 2 days old; s/ unknown parents, left at the home of Juan Antonio Cerna; gp/ Jose Maria Trugillo & Juana Maria Muñis.

Frame 1684, #41
MUÑIS, Lorensa Maria de los Angeles
bap 10 Dec 1836, 5 days old; d/ Faustino Muñis & Antonia Lucero, parishioners; gp/ Juan Christoval Muñis & Maria Antonia Tafolla.

GARCIA, Maria del Rallo Concepcion
bap 11 Dec 1836, 4 days old; d/ Juan Garcia & Maria Ysabel Garcia, parishioners; ap/ Tomas Garcia & Bernarda Carbajal; am/ Ramon Garcia & Acension Lopes; gp/ Jose Gonsales & Maria de la Lus Gonsales.

Frames 1684-1685
GALLEGO, Maria Guadalupe
bap 12 Dec 1836, 4 days old; d/ Ycidro Gallego & Encarnacion Candelaria, parishioners; gp/ Diego Montolla & Jesus Lucero.

ARMIJO, Jose Guadalupe
bap 13 Dec 1836, 3 days old; natural s/ Carmen Armijo; gp/ Juan Armijo & Placida Armijo.

LUJAN, Maria Francisca Lucia (of Bernalillo)
bap 13 Dec 1836, 8 days old; legit d/ Eulogio Lujan & Juana Mora, parishioners of Sandia; gp/ Pedro Romero.

Frame 1686, #42
MONTOLLA, Maria Leocadia de los Dolores
bap 15 Dec 1836, 7 days old; legit d/ Don Diego Montolla & Doña Marta Gallego, parishioners of Sandia; ap/ Nerio Montolla & Manuela Sanches; am/ not stated; gp/ Tomas Montolla & Grabiela Tenorio.

GRIEGO, Maria Dolores
bap 15 Dec 1836, 8 days old; d/ Jose Griego & Soledad Garcia, parishioners; ap & am/ not stated; gp/ Antonio Trugillo & Dolores Trugillo.

GONSALES, Maria Polinaria (of Bernalillo)
bap 15 Dec 1836, 8 days old; legit d/ Juan Gonsales & Jacinta Martines, parishioners of Sandia; gp/ Doña Antonia Gonsales.

Frame 1687
NS, Jose Benito
bap 21 Dec 1836, 5 days old; s/ unknown parents; gp/ Jose Benito Alire & Maria Garcia.

GONSALES, Jose Melquiades
bap 23 Dec 1836, 8 days old; s/ Francisco Gonsales & Maria Antonia Garcia; gp/ Sabino Gonsales & Maria de Jesus Luna.

Frames 1687-1688, #43
GABALDON, Jose de Jesus Ladislao
bap 28 Dec 1836, 2 days old; legit s/ Nepomuceno Gabaldon & Barbara Mestas, parishioners; ap/ not stated; am/ Don Ignacio Mestas & Doña Guadalupe Duran; gp/ Don Bisente Domingues & Doña Mariana Loera.

CASTILLO, Maria Barbara de los Dolores (of Bernalillo)
bap 7 Jan 1837, 6 days old; d/ Jose Felipe Castillo & Doña Jesus Perea, parishioners of the mission of Sandia; ap/ Don Antonio Jose Castillo & Doña Guadalupe Pino; am/ Don Pedro Jose Perea & Doña Barbara Romero; gp/ Don Antonio Jose Chabes & Doña Dolores Perea.

Frame 1688-1689
JARAMILLO, Maria Beneranda
bap 11 Jan 1837, 3 days old; d/ Ysidro Jaramillo & Catarina Mestas, parishioners; ap & am/ not stated; gp/ Catarina Sanches.

GALLEGO, Maria Juana
bap 18 Jan 1837, 3 days old; d/ Jose Anastacio Gallego & Soledad Candelaria, parishioners; ap & am/ not stated; gp/ Pedro Aranda & Rosalia Jaramillo.

ORTEGA, Maria Sebastiana
bap 20 Jan 1837, 2 days old; natural d/ Rosalia Ortega; gp/ Doña Ygnacia Basan.

Frames 1689-1690, #44
DURAN, Jose Bartolo
bap 23 Jan 1837, 4 days old; legit s/ Juan Rafael Duran & Josefa Apodaca; ap/ Teodoro Duran & Juana Garcia; am/ Jose Apodaca & Gertrudis Lopes; gp/ Bartolo Apodaca & Soledad Telles.

BURTIERRES, Anisteo de Jesus
bap 23 Jan 1837, 3 days old; s/ Pablo Burtierres & Juana Sena, parishioners; ap/ Miguel Burtierres & Maria Ysidora Armijo; am/ not stated gp/ Santiago Trujillo & Ana Maria Burtierres.

NS, Maria del Refugio
bap 25 Jan 1837; Navajo Indian, d/ unknown parents; in the household of Don Juan Armijo & Doña Ana Maria Gabaldon; gp/ Don Pedro Madraiga & Doña Antonia Ortis.

Frame 1691
BURTIERRES, Jose Ramon Anastacio (of Corrales)
bap 28 Jan 1837, 6 days old; legit s/ Juan Jose Burtierres & Rita Cordoba, parishioners of Sandia; gp/ Jose Rafael Garcia & Maria del Rosario Martines.

TENORIO, Jose Ynes
bap 28 Jan 1837, 5 days old; legit s/ Jose Francisco Tenorio & Rita Gurule, parishioners; gp/ Jose Rafael Garcia & Maria del Rosario Martines.

Frame 1692, #45
SANCHES, Maria del Refugio
bap 28 Jan 1837, 3 days old; legit d/ Manuel Sanches & Guadalupe Jaramillo, parishioners; gp/ Jose Dolores Chabes & Nicanora Garcia.

NOANES, Maria Paula
bap 29 Jan 1837, 4 days old; d/ Salbador Noanes & Maria Guadalupe Garcia, parishioners; ap/ Geronimo Nuanes & Barbara Maese; am/not stated; gp/ Don Tadeo Garcia & Doña Antonia Griego.

Frames 1692-1693
TAFOLLA, Maria Alfonsa
bap 29 Jan 1837, 3 days old; legit s/ Domingo Tafolla & Ana Maria Martines, parishioners; ap & am/ not stated; gp/ Manuel Garcia & Rafaela Rael.

GARCIA, Maria Josefa
bap 1 Feb 1837, 8 days old; natural d/ Francisca Garcia; gp/ Doña Maria de la Luz Lopez.

CANDELARIA, Maria Alfonsa
bap 1 Feb 1837, 10 days old; d/ Julian Candelaria & Gregoria Candelaria, parishioners; ap & am/ not stated; gp/ Jose Gomes & Gregoria Griego.

Frame 1694, #46
PEREA, Juan Pablo (of Sandia Pueblo)
bap 3 Feb 1837, 10 days old; s/ Domingo Perea & Maria Josefa Salasar, natives of the pueblo; gp/ Juan Pedro (Cilba) & Concepcion Cilba.

NS, Pascual (of Sandia Pueblo)
bap 3 Feb 1837, 1 month old; s/ unknown parents of the pueblo; gp/ Juan Crus & Petrona NS.

MONTOLLA, Maria Candelaria
bap 5 Feb 1837, 3 days old; d/ Bicente Montolla & Maria Josefa Martines, parishioners; ap/ Pedro Montolla & Encarnacion Luna; am/ Pedro Martines & Dolores Beitia; gp/ Don Ramon Aragon & Doña Ana Maria Cordoba.

Frame 1695, #47
GAUNA, Jose Guadalupe
bap 5 Feb 1837, 1 month old; s/ Juan Gauna & Maria Sandobal, parishioners of Sandia; gp/ Francisco Martines & Encarnacion Lucero.

GARCIA, Blas Antonio
bap 5 Feb 1837, 2 days old; s/ Juan Garcia & Juana Victoria NS, parishioners; ap/ Juan Jose Garcia & Francisca Candelaria; am/ not stated; gp/ Blas Garcia & Maria Ralles Apodaca.

Frame 1696, #48
NS, Maria Rosa
bap 6 Feb 1837, 9 days old; d/ unknown parents, placed in the home of Juan Pablo Apodaca; gp/ Juan Esteban Jaramillo & Relles Armijo.

PEREA, Maria Candelaria
bap 7 Feb 1837, 7 days old; legit d/ Salbador Perea & Gabriela Candelaria, parishioners; ap/ Jose Perea & Victoria Garcia; am/ Ygnacio Candelaria & Maria Chabes; gp/ Manuel Gonsales & Maria Rita Rael.

NS, Jose Antonio
bap 7 Feb 1837, 8 days old; s/ unknown parents, born in home of Geronimo Jaramillo; gp/ Pablo Sabedra.

Frame 1697
ARMIJO, Maria Dolores
bap 11 Feb 1837, 2 days old; d/ Don Juan Armijo & Doña Paula Jaramillo, parishioners; ap/ Santiago Armijo & Maria Petra Perea; am/ Miguel Antonio Jaramillo & Lorensa Lucero; gp/ Don Bicente Domingues & Doña Mariana Loera.

GARCIA, Maria Rumalda
bap 12 Feb 1837, 4 days old; d/ Francisco Garcia & Relles Candelaria, parishioners; ap/ Juan Garcia & Maria Ysabel Montolla; am/ Jose Tomas Candelaria & Ana Maria Gallego; gp/ Bartolo Perea & Josefa Candelaria.

Frame 1698, #49
ARMIJO, Maria del Rallo Petronila
bap 13 Feb 1837, 15 days old; d/ Jose Miguel Armijo & Antonia Chrispin, parishioners; ap & am/ not stated; gp/ Pablo Baca & Beginia Burtierres.

GARCIA, Jose Blas
bap 13 Feb 1837, 12 days old; legit s/ Pablo Garcia & Antonia Martines, parishioners; ap/ not stated; am/ Ysidro Martines & Doña Maria Montaño; gp/ Sabino Gonsales & Maria de Jesus Luna.

GONSALES, Maria Candelaria
bap 13 Feb 1837, 12 days old; d/ Jose Gonsales & Francisca Garcia, parishioners; ap/ Felipe Gonsales & Maria Gurule; am/ Juan Garcia & Maria Chabes; gp/ Don Hilario Gonsales & Maria Rita Rael.

Frame 1699
MONTOLLA, Jose Rumaldo
bap 14 Feb 1837, 3 days old; s/ Francisco Montolla & Acencion Garcia, parishioners; ap/ Jose Miguel Montolla & Catarina Lucero; am/ Jose Manuel Garcia & Josefa Chabes; gp/ Bautista Gonsales & Guadalupe Ruis.

NS, Maria Feliciana
bap 14 Feb 1837, 4 days old; d/ unknown parents, born at the home of Maria Jaramillo; gp/ Pablo Lucero & Maria Ynes Ruis.

Frames 1699-1700, #50
SANDOBAL, Juan Jose Desiderio
bap 14 Feb 1837, 4 days old; s/ Dolores Sandobal & Juana Trugillo, parishioners; ap/ Juan Sandobal & Josefa Apodaca; am/ Baltasar Trugillo & Teresa Gallego; gp/ Rafael Trugillo & Gertrudes Gurule.

MONTOLLA, Maria Rallo
bap 14 Feb 1837, 3 days old; legit d/ Jose Montolla & Maria Loreta Arias, parishioners; ap/ Juan Montolla & Rita Valencia; am/ Felipe Arias & Antonia Griego; gp/ Juan Gurule & Gregoria Arias.

SANCHES, Jose Amador
bap 14 Feb 1837, 2 days old; legit s/ Dolores Sanches & Juana Candelaria, parishioners; ap/ Manuel Sanches & Ana Maria Lopes; am/ not stated; gp/ Petra Sanches.

Frame 1701
GURULE, Maria Candelaria
bap 15 Feb 1837, 3 days old; legit d/ Marcelo Gurule & Petra Burtieres, parishioners; ap & am/ not stated; gp/ Lasaro Torres & Micaela Arias.

LOPES, Maria Nicola Lugarda
bap 15 Feb 1837, 4 days old; legit d/ Jose Cleto Lopes & Dolores Candelaria, parishioners; ap & am/ not stated; gp/ Lorenso Lucero & Maria Ynes Ruiz.

PEREA, Maria Trinidad
bap 15 Feb 1837, 3 days old; natural d/ Dolores Perea; gp/ Ysidora Lopes.

Frame 1702, #51
CANDELARIA, Maria de la Luz
bap 15 Feb 1837, 3 days old; legit d/ Jose Pablo Candelaria & Maria Antonia Sandobal, parishioners; ap/ not stated; am/ Esteban Sandobal & Tomasa Duran; gp/ Don Juan Gil & Doña Maria de la Lus Lopes.

PEREA, Jose Polinario
bap 16 Feb 1837, 4 days old; s/ Juan Jose Perea & Francisca Tafolla, parishioners; ap/ not stated; am/ Ygnacio Tafolla & Maria Antonia Baca; gp/ Gaspar Atencio & Maria Ysabel Chabes.

Frame 1703
MONTOLLA, Rafael Gregorio
bap 17 Feb 1837, 3 days old; legit s/ Jose Maria Montolla & Clara Armijo, parishioners; ap/ not stated; am/ Don Lucas Armijo & Doña Barbara Ortiz; gp/ Christobal Armijo & Beneranda Ortiz.

PADILLA, Jose Dolores
bap 22 Feb 1837, 6 days old; legit s/ Jose Manuel Padilla & Maria Antonia Otero, parishioners; ap & am/ not stated; gp/ Juan Jose Sanches & Antonia Rita Luna.

GALLEGO, Maria Guadalupe
bap 22 Feb 1837, 7 days old; legit d/ Christobal Gallego & Maria del Carmen Romero, parishioners; ap & am/ not stated; gp/ Juan Luna & Maria Guadalupe Luna.

Frame 1704, #52
NS, Juan Felipe
bap 22 Feb 1837, 4 days old; s/ unknown parents; gp/ Julian Padilla & Albina Gurule.

ROMERO, Maria Ramona
bap 24 Feb 1837, 5 days old; legit d/ Baltazar Romero & Paula Lucero, parishioners; ap/ Miguel Antonio Romero & Paula Garcia; am/ not stated; gp/ Juan Jose Sanches & Antonia Rita Luna.

Frame 1705
GARCIA, Maria Dolores
bap 24 Feb 1837, 6 days old; d/ Manuel Garcia & Concecion Lopez, parishioners; ap/ Pedro Garcia & Maria Analla; am/ not stated; gp/ Pablo Armijo & Nicolasa Burtierres.

NS, Jose Miguel
bap 26 Feb 1837, 8 days old; s/ unknown parents, born in the home of Rafaela Garcia; gp/ Manuel Cerna & Ana Maria Garcia.

BURTIERRES, Maria del Rallo Manuela
bap 27 Feb 1837, 10 days old; d/ Esteban Burtierres & Quiteria Burtierres, parishioners; gp/ Diego Sanches & Juana Maria Gallego.

Frame 1706, #53
LOPEZ, Maria del Rallo de Jesus
bap 3 Mar 1837, 4 days old; d/ Jose Bernabe Lopez & Cipriana Perea, parishioners; ap & am/ not stated; gp/ Miguel Quinones & Tomasa Lopes.

GRIEGO, Maria Sesaria de los Dolores
bap 4 Mar 1837, 8 days old; d/ Pablo Griego & Juana Montolla, parishioners; ap/ Felipe Griego & Margarita Gonsales; am/ Juan Montolla & Maria de Jesus Lucero; gp/ Ambrocio Gonsales & Grabiela Gonsales.

Frame 1707
GURULE, Maria Nazaria
bap 5 Mar 1837, 8 days old; legit d/ Santiago Gurule & Rita Ginso, parishioners; ap & am/ not stated; gp/ Antonio Felis Garcia & Ana Maria Mestas.

MARTINES, Jose Antonio (of Bernalillo)
bap 6 Mar 1837, 11 days old; s/ Leonicio Martines & Soledad Jaramillo, parishioners of Sandia; ap/ Antonio Martines & Teresa Burtierres; am/ Christobal Jaramillo & Elena Chabes; gp/ Juan Antonio Rael & Soledad Miera.

NS, Maria Albina de Jesus
bap 7 Mar 1837; Navajo of the household of Don Julian Tenorio; gp/ Rosalia Tenorio.

Frame 1708, #54
CORDOBA, Juan de Dios
bap 8 Mar 1837, 8 days old; s/ Bautista Cordoba & Manuela Cerna, parishioners; ap/ Nicolas Cordoba & Maria Ygnacia Garcia; am/ Juan Cerna & Barbara Gallego; gp/ Pablo Martines & Maria Antonia Griego.

NS, Maria Rita de los Dolores
bap 8 Mar 1837, 7 days old; d/ unknown parents; gp/ Bernardo Apodaca & Dolores Torres.

Frames 1708-1709
OTERO, Maria Lucretia
bap 8 Mar 1837, 8 days old; d/ Santiago Otero & Ana Maria Samora, parishioners; ap/ Julian Otero & Manuela Padilla; am/ Jose Samora & Rafaela Martines; gp/ Jose Lucero & Juana Samora.

CANDELARIA, Maria Placida
bap 10 Mar 1837, 6 days old; d/ Manuel Candelaria & Francisca Griego, parishioners; ap/ Juan Bicente Candelaria & Maria Candelaria Lobato; am/ not stated; gp/ Jose Parras & Maria Juliana Candelaria.

Frames 1709-1710, #55
GARCIA, Melquiades de Jesus
bap 12 Mar 1837, 3 days old; s/ Jose Antonio Garcia & Ygnacia Candelaria, parishioners; ap/ Felis Garcia & Maria Ysabel Lopes; am/ not stated; gp/ Francisco Torres & Dolores Torres.

NS, Ygnacio de Jesus
bap 12 Mar 1837, 5 days old; s/ unknown parents; gp/ Doña Trinidad Gabaldon.

ARANDA, Maria Teresa de Jesus
bap 13 Mar 1837, 3 days old; d/ Pedro Aranda & Rosalia Jaramillo, parishioners; ap/ Antonio Aranda & Antonia Teresa Romero; am/ Jose Miguel Jaramillo & Antonia Maria Poblano; gp/ Francisco Aranda & Juana Aranda.

Frames 1710-1711
CANDELARIA, Maria Eulogia
bap 14 Mar 1837, 4 days old; d/ Francisco Candelaria & Manuela Gallego; ap/ Ygnacio Candelaria & Maria Luisa Garcia; am/ Martin Gallego & Manuela Garcia; gp/ Manuel Candelaria & Ana Maria Trugillo.

NS, Maria Polinaria
bap 14 Mar 1837, 8 days old; d/ unknown parents, b. in the house of Don Santiago Gonzales; gp/ Ambrosio Gonsales & Grabiela Gonsales.

ARIAS, Jose Antonio de Jesus
bap 15 Mar 1837, 4 days old; s/ Juan Christoval Arias & Tomasa Martines, parishioners; ap/ Pablo Arias & Encarnacion Valencia; am/ Baltasar Martines & Maria Antonia Griego; gp/ Don Juan de Dios Chabes & Doña Monica Lucero.

Frame 1712
NS, Maria Altagracia
bap 15 Mar 1837, 2 days old; d/ unknown parents, left at the home of Pablo Sabedra; gp/ Salbador Martines & Maria Altagracia Martines.

SALASAR, Maria del Refugia
bap 18 Mar 1837, 3 days old; d/ Manuel Salasar & Francisca Trugillo, parishioners; ap & am/ not stated; gp/ Pedro Antonio Montolla & Rosa Montolla.

DURAN, Jose Agapito
bap 18 Mar 1837, 2 days old; legit s/ Francisco Duran & Bernarda Gurule; ap & am/ not stated; gp/ Manuel Muñis & Josefa Candelaria.

Frame 1713
NS, Antonio Jose
bap 19 Mar 1837, 10 days old; s/ unknown parents, left at the home of Juliana Montaño; gp/ Jose Griego & Manuela Barrela.

TORRES, Jose Relles
bap 20 Mar 1837, 2 days old; s/ Francisco Torres & Juliana Montolla, parishioners; ap & am/ not stated; gp/ Salbador Cena & Barbara Burtierres.

BURTIERRES, Jose Encarnacion
bap 25 Mar 1837, 6 days old; s/ Jose Burtierres & Gertrudis Gomes, parishioners; gp/ Jose Antonio Martines & Quiteria Griego.

Frame 1714, #5
NS, Maria del Rallo de Jesus
bap 25 Mar 1837; d/ unknown parents, Indian in the household of Don Blas Lucero; gp/ Doña Elena Domingues.

JARAMILLO, Jose Domingo
bap 27 Mar 1837, 3 days old; legit s/ Juan Crus Jaramillo & Manuela Mestas, parishioners; ap & am/ not stated; gp/ Antonio Analla & Tomasa Tafolla.

Frame 1715
NS, Jose Leandro (of Sandia Pueblo)
bap 29 Mar 1837, 8 days old; s/ unknown parents of Sandia Pueblo; gp/ Luciano Manchego & Guadalupe NS of Sandia Pueblo.

NS, Maria Dolores
bap 30 Mar 1837, 15 days old; d/ unknown parents; gp/ Juana Chabes.

LUCERO, Maria Andrea
bap 30 Mar 1837, 1 month old; d/ Juan Lucero & Maria Gertrudes Garcia, parishioners; ap & am/ not stated; gp/ Jose Maria Martines & Maria Luciana Martines.

Frame 1716, #59
GRIEGO, Jose Teodoro
bap 6 Apr 1837, 5 days old; s/ Jose Tomas Griego & Monica Santillanes, parishioners; ap/ Miguel Griego & Petra Candelaria; am/ Antonio Santillanes & Geralda Garcia; gp/ Juan Calletano Garcia & Maria Francisca Santillanes.

GONSALES, Maria Francisca
bap 7 Apr 1837, 8 days old; d/ Juan Albino Gonsales & Balbina Lopes, parishioners; ap/ Juan Domingo Gonsales & Maria Archuleta; am/ Gaspar Lopes & Rosalia Duran; gp/ Mariano Gonsales & Maria de Jesus Luna.

TRUGILLO, Jose Rafael
bap 11 Apr 1837, 1 day old; legit s/ Santiago Trugillo & Maria Salome Burtierres; ap/ Jose Trugillo & Soledad Balencia; am/ Miguel Burtierres & Gregoria Armijo; gp/ Rafael Armijo & Soledad Peña.

Frame 1717
GARCIA, Juan Jose Nepomuceno
bap 11 Apr 1837, 2 days old; legit s/ Ambrocio Garcia & Ledibina Sandobal, parishioners; Felis Garcia & Maria Ysabel Lopes; am/ not stated; gp/ Jose Rael & Josefa Vigil.

SANCHES, Maria Clara
bap 12 Apr 1837, 4 days old; legit d/ Christobal Sanches & Concepcion Valencia, parishioners; ap/ not stated; am/ Juan Domingo Valencia & Maria Ygnacia Salasar; gp/ Mariano Lucero & Marcelina Valencia.

Frames 1717-1718, #60
GALLEGO, Juan Domingo
bap 15 Apr 1837, 7 days old; legit s/ Bacilio Gallego & Clara Peña, parishioners; ap/ Antonio Jose Gallego & Madalena Romero; am/ Agustin Peña & Dolores Montolla; gp/ Juan Gallego & Gertrudis Gallego.

GURULE, Maria Juliana
bap 16 Apr 1837, 4 days old; d/ Lorenso Gurule & Maria Ycidora Noanes, parishioners; ap/ not stated; am/ Geronimo Noanes & Barbara Maese; gp/ Bernardo Valencia & Maria Martin.

NS, Jose Caledonio
bap 16 Apr 1837, 2 days old; s/ unknown parents, left at the home of Pedro Burtierres; gp/ Jose Sanches & Juliana Burtierres.

Frame 1719
NS, Maria del Rallo Juana
bap 19 Apr 1837, 2 days old; d/ unknown parents, left at the home of Doña Soledad Armijo; gp/ Don Teodoro Armijo & Doña Soledad Armijo.

NS, Antonio Perfecto
bap 19 Apr 1837, 2 days old; s/ unknown parents, left at the home of Don Felis Garcia; gp/ Pedro Armijo & Maria de la Luz Garcia.

SANCHES, Jose Toribio
bap 23 Apr 1837, 3 days old; s/ Juan Sanches & Maria Guadalupe Chabes, parishioners; ap/ Alonso Rael & Josefa Tenorio; am/ not stated; gp/ Juan Montolla & Juana Martines.

Frame 1720, #71
BURTIERRES, Jose Aniceto
bap 23 Apr 1837, 3 days old; s/ Juan Burtierres & Manuela Lopes, parishioners; ap/ Miguel Burtierres & Maria Cimona Gallego; am/ Tomas Lopes & Maria Candelaria; gp/ Felipe Samora & Juana Mora.

NS, Jose de Jesus
bap 23 Apr 1837, 3 days old; s/ unknown parents; gp/ Mateo Lopes & Maria Manuela Montolla

Frames 1720-1721, #61
LOPES, Maria del Rallo
bap 24 Apr 1837, 4 days old; d/ Juan Christobal Lopes & Rita Candelaria, parishioners; ap/ Gregorio Sedillo & Juana Candelaria; am/ not stated; gp/ Juan Chabes & Josepha Chabes.

GONSALES, Juan Bautista
bap 26 Apr 1837, 8 days old; s/ Francisco Gonsales & Maria Petra Gonsales, parishioners; ap/ Antonio Gonsales & Maria Gertrudis Gurule; am/ Antonio Gonsales & Juana Sandobal; gp/ Juan Christobal Montolla & Monica Gonsales.

NS, Juan George Anastacio
bap 27 Apr 1837, 10 days old; s/ unknown parents, left at the home of Don Victorio Sedillo; gp/ Pedro Sedillo & Francisca Chabes.

Frame 1722
MONTOLLA, Jose Gregorio
bap 12 Apr 1837, 4 days old; legit s/ Julian Montolla & Dolores Lopes, parishioners; ap/ Luis Montolla & Gregoria Ginso; am/ not stated; gp/ Ynes Ruis.

GARCIA, Jose Macimo
bap 12 Apr 1837, 1 day old; legit s/ Juan Rafael Garcia & Encarnacion Lucero, parishioners; ap/ Juan Rafael Garcia & Manuela Muñis; am/ Gregorio Lucero & Maria Lopes; gp/ Juan Rafael Garcia & Manuela Muñis.

Frames 1722-1723
NS, Maria Dolores
bap 19 Apr 1837, 2 days old; d/ unknown parents, placed in the hose of Doña Bartola Apodaca; gp/ Don Bartolo Apodaca & Doña Soledad Telles.

CANDELARIA, Antonio Jose
bap 15 Apr 1837, 1 day old; legit s/ Juan Bicente Candelaria & Candelaria Lobato, parishioners; ap/ Juan Candelaria & Maria Dolores Candelaria; am/ not stated; gp/ Manuel Analla & Felipa Martines.

JARAMILLO, Jose Ysidro
bap 15 Apr 1837, 2 days old; s/ Marcos Jaramillo & Ana Maria Garcia, parishioners; ap/ Christobal Jaramillo & Elena Chabes; am/ Diego Garcia & Ramona Candelaria; gp/ Juan Jose Santillanes & Josefa Garcia.

Frame 1724, #63
MARTINES, Jose Antonio
bap 27 Apr 1837, 2 days old; s/ Gregorio Martines & Gregoria Gurule, parishioners; ap/ Miguel Martines & Doroteo Gallego; am/ not stated; gp/ Antonio Burtierres & Guadalupe Garcia.

NS, Mariana de Jesus
bap 28 Apr 1837, 5 days old; d/ unknown parents, left at the home of Antonio Lopes; gp/ Juan Ysidro Gonsales & Maria del Rosario Duran.

Frames 1724-1725
ROMERO, Antonio Maria
bap 3 May 1837, 2 days old; s/ Jose Miguel Romero & Maria Ygnacia Montaño, parishioners; ap/ Miguel Antonio Romero & Juana Garcia; am/ Salbador Montaño & Gregoria Chabes; gp/ Don Antonio Maria Garcia & Juana Montolla.

NS, Maria de Jesus
bap 7 May 1837, 3 days old; d/ unknown parents; gp/ Joaquin Luna & Manuela Romero.

NS, Juan Miguel
bap 8 May 1837, 5 days old; s/ unknown parents; gp/ Bartolo Lobato & Maria Matilde Duran.

Frame 1726, #64
JARAMILLO, Domingo
bap 15 May 1837, 3 days old; legit s/ Manuel Jaramillo & Maria Gertrudis Mestas; ap/ Jose Miguel Jaramillo & Doña Ana Maria Ortega; am/ not stated; gp/ Mariano Ulibarri & Juana Otero.

NS, Maria Gertrudes
bap 20 May 1837, 3 days old; d/ unknown parents, left at the home of Don Andres Lucero; gp/ Don Andres Lucero & Doña Lorenza Lucero.

Frame 1727
NS, Maria Trinidad
bap 22 May 1837, 7 days old; d/ unknown parents; gp/ Jose Anastacio Cordoba & Manuela Garcia.

MONTOLLA, Domingo
bap 21 May 1837, 8 days old; s/ Juan Bautista Montolla & Juana Rafaela Aragon, parishioners; ap/ Juan Montolla & Rita Lopes; am/ Juan Domingo Aragon & Juana Garcia; gp/ Miguel Garcia & Rosalia Barrela.

Frames 1727-1728, #65
BURTIERRES, Maria Benigna
bap 23 May 1837, 3 days old; d/ Leonardo Burtierres & Soledad Garcia, parishioners; ap/ Santiago Burtierres & Guadalupe Santillanes; am/ not stated; gp/ Don Jose Armijo.

MESTAS, Maria Beneranda
bap 30 May 1837, 3 days old; d/ Ambrosio Mestas & Nepomucena Gonsales, parishioners; ap/ Ygnacio Mestas & Guadalupe Duran; am/ not stated; gp/ Juan Griego & Estefana Garcia.

PEREA, Jose Ygnacio Nepomuceno
bap 31 May 1837, 3 days old; legit s/ Francisco Perea & Paula Sandoval, parishioners; ap/ Rafael Perea & Carmen Romero; am/ Jose Sandoval & Petra Sabedra; gp/ Don Ygnacio Ruis & Doña Ysidora Lopes.

Frame 1729
NS, Jose Manuel
bap 2 Jun 1837; s/ unknown parents, left at the home of Maria Justa Romero; gp/ Manuel Perea & Gertrudis Gurule.

LUCERO, Maria Ysabel
bap 3 Jun 1837, 3 days old; d/ Francisco Lucero & Manuela Aragon, parishioners; ap/ Juan Lucero & Maria Justa Pino; gp/ Antonio Jose Martines & Maria Luciana Lucero.

Frame 1730, #80
PROBENCIO, Maria Petra
bap 3 Jun 1837, 2 days old; d/ Jose Probencio & Juana Carabajal, parishioners; ap/ not stated; am/ Miguel Carabajal & Jacinta Lopes; gp/ Pedro Lopes & Petra Lopes.

NS, Jose Quirino
bap 4 Jun 1837, 4 days old; s/ unknown parents, left at the home of Don Torribio Sedillo; gp/ Francisco Sanchez.

Frames 1730-1731
BACA, Maria Quirina
bap 6 Jun 1837, 3 days old; d/ Don Jose Baca & Maria Antonia Garcia, parishioners; ap/ Juan Domingo Baca & Maria Getrudes Ortiz; am/ Salbador Garcia & Maria Chabes; gp/ Don Salbador Jaramillo.

LAURIANO, Maria Juana
bap 10 Jun 1837, 2 days old; legit d/ Juan Lauriano & Antonia Sanches, parishioners; gp/ Gregorio Apodaca & Catarina Apodaca.

SALASAR, Antonio
bap 11 Jun 1837, 2 days old; legit s/ Lucas Salazar & Rosalia Jinso, parishioners; gp/ Felipe Aragon & Ana Maria Aragon.

LUJAN, Antonio Jose
bap 15 Jun 1837; legit s/ Jose Maria Lujan & Dolores Duran, parishioners; gp/ Don Jose Armijo & Doña Barbara Ortiz.

Frame 1732, #67
SANDOBAL, Juan Antonio
bap 15 Jun 1837, 4 days old; legit s/ Antonio Sandobal & Maria Dolores Montolla; gp/ Juan Luna & Concepcion Luna.

LUNA, Antonio Jose
bap 18 Jun 1837, 3 days old; legit s/ Francisco Luna & Concepcion Sena, parishioners; gp/ Mariano
Gonzalez & Maria Archuleta.

NS, Jose Pablo
bap 18 Jun 1837, 3 days old; s/ unknown parents; gp/ Guadalupe Chaves & Maria Leonarda Padilla.

Frame 1733
MARES, Pedro Antonio
bap 2 Jul 1837, 4 days old; s/ Ramon Mares & Maria de la Lus Jaramillo, parishioners; ap/ Juan Pablo
Mares & Ana Maria Noanes; am/ Ramon Jaramillo & Relles Armijo; gp/ Santiago Trugillo & Maria
Salome Burtierres.

GARCIA, Maria de Jesus
bap 2 Jul 1837, 2 days old; d/ Rumaldo Garcia & Ana Maria Arias, parishioners; gp/ Albino Gonsales &
Balbina Lopes.

Frames 1733-1734, #68
NS, Maria del Refugio
bap 7 Jul 1837, 8 days old; d/ unknown parents; gp/ Maria Josefa Griego.

NS, Jose Anisteo de Jesus
bap 8 Jul 1837, 2 days old; s/ unknown parents, left at the home of Don Diego Lopes; gp/ Doña Maria de
la Lus Lopes.

CONTRERAS, Juan Christobal
bap 9 Jul 1837, 3 days old; legit s/ Juan Francisco Contreras & Mariana Cordoba, parishioners; ap & am/
not stated; gp/ Juan Apodaca & Maria Ysabel Sanches.

Frame 1735
NOANES, Pedro Jose
bap 14 Jul 1837, 4 days old; legit s/ Santiago Noanes & Maria Manuela Atencio, parishioners; ap/
Geronimo Noanes & Barbara Noanes; am/ Gaspar Atencio & Maria Ysabel Chaves; gp/ Juan Domingo
Sandobal & Maria Concepcion Montolla.

MONTOLLA, Epimenio de Jesus
bap 14 Jul 1837, 3 days old; s/ Don Juan Montolla & Clara Jaramillo, parishioners; ap/ not stated; am/
Ramon Jaramillo & Relles Armijo; gp/ Don Blas Lucero & Doña Benita Domingues.

Frame 1736, #69
GARCIA, Maria de Rallo
bap 14 Jul 1837, 6 days old; d/ Juan Garcia & Francisca Gurule, parishioners; gp/ Jose Manuel Gonsales
& Francisca Garcia.

NS, Jose Concepcion
bap 18 Jul 1837, 7 days old; s/ unknown parents, left at the home of Juan Ygnacio Garcia; gp/ Jose
Dolores Samora & Soledad Garcia.

GALLEGO, Juan Nepomuceno
bap 18 Jul 1837, 3 days old; s/ Juan Antonio Gallego & Petra Lopes, parishioners; ap/ not stated; am/ Bernardo Lopes & Relles Lujan, gp/ Juan Nepomuceno Carbajal & Maria Francisca Carbajal.

Frame 1737
APODACA, Maria del Carmen
bap 20 Jul 1837, 3 days old; d/ Julian Apodaca & Antonia Griego, parishioners; ap & am/ not stated; gp/ Diego Romero & Juliana Montaño.

ALIRI, Felipe Santiago
bap 27 Jul 1837, 3 days old; s/ Jose Benito Aliri & Juana Garcia, parishioners; ap & am/ not stated; gp/ Ramon Romero & Juana Maria Romero.

Frames 1737-1738, #70
GARCIA, Maria de Jesus
bap 29 Jul 1837, 6 days old; d/ Jose Gregorio Garcia & Petra Gonsales, parishioners; ap & am/ not stated; gp/ Sabino Gonsales & Maria de Jesus Luna.

BACA, Salbador Antonio
bap 29 Jul 1837, 3 days old; legit s/ Antonio Baca & Manuela Lucero, parishioners; ap/ Rafael Baca & Juana Reta Candeleria; am/ Alfonso Lucero & Manuela Chrispin; gp/ Salbador Martines & Maria Alta Gracia Martines.

JARAMILLO, Jose Domingo de Jesus
bap 4 Aug 1837, 4 days old; s/ Luciano Jaramillo & Loreta Rael, parishioners; ap/ not stated; am/ Juan Rael & Maria Gurule; gp/ Juana Garcia.

Frame 1739
GRIEGO, Maria del Rallo Ysabel
bap 5 Aug 1837, 3 days old; legit d/ Hilario Griego & Maria de Jesus Garcia, parishioners; ap/ Pablo Griego & Maria Ysidora Apodaca; am/ Jose Garcia & Marta Duran; gp/ Jose Maria Chabes & Maria Ysabel Apodaca.

CANDELARIA, Jose Ygnacio
bap 6 Aug 1837, 3 days old; legit s/ Jose Candelaria & Juana Garcia, parishioners; ap & am/ not stated; gp/ Jose Antonio Martines & Quiteria Griego.

Frame 1740
NS, Juan Domingo
bap 6 Aug 1837, 4 days old; s/ unknown parents, left at the home of Maria Antonia Griego; gp/ Jose Pablo Martines & Maria Ycidora Arias.

CHABES, Juan Agustin
bap 8 Sep 1837, 1 month old; legit s/ Pedro Chabes & Encarnacion Gonsales, parishioners; ap/ Tomas Chabes & Tomasa Padilla; am/ Antonio Gonsales & Micaela Sandobal; gp/ Deciderio Garcia & Maria Gregoria Candelaria.

NS, Jose Antonio
bap 8 Sep 1837, 10 days old; s/ unknown parents; gp/ Manuel Perea & Juliana Santillanes.

Frame 1741
GARCIA, (No Name)
bap 8 Sep 1837, 8 days old; legit s/ Juan Garcia & Francisca Santillanes, parishioners; ap/not stated; am/ Luciano Santillanes & Maria Duran; gp/ Asencio Griego & Ana Maria Salazar.

GRIEGO, Maria Peregrina
bap 9 Sep 1837, 1 month old; legit d/ Rafael Griego & Barbara Apodaca, parishioners; gp/ Don Juan Armijo & Doña Paula Jaramillo.

PEREA, Juana Agustin
bap 10 Sep 1837, 4 days old; legit s/ Bartolo Perea & Josefa Candelaria, parishioners; gp/ Jose Maria Sandobal & Maria Teresa Luna.

Frame 1742, #72
NS, Maria Peregrina de los Dolores
bap 11 Sep 1837, 8 days old; d/ unknown parents; gp/ Miguel Antonio Jaramillo & Lorenza Lucero.

SANCHES, Manuel Antonio
bap 12 Sep 1837, 2 days old; legit s/ Nepomuceno Sanches & Maria Dolores Chabes, parishioners; ap/ Felis Sanches & Ana Maria Aguirre; am/ Antonio Chabes & Manuela Garcia; gp/ Juan Chabes & Teodora Chabes.

PEREA, Manuel Antonio
bap 12 Sep 1837, 7 days old; s/ Juan Perea & Cruz Duran, parishioners; ap/ Francisco Perea & Feliciana Martines; am/ Pedro Duran & Josefa Antonia Jaramillo, gp/ Manuel Antonio Perea & Gregoria Duran.

Frame 1743
GURULE, Maria Concepcion
bap 15 Sep 1837, 2 days old; legit d/ Jose Grabiel Gurule & Maria Nicolasa Luna, parishioners; ap/ Jose Grabiel Gurule & Ana Maria Gonsalez; am/ Ycidro Luna & Manuela Candelaria; gp/ Domingo Sanches & Maria de la Lus Perea.

CHRESPIN, Jose Francisco Cornelio
bap 17 Sep 1837, 3 days old; legit s/ Juan Andres Chrespin & Rosalia Lucero, residents of Albuquerque; gp/ Salbador Pacheco & Rosalia Lucero.

Frame 1744
GUTIERRES, Jose Campos Concepcion
bap 19 Sep 1837, 11 days old; legit s/ Jose Antonio Gutierres & Ysabel Griego, residents of Albuquerque; ap/ not stated; am/ Jose Griego & Gertrudis Valencia; gp/ Felipe Martines & Quiteria Griego, of los Gallegos.

Frame 1745, #73
MUÑIZ, Jesus Maria
bap 17 Sep 1837, 4 days old; legit s/ Juan Christobal Muñiz & Ana Maria Pacheco, residents of Albuquerque; ap/ not stated; am/ Geronimo Pacheco & Pascuala Sanches; gp/ Diego Lopes & Juliana Chabes.

SUAREZ, Jose Mateo
bap 23 Sep 1837, 3 days old; legit s/ Mateo Suarez & Guadalupe Griego, residents of Alameda; ap/ Calletano Suarez & Maria Antonia Velasquez; am/ Paublo Griego & Maria Ysidora Apodaca; gp/ Manuel Apodaca & Maria Gertrudis Apodaca.

NS, Maria Placida
bap 23 Sep 1837, 2 days old; d/ unknown parents, in the household of Don Juan Armijo; gp/ Marcelo Gurule & Maria Edubige Gomes.

Frame 1746
ARMIJO, Jose Ericeo
bap 27 Sep 1837, 1 day old; legit s/ Ygnacio Armijo & Francisca Cisneros, residents of Alameda; ap/ Santiago Armijo & Rosalia Garcia; am/ Francisco Cisneros & Juana Duran; gp/ Santiago Trujillo & Maria Salome Burtierres.

GONZALES, Juan Christobal
bap 29 Sep 1837, 3 days old; legit s/ Sabino Gonzales & Maria de la Luz Montolla, residents of Alameda; ap & am/ not stated; gp/ Julian Padilla & Rosa Padilla.

Frame 1747, #74
APODACA, Maria Rosa (of Alameda)
bap 22 Oct 1837, 4 days old; legit d/ Juan Apodaca & Maria de la Luz Padilla; ap/ Rafael Apodaca & Juana Maria Romero; am/ Julian Padilla & deceased Juana Maria Padilla; gp/ Dolores Padilla & Maria Rosa de los Dolores Padilla, residents of Alameda.

NS, Jose Manuel (of San Antonio)
bap 22 Oct 1837, 5 years old; native Navajo Indian, from the home of Andres Lucero & Tomasa Garcia; gp/ Desiderio (Lucero) & Maria Gertrudis Lucero.

Frames 1747 - 1748
ANAYA, Maria Seferina (of los Griegos)
bap 22 Oct 1837, 2 days old; legit d/ Rafael Anaya & Ynes Gurule; ap/ deceased Felipe Anaya & Dolores Torres; am/ Juan Cristoval Gurule & Maria Ygnacia Martines; gp/ Miguel Quiñoes & Polonia Marques, residents of los Griegos.

GARCIA, Neri (of los Griegos)
bap 30 Oct 1837, 1 month old; natural s/ Catarina Garcia; am/ Juan Garcia & Gertrudis Gallegos; gp/ Juan de Luis Armenta & Maria Manuela Padia.

DURAN, Maria Santos (of Los Duranes)
bap 31 Oct 1837, 2 days old; natural d/ Margarita Duran, residents of los Duranes; am/ Salvador Duran & Balbaneda Garcia, deceased; gp/ Juan Lucero & Manuela Sabedra, residents of Albuquerque.

Frame 1749, #75
CASTILLO, Maria Concepcion (of Corrales)
bap 7 Oct 1837, 3 days old; legit d/ Juan Castillo & Catarina Garcia, parishioners; ap/ Antonio Jose Castillo & Quiteria Chabes; am/ Antonio Garcia & Francisca Gonsales; gp/ Nicolas Sandobal & Concepcion Armijo.

ANALLA, Santiago (of Atrisco)
bap 7 Oct 1837, 3 days old; legit s/ Jose Rosalio Analla & Teresa Candelaria, parishioners; ap/ Manuel Analla & Sidora Gonsales; am/ Juan Pablo Candelaria & Guadalupe Herrera; gp/ Miguel Jaramillo & Estefana Herrera.

Frames 1749-1750
ALFAROS, Maria Dolores
bap 22 Oct 1837, 3 days old; d/ Guadalupe Alfaros & Maria Paula Garcia, parishioners; ap/ Juan Alfaros & Maria Lopes; am/ Juan Manuel Garcia & Manuela Perea; gp/ Santiago Romero & Maria Dolores Candelaria.

APODACA, Maria Rosa (of Alameda)
Bap 22 Oct 1837, 4 days old; legit d/ Juan Apodaca & Maria de la Lus Padilla; ap/ Rafael Apodaca & Juana Maria Romero, of Alameda; am/ Julian Padilla & Juana Maria Padilla; gp/ Jose Dolores Padilla & Maria Dolores Padilla.

LUCERO, Maria Begnina
bap 12 Nov 1837, 4 days old; legit d/ Sebastian Lucero & Maria Nicolasa Ramires, residents of Alameda; ap/ Eusebio Lucero & Josefa Garcia; am/ Antonio Ramires & Ysabel Griego; gp/ Felis Sanches & Sebastian Sena.

Frame 1751, #76
LUCERO, Maria del Carmel (of Alameda)
bap 12 Nov 1837, 8 days old; legit d/ Juan Lucero & Micaela Trugillo; ap/ Miguel Lucero & Maria Dimas Aragon; am/ Juan Antonio Trugillo & Maria Juana Montoya; gp/ Jose Gabriel Gurule & Maria Nicolasa Luna, residents of Alameda.

GONSALES, Jesus Maria (of Alameda)
bap 12 Nov 1837, 4 days old; legit d/ Juan de la Crus Gonsales & Maria de Jesus Moya, residents of Alameda; ap/ Francisco Gonsales & Barbara Basques; am/ Eusebio Moya & Gregoria Garcia; gp/ Jesus Moya & Juana Moya, residents of the same.

TRUGILLO, Maria Antonia
bap 12 Nov 1837, 6 days old; legit d/ Antonio Trugillo & Marta Crespin; ap/ Juan Trugillo & Manuela Apodaca; am/ Juan Crespin & Magdalena Martines; gp/ Juan Pablo Sanches & Maria Antonia Lucero.

Frame 1752
VALDES, Maria Teodora (of los Ranchos)
bap 19 Nov 1837, 13 days old; legit d/ Luciano Valdes & Maria Seberiana Gallegos; ap/ Jose Valdes & Gertrudis Chaves; am/ Jose Mariano Gallegos & Maria Teodora Romero; gp/ Nasario Gonsales & Maria Lugarda Garcia.

JARAMILLO, Maria de las Nieves (of Ranchos of Atrisco)
bap 20 Nov 1837, 5 days old; legit d/ Manuel Jaramillo & Maria Dolores Lopes; ap/ Manuel Jaramillo & Juana Montoya; am/ Agustin Lopes & Francisca Garcia; gp/ Jose Jaramillo & Maria Nieves Chaves.

ANAYA, Manuel Antonio (of Atrisco)
bap 26 Nov 1837, 9 days old; legit s/ Salvador Anaya & Barbara Sanches; ap/ Pedro Anaya & Dolores (blank); am/ Manuel Sanches & Dolores Chaves; gp/ Manuel Sanches & Maria Marselina Sanches, of Atrisco.

Frames 1752-1753, #77
MESTAS, Rafaela (of Atrisco)
bap 26 Nov 1837, 5 days old; legit d/ Manuel Mestas & Ysidora Corris; ap & am/ (left blank); gp/ Jose Rafael Martines & Mariana Sisneros, residents of Atrisco.

NS, Maria Clara
bap 20 Nov 1837, 2 years old; native of the Navajo, left at the home of Don Juan Armijo; gp/ Don Juan Armijo & Doña Juana Sista Armijo, residents of Atrisco.

MOYA, Maria del Rosario
bap 28 Nov 1837, 2 days old; natural d/ Josefa Moya; am/ Acencio Moya & Juana Sandoval; gp/ Juan Gil & Doña Luz Lopes, residents of Albuquerque.

GURULE, Santa Ana
bap 3 Dec 1837, 6 days old; legit d/ Nicolas Gurule & Simona Martines; ap/ Antonio Gurule & Maria Antonia Gurule; am/ Jose Martines & Rosa Montoya; gp/ Jesus Griego & Marselina Griego, residents of los Ranchos.

ARCHIBEQUE, Jose Francisco Carso (of Bernalillo)
bap 3 Dec 1837, 5 days old; legit s/ Marselino Archibeque & Maria Juana Gallegos; ap/ Agustin Archibeque & Manuela Chaves; am/ Joaquin Salasar & Maria Bicenta Gallegos; gp/ Jose Maria (Salasar) & Maria Manuela Salasar, residents of Bernalillo.

Frame 1754
GRIEGO, Francisco
bap 5 Dec 1837, 5 days old; natural s/ Simona Griego; am/ Ana Maria Griego; gp/ Jose Miguel Nuanes & Juana Andrea Nuanes, residents of los Griegos.

ESPINOSA, Maria Begnina (of San Antonio)
bap 14 Dec 1837, 14 days old; legit d/ Nepomuceno Espinosa & Socorro Gutierres; ap/ Lorenso Espinosa & Maria Natividad Mascareñas; am/ Juan Pablo Gonsales & Ana Maria Ylisarri; gp/ Jose de Jesus Apodaca & Maria Antonia Gutierres.

ANAYA, Guadalupe (of Ranchos of Atrisco)
bap 14 Dec 1837, 3 days old; legit d/ Juan Anaya & Francisca Montaño; ap/ Manuel Anaya & Maria Antonia Apodaca; am/ Pedro Montaño & Josefa Martines; gp/ Julian Sedillo & Juana Rosa Candelaria, residents of los Ranchos.

Frames 1754-1755
JINSO, Leocadia (of San Antonio)
bap 17 Dec 1837, 8 days old; legit d/ Santiago Jinso & Manuela Anaya; ap/ Diego Antonio Ginso & Rosalia Chaves; am/ Miguel Anaya & (blank); gp/ Antonio Gutierres & Guadalupe Garcia, residents of los Griegos.

CANDELARIA, Eulalia (of Atrisco)
bap 14 Dec 1837, 4 days old; legit d/ Jesus Maria Candelaria & Ysabel Chaves; ap/ Jose Candelaria & Tomasa Padia; am/ Juan Antonio Chaves & Gertrudis Torres; gp/ Juan Ortega & Estefana Ortega.

SANCHES, Juana Maria de Rallo (of Alameda)
bap 20 Dec 1837, 3 days old; legit d/ Francisco Sanches & Juana Cordova; ap/ Gabriel Sanches & Juana Sedillo; am/ Carlos Cordova & Juana Duran; gp/ Ygnacio Gutierres & Maria Bentura Gurule, residents of Alameda.

Frames 1755-1756
ANAYA, Jose Ygnacio
bap 28 Dec 1837, 4 days old; legit s/ Cayetano Anaya & Manuela Antonia Perea; ap/ Antonio Anaya & Ramona Tafoya; am/ Bentura Perea & Juana Lopes; gp/ Juan Rafael Garcia & Encarnacion Lucero, from the same place.

GARCIA, Tomas de Aquino (of los Candelarias)
bap 29 Apr 1837, 2 days old; legit s/ Juan Pablo Garcia & Gregoria Chaves, parishioners; ap/ Juan Garcia & Juana Barbera NS; am/ Juan Jose Chaves & Francisca Gonzales; gp/ Jose Rafael Lopes & Luisa Chaves, all residents of los Candelarias.

PRIMO, Jose Manuel
bap 4 Jan 1838, 4 days old; natural s/ Nicanora Primo; am/ Leonardo Primo & Ana Maria Chaves; gp/ Don Juan Gil & Doña Lus Lopes.

Frames 1756-1757, #79
GARCIA, Maria Juliana
bap 7 Jan 1838, 7 days old; legit d/ Ambrosio Garcia & Catarina Armijo; ap/ Martin Garcia & Ana Maria Apodaca; am/ Rafael Armijo & Soledad de la Peña; gp/ Ramon Mares & Marta de la Lus NS.

GARCIA, Maria Juliana
bap 7 Jan 1838, 3 days old; legit d/ Juan Garcia & Rita Lopes; ap/ Agustin Garcia & Ana Maria Apodaca; ap/ Luis Lopes & Antonia Lopes; gp/ Felipe Gallegos & Lucia Griego, residents of los Candelarias.

ARAGON, Jose Norberto
bap 8 Jan 1838, 10 days old; legit s/ Eusebio Aragon & Miguela Santillanes; ap/ Jose Manuel Aragon & Barbara Chaves; am/ Guadalupe Santillanes & Miguela Carrio; gp/ Diego Antonio Chaves & Maria Seferina Chaves.

SAMORA, Maria Pabla
bap 16 Jan 1838, 4 days old; legit d/ Balentino Samora & Ana Maria Gurule; ap/ Juan Samora & Juliana Montaño; am/ Felipe Gurule & Juana Gutierres; gp/ Manuel Barela & Vicenta Gallego.

Frames 1757-1758
GUTIERRES, Jose Alvino
bap 16 Jan 1838, 20 days old; natural s/ Petrona Gutierres; am/ Ysidro Gutierres & Dolores Martines; gp/ Antonio Gutierres & Maria Eduvigen Gomes.

TENORIO, Maria Trinidad
bap 17 Jan 1838, 14 days old; legit d/ Jose Maria Tenorio & Ramona Romero; ap/ Manuel Tenorio & Antonia Analla; gp/ Manuel Gurule & Juana Gutierres, residents of los Ranchos.

DURAN, Jose de los Reyes
bap 19 Jan 1838, 5 days old; natural s/ Juana Duran; am/ Mateo Duran & Maria Antonia Muñis; gp/ Jose Tomas Contreras & Pabla Chaves, residents of los Duranes.

MARTIN, Jose Antonio (of Griegos)
bap 21 Jan 1838, 5 days old; legit s/ Juan Martin & Alfonsa Olguin; ap/ Miguel Martines & Dorotea Gallego; am/ Francisco Olguin & Soledad Garcia; gp/ Jose Antonio Martines & Quiteria Griego.

Frame 1759, #80
GRIEGO, Pedro Jose
bap 21 Jan 1838, 3 days old; legit s/ Manuel Griego & Catarina Samora, residents of los Gallegos; ap/ Blas Griego & Maria Rosa Chabes; am/ Francisco Samora & Maria Ygnacia Balencia; gp/ Jose Manuel Montaño & Guadalupe Garcia.

PEREA, Maria Ygnes
bap 21 Jan 1838, 4 days old; natural d/ Dolores Perea; am/ Jose Miguel Perea & Manuel NS; gp/ Pablo Sisneros & Francisca Ruiz, residents of this plaza of Albuquerque.

Frames 1759-1760
GRIEGO, Jose Anastacio (of los Ranchos)
bap 26 Jan 1838, 6 days old; legit s/ Juan Ysidor Griego & Maria Bentura Lucero; ap/ Francisco Griego & Maria Antonia Serna; am/ Juan Lucero & Maria Antonia Martines; gp/ Francisco Lucero & Ygnes Montolla.

NS, Visente Antonio
bap 26 Jan 1838, 4 days old; natural s/ Maria NS, Comanche, native of San Antonio de Mestas; am/ not stated; gp/ Salbador Antonio Tafolla & Maria de la Lus Montolla.

TRUJILLO, Jose Ygnacio
bap 27 Jan 1838, 4 days old; legit s/ Pedro Antonio Trujillo & Maria Ocario Sanchis, ap/ Juan Jose Trujillo & Maria de Carmen Tafolla; am/ Domingo (Candelaria) & Maria de la Lus Candelaria, residents of Alameda.

Frame 1760-1761, #81
SAMORA, Juana Maria
bap 28 Jan 1838, 8 days old; legit d/ Christoval Samora & Anamaria Martines; ap/ Juan Samora & Juliana Montaño; am/ Felipe Martines & Francisca Samora; gp/ Antonio de Jesus Sandoval & Teresa Luna, all residents of los Ranchos.

ANALLA, Maria Francisca
bap 29 Jan 1838, 2 days old; legit d/ Manuel Analla & Felipa Martines; ap/ Felipe Analla & Dolores Torres; am/ Pedro Martines & Juana Garcia; gp/ Miguel Antonio Griego & Maria Ysidora Griego, of the plaza of los Griegos.

DURAN, Maria Petrona
bap 31 Jan 1838, 2 days old; legit d/ Casimiro Duran & Juana Sandobal, residents of this jurisdiction; ap/ Teodoro Duran & Maria Lucero; am/ Jose Sandobal & Petrona Sabedra; gp/ Francisco Antonio Sandobal & Maria Lucero, all residents of the same.

Frame 1762
ANAYA, Juan Jose
bap 6 Feb 1838, 11 days old; natural s/ Soledad Anaya, resident; am/ Jose Anaya & Dolores Lopes; gp/ Juan Apodaca & Maria Ysabel Sanches, residents of the same.

GAUNA, Jose de los Reyes
bap 8 Feb 1838, 1 month old; s/ Juan Gauna & Maria Sandoval; ap/ Juachin Gauna & Barbara Bernal; am/ Juan Francisco Sandoval & Juana Archibecco; gp/ Juan Pedro Marques & Juana Miguela Sandoval, residents of Corrales.

Frames 1762-1763, #82
GURULE, Maria Ylaria
bap 8 Feb 1838, 1 month old; legit d/ Juan Gurule & Maria Manuela Gutierres, ap/ Jose Gurule & Dolores Gauna; am/ not stated; gp/ Juan Montoya & Maria Rita Montoya, residents of Corrales.

LUCERO, Jose Guadalupe Nicanor
bap 9 Feb 1838, 8 days old; s/ Juan Jose Lucero & Gertrudis Chabes; ap/ Diego Lucero & Maria Antonia Armijo; am/ Francisco Chabes & Maria Alfonsa Armijo; gp/ Juan Antonio Rael & Rafaela Rael, residents of Alameda.

CHABES, Blas
bap 9 Feb 1838, 7 days old; s/ Romualdo Chabes & Barbara Trujillo; ap/ Estanislado Chabes & Soledad Ortega; am/ Jose Trujillo & Soledad Balencia; gp/ Antonio Trujillo & Dolores Trujillo, residents of los Ranchos.

Frames 1763-1764
GRIEGO, Juana Maria
bap 9 Feb 1838, 11 days old; d/ Jose Gabriel Griego & Maria Elogia Romero; ap/ Francisco Griego & Gertrudis Gallego; am/ Luis Romero & Maria Juana Aragon; gp/ Juan Nepomuceno Montolla & Maria de Jesus Lucero.

MONTOLLA, Jose Blas
bap 10 Feb 1838, 7 days old; legit s/ Christoval Montolla & Monica Gonsales; ap/ Felipe Montolla & Maria de la Luz Lopes; am/ Juan Gonsales & Maria Antonia Armijo; gp/ Juan Jose Sanchis & Antonia Rita Luna, residents of los Ranchos.

CORDOVA, Maria Juana
bap 11 Feb 1838, 4 days old; legit d/ Jose Cordova & Maria Manuela Garcia; ap/ Nicolas Cordova & Maria Ygnacia Duran; am/ Juan Esteban Garcia & Maria Paula Perea; gp/ Rafael Montolla & Maria Ramona Montolla.

Frame 1765, #83
GUTIERRES, Jose Desiderio
bap 11 Feb 1838, 11 days old; legit s/ Cruz Gutierres & Guadalupe Jaramillo, residents of Bernalillo; ap/ Pedro Gutierres & Maria Francisca Griego; am/ Mariano Jaramillo & Maria Martines; gp/ Juan Martines & Maria Rita Gutierres, residents of the same.

CHAVES, Yldefonso Desiderio
bap 11 Feb 1838, 20 days old; legit s/ Felipe Chaves & Maria Desideria Muñis, residents of Bernalillo; ap/ Jose Rafael Chaves & Ysidora Gutierres; am/ Lucrecio Muñis & Maria Guadalupe Sanches; gp/ Jesus Maria Salazar & Maria Vicenta Gallegos, residents of the same.

Baptisms – Albuquerque, New Mexico
1829–1850

Frame 1766
TRUJILLO, Maria Antonia
bap 12 Feb 1838, 7 days old; d/ Mariano Trujillo & Maria Luisa Cordoba; ap/ Marcos Trujillo & Juana Castela; am/ Marcos Cordoba & Rafaela Garcia, residents of Alameda; gp/ Agustin Sandoval & Francisca Romero.

GRIEGO, Blas Jose (of los Ranchos)
bap 12 Feb 1838, 8 days old; legit s/ Jose Griego & Paula Analla; ap & am/ not stated; gp/ Lucas Romero & Rosa Romero.

Frame 1767, #84
SANCHES, Deciderio
bap 18 Feb 1838, 8 days old; legit s/ Antonio Sanches & Maria Magdalena Grigo; ap/ Antonio Jose Sanches & Sebastiana Ortega; am/ Miguel Griego & Gertrudis Olgin; gp/ Jose Antonio Garcia & Tomasa Griego.

GARCIA, Balentina
bap 18 Feb 1838, 5 days old; legit d/ Juan Garcia & Maria Juana Chaves; ap/ Francisco Garcia & Manuela Gonsales; am/ Juaquin Chaves & Barbara Armijo; gp/ Felipe Garcia & Barbara Garcia.

SANCHES, Antonio Jose
bap 20 Feb 1838, 5 days old; legit s/ Ysidro Sanches & Catalina Mestas; ap & am/ not stated; gp/ Antonio Anaya & Tomasa Tafoya.

Frame 1768
ESPINOSA, Jose Albino
bap 21 Feb 1838, 8 days old; legit s/ Antonio Espinosa & Geralda Perea; ap & am/ not stated; gp/ Jose Joaquin Montaño & Maria Duran.

BACA, Rumaldo
bap 22 Feb 1838; s/ Lorensa Baca & unknown father; gp/ Juan Nepomuceno Sanches & Dolores Chaves.

ARCHIVEQUE, Maria Begnina
bap 23 Feb 1838, 8 days old; legit d/ Juan Archiveque & Magdalena Gonsales; ap/ Agustin Archiveque & Manuela Chabes; am/ Rafael Gonsales & grandmother not stated; gp/ Juan Jose Gonsales & Encarnacion Perea.

Frame 1769, #85
RAMIRES, Jose Romulo Nestor (of Bernalillo)
bap 27 Feb 1838; legit s/ Antonio Ramires & Maria Loreta Garcia; ap/ Jose Ramires & Maria Jesus Tenorio; am/ Alonso Garcia & Maria Josefa Gallegos; gp/ Vicente Montoya & Maria Antonia Garcia.

SAMORA, Maria Gabriela (of Corrales)
bap 27 Feb 1838, 8 days old; legit d/ Nepomucena Samora & Guadalupe Duran; ap & am/ not stated; gp/ Diego Antonio Chabes & Maria Bibiana Chabes.

GARCIA, Juan Albino
bap 2 Mar 1838, 5 days old; legit s/ Manuel Garcia & Tomasa Sena; ap & am/ not stated; gp/ Anastacio Barela & Rafaela Garcia.

Frame 1770
SENA, Juan Pablo
bap 5 Mar 1838, 5 days old; legit s/ Miguel Sena & Ysidora Garcia; ap/ Francisco Sena & Manuela Martin; am/ Juan Jose Garcia & Francisca Gallego; gp/ Deciderio Garcia & Nepomucena Candelaria.

TORRES, Nestor
bap 5 Mar 1838, legit s/ Manuel Torres & Ana Maria Garcia; ap & am/ not stated; gp/ Pedro Aranda & Rosalia Jaramillo.

GURULE, Juan Pablo
bap 6 Mar 1838, 8 days old; legit s/ Antonio Gurule & Maria Guadalupe Padilla; ap & am/ not stated; gp/ Juan Apodaca & Maria de la Luz Padilla.

Frame 1771, #86
GONSALES, Maria Paubla
bap 6 Mar 1838, 5 days old; d/ Antonio Gonsales & Juana Garcia; ap/ Leonicio Gonsales & Rafaela Martin; am/ Antonio Garcia & Margarita Rael; gp/ Salbador Antonio Tafoya & Juana Maria Lucero.

CANDELARIA Maria Antonia
bap 7 Mar 1838, 5 days old; legit d/ Enrriques Candelaria & Ysabel Garcia; ap/ Antonio Candelaria & Manuela Rael; am/ Juan de Jesus Garcia & Rosa Sabedra; gp/ Lasaro Candelaria & Maria Antonia Garcia.

ARMIJO, Maria Manuela Casimira
bap 7 Mar 1838, 3 days old; legit d/ Don Juan Cristobal Armijo & Doña Juana Chabes; ap/ Don Juan Armijo & Rosalia Ortega; am/ Don Francisco Chabes & Doña Ana Maria Castillo; gp/ Don Jose Maria Gutierres & Doña Manuela Chabes.

Frame 1772
OTERO, Juan Eusebio de Jesus
ORTEGA, Juan Eusebio de Jesus (in margin)
bap 8 Mar 1838, 5 days old; legit s/ Santiago Otero & Maria Samora; ap & am/ not stated; gp/ Jose Santos Gonsales & Dolores Gonsales.

LUSERO, Maria Dolores
bap 9 Mar 1838, 8 days old; s/ Jose Nieves Lusero & Maria Eulogia Sabedra; gp/ Jose Desiderio Lusero & Maria Gertrudis Lusero.

GARCIA, Jose Domingo
bap 10 Mar 1838, 5 days old; legit s/ Juan Garcia & Ysabel Gurule; ap & am/ not stated; gp/ Antonio Jose Lusero & Maria Gertrudis Lusero.

Frame 1773, #87
CANDELARIA, Maria Juana del Refugio
bap 10 Mar 1838, 3 days old; legit d/ Rafael Candelaria & Maria Antonio Garcia; ap/ Antonio Candelaria & Ana Maria Salazar; am/ Felis Garcia & Ysabel Lopes; gp/ Jose Lucero & Maria Gertrudis Gutierres.

SANTILLANES, Juan Miguel
bap 11 Mar 1838, 8 days old; legit s/ Diego Santillanes & Maria Juana Garcia; ap/ Juan Miguel Santillanes & Micaela Gonsales; am/ Antonio Garcia & Margarita Rael; gp/ Juan Miguel Garcia & Maria Gertrudis Apodaca.

Frames 1773-1774
CHABES, Dolores Hemeteria (of Los Padillas)
bap 12 Mar 1838; legit d/ Don Jose Chabes & Doña Manuela Armijo; ap/ Don Francisco Chabes & Doña Ana Maria Castillo; am/ Don Juan Armijo & Doña Rosalia Ortega; gp/ Don Mariano Chabes & Doña Dolores Perea.

BACA, Jose Maria
bap 13 Mar 1838; legit s/ Diego Baca & Francisca Samora; ap/ Jose Antonio Baca & Lus Garcia; am/ Juan Antonio Samora & Rafaela Muñis; gp/ Pablo Sisneros & Gertrudis Lopes.

CANDELARIA, Manuel Antonio
bap 15 Mar 1838; legit s/ Francisco Antonio Candelaria & Lorensa Padilla; ap/ Juan Candelaria & Teresa Chabes; am/ Diego Antonio Padilla & Manuela Aguirre; gp/ Manuel Antonio Sanches & Maria Josefa Apodaca.

Frame 1775, #88
ARAGON, Antonio
bap 16 Mar 1838; legit s/ Martin Aragon & Maria Gonsales; ap & am/ not stated; gp/ Crescencio (Aragon) & Encarnacion Aragon.

MORA, Jose Matias
bap 18 Mar 1838; legit s/ Esteban Mora & Juana Maria Griego; ap & am/ not stated; gp/ Anastacio Lusero & Juana Duran.

GALLEGO, Maria Gabriela
bap 19 Mar 1838, legit d/ Antonio Gallego & Maria Petra Padilla; ap & am/ not stated; gp/ Jose Manuel Gurule & Maria Toribia Gurule.

Frame 1776
GRIEGO, Jose Benito (twin)
GRIEGO, Maria Benigna (twin)
bap 22 Mar 1838; legit ch/ Juan Antonio Griego & Maria Candelaria Luna; ap/ Felipe Griego & Margarita Gonsales; am/ Ysidro Luna & Manuela Candelaria; first gp/ Tadeo Garcia & Barbara Griego; second gp/ Jose Domingo Griego & Maria Juana Montoya.

CHABES, Jose de la Lus
bap 22 Mar 1838; legit s/ Juan de Dios Chabes & Monica Lusero; ap & am/ not stated; gp/ Mariano Lusero & Marselina Balencia.

GONSALES, Jose de Jesus
bap 23 Mar 1838; legit s/ Antonio Maria Gonsales & Micaela Lusero; ap & am/ not stated; gp/ Jesus Maria Truxillo & Maria Lorensa Lusero.

Frame 1777, #89
ARAGON, Ana Maria Agapita
bap 25 Mar 1838; legit d/ Juan Rafael Aragon & Catarina Sabedra; ap & am/ not stated; gp/ Jose Dolores (Perea) & Paubla Perea.

CHABES, Pedro Antonio
bap 25 Mar 1838; legit s/ Blas Chabes & Gertrudis Sandobal; ap & am/ not stated; gp/ Antonio Montoya & Rosa Montoya.

Frames 1777-1778
GRIEGO, Abran
bap 26 Mar 1838; s/ Maria Dimas Griego & unknown father; gp/ Luis Mares & Teresa Garcia.

MARTIN, Maria Vitoria
bap 28 Mar 1838; legit d/ Jose Martin & Gertrudis Salasar; ap & am/ not stated; gp/ Miguel Arias & Maria Ygnacia Salasar.

NIETO, Teodoro de Jesus
bap 28 Mar 1838; legit s/ Juan Rafael Nieto & Juana Gregoria Jaramillo; ap/ Juan Rafael Nieto & Gertrudis Salasar; am/ Julian Jaramillo & Juana Arias; gp/ Manuel Sisneros & Mariana Sisneros.

GONSALES, Maria Soledad
bap 30 Mar 1838; legit d/ Juan Bautista Gonsales & Ana Maria Otero; ap & am/ not stated; gp/ Santiago Otero & Manuela Antonia Padilla.

Frame 1779, #90
ANSURES, Miguel Antonio
bap 30 Mar 1838; legit s/ Rafael Ansures & Catalina Lujan; ap & am/ not stated; gp/ Antonio Anaya & Guadalupe Anaya.

MARTIN, Maria Balbina
bap 2 Apr 1838; legit d/ Felipe Martin & Victoria Arias; ap/ Felipe Martin & Juana Truxillo; am/ Miguel Arias & Gregoria Martin; gp/ Diego Romero & Juliana Montaño.

TORRES, Jose Anastacio
bap 2 Apr 1838; legit s/ Juan Torres & Ysabel Gutierres; ap & am/ not stated; gp/ Miguel Garcia & Tomasa Olguin.

Frame 1780
PEREA, Maria Clara
bap 2 Apr 1838; legit d/ Manuel Perea & Gertrudis Gurule; ap & am/ not stated; gp/ Antonio Santillanes & Pabla Contreras.

ARMIJO, Antonio Maria de Jesus
bap 2 Apr 1838; legit s/ Pedro Armijo & Maria de la Lus Garcia; ap/ Pablo Armijo & Josefa Chabes; am/ Felis Garcia & Ysabel Lopes; gp/ Antonio Maria Garcia & Maria Juana Montaño.

GARCIA, Juana
bap 8 Apr 1838; legit d/ Julian Garcia & Juana Aragon; ap/ Juan Antonio Garcia & Francisca Gonsales; am/ Jose Manuel Aragon & Teresa Barbero NS; gp/ Juan Apodaca & Maria Ysabel Sanches.

Frames 1780-1781, #91
LAURIANO, Jose Dolores
bap 8 Apr 1838; legit s/ Jose Lauriano & Rosalia Baca; ap & am/ not stated; gp/ Juan Barela & Maria Josefa Chabes.

SAMORA, Jose Selestino de los Dolores
bap 8 Apr 1838; legit s/ Jose Samora & Josefa Griego; ap/ Francisco Samora & Maria Ygnacia Belencia; am/ Jose Miguel Griego & Dolores Garcia; gp/ Diego Romero & Juliana Montaño.

GURULE, Maria Nicolasa
bap 11 Apr 1838, 5 days old; legit d/ Diego Gurule & Maria Teresa Gutierres; ap & am/ not stated; gp/ Blas Muñis & Ana Maria Pacheco.

Frames 1781-1782
GALLEGO, Maria Dolores de la Merced
bap 14 Apr 1838, 3 days old; legit d/ Francisco Gallego & Maria Tomasa Candelaria; ap & am/ not stated; gp/ Jose Maria Mares & Maria Apolonia Mares.

APODACA, Maria Soledad
bap 14 Apr 1838, 8 days old; legit d/ Rafael Apodaca & Barbara Molina; ap & am/ not stated; gp/ Bartolo Apodaca & Soledad Telles.

ARMIJO, Juan Antonio
bap 15 Apr 1838, 3 days old; legit s/ Manuel Armijo & Maria Soledad Garcia; ap & am/ not stated; gp/ Salbador Perea & Maria Gabriela Candelaria.

CARABAJAL, Maria Tomasa
bap 15 Apr 1838, 8 days old; legit d/ Manuel Carabajal & Teresa Sanches; ap & am/ not stated; gp/ Jose Moya & Dolores Sanches.

Frame 1783, #92
NS, Maria Apolonia
bap 15 Apr 1838, 5 days old; d/ unknown parents; gp/ Maria Marta Urtado.

GONSALES, Leonor
bap 22 Apr 1838, 3 days old; legit d/ Ylario Gonsales & Maria Rita Rael; ap/ Felipe Gonsales & Maria de la Lus Gurule; am/ Antonio Rael & Francisca Padilla; gp/ Jose Gonsales & Francisca Santillanes.

SABEDRA, Jose Nestor
bap 22 Apr 1838; legit s/ Manuel Sabedra & Elena Duran; ap & am/ not stated; gp/ Jose Gregorio Garcia & Maria Petra Gonsales.

Frames 1783-1784
SABEDRA, Maria Antonia
bap 23 Apr 1838, 5 days old; legit d/ Juan Cristobal Sabedra & Maria Monica Sanches; ap & am/ not stated; gp/ Juan Garcia & Maria Antonia Chabes.

NS, Jose Andres (Indian)
bap 23 Apr 1838; s/ Feliciana NS & father unknown, an Indian; gp/ Juan de Dios Mestas & Maria Marselina Gabaldon.

GARCIA, Maria Clara Aniseta
bap 23 Apr 1838, 3 days old; legit d/ Felis Garcia & Maria Carmen Maestas; ap & am/ not stated; gp/ Juan Garcia & Ana Maria Maestas.

TRUXILLO, Maria Juana Beneranda
bap 29 Apr 1838, 5 days old; legit d/ Francisco Truxillo & Guadalupe Chabes; ap & am/ not stated; gp/ Felis Sanches & Maria Sebastiana Sena.

Frame 1785, #92
MADRID, Jose Marcos
bap 29 Apr 1838, 2 days old; legit s/ Cristobal Madrid & Rosalia Medina; ap & am/ not stated; gp/ Nepomuceno Ortega & Maria Tomasa Basan.

NS, Maria Dolores
bap 29 Apr 1838, 3 days old; d/ unknown parents; gp/ Mariano Chabes & Felipa Garcia.

SEDILLO, Jose Balerio
bap 29 Apr 1838, 3 days old; legit s/ Toribio Sedillo & Ysabel Sanches; ap & am/ not stated; gp/ Jose Rafael Baca & Maria Paubla Baca.

GALLEGO, Pedro Antonio
bap 1 May 1838, 3 days old; legit s/ Jose Anastacio Gallego & Maria Soledad Candelaria; ap/ Jose Gallego & Manuela Gurule; am/ Francisco Antonio Candelaria & Manuela Aguirre; gp/ Salbador Jaramillo & Maria Gertrudis Baca.

Frame 1786
LUJAN, Maria Prudencia
bap 2 May 1838, 5 days old; legit d/ Miguel Lujan & Rita Sandobal; ap & am/ not stated; gp/ Jose Jaramillo & Paubla Jaramillo.

APODACA, Maria Cruz Altagracia
bap 3 May 1838, 8 days old; legit d/ Juan Apodaca & Manuela Gurule; ap & am/ not stated; gp/ Jose Manuel Noanes & Maria Paubla Candelaria.

GUTIERRES, Maria Prudencia
bap 3 May 1838, 2 days old; legit d/ Agustin Alberto Gutierres & Josefa Gurule; ap & am/ not stated; gp/ Jose Gonsales & Francisca Gonsales.

GRIEGO, Manuel Antonio
bap 6 May 1838, 3 days old; legit s/ Domingo Griego & Rafaela Martin; gp/ Rafael Gallegos & Rosalia Gallego.

Frame 1787, #93
CHABES, Salabor Antonio
bap 7 May 1838, 3 days old; legit s/ Juan Chabes & Maria Yldefonsa Duran; ap & am/ not stated; gp/ Rafael Montoya & Maria Ramona Montoya.

MARTINES, Miguel Antonio
bap 12 May 1838, 2 days old; legit s/ Jose Antonio Martines & Quiteria Griego; ap & am/ not stated; gp/ Juan Antonio Garcia & Maria Gregoria Candelaria.

CHABES, Pedro Antonio
bap 12 May 1838, 5 days old; legit s/ Miguel Chabes & Decideria Gurule; ap & am/ not stated; gp/ Tomas Tafoya & Soledad Montoya.

CHABES, Maria Juana Nepomucena
bap 16 May 1838, 8 days old; legit d/ Toribio Chabes & Lorensa Perea; gp/ Manuel Carbajal & Maria Ramona Perea.

Frame 1788
GURULE, Maria Trenidad
bap 16 May 1838, 5 days old; d/ Maria Juana Gurule & unknown father; gp/ Jose Lopes & Cipriana Perea.

CHABES, Maria Bonifacia
bap 19 May 1838, 2 days old; legit d/ Gabriel Chabes & Yldefonsa Sena; gp/ Salbador Perea & Gabriela Candelaria.

TRUXILLO, Ana Maria Estanislada
bap 19 May 1838, 5 days old; legit d/ Jose Ignacio Truxillo & Maria Rita Lujan; gp/ Pedro Antonio Truxillo & Ana Maria Noanes.

GARCIA, Andres Antonio
bap 19 May 1838, 8 days old; legit s/ Salbador Garcia & Juana Perea; ap & am/ not stated; gp/ Concepcion Lopes.

Frame 1789, #94
SANCHES, Maria Luisa del Rosaria Celestina
bap 21 May 1838, 5 days old; legit d/ Gabriel Sanches & Rafaela Ruis; ap/ Antonio Jose Sanches & Rosalia Martin; am/ Lorenso Ruis & Urbana Ydalgo; gp/ Don Gregorio Ortiz & Doña Clara Sarracino.

NS, Jose Deciderio
bap 23 May 1838, 2 days old; s/ Concepcion NS, Indian & unknown father; gp/ Francisco Armijo & Soledad Armijo.

CHABES, Maria Felipa
bap 27 May 1838, 3 days old; d/ Rita Chabes & unknown father; gp/ Antonio Jose Baldonado & Maria Rafaela Blea.

SANDOBAL, Pedro Miguel Bernardino
bap 27 May 1838, 4 days old; s/ Jose Angel Sandobal & Gertrudes Rael; ap & am/ not stated; gp/ Rafael Montoya & Maria Ramona Montoya.

Frame 1790, #94
TAFOYA, Maria Concepcion
bap 28 May 1838, 5 days old; legit d/ Domingo Tafoya & Ana Maria Martin; ap/ Juan Ygnacio Tafoya & Maria Antonia Baca; am/ Antonio Jose Martin & Luciana Lusero; gp/ Salbador Tafoya & Juana Maria Lusero.

CHABES, Juan de Jesus
bap 29 May 1838, 3 days old; legit s/ Jose Dolores Chabes & Nicanora Garcia; ap & am/ not stated; gp/ Alejo Garcia & Gracia Garcia.

SANDOBAL, Pedro Jose
bap 31 May 1838, 2 days old; s/ Rosalia Sandobal & unknown father; gp/ Francisco Rael & Maria Manuela Rael.

GONSALES, Salbador Manuel
bap 14 Jun 1838, 2 days old; s/ Rafael Gonsales & Maria Juana Aragon; ap & am/ not stated; gp/ Francisco Lusero & Maria Manuela Aragon.

Frame 1791, #95
GONSALES, Juan Nepomuseno
bap 16 Jun 1838, 2 days old; legit s/ Ysidro Gonsales & Maria Duran; ap & am/ not stated; gp/ Maria Antonia Perea.

CANDELARIA, Bernabe
bap 17 Jun 1838, 8 days old; legit s/ Manuel Candelaria & Ana Maria Truxillo; ap & am/ not stated; gp/ Antonio Truxillo & Gregoria Truxillo.

GUTIERRES, Jose Vitor
bap 17 Jun 1838, 2 days old; legit s/ Juan Cristobal Gutierres & Manuela Garcia; ap & am/ not stated; gp/ Baltasar Martin & Soledad Martin.

SANDOBAL, Maria Juliana
bap 24 Jun 1838, 3 days old; legit d/ Jose Miguel Sandobal & Antonia Rosa Lusero; ap & am/ not stated; gp/ Miguel Antonio Gutierres & Maria Albina Santillanes.

Frame 1792
GARCIA, Maria Ana
bap 2 Jul 1838, 3 days old; d/ Francisco Garcia & Josefa Padilla; ap & am/ not stated; gp/ Bartolo Lobato & Matilde Duran.

CANDELARIA, Maria Rosario de los Dolores
bap 4 Jul 1838, 1 day old; legit d/ Tomas Candelaria & Maria Gertrudis Gabaldon; ap & am/ not stated; gp/ Juan (Armijo) & Juana Armijo.

GARCIA, Juan Christobal
bap 15 Jul 1838, 3 days old; legit s/ Manuel Garcia & Barbara Lopes; ap & am/ not stated; gp/ Vicente Luna & Bibiana Chabes.

MONTOYA, Maria Concepcion
bap 19 Jul 1838, 2 days old; legit d/ Miguel Montoya & Refugio Baca; ap/ Nerio Montoya & Crus Urbana; am/ Roman Baca & Manuela Martin; gp/ Jose Rael & Nepomusena Rael.

Frame 1793, #96
GARCIA, Maria Ana de los Dolores
bap 19 Jul 1838, 2 days old; legit d/ Juan Garcia & Juana Maria Sanches; ap/ Felis Garcia & Ysabel Lopes; am/ Vicente Sanches & Ana Maria Mestas; gp/ Mariano Armijo & Gabriela Jaramillo.

ARIAS, Jose Antonio
bap 26 Jul 1838, 2 days old; legit s/ Yldefonso Arias & Juana Mora; ap & am/ not stated; gp/ Luis Mares
& Teresa Garcia.

LUSERO, Maria Buenabentura
bap 29 Jul 1838, 7 days old; legit d/ Antonio Lusero & Petrona Truxillo; ap & am/ not stated; gp/
Manuela Sandobal.

APODACA, Ana Maria
bap 28 Jul 1838, 2 days old; legit d/ Pablo Apodaca & Apolonia Sarracino; ap & am/ not stated; gp/ Jose
Gonsales & Maria Felipa Gonsales.

Frame 1794
NS, Maria Estefana
bap 3 Aug 1838, 1 day old; d/ Guadalupe NS, an Indian & unknown father; gp/ Diego Sanches & Maria
Dolores Mora.

OTERO, Maria Trenidad
bap 8 Aug 1838, 2 days old; legit d/ Juan Otero & Rosalia Jaramillo; ap & am/ not stated; gp/ Ambrocio
Lopes & Juana Lopes.

SANCHES, Maria Clara
bap 13 Aug 1838, 1 day old; legit d/ Francisco Sanches & Juana Gutierres; ap & am/ not stated; gp/ Felis
Ortega & Maria Reyes Montaño.

MONTAÑO, Maria del Carmen
bap 13 Aug 1838, 3 days old; legit d/ Antonio Jose Montaño & Rita Luna; ap & am/ not stated; gp/ Felipe
Duran & Maria Ynes Luna.

Frames 1794-1795, #97
SANDOVAL, Jose Anastacio Polito
bap 16 Aug 1838, 2 days old; legit s/ Jose Dolores Sandobal & Juana Truxillo; ap & am/ not stated; gp/
Santiago Truxillo & Maria Juana Sandobal.

MONTOYA, Adolfo de Jesus
bap 16 Aug 1838, 1 day old; legit s/ Francisco Montoya & Maria de Jesus Armijo; ap & am/ not stated;
gp/ Pablo Ruis & Ana Maria Ruis.

GONSALES, Maria Marselina
bap 18 Aug 1838, 1 day old; legit d/ Juan Gonsales & Ana Maria Sandobal; ap & am/ not stated; gp/
Ramon Rael & Dolores Chabes.

CORDOBA, Pedro
bap 19 Aug 1838, 3 days old; legit s/ Leonicio Cordoba & Juana Sanches; gp/ Jose Maria Aragon &
Dolores Sanches.

GUTIERRES, Jose Maximiano
bap 20 Aug 1838, 3 days old; legit s/ Estanislado Gutierres & Apolonia Gonsales; ap/ Juan Gutierres &
Guadalupe Chabes; am/ Lorenso Gonsales & Teodora Salasar; gp/ Jose Miguel Mares & Ana Maria
Noanes.

Frame 1796
NS, Trenidad
bap 23 Aug 1838, 2 days old; d/ Dolores NS, an Indian & unknown father; gp/ Juan Barela & Catarina Ortiz.

GUTIERRES, Juan Eluterio
bap 23 Aug 1838, 2 days old; s/ Maria Felipa Gutierres & unknown father; gp/ Jose Maria Tenorio & Maria Ramona Sisneros.

CANDELARIA, Edubigen del Refugio
bap 23 Aug 1838, 3 days old; legit d/ Juan Candelaria & Ascencion Garcia; gp/ Manuel Gregorio Jaramillo & Maria Josefa Garcia.

CANDELARIA, Rosalia
bap 24 Aug 1838, 2 days old; legit d/ Casimiro Candelaria & Matilde Griego; ap & am/ not stated; gp/ Jose Antonio Montaño & Maria Micaela Santillanes.

GARCIA, Manuela Reyes
bap 25 Aug 1838, 5 days old; legit d/ Vicente Garcia & Paubla Chabes; ap & am/ not stated; gp/ Ygnacio Romero & Juana Maria Romero.

Frame 1797, #98
NS, Maria Juana
bap 30 Aug 1838, 3 days old; d/ Dolores NS, Indian & unknown father; gp/ Antonio Maria Garcia & Juana Montaño.

CHABES, Teofilo
bap 2 Sep 1838, 5 days old; legit s/ Jose Maria Chabes & Ysabel Apodaca; ap & am/ not stated; gp/ Jose Chabes & Rosalia Tenorio.

LUSERO, Ana Maria
bap 5 Sep 1838, 3 days old; legit d/ Jose Maria Lusero & Dolores Griego; ap/ Jose Lusero & Encarnacion Gonsales; am/ Jose Griego & Gertrudis Balencia; gp/ Ylario Gonsales & Maria Rita Rael.

NS, Maria Dolores
bap 10 Sep 1838, 3 days old; d/ unknown parents; gp/ Jose Dolores Mares & Maria Rita Perea.

MUÑIS, Antonio Jose Trenidad
bap 10 Sep 1838, 8 days old; legit s/ Manuel Muñis & Maria Josefa Candelaria; ap & am/ not stated; gp/ Juan Jose Garcia & Maria Petra Teyes.

Frame 1798
LUJAN, Maria Luisa de Jesus
bap 10 Sep 1838, 3 days old; legit d/ Pablo Lujan & Juana Maria Truxillo; ap & am/ not stated; gp/ Salbador Arias & Maria Ysidora Arias.

CARBAJAL, Nepomuceno
bap 4 Oct 1838, 9 days old; legit s/ Juan Pedro Carbajal & Gertrudis Gonsales; ap & am/ not stated; gp/ Antonio Ruis & Petra Maldonado.

NS, Justa
bap 3 Oct 1838, 9 days old; d/ unknown parents; gp/ Mateo Suares & Guadalupe Griego.

LUSERO, Francisco Trenidad
bap 4 Oct 1838, 1 day old; legit s/ Lorenso Lusero & Ygnes Ruis; ap/ Juan Lusero & Francisca Tafoya; am/ Lorenso Ruis & Ascencion Jaramillo; gp/ Jesus Armijo & Mariana Sarracino.

Frame 1799, #99
PACHECO, Maria Ysabel
bap 5 Oct 1838, 20 days old; legit d/ Jose Antonio Pacheco & Juliana Santillanes; ap/ Salbador Pacheco & Juana Torres; am/ Luciano Santillanes & Gertrudis Duran; gp/ Juan Apodaca & Maria Ysabel Sanches.

CANDELARIA, Juana Maria
bap 6 Oct 1838, 8 days old; legit d/ Vicente Candelaria & Maria Reyes Griego; ap/ Lorenso Candelaria & Maria Antonia Montaño; am/ Antonio Griego & Antonia Garcia; gp/ Francisco Romero & Juana Maria Romero.

ARMIJO, Juan Bautista
bap 6 Oct 1838, 16 days old; s/ unknown parents, left at the home of Jose Armijo; gp/ Felis Ortega & Maria Reyes Montaño.

PADILLA, Maria Francisca
bap 7 Oct 1838, 16 days old; legit d/ Baltasar Padilla & Juana Garcia; ap & am/ not stated; gp/ Felipe Aragon & Gertrudis Garcia.

Frame 1800
GARCIA, Gertrudis
bap 7 Oct 1838, 20 days old; legit d/ Juan Garcia & Concepcion Anaya; ap/ Juan Jesus Garcia & Rosa Sabedra; am/ Miguel Anaya & Micaela Urban; gp/ Bibian Sabedra & Josefa Sabedra.

MONTOYA, Maria Francisca
bap 8 Oct 1838, 5 days old; legit d/ Juan Reyes Montoya & Gertrudis Moya; ap & am/ not stated; gp/ Jose Manuel Gurule & Maria Toribia Gurule.

SANCHES, Juan Jose
bap 10 Oct 1838, 5 days old; legit s/ Juan Sanches & Manuela Gonsales; ap/ Felipe Sanches & Ygnes Garcia; am/ Jose Manuel Gonsales & Maria Antonia Lobato; gp/ Bartolo Apodaca & Soledad Telles.

TORRES, Jesus Maria
bap 30 Oct 1838, 15 days old; legit s/ Felipe Torres & Maria Bernardina Garcia; ap/ Salbador Torres & Gertrudes Baca; am/ Francisco Garcia & Maria Reyes Candelaria; gp/ Francisco Antonio Garcia & Maria Gregoria Candelaria.

ORTIZ, Jose Rafael (twin)
ORTIZ, Teofilo (twin)
bap 31 Oct 1838, 8 days old; ch/ Margarita Ortiz & unknown father; first gp/ Jose Armijo & Concepcion Ortiz; second gp/ Pablo Ruis & Clara Armijo.

Frame 1801, #100
APODACA, Maria Monica de los Dolores
bap 1 Nov 1838, 8 days old; legit d/ Juan Antonio Apodaca & Petra Ballejos; ap & am/ not stated; gp/ Jose Gomes & Maria Antonia Gomes.

NS, Jose Agapito (Indian)
bap 1 Nov 1838, 9 days old; s/ Maria NS, an Indian, & unknown father; gp/ Juan Baca & Tomasa Lopes.

ABILA, Jose Rafael
bap 2 Nov 1838, 5 days old; legit s/ Miguel Abila & Lugarda Montoya; ap & am/ not stated; gp/ Manuel Garcia & Rafaela Rael.

CARRILLO, Juan Rafael
bap 2 Nov 1838, 4 days old; legit s/ Antonio Carrillo & Juana Jaramillo; gp/ Juan Barreras & Maria Marques.

Frames 1801-1802
LAURIANO, Rafael Antonio
bap 2 Nov 1838, 8 days old; legit s/ Juan Cristobal Lauriano & Rita Candelaria; ap & am/ not stated; gp/ Jose Benabides & Maria Antonia Benabides.

APODACA, Juan Nepomuseno
bap 2 Nov 1838, 3 days old; legit s/ Juan Antonio Apodaca & Petrona Ballejo; ap/ Damiano Apodaca & Vitoria Samora; am/ Salbador Ballejos & Barbara Duran; gp/ Jose Antonio Gutierres & Maria Edubigen Gomes.

PEREA, Maria Serafina
bap 2 Nov 1838, 3 days old; legit d/ Pedro Antonio Perea & Francisca Sena; ap/ Bartolo Perea & Quiteria Romero; am/ Jose Maria Sena & Vicenta Perea; gp/ Felis Sanches & Sebastiana Sena.

APODACA, Jose Alejandro
bap 4 Nov 1838, 7 days old; legit s/ Jose Manuel Apodaca & Maria Luisa Aragon; gp/ Tomas Tafoya & Soledad Montoya.

LUSERO, Maria del Rosario
bap 4 Nov 1838, 2 days old; legit d/ Jose Miguel Lusero & Maria Manuela Garcia; ap/ Jose Miguel Lusero & Maria Dimas Aragon; am/ Jose Antonio Garcia & Soledad Sandobal; gp/ Ramon Romero & Maria Juana Romero.

Frame 1803, #200
TORRES, Maria Monica
bap 4 Nov 1838, 8 days old; legit d/ Juan Torres & Maria Dolores Gutierres; ap & am/ not stated; gp/ Pedro Contreras & Monica Contreras.

LUSERO, Maria Luciana
bap 7 Nov 1838, 5 days old; legit d/ Hermegildo Lusero & Maria Francisca Sanches; ap & am/ not stated; gp/ Juan Montoya & Maria Luciana Martin.

MOYA, Manuel
bap 9 Nov 1838, 7 days old; legit s/ Jose Moya & Maria Sanches; gp/ Jose Chabes & Josefa Chabes.

SABEDRA, Juan Jesus
bap 9 Nov 1838, 3 days old; s/ Guadalupe Sabedra & unknown father; gp/ Juan Armijo & Placida Armijo.

Frames 1803-1804
TRUXILLO, Jose Hemeterio
bap 9 (no month) 1838, 5 days old; legit s/ Nepomuseno Truxillo & Maria Josefa Garcia; ap & am/ not stated; gp/ Miguel Gonsales & Maria Rita Truxillo.

LUSERO, Jose Andres
bap 11 Nov 1838, 5 days old; legit s/ Jose Miguel Lusero & Andrea Pacheco; ap & am/ not stated; gp/ Miguel Sanches & Barbara Sanches.

NS, Jose Maria
bap 11 Nov 1838; s/ unknown Navajo Indians; gp/ Juan Barela & Maria Antonia Griego.

GURULE, Maria Marselina
bap 11 Nov 1838, 7 days old; legit d/ Manuel Gurule & Rafaela Padilla; ap/ Domingo Gurule & Ana Maria Gonsales; am/ Jose Manuel Padilla & Maria Antonia Otero; gp/ Ramon Otero & Dolores Padilla.

BARELA, Andrea
bap 19 Nov 1838, 5 days old; legit d/ Manuel Barela & Vicenta Gallego; ap & am/ not stated; gp/ Miguel Montaño & Rosalilla Jaramillo.

Frame 1805, #300
GARCIA, Ambrocio de Jesus
bap 19 Nov 1838, 8 days old; s/ Cristobal Garcia & Rosalia Montaño; gp/ Jose Armijo & Placida Armijo.

HERRERA, Gregoria
bap 20 Nov 1838, 7 days old; legit d/ Jose Herrera & Barbara Garcia; ap & am/ not stated; gp/ Jose Anastacio Noanes & Barbara Gurule.

GARCIA, Felipe Neri
bap 21 Nov 1838, 5 days old; legit s/ Cleto Garcia & Nicolasa Duran; ap & am/ not stated; gp/ Antonio Duran & Maria Rosalia Duran.

LUSERO, Jose Maria
bap 22 Nov 1838, 7 days old; legit s/ Jose Ygnacio Lusero & Dolores Romero; ap & am/ not stated; gp/ Jose Maria Gonsales & Gertrudis Garcia.

Frames 1805-1806
SANCHES, Maria Josefa
bap 23 Nov 1838, 5 days old; legit d/ Juan Jose Sanches & Candelaria Sedillo; ap & am/ not stated; gp/ Bernardino Anaya.

GARCIA, Juan Nepomuceno
bap 23 Nov 1838, 5 days old; legit s/ Miguel Garcia & Rosalia Barela; ap/ Luis Garcia & Tomasa Olguin; am/ Santiago Barela & Juana Aranda; gp/ Ramon Gallego & Rosalia Montaño.

GARCIA, Jose Jesus
bap 23 Nov 1838, 8 days old; legit s/ Antonio Garcia & Tomasa Griego; ap & am/ not stated; gp/ Miguel Arias & Marcelina Balencia.

ARIAS, Juana Catarina
bap 24 Nov 1838, 2 days old; legit d/ Juan Domingo Arias & Maria Juliana Lusero; gp/ Tadeo Garcia & Barbara Antonia Griego.

ORTEGA, Maria de la Crus
bap 24 Nov 1838, 3 days old; d/ Maria Antonia Ortega & unknown father; gp/ Manuel Truxillo & Maria Dolores Muñis.

AASF, Reel #2
B-8 (Box 7a) 1838–1842

Frame 1808, #1
CHAVES, Maria Rosalia
bap 30 Nov 1838, 2 days old; legit d/ Jose Antonio Chaves & Dolores Candelaria; ap & am/ not stated; gp/ Juan Barela & Rosalia Baca.

GURULE, Juan de la Crus Andres
bap 30 Nov 1838, 8 days old; legit s/ Marselo Gurule & Petra Gutierres; ap/ Antonio Gurule & Maria Antonia Montaño; am/ Francisco Gutierres & Manuela Bernal; gp/ Jose Antonio Garcia & Ygnacia Basan.

NS, Juan Andres
bap 1 Dec 1838; s/ unknown parents; gp/ Maria Guadalupe Otero.

NS, Maria Trinidad
bap 12 Dec 1838; d/ unknown, Indian woman at home of Don Juan Armijo; gp/ Amador Armijo & Doña Ana Maria Gabaldon.

GONSALES, Maria Leocadia Nestora
bap 12 Dec 1838, 8 days old; legit d/ Esteban Gonsales & Dolores Arias; ap & am/ not stated; gp/ Ramon Candelaria & Juana Candelaria.

Frame 1809
TRUXILLO, Juan
bap 19 Dec 1838, 3 days old; legit s/ Santiago Truxillo & Juana Sandobal; ap & am/ not stated; gp/ Antonio Jose Baldonado & Maria de la Lus Rael.

SANCHES, Manuel
bap 29 Dec 1838, 2 days old; legit s/ Domingo Sanches & Maria Dolores Perea; ap & am/ not stated; gp/ Rafael Apodaca & Ana Maria Romero.

GUTIERRES, Maria Barbara
bap 29 Dec 1838, 5 days old; legit d/ Salbador Gutierres & Nicolasa Cordoba; ap & am/ not stated; gp/ Antonio Sandoval & Maria Gertrudis Santillanes.

BACA, Manuel Antonio
bap 6 Jan 1839, 2 days old; legit s/ Juan Domingo Baca & Maria Dolores Gutierres; ap & am/ not stated;
gp/ Diego Antonio Chaves & Tomasa Apodaca.

TRUXILLO, Luciano
bap 4 Jan 1839, 2 days old; s/ unknown father & Guadalupe Truxillo; gp/ Antonio Truxillo & Gregoria
Truxillo.

Frame 1810, #2
MARTIN, Maria Albina
bap 7 Jan 1839, 5 days old; d/ Dolores Martin & unknown father; gp/ Antonio Peña & Teresa Arias.

MORA, Maria Natividad
bap 13 Jan 1839, 3 days old; legit d/ Luciano Mora & Manuela Truxillo; ap & am/ not stated; gp/ Felipe
Mora & Maria Antonia Mora.

ROMERO, Maria Ygnacia
bap 15 Jan 1839, 5 days old; legit d/ Manuel Romero & Maria Petra Apodaca; gp/ Francisco Apodaca &
Maria Ygnacia Lopes.

HERRERA, Jose Fulgencio
bap 18 Jan 1839, 2 days old; legit s/ Salbador Herrera & Maria Ygnacia Chaves; gp/ Salbador Jaramillo &
Gertrudis Baca.

Frame 1811
MOYA, Maria Antonia
bap 18 Jan 1839, 3 days old; legit d/ Juan Andres Moya & Maria Ygnacia Sanches; ap & am/ not stated;
gp/ Salvador Jaramillo & Maria Gertrudis Baca.

GRIEGO, Jesus Maria
bap 23 Jan 1839, 7 days old; legit s/ Ylario Griego & Maria Jesus Garcia; ap & am/ not stated; gp/ Juan
Apodaca & Francisca Apodaca.

TRUXILLO, Maria Beneranda
bap 23 Jan 1839, 3 days old/ legit d/ Pablo Truxillo & Lus Gallego; ap & am/ not stated; gp/ Antonio
Sanches & Manuela Gonsales.

GARCIA, Maria Luisa
bap 24 Jan 1839, 5 days old; legit d/ Manuel Garcia & Ylaria Lucero; ap & am/ not stated; gp/ Jesus
Armijo & Beneranda Sanches.

Frame 1812, #3
GALLEGO, Vicente
bap 28 Jan 1839, 3 days old; legit s/ Antonio Gallego & Petra Padilla; gp/ Jose Dolores Padilla & Maria
Rosa Padilla.

GUTIERRES, Juan Cristobal
bap 31 Jan 1839, 2 days old; legit s/ Ylario Gutierres & Nicolasa Garcia; ap & am/ not stated; gp/ Jose
Mariano Garcia & Maria Agustina Garcia.

BARELA, Pedro Nolasco
bap 1 Feb 1839, 3 days old; legit s/ Antonio Barela & Catarina Ortiz; ap & am/ not stated; gp/ Doña Dolores Ortiz.

MARTIN, Paubla
bap 1 Feb 1839, 3 days old; legit d/ Jose de la Crus Martin & Vitoria Gabaldon; ap & am/ not stated; gp/ Jose Maria Griego & Maria Ysidora Griego.

Frame 1813
GALLEGO, Maria Candelaria
bap 2 Feb 1839, 2 days old; legit d/ Ramon Gallego & Rosalia Montaño; ap/ Antonio Gallego & Madalena Garcia; am/ Antonio Montaño & Micaela Santillanes; gp/ Juan Cristobal Armijo & Ana Maria Chaves.

GRIEGO, Maria Balbina
bap 5 Feb 1839; d/ Juana Griego & unknown father; gp/ Jose Mansanares & Maria Estefana Jaramillo.

SANCHES, Blas de Jesus
bap 7 Feb 1839, 2 days old; legit s/ Apolonio Sanches & Juana Maria Arias; ap & am/ not stated; gp/ Juan Christobal Arias & Tomas Martin.

APODACA, Rumaldo
bap 9 Feb 1839, 3 days old; legit s/ Salbador Apodaca & Clara Gutierres; ap & am/ not stated; gp/ Vicente Sanches & Ana Maria Maestas.

Frame 1814, #4
CANDELARIA, Antonio Ygnacio
bap 10 Feb 1839, 12 days old; legit s/ Pablo Candelaria & Madalena Garcia; ap & am/ not stated; gp/ Jose Manuel Noanes & Ysabel Sisneros.

DURAN, Juan
bap 10 Feb 1839, 4 days old; legit s/ Casimiro Duran & Juana Sandobal; ap/ Teodoro Duran & Maria Lusero; am/ Jose Sandobal & Petrona Sabedra; gp/ Diego Lopes & Juana Lopes.

HERRERA, Juan
bap 10 Feb 1839, 3 days old; legit s/ Juan Herrera & Barbara Jaramillo; gp/ Antonio Jose Chaves & Ysidora Chaves.

ARCHULETA, Pedro
bap 13 Feb 1839, 3 days old; legit s/ Pedro Archuleta & Teresa Chaves; gp/ Erban Mora & Juana Maria Griego.

APODACA, Maria Dolores
bap 19 Feb 1839, 5 days old; legit d/ Rafael Apodaca & Estefana Salazar; ap & am/ not stated; gp/ Leonicio Sandobal & Maria Juana Martin.

Frame 1815
GUTIERRES, Maria Benina de Jesus
bap 19 Feb 1839, 2 days old; legit d/ Estevan Gutierres & Quiteria Montoya; ap & am/ not stated; gp/ Juan Domingo Garcia & Maria Guadalupe Garcia.

GARCIA, Jose Gregorio
bap 23 Feb 1839, 3 days old; legit s/ Alejo Garcia & Maria Gracia Garcia; ap & am/ not stated; gp/
Manuel Geronimo Jaramillo & Maria Josefa Garcia.

NS, Maria Anastacia
bap 24 Feb 1839; in the household of Pablo Martin; gp/ Pablo Martin & Maria Cecilia Candelaria.

Frames 1815-1816, 35
SANCHES, Maria Guadalupe
bap 24 Feb 1839, 3 days old; d/ Catarina Sanches & unknown father; gp/ Don Gregorio Ortiz &
Beneranda Sanches.

ANAYA, Seberiano de Jesus
bap 27 Feb 1839, 7 days old; s/ Dolores Anaya & unknown father; gp/ Juan Cristobal (Arias) & Maria
Ysidora Arias.

SALAZAR, Jose Nestor
bap 28 Feb 1839, 3 days old; legit s/ Manuel Salazar & Francisca Truxillo; ap & am/ not stated; gp/
Hermeregildo Lusero & Maria Francisca Sanches.

GRIEGO, Biterbo de Jesus
bap 8 Mar 1839, 2 days old; legit s/ Gregorio Griego & Francisca Apodaca; ap/ Jose Maria Griego &
Candelaria Armijo; am/ Juan Apodaca & Manuela Gurule; gp/ Francisco Armijo & Rosalia Armijo.

Frames 1816-1817
ROMERO, Maria Gregoria
bap 17 Mar 1839, 2 days old; legit d/ Antonio Jose Romero & Guadalupe Garcia; ap/ Miguel Antonio
Romero & Juana Garcia; am/ Juan Jose Garcia & Francisca Gonsales; gp/ Ramon Samora & Gregoria
Candelaria.

SANCHES, Maria
bap 21 Mar 1839, 5 days old; d/ Domingo Sanches & Perfecta Montoya; ap & am/ not stated; gp/ Jose
Montoya & Maria Ygnacia Montoya.

APODACA, Jose Maria (twin)
APODACA, Jose Maria (twin)
bap 21 Mar 1839, 4 days old & named the same; s/ Jose Bentura Apodaca & Dolores Torres; ap/ Jose
Apodaca & Gertrudis Lucero; am/ Lorenso Torres & Juana Nepomucena Ruis; first gp/ Manuel Antonio
Apodaca & Maria Gertrudis Apodaca; second gp/ Jose Rafael Apodaca & Juana Nepomucena Ruis.

Frame 1818, #6
NS, Jose Gabriel
bap 24 Mar 1839, 5 days old; s/ Guadalupe NS, Indian; gp/ Blas Lusero & Gertrudis Lusero.

SANCHES, Jose Gabriel
bap 24 Mar 1839, 3 days old; s/ Cristobal Sanches & Maria Concepcion Balencia; ap & am/ not stated;
gp/ Diego Antonio Romero & Benina Samora.

NS, Maria Clara
bap 24 Mar 1839; of the Navajo Nation; gp/ Jose Chaves & Benina Chaves.

ARMIJO, Eugenio
bap 24 Mar 1839, 3 days old; s/ Jesus Armijo & Monica Pacheco; ap & am/ not stated; gp/ Juan Pacheco & Petra Lopes.

Frames 1818-1819
APODACA, Donaciano Incarnacion
bap 25 Mar 1839, 5 days old; legit s/ Francisco Apodaca & Tomasa Barela; ap & am/ not stated; gp/ Jose Ramon Rael & Maria Barbara Apodaca.

MARES, Jose Leonicio
bap 27 Mar 1839, 5 days old; legit s/ Jose Manuel Mares & Maria Francisca Candelaria; ap & am/ not stated; gp/ Jose Baca & Maria Antonia Garcia.

PEREA, Antonio Maria Ruperto
bap 31 Mar 1839, 5 days old; legit s/ Juan Jose Perea & Francisca Tafoya; ap/ Bentura Perea & Juana Lopes; am/ Juan Ygnacio Tafoya & Maria Antonia Baca; gp/ Antonio Maria Garcia & Maria Juana Montaño.

NS, Maria Dolores de la Trenidad
bap 31 Mar 1839; parvula Indian; gp/ Don Antonio Jose Chaves & Doña Barbara Armijo.

Frame 1819-1820, #7
BALDONADO, Juan Pablo
bap 31 Mar 1839, 5 days old; legit s/ Antonio Jose Baldonado & Maria Lus Rael; ap/ Juan Baldonado & Manuela Aragon; am/ Juan Antonio Rael & Maria Soledad Miera; gp/ Ygnacio Miera & Quiteria Rael.

GALLEGO, Juana Maria Pelagia
bap 31 Mar 1839, 3 days old; legit d/ Bacilio Gallego & Clara Peña; ap/ Jose Gallego & Madalena Garcia; am/ Agustin Peña & Dolores Chavez; gp/ Don Juan Cristobal Armijo & Doña Juana Maria Chaves.

SABEDRA, Jose Miguel
bap 31 Mar 1839, 3 days old; s/ Maria Antonia Sabedra & unknown father; gp/ Bibian Sabedra & Josefa Sabedra.

BENABIDES, Jesus Maria
bap 31 Mar 1839, 4 days old; legit s/ Juan Manuel Benabides & Juana Padilla; ap & am/ not stated; gp/ Jesus Maria Candelaria & Ysabel Torres.

Frames 1820-1821
CORDOBA, Maria Benina de los Dolores
bap 2 Apr 1839, 3 days old; legit d/ Juan Cordoba & Juana Griego; ap & am/ not stated; gp/ Juan Nepomuceno Gutierres & Ana Maria Montoya.

SANTILLANES, Maria Abrana
bap 9 Apr 1839, 3 days old; legit d/ Jose Miguel Santillanes & Josefa Martines; ap/ Miguel Santillanes & Josefa Martines; am/ Antonio Martines & Manuela Truxillo; gp/ Miguel Antonio Santillanes & Juana Balbaneda Lucero.

CANDELARIA, Jose Tiofilo
bap 9 Apr 1839, 2 days old; legit s/ Jose Pablo Candelaria & Manuela Antonia Sandobal; ap & am/ not stated; gp/ Jose Ramon Apodaca & Maria Manuela Candelaria.

ARANDA, Maria Vicenta del Rayo
bap 11 Apr 1839, 3 days old; legit d/ Pedro Aranda & Rosalia Jaramillo; ap/ Antonio Aranda & Teresa Romero; am/ Miguel Jaramillo & Ana Maria Ortega; gp/ Miguel Saens & Maria Ygnacia Salazar.

Frame 1822, #8
MUÑIS, Maria Vicenta
bap 12 Apr 1839; legit d/ Blas Muñis & Maria Ygnacia Martin; ap & am/ not stated; gp/ Vicente Otero & Maria Guadalupe Otero.

SANCHES, Manuel Antonio
bap 18 Apr 1839, 6 days old; legit s/ Manuel Sanches & Maria Antonia Jaramillo; ap & am/ not stated; gp/ Jose Montaño.

APODACA, Gabrel
bap 21 Apr 1839, 30 days old; legit s/ Santos Apodaca & Maria Estanislada Espinosa; ap & am/ not stated; gp/ Francisco Antonio Gonsales & Maria Estefana Arteaga.

Frames 1822-1823
MONTAÑO, Maria Perfecta
bap 29 Apr 1839, 7 days old; legit d/ Pedro Montaño & Maria Nepomucena Muñis; ap & am/ not stated; gp/ Felipe Mora & Benina Samora.

NS, Manuel Antonio
bap 30 Apr 1839, 12 days old; s/ unknown parents; gp/ Juan Gutierres & Concepcion Arias.

NS, Juana Maria (Indian)
bap 1 May 1839; Navajo in the household of Antonio Sandobal; gp/ Jose Lueras & Estefana Ortega.

GALLEGO, Maria de la Crus
bap 3 May 1839, 5 days old; d/ Paubla Gallego & unknown father; gp/ Juan Bautista Gutierres & Teresa Gutierres.

Frames 1823-1824, #9
APODACA, Asencion
bap 10 May 1839, 3 days old; s/ Catalina Apodaca & unknown father; gp/ Juan Armijo & Placida Armijo.

LUCERO, Jose Gregorio
bap 12 May 1839, 8 days old; s/ Jose Lucero & Ana Maria Samora; gp/ Santiago Nuanes & Maria Manuela Atencio.

ORTEGA, Maria Dominga
bap 15 May 1839, 4 days old; d/ Paubla Ortega; gp/ Francisco Lucero & Ygnacia Basan.

GARCIA, Jose Francisco
bap 15 May 1839, 5 days old; legit s/ Manuel Garcia & Rafaela Rael; ap & am/ not stated; gp/ Jose Rafael Miera & Maria Juana Montoya.

Frame 1825
MOYA, Maria Dolores
bap 15 May 1839, 5 days old; d/ Juana Moya & unknown father; gp/ Juliana Chaves.

PEÑA, Maria Candelaria
bap 18 May 1839, 3 days old; legit d/ Antonio Peña & Juana Arias; ap & am/ not stated; gp/ Jose Mansanares & Maria Estefana Jaramillo.

GRIEGO, Maria Antonia
bap 18 May 1839, 2 days old; d/ Marcelina Griego & unknown father; gp/ Salbador Romero & Rosa Romero.

Frames 1825-1826, #10
ARMIJO, Maria Juana Alta Gracia
bap 19 May 1839, 2 days old; legit d/ Jose Miguel Armijo & Maria Dolores Martin; ap & am/ not stated; gp/ Jose Ramon Mares & Maria de la Lus Jaramillo.

MARTIN, Salbador Antonio
bap 2 Jun 1839, 3 days old; legit s/ Antonio Jose Martin & Luciana Lucero; ap & am/ not stated; gp/ Salbador Sanches & Maria Olalla Tafoya.

HERRERA, Maria Quiteria
bap 2 Jun 1839, 5 days old; legit d/ Manuel Herrera & Maria Benigna Chaves; ap & am/ not stated; gp/ Domingo Sanches & Quiteria Gonsales.

Frames 1826-1827
TAFOYA, Jose Antonio
bap 4 Jun 1839, 7 days old; legit s/ Tomas Tafoya & Soledad Montoya; ap & am/ not stated; gp/ Ygnacio Martin & Guadalupe Padilla.

NS, Ambrocio
bap 6 Jun 1839, 3 days old; s/ Josefa NS, Indian, gp/ Jose de Jesus Gonsales & Guadalupe Chaves.

BARELA, Juan Antonio
bap 13 Jun 1839, 2 days old; legit s/ Anastacio Barela & Rafaela Garcia; ap & am/ not stated; gp/ Jose Antonio Garcia & Tomasa Griego.

NS, Maria Selestina
bap 16 Jun 1839, 3 days old; d/ Rosalia NS, Indian & unknown father; gp/ Doña Ygnacia Basan.

Frame 1828, #11
GRIEGO, Juan Pedro
bap 7 Jul 1839, 5 days old; legit s/ Juan Griego & Estefana Gonsales; ap & am/ not stated; gp/ Juan Montoya & Luciana Martin.

CANDELARIA, Maria Eulogia de Jesus
bap 19 Jul 1839, 2 days old; legit d/ Pedro Candelaria & Dolores Duran; gp/ Jose Manuel Perea & Francisca Perea.

CANDELARIA, Josefa
bap 19 Jul 1839, 5 days old; d/ Ysabel Candelaria & unknown father; gp/ Jose Ygnacio Candelaria & Niebes Gutierres.

Frames 1828-1829
DURAN, Mariana
bap 22 Jul 1839, 5 days old; legit d/ Salbador Duran & Josefa Candelaria; ap/ Miguel Duran & Ygnes Griego; am/ Bernardo Candelaria & Marta Barbero NS; gp/ Pedro Antonio (Contreras) & Monica Contreras.

LOPEZ, Fernando
bap 28 Jul 1839, 3 days old; legit s/ Lasaro Lopes & Gertrudis Santillanes; ap/ Jesus Lopes & Barbara Jaramillo; am/ Guadalupe Santillanes & Micaela Carrillo; gp/ Eusebio Santillanes & Micaela Santillanes.

TORRES, Jesus Maria Polinario
bap 29 Jul 1839, 2 days old; s/ Maria Reyes Torres & unknown father; gp/ Antonio Jose Griego & Gertrudes Balencia.

Frames 1829-1830, #12
ROMERO, Juan Christobal Eulogio
bap 30 Jul 1839, 8 days old; legit s/ Antonio Romero & Encarnacion Balencia; ap/ Jose Antonio Romero & Vitoria Garcia; am/ Juan Domingo Balencia & Maria Ygnacia Salazar; gp/ Diego Romero & Maria Ygnacia Balencia.

SANTILLANES, Jose Leon de Jesus
bap 30 Jul 1839, 3 days old; legit s/ Antonio Santillanes & Balbaneda Lucero; ap & am/ not stated; gp/ Francisco Antonio Santillanes & Juana Truxillo.

GARCIA, Maria Luisa
bap 2 Aug 1839, 2 days old; legit d/ Juan Garcia & Ysabel Garcia; ap/ Tomas Garcia & Bernarda Tafoya; am/ Ramon Garcia & Acencion Lopes; gp/ Jesus Armijo & Francisca Sanches.

PEREA, Maria Teodora de Jesus
bap 4 Aug 1839, 2 days old; legit d/ Manuel Perea & Gregoria Duran; ap & am/ not stated; gp/ Ysidro Luna & Teodora Peña.

Frame 1831
MONTOYA, Pedro Miguel
bap 4 Aug 1839, 5 days old; legit s/ Rafael Montoya & Ana Maria Duran; ap/ Pedro Montoya & Maria Luna; am/ Salbador Duran & Ana Maria Candelaria; gp/ Antonio Maria Garcia & Juana Montaño.

GARCIA, Manuel Antonio
bap 18 Aug 1839, 2 days old; s/ Maria Eleuteria Garcia & unknown father; gp/ Jose Maria Perea & Maria Apolonia Chaves.

CASTILLO, Jose Miguel
bap 20 Aug 1839, 4 days old; legit s/ Juan Miguel Castillo & Rosalia Martin; ap/ Antonio Jose Castillo & Quiteria Chaves; am/ Ysidoro Martin & Maria Dorotea Montaño; gp/ Manuel Contreras & Luisa Contreras.

Frame 1832, #13
DURAN, Maria Clara
bap 6 Sep 1839, 3 days old; legit d/ Manuel Duran & Manuela Muñis; ap & am/ not stated; gp/ Clara Armijo.

DURAN, Miguel Antonio
bap 6 Sep 1839, 3 days old; legit s/ Juan Rafael Duran & Josefa Apodaca; ap/ Teodora Duran & Maria Garcia; am/ Jose Apodaca & Gertrudis Jaramillo; gp/ Francisco Sandobal & Ana Maria Lusero.

GOMES, Jose Albino
bap 7 Sep 1839, 2 days old; s/ Maria Gomes & unknown father; gp/ Juana Candelaria.

Frame 1833
MONTOYA, Maria Juana
bap 9 Sep 1839, 5 days old; legit d/ Juan Montoya & Maria Lina Cordoba; ap & am/ not stated; gp/ Juan Jose Cordoba & Catarina Lusero.

JARAMILLO, Bartolo
SEDILLO, Bartolo
bap 11 Sep 1839, 8 days old; s/ Petra Jaramillo & unknown father; gp/ Antonio Lauriano & Rosalia Jaramillo. [Note: Bartolo later used the last name Sedillo of his step-father, Pedro Sedillo.]

GUTIERRES, Lorenso
bap 15 Sep 1839, 5 days old; legit s/ Agustin Gutierres & Josefa Gurule; ap & am/ not stated; gp/ Lasaro Torres & Juana Micaela Arias.

MARTIN, Bartolo
bap 17 Sep 1839, 8 days old; legit s/ Pablo Martin & Francisca Moya; ap & am/ not stated; gp/ Juan de Jesus Armenta & Maria Marselina Martin.

Frame 1834, #14
MONTAÑO, Maria Teodora
bap 19 Sep 1839, 3 days old; legit d/ Manuel Montaño & Guadalupe Jaramillo; ap & am/ not stated; gp/ Juan Ascencio Garcia & Maria Teodora Padilla.

SAMORA, Lino
bap 23 Sep 1839, 7 days old; legit s/ Jose Dolores Samora & Soledad Garcia; ap/ Juan Francisco Samora & Ygnacia Balencia; am/ Juan Ygnacio Garcia & Juana Mirabal; gp/ Juan Gallego & Gertrudis Gallego.

SANDOBAL, Maria Polinaria
bap 26 Sep 1839, 5 days old; legit d/ Domingo Sandobal & Concepcion Montoya; ap/ Juan Sandobal & Ygnacia Gonsales; am/ Pedro Montoya & Maria Luna; gp/ Jose Gonsales & Francisca Antonia Santillanes.

Frame 1835
GARCIA, Manuel Antonio
bap 29 Sep 1839, 2 days old; legit s/ Julian Garcia & Juana Lorensa Aragon; ap & am/ not stated; gp/ Diego Antonio Lopes & Maria Geralda Duran.

Baptisms – Albuquerque, New Mexico
1829–1850

GALLEGO, Manuel Antonio
bap 29 Sep 1839, 8 days old; legit s/ Juan Gallego & Maria de la Rosario Garcia; ap & am/ not stated; gp/ Manuel Sanches & Maria Soledad Sanches.

APODACA, Jose Rafael
bap 5 Oct 1839, 1 day old; legit s/ Jose Antonio Apodaca & Maria Barbara Benabides; ap & am/ not stated; gp/ Juan Sanches & Maria Dolores Sanches.

Frames 1835-1836, #15
MARES, Maria Salome
bap 7 Oct 1839, 5 days old; d/ Ramon Mares & Maria de la Lus Armijo; ap & am/ not stated; gp/ Jose Antonio Martin & Maria Francisca Padilla.

GUTIERRES, Maria Teresa
bap 19 Oct 1839, 3 days old; d/ Maria Juana Gutierres & unknown father; gp/ Maria Julian Gurule.

GARCIA, Pedro Antonio
bap 20 Oct 1839, 8 days old; legit s/ Juan Rafael Garcia & Encarnacion Lusero; ap & am/ not stated; gp/ Gregorio Lusero & Marta Lopes.

NS, Jose Rafael
bap 27 Oct 1839, 3 days old; s/ Dolores NS, Indian & unknown father; servant of Don Antonio Sandobal; gp/ Juan Ortega & Estefana Ortega.

Frame 1837
CRESPIN, Maria Petra
bap 27 Oct 1839, 5 days old; legit d/ Juan Andres Crespin & Rosalia Lucero; ap & am/ not stated; gp/ Juan Apodaca & Maria Ysabel Sanches.

ARMIJO, Maria Rafaela Evarista
bap 28 Oct 1839, 5 days old; legit d/ Don Juan Christobal Armijo & Doña Juana Maria Chaves; ap/ Don Juan Armijo & Doña Rosalia Ortega; am/ Don Francisco Chaves & Doña Ana Maria Castillo; gp/ Don Jose Armijo & Doña Maria Magdalena Romero.

SANCHES, Jesus Maria Benseslao
bap 31 Oct 1839, 8 days old; legit s/ Juan Jose Sanches & Rosalia Martin; ap & am/ not stated; gp/ Jose Gabrel Sanches & Rafaela Ruis.

Frame 1838, #16
GARCIA, Jose Amado
bap 5 Nov 1839, 8 days old; legit s/ Cleto Garcia & Maria Nicolasa Duran; ap/ Juan Maria Garcia & Maria Antonia Anaya; am/ Manuel Duran & Manuela Muñis, gp/ Antonio Duran & Maria Rosalia Duran.

GARCIA, Maria Andrea
bap 9 Nov 1839, 5 days old; legit d/ Juan Garcia & Ynes Serna; ap/ Juan Ygnacio Garcia & Juana Mirabal; am/ Tomas Serna & Rafaela Garcia; gp/ Juan Rafael Serna & Rosalia Serna.

TRUXILLO, Maria del Refugio
bap 11 Nov 1839, 8 days old; legit d/ Benancio Truxillo & Juana Salasar; ap/ Jose Antonio Truxillo & Maria Gallego; am/ Bernardo Salasar & Barbara Lopes; gp/ Gabrel Sanches & Rafaela Ruis.

GARCIA, Jose Roman
bap 11 Nov 1839, 2 days old; legit s/ Juan Garcia & Juana Vitoria Garcia; ap & am/ not stated; gp/ Roman Apodaca & Maria Manuela Candelaria.

Frame 1839
CANDELARIA, Manuel Antonio
bap 13 Nov 1839, 3 days old; legit s/ Jose Rafael Candelaria & Dolores Baca; ap & am/ not stated; gp/ Manuel Lusero & Maria Juana Baca.

MARTIN, Monica
bap 13 Nov 1839, 2 days old; d/ Josefa Martin & unknown father; gp/ Jose Armijo & Maria Placida Armijo.

GALLEGO, Pedro Antonio
bap 17 Nov 1839, 3 days old; s/ Maria Juliana Gallego & unknown father; gp/ Antonio Gallego & Maria Petra Padilla.

Frames 1839-1840, #17
TAFOYA, Juan Andres
bap 17 Nov 1839, 2 days old; s/ Manuela Tafoya & unknown father; gp/ Mariano Chaves & Maria Dolores Chaves.

GURULE, Jose Ysabel
bap 19 Nov 1839, 3 days old; legit s/ Lorenso Gurule & Ysidora Noanes; ap & am/ not stated; gp/ Pedro Griego & Maria Simona Griego.

LOPES, Maria de Carmen
bap 19 Nov 1839, 2 days old; legit d/ Jose Lopes & Rosalia Garcia; ap & am/ not stated; gp/ Teodoro Lopes & Maria Cruz Romero.

BACA, Jose Gregorio
bap 22 Nov 1839, 5 days old; legit s/ Manuel Baca & Maria Guadalupe Garcia; ap & am/ not stated; gp/ Juan Jose Apodaca & Maria de la Lus Padilla.

Frame 1841
GABALDON, Clemente Rafael
bap 22 Nov 1839, 3 days old; legit s/ Nepomuceno Gabaldon & Barbara Maestas; ap & am/ not stated; gp/ Manuel Armijo & Juana Armijo.

GARCIA, Jesus Maria y Jose
bap 23 Nov 1839, 5 days old; legit s/ Salbador Garcia & Rosa Gutierres; ap & am/ not stated; gp/ Antonio Jose Armijo & Placida Armijo.

MONTOYA, Pedro Miguel
bap 27 Nov 1839, 3 days old; legit s/ Juan Montoya & Maria Martin; ap & am/ not stated; gp/ Ygnacio Gurule & Maria Bentura Aragon.

Frames 1841-1842, #18
GUTIERRES, Santiago
bap 29 Nov 1839, 2 days old; legit s/ Juan Gutierres & Manuela Lopes; ap & am/ not stated; gp/ Manuel Garcia & Concepcion Lopes.

GARCIA, Juan Andres
bap 30 Nov 1839, 5 days old; legit s/ Jose Antonio Garcia & Maria Dolores Mora; ap & am/ not stated; gp/ Felipe Mora & Maria Antonia Mora.

GONSALES, Maria Rafaela
bap 1 Dec 1839, 2 days old; legit d/ Jose Gonsales & Maria Francisca Antonia Santillanes; ap/ Francisco Gonsales & Tomasa Sena; am/ Nicolas Santillanes & Maria Luisa Garcia; gp/ Rafael Apodaca & Juana Maria Romero.

MAESTAS, Maria Dolores de Guadalupe
bap 1 Dec 1839, 2 days old; legit d/ Ambrocio Maestas & Nepomucena Gonsales; ap & am/ not stated; gp/ Juan Felipe Lobato & Manuela Maestas.

Frame 1843
SALASAR, Jesus Maria
bap 4 Dec 1839, 6 days old; legit s/ Juan Salasar & Madalena Garcia; ap & am/ not stated; gp/ Jose Ramon Tenorio & Maria Josefa Tenorio.

MARTIN, Maria Dolores
bap 8 Dec 1839, 5 days old; d/ Pablo Martin & Maria Cecilia Candelaria; ap/ Jose Martin & Juana Griego; am/ Esteban Candelaria & Maria Jesus Luna; gp/ Esteban Candelaria & Maria Jesus Luna.

MARTIN, Nicolas
bap 12 Dec 1839, 9 days old; legit s/ Jose Martin & Maria Gertrudis Nieto; ap/ Jose Martin & Rosalia Lusero; am/ none; gp/ Francisco Lusero & Ygnes Montoya.

Frame 1844, #19
SANIS, Maria Guadalupe
bap 12 Dec 1839; legit d/ Ramon Sanis & Margarita Pacheco; ap & am/ not stated; gp/ Juan Garcia & Francisca Candelaria.

GUTIERRES, Barbara
bap 12 Dec 1839, 5 days old; d/ Miguel Gutierres & Ysabel Griego; ap & am/ not stated; gp/ Mariano Martin & Ludubina Martin.

GURULE, Nicolasa
bap 12 Dec 1839, 5 days old; legit d/ Jose Pablo Gurule & Estefana Rael; ap & am/ not stated; gp/ Yldefonso Sanis & Juana Sanis.

Frame 1844-1845
SANCHES, Jose Guadalupe
bap 13 Dec 1839, 3 days old; s/ Maria Sanches & unknown father; gp/ Manuel Sanches & Maria Petra Sanches.

GARCIA, Maria Guadalupe de Altagracia
bap 17 Dec 1839, 5 days old; d/ Juan Cristobal Garcia & Maria Rita Lopes; ap/ Martin Garcia & Ana Maria Apodaca; am/ Luis Lopes & Antonia Lusero; gp/ Jose Rafael Gutierres & Juana de los Reyes Gutierres.

GARCIA, Maria Soledad
bap 25 Dec 1839, 5 days old; legit d/ Cristobal Garcia & Rosalia Montaño; ap/ Jose Maria Garcia & Juana Lusero; am/ Salbador Montaño & Gregoria Chaves; gp/ Jose Antonio Garcia & Doña Begnina Chaves.

GARCIA, Jose Demitrio
bap 25 Dec 1839, 3 days old; s/ Diego Garcia & Gregoria Cordova; ap & am/ not stated; gp/ Jose Antonio Garcia & Doña Maria Ygnacia Basan.

Frame 1846, #20
TORRES, Jose Antonio
bap 25 Dec 1839, 2 days old; legit s/ Benito Torres & Maria Santos Garcia; ap & am/ not stated; gp/ Luciano Santillanes & Juana Torres.

CONTRERAS, Maria Guadalupe (of Alameda)
bap 12 Dec 1830, 6 days old; d/ Tomas Contreras & Paula Chaves; gp/ Jose Chaves & Francisca Montoya.

GARCIA, Barbara
bap 25 Dec 1839, 6 days old; d/ Ygnacia Garcia & unknown father; gp/ Julian Lopes & Barbara Carbajal.

CANDELARIA, Jose Albino
bap 26 Dec 1839, 8 days old; s/ Manuel Candelaria & Ana Maria Truxillo; ap/ Esteban Candelaria & Maria Jesus Luna; am/ Jose Truxillo & Soledad Balencia; gp/ Miguel Sanis & Maria Ygnacia Salasar.

Frame 1847
NS, Jose de la Lus
bap 26 Dec 1839, 5 days old; s/ Guadalupe NS, Indian & unknown father, servant of Santiago Armijo; gp/ Don Blas Lusero & Doña Gabriela Jaramillo.

BACA, Maria Albina
bap 26 Dec 1839, 8 days old; legit d/ Simon Baca & Lorensa Griego; ap & am/ not stated; gp/ Benito Alire & Juana Garcia.

ANAYA, Juan Jose
bap 27 Dec 1839, 3 days old; legit s/ Jose Anaya & Josefa Moya; ap/ Antonio Anaya & Tomasa Tafoya; am/ Ascencio Moya & Juana Sandobal; gp/ Marcos Ruis & Balbina Candelaria.

Frames 1847-1848
NS, Jesus Jose
bap 27 Dec 1839; s/ unknown parents; gp/ Antonio Anaya & Manuela Anaya.

ABILA, Maria Guadalupe de los Angeles
bap 30 Dec 1839, 15 days old; d/ Miguel Abila & Lugarda Montoya; ap & am/ not stated; gp/ Pedro Candelaria & Petra Candelaria.

GARCIA, Maria Petra
bap 31 Dec 1839, 3 days old; legit d/ Antonio Garcia & Gregoria Candelaria; ap/ Juan Garcia & Ysabel Romero; am/ Ygnacio Candelaria & Concepcion Chaves; gp/ Juan Esteban Sanches & Maria de la Lus Perea.

ORTEGA, Jose Manuel
bap 2 Jan 1840, 2 days old; s/ Felis Ortega & Reyes Montaño; ap/ Felis Ortega & Reyes Morales; am/ Juan Andres Montaño & Josefa Griego; gp/ Deciderio Lusero & Gertrudis Lucero.

Frame 1849
GALLEGO, Maria Manuela
bap 3 Jan 1840, 3 days old; d/ Juan Antonio Gallego & Maria Petra Lopes; ap & am/ not stated; gp/ Juan Apodaca & Maria Ysabel Sanches.

GARCIA, Jose Martiniano
bap 7 Jan 1840, 7 days old; legit s/ Ambrocio Garcia & Lubina Sanches; ap & am/ not stated; gp/ Juan Andres Moya & Simona Sanches.

GUTIERRES, Manuela
bap 8 Jan 1840, 7 days old; d/ Facundo Gutierres & Rosalia Gallego; gp/ Jose Angel Sanches & Juana Gonsales.

Frame 1850, #22
MONTOYA, Jose de los Reyes
bap 8 Jan 1840, 5 days old; s/ Juan Bautista Montoya & Juana Rafaela Aragon; ap & am/ not stated; gp/ Jose Montoya & Loreta Arias.

GARCIA, Manuel Antonio
bap 9 Jan 1840, 3 days old; s/ Maria Luisa Garcia & unknown father; gp/ Manuel Garcia & Josefa Garcia.

GARCIA, Jose Nasario
bap 10 Jan 1840, 5 days old; s/ Dolores Garcia & unknown father; gp/ Salbador Lopes & Maria Manuela Anaya.

Frame 1851
CANDELARIO, Trenidad
bap 12 Jan 1840, 3 days old; d/ Baltasar Candelario & Maria Marques; ap & am/ not stated; gp/ Rafael Armijo & Josefa Chaves.

GUTIERRES, Maria Rufina Alta Gracia
bap 15 Jan 1840, 2 days old; d/ Teresa Gutierres & unknown father; gp/ Jose Francisco Noanes & Maria Antonia Candelario.

CARABAJAL, Juana Maria Alta Gracia
bap 17 Jan 1840, 2 days old; d/ Francisca Carabajal & unknown father; gp/ Juana Maria Montaño.

SANIS, Juan Pablo
bap 17 Jan 1840, 5 days old; s/ Jose Sanis & Maria Martina Truxillo; ap & am/ not stated; gp/ Mariano Sandoval & Maria Edubigen Garcia.

Frame 1852, #23
ARANDA, Maria Antonia Fabiana
bap 20 Jan 1840, 3 days old; legit d/ Francisco Aranda & Maria Bentura Montaño; ap/ Antonio Aranda & Antonia Teresa Romero; am/ Toribio Montaño & Ana Maria Serbantes; gp/ Mariano Ysisarri & Doña Juana Otero.

SAMORA, Jose Genaro
bap 20 Jan 1840, 7 days old; s/ Cristobal Samora & Ana Maria Martin; ap/ Juan Samora & Juliana Montaño; am/ Felipe Martin & Francisca Mora; gp/ Don Jose de Valle & Ludubina Martin.

Frames 1852-1853, #23
ANAYA, Jose Marselo
bap 21 Jan 1840, 3 days old; s/ Jose Miguel Anaya & Maria Antonia Garcia; ap & am/ not stated; gp/ Jose Antonio Tafoya & Petra Garcia.

NS, Jose Antonio
bap 22 Jan 1840, 2 days old; s/ Maria del Carmen NS, Indian servant of Don Ambrocio Armijo, & unknown father; gp/ Jose de los Reyes Sabedra & Maria Guadalupe Sabedra.

GARCIA, Sebastian
bap 24 Jan 1840, 5 days old; s/ Pablo Garcia & Maria Antonia Martin; ap & am/ not stated; gp/ Jose Gregorio Garcia & Maria Petra Gonsales.

GARCIA, Jose de la Paz
BACA, Jose de la Paz
bap 24 Jan 1840, 5 days old; s/ Rosalia Garcia & unknown father; gp/ Pedro Aranda & Rosalia Jaramillo. [Note in margin: the surname Baca was added later.]

Frame 1854, #24
SABEDRA, Placida
bap 27 Jan 1840, 3 days old; legit d/ Francisco Sabedra & Maria Dolores Garcia; ap/ Juan Cristobal Sabedra & Paubla Duran; am/ Jose Antonio Garcia & Ygnacia Candelario; gp/ Antonio Jose Armijo & Placida Armijo.

MONTAÑO, Jose Anastacio
bap 27 Jan 1840, 7 days old; s/ Toribio Montaño & Marselina Baca; ap/ Jose Miguel Montaño & Rosalia Griego; am/ Diego Baca & Francisca Samora; gp/ Pedro Antonio Gutierres & Maria Gregoria Gutierres.

Frames 1854-1855
MORA, Jose Abelino
bap 27 Jan 1840, 5 days old; s/ Esteban Mora & Juana Maria Griego; ap/ Ysidro Mora & Juana Marques; am/ Francisco Griego & Maria Antonia Serna; gp/ Roque Jaramillo & Monica Lusero.

APODACA, Maria Guadalupe de Jesus
bap 1 Feb 1840, 2 days old; legit d/ Juan Apodaca & Maria Ysabel Sanches; ap & am/ not stated; gp/ Juan Felipe Maestas & Maria Marselina Gabaldon.

GURULE, Maria Beneranda
bap 3 Feb 1840, 8 days old; legit d/ Jose Gabriel Gurule & Maria Nicolasa Luna; ap & am/ not stated; gp/ Felis Sanches & Maria Sebastiana Sena.

BACA, Maria Petra
bap 4 Feb 1840, 6 days old; legit d/ Antonio Baca & Manuela Lusero; ap & am/ not stated; gp/ Pascual Candelario & Guadalupe Baca.

Frame 1856, #25
PADILLA, Maria Edubigen
bap 5 Feb 1840, 3 days old; d/ Maria Catalina Padilla & unknown father; gp/ Antonio Gallego & Maria Petra Padilla.

PADILLA, Maria Candelaria
bap 5 Feb 1840, 5 days old; d/ Barbara Padilla & unknown father; gp/ Manuel Padilla & Rosa Padilla.

NS, Juan Seberiano
bap 8 Feb 1840, 3 days old; s/ unknown parents; gp/ Salbador Noanes & Guadalupe Garcia.

ANAYA, Apolonio
bap 11 Feb 1840, 2 days old; legit s/ Felis Anaya & Maria Cecilia Gurule; ap & am/ not stated; gp/ Antonio Muñis & Josefa Candelario.

Frame 1857
LOPES, Ygnacio
bap 11 Feb 1840, 3 days old; legit s/ Bernabel Lopes & Cipriana Perea; ap & am/ not stated; gp/ Antonio Anaya & Catalina Griego.

ANAYA, Jose Deciderio
bap 12 Feb 1840, 2 days old; legit s/ Juan Anaya & Dolores Montaño; ap & am/ not stated; gp/ Gregorio Jaramillo & Josefa Garcia.

MARIÑO, Jose Emeterio
bap 16 Feb 1840, 3 days old; legit s/ Juan Mariño & Maria de la Crus Gurule; ap & am/ not stated; gp/ Francisco Rael & Maria Gregoria Romero.

Frame 1858, #26
SERNA, Maria Faustina
bap 17 Feb 1840; legit d/ Antonio Maria Serna & Micaela Griego; ap & am/ not stated; gp/ Diego Sanches & Francisca Sanches.

GRIEGO, Jose Rumaldo
bap 17 Feb 1840, 4 days old; legit s/ Juan Ysidoro Griego & Maria Bentura Lusero; ap/ Francisco Griego & Maria Antonia Serna; am/ Juan Lusero & Antonia Martin; gp/ Jose Griego & Maria Manuela Gallego.

SANTILLANES, Maria Agustina
bap 17 Feb 1840, 3 days old; legit d/ Miguel Santillanes & Josefa Martin, gp/ Jose Dolores Sandobal & Ana Truxillo.

Frame 1859
ABEYTA, Maria Filomena Alta Gracia
bap 17 Feb 1840, 4 days old; legit d/ Felis Abeyta & Juliana Atencio; ap/ Juan Crus Abeyta & Juana Peralta; am/ Gaspar Atencio & Ysabel Chaves; gp/ Cristobal Apodaca & Ysabel Garcia.

CANDELARIO, Benigna
bap 18 Feb 1840, 3 days old; legit d/ Jesus Maria Candelario & Ysabel Chaves; ap/ Jose Candelario & Tomasa Padilla; am/ Juan Antonio Chaves & Gertrudes Torres; gp/ Miguel Antonio Sandobal & Soledad Telles.

ESPINOSA, Jose Francisco Balentin
bap 19 Feb 1840, 6 days old; s/ Nepomuceno Espinosa & Maria de Socorro Gutierres; ap & am/ not stated; gp/ Pedro Baca & Rosalia Baca.

Frame 1860, #27
GUTIERRES, Jose Antonio
bap 19 Feb 1840, 5 days old; legit s/ Estevan Gutierres & Quiteria Montoya; ap & am/ not stated; gp/ Diego Antonio Garcia & Paubla Salasar.

LUSERO, Maria Soledad
bap 20 Feb 1840, 6 days old; legit d/ Juan Jose Lusero & Maria Gertrudis Chabes; ap & am/ not stated; gp/ Manuel Garcia & Soledad Miera.

LOPES, Jose Euleuterio
bap 21 Feb 1840, 2 days old; legit s/ Felipe Lopes & Juliana Torres; ap & am/ not stated; gp/ Juan Ysidoro (Griego) & Maria Agustina Griego.

Frame 1861
GRIEGO, Lorensa
bap 23 Feb 1840, 4 days old; legit d/ Manuel Griego & Catalina Samora; ap/ Blas Griego & Maria Antonia Chaves; am/ Francisco Samora & Maria Ygnacia Balencia; gp/ Jose Truxillo & Maria Gregoria Truxillo.

MARTINES, Maria Juliana
bap 23 Feb 1840, 2 days old; legit d/ Gregorio Martines & Gregoria Candelario; ap & am/ not stated; gp/ Jose Rafael Duran & Maria Lugarda Duran.

Frames 1861-1862, #28
ARIAS, Maria Josefa
bap 25 Feb 1840, 5 days old; legit d/ Atanacio Arias & Francisca Jaramillo; ap & am/ not stated; gp/ Francisco Abila & Teresa Arias.

LOPES, Gregorio
bap 27 Feb 1840, 3 days old; legit s/ Jose Cleto Lopes & Dolores Garcia; ap & am/ not stated; gp/ Gregorio Apodaca & Catalina Apodaca.

LUSERO, Pedro Antonio Albino
bap 29 Feb 1840, 5 days old; s/ Francisco Lusero & Manuela Aragon; ap & am/ not stated; gp/ Pedro Antonio Garcia & Maria Antonia Tafoya.

Frame 1863
NOANES, Pablo Roman
bap 29 Feb 1840, 3 days old; s/ Andres Noanes & Juana Armijo; ap & am/ not stated; gp/ Pablo Carrillo & Maria Petra Santillanes.

Baptisms – Albuquerque, New Mexico
1829–1850

GARCIA, Jose Domingo Florencio
bap 1 Mar 1840, 8 days old; s/ Francisco Garcia & Maria Juliana Gurule; ap/ Simon Garcia & Maria Josefa Otero; am/ Juan Jose Gurule & Andrea Balencia; gp/ Jose Francisco Rael & Maria Toribia Rael.

MAESTAS, Maria Juliana
bap 1 Mar 1840, 15 days old; legit d/ Rafael Maestas & Juana Lopes; ap & am/ not stated; gp/ Ygnacio Truxillo & Manuela Sandobal.

Frame 1864, #29
ARIAS, Maria Rufina Cesaria
bap 1 Mar 1840, 5 days old; legit d/ Juan Cristobal Arias & Tomasa Martines; ap/ Pablo Arias & Encarnacion Balencia; am/ Baltasar Martines & Maria Antonia Griego; gp/ Francisco Ortega & Maria Ygnacia Basan.

GURULE, Donaciano
bap 1 Mar 1840, 3 days old; legit s/ Juan Antonio Gurule & Guadalupe Padilla; ap & am/ not stated; gp/ Jose Gurule & Maria Nicolasa Luna.

GONSALES, Jose Florencio
bap 2 Mar 1840, 9 days old; s/ Santiago Gonsales & Maria Manuela Aragon; ap/ Juan Gonsales & Maria Antonia Armijo; am/ Manuel Aragon & Mariana Sanches; gp/ Jose Martines & Maria Antonia Gonsales.

Frame 1865
SUARES, Eusebia
bap 9 Mar 1840, 4 days old; d/ Pedro Suares & Petra Carabajal; ap & am/ not stated; gp/ Juan Armijo & Juana Armijo.

PAIS, Eusebio
bap 9 Mar 1840, 7 days old; s/ Andres Pais & Albina Gurule; ap & am/ not stated; gp/ Jose Rael & Manuela Rael.

LOPES, Jose Tomas
bap 9 Mar 1840, 3 days old; s/ Luciana Lopes & unknown father; gp/ Jose Ygnacio Candelario & Niebes Gutierres.

Frames 1865-1866, #30
CHAVES, Vitor Bensenlao
bap 9 Mar 1840, 3 days old; s/ Rumaldo Chaves & Barbara Truxillo; ap/ Estanislado Chaves & Soledad Ortega; am/ Jose Truxillo & Soledad Balencia; gp/ Don Gregorio Ortiz & Doña Clara Sarracino.

CHAVES, Maria Francisca
bap 11 Mar 1840, 2 days old; d/ Jose Maria Chaves & Maria Ysabel Apodaca; ap/ Jose Chaves & Catalina Baldonado; am/ Francisco Apodaca & Tomasa Barela; gp/ Francisco Apodaca & Josefa Apodaca.

CORDOBA, Maria Rufina
bap 11 Mar 1840, 16 days old; d/ Juana Cordoba & unknown father; gp/ Ygnacio Romero & Guadalupe Garcia.

Frames 1866-1867
MOYA, Jose Gregorio
bap 14 Mar 1840, 4 days old; s/ Jironimo Moya & Maria Jesus Martin; ap & am/ not stated; gp/ Jose Antonio Balencia & Juliana Gutierres.

MORALES, Maria Antonia del Refugio
bap 16 Mar 1840, 3 days old; d/ Jose Antonio Morales & Juana Romero; ap & am/ not stated; gp/ Jose Maria Jaramillo & Estefana Jaramillo.

PINEDA, Manuel Antonio
bap 16 Mar 1840, 5 days old; s/ Miguel Antonio Pineda & Ana Maria Gonsales; ap & am/ not stated; gp/ Sinforiana Madrid.

GONSALES, Antonio Jose
bap 17 Mar 1840, 3 days old; s/ Ylario Gonsales & Maria Rita Rael; ap/ Felipe Gonsales & Maria de la Lus Gurule; am/ Antonio Rael & Francisca Padilla; gp/ Jose Antonio Garcia & Tomasa Griego.

Frame 1868, #31
BARELA, Maria Josefa (twin)
bap 17 Mar 1840, 2 days old; d/ Manuel Barela & Visenta Gallego; ap/ Santiago Barela & Juana Aranda; am/ Juan Gallego & Manuela Gurule; gp/ Jose Antonio Garcia & Juana Aranda. [Note: See also entry below.]

BARELA, Maria Gabriela (twin)
bap 17 Mar 1840, 2 days old; d/ Manuel Barela & Vicenta Gallego; ap/ Santiago Barela & Juana Aranda; am/ Juan Gallego & Manuela Gurule; gp/ Juan Gallego & Gertrudes Gallego. [Note: See also entry above.]

Frames 1868-1869
CANDELARIO, Jose Gabriel
bap 18 Mar 1840, 3 days old; s/ Julian Candelario & Ana Maria Garcia; ap & am/ not stated; gp/ Juan Lusero & Manuel Gurule.

APODACA, Maria Gabrela
bap 18 Mar 1840, 3 days old; d/ Julian Apodaca & Maria Antonia Griego; ap & am/ not stated; gp/ Jose Maria Griego & Maria Guadalupe Mora.

SUARES, Maria Alta Gracia
bap 18 Mar 1840, 2 days old; d/ Mateo Suares & Guadalupe Griego; ap/ Calletano Suares & Maria Antonia Belasques; am/ Pablo Griego & Ysidora Apodaca; gp/ Salbador Antonio Martin & Ana Maria Alta Gracia NS.

Frame 1870, #32
MONTOYA, Gabriel
bap 19 Mar 1840, 3 days old; s/ Juan Montoya & Clara Jaramillo; ap & am/ not stated; gp/ Juan Armijo & Juana Armijo.

LOPES, Jesus Jose
bap 19 Mar 1840, 2 days old; s/ Pascual Lopes & Antonia Maestas; ap & am/ not stated; gp/ Juan Nepomuceno Perea & Francisca Garcia.

GARCIA, Jose Longino
bap 20 Mar 1840, 6 days old; s/ Rumaldo Garcia & Ana Maria Arias, ap & am/ not stated; gp/ Yldefonso Sanis & Juana Garcia.

Frames 1870-1871
SISNEROS, Benito Donaciano de Jesus
bap 22 Mar 1840, 5 days old; s/ Pablo Roman Sisneros & Maria Francisca Ruis; ap/ Francisco Sisneros & Juana Maria Candelaria; am/ Antonio Ruis & Maria Ysabel Armijo; gp/ Antonio Truxillo & Gregoria Truxillo.

GARCIA, Maria Soledad
bap 24 Mar 1840, 3 days old; d/ Dolores Garcia & unknown father; ap & am/ not stated; gp/ Juan Cristobal Rael & Maria Juliana Rael.

MARTIN, Maria Benina
bap 24 Mar 1840, 7 days old; d/ Jose Antonio Martin & Quiteria Griego; ap & am/ not stated; gp/ Jose Griego & Maria Manuela Gallego.

Frames 1871-1872, #33
TENORIO, Maria Encarnacion
bap 24 Mar 1840, 3 days old, d/ Jose Maria Tenorio & Maria Ramona Sisneros; ap/ Salbador Tenorio & Maria Antonia Anaya; am/ Antonio Sisneros & Maria Manuela Sisneros; gp/ Don Andres Ortega & Doña Juana Garcia.

GRIEGO, Maria Encarnacion
bap 28 Mar 1840, 4 days old; d/ Jose Griego & Manuela Gallego; ap/ Miguel Griego & Gertrudis Olguin; am/ Martin Gallego & Guadalupe Garcia; gp/ Jose Antonio Garcia & Tomasa Griego.

LUJAN, Jose Bidal Sisto
bap 27 Mar 1840, 2 days old; s/ Jose Maria Lujan & Dolores Duran; ap & am/ not stated; gp/ Jose Armijo & Clara Armijo.

Frame 1873
NOANES, Manuel Antonio
bap 1 Apr 1840, 4 days old; s/ Jose Manuel Noanes & Mariana Sisneros; ap & am/ not stated; gp/ Manuel Antonio Muñis & Maria Josefa Candelaria.

CHAVES, Maria Benina
bap 2 Apr 1840, 5 days old; d/ Patricio Chaves & Maria Gertrudes Sanches; ap & am/ not stated; gp/ Manuel Garcia & Maria Josefa Duran.

GARCIA, Maria Francisca Paubla
bap 5 Apr 1840, 3 days old; d/ Francisco Garcia & Manuela Carrillo; ap & am/ not stated; gp/ Juan Antonio Lopes & Maria Antonia Gonsales.

Frame 1874, #34
ANAYA, Maria Francisca Paubla
bap 6 Apr 1840, 3 days old; d/ Jose Rosario Anaya & Teresa Candelaria; ap & am/ not stated; gp/ Juan (Anaya) & Maria Josefa Anaya.

GARCIA, Jose Candido
bap 7 Apr 1840, 2 days old; s/ Bernardo Garcia & Maria Antonia Lopes; ap & am/ not stated; gp/ Pedro Contreras & Monica Contreras.

SISNEROS, Maria Jesus Dolores
bap 7 Apr 1840, 2 days old; d/ Maria Ysabel Sisneros & unknown father; gp/ Juan Jose Garcia & Maria Petra Telles.

Frames 1874-1875
APODACA, Maria Vitoriana (of Ysleta Mission)
bap 8 Apr 1840, 13 days old; s/ Gregorio Apodaca & Manuela Torres; ap & am/ not stated; gp/ Jose Andres Lobato & Soledad Chaves.

GRIEGO, Begnino (of Ysleta Mission)
bap 8 Apr 1840, 3 days old; s/ Vicente Griego & Guadalupe Rubin; ap & am/ not stated; gp/Antonio Jaramillo & Simona Bernal.

GONSALES, Jose Francisco Pelagio
bap 9 Apr 1840, 6 days old; s/ Ysidro Gonsales & Maria del Rosario Griego; ap & am/ not stated; gp/ Jose Francisco Apodaca & Maria Manuela Anaya.

Frames 1875-1876, #35
PEÑA, Jose Maria (of Ysleta Mission)
bap 12 Apr 1840, 8 days old; s/ Rafael Peña & Maria Catalina Aguirre; ap/ Mariano Peña & Soledad Garcia; am/ Francisco Aguirre & Maria Bibiana Pacheco; gp/ Mateo Peña & Maria Barbara Yturrieta.

TRUXILLO, Leon Selso
bap 12 Apr 1840, 3 days old; s/ Santiago Truxillo & Maria Gutierres; ap/ Jose Truxillo & Soledad Balencia; am/ Miguel Gutierres & Gregoria Armijo; gp/ Juan de Dios Chaves & Monica Lusero.

GARCIA, Julian
bap 13 Apr 1840, 2 days old; s/ Jose Antonio Garcia & Polinaria Salazar; ap/ Felis Garcia & Maria Ysabel Lopes, am/ Juan Cristobal Salazar & Micaela Montoya; gp/ Felis Garcia & Ysabel Lopes.

Frames 1876-1877
SANCHES, Teodoro Caciano
bap 14 Apr 1840, 14 days old; s/ Domingo Sanches & Quiteria Gonsales; ap/ Jose Sanches & Gregoria Rael; am/ Juan Gonsales & Barbara Castillo; gp/ Felis Sanches & Sebastiana Sena.

SEDILLO, Antonio Jose
bap 14 Apr 1840, 2 days old; s/ Julian Sedillo & Cipriana Garcia; ap & am/ not stated; gp/ Salbador Herrera & Manuela Garcia.

GUTIERRES, Maria Teresa de Jesus
bap 14 Apr 1840, 5 days old; d/ Juan Gutierres & Juana Marques; ap & am/ not stated; gp/ Diego Gurule & Teresa Mares.

MARQUES, Maria de la Lus
bap 15 Apr 1840, 8 days old; d/ Antonio Marques & Dolores Toledo; ap & am/ not stated; gp/ Jose Gonsales & Maria de la Lus Gonsales.

Frame 1878, #36
GRIEGO, Jose Toribio Dolores
bap 19 Apr 1840, 4 days old; s/ Geronimo Griego & Maria Albina Lusero; ap/ Miguel Griego &
Gertrudes Olgin; am/ Juan Lusero & Maria Antonia Martines; gp/ Juan Lusero & Juana Lusero.

MARTINES, Fernando
bap 23 Apr 1840, 8 days old; s/ Jose Antonio Martines & Maria Antonia Belasques; ap & am/ not stated;
gp/ Juan Samora & Gertudis Balencia.

CORDOBA, Maria Rufina
bap 23 Apr 1840, 8 days old; d/ Marcos Cordoba & Gertrudis Duran; ap & am/ not stated; gp/ Jose
Montoya & Maria Ygnacia Montoya.

Frame 1879
GRIEGO, Ygnes
bap 23 Apr 1840, 3 days old; d/ Jose Griego & Soledad Candelario; ap & am/ not stated; gp/ Jose Armijo
& Maria Guadalupe Peralta.

TRUXILLO, Jose
bap 25 Apr 1840, 5 days old; s/ Pablo Truxillo & Maria de la Lus Gallego; ap & am/ not stated; gp/
Francisco Martines & Maria Petrona Martines.

Frames 1879-1880, #37
GONSALES, Maria Edubigen de los Dolores
bap 1 May 1840, 7 days old; legit d/ Francisco Gonsales & Maria Petra Sandobal; gp/ Jose Narsiso Garcia
& Francisca Aragon.

PEREA, Felipe Ladislado Nepomuseno
bap 1 May 1840, 5 days old; legit s/ Francisco Perea & Pabla Sandobal; ap/ Rafael Perea & Carmen
Sandobal; am/ Jose Sandobal & Petra Sabedra; gp/ Jose Lusero & Gertrudes Gutierres.

MARTIN, Jose Patrocinio
bap 2 May 1840, 7 days old; s/ Dolores Martin & unknown father; gp/ Jose Lopes & Gregoria Martin.

Frames 1880-1881
SANCHES, Pedro (of Ysleta Mission)
bap 2 May 1840, 3 days old; s/ Juan Sanches & Juana Martines; ap & am/ not stated; gp/ Antonio
Jaramillo & Simona Bernal.

CHAVES, Jesus Maria
bap 2 May 1840, 3 days old; legit s/ Jose Chaves & Lus Olona; ap/ Estanislado Chaves & Soledad Otero;
am/ Miguel Olona & Barbara Sanches; gp/ Juan de Dios Chaves & Monica Lusero.

MONTAÑO, Maria del Carmen
bap 3 May 1840, 2 days old; d/ Antonio Montaño & Josefa Lusero; ap & am/ not stated; gp/ Jesus Lusero
& Barbara Antonia Torres.

Frame 1882, #38
BACA, Maria Juana
bap 3 May 1840, 3 days old; d/ Don Jose Baca & Maria Antonia Garcia; ap/ Juan Domingo Baca & Ana Gertrudes Ortiz; am/ Salbador Garcia & Toribia Chaves; gp/ Jose Armijo & Maria Guadalupe Chaves.

DURAN, Maria Tomasa
bap 9 May 1840, 7 days old; d/ Juana Duran & unknown father; gp/ Manuel Carabajal & Maria Ramona Perea.

PINEDA, Blas Antonio
bap 10 May 1840, 5 days old; legit s/ Nepomuseno Pineda & Josefa Truxillo; gp/ Jose Narciso & Francisca Aragon

Frame 1883
JARAMILLO, Jose Abran
bap 10 May 1840, 3 days old; legit s/ Manuel Jaramillo & Gertrudis Maestas; ap/ Miguel Jaramillo & Ana Maria Ortega; am/ Mariano Maestas & Guadalupe Chaves; gp/ Blas Lusero & Gertrudis Lusero.

MOYA, Reymundo
bap 13 May 1840, 3 days old; legit s/ Francisco Moya & Juana Lopes; ap/ Asencio Moya & Juana Sandobal; am/ Leonardo Lopes & Juana Maria Arroyos; gp/ Ramon Balencia & Refugio Ortiz.

BALENCIA, Jose Miguel
bap 19 May 1840, 8 days old; legit s/ Juan Balencia & Maria Guadalupe Candelario; ap & am/ not stated; gp/ Jose de la Cruz Gurule & Maria Encarnacion Gurule.

Frame 1884, #39
SANCHES, Juan Nepomenceno
bap 16 May 1840, 8 days old; legit s/ Dolores Sanches & Juana Candelario; gp/ Juan Nepomuseno Carabajal & Juana Maria Carabajal.

MARTINES, Maria Dolores
bap 19 May 1840, 5 days old; legit d/ Jose Maria Martines & Catalina Garcia; ap & am/ not stated; gp/ Juan Torres & Maria Dolores Gutierres.

GUTIERRES, Pedro Antonio
bap 2 Jun 1840, 9 days old; s/ Rosa Gutierres & unknown father; gp/ Jose Gregorio Garcia & Maria Petra Gonsales.

Frames 1884-1885
GALLEGO, Maria del Rayo
bap 2 Jun 1840, 8 days old; d/ Juan Gallego & Manuela Gurule; ap & am/ not stated; gp/ Jose Gonsales & Francisca Antonia Santillanes.

GUTIERRES, Jose Aristeo de Jesus
bap 3 Jun 1840, 16 days old; legit s/ Felipe Gutierres & Maria Lorensa Jaramillo; ap & am/ not stated; gp/ Miguel Antonio Candelario & Maria Ynes Candelario.

GARCIA, Amado de Jesus
bap 3 Jun 1840, 8 days old; legit s/ Antonio Felis Garcia & Carmen Sanches; ap/ Felis Garcia & Maria Ysabel Lopes; am/ Vicente Sanches & Ana Maria Maestas; gp/ Antonio Maria Garcia & Maria Juana Montaño.

Frames 1885-1886, #40
SANDOBAL, Felipe
bap 3 Jun 1840, 5 days old; legit s/ Jose Angel Sandobal & Maria Gertrudes Gonsales; ap & am/ not stated; gp/ Juan Domingo Sandobal & Maria Concepcion Montoya.

SAISN, Maria Fernanda
bap 4 Jun 1840, 6 days old; legit d/ Francisco Saisn & Refugio Gutierres; ap/ Salbador Saisn & Juana Maria Aragon; am/ Salbador Gutierres & Niculasa Cordoba; gp/ Felis Cordoba & Rosa Garcia.

SANDOBAL, Felipe
bap 4 Jun 1840, 6 days old; legit s/ Antonio Sandobal & Maria Candelario; ap & am/ not stated; gp/ Manuel Candelario & Ana Maria Truxillo.

TRUXILLO, Jose Antonio Epitafio
bap 4 Jun 1840, 12 days old; legit s/ Manuel Truxillo & Dolores Muñis; ap & am/ not stated; gp/ Pablo Garcia & Maria Gertrudes Garcia.

Frame 1887
GRIEGO; Maria Paubla
bap 6 Jun 1840, 4 days old; d/ Pedro Asencio Griego & Ana Maria Salasar; ap/ Jose Maria Griego & Candelaria Armijo; am/ Torivio Salasar & Polinaria Gutierres; gp/ Baltasar Romero & Maria Paubla Lusero.

SANCHES, Maria Quirina
bap 7 Jun 1840, 5 days old; legit d/ Antonio Sanches & Magdalena Griego; ap/ Jose Antonio Sanches & Sebastiana Ortega; am/ Miguel Griego & Gertrudes Olgin; gp/ Rumaldo Chaves & Barbara Truxillo.

RAEL, Maria Soledad
bap 7 Jun 1840, 20 days old; d/ Maria Bitoria Rael & unknown father; gp/ Manuel Garcia & Maria Josefa Duran.

Frame 1888, #41
LOPES, Juana Maria
bap 8 Jun 1840, 8 days old; legit d/ Juan Lopes & Soledad Garcia; ap & am/ not stated; gp/ Jose Dolores Apodaca & Maria Ygnacia Garcia.

CORDOBA, Antonio Jose Quirino
bap 8 Jun 1840, 5 days old; legit s/ Dionicio Cordoba & Juana Sanches; ap/ Marcos Cordoba & Rafaela Garcia; am/ Jose Sanches & Gregoria Rael; gp/ Felipe Garcia & Lus Rael.

SANCHES, Maria de los Angeles
bap 8 Jun 1840, 8 days old; d/ Diego Antonio Sanches & Juana Maria Gallego; ap/ Antonio Jose Sanches & Maria Rosalia Martines; am/ Juan Gallego & Manuela Gurule; gp/ Gabriel Sanches & Rafaela Ruis.

Frame 1889
APODACA, Maria Maximiana
bap 10 Jun 1840, 5 days old; legit d/ Juan Apodaca & Maria de la Lus Padilla; ap & am/ not stated; gp/ Jose Domingo Romero & Maria Petra Padilla.

LUSERO, Maria Antonia
bap 13 Jun 1840, 5 days old; legit d/ Jose Ygnacio Lucero & Dolores Romero; ap & am/ not stated; gp/ Anselmo Baldonado & Bibiana Gonsales.

CHAVES, Pablo
bap 13 Jun 1840, 3 days old; s/ Juana Chaves & unknown father; gp/ Juan Jose Gonsales & Encarnacion Perea.

Frames 1889-1890, #42
PADILLA, Ana Quiteria de Jesus
bap 14 Jun 1840, 3 days old; legit d/ Vitoriano Padilla & Ramona Castillo; ap/ Diego Padilla & Rita Abila; am/ Juan Castillo & Juana Catalina Garcia; gp/ Don Fernando Ortiz & Doña Dolores Ortiz.

GARCIA, Juan Bernabel
bap 15 Jun 1840, 5 days old; legit s/ Juan Garcia & Juana Maria Armijo; ap & am/ not stated; gp/ Antonio Garcia & Ana Maria Maestas.

PEREA, Manuel Antonio
bap 18 Jun 1840, 6 days old; legit s/ Bartolo Perea & Josefa Candelario; ap & am/ not stated; gp/ Rafael Montoya & Ana Maria Duran.

DURAN, Maria Juana
bap 27 Jun 1840, 3 days old; legit d/ Francisco Duran & Bernarda Gurule; ap & am/ not stated; gp/ Polinario Perea & Ysidora Perea.

Frame 1891, #42
ARMIJO, Maria Ysabel Estanislada
bap 28 Jun 1840, 2 days old; d/ Pedro Armijo & Maria de la Lus Garcia; ap & am/ not stated; gp/ Ambrocio Garcia & Maria Ludabina Sandobal.

PACHECO, Maria Dolores
bap 1 Jul 1840, 8 days old; d/ Francisco Esteban Pacheco & Manuela Truxillo; ap & am/ not stated; gp/ Pablo Armijo & Dolores Garcia.

SALASAR, Juan Paublo
bap 1 Jul 1840, 6 days old; s/ Manuel Salasar & Francisca Truxillo; ap & am/ not stated; gp/ Jose Higinio Lusero & Maria Rita Lusero.

Frames 1891-1892, #43
TORRES, Maria Filomena
bap 6 Jul 1840, 5 days old; d/ Francisco Torres & Maria Juliana Sanches; ap & am/ not stated; gp/ Diego Antonio Romero & Maria Nepomusena Muñis.

TORRES, Maria Francisca
bap 12 Jul 1840, 7 days old; d/ Benito Torres & Gertrudes Griego; ap & am/ not stated; gp/ Juan Francisco Moya & Ludubina Moya.

SANCHES, Maria de la Paz
bap 16 Jul 1840, 4 days old; d/ Francisca Sanches & unknown father; gp/ Don Ysidro Ortiz & Doña Sinforiana Madrid.

GARCIA, Maria Dolores del Rayo
bap 18 Jul 1840, 2 days old; d/ Maria Lorensa Garcia & unknown father; gp/ Jose Sabedra & Francisca Garcia.

Frame 1893
SUARES, Justa Rufina
bap 20 Jul 1840, 2 days old; legit d/ Calletano Suares & Cesaria Carabajal; ap/ Francisco Suares & Gertrudes Duran; am/ Miguel Carabajal & Jasinta Lopes; gp/ Don Mariano Armijo & Doña Gabrela Jaramillo.

JARAMILLO, Jose Manuel
bap 20 Jul 1840, 12 days old; legit s/ Ylario Jaramillo & Euguenia Ortega; ap & am/ not stated; gp/ Jose Lusero & Juana Lusero.

BUSTAMANTE, Maria Apolonia
bap 8 Aug 1840, 3 days old; legit d/ Carpio Bustamante & Guadalupe Larrañaga; ap/ Bernardo Bustamante & Maria Anastacia Griego; am/ Mariano Larrañaga & Maria de Jesus Ortiz; gp/ Miguel Abila & Maria Lugarda Montoya.

Frame 1894, #44
SERNA, Francisco Roman
bap 9 Aug 1840, 5 days old; legit s/ Francisco Serna & Dolores Griego; ap/ Antonio Serna & Bibiana Fernandes; am/ Juan Griego & Maria del Carmen Gomes; gp/ Juan Ysidoro Griego & Maria Bentura Lusero.

PEÑA, Lorenso
bap 10 Aug 1840, 2 days old; legit s/ Ramon Peña & Rosalia Gurule; ap & am/ not stated; gp/ Francisco Lusero & Ygnes Montoya.

TAFOYA, Jose Antonio
bap 10 Aug 1840, 3 days old; legit s/ Domingo Tafoya & Ana Maria Martin; ap/ Juan Ygnacio Tafoya & Maria Antonia Baca; am/ Antonio Jose Martin & Maria Luciana Lusero; gp/ Tomas Tafoya & Soledad Montoya.

Frame 1895
OTERO, Juan Jose
bap 18 Aug 1840; legit s/ Juan Otero & Rosalia Jaramillo; ap & am/ not stated; gp/ Juan Jose Jaramillo & Trenidad Otero.

GRIEGO, Jose Librado
bap 23 Aug 1840, 3 days old; legit s/ Simon Griego & Ana Maria Perea; ap & am/ not stated; gp/ Felipe Martin & Josefa Martin.

DURAN, Juana Maria
bap 23 Aug 1840, 5 days old; d/ Rosalia Duran & unknown father; gp/ Jose Mansanares & Maria Estefana Jaramillo.

Frames 1895-1896, #45
CHAVES, Juana (twin)
CHAVES, Maria de la Lus (twin)
bap 27 Aug 1840, 2 days old; legit d/ Juan Chaves & Micaela Sanches; ap/ Jose Maria Chaves & Maria Ygnacia Jaramillo; am/ Felis Sanches & Ana Maria Aguirre; first gp/ Diego Lopes & Juliana Chaves; second gp/ Jesus Lopes & Juana Armijo.

CANDELARIA, Maria Guadalupe
bap 28 Aug 1840, 3 days old; legit d/ Salbador Candelaria & Maria de Jesus Padilla; ap & am/ not stated; gp/ Jose Castillo & Maria Guadalupe Padilla.

BACA, Maria Rosa
bap 30 Aug 1840, 5 days old; legit d/ Juan Baca & Maria Rafaela Cordoba; ap & am/ not stated; gp/ Jose Apodaca & Maria Juana Apodaca.

Frame 1897
GUTIERRES, Maria Nepomusena
bap 30 Aug 1840, 2 days old; legit d/ Francisco Gutierres & Maria Manuela Montoya; ap & am/ not stated; gp/ Juan Jose Garcia & Maria Manuela Salazar.

NS, Amador
bap 1 Sep 1840, 3 days old; s/ Dolores NS, Indian of Juan Barela & unknown father; gp/ Francisco Antonio Romero & Quiteria Moya.

MONTOYA, Paubla
bap 9 Sep 1840, 9 days old; legit d/ Miguel Montoya & Refugio Baca; ap & am/ not stated; gp/ Juan Chaves & Paubla Chaves.

Frame 1898, #46
MONTOYA, Rosa
bap 10 Sep 1840, 6 days old; d/ Dolores Montoya & unknown father; gp/ Manuel Candelario & Ana Maria Truxillo.

MONTOYA, Maria Barbara
bap 11 Sep 1840, 5 days old; legit d/ Jose Rafael Montoya & Maria Gertrudes Chaves; gp/ Roman Apodaca & Micaela Sanches.

PADILLA, Epitafio
bap 13 Sep 1840, 4 days old; legit s/ Baltasar Padilla & Juana Garcia; ap & am/ not stated; gp/ Don Pedro Aranda & Doña Rosalia Jaramillo.

CANDELARIO, Juan Paublo
bap 13 Sep 1840, 4 days old; s/ Paubla Candelario & unknown father; gp/ Francisco Griego & Maria Soledad Anaya.

Frame 1899
BACA, Maria Soledad Natividad
bap 14 Sep 1840, 8 days old; legit d/ Ramon Baca & Maria del Rosario Marques; ap/ Pedro Baca & Maria Antonia Gallego; am/ Juan Marques & Petra Chaves; gp/ Antonio Truxillo & Gregoria Truxillo.

GRIEGO, Maria Gertrudes de la Cruz
bap 14 Sep 1840, 2 days old; legit d/ Ylario Griego & Maria de Jesus Garcia; ap & am/ not stated; gp/ Julian Griego & Maria Candida Griego.

GARCIA, Maria Soledad Amada
bap 16 Sep 1840, 3 days old; legit d/ Ambrocio Garcia & Catalina Armijo; ap/ Martin Garcia & Ana Maria Apodaca; am/ Rafael Armijo & Soledad Peña; gp/ Juan Pablo Gutierres & Josefa Martines.

Frame 1900, #47
GARCIA, Jose Tomas
bap 18 Sep 1840, 3 days old; legit s/ Deciderio Garcia & Nepomusena Candelario; ap/ Juan Garcia & Ysabel Romero; am/ Ygnacio Candelario & Concepcion Chaves; gp/ Ygnacio Candelario & Maria Luisa Garcia.

NS, Juana Lina
bap 1 Oct 1840, 8 days old; d/ Dolores NS, Indian servant, & unknown father; gp/ Juan Cristoval Garcia & Juana Maestas.

GALLEGO, Jose Agapito
bap 2 Oct 1840, 15 days old; legit s/ Francisco Gallego & Maria Tomasa Candelario; ap & am/ not stated; gp/ Jose Vitoriano Griego & Maria Jesus Candelario.

Frame 1901
SABEDRA, Maria Miquela de los Dolores
bap 2 Oct 1840, 3 days old; d/ Guadalupe Sabedra & unknown father; gp/ Jose Montoya & Dolores Garcia.

PEREA, Maria Antonia
bap 2 Oct 1840, 3 days old; d/ Dolores Perea & unknown father; gp/ Jose Armijo & Maria Placida Armijo.

NS, Antonio
bap 4 Oct 1840; s/ Francisca NS, Indian of Maria Antonia Griego & unknown father; gp/ Rafael Garcia & Tomasa Martines.

CANDELARIO, Juana Maria
bap 6 Oct 1840, 1 day old; legit d/ Rumaldo Candelario & Josefa Garcia; ap & am/ not stated; gp/ Antonio Jose Santillanes & Manuela Garcia.

Frame 1902, #48
MUÑIS, Jose Ygnacio Nepomuseno
bap 6 Oct 1840, 5 days old; s/ Juan Cristobal Muñis & Ana Maria Pacheco; ap/ Jose Maria Muñis & Barbara Garcia; am/ Gregorio Pacheco & Pascuala Sanches; gp/ Bernardo Balencia & Ana Maria Aragon.

LUSERO, Gabriela
bap 9 Oct 1840, 2 days old; legit d/ Jose de las Nieves Lusero & Eulogia Sabedra; ap/ Andres Lusero & Tomasa Garcia; am/ Francisco Sabedra & Maria de la Lus Chaves; gp/ Mariano Armijo & Gabriela Jaramillo.

SANDOBAL, Maria Juana
bap 11 Oct 1840, 3 days old; legit d/ Encarnacion Sandobal & Rosalia Baldonado; ap & am/ not stated; gp/ Jose Apodaca & Maria Juana Apodaca.

GURULE, Maria Lina Toribia
bap 11 Oct 1840, 5 days old; legit d/ Manuel Gurule & Getrudes Perea; ap & am/ not stated; gp/ Ygnacio Sanches & Maria Juliana Chaves.

Frame 1903
GUTIERRES, Teresa
bap 15 Oct 1840, 2 days old; legit d/ Mariano Gutierres & Juana Lusero; ap/ Pedro Antonio Gutierres & Guadalupe Garcia; am/ Juan Lusero & Barbara Candelario; gp/ Antonio Noanes & Maria Candelaria Griego.

MAES, Juan de la Paz
bap 22 Oct 1840, 8 days old; legit s/ Vicente Maes & Maria Petrona Griego; ap & am/ not stated; gp/ Jose Santos Herrera & Maria Juana Lusero.

APODACA, Maria Alta Gracia
bap 23 Oct 1840, 3 days old; legit d/ Ramon Apodaca & Manuela Candelaria; ap/ Jose Antonio Apodaca & Ysabel Martin; am/ Paublo Candelaria & Andrea Gutierres; gp/ Salbador Antonio Martin & Maria Alta Gracia Martin.

Frame 1904, #49
JARAMILLO, Mariano
bap 27 Oct 1840, 12 days old; legit s/ Fernando Jaramillo & Petra Sanches; ap & am/ not stated; gp/ Mariano Ruis & Guadalupe Jaramillo.

NS, Antonio Jose
bap 28 Oct 1840, 3 days old; s/ Rita NS, Indian servant of Don Antonio Sandobal, & unknown father; gp/ Jesus Maria Baca & Maria del Rosario Marques.

CHAVES, Jose Crespin
bap 30 Oct 1840, 6 days old; legit s/ Pedro Chaves & Margarita Montoya; ap & am/ not stated; gp/ (not stated) & Balsa Cordoba.

Frame 1905
CANDELARIA, Maria Nicolasa
bap 7 Nov 1840, 2 days old; d/ Maria Concepcion Candelaria & unknown father; gp/ Vicente Candelario & Maria Andrea Gallego.

GARCIA, Pedro
bap 8 Nov 1840, 3 days old; legit s/ Jose Manuel Garcia & Apolonia Anaya; ap & am/ not stated; gp/ Juan de la Crus Gonsales & Maria Jesus Moya.

GARCIA, Jose Santos Abran
bap 8 Nov 1840, 8 days old; legit s/ Jose Alexo Garcia & Maria Gracia Garcia; ap & am/ not stated; gp/ Dolores Lopes & Maria Paubla Perea.

Frames 1905-1906, #50
NOANES, Carlos
bap 10 Nov 1840, 6 days old; legit s/ Salbador Noanes & Maria Guadalupe Garcia; ap/ Francisco Noanes & Maria Barbara Maes; am/ Juan Garcia & Maria Ysabel Romero; gp/ Jose Anastacio Noanes & Barbara Gurule.

SANTILLANES, Antonio Jose Santos
bap 11 Nov 1840, 12 days old; legit s/ Diego Santillanes & Maria Juana Garcia; ap/ Juan Miguel Santillanes & Micaela Gonsales; am/ Antonio Garcia & Margarita Rael; gp/ Antonio Garcia & Juana Sanis.

NS, Jose Manuel
bap 11 Nov 1840, 11 days old; s/ unknown parents; gp/ Juan Manuel Benabides & Juana Lopes.

Frames 1906-1907
SEDILLO, Juan Ylario de Jesus
bap 12 Nov 1840, 9 days old; legit s/ Toribio Sedillo & Ysabel Sanches; ap/ Antonio Felis Sedillo & Antonia Narcisa Baca; am/ Jose Ramos Sanches & Juana Barbara Montoya; gp/ Don Juaquin Alejandro Basan & Doña Maria Dolores Sedillo.

LUSERO, Pedro Antonio
bap 15 Nov 1840, 8 days old; legit s/ Andres Lusero & Francisca Salasar; ap/ Juan Lusero & Justa Pino; am/ Julian Salasar & Guadalupe Rael; gp/ Pedro Martin & Paubla Martin.

LOPES, Maria Petra
bap 16 Nov 1840, 2 days old; d/ Catalina Lopes & unknown father; gp/ Manuel Carabajal & Barbara Carabajal.

CHAVES, Carlos
bap 17 Nov 1840, 8 days old; s/ Miguel Chaves & Decideria Gurule; ap & am/ not stated; gp/ Ramon Rael & Decideria Ortiz.

Frame 1908, #51
NS, Maria Ramona
bap 19 Nov 1840, 5 days old; d/ unknown parents; gp/ Francisco Mata & Maria Concepcion Pando.

LUSERO, Juan de los Reyes
bap 24 Nov 1840, 5 days old; s/ Ramon Lusero & Leocadia Sanches; ap & am/ not stated; gp/ Jose Rafael Gutierres & Juana de los Reyes Gutierres.

ARIAS, Maria Ygnacia
bap 25 Nov 1840, 6 days old; d/ Concepcion Arias & unknown father; gp/ Francisco Lusero & Ygnes Montoya.

Frame 1909
CHAVES, Juan Jose de los Dolores
bap 25 Nov 1840, 7 days old; s/ Juan de Dios Chaves & Monica Lusero; ap/ Estanislado Chaves &
Soledad Ortega; am/ Mariano Lusero & Marselina Balencia; gp/ Miguel Sanis & Maria Ygnacia Salasar.

GRIEGO, Maria Seferina
bap 27 Nov 1840, 3 days old; d/ Jose Griego & Paubla Anaya; ap & am/ not stated; gp/ Salvador
Jaramillo & Francisca Jaramillo.

GARCIA, Maria de la Lus
bap 27 Nov 1840, 2 days old; d/ Bartolo Garcia & Juana Maria Padilla; ap/ Juan Garcia & Barbara
Chaves; am/ Diego Antonio Padilla & Manuela Aguirre; gp/ Jose Mares & Dolores Mares.

Frame 1910, #52
CANDELARIO, Maria Olimpia
bap 28 Nov 1840, 6 days old; d/ Enriques Candelario & Ysabel Garcia; ap & am/ not stated; gp/
Francisco Antonio Romero & Quiteria Moya.

ARCHIBEQUE, Pablo Antonio
bap 28 Nov 1840, 3 days old; s/ Josefa Archibeque & unknown father; gp/ Manuel Garcia & Dolores
Garcia.

JARAMILLO, Jose Ramon
bap 28 Nov 1840, 6 days old; s/ Augustin Jaramillo & Francisca Garcia; ap/ Juan Jaramillo & Rosa
Gutierres; am/ Juan de Jesus Garcia & Rosa Sabedra; gp/ Jesus Gallego & Maria Rosario Garcia.

Frame 1911
TORRES, Facundo
bap 28 Nov 1840, 3 days old; s/ Felipe Torres & Maria Garcia; ap/ Jose Torres & Gertrudis Barreras; am/
Francisco Garcia & Maria Reyes Candelaria; gp/ Ylario Garcia & Rafaela Garcia.

ARMIJO, Maria Andrea
bap 28 Nov 1840, 3 days old; d/ Rafaela Armijo & Josefa Ca(smeared); gp/ Jose Lueras & Josefa Chaves.

GUTIERRES, Jose de Jesus Santiago
bap 28 Nov 1840, 10 days old; s/ Jose Maria Gutierres & Manuela Antonia Mares; ap/ Don Juan Jose
Gutierres & Doña Dolores Montoya; am/ Francisco Chaves & Ana Maria Castillo; gp/ Juan Gutierres &
Barbara Chaves.

Frame 1912, #53
ANSURES, Andrea
bap 28 Nov 1840, 3 days old; d/ Teodora Ansures & unknown father; gp/ Dolores Lusero & Petra Lusero.

ANALLA, Maria Andrea
bap 30 Nov 1840; d/ Miguel Analla & Maria Lopes; ap & am/ not stated; gp/ Jose Ramon Sanches &
Manuela Tapia.

LUSERO, Julian Antonio
bap 4 Dec 1840, 7 days old; s/ Jose Miguel Lusero & Maria Manuela Garcia; ap/ Miguel Lusero & Maria Dimas Aragon; am/ Jose Antonio Garcia & Soledad Sandoval; gp/ Jose Manuel Herrera & Maria de la Lus Sandobal.

Frame 1913
ANALLA, Francisco Gabriel
bap 5 Dec 1840, 3 days old; s/ Rafael Analla & Ynes Gurule; ap & am/ not stated; gp/ Francisco Armijo & Maria Petra Perea.

MARTIN, Antonio Nicolas
bap 6 Dec 1840, 8 days old; s/ Felipe Martin & Vitoria Sanis; ap/ Felipe Martin & Juana Truxillo; am/ Miguel Sanis & Ana Gregoria Martines; gp/ Juan Tomas Aragon & Maria Gertrudis Garcia.

DURAN, Barbara
bap 6 Dec 1840, 3 days old; d/ Casimiro Duran & Juana Sandobal; ap & am/ not stated; gp/ Jose Armijo & Maria Placida Armijo.

Frame 1914, #54
GALLEGO, Andres
bap 6 Dec 1840, 6 days old; legit s/ Jesus Gallego & Maria Dolores Rodriguez; ap & am/ not stated; gp/ Paublo Gonzales & Maria Gertrudes Aragon.

ORTIZ, Petra
bap 7 Dec 1840, 4 days old; legit d/ Don Ysidro Ortiz & Doña Sinforiana Madrid; ap/ Don Francisco Ortiz & Doña Maria Garcia; am/ Dolores Madrid & Doña Crisanta Domingues; gp/ Don Fernando Ortiz & Doña Jacinta Serrano.

GUTIERRES, Abad
bap 8 Dec 1840, 3 days old; legit s/ Jose Gutierres & Gertrudes Gomes; ap/ Jose Gutierres & Juana Lopes; am/ Francisco Gomes & Mariana Dias; gp/ Jose Toribio Truxillo & Maria Dolores Truxillo.

Frame 1915
CANDELARIA, Maria Eligia
bap 11 Dec 1840, 11 days old; legit d/ Vicente Candelaria & Ana Maria Chaves; ap/ Francisco Candelaria & Lus Armijo; am/ Geronimo Chaves & Encarnacion Gonsales; gp/ Ambrocio Gonsales & Gabriela Gonsales.

SALASAR, Jose Sabas
bap 12 Dec 1840, 8 days old; legit s/ Miguel Salasar & Maria Apolonia Padilla; ap & am/ not stated; gp/ Esteban Mora & Juana Maria Griego.

ROMERO, Antonio Abad
bap 13 Dec 1840, 3 days old; legit s/ Lino Romero & Josefa Garcia; ap/ Luis Jose Romero & Juana Aragon; am/ Antonio Garcia & Francisca Gonsales; gp/ Don Ramon Aragon & Doña Ana Maria Cordoba.

ARAGON, Maria Barbara
bap 13 Dec 1840, 5 days old; d/ Maria Gertrudis Aragon & unknown father; gp/ Francisco Sanches.

Frame 1916, #55
MARTIN, Jose Concepcion
bap 14 Dec 1840, 8 days old; legit s/ Paublo Martin & Francisca Ortiz; ap & am/ not stated; gp/ Felipe Lopes & Maria Juliana Torres.

GARCIA, Jose Guadalupe
bap 16 Dec 1840, 5 days old; legit s/ Jose Manuel Garcia & Barbara Carbajal; ap & am/ not stated; gp/ Jose Dolores Apodaca & Maria Ygnacia Garcia.

GARCIA, Jose Atanacio
bap 17 Dec 1840, 3 days old; legit s/ Manuel Garcia & Maria Rafaela Rael; ap & am/ not stated; gp/ Jose Maria Miera & Maria de la Lus Lopes.

Frame 1917
GARCIA, Maria Ysabel
bap 18 Dec 1840, 5 days old; legit d/ Antonio Maria Garcia & Juana Montaño; ap/ Felis Garcia & Ysabel Lopes; am/ Salbador Montaño & Gregoria Chaves; gp/ Juan Garcia & Juana Maria Maestas.

ARAGON, Jose de Jesus
bap 19 Dec 1840, 6 days old; s/ Juan Rafael Aragon & Catarina Sabedra; gp/ Francisco Jiron & Maria Aragon.

Frames 1917-1918, #56
NIETO, Albino
bap 20 Dec 1840, 3 days old; s/ Ana Maria Nieto & unknown father; gp/ Ramon Candelario & Ana Maria Truxillo.

GUTIERRES, Juana
bap 25 Dec 1840, 3 days old; legit d/ Ylario Gutierres & Nicolas Garcia; ap & am/ not stated; gp/ Felipe Gutierres & Lorensa Jaramillo.

MUÑIS, Maria Manuela de Jesus
bap 25 Dec 1840, 2 days old; legit d/ Manuel Muñis & Josefa Candelario; ap & am/ not stated; gp/ Jose Rafael Duran & Maria Rosa Gurule.

Frames 1918-1919
SANCHES, Jesus Jose
bap 26 Dec 1840, 5 days old; s/ Maria Sanches & unknown father; gp/ Jesus Jose Apodaca & Dolores Torres.

TAFOYA, Juana Maria
bap 28 Dec 1840, 3 days old; legit d/ Jose Antonio Tafoya & Petra Garcia; ap/ Jose Antonio Tafoya & Guadalupe Duran; am/ Juan Rafael Garcia & Manuela Muñis; gp/ Doña Dolores Ortiz.

APODACA, Juana Maria
bap 4 Jan 1841, 2 days old; legit d/ Jose Francisco Apodaca & Maria Nicolasa Gurule; ap/ Nicolas Apodaca & Maria de la Luz Garcia; am/ Ygnacio Gurule & Maria Apolonia Nieto; gp/ Ygnacio Gurule & Maria Bentura Aragon.

Frame 1920, #57
CARABAJAL, Salbador Manuel
bap 4 Jan 1841, 8 days old; legit s/ Juan Pedro Carabajal & Gertrudes Gonsales; gp/ Rafael Armijo &
Doña Rosalia Mastas.

NOANES, Jose Donaciano de los Reyes
bap 7 Jan 1841, 5 days old; legit s/ Santiago Noanes & Maria Manuela Atencio; ap & am/ not stated; gp/
Antonio Baldonado & Maria Tomasa Gonsales.

NOANES, Juan Pablo
bap 15 Jan 1841, 2 days old; legit s/ Antonio Noanes & Maria Candelaria Griego; ap/ Jose Manuel
(Noanes) & Paubla Candelaria; am/ Jose Maria Griego & Maria Guadalupe Mora; gp/ Jose Maria Griego
& Guadalupe Mora.

Frame 1921
GARCIA, Maria Alta Gracia
bap 17 Jan 1841, 9 days old; legit d/ Miguel Garcia & Rosalia Barela; ap & am/ not stated; gp/ Don
Mariano Ysisarri & Doña Juana Otero.

TRUXILLO, Jesus Maria
bap 17 Jan 1841; 8 days old; s/ Guadalupe Truxillo & unknown father; gp/ Juan Antonio (Gonsales) &
Maria Tomasa Gonsales.

Frames 1921-1922, #58
JARAMILLO, Jose Pablo
bap 17 Jan 1841, 8 days old; legit s/ Manuel Gregorio Jaramillo & Josefa Garcia; ap/ Agustin Jaramillo &
Getrudes Salasar; am/ Jose Garcia & Gertrudes Lauriana; gp/ Toribio Sedillo & Maria Ysabel Sanches.

LOVATO, Francisco
bap 17 Jan 1841, 8 days old; legit s/ Juan Lovato & Manuela Rael; ap/ Juan Lovato & Maria Casados;
am/ Antonio Rael & Francisca Padilla; gp/ Francisco Rael & Gregoria Romero.

HERRERA, Antonio Jose
bap 19 Jan 1841, 8 days old; legit s/ Jose Santos Herrera & Maria Juana Lusero; ap & am/ not stated; gp/
Juan Lente & Maria de los Angeles Bellejos

CANDELARIA, Juan Felipe de Jesus
bap 19 Jan 1841, 8 days old; legit s/ Maria Candelaria & unknown father; gp/ Juan Felipe Lovato &
Manuela Maestas.

Frame 1923
GARCIA, Maria Placida Leon
bap 20 Jan 1841, 8 days old; legit d/ Maria Juana Garcia & unknown father; gp/ Juan Christoval Rael &
Maria Juliana Rael.

BALENCIA, Juan Pablo
bap 27 Jan 1841, 8 days old; legit s/ Bernardo Balencia & Juana Aragon; ap/ Juan Domingo Balencia &
Paubla Martines; am/ Tomas Aragon & Gertrudes Garcia; gp/ Jose Montolla & Teresa Miera.

GONSALES, Maria Concepsion
bap 29 Jan 1841, 7 days old; d/ Juan Gonsales & Ygnacia Montolla; ap & am/ not stated; gp/ Francisco Rael & Gregoria Romero.

Frame 1924, #59
ALFAROS, Juan Pablo
bap 28 Jan 1841, 4 days old; legit s/ Guadalupe Alfaros & Dolores Garcia; ap/ Jose Maria Alfaros & Maria Mata; am/ Juan Manuel Garcia & Manuela Perea; gp/ Gabriel Sanches & Rafaela Ruis.

GONSALES, Jose Manuel Vicente
bap 29 Jan 1841, 5 days old; s/ Monica Gonsales & unknown father; gp/ Juan Antonio Rael & Maria de la Lus Rael.

Frame 1925
GARCIA, Placida
bap 4 Feb 1841, 20 days old; legit d/ Antonio Garcia & Tomasa Griego; ap/ Juan Cristobal Garcia & Encarnacion Romero; am/ Miguel Griego & Gertrudes Olguin; gp/ Blas Lucero & Gabrela Jaramillo.

CHAVES, Jose Ramon
bap 6 Feb 1841, 4 days old; legit s/ Antonio Chaves & Maria Ygnacia Maestas; ap/ Geronimo Chaves & Maria Encarnacion Gonsales; am/ Jose Mariano Montoya & Maria Reyes Maestas; gp/ Ramon Aragon & Ana Maria Cordova.

MONTAÑO, Paublo Antonio
bap 8 Feb 1841, 8 days old; legit s/ Torivio Montaño & Marselina Baca; ap & am/ not stated; gp/ Jose Sabedra & Maria Guadalupe Sabedra.

Frame 1926, #60
GUTIERRES, Rumaldo de Jesus
bap 9 Feb 1841, 3 days old; legit s/ Juan Nepomuceno Gutierres & Maria Francisca Anaya; ap/ Juan Miguel Gutierres & Maria Nieves Chaves; am/ Manuel Anaya & Maria Antonia Apodaca; gp/ Juan Andres Moya & Maria Cimona Sanchez.

MARTINES, Jose Deciderio
bap 11 Feb 1841, 3 days old; s/ Juan Martines & Yldefonsa Olguin; ap & am/ not stated; gp/ Jose Leonardo Candelaria & Francisca Gonsales.

SANCHES, Miguel Antonio
bap 16 Feb 1841, 4 days old; s/ Dolores Sanches & unknown father; gp/ Julian Lopes & Barbara Carabajal.

Frame 1927
SANDOVAL, Jose Romulo
bap 17 Feb 1841, 8 days old; legit s/ Jose Miguel Sandoval & Antonia Rosa Lusero; ap & am/ not stated; gp/ Esteban Candelaria & Maria Jesus Luna.

MORA, Julian
bap 18 Feb 1841, 8 days old; legit s/ Luciano Mora & Maria Manuela Antonia Truxillo; ap & am/ not stated; gp/ Vicente Samora & Manuela Lusero.

ROMERO, Manuel
bap 19 Feb 1841, 6 days old; s/ Sista Romero & unknown father; gp/ Antonio Gutierres & Maria
Eduvigen Gomes.

GUTIERRES, Maria Nestora
bap 19 Feb 1841, 6 days old; d/ Juan Gutierres & Maria Josefa Anaya; ap & am/ not stated; gp/ Jose
Antonio Garcia & Maria Ysabel Gallego.

Frame 1928, #61
GARCIA, Maria Juliana
bap 20 Feb 1841, 8 days old; legit d/ Jose Gregorio Garcia & Petra Gonsales; ap/ Juan Ygnacio Garcia &
Juana Mirabal; am/ Jose Gonsales & Francisca Garcia; gp/ Esteban Gonsales & Maria Dolores Arias.

NS, Maria Dolores
bap 25 Feb 1841, 8 days old; d/ Manuela NS, Indian, & unknown father; gp/ Manuel Benavides & Maria
Apodaca.

SANCHES, Lorensa
bap 25 Feb 1841, 8 days old; legit d/ Apolonio Sanches & Juana Maria Arias; ap & am/ not stated; gp/
Antonio Jose Armijo & Placida Armijo.

CHAVES, Jesus Jose Matias
bap 25 Feb 1841, 8 days old; legit s/ Deciderio Chaves & Concepcion Ortis; ap & am/ not stated; gp/ Don
Gregorio Ortis & Beneranda Sanches.

ANAYA, Jose Nestor
bap 27 Feb 1841, 8 days old; legit s/ Jose Anaya & Josefa Moya; ap/ Antonio Anaya & Tomasa Ansures;
am/ Asencio Moya & Juana Tenorio; gp/ Juan Apodaca & Ysabel Sanches.

Frame 1929
GRIEGO, Maria Sesaria
bap 27 Feb 1841, 8 days old; legit d/ Gregorio Griego & Maria Francisca Apodaca; ap/ Jose Maria Griego
& Candelaria Armijo; am/ Juan Apodaca & Maria Manuela Gurule; gp/ Julian Apodaca & Maria Antonia
Griego.

MONTAÑO, Felipe
bap 28 Feb 1841, 8 days old; legit s/ Antonio Jose Montaño & Maria Rita Luna; ap/ Jose Montaño &
Miguela Santillanes; am/ Ysidro Luna & Maria Manuela Candelaria; gp/ Jose Graviel Gurule & Maria
Nicolasa Luna.

CANDELARIA, Jose Francisco Pelagio
bap 1 Mar 1841, 8 days old; legit s/ Jesus Maria Candelaria & Maria Ysabel Chaves; ap & am/ not stated;
gp/ Jose Francisco Apodaca & Maria Ygnacia Lopes.

LOPES, Vicente Antonio
bap 6 Mar 1841, 8 days old; legit s/ Leonicio Lopes & Gertrudes Perea; ap/ Luis Lopes & Antonia Nina
NS; am/ Simon Perea & Guadalupe Duran; gp/ Jose Antonio Garcia & Maria Ysavel Gallego.

Frame 1930, #62
CARRILLO, Antonio Maria
bap 12 Mar 1841, 8 days old; s/ Manuela Carrillo & unknown father; gp/ Juan Christobal Muñis & Ana Maria Pacheco.

DURAN, Dolores
bap 15 Mar 1841, 8 days old; legit d/ Salvador Duran & Maria Garcia; ap/ Felipe Duran & Juana Gonsales; am/ Miguel Garcia & Rosalia Lusero; gp/ Antonio Truxillo & Dolores Truxillo.

GARCIA, Maria Carmen
bap 15 Mar 1841, 8 days old; legit d/ Juan Miguel Garcia & Guadalupe Montaño; ap/ Antonio Garcia & Margarita Rael; am/ Jose Montaño & Francisca Gonsales; gp/ Baltasar Romero & Paubla Lusero.

NS, Jose Estanislado
bap 15 Mar 1841, 8 days old; s/ unknown parents; gp/ Jose Alejandro Lusero & Maria Rita NS.

GONSALES, Jose Francisco
bap 15 Mar 1841, 8 days old; legit s/ Crus Gonsales & Maria de Jesus Moya; ap/ Jose Francisco Gonsales & Barbara Basques; am/ Eusebio Moya & Gregoria Garcia; gp/ Guadalupe Alfaro & Paubla Garcia.

CARABAJAL, Maria Nestora
bap 15 Mar 1841, 8 days old; legit d/ Hermenegildo Carabajal & Margarita Duran; ap & am/ not stated; gp/ Ysidro Luna & Maria Teodora de la Peña.

Frame 1931
RUIS, Jesus Maria Trinidad
bap 15 Mar 1841, 8 days old; s/ Ana Maria Ruis & unknown father; gp/ Jesus Armijo & Marina Sarracino.

GARCIA, Francisco
bap 16 Mar 1841, 8 days old; legit s/ Manuel Garcia & Ylaria Lusero; ap/ Tomas Garcia & Bernarda Garcia; am/ Gregorio Lusero & Marta Lopes; gp/ Francisco Lopes & Petra Lopes.

ABEYTA, Grabiela de Jesus
bap 22 Mar 1841, 6 days old; d/ Felipe Abeyta & Maria Juliana Atencio; ap/ Hermenegildo Abeyta & Maria Josefa Aguilar; am/ Gaspar Atencio & Maria Ysabel Chaves; gp/ Jose Mateo Armijo & Maria Rosalia Armijo.

BARELA, Barbara
bap 22 Mar 1841, 5 days old; legit d/ Antonio Barela & Catarina Ortis; ap/ Juan Barela & Josefa Chaves; am/ Lorenso Ortis & Maria Rafaela Ruis; gp/ Miguel Antonio Candelario & Barbara Apodaca.

BARELA, Mariano Luis
bap 22 Mar 1841, 8 days old; legit s/ Manuel Barela & Visenta Gallego; ap/ Santiago Barela & Juana Aranda; am/ Juan Gallego & Maria Manuela Gurule; gp/ Mariano Ysisarri & Juana Otero.

Frame 1932, #63
GALLEGO, Juan Paublo
bap 23 Mar 1841, 8 days old; legit s/ Basilio Gallego & Clara Peña; ap/ Antonio Jose Gallego & Madalena Garcia; am/ Agustin Peña & Dolores Chaves; gp/ Ramon Candelaria & Manuela Martin.

ABILA, Jose Abran
bap 27 Mar 1841, 8 days old; legit s/ Jose Miguel Abila & Lugarda Montolla; ap & am/ not stated; gp/
Bibiano Sabedra & Josefa Sabedra.

GALLEGO, Jose Manuel
bap 27 Mar 1841, 8 days old; legit s/ Rumaldo Gallego & Maria Gregoria Gutierres; ap & am/ not stated;
gp/ Jose Manuel Truxillo & Maria Juliana Martines. [Note: See also record below.]

GALLEGO, Jose Manuel
bap 28 Mar 1841, 6 days old; legit s/ Rumaldo Gallego & Maria Gregoria Gutierres; ap/ Juan Gallego &
Francisca Montaño; am/ Pedro Antonio Gutierres & Guadalupe Garcia; gp/ Jose Manuel Truxillo &
Maria Juliana Martines. [Note: See also record above.]

Frames 1932-1933
SAMORA, Juan Christobal
bap 28 Mar 1841, 8 days old; legit s/ Jose Manuel Samora & Luisa Aragon; ap/ Juan Samora & Margarita
Barela; am/ Juan de Jesus Aragon & Rosalia Gonsales; gp/ Jose Rael & Decideria Ortiz.

GARCIA, Manuela Antonia
bap 30 Mar 1841, 7 days old; legit d/ Jose Edubigen Garcia & Nepomusena Rael; ap/ Andres Garcia &
Juana Torres; am/ Antonio Rael & Francisca Padilla; gp/ Felipe Gonsales & Decideria Gonsales.

GRIEGO, Paubla
bap 30 Mar 1841, 7 days old; d/ Juana Gregoria Griego & unknown father; gp/ Juan Chaves & Paubla
Chaves.

GARCIA, Jose Teodoro
bap 2 Apr 1841, 6 days old; legit s/ Jose Antonio Garcia & Polinara Salasar; ap/ Felis Garcia & Ysabel
Lopes; am/ Juan Cristoval Salasar & Maria Miguela Montoya; gp/ Juan Cristobal (Montoya) & Maria
Migz fuela Montoya.

CANDELARIA, Manuel
bap 4 Apr 1841, 5 days old; legit s/ Paublo Candelaria & Magdalena Garcia; ap & am/ not stated; gp/
Manuela Sandoval.

Frame 1934, #64
NS, Ysidro
bap 5 Apr 1841, 8 days old; s/ unknown parents; gp/ Jose Juaquin Olgin & Maria Micaela Belasques.

SANCHES, Eusebio
bap 6 Apr 1841, 8 days old; s/ Domingo Sanches & Quiteria Gonsales; ap/ Jose Sanches & Gregoria Rael;
am/ Juan Gonsales & Barbara Castillo; gp/ Paublo Garcia & Gregoria Rael.

TAPIA, Maria Juana
bap 7 Apr 1841, 4 days old; legit d/ Manuel Tapia & Albina Gallego; ap & am/ not stated; gp/ Jose Lopes
& Trinidad Lopes.

LOPES, Maria Vicenta
bap 10 Apr 1841, 2 days old; legit d/ Juan Cristoval Lopes & Maria Rita Candelaria; ap & am/ not stated;
gp/ Miguel Lopes & Maria Nicanora Garcia.

BARELA, Juana
bap 11 Apr 1841, 4 days old; legit d/ Anastacio Barela & Rafaela Garcia; ap/ Santiago Barela & Juana Aranda; am/ Tadeo Garcia & Jacinta Candelario; gp/ Pedro Aranda & Rosalia Jaramillo.

TORRES, Maria de Jesus
bap 11 Apr 1841, 3 days old; legit d/ Juan Torres & Ysabel Gutierres; ap & am/ not stated; gp/ Jose Albino Garcia & Maria Juana de Jesus Garcia.

Frame 1935
CASTILLO, Juan Bautista Leon
bap 15 Apr 1841, 2 days old; legit s/ Juan Miguel Castillo & Rosalia Martines; ap/ Antonio Castillo & Quiteria Chaves; am/ Ysidro Martines & Dorotea Montaño; gp/ Ylario Gonsales & Maria Rita Rael.

JARAMILLO, Maria Guadalupe
bap 15 Apr 1841, 4 days old; legit d/ Lusiano Jaramillo & Lorensa Rael; ap & am/ not stated; gp/ Pasqual Montoya & Maria de la Crus Martin.

GRIEGO, Juan Nepomuseno Aniceto
bap 17 Apr 1841, 8 days old; s/ Juan Ysidro Griego & Juana Garcia; ap & am/ not stated; gp/ Alejandro Duran & Quiteria Garcia.

HERRERA, Maria Quirina
bap 18 Apr 1841, 7 days old; legit s/ Salbador Herrera & Maria Ygnacia Chaves; ap/ Vicente Herrera & Maria Antonia Montaño; am/ Antonio Chaves & Manuela Garcia; gp/ Jose Anastacio Gallego & Soledad Candelario.

PINEDA, Juan Andres
bap 18 Apr 1841, 3 days old; legit s/ Nepomuseno Pineda & Josefa Truxillo; ap & am/ not stated; gp/ Juan Andres Lusero & Francisca Salasar.

Frame 1936, #65
GRIEGO, Maria Anastacia Nicanora
bap 19 Apr 1841, 8 days old; legit d/ Antonio Griego & Luduvina Martin; ap & am/ not stated; gp/ Juan Griego & Encarnacion Griego.

NS, Maria Antonia de Jesus
bap 22 Apr 1841, 2 days old; d/ unknown parents; gp/ Juana Jaramillo.

GARCIA, Salbador Gorge
bap 23 Apr 1841, 4 days old; legit s/ Salvador Garcia & Juana Romero; ap/ Jose Antonio Garcia & Juana Sandoval; am/ Santiago Romero & Dolores Candelaria; gp/ Nerio Gonsalez & Maria Rita Rael.

CHAVES, Bartolo
bap 25 Apr 1841, 3 days old; legit s/ Jose Dolores Chaves & Nicanora Garcia; ap/ Gabrien Chaves & Maria de Jesus Armijo; am/ Juan de Jesus Garcia & Rosa Sabedra; gp/ Bartolo Garcia & Juana Maria Padilla.

Frame 1937
PEÑA, Pedro Antonio
bap 3 May 1841, 5 days old; legit s/ Antonio Peña & Juana Arias; ap & am/ not stated; gp/ Juan Nepomuseno Mansanares & Maria Agustina Mansanares.

NS, Maria Petra
bap 3 May 1841, 3 days old; d/ unknown parents; gp/ Maria Manuela Antonia Perea.

NS, Jose de la Crus
bap 5 May 1841, 5 days old; s/ unknown parents; gp/ Juan Tafoya & Juliana Chaves.

Frames 1937-1938, #66
ANAYA, Maria Antonia
bap 6 May 1841, 4 days old; legit d/ Felis Anaya & Cesilia Gurule; ap & am/ not stated; gp/ Cleto Anaya & Blasa Duran.

NS, Jose Atanacio
bap 6 May 1841, 8 days old; s/ unknown parents; gp/ Juan Gutierres & Maria Josefa Anaya.

DURAN, Gregoria Amadora
bap 9 May 1841, 7 days old; legit d/ Juan Duran & Ysabel Griego; ap & am/ not stated; gp/ Manuel Candelario & Ana Maria Truxillo.

GARCIA, Jose Gregorio
bap 9 May 1841, 8 days old; legit s/ Pablo Garcia & Antonia Martin; ap & am/ not stated; gp/ Juan Garcia & Ygnes Serna.

Frame 1939
APODACA, Maria Prudencia Tiburcia
bap 11 May 1841, 3 days old; legit d/ Salbador Apodaca & Clara Gutierres; ap/ Nicolas Apodaca & Lus Garcia; am/ Francisco Gutierres & Candelaria Martin; gp/ Lucas Garcia & Juana Garcia.

BACA, Jose de la Crus
bap 12 May 1841, 8 days old; legit s/ Juan Domingo Baca & Dolores Rael; ap & am/ not stated; gp/ Juan Gutierres & Juana Gutierres.

Frame 1940, #67
GARCIA, Maria Bonifacia
bap 15 May 1841, 2 days old; legit d/ Salbador Garcia & Soledad Candelario; ap & am/ not stated; gp/ Jesus Lopes & Juana Armijo.

LOPES, Bonafacio Paublin
bap 15 May 1841, 2 days old; legit s/ Francisco Lopes & Francisca Luna; ap/ Paublin Lopes & Ana Garcia; am/ Ysidro Luna & Manuela Candelario; gp/ Mariano Garcia & Andrea Carabajal.

GONSALES, Jose Rafael
bap 16 May 1841, 5 days old; legit s/ Baltasar Gonsales & Maria Marques; gp/ Rafael Chaves & Maria Nepomusena Apodaca.

Baptisms – Albuquerque, New Mexico
1829–1850

Frames 1940-1941
MARTIN, Jose de la Lus
bap 18 May 1841, 8 days old; legit s/ Antonio Jose Martin & Maria Luciana Lusero; ap/ Vicente Martin & Ysabel Baldonado; am/ Juan Lusero & Justa Pino; gp/ Gabrel Sanches & Rafaela Ruis.

GONSALES, Maria Concepcion
bap 21 May 1841, 2 days old; legit d/ Francisco Gonsales & Maria Antonia Garbiso; ap/ Felipe Gonsales & Maria de la Lus Lusero; am/ Antonio Garbiso & Maria de la Lus Garcia; gp/ Rafael Montoya & Maria Ramona Montoya.

MOLLA, Jose Rumaldo
bap 24 May 1841, 6 days old; s/ Jose Maria Molla & Dolores Sanis; ap/ Eusebio Molla & Maria Duran; am/ Salbador Sanis & Juana Maria Aragon; gp/ Jose Maria Truxillo & Maria Lorensa Lusero.

Frames 1941-1942, #68
LUSERO, Jose Domingo
bap 25 May 1841, 8 days old; legit s/ Jose Miguel Lusero & Andrea Pacheco; ap & am/ not stated; gp/ Jose Manuel Martin & Concepcion Pando.

LUSERO, Barbara
bap 28 May 1841, 5 days old; legit d/ Rubi Lusero & Dolores Balencia; gp/ Francisco Rael & Gregoria Romero.

BERNAL, Manuel Antonio
bap 29 May 1841, 3 days old; legit s/ Jose Maria Bernal & Estefana Jaramillo; ap & am/ not stated; gp/ Manuel Gregorio Jaramillo & Josefa Garcia.

Frame 1943
NS, Maria Dolores
bap 30 May 1841, 5 days old; infant, Ute Indian; gp/ Don Mariano Ysisarre & Doña Juana Otero.

NS, Jose
bap 31 May 1841, 5 days old; s/ unknown parents; gp/ Jose Ygnes Chaves & Rufina Apodaca.

GONSALES, Jose Rafael
bap 3 Jun 1841, 8 days old; legit s/ Rafael Gonsales & Maria Jesus Aragon; ap/ Manuel Gonsales & Toribia Armijo; am/ Tadeo Aragon & Maria Luisa Balencia; gp/ Guadalupe Alfaro & Maria Paubla Garcia.

Frame 1944, #69
SALAZAR, Jose Nestor
bap 4 Jun 1841, 4 days old; legit s/ Juan Salazar & Ramona Sanches; ap/ Torribio Salazar & Polinaria Perea; am/ Jose Sanches & Gregoria Rael; gp/ Julian Sanches & Maria Candelario.

JARAMILLO, Maria Josefa de los Reyes
bap 5 Jun 1841, 5 days old; legit d/ Juan Esteban Jaramillo & Francisca Perea; ap/ Ramon Jaramillo & Maria Juana de los Reyes Armijo; am/ Jose Manuel Perea & Maria Rosalia Duran; gp/ Juan Pablo Gutierres & Maria Josefa Martines.

Frames 1944-1945
LAURIANO, Maria Rafaela Marselina
bap 5 Jun 1841, 5 days old; legit d/ Teodoro Lauriano & Josefa Chaves; ap/ Manuel Lauriano & Maria Crus Romero; am/ Agustin Chaves; gp/ Jose Rafael (Montoya) & Candelaria Montoya.

MONTOYA, Trenidad Doroteo del Rosario
bap 8 Jun 1841, 3 days old; legit s/ Jose Maria Montoya & Clara Armijo; ap/ Pablo Montoya & Reyes (blank); am/ Lucas Armijo & Barbara Ortiz; gp/ Salbador Herrera & Maria Ygnacia Chaves.

NS, Manuel Bonifacio
bap 10 Jun 1841, 5 days old; s/ unknown parents; gp/ Juan de Dios Chaves & Monica Lusero.

Frame 1946, #70
PEREA, Maria del Carmen
bap 10 Jun 1841, 3 days old; legit d/ Manuel Perea & Juana Sanis; ap/ Francisco Perea & Manuela Candelario; am/ Yldefonso Sanis & Juana Garcia; gp/ Jose Angel & Paubla Garcia.

LUSERO, Francisco
bap 10 Jun 1841, 5 days old; legit s/ Hermenegildo Lusero & Francisca Sanches; ap/ Jose Lucero & Juliana Gonsales; am/ Felipe Sanches & Ana Maria Truxillo; gp/ Francisco Rael & Gregoria Romero.

Frames 1946-1947
TORRES, Maria Antonia
bap 19 Jun 1841, 5 days old; legit d/ Juan Torres & Dolores Gonsales; ap & am/ not stated; gp/ Jose Maria Griego & Guadalupe Mora.

GALLEGO, Juan Albino
bap 3 Jul 1841, 4 days old; legit s/ Jose Pablo Gallego & Juana Garcia; ap & am/ not stated; gp/ Francisco Mora & Josefa Mora.

GARCIA, Ana Maria
bap 5 Jul 1841, 5 days old; d/ Juan Garcia & Juana Maria Chaves; ap/ Francisco Garcia & Manuela Gonsales; am/ Juaquin Chaves & Barbara Armijo; gp/ Ramon Antonio Garcia & Paubla Salasar.

Frame 1948, #71
SANCHES, Jose Refugio
bap 7 Jul 1841, 4 days old; legit s/ Domingo Sanches & Maria de la Lus Perea; ap/ Jose Sanches & Josefa Griego; am/ Francisco Perea & Manuela Candelario; gp/ Rafael Gutierres & Gregoria Armijo.

GARCIA, Juan Manuel
bap 11 Jul 1841, 8 days old; legit s/ Alejo Garcia & Gracia Garcia; ap/ Juan de Jesus Garcia Jurado & Maria Rosa Sabedra; am/ Juan Asencio Garcia de Noriega & Barbara Chaves; gp/ Manuel Maestas & Maria Antonia Garcia.

GURULE, Jose Pedro
bap 12 Jul 1841, 5 days old; legit s/ Jose Pablo Gurule & Maria Ygnacia Perea; ap/ Salbador Gurule & Maria Manuela Garcia; am/ Miguel Perea & Juana Garcia; gp/ Juan Gurule & Gregoria Arias.

Frame 1949
ARMENTA, Jose Bentura (of Chilili)
bap 22 Jul 1841, 6 days old; legit s/ Jose Ygnes Armenta & Maria Bibiana Gallego; ap/ Matias Armenta
& Maria Francisca Martin; am/ Rafael Gallego & Barbara Gonsales; gp/ Salbador Tafoya & Juana Maria
Lusero.

NS, Maria Carlos
bap 25 Jul 1841, 4 years old; Navajo, d/ unknown parents; gp/ Tomas Candelario & Maria Dolores
Armijo.

Frames 1949-1950, #72
TAFOYA, Maria Apolinaria Antonia
bap 30 Jul 1841, 5 days old; legit d/ Tomas Tafoya & Soledad Montoya; ap/ Juan Ygnacio Tafoya &
Maria Antonia Baca; am/ Juan Reyes Montoya & Maria Gertrudes Moya; gp/ Juan Antonio Garcia &
Maria Gregoria Candelario.

MARTIN, Apolinario
bap 4 Aug 1841, 8 days old; legit s/ Jose Gregorio Martin & Maria Gertrudes Salasar; ap & am/ not
stated; gp/ Jose Manuel Martin & Rosalia Lusero.

GABALDON, Jose de las Niebes
bap 7 Aug 1841, 2 days old; s/ Miguel Gabaldon & Juana Lopes; ap/ Ygnacio Gabaldon & Micaela
Sanches; am/ Antonio Lopes & Micaela Jaramillo; gp/ Juan Andres Moya & Manuela Moya.

Frames 1950-1951
NARANJO, Maria Eligia
bap 8 Aug 1841, 3 days old; legit s/ Monico Naranjo & Guadalupe Barreras; ap & am/ not stated; gp/
Juan Antonio Candelaria & Maria Antonia Sena.

BACA, Juan Jose
bap 8 Aug 1841, 5 days old; s/ Sabino Baca & Maria Tomasa Lopes; ap & am/ not stated; gp/ Reyes
Belarde & Ana Maria Candelaria.

GARCIA, Manuel Antonio Alta Gracia
bap 10 Aug 1841, 5 days old; s/ Salbador Garcia & Reyes Lopes; ap & am/ not stated; gp/ Agustin Lobato
& Manuela Mestas.

Frame 1952, #73
CANDELARIA, Maria Trinidad
bap 15 Aug 1841, 8 days old; s/ Manuel Candelaria & Francisca Griego; ap & am/ not stated; gp/ Manuel
Antonio Pineda & Ana Maria Duran.

GONSALES, Teodocio de Jesus
bap 16 Aug 1841, 4 days old; s/ Antonio Gonsales & Maria Clara Garcia; ap/ Jose Antonio Gonsales &
Maria Barbara Candelaria; am/ Francisco Garcia & Maria Soledad Lopes; gp/ Pablo Sisneros & Francisca
Ruis.

ROMERO, Jose Nestor
bap 24 Aug 1841, 8 days old; s/ Domingo Romero & Petra Padilla; ap & am/ not stated; gp/ Manuel
Garcia & Rafaela Rael.

Baptisms – Albuquerque, New Mexico
1829–1850

Frame 1953
NS, Juana
bap 29 Aug 1841; Ute Indian, d/ unknown parents; gp/ Don Ambrocio (Armijo) & Doña Placida Armijo.

GONSALES, Jose Polonio
bap 2 Sep 1841, 9 days old; legit s/ Francisco Gonsales & Petra Gonsales; ap/ Antonio Gonsales & Maria Gertrudis Gurule; am/ Antonio Gonsales & Juana Sandoval; gp/ Agustin Padilla & Maria Dolores Gonsales, residents of Chilili.

BENABIDES, Rosa
bap 3 Sep 1841, 5 days old; legit d/ Juan Manuel Benabides & Juana Lopes; ap/ Manuel Benabides & Pascuala Gutierres; am/ Mateo Lopes & Manuela Padilla; gp/ Ramon Baca & Maria del Rosario Marques.

Frame 1954, #74
CHAVES, Jesus Maria
bap 3 Sep 1841, 8 days old; s/ Juan Chaves & Maria Yldefonsa Duran; ap/ Blas Chaves & Ana Maria Sanches; am/ Salbador Duran & Ana Maria Candelaria; gp/ Diego Luna & Maria Paubla Perea.

NOLAN, Antonio Venceslao
bap 4 Sep 1841, b. 8 Jul; legit s/ Gerbacio Nolan & Dolores Lalanda; ap/ Francisco Nolan & Angelica Curina; am/ Juan Bautista Lalanda & Apolonia Lusero, residents of Santa Fe; gp/ Don Antonio Sandoval & Doña Yrinea Nolan.

NS, Daniel
bap 4 Sep 1841; child, Ute Indian of Don Antonio Sandobal; gp/ Don Francisco Sarracino.

Frames 1954-1955
GUTIERRES, Gabriela
bap 5 Sep 1841, 9 days old; legit d/ Juan Pablo Gutierres & Josefa Martines; ap/ Miguel Gutierres & Gregoria Armijo; am/ Antonio Martines & Monica Jaramillo; gp/ Blas Lusero & Rosalia Tenorio.

GRIEGO, Vitoriano
bap 5 Sep 1841, 3 days old; s/ Ysabel Griego & unknown father; gp/ Felipe Torres & Bernardina Garcia.

SAMORA, Jose Regino
bap 9 Sep 1841, 7 days old; legit s/ Felipe Samora & Gertrudes Gallego; ap/ Francisco Samora & Ygnacia Valencia; am/ Antonio Jose Gallego & Maria Madalena Garcia; gp/ Francisco Ortega & Maria Ygnacia Basan.

Frames 1955-1956, #75
SANCHES, Maria Soledad del Rayo
bap 9 Sep 1841, 8 days old; legit d/ Francisco Sanches & Juana Martines; ap & am/ not stated; gp/ Matias Armijo & Soledad Armijo.

SANCHES, Gabriela
bap 9 Sep 1841, 3 days old; legit d/ Domingo Sanches & Perfecta Montoya; ap & am/ not stated; gp/ Manuel Candelario & Ana Maria Truxillo.

LOPES, Francisco Antonio
bap 10 Sep 1841, 5 days old; legit s/ Jose Lopes & Maria Rosalia Serna; ap & am/ not stated; gp/ Francisco Lusero & Ygnes Montoya.

NS, Maria Trenidad
bap 10 Sep 1841, 2 days old; d/ Maria Antonia NS, Indian, & unknown father; gp/ Paublin NS.

Frame 1957
BALDONADO, Antonio Jose
bap 14 Sep 1841, 7 days old; legit s/ Juan Antonio Baldonado & Tomasa Lopes; ap & am/ not stated; gp/ Salbador Armijo & Maria Placida Armijo.

SANCHES, Jose
bap 15 Sep 1841, 5 days old; s/ Michaela Sanches & unknown father; gp/ Salbador Romero & Francisca Chaves.

RAEL, Maria Decideria
bap 17 Sep 1841, 4 days old; legit d/ Juan Rael & Ana Maria Sandobal; ap & am/ not stated; gp/ Antonio Sandobal & Maria Decideria Candelario.

Frame 1958, #76
ANAYA, Maria Rosalia Alta Gracia
bap 23 Sep 1841, 3 days old; legit d/ Manuel Anaya & Felipa Martines; ap/ Felipe Anaya & Dolores Torres; am/ Pedro Martines & Juana Garcia; gp/ Francisco Candelario & Maria Ysabel Garcia.

BACHICHA, Maria Lina Alta Gracia
bap 27 Sep 1841, 7 days old; legit d/ Manuel Bachicha & Gregoria Lusero; ap & am/ not stated; gp/ Felipe Aragon & Rosalia Montaño.

SANCHES, Jose Mauricio
bap 29 Sep 1841, 8 days old; legit s/ Nasario Sanches & Candelaria Baca; ap/ Antonio Sanches & Rosalia Martin; am/ Juan Jose Baca & Gertrudes Castillo; gp/ Felis Sanches & Sebastiana Sena.

Frames 1958-1959
CORDOBA, Maria Francisca
bap 4 Oct 1841, 5 days old; legit d/ Juan Cordoba & Juana Griego; ap/ Jose Antonio Cordoba & Maria Quiteria Chaves; am/ Francisco Griego & Maria Antonia Montoya; gp/ Juan Montoya & Dolores Montoya.

GONZALES, Maria Juana
bap 4 Oct 1841, 7 days old; d/ Ramona Gonzales & unknown father; gp/ Pablo Griego & Maria Juana Montoya.

APODACA, Maria Gabriela
bap 8 Oct 1841, 3 days old; legit d/ Francisco Apodaca & Tomasa Barela; ap/ Jose Apodaca & Gertrudes Lusero; am/ Juan Barela & Josefa Chaves; gp/ Juan Apodaca & Ysabel Sanches.

GRIEGO, Maria Clara Guadalupe
bap 10 Oct 1841, 2 days old; legit d/ Rafael Griego & Barbara Apodaca; ap/ Rafael Griego & Ana Maria Lopes; am/ Jose Apodaca & Josefa Lucero; gp/ Don Gregorio Ortiz & Doña Maria Clara Saracino.

Frame 1960, #77
GARCIA, Antonio Jose de Jesus
bap 15 Oct 1841, 7 days old; legit s/ Juan Rafael Garcia & Encarnacion Lusero; ap/ Juan Rafael Garcia & Manuela Muñis; am/ Gregorio Lusero & Marta Lopes; gp/ Lionicio Lopes & Gertrudes Perea.

GARCIA, Jose Eduardo
bap 16 Oct 1841, 3 days old; legit s/ Diego Garcia & Serafina Candelario; ap/ Manuel Garcia; am/ Salbador Candelario & Rita Sanches; gp/ Don Francisco Ortega & Doña Ygnacia Basan.

LOPES, Julian Antonio
bap 16 Oct 1841, 5 days old; legit s/ Felipe Lopes & Juliana Torres; ap/ Juan Lopes & Rosa Jaramillo; am/ Pedro Torres & Guadalupe Garcia; gp/ Jose Ortega & Paubla Ortega.

Frames 1960-1961
CHAVES, Jose Dabid
bap 20 Oct 1841, 3 days old; legit s/ Diego Chaves & Maria Eluteria Garcia; ap/ Geronimo Chaves & Encarnacion Gonsales; am/ Antonio Garcia & Margarita Rael; gp/ Juan Miguel Garcia & Guadalupe Garcia.

GARCIA, Jose Eleno
bap 21 Oct 1841, 8 days old; legit s/ Juan Cristobal Garcia & Maria Rita Lopes; ap/ Martin Garcia & Ana Maria Apodaca; am/ Luis Lopes & Antonia Lusero; gp/ Juan Pablo Gutierres & Maria Josefa Martines.

SALASAR, Apolonia
bap 24 Oct 1841, 8 days old; legit d/ Juan Salasar & Juana Garcia; ap & am/ not stated; gp/ Blas Lusero & Rosalia Tenorio.

GARCIA, Jose Rafael
bap 24 Oct 1841, 3 days old; legit s/ Julian Garcia & Maria Gomes; ap & am/ not stated; gp/ Miguel Noanes & Ana Maria Perea.

Frame 1962, #78
GARCIA, Maria del Socorro
bap 29 Oct 1841, 4 days old; legit d/ Jose Rafael Garcia & Maria Dolores Chaves; ap & am/ not stated; gp/ Manuel Candelario & Juliana Candelario.

HERRERA, Jose Maria
bap 3 Nov 1841, 5 days old; legit s/ Juan Herrera & Barbara Jaramillo; ap/ Vicente Herrera & Maria Antonia Montaño; am/ Miguel Jaramillo & Gertrudes Griego; gp/ Jose Rosario Anaya & Teresa Candelario.

GARCIA, Jose de los Reyes
bap 4 Nov 1841, 7 days old; legit s/ Benito Garcia & Felipa Gallego; ap & am/ not stated; gp/ Juan Pacheco & Juliana Gutierres.

GONSALES, Ana Maria Bibiana
bap 5 Nov 1841; legit d/ Esteban Gonsales & Dolores Arias; ap & am/ not stated; gp/ Ramon Candelario & Ana Maria Truxillo.

Frame 1963
MOYA, Nemecia Beneranda
bap 6 Nov 1841, 3 days old; legit d/ Juan Andres Moya & Simona Sanches; ap & am/ not stated; gp/ Juan Sanches & Beneranda Sanches.

GRIEGO, Jose Carlos
bap 8 Nov 1841, 4 days old; legit s/ Geronimo Griego & Maria Albina Lusero; ap/ Miguel Griego & Gertrudes Olgin; am/ Juan Lusero & Maria Antonia Martines; gp/ Anastacio Lusero & Maria Reyes Lusero.

PEREA, Jose Santos
bap 9 Nov 1841, 5 days old; s/ Juana Perea & unknown father; gp/ Nestor Garcia & Ana Maria Garcia.

Frame 1964, #79
MAESTAS, Maria Rafaela Abelina Candelaria
bap 12 Nov 1841, 3 days old; legit d/ Mariano Maestas & Catarina Aragon; ap/ Pedro Maestas & Maria Antonia Duran; am/ Manuel Aragon & Mariana Sanches; gp/ Manuel Armijo & Ana Maria Gabaldon.

MARTIN, Maria Teodocia
bap 14 Nov 1841, 3 days old; legit d/ Juan Pablo Martin & Maria Cecilia Candelario; ap/ Jose Martin & Juana Griego; am/ Esteban Candelario & Maria Jesus Luna; gp/ Rafael Apodaca & Juana Maria Romero.

ARMIJO, Jose Eugenio
bap 17 Nov 1841, 3 days old; s/ Don Juan Cristobal Armijo & Doña Juana Chaves; ap/ Don Juan Armijo & Doña Rosalia Ortega; am/ Don Francisco Chaves & Doña Ana Maria Castillo; gp/ Don Juan Armijo & Doña Dolores Perea.

GARCIA, Maria Ysabel
bap 18 Nov 1841, 3 days old; legit d/ Ambrocio Garcia & Catarina Armijo; ap/ Martin Garcia & Anna Maria Apodaca; am/ Rafael Armijo & Soledad Peña; gp/ Francisco Armijo & Francisca Sisneros.

Frame 1965
BARRANCA, Jose Nicanor
bap 21 Nov 1841, 3 days old; legit s/ Felipe Barranca & Nicolasa Cordoba; ap & am/ not stated; gp/ Juan Jose Apodaca & Maria de la Lus Padilla.

BACA, Maximo
bap 28 Nov 1841, 12 days old; legit s/ Manuel Baca & Tomasa Apodaca; ap & am/ not stated; gp/ Ramon Candelaria & Ana Maria Truxillo.

GARCIA, Maria Guadalupe
bap 28 Nov 1841, 8 days old; legit d/ Juan Garcia & Juana Montaño; ap/ Juan Garcia & Juana Candelario; am/ Juan Jose Montaño & Francisca Gonsales; gp/ Juan Miguel Garcia & Guadalupe Montaño.

Frame 1966, #80
MARES, Jose Esteban
bap 28 Nov 1841, 8 days old; s/ Ramon Mares & Lus Jaramillo; ap/ Paublo Mares & Ana Maria Nuanes; am/ Ramon Jaramillo & Reyes Armijo; gp/ Leonardo Candelario & Francisca Gonsales.

MARTIN, Clemente
bap 28 Nov 1841, 8 days old; s/ Miguel Antonio Martin & Francisca Carabajal; ap/ Rafael Martin & Manuela Anaya; am/ Juan Pedro Carabajal & Gertudes Gonsales; gp/ Jose Garcia & Dolores Garcia.

GARCIA, Juan Nepomuceno
bap 29 Nov 1841, 8 days old; legit s/ Juan Garcia & Consepcion Anaya; ap & am/ not stated; gp/ Juan Candelario & Ana Maria Candelario.

ORTIZ, Genara
bap 5 Dec 1841, 3 days old; d/ Don Ysidro Ortiz & Doña Sinforiana Madrid; ap/ Don Francisco Ortiz & Doña Maria Garcia; am/ Don Dolores Madrid & Doña Crisanta Domingues; gp/ Don Fernando Ortiz & Doña Dolores Ortiz.

Frame 1967
LOBATO, Maria Dolores
bap 5 Dec 1841, 8 days old; legit d/ Agustin Lobato & Juliana Candelaria; ap & am/ not stated; legit gp/ Antonio Anaya & Maria Manuel(a) Anaya.

GURULE, Maria Bibiana
bap 8 Dec 1841, 8 days old; legit d/ Jose de la Cruz Gurule & Maria Juana Gutierres; ap & am/ not stated; gp/ Jose Santos Gonsales & Maria Guadalupe Otero.

GARCIA, Ambrocio
bap 9 Dec 1841, 8 days old; legit s/ Julian Garcia & Juana Aragon, ap/ Juan Jose Garcia & Francisca Bustos; am/ Jose Manuel Aragon & Teresa Candelario; gp/ Juan Rafael Garcia & Manuela Muñis.

Frames 1967-1968, #81
MORALES, Maria Andrea Dolores
bap 11 Dec 1841, 8 days old; d/ Jose Morales & Juana Romero; gp/ Manuel Jaramillo & Dolores Jaramillo.

NS, Maria Ysidora
bap 13 Dec 1841, 8 days old; d/ unknown parents; gp/ Jose Mansanares & Maria Estefana Jaramillo.

MARQUES, Jose
bap 14 Dec 1841, 8 days old; legit s/ Jose Marques & Francisca Torres; ap & am/ not stated; gp/ Ygnes Chaves & Serafina Apodaca.

CHAVES, Juana Rufina
bap 19 Dec 1841, 8 days old; legit d/ Rumaldo Chaves & Barbara Truxillo; ap/ Estanislado Chaves & Soledad Ortega; am/ Jose Truxillo & Soledad Balencia; gp/ Jose Armijo & Juana Armijo.

Frame 1969
APODACA, Maria Concepcion
bap 23 Dec 1841, 8 days old; legit d/ Francisco Apodaca & Nicolasa Gurule; ap/ Nicolas Apodaca & Lus Garcia; am/ Ygnacio Gurule & Apolonia Salazar; gp/ Jose Cleto Lusero & Maria Gabriela Candelario.

GRIEGO, Jose Emiterio
bap 23 Dec 1841, 8 days old; legit s/ Jose Tomas Griego & Monica Contreras; ap/ Miguel Griego & Petrona Candelario; am/ Jose Tomas Contreras & Paubla Chaves; gp/ Luciano Santillanes & Gertrudes Duran.

JARAMILLO, Maria Ysabel
bap 26 Dec 1841, 8 days old; legit d/ Salvador Jaramillo & Gertrudes Baca; ap/ Geronimo Jaramillo & Gertrudis Apodaca; am/ Jose Baca & Maria Antonia Garcia; gp/ Jose Maria Chaves & Maria Ysabel Apodaca.

Frame 1970, #82
GRIEGO, Juan Narciso
bap 26 Dec 1841, 8 days old; legit s/ Agustin Griego & Maria Josefa Gurule; ap & am/ not stated; gp/ Maria Barbara Cordoba.

LUSERO, Dolores Alta Gracia
bap 27 Dec 1841, 8 days old; d/ Rosalia Lusero & unknown father; gp/ Antonio Anaya & Tomasa Tafolla.

PADILLA, Maria Josefa
bap 28 Dec 1841, 8 days old; legit d/ Juan Jose Padilla & Barbara Gallego; ap & am/ not stated; gp/ Manuel Barela & Vicenta Gallego.

GALLEGO, Jose Lasaro
bap 29 Dec 1841; legit s/ Jesus Gallego & Maria Rosaria Garcia; ap & am/ not stated; gp/ Jose Garcia & Juana Maria Garcia.

Frame 1971
BACA, Maria Soledad
bap 30 Dec 1841, 8 days old; legit d/ Ramon Baca & Maria Marques; ap & am/ not stated; gp/ Manuel Apodaca & Barbara Molina.

GARCIA, Maria Guadalupe
bap 4 Jan 1842; d/ Juan Garcia & Maria Ygnes Apodaca; ap & am/ not stated; gp/ Monico Nagena & Guadalupe Barreras.

MARTINES, Maria Reyes Alta Gracia
bap 5 Jan 1842, 8 days old; d/ Maria Catalina Martines & unknown father; gp/ Manuel Garcia & Maria Barbara Martin.

Frame 1972, #83
MESTAS, Maria Manuela
bap 9 Jan 1842, 8 days old; legit d/ Ambrocio Mestas & Juliana Gonsales; ap & am/ not stated; gp/ Juan Garduño & Ana Maria Pais.

ROMERO, Miguel
bap 10 Jan 1842, 8 days old; legit s/ Francisco Romero & Marcelina Griego; ap & am/ not stated; gp/ Mariano Martin & Luduvina Martines.

GARCIA, Jose David
bap 10 Jan 1842, 8 days old; legit s/ Cleto Garcia & <u>Niculasa</u> Duran; ap/ Juan Garcia & Antonia Anaya,
am/ Manuel Duran & Manuela Muñis; gp/ Julian Garcia & Juana Lorenza Aragon.

MARTIN, Maria Miquela
bap 11 Jan 1842, 8 days old; legit d/ Antonio Martin & Manuela Candelaria; ap/ Manuel Martin & Luz
Griego; am/ Miguel Candelario & Rafaela Garcia; gp/ Jose Miguel Montaño & Barbara Garviso.

Frames 1972-1973
APODACA, Maria Rosario de los Dolores
bap 12 Jan 1842, 8 days old; legit d/ Gregorio Apodaca & Lugarda Duran; ap & am/ not stated; gp/ Jose
Dolores Lusero & Petra Lusero.

MOLLA, Maria del Rayo
bap 17 Jan 1842, 8 days old; d/ Dolores Molla & unknown father; gp/ Francisco Moya & Juana Lopes.

MARTIN, Antonio Jose
bap 19 Jan 1842, 8 days old; legit s/ Gregorio Martin & Gregoria Candelario; ap & am/ not stated; gp/
Juan Torres & Maria Dolores Gutierres.

ARMIJO, Jose David
bap 20 Jan 1842, 8 days old; legit s/ Teodoro Armijo & Paubla Jaramillo; ap/ Santiago Armijo & Maria
Petra Perea; am/ Miguel Antonio Jaramillo & Lorenza Lucero y Garcia; gp/ Vicente Maes & Petrona
Anaya.

Frames 1973-1974, #84
LOPES, Maria Alta Gracia
bap 21 Jan 1842, 8 days old; legit d/ Vicente Lopes & Rafaela Duran; ap/ Ramon Lopes & Reyes
Jaramillo; am/ Juan Rafael Duran & Josefa Apodaca; gp/ Juan Apodaca & Maria Ysabel Sanches.

LUSERO, Jose Maria
bap 26 Jan 1842, 8 days old; s/ Rita Lusero & unknown father; gp/ Lagos Gurule & Maria Encarnacion
Gurule.

MONTOLLA, Jose de la Paz Nolasco
bap 28 Jan 1842, 8 days old; legit s/ Jose Montolla & Loreta Arias; ap & am/ not stated; gp/ Jose
Guadalupe Chaves & Maria Leonarda Padilla.

RAEL, Tomasa
bap 28 Jan 1842, 8 days old; d/ Estefana Rael & unknown father; gp/ Anastacio Barela & Tomasa Garcia.

ORTEGA, Jesus Maria
bap 28 Jan 1842, 8 days old; s/ Paubla Ortega, Indian of Don Andres Ortega, & unknown father; gp/ Juan
de la Cruz Basan & Maria de la Luz Basan.

Frame 1975
GARCIA, Jose Ygnacio
bap 26 Jan 1842, 8 days old; legit s/ Antonio Feliz Garcia & Carmen Sanches; ap/ Feliz Garcia & Ysabel
Sandoval; am/ Antonio Sanches & Ana Maria Duran; gp/ Jose Ygnacio Candelario & Nieves Ortiz.

ORTEGA, Miguel Antonio
bap 29 Jan 1842, 8 days old; s/ Rosa Ortega & unknown father; gp/ Jose Maria Griego & Juana Gutieres.

GUTIERRES, Sinforiana de Jesus
bap 6 Jan 1842, 8 days old; d/ Maria Teresa Gutierres & unknown father; gp/ Paublo Sisneros & Maria Francisca Ruis.

CHAVES, Juan de Dios
bap 6 Jan 1842, 8 days old; legit s/ Jose Chaves & Lus Olona; ap/ Estanisla Chaves & Soledad Ortega; am/ Miguel Olona & Barbara Sanches; gp/ Pedro Aranda & Rosalia Jaramillo.

Frame 1976, #85
NS, Jose Telesforo
bap 7 Jan 1842, 8 days old; s/ Rita NS, Indian of Don Antonio Sandoval; gp/ Antonio Maria Lusero & Filomena Lusero.

HERRERA, Juana
bap 8 Jan 1842, 6 days old; legit d/ Jose Herrera & Maria de la Luz Sandoval; ap/ Jose Andres Herrera & Dolores Garcia; am/ Miguel Sandoval & Manuela Gonsales; gp/ Ambrocio Garcia & Maria Luduvina Sandoval.

NS, Apolonia Alta Gracia
bap 9 Feb 1842, 6 days old; d/ unknown parents; gp/ Juan Gutierres & Maria Gregoria Armijo.

NS, Manuel
bap 9 Feb 1842, 3 days old; s/ unknown parents; gp/ Jose Dolores Samora & Soledad Garcia.

AASF, Reel #2
B-9 (Box 7a) 1842-1846

Frame 1978, #1
PACHECO, Maria Juana
bap 13 Feb 1842, 8 days old; d/ Dolores Pacheco & unknown father; gp/ Juan Sedillo & Juana Carabajal.

CANDELARIO, Maria Dolores
bap 13 Feb 1842, 8 days old; legit d/ Rafael Candelario & Antonia Garcia; ap/ Antonio Candelario & Maria Anaya; am/ Feliz Garcia & Ysabel Lopes; gp/ Manuel Montoya & Dolores Garcia.

LUSERO, Juan Cristobal
bap 15 Feb 1842, 8 days old; legit s/ Francisco Lusero & Vicenta Martin; ap & am/ not stated; gp/ Juan Montoya & Juana Maria Lusero.

HERRERA, Placida
bap 15 Feb 1842; legit d/ Manuel Herrera & Benina Chaves; ap/ Vicente Herrera & Maria Antonia Montaño; am/ Antonio Chaves & Manuela Garcia; gp/ Blas Chaves & Paubla Chaves.

Frame 1979
BARELA, Jose Desiderio Romulo
bap 16 Feb 1842, 8 days old; legit s/ Jesus Barela & Maria Antonia Lovato; ap/ Juan Andres Barela & Barbara Gallego; am/ Juan Nerio Lobato & Maria Dolores Sedillo; gp/ Antonio Jaramillo & Simona Bernal, of Ysleta.

CHAVES, Maria Faustina
bap 16 Feb 1842, 8 days old; legit d/ Francisco Chaves & Juana Rubin; ap/ Antonio Chaves & Petra Chaves; am/ Manuel Rubin & Juana Gutierres; gp/ Jose Antonio Chaves & Petra Chaves.

GUTIERRES, Deciderio
bap 16 Feb 1842, 8 days old; legit s/ Juan Gutierres & Josefa Anaya; ap & am/ not stated; gp/ Salvador Herrera & Maria Ygnacia Chaves.

CORDOVA, Jose Eliseo
bap 17 Feb 1842, 8 days old; s/ Juana Cordova & unknown father; gp/ Santiago Alari & Juana Garcia.

Frames 1979-1980, #2
SISNEROS, Juana Maria Altagracia
bap 17 Feb 1842, 8 days old; legit d/ Paublo Sisneros & Francisca Ruis; ap/ Francisco Sisneros & Juana Maria Candelaria; am/ Antonio Ruis & Ysabel Armijo; gp/ Jose Ramon Mares & Maria de la Lus Jaramillo.

NS, Maria Apolonia
bap 17 Feb 1842, 8 days old; d/ unknown parents; gp/ Jose Ambrocio Martin & Maria Apolonia Martin.

SEDILLO, Josefa
bap 17 Feb 1842, 8 days old; legit d/ Blas Sedillo & Dolores Candelario; ap/ Tomas Sedillo & Tomasa Garcia; am/ Juan Ysidoro Candelario & Gertrudes Jaramillo; gp/ Pedro Lopes & Guadalupe Candelario.

CHAVES, Polidoro Romulo
bap 20 Feb 1842, 8 days old; legit s/ Jose Maria Chaves & Maria Ysabel Apodaca; ap/ Jose Chaves & Catalina Baldonado; am/ Francisco Apodaca & Tomasa Barela; gp/ Manuel Apodaca & Maria Getrudes Apodaca.

LOPES, Jose Deciderio
bap 22 Feb 1842, 8 days old; s/ Jose Angel Lopes & Ana Maria Marques; ap/ Manuel Lopes & Encarnacion Duran; am/ Diego Marques & Ana Maria Belarde; gp/ Jose Armijo & Maria Guadalupe Chaves.

SANCHES, Donaciano
bap 23 Feb 1842, 8 days old; legit s/ Juan Sanches & Guadalupe Chaves; ap & am/ not stated; gp/ Jose Tenorio & Ana Maria Tenorio.

Frame 1981
LUSERO, Maria Carlota
bap 23 Feb 1842, 8 days old; legit d/ Blas Lusero & Rosalia Tenorio; ap/ Andres Lusero & Tomasa Garcia; am/ Julian Tenorio & Benina Chaves; gp/ Tomas Martines & Maria Antonia Tenorio.

SABEDRA, Paubla
bap 24 Feb 1842, 6 days old; legit d/ Francisco Sabedra & Dolores Garcia; ap/ Juan Cristobal Sabedra & Paubla Duran; am/ Jose Antonio Garcia & Ygnacia Candelario; gp/ Pedro Lopes & Guadalupe Candelario.

LUSERO, Faustino
bap 26 Feb 1842, 8 days old; legit s/ Ygnacio Lusero & Dolores Montoya; ap & am/ not stated; gp/ Juan Padilla & Dolores Ortega.

LOVATO, Antonio Jose
bap 27 Feb 1842, 8 days old; legit s/ Jose Lovato & Manuela Rael; ap/ Juan Lovato & Maria Casados; am/ Antonio Rael & Francisca Padilla; gp/ Juan Jose Sanches & Rita Luna.

BACA, Maria Manuela
bap 27 Feb 1842, 8 days old; legit d/ Simon Baca & Lorenza Candelario; ap & am/ not stated; gp/ Luis Madrid & Maria Manuela Gallego.

Frame 1982, #3
SABEDRA, Maria de la Luz de los Dolores
bap 1 Mar 1842, 8 days old; d/ Lucas Sabedra & Luisa Duran; ap & am/ not stated; gp/ Jose Dolores Lusero & Petra Lusero.

TORRES, Nestor
bap 2 Mar 1842, 6 days old; s/ Francisco Torres & Juliana Montaño; ap & am/ not stated; gp/ Miguel Garcia & Juana Maria Garcia.

RUBI, Jose
bap 2 Mar 1842, 8 days old; legit s/ Rafael Rubi & Encarnacion Anaya; ap & am/ not stated; gp/ Tomas Pacheco & Maria Jaramillo.

MARTIN, Nestor
bap 3 Mar 1842, 8 days old; legit s/ Jose Antonio Martin & Quiteria Griego; ap/ Jose Martin & Maria Antonia Gallego; am/ Miguel Griego & Getrudis Olgin; gp/ Juan Domingo Valencia & Paubla Martines.

Frames 1982-1983
RAEL, Maria Nestora
bap 7 Mar 1842, 8 days old; legit d/ Cristobal Rael & Gregoria Lopes; ap/ Juan Rael & Maria Gurule; am/ Jose Miguel Lopes & Maria Manuela Sanches; gp/ Dolores Lopes & Paubla Lopes.

PADILLA, Maria Paubla Emateria
bap 7 Mar 1842, 8 days old; legit d/ Gregoria Padilla & unknown father; gp/ Jose Lucas Mora & Maria Luiza Gonsales.

ARIAS, Pedro Jose
bap 7 Mar 1842, 8 days old; legit s/ Atanacio Arias & Francisca Jaramillo; ap/ Paublo Arias & Encarnacion Balencia; am/ Julian Jaramillo & Ysabel Gurule; gp/ Pedro Jose Lusero & Maria Rufina Lusero.

SANCHES, Manuel Antonio
bap 7 Mar 1842, 8 days old; legit s/ Juan Sanches & Juana Martines; ap & am/ not stated; gp/ Manuel Antonio Peña & Soledad Lopes.

BACA, Antonio Teresa de Jesus
bap 7 Mar 1842, 8 days old; legit s/ Antonio Baca & Maria Manuela Lusero; ap & am/ not stated; gp/ Jose Anaya & Antonia Teresa de Jesus Candelario.

Frame 1984, #4
CHAVES, Tomasa
bap 10 Mar 1842, 8 days old; legit d/ Salvador Chaves & Josefa Belarde; ap/ Domingo Chaves & Manuela Aguirre; am/ Juan Cruz Belarde & Juana Sanches; gp/ Antonio Jaramillo & Simona Bernal.

NS, Maria de los Angeles
bap 10 Mar 1842, 8 days old; d/ unknown parents; gp/ Juan Montolla & Ana Maria Sanches.

ORTEGA, Maria Nestora
bap 11 Mar 1842; d/ Rosalia Ortega, Indian of Don Andres Ortega & unknown father; gp/ Salbador Tenorio & Maria Gregoria Garcia.

LOVATO, Maria de Jesus
bap 14 Mar 1842, 8 days old; legit d/ Juan Felipe Lovato & Manuela Maestas; ap/ Juan Lovato & Ana Maria Casados; am/ Ygnacio Maestas & Guadalupe Duran; gp/ Bentura Apodaca & Maria Dolores Torres.

GARCIA, Salbador Eulogio
bap 17 Mar 1842, 3 days old; legit s/ Francisco Garcia & Juliana Rael; ap/ Simon Garcia & Josefa Padilla; am/ Juan Rael & Maria Gurule; gp/ Salbador Martin & Clara Gutierres.

Frames 1984-1985
NS, Placida de los Dolores
bap 18 Mar 1842, 5 days old; in the home of Juan Nuanes, d/ unknown parents; gp/ Juan Nuanes & Dolores Gonsales.

SERNA, Jose
bap 18 Mar 1842, 8 days old; legit s/ Antonio Maria Serna & Cruz Sanches; ap & am/ not stated; gp/ Manuel Garcia & Juana Maria Chaves.

APODACA, Juana Maria
bap 19 Mar 1842, 8 days old; legit d/ Juan Apodaca & Lus Padilla; ap/ Rafael Apodaca & Juana Maria Romero; am/ Julian Padilla & Ana Maria Padilla; gp/ Felis Sanches & Sebastiana Sena.

SANCHES, Jose Dolores
bap 20 Mar 1842, 8 days old; legit s/ Jose Sanches & Paubla Garcia; ap & am/ not stated; gp/ Anastacio Barela & Rafaela Garcia.

GALLEGO, Maria Quiteria
bap 20 Mar 1842, 8 days old; legit d/ Jose Anastacio Gallego & Maria Soledad Candelario; ap/ Juan Gallego & Maria Antonia Gurule; am/ Jose Francisco Candelario & Lorenza Padilla; gp/ Antonio Gallego & Maria Petra Padilla.

Frame 1986, #5
APODACA, Jose Benito
bap 21 Mar 1842, 8 days old; legit s/ Lionicio Apodaca & Crus Torres; ap & am/ not stated; gp/ Felipe Mora & Reyes Torres.

LOPES, Juan Nepomuceno Otabiano (twin)
LOPES, Jose Paublo (twin)
bap 24 Mar 1842; legit twin s/ Jose Cleto Lopes & Dolores Candelario; ap & am/ not stated; first gp/ Amador Candelario & Maria Armijo; second gp/ Juan Cristobal Garcia & Juana Mestas.

SANCHES, Jose Mariano Ruperto
bap 27 Mar 1842, 8 days old; legit s/ Antonio Sanches & Madalena Griego; ap/ Antonio Jose Sanches & Sebastiana Ortega; am/ Miguel Griego & Gertrudis Olgin; gp/ Mariano Ysisarre & Juana Otero.

GALLEGO, Jose de Jesus
bap 27 Mar 1842, 8 days old; legit s/ Bacilio Gallego & Clara Peña; ap/ Antonio Gallego & Madalena Garcia; am/ Agustin Peña & Dolores Chaves; gp/ Juan Domingo Balencia & Paubla Martines.

GONSALES, Jose Antonio
bap 27 Mar 1842, 8 days old; legit s/ Jose Agaton Gonsales & Ynes Sanches; ap/ Francisco Gonsales & Antonia Garviso; am/ Antonio Sanches & Mariana Griego; gp/ Jose Antonio Martin & Quiteria Griego.

Frame 1987
MONTAÑO, Maria Josefa
bap 27 Mar 1842, 8 days old; legit d/ Jose Montaño & Guadalupe Garcia; ap/ Jose Montaño & Miquela Santillas; am/ Julian Garcia & Barbara Serna; gp/ Juan Antonio Garcia & Paubla Garcia.

SANIS, Jose Dolores Ruperto
bap 27 Mar 1842, 6 days old; legit s/ Jose Sanis & Martina Truxillo; ap/ Salbador Sanis & Juana Aragona; am/ Mariano Truxillo & Luisa Cordoba; gp/ Julian Sanches & Juana Candelario.

JARAMILLO, Clara
bap 27 Mar 1842, 8 days old; legit d/ Leonardo Jaramillo & Petra Sanches; ap/ Miguel Jaramillo & Gertrudes Candelario; am/ Juan Andres Sanches & Josefa Martines; gp/ Juan Herrera & Barbara Jaramillo.

ARANDA, Jose
bap 2 Apr 1842, 8 days old; legit s/ Francisco Aranda & Bentura Montaño; ap/ Antonio Aranda & Teresa Garcia; am/ Torivio Montaño & Ana Maria Candelario; gp/ Ramon Gallego & Rosalia Montaño.

ARIAS, Maria Jesus
bap 2 Apr 1842, 8 days old; legit d/ Juan Cristobal Arias & Tomasa Martines; ap/ Paublo Arias & Encarnacion Balencia; am/ Baltasar Martines & Maria Antonia Griego; gp/ Jose Antonio Montaño & Maria Antonia Griego.

Frame 1988, #6
LUSERO, Maria Juana
bap 3 Apr 1842, 8 days old; legit d/ Francisco Lusero & Manuela Aragon; ap/ Juan Lusero & Gertrudes Pino; am/ Tadeo Aragon & Maria Luisa Balencia; gp/ Jose Miguel Santillanes & Maria Josefa Martines.

MARTIN, Nestora
bap 3 Apr 1842, 8 days old; legit d/ Jose Martin & Rosalia Lusero; ap & am/ not stated; gp/ Paublo Gallego & Rosalia Jinso.

GRIEGO, Teodoro
bap 3 Apr 1842, 8 days old; legit s/ Simon Griego & Ana Maria Perea; ap & am/ not stated; gp/ Anastacio Barela & Rafaela Garcia.

MONTOYA, Estaquio Nicanor
bap 3 Apr 1842, 8 days old; legit s/ Juan Montoya & Clara Jaramillo; ap/ Bartolo Montoya & Ysidora Garcia; am/ Ramon Jaramillo & Reyes Armijo; gp/ Juan Antonio Rael & Soledad Miera.

NS, Jose Antonio
bap 4 Apr 1842, 8 days old; s/ unknown parents; gp/ Josefa Baca.

Frame 1989
TRUXILLO, Maria Francisca
bap 5 Apr 1842, 8 days old; legit d/ Paublo Truxillo & Lus Gallego; ap/ Juan Antonio Truxillo & Juana Montoya; am/ Jose Miguel Gallego & Dolores Martin; gp/ Manuel Candelario & Ana Maria Truxillo.

PADILLA, Jose Antonio
bap 9 Apr 1842, 8 days old; legit s/ Juan Padilla & Rosalia Chaves; ap/ Paublo Padilla & Felipa Garcia; am/ Agustin Chaves & Juana Sanches; gp/ Jose Antonio Montoya & Juana Maria Chaves.

SAMORA, Vicente
bap 10 Apr 1842, 8 days old; legit s/ Pablo Samora & Pascuala Baca; gp/ Pedro Aranda & Rosalia Jaramillo.

SANCHES, Jose de Jesus Perfidio
bap 10 Apr 1842, 8 days old; legit s/ Manuel Sanches & Maria Antonia Jaramillo; ap/ Antonio Sanches & Rosalia Martin; am/ Francisco Jaramillo & Guadalupe Duran; gp/ Pedro Antonio Perea & Sebastiana Sena.

SABEDRA, Ambrocio
bap 12 Apr 1842, 6 days old; s/ Guadalupe Sabedra & unknown father; gp/ Jose Armijo & Placida Armijo.

GUTIERRES, Ambrocio
bap 12 Apr 1842, 8 days old; legit s/ Juan Gutierres & Manuela Lopes; ap/ Miguel Gutierres & Simona Griego; am/ Tomas Lopes & Ygnacia Garcia; gp/ Torivio Montaño & Marselena Baca.

Frame 1990, #7
SANCHES, Maria Leonor
bap 12 Apr 1842, 6 days old; legit d/ Francisco Sanches & Manuela Sanches; ap/ Grabiel Sanches & Juana Sedillo; am/ Ramos Sanches & Juana Barbara Montoya; gp/ Jose Armijo & Maria Guadalupe Chaves.

SEDILLO, Maria Apolonia
bap 12 Apr 1842, 8 days old; legit d/ Pedro Sedillo & Petra Gutierres; ap/ Paublo Sedillo & Madalegna Candelario; am/ Paublo Gutierres & Concecion Lopes; gp/ Salbador Lopes & Ygnacia Lopes.

CANDELARIO, Beneranda Refugio
bap 13 Apr 1842, 8 days old; legit d/ Juan Candelario & Augustina Garcia; ap & am/ not stated; gp/ Juan Ysidoro Griego & Juana Garcia.

GRIEGO, Antonio Maria (twin)
GRIEGO, Feliciana (twin)
bap 13 Apr 1842, 8 days old; legit twin ch/ Juan Antonio Griego & Candelaria Luna; ap/ Felipe Griego & Margarita Gonsales; am/ Ysidro Luna & Manuela Candelaria; first gp/ Martin Gallego & Guadalupe Garcia; second gp/ Deciderio Garcia & Nepumusena Candelario.

ROMERO, Jose Francisco
bap 13 Apr 1842, 8 days old; legit s/ Lino Romero & Josefa Garcia; ap/ Luis Romero & Juana Aragon; am/ Antonio Garcia & Francisca Gonsales; gp/ Francisco Armijo & Josefa Aragon.

Frame 1991
MOYA, Jose Leon
bap 13 Apr 1842, 8 days old; legit s/ Juan Francisco Moya & Paubla Anaya; ap & am/ not stated; gp/ Francisco Armijo & Soledad Armijo.

NS, Jesus Jose
bap 14 Apr 1842, 3 days old; s/ unknown parents; gp/ Francisco Antonio Romero & Quiteria Moya.

SANCHES, Jose Alexo
bap 15 Apr 1842, 8 days old; legit s/ Manuel Sanches & Guadalupe Jaramillo; ap & am/ not stated; gp/ Jose Alexo Garcia & Maria Garcia.

GARCIA, Jose Maria Hermenegildo
bap 15 Apr 1842, 8 days old; legit s/ Juan Garcia & Ysabel Garcia; ap & am/ not stated; gp/ Jose Armijo & Juana Armijo.

SANDOVAL, Juan Maria
bap 10 Apr 1842, 8 days old; legit s/ Encarnacion Sandoval & Rosalia Baldonado; ap & am/ not stated; gp/ Ramon Gonsales & Ana Maria Sandoval.

Frame 1992, #8
ANAYA, Jose Anastacio
bap 17 Apr 1842, 8 days old; legit s/ Juan Anaya & Dolores Sanches; ap & am/ not stated; gp/ Jose Niebes Lusero & Maria Eulogia Sabedra.

BALENCIA, Maria Placida
bap 17 Apr 1842, 8 days old; legit d/ Bernardo Balencia & Ana Maria Aragon; ap/ Juan Domingo Balencia & Paubla Martin; am/ Juan Tomas Aragon & Getrudes Samora; gp/ Lorenso Montaño & Juana Montaño.

SANDOBAL, Victoriano
bap 17 Apr 1842, 8 days old; legit s/ Jose Sandobal & Juana Carrillo; ap/ Juan Francisco Sandobal & Juana Aragon; am/ Miguel Antonio Carrillo & Catalina Gonsales; gp/ Paublo Lusero & Ygnes Lopes.

CORDOBA, Maria Leonor
bap 18 Apr 1842, 8 days old; legit d/ Domingo Cordoba & Consepcion Aragon; ap/ Diego Cordoba & Juliana Santillanes; am/ Eusebio Aragon & Miquela Garcia; gp/ Francisco Rael & Gregoria Romero.

CANDELARIA, Jose Rafael
bap 22 Apr 1842, 8 days old; legit s/ Jesus Maria Candelaria & Ysabel Chaves; ap & am/ not stated; gp/ Manuel Garcia & Rafaela Rael.

Frame 1993
RAEL, Antonio
bap 22 Apr 1842, 6 days old; legit s/ Jose Rael & Decideria Ortiz; ap/ Antonio Rael & Francisca Padilla; am/ Matias Ortiz & Dolores Chaves; gp/ Francisco Rael & Gregoria Romero.

LUSERO, Maria Soledad
bap 22 Apr 1842, 8 days old; legit d/ Jesus Lusero & Maria Ysabel Aragon; ap & am/ not stated; gp/ Jose Antonio Padilla & Maria Monica Apodaca.

GARCIA, Manuel Gregorio Bisente
bap 22 Apr 1842, 6 days old; legit s/ Manuel Garcia & Ylaria Lusero; ap & am/ not stated; gp/ Juan Felipe Mestas & Maria Marcelina Gavaldon.

GURULE, Marcos
bap 24 Apr 1842, 7 days old; legit s/ Juan Gurule & Manuela Lopes; ap & am/ not stated; gp/ Juan Montoya & Maria Dolores Montoya.

MARTIN, Maria Placida de Jesus
bap 24 Apr 1842, 7 days old; legit d/ Jose Martin & Dolores Lusero; ap & am/ not stated; gp/ Nicolas Gurule & Maria Acina Martines.

GARCIA, Maria Placida Alta Gracia
bap 24 Apr 1842, 7 days old; legit d/ Francisco Garcia & Petra Lopes; ap/ Jose Antonio Garcia & Ygnacia Candelario; am/ Francisco Lopes & Rosalia Duran; gp/ Feliz Garcia & Maria Ysabel Lopes.

Frame 1994, #9
DURAN, Maria Aniceta
bap 25 Apr 1842, 5 days old; legit d/ Antonio Duran & Tomasa Gutierres; ap/ Mateo Duran & Antonia Muñis; am/ Francisco Gutierres & Manuela Bernala; gp/ Pedro Gutierres & Concepcion Gutierres.

SALAZAR, Nepumuceno
bap 25 Apr 1842, 5 days old; legit s/ Luis Salazar & Juliana Garcia; ap/ Christobal Salazar & Miquela Gonsales; am/ Andres Garcia & Juana Torres; gp/ Ramon Garcia & Maria Paubla Salasar.

NS, Maria Eulogia
bap 16 Apr 1842, 8 days old; d/ unknown parents; gp/ Juan Sais & Ygnes Sais.

GUTIERRES, Maria Aniseta
bap 16 Apr 1842, 8 days old; d/ Petrona Gutierres & unknown father; gp/ Jose Dolores Samora & Soledad Garcia.

APODACA, Maria Toribia
bap 27 Apr 1842, 3 days old; legit d/ Jesus Apodaca & Dolores Lopes; ap & am/ not stated; gp/ Jose Baca & Josefa Sabedra.

Frame 1995
GALLEGO, Jose Aniceto
bap 30 Apr 1842, 8 days old; legit s/ Ramon Gallego & Rosalia Montaño; ap/ Antonio Jose Gallego & Maria Madalena Garcia; am/ Toribio Montaño & (blank space); gp/ Pedro Aranda & Rosalia Jaramillo.

GUTIERRES, Vidal Balerio
bap 30 Apr 1842, 8 days old; legit s/ Juan Gutierres & Francisca Anaya; ap & am/ not stated; gp/ Paublo Armijo & Dolores Garcia.

LOPES, Juana Nepomucena
bap 1 May 1842, 8 days old; legit d/ Jose Lopes & Sipriana Anaya; ap & am/ not stated; gp/ Juan Nepomuseno Ortega & Maria Luisa Ortega.

OLGIN, Maria Rosalia
bap 1 May 1842, 8 days old; legit d/ Geronimo Olgin & Vitoria Gavaldon; ap & am/ not stated; gp/ Cristoval Apodaca & Ysabel Garcia.

GARCIA, Pedro
bap 1 May 1842, 8 days old; legit s/ Antonio Garcia & Gregoria Candelario; ap/ Juan Garcia & Ysabel Romero; am/ Ygnacio Candelario & Concepcion Chaves; gp/ Vicente Luna & Bibiana Chaves.

Frame 1996, #10
PEÑA, Jose Anastacio
bap 1 May 1842, 8 days old; legit s/ Antonio Peña & Juana Arias; ap & am/ not stated; gp/ Julian Sanches & Juana Candelaria.

NS, Pedro
bap 1 May 1842, 8 days old; s/ unknown parents; gp/ Miguel Lopes & Rosalia Garcia.

MORA, Jose Antonio
bap 2 May 1842, 7 days old; legit s/ Esteban Mora & Juana Maria Griego; ap/ Ysidro Mora & Juana Marquez; am/ Francisco Griego & Antonia Serna; gp/ Jose Angel & Paubla Garcia.

LUJAN, Jose Amador
bap 6 May 1842, 8 days old; legit s/ Juan Antonio Lujan & Maria Fabiana Sandoval; ap & am/ not stated; gp/ Ygnacio Truxillo & Juana Rita Lujan.

JARAMILLO, Jose Crus Leon
bap 7 May 1842, 6 days old; legit s/ Juan Jose Jaramillo & Trinidad Otero; ap & am/ not stated; gp/ Diego Antonio Lovato & Maria Matilde Duran.

Frame 1997
GRIEGO, Juan Bautista
bap 8 May 1842, 8 days old; legit s/ Juan Griego & Isabel (blank space); ap & am/ not stated; gp/ Yldefonso Sanis & Juana Garcia.

NS, Jose Maria
bap 9 May 1842, 6 days old; legit s/ Candelaria NS & unknown father; gp/ Juan Antonio Baldonado & Maria Tomasa Gonsales.

GURULE, Maximo
bap 11 May 1842, 8 days old; legit s/ Juan Antonio Gurule & Guadalupe Padilla; ap & am/ not stated; gp/ Dolores Gallego & Manuela Gurule.

ABEYTA, Jose Bernardino
bap 13 May 1842, 7 days old; legit s/ Feliz Abeyta & Maria Juliana Atencio; ap & am/ not stated; gp/ Jose Miguel Mares & Maria Antonia Candelario.

CORDOVA, Maria Edubigen
bap 13 May 1842, 8 days old; legit d/ Ramon Cordova & Maria Juana Rael; ap & am/ not stated; gp/ Feliz Cordova & Rosa Garcia.

Frame 1997-1998, #11
GARCIA, Jesus Maria (twin)
GARCIA, Ana Maria Dominga Trinidad (twin)
bap 13 May 1842, 8 days old; legit ch/ Antonio Maria Garcia & Juana Montaño; ap/ Feliz Garcia & Ysabel Lopes; am/ Salvador Montaño & Gregoria Chaves; first gp/ Juan Garcia & Francisca Garcia; second gp/ Juan Apodaca & Maria Ysabel Sanches.

HERRERA, Maria Dimas (of Seboyeta)
bap 18 May 1842, 8 days old; legit d/ Gregorio Herrera & Paubla Peralta; ap & am/ not stated; gp/ Antonio Jose Lusero & Maria Gertrudes Chaves.

LUSERO, Maria Leonor (of Seboyeta)
bap 18 May 1842, 8 days old; legit d/ Antonio Jose Lusero & Gertrudes Chaves; ap/ Andres Lusero & Gertrudes Chaves; am/ Miguel Chaves & Josefa Peralta; gp/ Blas Lucero & Rosalia Tenorio.

CHAVES, Jose Francisco Ruperto (of Seboyeta)
bap 18 May 1842, 8 days old; legit s/ Francisco Chaves & Andrea Sanches; ap/ Antonio Chaves & Magdalena Salaises; am/ Ramon Sanches & Juana Barbara Montoya; gp/ Francisco Sanches & Maria Manuela Sanches.

MARTIN, Dolores
bap 21 May 1842, 6 days old; legit s/ Francisco Martin & Encarnacion Garcia; ap & am/ not stated; gp/ Ubaldo Garcia & Ana Maria Montoya.

Frame 1999
TAFOLLA, Jose Trinidad
bap 22 May 1842, 8 days old; legit s/ Domingo Tafolla & Ana Martin; ap/ Ygnacio Tafolla & Manuela Baca; am/ Jose Martin & Luciana Lusero; gp/ Juan Gonsales & Luz Rael.

LUSERO, Maria Decideria
bap 23 May 1842, 8 days old; legit d/ Juan Andres Lusero & Francisca Salazar; ap & am/ not stated; gp/ Jose Gonsales & Juliana Gutierres.

NUANES, Jose Deciderio
bap 23 May 1842, 8 days old; legit s/ Santiago Nuanes & Manuela Atencio; ap & am/ not stated; gp/ Juan Nuanes & Dolores Gonsales.

NS, Maria Urbana
bap 29 May 1842, 8 days old; d/ unknown parents; gp/ Francisco Lusero & Ygnes Montoya.

BUGANDA, Maria Juana Nepomucena
bap 30 May 1842, 6 days old; legit d/ Miguel Buganda & Maria Simona Lucero; ap & am/ not stated; gp/ Maria Aragona.

GARCIA, Estanislado
bap 30 May 1842, 6 days old; legit s/ Rumaldo Garcia & Ana Maria Arias; ap & am/ not stated; gp/ Jose Mansanares & Maria Estefana Jaramillo.

Frame 2000, #12
GRIEGO, Felicitas
bap 30 May 1842, 7 days old; d/ Jose Griego & Manuela Martin; ap & am/ not stated; gp/ Julian Tenorio & Venina Chaves.

PEREA, Maria Dorotea
bap 5 Jun 1842, 7 days old; legit d/ Antonio Perea & Candelaria Garcia; ap & am/ not stated; gp/ Antonio Garcia & Juana Sanis.

OTERO, Trinidad (of Chilili)
bap 6 Jun 1842, 8 days old; legit s/ Juan Otero & Maria Rosalia Jaramillo; ap & am/ not stated; gp/ Agustin Padilla & Clara Padilla.

NS, Antonio Jose
bap 12 Jun 1842, 8 days old; legit s/ unknown parents; gp/ Polinario Perea & Ysidora Perea.

GRIEGO, Maria Antonia
bap 15 Jun 1842, 7 days old; legit d/ Pedro Griego & Ana Maria Salasar; ap & am/ not stated; gp/ Jose Miguel Montaño & Maria Barbara Garbiso.

Frames 2000-2001
ORTEGA, Maria Josefa Juliana
bap 24 Jun 1842, 8 days old; legit d/ Don Juan Christobal Ortega & Doña Maria de la Lus Basan; ap/ Don Juan Andres Ortega & Doña Juana Andrea Garcia; am/ Don Ygnacio Basan & Doña Antonia Gutierres; gp/ Don Andres Ortega & Doña Ygnacia Basan.

NS, Salbador
bap 26 Jun 1842, 3 days old; s/ unknown parents; gp/ Paublo Armijo & Gertrudes Lusero.

GUTIERRES, Maria Filomina Maximiana
bap 26 Jun 1842, 8 days old; legit d/ Mariano Gutierres & Juana Ginnsa; ap & am/ not stated; gp/ Francisco Candelario & Maria Ysabel Garcia.

Baptisms – Albuquerque, New Mexico
1829–1850

PAIS, Juan Bautista
bap 27 Jun 1842, 8 days old; legit s/ Andres Pais & Albina Gurule; ap & am/ not stated; gp/ Domingo Sanches & Maria de la Luz Perea.

GARCIA, Ygnacia
bap 2 Jul 1842, 8 days old; legit d/ Ylario Garcia & Martina Griego, ap/ Francisco Garcia & Reyes Candelario; am/ Jose Griego & Gertrudes Garcia; gp/ Rumaldo Chaves & Barbara Truxillo.

Frames 2001-2002, #13
ORTEGA, Maria Alta Gracia
bap 3 Jul 1842; legit d/ Jose Maria Ortega & Juana Duran; ap & am/ not stated; gp/ Jose Miguel Lusero & Petra Muñis.

MONTOYA, Maria Estanislada Josefa
bap 4 Jul 1842, 8 days old; legit d/ Vicente Montoya & Josefa Martines; ap & am/ not stated; gp/ Marcos Sanches Vergara & Josefa Sanches Vergara.

SANCHEZ, Luis Jose
bap 4 Jul 1842, 8 days old; legit s/ Domingo Sanchez & Quiteria Gonzales; gp/ Sabino Gonzales & Barbara Castillo.

HERRERA, Jose Rafael Tranquilo
bap 16 Jul 1842, 8 days old; legit s/ Felipe Herrera & Juana Garcia; ap/ Vicente Herrera & Maria Antonia Montaño; am/ Francisco Garcia & Guadalupe Otero; gp/ Salbador Sanches & Olaya Tafolla.

GARCIA, Ana Maria
bap 25 Jul 1842, 8 days old; legit d/ Salbador Garcia & Juana Romero; ap/ Jose Antonio Garcia & Soledad Sandobal; am/ Santiago Romero & Dolores Candelario; gp/ Jose Dolores Sandoval & Gregoria Romero.

Frames 2002-2003
PACHECO, Maria Antonia
bap 25 Jul 1842, 8 days old; legit d/ Juan Pacheco & Juliana Gallego; ap & am/ not stated; gp/ Paublo Gonsales & Maria Getrudes Aragon.

CANDELARIO, Maria Josefa
bap 29 Jul 1842; legit d/ Ramon Candelario & Maria Perfecta Garcia; gp/ Antonio Arias & Maria Gurule.

GARCIA, Maria Marta
bap 29 Jul 1842, 8 days old; legit d/ Gregorio Garcia & Francisca Sanches; ap & am/ not stated; gp/ Simon Griego & Ana Maria Baca.

ALFAROS, Ana Maria
bap 29 Jul 1842, 8 days old; legit d/ Guadalupe Alfaros & Paubla Garcia; ap/ Miguel Alfaros & Juana Mata; am/ Manuel Garcia & Manuela Perea; gp/ Jose Luis Garcia & Maria Manuela Perea.

NS, Jose de Jesus Maria
bap 2 Aug 1842, 8 days old; s/ unknown parents; gp/ Jesus Apodaca & Dolores Torres.

SUARES, Mariano
bap 2 Aug 1842, 8 days old; legit s/ Pedro Suares & Petra Carabajal; ap & am/ not stated; gp/ Mariano Armijo & Grabiela Jaramillo.

Frame 2004, #14
NS, Jesus Maria de los Dolores
bap 3 Aug 1842, 8 days old; s/ unknown parents; gp/ Francisco Mata & Francisca Lopes.

PEÑA, Maria Petra
bap 7 Aug 1842; legit d/ Ramon Peña & Rosalia Ginso; ap/ Jose Antonio Peña & Barbara Montaño; am/ Jose Paublito Ginso & Getrudes Gurule; gp/ Juan Ysidoro Griego & Bentura Lusero.

MONTOLLA, Ygnacia Romana
bap 14 Aug 1842, 8 days old; legit d/ Juan Bautista Montolla & Juana Rafaela Aragon; ap/ Juan Montolla & Maria Rosa Balencia; am/ Juan Andres Aragon & Maria Manuela Brito; gp/ Antonio Aban Aragon & Maria Gracia Vigil.

GARCIA, Maria Clara Polita
bap 14 Aug 1842, 8 days old; legit d/ Ambrocio Garcia & Delubina Sandobal; ap/ Feliz Garcia & Ysabel Lopes; am/ Miguel Sandoval & Manuela Gonsales; gp/ Salbador Sanches & Olalla Tafolla.

MOLINA, Maria Polita Casiana
bap 15 Aug 1842, 8 days old; legit d/ Pedro Molina & Maria Manuela Sanches; ap/ Miguel Molina & Gertrudes Gutierres; am/ Manuel Sanches & Simona Anaya; gp/ Jose Luera & Getrudes Apodaca.

NUANES, Maria Concepcion
bap 15 Aug 1842, 8 days old; unknown parents; gp/ Miguel Nuanes & Carmen Gomes.

Frame 2005
SABEDRA, Teodocio
bap 18 Aug 1842, 8 days old; legit s/ Miguel Sabedra & Nestora Montolla; ap/ Francisco Sabedra & Maria Chaves; am/ Antonio Montoya & Florentina Ortiz; gp/ Jose Nestor Montoya & Florentina Ortiz.

GURULE, Juan Esteban
bap 19 Aug 1842, 8 days old; legit s/ Marselo Gurule & Maria Petra Gutierres; ap & am/ not stated; gp/ Diego Antonio Garcia & Maria Paubla Salazar.

GUTIERRES, Jose Nestor
bap 22 Aug 1842, 8 days old; legit s/ Paublo Gutierres & Petra Muñis; ap/ Ysidro Gutierres & Dolores Griego; am/ Francisco Muñis & Justa Romero; gp/ Mariano Chaves & Monica Romero.

TAPIA, Maria Elena (twin)
TAPIA, Maria Sinforiana (twin)
bap 22 Aug 1842, 8 days old; legit d/ Manuel Tapia & Maria Antonia Armenta; ap/ Ygnacio Tapia & Juana Montaño; am/ Jose Maria Armenta & Ygnacia Martin; first gp/ Diego Romero & Nepomusena Muñis; second gp/ Pedro Lusero & Encarnacion Anaya.

Frame 2006, #15
MONTOYA, Maria Nieves (of Sandia)
bap 23 Aug 1842, 8 days old; legit d/ Tomas Montoya & Juana Gutierres; ap/ Jose Miguel Montoya & Caterina Lusero; am/ Manuel Gutierres & Trinidad Gonsales; gp/ Paublo Lusero & Luisa Flores.

CANDELARIA, Maria de la Lus
bap 26 Aug 1842, 8 days old; legit d/ Julian Candelaria & Juana Maria Garcia; ap & am/ not stated; gp/ Diego Antonio Garcia & Geralda Perea.

MORALES, Luis
bap 29 Aug 1842, 8 days old; legit s/ Jose Antonio Morales & Juana Romero; ap & am/ not stated; gp/ Juan Garcia & Maria Concepcion Anaya.

ARMIJO, Maria Seferina
bap 29 Aug 1842, 8 days old; legit d/ Francisco Armijo & Josefa Aragon; ap/ Santiago Armijo & Maria Petra Perea; am/ Fernando Aragon & Encarnacion Valdes; gp/ Francisco Aragon & Francisca Aragon.

NS, Maria Sesaria
bap 29 Aug 1842, 8 days old; d/ unknown parents; gp/ Bartolo Apodaca & Soledad Telles.

MORA, Felipe Leonicio
bap 30 Aug 1842, 8 days old; legit s/ Felipe Mora & Reyes Torres; ap & am/ not stated; gp/ Felipe Torres & Bernardina Garcia.

Frame 2007
NS, Maria Rafaela
bap 30 Aug 1842, 8 days old; d/ unknown parents; gp/ Mariano Apodaca & Rafaela Apodaca.

SUARES, Ana Maria Dolores
bap 30 Aug 1842, 8 days old; legit d/ Mateo Suares & Guadalupe Griego; ap & am/ not stated; gp/ Rumaldo Griego & Francisca Apodaca.

NS, Maria Josefa
bap 31 Aug 1842, 8 days old; Ute Indian, in the house of house of Juan Domingo Valencia; gp/ Diego Antonio Samora & Ygnacia Valencia.

NS, Maria Bartola
bap 2 Sep 1842, 8 days old; d/ unknown parents; gp/ Paublo Sisneros & Francisca Ruis.

SANDOVAL, Juana Maria
bap 3 Sep 1842, 8 days old; legit d/ Jose Sandoval & Antonia Rael; ap/ Miguel Sandoval & Manuela Gurule; am/ Antonio Rael & Francisca Padilla; gp/ Salbador Garcia & Gregoria Romero.

MUÑIS, Maria Rita
bap 9 Sep 1842, 8 days old; legit d/ Francisco Muñis & Teodora Sanis; ap/ Jose Maria Muñis & Barbara Samora; am/ Miguel Sanis & Gregoria Martin; gp/ Ylario Gonsales & Maria Rita Rael.

Frame 2008, #16
LUSERO, Nicolas Tolentino
bap 13 Sep 1842, 8 days old; legit s/ Jose Nieves Lusero & Maria Eulogia Savedra; ap/ Andres Lusero & Tomasa Garcia; am/ Francisco Sabedra & Maria de la Luz Chaves; gp/ Antonio Sabedra & Nestora Montoya.

TENORIO, Jose Tranquilino
bap 14 Sep 1842, 8 days old; legit s/ Jose Maria Tenorio & Ramona Sisneros; ap/ Manuel Tenorio & Antonia Anaya; am/ Antonio Sisneros & Manuela Romero; gp/ Maria de los Angeles Ortega.

NS, Maria Soledad
bap 18 Sep 1842, 8 days old; Ute Indian, in the house of Don Rosalio Mestas; gp/ Marcos Ruis & Balbina Candelario.

SALAZAR, Maria Agustina
bap 20 Sep 1842, 8 days old; legit d/ Manuel Salazar & Francisca Truxillo; ap & am/ not stated; gp/ Vicente Gallego & Ana Maria Jaramillo.

NS, Juan Gil Abad (of Atrisco)
bap 24 Sep 1842, 8 days old; legit s/ Manuela NS, Indian in the house of Luciano Sedillo; gp/ Jose Maria Telles & Monica Chaves.

Frame 2009
NS, Maria Juana
bap 26 Sep 1842, 8 days old; Ute Indian, in the house of Agustin Padilla; gp/ Agustin Padilla & Dolores Gonsales.

SAMORA, Encarnacion
bap 29 Sep 1847, 8 days old; legit d/ Ramon Samora & Gregoria Candelario; ap/ Miguel Samora & Marcelina Gallego; am/ Jose Candelario & Francisca Gonsales; gp/ Dolores Garcia & Ygnacia Samora.

ARMIJO, Ana Maria
bap 30 Sep 1842, 8 days old; legit d/ Pedro Armijo & Luz Garcia; ap & am/ not stated; gp/ Juan Garcia & Juana Maria Mestas.

BAROS, Juan Nepomuseno
bap 2 Oct 1842, 8 days old; legit s/ Ramon Baros & Bibiana Montoya; ap/ Juan Antonio Baros & Ana Maria Nieto; am/ Juan Montoya & Ygnes Garcia; gp/ Esteban Gutierres & Maria Quiteria Montolla.

NUANES, Jose Manuel
bap 3 Oct 1842, 8 days old; legit s/ Antonio Nuanes & Maria Candelaria Griego; ap/ Jose Manuel Nuanes & Maria Paubla Duran; am/ Jose Maria Griego & Maria Guadalupe Mora; gp/ Juan Calletano Garcia & Maria Juana Andrea Nuanes. [Note: "26 Aug" entered in the right margin by "8 days old."]

Frames 2009-2010, #17
MARES, Juan Paublo de Jesus
bap 5 Oct 1842, 8 days old; legit s/ Nicolas Mares & Manuela Garcia; ap & am/ not stated; gp/ Luis Mares & Teresa Garcia.

NS, Jose Urigido
bap 9 Oct 1842, 8 days old; s/ unknown parents; gp/ Agustin Sisneros.

MORA, Maria del Pilar
bap 13 Oct 1842, 8 days old; legit d/ Jose Mora & Maria Sanis; ap/ Juan Esteban Mora & Maria Luisa Gutierres; am/ Miguel Sanis & Gregoria Martin; gp/ Mariano Martin & Maria Ygnacia Salasar.

NUANES, Maria Carlos
bap 16 Oct 1842, 8 days old; legit d/ Miguel Nuanes & Dolores Griego; ap/ Jose Manuel Griego & Paubla Candelario; am/ Juan Griego & Carmen Gomes; gp/ Toribio Nuanes & Clofia Armijo.

ARAGON, Lorenzo
bap 16 Oct 1842, 8 days old; legit s/ Aban Aragon & Maria Rodrigues; ap & am/ not stated; gp/ Jose Antonio Garcia & Rosalia Jaramillo.

GUTIERRES, Jose Leonicio
bap 16 Oct 1842, 8 days old; legit s/ Ygnacio Gutierres & Ana Maria Valencia; gp/ Juana Candelario.

Frame 2011
NS, Tomasa
bap 16 Oct 1842, 8 days old; d/ unknown parents; gp/ Antonio Duran & Maria Gregoria Sanches.

LUSERO, Jose Florentino
bap 16 Oct 1842, 7 days old; legit s/ Ygnacio Lusero & Josefa Lopes; ap/ Gregorio Lusero & Marta Lopes; am/ Francisco Lopes & Rosalia Duran; gp/ Gregorio Lusero & Josefa Lusero.

APODACA, Jose Paublo
bap 16 Oct 1842, 5 days old; legit s/ Julian Apodaca & Antonia Griego; ap/ Jose Apodaca & Magdalena Perea; am/ Miguel Griego & Petrona Candelario; gp/ Salbador Candelario & Getrudes Lopes.

TAFOLLA, Manuel Antonio
bap 18 Oct 1842, 6 days old; legit s/ Jose Antonio Tafolla & Petra Garcia; ap/ Jose Antonio Tafolla & Maria Guadalupe Duran; am/ Juan Rafael Garcia & Maria Manuela Duran; gp/ Nicolas Mares & Manuela Garcia.

CANDELARIO, Jose Pedro
bap 19 Oct 1842, 8 days old; legit s/ Rumaldo Candelario & Josefa Garcia; ap & am/ not stated; gp/ Diego Antonio Garcia & Geralda Garcia.

SABEDRA, Maria Tomasa
bap 19 Oct 1842, 8 days old; legit d/ Juan Sabedra & Ysabel Lopes; ap & am/ not stated; gp/ Juan Apodaca & Getrudes Apodaca.

Frame 2012, #18
LOPES, Clara
bap 22 Oct 1842, 7 days old; legit d/ Francisco Lopes & Guadalupe Perea; ap/ Bernardo Lopes & Reyes Lujan; am/ Jose Miguel Perea & Manuela Sanches; gp/ Don Gregorio Ortis & Francisca Sanches.

NS, Mariano
bap 24 Oct 1842, 8 days old; s/ unknown parents; gp/ Paublo Gutierres & Maria Petra Muñis.

MONTAÑO, Jose Antonio
bap 24 Oct 1842, 8 days old; legit s/ Toribio Montaño & Marcelina Baca; ap & am/ not stated; gp/ Benito Torres & Trinidad Gutierres.

NS, Rafaela
bap 25 Oct 1842, 8 days old; d/ unknown parents; gp/ Fernando Gutierres & Rafaela Rael.

GRIEGO, Maria Simona de Jesus
bap 29 Oct 1842, 8 days old; legit d/ Deciderio Griego & Guadalupe Candelario; ap & am/ not stated; gp/ Gregorio Griego & Francisca Candelario.

Frame 2013
NS, Maria Florentina
bap 8 Nov 1842, 8 days old; d/ unknown parents; gp/ Manuel Tenorio & Ana Teresa Gallego.

NS, Jose
bap 9 Nov 1842, 8 days old; s/ unknown parents; gp/ Miguel Antonio Candelario & Barbara Apodaca.

GRIEGO, Teodocio
bap 10 Nov 1842, 7 days old; d/ Juan Ysidoro Griego & Dolores Lusero; ap & am/ not stated; gp/ Juan Montoya & Juana Lusero.

GURULE, Jose Domingo
bap 13 Nov 1842, 6 days old; legit s/ Manuel Gurule & Maria Getrudes Perea; ap/ Domingo Gurule & Maria Gonsales; am/ Antonio Perea & Maria Juliana Chaves; gp/ Juan Cristoval Gurule & Ana Maria Gurule.

NS, Maria Manuela
bap 13 Nov 1842, 8 days old; d/ unknown parents; gp/ Paublo Gallego & Rosalia Gallego.

NS, Maria Paubla
bap 13 Nov 1842; gp/ Juan Gutierres & Gregoria Armijo.

Frame 2014, #19
NS, Juan Ramon
bap 13 Nov 1842, 8 days old; s/ unknown parents; gp/ Manuela Moya.

TRUXILLO, Jose Teodoro
bap 20 Nov 1842, 8 days old; legit s/ Jose Truxillo & Maria Petra Aragon; ap & am/ not stated; gp/ Jose Dolores Nieto & Maria Getrudes Garcia.

GONSALES, Salbador Antonio Trinidad
bap 20 Nov 1842, 7 days old; legit s/ Ylario Gonsales & Maria Rita Rael; ap/ Felipe Gonsales & Maria de la Luz Gurule; am/ Antonio Rael & Francisca Padilla; gp/ Cecilio Montoya & Ana Maria Duran.

NS, Maria Trinidad
bap 20 Nov 1842; child in the household of Jose Antonio Garcia; gp/ Jose Antonio Garcia.

SAMORA, Maria Cicilia
bap 28 Nov 1842, 6 days old; legit d/ Cristoval Samora & Ana Maria Martin; ap/ Juan Samora & Juliana Montaño; am/ Felipe Martin & Francisca Martin; gp/ Bentura Montaño & Antonio Jose Aranda.

GARCIA, Jose David
bap 28 Nov 1842, 8 days old; legit s/ Cleto Garcia & Niculasa Duran; ap/ Juan Garcia & Antonia Anaya, am/ Manuel Duran & Manuela Muñis; gp/ Jose Leonardo Candelario & Francisca Gonsales.

Frame 2015
TRUXILLO, Jose Teodoro
bap 28 Nov 1842, 8 days old; legit s/ Jose Truxillo & Maria Petra Garcia; ap & am/ not stated; gp/ Jose Dolores Nieto & Maria Getrudes Gracia.

CANDELARIO, Juan Facundo
bap 28 Nov 1842, 8 days old; legit s/ Agustin Candelario & Dolores Sanches; ap/ Manuel Candelario & Gregoria Chaves; am/ Felipe Sanches & Getrudes Anaya; gp/ Jesus Maria Baca & Maria Lugarda Baca.

SANCHES, Maria Juana
bap 28 Nov 1842, 7 days old; legit d/ Dolores Sanches & Juana Candelario; ap/ Manuel Sanches & Ana Maria Lopes; am/ Paublo Candelario & Andrea Montoya; gp/ Jose Paublo Candelario & Apolonia Candelario.

NS, Maria Ramona Dolores
bap 28 Nov 1842, 8 days old; d/ unknown parents; gp/ Tomasa Moya.

MAES, Maria Soledad
bap 28 Nov 1842, 8 days old; legit d/ Vicente Maes & Petrona Griego; ap & am/ not stated; gp/ Francisco Moya & Paubla Anaya.

Frames 2015-2016, #20
OLGUIN, Jose Ysabel
bap 28 Nov 1842, 8 days old; legit s/ Miguel Olguin & Maria Luisa Montoya; ap/ Juaquin Olguin & Maria Micaela Belasques; am/ Ramon Montoya & Antonia Armijo; gp/ Juaquin Olguin & Maria Micaela Belasques.

NS, Jose Nestor
bap 28 Nov 1842, 8 days old; s/ unknown parents; gp/ Paublo Sisneros & Francisca Ruis.

CANDELARIO, Jose
bap 1 Dec 1842, 8 days old; legit s/ Manuel Candelario & Ana Maria Truxillo; ap/ Esteban Candelario & Maria de Jesus Pina; am/ Jose Truxillo & Soledad Balencia; gp/ Estevan Candelario & Maria de Jesus Luna.

BARELA, Juan Esteban
bap 1 Dec 1842, 6 days old; legit s/ Paublo Barela & Paubla Garcia; ap/ Santiago Barela & Juana Aranda; am/ Juan Antonio Garcia & Gregoria Candelario; gp/ Deciderio Garcia & Nepomucena Candelario.

LUSERO, Maria Benigna
bap 1 Dec 1842, 6 days old; legit d/ Juan Antonio Lusero & Dolores Sanches; ap & am/ not stated; gp/ Manuel Herrera & Benigna Chaves.

NS, Andrea de la Trinidad
bap 1 Dec 1842, 8 days old; d/ unknown parents; gp/ Gregorio Chaves & Ysidra Chaves.

Frame 2017
MONTOYA, Maria Dolores
bap 5 Dec 1842, 8 days old; legit d/ Manuel Montoya & Rosa Santillanes; ap & am/ not stated; gp/ Salvador Sandobal & Juana Truxillo.

TORRES, Juan Andres
bap 11 Dec 1842, 8 days old; legit s/ Felipe Torres & Bernardina Garcia; ap & am/ not stated; gp/ Jose Angel Sanches & Paubla Garcia.

LOPES, Maria del Carmen
bap 11 Dec 1842, 5 days old; legit d/ Manuel Lopes & Manuela Ginso; ap/ Bernardo Lopes & Reyes Lujan; am/ Santiago Ginso & Manuela Anaya; gp/ Juan Apodaca & Ysabel Sanches.

TRUXILLO, Maria Guadalupe
bap 18 Dec 1842, 8 days old; legit d/ Santiago Truxillo & Maria Gutierres; ap/ Jose Truxillo & Maria Soledad Balencia; am/ Miguel Gutierres & Maria Gregoria Armijo; gp/ Jose Truxillo & Maria Gregoria Truxillo.

GARCIA, Jose Lacio
bap 11 Dec 1842, 8 days old; legit s/ Dolores Garcia & Maria Ygnacia Samora; ap/ Ysidro Garcia & Getrudes Sanches; am/ Miguel Samora & Marcelina Gallego; gp/ Juan Samora & Manuela Martin.

PEREA, Juan Pedro
bap 18 Dec 1842, 8 days old; legit s/ Antonio Perea & Maria Juliana Chaves; gp/ Jose Miguel Chaves & Maria Decideria Gurule.

Frame 2018, #25
GARCIA, Felipe de Jesus
bap 12 Feb 1843, 6 days old; legit s/ Miguel Garcia & Rosalia Barela; ap/ Luis Garcia & Tomasa Olguin; am/ Santiago Barela & Juana Aranda; gp/ Francisco Aranda & Bentura Montoya.

NS, Jose Mariano
bap 12 Feb 1843, 8 days old; s/ unknown parents; gp/ Salbador Martin & Soledad Telles.

APODACA, Antonio Apolonio de Jesus
bap 12 Feb 1843, 8 days old; legit s/ Gregorio Apodaca & Lugarda Duran; ap/ Ramon Apodaca & Rafaela Lopes; am/ Rafael Duran & Rosa Gurule; gp/ Antonio Santillanes & Paubla Contreras.

PADILLA, Juan de los Reyes
bap 12 Feb 1843, 7 days old; legit s/ Jose Padilla & Simona Apodaca; ap & am/ not stated; gp/ Diego Gurule & Maria Teresa Gutierres.

RAEL, Maria Serafina Erinea
bap 22 Feb 1843, 8 days old; legit d/ Santiago Rael & Serafina Martin; ap/ Eusebio Rael & Rosa Montoya; am/ Bernardo Martin & Candelaria Chaves; gp/ Juan Gonsales & Lus Rael.

Frames 2018-2019
BACA, Jesus Jose
bap 26 Feb 1843, 7 days old; legit s/ Domingo Baca & Dolores Rael; ap & am/ not stated; gp/ Manuel Carabajal & Barbara Carabajal.

CHAVES, Jose Justo
bap 26 Mar 1843, 8 days old; legit s/ Jose Antonio Chaves & Dolores Candelario; ap & am/ not stated; gp/ Jose Candelario & Maria Antonia Garcia.

MARQUES, Afermin de Jesus Maria y Jose
bap 26 Mar 1843, 8 days old; legit s/ Jose Marques & Francisca Torres; ap & am/ not stated; gp/ Juan Garcia & Candelaria Gonsales.

GARCIA, Antonio Jose Nestor
bap 26 Mar 1843, 8 days old; legit s/ Jose Deciderio Garcia & Maria Nepomucena Candelario; ap/ Juan Garcia & Maria Ysabel Romero; am/ Ygnacio Candelario & Maria Concepcion Chaves, gp/ Jose Cleto Lusero & Maria Grabiela Candelario.

LOPES, Juana
bap 26 Mar 1843, 5 days old; d/ Dolores Lopes; gp/ Francisco Lopes & Trinidad Ruis.

NS, Juan
bap 28 Mar 1843, 8 days old; s/ unknown parents; gp/ Pedro Antonio Montoya.

Frame 2020, #24
LOPES, Placida
bap 29 Mar 1843, 8 days old; legit d/ Pedro Lopes & Maria Guadalupe Candelario; ap/ Francisco Lopes & Rosalia Duran; am/ Francisco Antonio Candelario & Lorenza Padilla; gp/ Salbador Armijo & Placida Armijo.

VARELA, Mariano Epifanio
bap 9 Apr 1843, 6 days old; legit s/ Anastacio Varela & Rafaela Garcia; ap/ Santiago Varela & Juana Aranda; am/ Tadeo Garcia & Jacinta Perea; gp/ Don Mariano Yrisarra & Doña Juana Otero.

NS, Manuela Antonia
bap 9 Apr 1843, 8 days old; d/ unknown parents; gp/ Diego Antonio Chaves & Concepcion Apodaca.

SANCHES, Teresa de Jesus
bap 10 Apr 1843, 5 days old; legit d/ Salvador Sanches & Olaya Tafolla; ap/ Bartolo Sanches & Rafaela Lopes; am/ Juan Ygnacio Tafolla & Antonia Baca; gp/ Manuel Garcia & Rafaela Rael.

MONTAÑO, Jose Manuel
bap 13 Apr 1843, 7 days old; legit s/ Jose Antonio Montaño & Maria Josefa Lusero; ap & am/ not stated; gp/ Jose Cleto Lusero & Maria Grabiela Candelario.

Frames 2020-2021
PEREA, Maria Juana
bap 15 Apr 1843, 7 days old; legit d/ Francisco Perea & Paubla Sandoval; ap/ Rafael Perea & Carmen Romero; am/ Jose Sandobal & Petrona Sabedra; gp/ Jose Perea & Francisca Perea.

Baptisms – Albuquerque, New Mexico
1829–1850

CARRILLO, Maria Dolores
bap _ Apr 1843, 8 days old; legit d/ Salbador Carrillo & Juana Griego; ap & am/ not stated; gp/ Felipe Torres & Teodora Torres. [Note: baptism day cut off at the margin.]

CANDELARIO, Maria Vicenta (of Atrisco)
bap 16 Apr 1843, 6 days old; legit d/ Salbador Candelario & Maria de Jesus Padilla; ap/ Juan Candelario & Jesusa Chaves; am/ Diego Antonio Padilla & Manuela Aguirre; gp/ Pedro Lopes & Guadalupe Padilla.

PADILLA, Ana Maria Nestora
bap 17 Apr 1843, 6 days old; legit d/ Manuel Padilla & Maria Ysidora Arias; ap/ Julian Padilla & Ana Maria Padilla; am/ Juan Cristobal Arias & Tomasa Martin; gp/ Juan Jose Apodaca & Maria de la Lus Padilla.

GOMES, Jose Toribio
bap 18 Apr 1843, 8 days old; legit s/ Juan Gomes & Juliana Gonsales; ap/ Antonio Gomes & Ygnacia Arias; am/ Juan Gonsales & Vitoria Garcia; gp/ Miguel Nuanes & Dolores Griego.

LOPES, Jose Aristeo
bap 19 Apr 1843, 8 days old; legit s/ Calletano Lopes & Juliana Jaramillo; ap & am/ not stated; gp/ Francisco Armijo & Rosalia Armijo.

Frames 2021-2022, #25
MOYA, Juan Nepomuceno
bap 26 Apr 1843, 8 days old; legit s/ Cristoval Moya & Maria Rufina Gallego; ap/ Grabiel Moya & Maria Antonia Urtado; am/ Rafael Gallego & Barbara Gonsales; gp/ Juan Maria Montoya & Juana Maria Moya.

BARELA, Filomena
bap 26 Apr 1843, 6 days old; legit d/ Manuel Barela & Vicenta Gallego; ap/ Santiago Barela & Juana Aranda; am/ Juan Galle(go) & Manuela Gurule; gp/ Miguel Garcia & Juana Nepomusena Garcia.

SANDOVAL, Jose Justo
bap 29 Apr 1843, 8 days old; s/ Tomas Sandoval & Gertrudes Armijo; ap & am/ not stated; gp/ Juan Andres Moya & Simona Sanches.

ARMIJO, Petra Aniseta
bap 30 Apr 1843, 8 days old; legit d/ Juan Cristoval Armijo & Juana Chaves; ap/ Juan Armijo & Rosalia Ortega; am/ Francisco Chaves & Ana Maria Castillo; gp/ Nicolas Armijo & Josefa Armijo.

SANDOVAL, Maria Bernardina Leonor
bap 2 May 1843, 8 days old; legit d/ Antonio Sandoval & Maria Decideria Candelario; ap/ Miguel Sandoval & Manuela Gonsales; am/ Esteban Candelario & Maria Jesus Luna; gp/ Ramon Candelario & Maria Jesus Luna.

MARTINES, Maria Petra
bap 3 May 1843, 7 days old; d/ Maria Francisca Martines & unknown father; gp/ Francisco Lusero & Ygnes Montoya.

Baptisms – Albuquerque, New Mexico
1829–1850

Frame 2023
SANCHES, Guadalupe Beneranda
bap 14 May 1843, 6 days old; legit d/ Catarina Sanches & unknown father; gp/ Don Diego Ortiz & Francisca Sanches.

BACA, Juana Catarina
bap 14 May 1843, 7 days old; legit d/ Juan Baca & Rafaela Cordova; ap/ Simon Baca & Ysavel Apodaca; am/ Nicolas Cordova & Ygnacia Duran; gp/ Jose Ygnacio Candelario & Maria Luisa Garcia.

GRIEGO, Juan
bap 14 May 1843, 7 days old; legit s/ Francisco Roman Griego & Soledad Sanches; ap/ Miguel Griego & Josefa Apodaca; am/ Ygnacio Sanches & Maria Manuela Anaya; gp/ Alejo Garcia & Maria Garcia.

GALLEGO, Jose Atanacio
bap 14 May 1843, 8 days old; legit s/ Francisco Gallego & Tomasa Candelario; ap & am/ not stated; gp/ Nicolas Mares & Maria Manuela Garcia.

CARABAJAL, Cristobal Maximo
bap 14 May 1843, 4 days old; legit s/ Juan Pedro Carabajal & Getrudes Gonsales; ap & am/ not stated; gp/ Manuel Antonio Candelario & Maria Manuela Serna.

BALENCIA, Juana de los Reyes
bap 14 May 1843, 7 days old; legit d/ Juan Balencia & Guadalupe Candelario; ap & am/ not stated; gp/ Juan Gutierres & Maria Juana Gutierres.

Frames 2023-2024, #26
CANDELARIO, Catalina de Jesus
bap 14 May 1843, 7 days old; d/ Juliana Candelario & unknown father; gp/ Paublo Sisneros & Francisca Ruis.

CHAVES, Marcos
bap 14 May 1843, 10 days old; legit s/ Miguel Chaves & Maria Decideria Gurule; ap & am/ not stated; gp/ Salvador Gurule & Ana Maria Gonsales.

PACHECO, Maria Nestora
bap 24 May 1843, 8 days old; legit d/ Francisco Pacheco & Manuela Truxillo; ap/ Francisco Pacheco & Marta Sandoval; am/ Antonio Jose Truxillo & Juliana Lusero; gp/ Santiago Padilla & Maria Francisca Padilla.

GONSALES, Jose Dolores
bap 25 May 1843, 7 days old; legit s/ Francisco Gonsales & Petra Gonsales; ap/ Antonio Gonsales & Getrudes Gurule; am/ Antonio Gonsales & Juana Sandoval; gp/ Jose Cicilio Montoya & Maria Ramona Montoya.

SANIS, Maria Ysidora
bap 25 May 1843, 7 days old; legit d/ Ramon Sanis & Margarita Pacheco; ap/ Salvador Sanis & Juana Maria Aragon; am/ Francisco Pacheco & Marta Sandoval; gp/ Jesus Maria Truxillo & Maria Lorensa Lusero.

CARABAJAL, Maria Josefa
bap 28 May 1843, 5 days old; legit d/ Hermenegildo Carabajal & Margarita Duran; ap & am/ not stated; gp/ Pedro Contreras & Maria Josefa Contreras.

Frame 2025
GONSALES, Maria Susana Bonifacia
bap 28 May 1843, 8 days old; legit d/ Sabino Gonsales & Encarnacion Valencia; ap/ Juan Gonsales & Barbara Castillo; am/ Juan Domingo Valencia & Maria Ygnacia Salasar, gp/ Juan Domingo Valencia & Paubla Martines.

ROMERO, Jose de Jesus
bap 28 May 1843, 6 days old; legit d/ Jose Manuel Romero & Marcelina Armijo; ap & am/ not stated; gp/ Pedro Molina & Manuela Anaya.

GURULE, Maria Manuela
bap 28 May 1843, 7 days old; legit d/ Santiago Gurule & Maria Rita Candelario; gp/ Jose Ramon Ginso & Maria Getrudes Gurule.

NUANES, Maria Trenidad
bap 28 May 1843, 7 days old; legit d/ Andres Nuanes & Estefana Candelario; ap & am/ not stated; gp/ Juan Cristoval Garcia & Susana Maria Mestas.

NS, Juan Ygnacio
bap 28 May 1843, 8 days old; s/ unknown parents; gp/ Maria Clara Armijo.

NS, Maria Trenidad
bap 28 May 1843, 5 days old; d/ unknown parents; gp/ Maria Ana Sarracino.

Frame 2026, #27
MONTAÑO, Pedro Antonio
bap 1 Jun 1843, 8 days old; legit s/ Lorenzo Montaño & Maria Petra Candelario; ap/ Jose Antonio Montaño & Manuela Antonia Martin; am/ Vicente Candelario & Ana Maria Chaves; gp/ Pedro Antonio Candelario & Maria Clara Candelario.

PEREA, Salbador
bap 8 Jun 1843, 8 days old; legit s/ Manuel Perea & Gregoria Duran; ap/ Francisco Perea & Luciana Martin; am/ Salbador Duran & Balbaneda Garcia; gp/ Vicente Luna & Bibiana Chaves.

GONSALES, Maria de la Lus
bap 10 Jun 1843, days old; legit d/ Santos Gonsales & Guadalupe Otero; ap/ Miguel Gonsales & Lus Garcia; am/ Julian Otero & Manuela Antonia Padilla; gp/ Jose Antonio Lopes & Juana Maria Lopes.

SANDOVAL, Maria Juana
bap 11 Jun, 6 days old; legit d/ Juan Sandoval & Justa Garcia; ap/ Jose Sandobal & Petronila (blank); am/ Juan Guadalupe Garcia & Dolores Candelario; gp/ Juan Nepomucena Carabajal & Maria Dolores Carabajal.

NS, Antonio Jose
bap 11 Jun 1843, 6 days old; s/ unknown parents; gp/ Jose Albino Duran & Juliana Garcia.

SANDOVAL, Jose Trenidad
bap 11 Jun 1843, 5 days old; legit s/ Francisco Sandoval & Maria Garcia; ap & am/ not stated; gp/ Tomas Candelario & Maria Armijo.

Frame 2027
CANDELARIO, Antonio Perfidio
bap 20 Jun 1843, 8 days old; legit s/ Vicente Candelario & Ana Maria Chaves; gp/ Eusebio Chaves & Bibiana Chabes.

BALDONADO, Juan Ygnacio
bap 24 Jun 1843, 7 days old; legit s/ Anselmo Baldonado & Bibiana Gonsales; ap/ Juan Domingo Baldonado & Maria Manuela Aragon; am/ Juan Gonsales & Barbara Castillo; gp/ Domingo Sanches & Quiteria Gonsales.

CANDELARIO, Estanislado Reyes
bap 2 Jul 1843, 8 days old; legit s/ Francisco Candelario & Ysabel Garcia; ap/ Casimiro Candelario & Matilde Griego; am/ Blas Garcia & Reyes Apodaca; gp/ Baltasar Martin & Dolores Apodaca.

NS, Petra
bap 5 Jul 1843, 3 days old; d/ unknown parents; gp/ Rafael Garcia & Maria Luisa Garcia.

CORDOVA, Maria Merced
bap 8 Jul 1843, 8 days old; legit d/ Juan Jose Cordova & Maria Dolores Gonsales; ap/ Manuel Cordova & Catarina Lusero; am/ Jose Gonsales & Maria Getrudes Chaves; gp/ Paublo Lusero & Catarina Lusero.

Frames 2027-2028, #28
MARQUES, Jose del Refugio
bap 9 Jul 1843, 8 days old; legit s/ Ramon Marques & Josefa Sierra; ap & am/ not stated; gp/ Jose Maria Griego & Guadalupe Mora.

TAFOYA, Maria Cisilia
bap 9 Jul 843, 6 days old; legit d/ Tomas Tafoya & Soledad Montoya; ap/ Juan Ygnacio Tafoya & Maria Antonia Baca; am/ Juan Montoya & Getrudes Moya; gp/ Juan Jose Sandoval & Rita Luna.

MONTOYA, Jesus Maria
bap 9 Jul 1843, 8 days old; legit s/ Jose Rafael Montoya & Getrudes Chaves; ap/ Jose Maria Montoya & Maria Luisa Padilla; am/ Agustin Chaves & Juana Sanches; gp/ Anastacio Montoya & Maria Anastacia Montoya.

SAMORA, Juan Cilirio
bap 9 Jul 843, 8 days old; legit s/ Jose Samora & Josefa Montaño; ap/ Francisco Samora & Maria Ygnacia Valencia; am/ Pedro Montaño & Nepomucena Muñis; gp/ Felipe Samora & Getrudes Gallego.

NS, Juan
bap 9 Jul 1843, 4 days old; s/ unknown parents; gp/ Manuel Antonio Muñis & Josefa Candelario.

GRIEGO, Juan Cristobal
bap 29 Jul 1843, 5 days old; legit s/ Miguel Griego & Juana Gutierres; ap/ Juan Domingo Griego & Gertrudes Candelario; am/ Bernardo Gutierres & Dolores Ortega; gp/ Juan Garcia & Juana Andrea Noanes.

Baptisms – Albuquerque, New Mexico
1829–1850

Frame 2029
LUCERO, Maria Marta
bap 6 Aug 1843, 6 days old; legit d/ Jose Maria Lucero & Maria Ygnacia Samora; ap/ Yldefonso Lucero
& Manuela Crespin; am/ Jose Samora & Rafaela Martin; gp/ Ambrocio Garcia & Maria Albina Sandoval.

SAVEDRA, Jose Meliton de Jesus
bap 9 Aug 1843, 8 days old; s/ Luis Savedra & Maria Luisa Duran; ap & am/ not stated; gp/ Jose Maria
Mares & Prudencia Mares.

BACA, Jose de las Niebes
bap 20 Aug 1843, 4 days old; s/ Mariano Baca & Dolores Garcia; ap & am/ not stated; gp/ Diego Lopes
& Juana Lopes.

LOPES, Maria del Refugio
bap 20 Aug 1843, 8 days old; legit d/ Teodoro Lopes & Josefa Chaves; ap/ Manuel Lopes & Cruz
Romero; am/ Agustin Chaves & Juana Sanches; gp/ Jose Antonio Montoya & Juana Maria Chaves.

ARAGON, Maria Monica
bap 3 Sep 1843, 3 days old; d/ Jose Manuel Aragon & Maria Ygnacia Margil; ap & am/ not stated; gp/
Francisco Lusero & Ynes Montoya.

Frame 2030, #29
CANDELARIO, Maria Gertrudes Felipa
bap 3 Sep 1843, 2 days old; d/ Manuel Candelario & Manuela Sandoval; ap & am/ not stated; gp/ Cleto
Lopes & Maria Altagracia Lopes.

BUSTAMANTE, Jose de los Reyes
bap 7 Sep 1843, 5 days old; s/ Carpio Bustamante & Guadalupe Larrañaga; ap/ Bernardo Bustamante &
Anastacia Griego; am/ Manuel Larrañaga & Maria de Jesus Ortiz; gp/ Antonio Sandoval & Ana Maria
Duran.

MARTINES, Juan Paublo
bap 10 Sep 1843, 7 days old; s/ Pablo Martines & Francisca Moya; ap & am/ not stated; gp/ Francisco
Moya & Paula Anaya.

NS, Ana Maria
bap 26 Sep 1843, 4 days old; d/ unknown parents; gp/ Juan Gutierres & Maria Josefa Anaya.

SALASAR, Maria Rosalia
bap 30 Sep 1843, 5 days old; d/ Juan Salasar & Maria Manuela Gurule; ap/ Julian Salasar & Gertrudes
Aragon; am/ Felipe Gurule & Juana Candelaria Gutierres; gp/ Juan Tomas Aragon & Juana Candelaria
Gutierres

Frame 2031
GARCIA, Maximiano
bap 8 Oct 1843, 6 days old; legit s/ Jose Antonio Garcia & Tomasa Griego; ap/ Juan Christoval Garcia &
Encarnacion Romero; am/ Miguel Griego & Gertrudis Olguin; gp/ Manuel Antonio Garcia & Gertrudis
Mestas.

LUCERO, Maria Gertrudis
bap 18 Oct 1843, 7 days old; legit d/ Blas Lucero & Rosalia Tenorio; ap/ Andres Lucero & Tomasa Garcia; am/ Julian Tenorio & Benigna Chaves; gp/ Deciderio Lucero & Cicilia Jaramillo.

NS, Maria Celestina
bap 22 Oct 1843, 3 days old; d/ unknown parents; gp/ Antonio Aragon & Maria Vigil.

HERRERA, Teodocio
bap 29 Oct 1843, 3 days old; s/ Juan Herrera & Barbara Jaramillo; ap/ Vicente Herrera & Maria Antonia Montaño; am/ Miguel Jaramillo & Gertrudis Griego; gp/ Jose Herrera & Ramona Herrera.

NS, Jose Aniceto
bap 29 Oct 1843, 2 days old; s/ unknown parents; gp/ Jose Rafael Duran & Maria Manuela Mascarenas.

NS, Julian
bap 29 Oct 1843, 6 days old; s/ unknown parents; gp/ Julian Lopes & Barbara Severina.

Frame 2032, #30
ARAGON, Antonio Jose
bap 29 Oct 1843, 8 days old; s/ Juan Rafael Aragon & Catalina Savedra; ap & am/ not stated; gp/ Manuel Savedra & Guadalupe Savedra.

GUTIERRES, Maria Eligia
bap 29 Oct 1843, 6 days old; d/ Juan Pablo Gutierres & Josefa Martines; ap/ Miguel Gutierres & Gregoria Armijo; am/ Jose Antonio Martines & Monica Jaramillo; gp/ Felis Sanchez & Lauriana Sena.

GURULE, Maria de Jesus
bap 30 Oct 1843, 4 days old; d/ Pablo Gurule & Maria Antonia Montoya; ap/ Ygnacio Gurule & Margarita Salazar; am/ Juan Montoya & Maria Leocadia Chaves; gp/ Jose Maria Sandoval & Teresa Luna.

GURULE, Juan Santos
bap 3 Nov 1843, 8 days old; s/ Pablo Gurule & Maria Antonia Mora; ap & am/ not stated; gp/ Manuel Mares & Rosalia Aranda.

MESTAS, Antonio Jose
bap 11 Nov 1843, 8 days old; s/ Pedro Mestas & Dolores Apodaca; ap/ Manuel Mestas & Guadalupe Otero; am/ Juan Apodaca & Ana Maria Sanches; gp/ Salvador Armijo & Placida Armijo.

Frame 2033
GARCIA, Maria de Jesus Trinidad Erculana
bap 11 Nov 1843, 7 days old; d/ Antonio Maria Garcia & Juana Montaño; ap/ Felis Garcia & Ysavel Lopes; am/ Salvador Montaño & Gregoria Chaves; gp/ Pablo Armijo & Dolores Armijo.

CEDILLO, Maria Santos
bap 12 Nov 1843, 9 days old; d/ Toribio Cedillo & Ysavel Sanches; gp/ Jose Sanches & Manuela Sanches.

MADRID, Maria Francisca
bap 12 Nov 1843, 5 days old; legit d/ Luis Madrid & Dolores Anaya; ap & am/ not stated; gp/ Francisco Santillanes & Dolores NS.

NS, Pedro
bap 12 Nov 1843, 3 days old; s/ unknown parents; gp/ Francisco Apodaca & Maria Petra Apodaca.

NS, Juan Pablo
bap 12 Nov 1843, 6 days old; s/ unknown parents; gp/ Juan Garcia & Juana Andrea Noanes.

Frame 2034, #21
SANIS, Maria Elena
bap 20 Dec 1842, 8 days old; legit d/ Francisco Sanis & Refugio Salasar; ap/ Salbador Sanis & Juana Maria Aragon; am/ Salbador Salasar & Nicolasa Cordova; gp/ Salbador Manuel Garcia & Ygnacia Maria Romero.

MONTAÑO, Jose Ynocencio
bap 31 Dec 1842, 8 days old; legit s/ Jose Montaño & Teresa Miera; gp/ Juan Gonsales & Lus Rael.

GARCIA, Damacia Guadalupe
bap 31 Dec 1842, 8 days old; legit d/ Salvador Garcia & Soledad Garcia; ap/ Guadalupe Garcia & Dolores Candelario; am/ Jose Antonio Garcia & Ygnacia Candelario; gp/ Perfecto Garcia & Dolores Garcia.

BARELA, Jose Francisco
bap 1 Jan 1843, 8 days old; legit s/ Antonio Barela & Catarina Ortis; ap/ Juan Barela & Josefa Chaves; am/ Lorenso Ortis & Rafaela Ruis; gp/ Jose Francisco Apodaca & Maria Ygnacia Lopes.

GARCIA, Maria Estefana
bap 1 Jan 1843, 8 days old; legit d/ Jose Garcia & Maria Griego; gp/ Atanacio Garcia & Dolores Candelario.

Frame 2035
CRESPIN, Paublo Antonio de Jesus
bap 5 Jan 1843, 8 days old; legit s/ Salvador Crespin & Reyes Lopes; ap & am/ not stated; gp/ Bartolo Sanches & Marcelina Sanches.

LOPES, Salbador Manuel
bap 5 Jan 1843, 8 days old; legit s/ Jesus Lopes & Juana Armijo; ap & am/ not stated; gp/ Jose Armijo & Placida Armijo.

TAFOLLA, Maria Reyes
bap 6 Jan 1843, 8 days old; legit d/ Francisca Tafolla & unknown father; gp/ Miguel Martines & Maria Dolores Ruis.

NS, Maria Plasida
bap 6 Jan 1843, 8 days old; d/ unknown parents; gp/ Jose Antonio Montaño.

GONZALES, Juan Andres
bap 22 Jan 1843, 8 days old; legit s/ Antonio Gonzales & Ana Maria Alire; ap/ Francisco Gonzales & Barbara Basques; am/ Manuel Alire & Dolores Romero; gp/ Juan Vijil & Apolonia Montoya.

Frames 2035-2036, #22
GURULE, Maria Anastacia Nestora
bap 22 Jan 1843, 8 days old; legit d/ Grabiel Gurule & Maria Nicolasa Luna; ap/ Jose Domingo Gurule & Ana Maria Gonsales; am/ Ysidro Luna & Manuela Candelario; gp/ Rafael Apodaca & Juana Maria Romero.

CORDOVA, Maria Marcelina
bap 22 Jan 1843, 8 days old; legit d/ Jose Cordova & Manuela Garcia; ap/ Nicolas Cordova & Maria Ygnacia Duran; am/ Juan Estevan Garcia & Maria Paubla Perea; gp/ Jose Manuel Gurule & Maria Gertrudes Perea.

BARRERAS, Juan Nepomuceno Crisostano
bap 29 Jan 1843, 8 days old; legit s/ Francisco Barreras & Bibiana Nuanes; ap/ Jose Antonio Barreras & Rafaela Samora; am/ Anastacio Nuanes & Barbara Gurule; gp/ Fernando Gutierres & Simona Nuanes.

CANDELARIO, Maria Petra
bap 29 Jan 1843, 8 days old; legit d/ Benito Candelario & Luciana Garcia; ap/ Juan Ysidro Candelario & Getrudes Jaramillo; am/ Juan Luiz Garcia & Leonarda Lopes; gp/ Manuel Ruis & Juliana Ruis.

NS, Francisco
bap 29 Jan 1843, 8 days old; s/ unknown parents; gp/ Jose Mansanar & Estefana Jaramillo.

SALAZAR, Carmen
bap 29 Jan 1843, 8 days old; legit d/ Serafin Salazar & Rafaela Garcia; ap & am/ not stated; gp/ Jesus Maria Gallego & Maria del Rosario Garcia.

Frame 2037
GONSALES, Maria Nestora Ramona
bap 5 Feb 1843, 8 days old; legit d/ Miguel Gonsales & Maria Rosa Montolla; ap & am/ not stated; gp/ Juan Nepomuceno Montolla & Maria de Jesus Lucero.

BACA, Jose Patrocinio
bap 5 Feb 1843, 7 days old; s/ Jose Polito NS & Rosalia Baca; ap & am/ not stated; gp/ Ancelmo Martines & Maria Luis Archuleta.

BACA, Maria Josefa
bap 5 Feb 1843, 8 days old; legit s/ Juan Jose Baca & Maria de la Luz Garcia; ap & am/ not stated; gp/ Jose de Jesus Gonsales & Ana Maria Duran.

GARCIA, Jose Leandro
bap 5 Feb 1843; legit s/ Jose Antonio Garcia & Polinaria Salasar; ap/ Felis Garcia & Maria Ysabel Lopes; am/ Juan Cristobal Salasar & Micaela Montoya; gp/ Francisco Sabedra & Maria Dolores Garcia.

ANAYA, Jose Nestor
bap 5 Feb 1843, 7 days old; legit s/ Jesus Anaya & Francisca Baca; ap/ Antonio Anaya & Tomasa Tafolla; am/ Diego Baca & Francisca Garcia; gp/ Antonio Anaya & Tomasa Tafolla.

Frame 2038, #31
GARCIA, Amador de Jesus
bap 12 Nov 1843, 8 days old; legit s/ Jose Antonio Garcia & Ysavel Gallego; ap/ Jose Francisco Garcia & Guadalupe Otero; am/ Joaquin Gallego & Maria Savedra; gp/ Felipe Herrera & Juana Herrera.

DURAN, Maria Benigna
bap 12 Nov 1843, 3 days old; legit d/ Antonio Duran & Tomasa Gutierres; ap/ Mateo Duran & Antonia Muñis; am/ Manuel Gutierres & Manuela Fernandes; gp/ Miguel Lopes & Maria Antonia Lopes.

ARMIJO, Maria
bap 12 Nov 1843, 6 days old; legit d/ Rafael Armijo & Josefa Chaves; ap & am/ not stated; gp/ Juan Rodrigues & Maria de la Luz Sanches.

GARCIA, Maria Ludubina (of Savino)
bap 24 Nov 1843, 6 days old; legit d/ Jose Garcia & Maria Concepcion NS; ap & am/ not stated; gp/ Antonio Martin & Ludubina Martin.

SANCHES, Maria Josefa de Jesus
bap 26 Nov 1843, 2 days old; legit d/ Cristoval Sanches & Concepcion Valencia; ap/ Felipe Sanches & Ana Maria Trujillo; am/ Juan Domingo Valencia & Ygnacia Salazar; gp/ Pedro Aranda & Rosalia Jaramillo.

Frame 2039
GRIEGO, Jose Gregorio
bap 26 Nov 1843, 6 days old; legit s/ Jose Tomas Griego & Monica Contreras; ap/ Miguel Griego & Petrona Candelario; am/ Jose Tomas Contreras & Maria NS; gp/ Ramon Gallegos & Rosalia Montaño.

TORRES, Jose Cisilio
bap 26 Nov 1843, 4 days old; legit s/ Benito Torres & Trinidad Gutierres; ap & am/ not stated; gp/ Jose Samora & Josefa Montaño.

ANAYA, Maria Catarina
bap 26 Nov 1843, 8 days old; legit d/ Jose Anaya & Josefa Moya; ap/ Antonio Anaya & Tomasa Ansures; am/ Asencio Moya & Juana Sandoval; gp/ Tomas Sandoval & Maria Gertrudis Armijo.

NS, Maria Guadalupe Abelina
bap 26 Nov 1843, 9 days old; d/ unknown parents; gp/ Jesus Gutierres & Josefa Mestas.

MARTIN, Maria Paula Dolores
bap 27 Nov 1843, 6 days old; legit d/ Miguel Antonio Martin & Maria Francisca Carbajal; ap/ Rafael Martin & Manuela Anaya; am/ Juan Pedro Carbajal & Gertrudes Gonsales; gp/ Pablo Armijo & Dolores Garcia.

Frame 2040, #32
SANCHES, Juan Jose
bap 28 Nov 1843, 3 days old; legit s/ Domingo Sanches & Perfecta Montoya; ap & am/ not stated; gp/ Paulino NS & Tomasa Sena.

NS, Jose Quirino
bap 28 Nov 1843, 6 days old; s/ unknown parents; gp/ Mateo Sanches Vergara & Manuelina Aragon.

MARTIN, Maria Elena
bap 30 Nov 1843, 4 days old; legit d/ Felipe Martin & Petrona Arias; ap/ Felipe Martin & Victoria Saens; am/ Miguel Arias; gp/ Antonio Martin & Ludubina Martin.

Note: The next several records are not sequential.

MARTIN, Pedro Maria
bap 26 Jul 1843, 5 days old; legit s/ Jose Martin & Maria Gertrudis Nieto; ap & am/ not stated; gp/ Pedro Lucero & Maria de Jesus Nieto.

LUCERO, Juana Maria del Refugio
bap 30 Jul 1843, 3 days old; legit d/ Diego Lucero & Dolores Lovato; ap/ Rafael Lucero & Barbara Montoya; am/ Jesus Lovato & Juana Paula Montoya; gp/ Juan Pablo Vegil & Apolonia Montoya.

Frame 2041
BACA, Ana Maria
bap 25 Jul 1843, 4 days old; legit d/ Ramon Baca & Guadalupe Garcia; ap/ Simon Baca & Rosalia Lucero; am/ Antonio Garcia & Margarita Rael; gp/ Pedro Martin & Maria Gertrudis Apodaca.

SANDOVAL, Jose Apolinario
bap 25 Jul 1843, 4 days old; legit s/ Juan Jose Sandoval & Gabriela Romero; ap & am/ not stated; gp/ Pablo Martin & Cisilia Candelaria.

ROMERO, Ana Maria Altagracia
bap 25 Jul 1843, 6 days old; legit d/ Ramon Romero & Dolores Chaves; ap/ Santiago Romero & Dolores Candelario; am/ Pedro Chaves & Margarita Montoya; gp/ Mariano Chaves & Bibiana Chaves.

GARCIA, Jose Cristino
bap 4 Aug 1843, 8 days old; legit s/ Dolores NS, Indian, and Felis Garcia; gp/ Francisca Lopes.

Frames 2041-2042, #33
NS, Manuel de Jesus
bap 15 Aug 1843, 5 days old; s/ unknown parents; gp/ Francisco Aragon & Francisca Aragon.

NS, Jose Francisco
bap 15 Aug 1843, 7 days old; s/ unknown parents; gp/ Francisco Aragon & Francisca Aragon.

GARCIA, Jose Catalino
bap 18 Aug 1843, 7 days old; legit s/ Miguel Garcia & Reyes Jaramillo; ap/ Pablo Garcia & Barbara Bernal; am/ Rafael Jaramillo & Josefa Rodrigues; gp/ Agustin Leal & Guadalupe Garcia.

NIETO, Jose Tiburcio
bap 19 Aug 1843, 5 days old; legit s/ Jose Dolores Nieto & Gertrudis Garcia; ap/ Juan Nieto & Petra Valdes; am/ Lagos Garcia & Juana Trujillo; gp/ Prudencio Garcia & Francisca Aragon.

GUTIERRES, Maria Clara
bap 23 Aug 1843, 8 days old; legit d/ Estanislao Gutierres & Apolonia Gonsales; ap/ Juan Gutierres & Guadalupe Chaves; am/ Lorenzo Gonsales & Teodora Salasar; gp/ Jose Domingo Romero & Ludubina Padilla.

Frame 2043
APODACA, Jose Anastacio
bap 25 Aug 1843, 7 days old; legit s/ Rafael Apodaca & Estefana Salasar; ap/ Francisco Apodaca & Soledad Garcia; am/ Juan Salasar & Manuela Trujillo; gp/ Felis Garcia & Carmen Mestas.

MOYA, Maria Manuela
bap 10 Sep 1843, 4 days old; legit d/ Jose Maria Moya & Maria Dolores Saens; gp/ Salvador Tenorio & Maria Luisa Trujillo.

LOVATO, Ana Maria
bap 11 Sep 1843, 3 days old; legit d/ Jose Lovato & Manuela Rael; ap/ Juan Lovato & Maria Casados; am/ Antonio Rael & Francisca Padilla; gp/ Felipe Lovato & Manuela Mestas.

SALASAR, Francisco
bap 7 Oct 1843, 8 days old; legit s/ Manuel Salasar & Francisca Jaramillo; gp/ Juan Armijo & Andrea Martin.

NS, Maria Teresa Placida
bap 15 Oct 1843, 5 days old; d/ unknown parents; gp/ Jose Montoya & Maria de la Lus Candelario.

Frame 2044, #34
ARAGON, Jesus Maria
bap 15 Oct 1843, 3 days old; legit s/ Jose Manuel Aragon & Quirina Sandoval; ap/ Eusebio Aragon & Micaela Sanches; am/ Juan Francisco Sandoval & Juana Archibeque; gp/ Francisco Aragon & Francisca Aragon.

GARCIA, Juan Nepomuceno
bap 5 Oct 1843, 3 days old; s/ Diego Garcia & Juliana Torres; gp/ Jose Martin & Juana Lucero.

GARCIA, Maria Francisca
bap 23 Oct 1843, 9 days old; legit d/ Manuel Garcia & Rafaela Rael; ap/ Miguel Garcia & Ana Maria Ballejos; am/ Juan Antonio Rael & Soledad Miera; gp/ Ygnacio Miera & Quiteria Rael.

NS, Maria Rosalia
bap 23 Oct 1843, 3 days old; d/ unknown parents; gp/ Marcelino Aragon & Rosalia Gonsales.

SANDOVAL, Maria Gertrudes Dolores
bap 23 Oct 1843, 2 days old; legit d/ Miguel Sandoval & Maria Rosa Lucero; gp/ Antonio Gutierres & Juana Maria Sandoval.

BACA, Teresa
bap 24 Oct 1843, 4 days old; legit d/ Jose Manuel Baca & Tomasa Apodaca; ap & am/ not stated; gp/ Manuel Baca & Guadalupe Garcia.

Frame 2045
GONSALES, Maria Francisca
bap 24 Oct 1843, 3 days old; legit d/ Manuel Gonsales & Ana Maria Alire; ap & am/ not stated; gp/ Jose Benito Alire & Juana Garcia.

GONSALES, Francisco
bap 7 Nov 1843, 2 days old; legit s/ Crus Gonsales & Maria de Jesus Moya; ap/ Francisco Gonsales & Barbara Basques; am/ Eusebio Moya & Gregoria Martines; gp/ Santiago Perea & Maria de la Lus Perea.

LUCERO, Maria Nestora de Jesus
bap 9 Nov 1843, 6 days old; d/ Dario Lucero & Paula Silva; ap/ Felipe Lucero & Maria Jesus Chaves; am/ Juan Jose Silva & Maria Juana Gutierres; gp/ Julian Rael & Maria Ygnacia Silva.

LUCERO, Damian
bap 25 Nov 1843, 8 days old; legit s/ Cleto Lucero & Gabriela Candelaria; ap/ Jose Lucero & Dolores Garcia; am/ Ygnacio Candelaria & Concepcion Chaves; gp/ Ignacio Candelaria & Maria Luisa Garcia.

Frames 2045-2046, #35
RAEL, Juana Nepomucena Altagracia
bap 16 Nov 1843, 9 days old; legit d/ Francisco Rael & Gregoria Romero; ap/ Antonio Rael & Francisca Padilla; am/ Antonio Romero & Ygnacio Montaño; gp/ Jose Sandoval & Francisca Padilla.

LUCERO, Ysavel
bap 19 Nov 1843, 8 days old; legit d/ Hermenegildo Lucero & Francisca Sanches; ap/ Roman Lucero & Feliciana Gonsales; am/ Felipe Sanches & Ana Maria Trujillo; gp/ Francisco NS & Ysabel NS.

NS, Maria Gregoria
bap 19 Nov 1843, 6 days old; d/ unknown parents; gp/ Jose Gutierres & Maria Dolores Gutierres.

LUCERO, Maria Concepcion
bap 8 Dec 1843, 8 days old; legit d/ Ramon Lucero & Leocadia Sanches; ap/ Miguel Lucero & Dimas Aragon; am/ Domingo Sanches & Luz Perea; gp/ Domingo Sanches & Luz Perea.

PADILLA, Maria Dolores
bap 8 Dec 1843, 5 days old; legit d/ Jose Antonio Padilla & Juana Gutierres; ap & am/ not stated; gp/ Francisco Gonsales & Dolores Gonsales.

Frames 2046-2047
NS, Antonio Jose
bap 8 Dec 1843, 6 days old; s/ unknown parents; gp/ Benigno Garcia & Paula Gonsales.

ARMENTA, Maria Petra
bap 8 Dec 1843, 3 days old; legit d/ Luis Armenta & Viviana Gallegos; ap & am/ not stated; gp/ Jose Gallego & Petra Perea.

CASTILLO, Jose Mariano Cicilio
bap 8 Dec 1843, 5 days old; legit s/ Jose Miguel Castillo & Rosalia Martin; ap/ Antonio Jose Castillo & Quiteria Chaves; am/ Ysidro Martin & Dorotea Montaño; gp/ Jose Antonio Garcia & Tomasa Griego.

JARAMILLO, Jose Rafael
bap 10 Dec 1843, 6 days old; legit s/ Gregorio Jaramillo & Josefa Garcia; ap & am/ not stated; gp/ Rafael Peña & Catarina Apodaca.

GARCIA, Maria Guadalupe
bap 10 Dec 1843, 4 days old; legit d Alejo Garcia & Gracia Garcia; ap/ Juan Garcia & Rosa Savedra; am/ Ascensio NS & Barbara Chaves; gp/ Jose Maria Jaramillo & Placida Jaramillo.

Frames 2047-2048, #36
SANCHES, Maria Francisca
bap 10 Dec 1843, 5 days old; legit d/ Manuel Sanches & Petra Chaves; ap/ Ygnacio Sanches & Manuela Anaya; am/ Jose Dolores Chaves & Nicanora Garcia; gp/ Jose Miguel Olguin & Luisa Montoya.

MARTINES, Juana Maria
bap 10 Dec 1843, 3 days old; legit d/ Pedro Martines & Gertrudis Apodaca; ap/ Jose Martines & Luciana Lucero; am/ Dionicio Apodaca & Maria Garcia; gp/ Salvador Tafoya & Juana Maria Lucero.

NS, Jose de Jesus Amador
bap 10 Dec 1843, 2 days old; s/ unknown parents; gp/ Damaso Griego & Manuela Carbajal.

CHAVES, Jose Sacramento
bap 10 Dec 1843, 5 days old; legit s/ Jose Dolores Chaves & Nicanora Garcia; ap/ Xabier Chaves & Maria de Jesus Armijo; am/ Juan Garcia & Rosa Savedra; gp/ Juan Garcia & Guadalupe Chaves.

GRIEGO, Maria Sinforiana
bap 12 Dec 1843, 3 days old; legit d/ Gregorio Griego & Francisca Apodaca; ap/ Jose Maria Griego & Francisca Armijo; am/ Juan Apodaca & Manuela Candelaria; gp/ Jose Samora & Josefa Montaño.

Frame 2049
LOPES, Maria Guadalupe
bap 12 Dec 1843, 6 days old; legit d/ Lasaro Lopes & Dolores Garcia; ap/ Salbador Lopes & Marta Cedillo; am/ Simon Garcia & Josefa Garcia; gp/ Ygnacio Lopes & Gertrudes Lopes.

MARTIN, Jose Melquiades
bap 14 Dec 1843, 6 days old; legit s/ Baltasar Martin & Dolores Apodaca; ap/ Jose Martin & Juana Griego; am/ Rafael Apodaca & Maria Romero; gp/ Rafael Apodaca & Maria Juana Apodaca.

BACHICHA, Salvador Antonio
bap 15 Dec 1843, 3 days old; legit s/ Manuel Bachicha & Gregoria Lusero; ap/ Juan Bachicha & Manuela Martin; am/ Jose Manuel Lusero & Francisca Garcia; gp/ Salvador Tafoya & Juana Maria Lusero.

GARCIA, Maria Juana Luisa
bap 17 Dec 1843, 8 days old; legit d/ Pablo Garcia & Gertrudis Sanches; ap/ Antonio Garcia & Maria Tafoya; am/ Jose Sanches & Gregoria Rael; gp/ Julian Sanches & Juana Candelario.

GARCIA, Jose de los Reyes
bap 17 Dec 1843, 6 days old; legit s/ Juan Garcia & Rita Lopes; ap/ Martin Garcia & Ana Maria Apodaca; am/ Luiz Lopes & Antonia Garcia; gp/ Francisco Armijo & Rosalia Armijo.

Frame 2050, #37
NS, Francisco
bap 17 Dec 1843, 6 days old; s/ unknown parents; gp/ Juan Griego & Marcelina Baca.

GUTIERRES, Maria Guadalupe
bap 17 Dec 1843, 5 days old; legit d/ Fernando Gutierres & Josefa Gonsales; ap/ Pedro Gutierres & Francisca Griego; am/ Juan Gonsales & Maria Antonia Armijo; gp/ Manuel Garcia & Rafael Rael.

ANAYA, Pablo
bap 17 Dec 1843, 2 days old; legit s/ Andres Anaya & Ana Maria Garcia; ap/ Juan Anaya & Francisca Baca; am/ Bautista Garcia & Luz Candelario; gp/ Pablo Armijo & Dolores Garcia.

MAREZ, Jose Balerio
bap 27 Dec 1843, 5 days old; legit s/ Manuel Marez & Dolores Duran; ap & am/ not stated; gp/ Dionicio Lopes & Gertrudis Perea.

NS, Jose Camilo de Jesus
bap 27 Dec 1843, 2 days old; d/ unknown parents; gp/ Jose Lucero & Maria Gertrudes Gutierres.

GUTIERRES, Manuel Antonio
bap 28 Dec 1843, 6 days old; legit s/ Juan Gutierres & Josefa Garcia; ap & am/ not stated; gp/ Damaso Garcia & Josefa Duran.

Frame 2051
GRIEGO, Maria Dolores
bap 28 Dec 1843, 2 days old; legit d/ Geronimo Griego & Albina Lucero; ap/ Miguel Griego & Gertrudis Olguin; am/ Juan Lucero & Antonia Griego; gp/ Jose Dolores Samora & Soledad Garcia.

NS, Maria Juana
bap 28 Dec 1843, 6 days old; d/ unknown parents; gp/ Jose Ynes Chaves & Maria Rufina Apodaca.

MUÑIS, Maria Luisa
bap 28 Dec 1843, 8 days old; legit d/ Manuel Muñis & Josefa Chaves; ap & am/ not stated; gp/ Pablo Garcia & Maria Petra Santillanes.

SANCHES, Jose Ynocencio Mellisos (twin)
SANCHES, Juan Ynocencio (twin)
bap 29 Dec 1843, 1 day old; legit ch/ Francisco Sanches & Maria Manuela Sanches; ap/ Gabriel Sanches & Juana Cedio; am/ Ramos Sanches & Juana Barbara Montoya; gp for both/ Jose Melquiades Chaves & Maria Josefa Chaves.

NS, Maria Concepcion
bap 29 Dec 1843, 5 days old; d/ unknown parents; gp/ Juan Cristoval Lucero & Juana Apodaca.

Frame 2052, #38
NS, Manuel Antonio
bap 2 Jan 1844, 3 days old; s/ unknown parents; gp/ Manuel Seberino & Dolores Pacheco.

ALARID, Donaciano de Jesus
bap 2 Jan 1844, 3 days old; legit s/ Gregorio Alarid & Juana Gonsales; ap & am/ not stated; gp/ Dionicio Atencio & Francisca Sanches.

NS, Natividad
bap 3 Jan 1844, 10 days old; d/ unknown parents; gp/ Jose Miguel Carrillo & Ana Maria Ballejos.

GARCIA, Manuel Antonio
bap 5 Jan 1844, 5 days old; legit s/ Salvador Garcia & Juana Romero; ap/ Antonio Garcia & Soledad Sandoval; am/ Santiago Romero & Dolores Candelario; gp/ Pablo Sisneros & Dolores Chaves.

SAMORA, Maria de los Reyes
bap 10 Jan 1844, 3 days old; legit d/ Ramon Samora & Gregoria Candelaria; ap/ Miguel Samora & Marcelina Gallegos; am/ Jose Candelaria & Francisca Gonsales; gp/ Miguel Gonsales & Clara Gutierres.

Frames 2052-2053
GALLEGO, Jose Nicanor
bap 10 Jan 1844, 5 days old; legit s/ Rumaldo Gallego & Gregoria Gutierres; am/ Juan Gallego & Francisca Gurule; am/ Antonio Gutierres & Guadalupe Garcia; gp/ Desiderio Griego & Guadalupe Apodaca.

GONSALES, Maria Marcelina Reyes
bap 10 Jan 1844, 5 days old; legit d/ Baltasar Gonsales & Maria Marques; ap & am/ not stated; gp/ Manuel Romero & Marcelina Armijo.

PEREA, Miguel Luciano
bap 10 Jan 1844, 5 days old; legit s/ Miguel Perea & Juana Garcia; ap & am/ not stated; gp/ Luciano Santillanes & Juliana Santillanes.

GARCIA, Jose
bap 13 Jan 1844, 8 days old; legit s/ Jose Garcia & Viviana Candelario; ap & am/ not stated; gp/ Juan Sanches & Luisa Sanches.

NS, Maria Narcisa
bap 17 Jan 1844, 8 days old; d/ unknown parents; gp/ Paulino Aldas & Tomasa Sena.

LEAL, Maria Benigna
bap 21 Jan 1844, 3 days old; legit d/ Agustin Leal & Guadalupe Garcia; ap/ Juan Domingo Leal & Beronica Cortes; am/ Juan Pablo Garcia & Carlota Bernal; gp/ Francisco Aragon & Francisca Aragon.

Frame 2054, #39
NS, Maria Eligia
bap 21 Jan 1844, 2 days old; d/ unknown parents; gp/ Felis Sanches & Sebastiana Sena.

OLGUIN, Jose de la Cruz
bap 21 Jan 1844, 5 days old; legit s/ Jose Miguel Olguin & Luisa Sanches; ap & am/ not stated; gp/ Manuel Herrera & Manuela Garcia.

LOPES, Barbara Nicanora
bap 21 Jan 1844, 8 days old; legit d/ Vicente Lopes & Barbara Duran; ap/ Ramon Lopes & Reyes Jaramillo; am/ Juan Rafael Duran & Josefa Apodaca; gp/ Cristoval Armijo & Barbara Ortis.

GARCIA, Maria Josefa de Jesus
bap 28 Jan 1844, 3 days old; legit d/ Salvador Garcia & Rosa Gutierres; ap & am/ not stated; gp/ Mateo Garcia & Ana Maria Tenorio.

SENA, Maria Juana
bap 1 Feb 1844, 6 days old; legit d/ Miguel Sena & Ysidora Garcia; ap/ Francisco Sena & Manuela
Martin; am/ Juan Jose Garcia & Francisca Gallego; gp/ Ramon Candelario & Maria Antonia Sena.

Frames 2054-2055
CANDELARIO, Miguel Antonio
bap 4 Feb 1844, 8 days old; legit s/ Jesus Maria Candelario & Maria Ysavel Chaves; ap & am/ not stated;
gp/ Bartolo Apodaca & Barvara Apodaca.

GONSALES, Jose Apolonio
bap 12 Feb 1844, 4 days old; legit s/ Jose Antonio Gonsales & Maria Clara Garcia; ap & am/ not stated;
gp/ Jose Maria Torres & Josefa Garcia.

MONTOYA, Maria Nestora
bap 13 Feb 1844, 2 days old; legit d/ Jose Montoya & Loreta Arias; ap & am/ not stated; gp/ Nasario
Gomes & Maria de la Lus Gomes.

NS, Maria Cesaria
bap 18 Feb 1844, in the house of Don Mariano Yrisarra & Doña Juana Otero; gp/ Manuel Yrisarra &
Josefa Yrisarra.

GARCIA, Juana Maria
bap 18 Feb 1844, 8 days old; legit d/ Juan Sisto Garcia & Maria Ynes Serna; ap/ Juan Ygnacio Garcia &
Juana Romero; am/ Tomas Serna & Rafaela Garcia; gp/ Jose Albino Garcia & Juana Garcia.

CANDELARIA, Jose Benito
bap 18 Feb 1844, 5 days old; legit s/ Romualdo Candelaria & Josefa Garcia; ap/ Juan Cristoval
Candelaria & Ysidora Garcia; am/ Diego Garcia & Ramona Candelaria; gp/ Juan Garcia & Maria Chaves.

Frame 2056, #40
SAVEDRA, Maria Andrea
bap 18 Feb 1844, 6 days old; legit d/ Francisco Savedra & Dolores Garcia; ap/ Jose Antonio Savedra &
Paula Duran; am/ Jose Antonio Garcia & Ygnacia Candelaria; gp/ Manuel Antonio Garcia & Altagracia
Garcia.

GARCIA, Maria Maximiana
bap 18 Feb 1844, 2 days old; legit d/ Rafael Garcia & Rosalia Garcia; ap/ Francisco Garcia &
Encarnacion Apodaca; am/ Juan Garcia & Victoria Garcia; gp/ Francisco Candelario & Ysavel Garcia.

MONTOYA, Maria Benigna
bap 19 Feb 1844, 5 days old; legit d/ Francisco Montoya & Asencion Garcia; ap/ Jose Miguel Montoya &
Catarina Lucero; am/ Jose Maria Garcia & Josefa Chacon; gp/ Pablo Griego & Maria Juana Montoya.

GRIEGO, Maria Juliana
bap 20 Jan 1844, 7 days old; legit d/ Domingo Griego & Manuela Lucero; ap/ Felipe Griego & Margarita
Garcia; am/ Diego Lucero & Dolores Lovato; gp/ Jose Marcos Lovato & Maria Nestora Lucero.

GURULE, Maria Gertrudis
bap 20 Feb 1844, 9 days old; legit d/ Vicente Gurule & Juana Candelaria; ap & am/ not stated; gp/ Jose
Lucero & Maria Getrudis Gutierres.

Frame 2057
MARTINES, Cesario
bap 25 Feb 1844, 10 days old; legit s/ Jose Martines & Quiteria Griego; ap & am/ not stated; gp/ Juan Cristoval Armijo & Juana Maria Chaves.

NS, Jose Porfirio
bap 25 Feb 1844, 5 days old; s/ unknown parents; gp/ Rafael Apodaca & Maria Juana Apodaca.

NS, Jose David
bap 25 Feb 1844, 3 days old; s/ unknown parents; gp/ Jose Cleto Lucero & Gabriela Candelario.

TAFOYA, Maria Clara
bap 28 Feb 1844, 6 days old; legit d/ Antonio Tafoya & Josefa NS; ap & am/ not stated; gp/ Mariano NS & Maria de San Juan.

LUCERO, Jose Emiterio
bap 6 Mar 1844, 5 days old; legit s/ Rubi Lucero & Dolores Griego; ap & am/ not stated; gp/ Basilio Gallego & Antonia Teresa Gallego.

Frame 2058, #41
SANDOVAL, Maria Soledad
bap 6 Mar 1844, 2 days old; legit s/ Juan Sandoval & Maria Justa Garcia; ap/ Jose Sandoval & Petrona Savedra; am/ Juan Garcia & Dolores Candelario; gp/ Salvador Garcia & Soledad Garcia.

CHAVES, Maria Barbara
bap 10 Mar 1844, 2 days old; legit d/ Pedro Chaves & Cristerna Lucero; ap/ Geronimo Chaves & Encarnacion Gonsales; am/ Hermenegildo Lucero & Francisca Sanches; gp/ Julian Gallego & Maria Rita Duran.

NS, Jesus Epigemio
bap 13 Mar 1844, 6 days old; s/ unknown parents; gp/ Salvador Lopes & Dolores Perea.

SAMORA, Miguel
bap 14 Mar 1844, 2 days old; legit s/ Pablo Samora & Pascuala Baca; ap & am/ not stated; gp/ Miguel Montaño & Petra Candelario.

LOPES, Jose Amador
bap 17 Mar 1844, 2 days old; legit s/ Vicente Lopes & Guadalupe Baca; ap & am/ not stated; gp/ Amador Candelario & Ana Maria Armijo.

Frames 2058-2059
NOANES, Jose Eusebio
bap 17 Mar 1844, 3 days old; legit s/ Salvador Noanes & Guadalupe Garcia; ap/ Geronimo Noanes & Barbara Maes; am/ Juan Garcia & Ysavel Romero; gp/ Juan Noanes & Dolores Gonsales.

NS, Jesus Maria
bap 17 Mar 1844, 2 days old; s/ unknown parents; gp/ Miguel Candelario & Maria Candelario.

CHAVES, Ana Maria
bap 17 Mar 1844, 5 days old; legit d/ Juan Chaves & Yldefonza Duran; ap & am/ not stated; gp/ Jose Cicilio Montoya & Maria Francisca Montoya.

MARTIN, Gregoria
bap 18 Mar 1844, 3 days old; legit d/ Pablo Martin & Cicilia Candelario; ap/ Jose Martin & Rosalia Garcia; am/ Esteban Candelario & Maria de Jesus Luna; gp/ Manuel Candelario & Ana Maria Trujillo.

MARES, Jose Luis
bap 19 Mar 1844, 6 days old; legit s/ Ramon Mares & Maria Lus Jaramillo; ap/ Juan Pablo Mares & Ana Maria Noanez; am/ Ramon Jaramillo & Reyes Armijo; gp/ Rafael Gutierres & Juana Gutierres.

Frame 2060, #42
NS, Jose Nicolas
bap 20 Mar 1844, 2 days old; s/ unknown parents; gp/ Marcelino Aragon & Rosalia Gonsales.

PEREA, Abran de Jesus
bap 24 Mar 1844, 5 days old; legit s/ Jose Maria Perea & Apolonia Chaves; ap/ Asencio Perea & Dolores Aranda; am/ Geronimo Chaves & Encarnacion Gonsales; gp/ Santiago Gonsales & Manuela Aragon.

GALLEGO, Maria Encarnacion
bap 28 Mar 1844, 5 days old; legit d/ Ramon Gallego & Rosalia Montaño, ap/ Antonio Gallego & Magdalena Garcia; am/ Toribio Montaño & Ana Maria Candelario; gp/ Rafael Gutierres & Gregoria Armijo.

CARRILLO, Maria Encarnacion
bap 8 Apr 1844, 2 days old; legit d/ Luis Carrillo & Manuela Lucero; ap & am/ not stated; gp/ Jose Dario Lucero & Paula Silva.

MONTOYA, Jose Maria
bap 12 Apr 1844, 8 days old; legit s/ Juan Montoya & Francisca Sanches; ap/ Juan Maria Montoya & Juana Silva; am/ Ygnacio Sanches & Barbara Aragon; gp/ Miguel Garcia & Josefa Sanches.

Frame 2061
CORDOVA, Apolonio
bap 14 Apr 1844, 3 days old; legit s/ Domingo Cordova & Concepcion Aragon; ap & am/ not stated; gp/ Juan Jose Cordoba & Dolores Lucero.

NORIEGA, Miguel
bap 17 Apr 1844, 8 days old; legit s/ Monico Noriega & Guadalupe Barreras; ap & am/ not stated; gp/ Antonio Martin & Ludubina Martin.

NS, Telesfora
bap 19 Apr 1844, 5 days old; d/ unknown parents; gp/ Lorenzo Montaño & Petra Candelario.

APODACA, Nestor
bap 22 Apr 1844, 3 days old; legit s/ Santos Apodaca & Estanislada Espinosa; ap/ Juan Apodaca & Estefana Crespin; am/ Jose Maria Espinosa & Matiana Garduño; gp/ Pablo Griego & Juana Montoya.

NS, Jose Ramon Seberiano
bap 22 Apr 1844, 5 days old; s/ unknown parents; gp/ Jose Francisco Tenorio & Maria Manuela Tenorio.

Frames 2061-2062, #43
NS, Antonio Epifanio
bap 22 Apr 1844, 6 days old; s/ unknown parents; gp/ Jose Gutierres & Trinidad Gutierres.

CORDOVA, Maria Exselsa
bap 23 Apr 1844, 6 days old; legit d/ Dionicio Cordova & Juana Sanches; ap/ Marcos Cordoba & Rafaela Garcia; am/ Jose Sanches & Gregoria Rael; gp/ Jose Gonsales & Monica Gonsales.

GARCIA, Maria Nestora
bap 26 Apr 1844, 4 days old; legit d/ Abad Garcia & Dimas Griego; ap & am/ not stated; gp/ Manuel Gurule & Juana Gurule.

SAENS, Juan Jose
bap 28 Apr 1844, 8 days old; legit s/ Juan Saens & Ramona Sanches; ap/ Paulin Saens & Manuela Gurule; am/ Jose Sanches & Gregoria Rael; gp/ Antonio Garcia & Juana Saens.

GARCIA, Felipe Neri
bap 28 Apr 1844, 8 days old; legit s/ Rumaldo Garcia & Ana Maria Arias; ap/ Juan Garcia & Josefa Guruled; am/ Juan Arias & Merced Gomes; gp/ Abad Duran & Gregoria Sanches.

LUCERO, Maria Marcelina
bap 3 May 1844, 2 days old; legit d/ Juan Andres Lucero & Francisca Salasar; ap/ Juan Lucero & Justa Pino; am/ Juan Salasar & Guadalupe Gonsales; gp/ Ysidro Santillanes & Barbara Gonsales.

Frame 2063
GURULE, Maria Gertudis
bap 3 May 1844, 8 days old; legit d/ Jabier Gurule & Altagracia Martines; ap/ Juan Gurule & Ygnacia Martines; am/ Rafael Martines & Manuela Anaya; gp/ Jose Lucero & Gertrudis Gutierres.

GARCIA, Ana Maria Filomena
bap 3 May 1844, 3 days old; legit d/ Juan Garcia & Juana Montaño; ap/ Juan Garcia & Juana NS; am/ Juan Montaño & Francisca Candelaria; gp/ Vicente Candelaria & Maria Reyes Griego.

NS, Gorge
bap 6 May 1844, 2 days old; s/ unknown parents; gp/ Jose Antonio Bustamante & Dolores Bustamante.

BALLEJOS, Jose de la Luz
bap 6 May 1844, 4 days old; legit s/ Santos Ballejos & Juana Lucero; ap & am/ not stated; gp/ Matias Armijo & Rosalia Armijo.

MONTOYA, Juan
bap 12 May 1844, 2 days old; legit s/ Vicente Montoya & Josefa Martines; ap/ Pedro Montoya & Maria Luna; am/ Pedro Martin & Dolores Abeita; gp/ Diego Martin & Marcelina Montoya.

Frame 2064, #44
GUERRA, Maria Gregoria
bap 12 May 1844, 6 days old; legit d/ Ambrosio Guerra & Nepomusena Gonsales; ap & am/ not stated;
gp/ Miguel Chaves & Decideria Gurule.

LUCERO, Maria Toribia
bap 14 May 1844, 8 days old; legit d/ Jose Miguel Lucero & Manuela Garcia; ap/ Miguel Lucero & Maria
Dimas Aragon; am/ Jose Antonio Garcia & Soledad Sandoval; gp/ Felis Cordoba & Rosa Garcia.

LOPES, Jose Antonio Abad
bap 15 May 1844, 8 days old; legit s/ Cleto Lopes & Maria Dolores Candelaria; ap/ Manuel Lopes &
Josefa Apodaca; am/ Pablo Candelaria & Andrea Montoya; gp/ Roman Apodaca & Manuela Candelaria.

LUCERO, Domingo
bap 15 May 1844, 2 days old; legit s/ Juan Cristoval Lucero & Juana Samora; ap & am/ not stated; gp/
Bernardo Valencia & Ana Maria Aragon.

VAROS, Maria Ysidora
bap 20 May 1844, 8 days old; legit d/ Roman Varos & Bibiana Montoya; ap & am/ not stated; gp/ Juan
Cruz Gonsales & Maria de Jesus Moya.

Frames 2064-2065
MARTIN, Jose Anastacio
bap 21 May 1844, 2 days old; legit s/ Jose Maria Martin & Rosario Montoya; ap/ Pedro Martin & Maria
de los Angeles Domingues; am/ Juan Maria Montoya & Juana Rael; gp/ Jesus Chaves & Maria Santos
Montoya.

ORTEGA, Maria Josefa Yrene
bap 22 May 1844; legit d/ Juan Cristoval Ortega & Maria de la Luz Basan; ap/ Andres Ortega & Maria
Andrea Garcia; am/ Ygnacio Basan & Apolonia Gutierres; gp/ Francisco Ortega & Ygnacia Basan.

SANCHES, Maria Victoria Dolores
bap 26 May 1844, 4 days old; legit d/ Juan Crus Sanches & Josefa Lucero; ap/ Jose Sanches & Juana
Garcia; am/ Jabier Lucero & Gertrudis Gonsales; gp/ Patricio Lucero & Bitoria Santillanes.

MOYA, Antonio
bap 30 May 1844, 4 days old; legit s/ Juan Francisco Moya & Paula Anaya; ap/ Victoriano Moya &
Teresa Martin; am/ Domingo Anaya & Dolores Griego; gp/ Antonio Trujillo & Dolores Trujillo.

CHAVES, Maria Candelaria
bap 13 Jun 1844, 6 days old; legit d/ Juan de Dios Chaves & Monica Lucero; ap/ Estanislao Chaves &
Soledad Ortega; am/ Mariano Lucero & Marcelina Valencia; gp/ Ambrocio Armijo & Candelaria Otero.

Frame 2066, #45
DURAN, Maria Antonia
bap 13 Jun 1844, 3 days old; legit d/ Salvador Duran & Josefa Candelaria; ap/ Miguel Duran & Ysabel
Griego; am/ Bernardo Candelaria & Marta Martines; gp/ Manuel Antonio Perea & Ana Gregoria Duran.

GALLEGO, Juan Francisco
bap 16 Jun 1844, 8 days old; legit s/ Bacilio Gallego & Clara Peña; ap & am/ not stated; gp/ Pedro Aranda & Rosalia Jaramillo.

CANDELARIA, Salvador Manuel
bap 16 Jun 1844, 2 days old; legit s/ Jesus Candelaria & Paula Chaves; ap & am/ not stated; gp/ Manuel Antonio Aragon & Maria Gallego.

NS, Juan Fortin
bap 16 Jun 1844, 5 days old; s/ unknown parents; gp/ Felipe Garcia & Josefa Garcia.

PACHECO, Antonio Jose
bap 16 Jun 1844, 7 days old; legit s/ Juan Pacheco & Juana Carbajal; ap/ Jose Pacheco & Juana Cedio; am/ Pedro Carbajal & Gertrudis Gonsales; gp/ Felipe Mestas & Marcelina Gavaldon.

Frames 2066-2067
APODACA, Maria Santa Ana
bap 20 Jun 1844, 2 days old; legit d/ Simon Apodaca & Josefa Sandoval; ap/ Rafael Apodaca & Estefana Salasar; am/ Miguel Sandoval & Manuela Gonsales; gp/ Jose Maria Herrera & Maria de la Luz Sandoval.

MADRID, Josefa
bap 21 Jun 1844, 6 days old; legit d/ Juan Madrid & Maria Sista Romero; ap & am/ not stated; gp/ Jose Guadalupe Ortega.

ALFARO, Victor Teodoro
bap 22 Jun 1844, 8 days old; legit s/ Guadalupe Alfaro & Paula Garcia; ap/ Juan Alfaro & Maria Lus Mata; am/ Juan Garcia & Manuela Perea; gp/ Antonio Garcia & Juana Saens.

CHAVES, Jose Luciano
bap 29 Jun 1844, 3 days old; legit s/ Jesus Chaves & Maria Montoya; ap/ Juan Chaves & Juliana Rael; am/ Juan Montoya & Luciana Martin; gp/ Diego Montoya & Barbara Aragon.

SALASAR, Jose Francisco
bap 30 Jun 1844, 8 days old; legit s/ Juan Salasar & Magdalena Montoya; ap & am/ not stated; gp/ Rafael Montoya & Rafaela Montoya.

Frames 2067-2068, #46
CRESPIN, Jose Pablo Estanislao
bap 30 Jun 1844, 4 days old; legit s/ Salvador Crespin & Reyes Lopes; ap & am/ not stated; gp/ Pablo Baca & Ana Maria Noanes.

MARTIN, Maria Decideria
bap 30 Jun 1844, 2 days old; legit d/ Vicente Martin & Reyes Anaya; ap & am/ not stated; gp/ Juan Mansanares.

GUTIERRES, Maria Tranquilina de los Reyes
bap 7 Jul 1844, 1 day old; legit d/ Eulogio Gutierres & Encarnacion Garcia; ap & am/ not stated; gp/ Jose Dolores Mares & Manuela Serna.

MUÑIS, Maria Barbara del Rosario
bap 7 Jul 1844, 6 days old; legit d/ Juan Cristoval Muñis & Ana Maria Pacheco; ap/ Jose Maria Muñis & Barbara Garcia; am/ Geronimo Pacheco & Pascuala Sanches; gp/ Blas Muñis & Ygnacia Martines.

APODACA, Maria Merced de Jesus
bap 13 Jul 1844, 3 days old; legit d/ Juan Apodaca & Dolores Lopes; ap/ Francisco Apodaca & Tomasa Barela; am/ Manuel Lopes & Crus Romero; gp/ Mateo Lopes & Josefa Lopes.

NS, Maria Merced
bap 14 July 1844, 3 days old; d/ unknown parents; gp/ Felipe Herrera & Juana Garcia.

Frame 2069
NS, Jose Ramon (of Cebolleta)
bap 14 Jul 1844, 1 day old; s/ unknown parents; gp/ Felipe Anaya & Francisca Anaya.

LUCERO, Francisca
bap 14 Jul 1844, 5 days old; legit d/ Ygnacio Lucero & Josefa Lopes; ap/ Gregorio Lucero & Marta Lopes; am/ Francisco Lopes & Rosalia Duran; gp/ Francisco Lopes & Francisca Luna.

GONSALES, Jose Felipe Lauriano
bap 25 Jul 1844, 8 days old, legit s/ Manuel Gonsales & Ana Maria Alire; ap & am/ not stated; gp/ Jose Tomas Montoya & Juana Maria Gutierres.

NS, Maria de los Dolores
bap 26 Jul 1844, 4 days old, Navajo child in the house of Don Ramon Gutierres; gp/ Salvador Garcia & Ana Rosa Gutierres.

NS, Maria Antonia
bap 28 Jul 1844, 6 days old; d/ unknown parents; gp/ Jose Benavides & Maria Antonia Apodaca.

Frame 2070, #47
NS, Jesus Maria y Jose
bap 28 Jul 1844, 3 days old; s/ unknown parents; gp/ Clemente Sanches & Juana Cedillo.

LOPES, Manuel Gregorio Rafael
bap 28 Jul 1844, 4 days old; legit s/ Francisco Lopes & Francisca Luna; ap/ Paulin Lopes & Ana Montaño; am/ Cidro Luna & Manuela Candelario; gp/ Gabriel Sanches & Clara Sarracino.

GRIEGO, Petra de los Angeles
bap 2 Aug 1844, 8 days old; legit d/ Juan Ysidoro Griego & Bentura Lucero; ap & am/ not stated; gp/ Jose Mares & Francisca Mares.

GONSALES, Maria Dolores
bap 4 Aug 1844, 2 days old; legit d/ Juan Gonsales & Maria Ygnacia Montaño; ap/ Francisco Gonsales & Maria Valencia; am/ Salvador Montaño & Barbara Olguin; gp/ Jose Montaño & Teresa Miera.

GUTIERRES, Nicolasa
bap 5 Aug 1844, 8 days old; legit d/ Simon Gutierres & Maria Gurule; ap & am/ not stated; gp/ Jose Dolores Samora & Soledad Garcia.

NS, Maria Juana
bap 11 Aug 1844; Navajo child in the household of Don Manuel Armijo; gp/ Mariano Ruis & Ramona Armijo.

Frame 2071
BENAVIDES, Benigna
bap 11 Aug 1844, 2 days old; legit d/ Juan Manuel Benavides & Juana Lopes; ap & am/ not stated; gp/ Jesus Candelaria & Paula Chaves.

GRIEGO, Maria Eligia
bap 18 Aug 1844, 7 days old; legit d/ Juan Griego & Dolores Cordoba; ap/ Francisco Griego & Josefa Sandoval; am/ Diego Cordoba & Juliana Santillanes; gp/ Felis Sanches & Severiana Luna.

CHAVES, Maria Estefana
bap 18 Aug 1844, 6 days old; legit d/ Jose Chaves & Juana Candelaria; ap/ Juan Chaves & Micaela Sanches; am/ Juan Candelaria & Ysidora Garcia; gp/ Juan Gutierres & Josefa Mares.

SAENS, Juana Maria
bap 18 Aug 1844, 3 days old; legit d/ Pedro Saens & Soledad Gutierres; ap/ Salvador Saens & Juana Aragon; am/ Salvador Gutierres & Nicolasa Cordova; gp/ Antonio Jose Sandoval & Dolores Sandoval.

MONTAÑO, Jose Eliseo
bap 23 Aug 1844, 5 days old; legit s/ Francisco Montaño & Juana Gutierres; ap & am/ not stated; gp/ Francisco Armijo & Soledad Armijo.

Frame 2072, #48
GONSALES, Maria Bernardina
bap 24 Aug 1844, 8 days old; legit d/ Estevan Gonsales & Dolores Arias; ap/ Juan Gonsales & Victoria Garcia; am/ Juan Domingo Arias & Juliana Lucero; gp/ Facundo Gutierres & Desideria Arias.

CANDELARIO, Lorenzo
bap 25 Aug 1844, 8 days old; legit s/ Miguel Antonio Candelario & Barvara Apodaca; ap & am/ not stated; gp/ Jose Benavides & Maria Candelario.

TAFOYA, Barbara
bap 26 Aug 1844, 2 days old; legit d/ Domingo Tafoya & Ana Maria Martin; ap & am/ not stated; gp/ Manuel Lucero & Paula Lucero.

PEREA, Bernardo
bap 26 Aug 1844, 3 days old; legit s/ Marcos Perea & Rosa Garcia; ap & am/ not stated; gp/ Marcos Sanches & Marcelina Aragon.

NS, Maria del Rosario
bap 28 Aug 1844; child of the Navajo nation in the household of Jose Fernando Gutierres; gp/ Jose Fernando Gutierres & Maria Juana Gonsales.

Frame 2073
TRUJILLO, Maria Eligia Jesus
bap 1 Sep 1844, 4 days old; legit d/ Pablo Trujillo & Maria de la Lus Gallego; ap/ Juan Antonio Trujillo & Juana Montoya; am/ Jose Miguel Gallego & Dolores Martines; gp/ Jose Sanches & Guadalupe Chaves.

LUCERO, Jose Quirino
bap 2 Sep 1844, 2 days old; legit s/ Francisco Lucero & Ynes Montoya; ap/ Juan Lucero & Maria Antonia Martin; am/ Juan Montoya & Rita Salazar; gp/ Miguel Garcia & Juana Nepomucena Garcia.

JARAMILLO, Maria de la Luz Geronima
bap 2 Sep 1844, 3 days old; legit d/ Manuel Jaramillo & Gertrudis Mestas; ap/ Miguel Jaramillo & Ana Maria Ortega; am/ Mariano Mestas & Guadalupe Chaves; gp/ Juan Cristoval Ortega & Maria de la Luz Basan.

GALLEGO, Ysidro
bap 5 Sep 1844, 1 day old; legit s/ Marcelino Gallego & Juana Salazar; ap/ Felipe Gallego & Maria Luisa Griego; am/ Miguel Salazar & Dolores Chaves; gp/ Ysidro Luna & Teodora Peña.

LOPES, Maria de Jesus Camilla
bap 5 Sep 1844, 2 days old; legit d/ Jesus Lopes & Juana Armijo; ap & am/ not stated; gp/ Lucas Gomes & Micaela Sanches.

Frames 2073-2074, #49
MONTOYA, Juan Nepomuceno
bap 10 Sep 1844, 5 days old; legit s/ Jose Maria Montoya & Dolores Gallego; ap & am/ not stated; gp/ Antonio Gallego & Catalina Chaves.

LUCERO, Maria Ygnacia Dolores
bap 12 Sep 1844, 2 days old; legit d/ Miguel Lucero & Bernarda Torres; ap/ Juan Antonio Lucero & Manuela Miera; am/ Jose Torres & Concepcion Trujillo; gp/ Juan Antonio Rael & Soledad Miera.

ARMIJO, Feliciana
bap 15 Sep 1844, 5 days old; legit d/ Juan Cristoval Armijo & Juana Chaves; ap/ Juan Armijo & Rosalia Ortega; am/ Francisco Chaves & Ana Maria Carrillo; gp/ Ambrocio Armijo & Candelaria Otero.

SANDOVAL, Jose Maria Tiburcio
bap 16 Sep 1844, 5 days old; legit s/ Jose Sandoval & Juana Carrillo; ap/ Francisco Sandoval & Juana Archibeque; am/ Juan Carrillo & Catalina Gutierres; gp/ Juan Jose Sandoval & Dolores Gonsales.

GONSALES, Maria de Jesus
bap 21 Sep 1844, 6 days old; legit s/ Francisco Gonsales & Petra Gonsales; ap/ Antonio Gonsales & Gertrudis Gurule; am/ Antonio Gonsales & Juana Sandoval; gp/ Jesus Maria Sandoval & Teresa Luna.

ROMERO, Nicolas
bap 21 Sep 1844, 7 days old; legit s/ Juan Romero & Refugia Flores; ap & am/ not stated; gp/ Diego Antonio Montoya & Maria Dolores Montoya.

Frame 2075
GARCIA, Lino
bap 24 Sep 1844, 8 days old; legit s/ Jose Luis Garcia & Marcelina Trujillo; ap/ Manuel Garcia & Manuela Perea; am/ Juan Antonio Trujillo & Juana Montoya; gp/ Juan Miguel Garcia & Guadalupe Montaño.

NS, Maria Merced Celestina
bap 26 Sep 1844, 4 days old; d/ unknown parents; gp/ Antonio Peña & Maria de Jesus Nieto.

MARTIN, Maria Francisca
bap 7 Oct 1844, 5 days old; legit d/ Juan Jose Martin & Nicolasa Sanches; ap/ Gaspar Martin & Francisca Atencio; am/ Ygnacio Sanches & Gabriela Aragon; gp/ Santiago Garcia & Marcelina Aragon.

NS, Juan Cristoval
bap 13 Oct 1844, 3 days old; s/ unknown parents; gp/ Juan Tafoya & Soledad Montoya.

GRIEGO, Maria Dolores
bap 13 Oct 1844, 2 days old; legit d/ Juan Antonio Griego & Candelaria Luna; ap/ Felipe Griego & Margarita Gonsales; am/ Ysidro Luna & Manuela Candelaria; gp/ Anastacio Varela & Rafaela Garcia.

Frame 2076, #50
CANDELARIO, Jose del Pilar
bap 15 Oct 1844, 2 days old; legit s/ Manuel Candelario & Ana Maria Trujillo; ap/ Esteban Candelario & Maria de Jesus Luna; am/ Jose Trujillo & Soledad Valencia; gp/ Jose Trujillo & Dolores Trujillo.

HERRERA, Manuel Antonio
bap 17 Oct 1844, 6 days old; legit s/ Jose Herrera & Maria de la Lus Sandoval; gp/ Andres Herrera & Dolores Garcia; am/ Miguel Sandoval & Manuela Gonsales; gp/ Salvador Tafoya & Juan Lucero.

PAIS, Maria Carlos
bap 17 Oct 1844, 3 days old; legit d/ Andres Pais & Albina Gurule; ap/ Leon Pais & Juana Arias; am/ Lagos Gurule & Juana Padilla; gp/ Francisco Rael & Gregoria Romero.

MORA, Jose Salome
bap 22 Oct 1844, 2 days old; legit d/ Estevan Mora & Juana Griego; ap/ Ysidro Mora & Juana Marques; am/ Francisco Griego & Antonia Serna; gp/ Antonio Martin & Maria Francisca Padilla.

VARELA, Maria Salome
bap 22 Oct 1844, 1 day old; legit d/ Pablo Varela & Paula Garcia; ap/ Santiago Varela & Juana Aranda; am/ Juan Antonio Garcia & Gregoria Candelario; gp/ Manuel Perea & Gabriela Candelario.

Frames 2076-2077
GARCIA, Maria Salome
bap 22 Oct 1844, 3 days old;/ d/ Juan Antonio Garcia & Gregoria Candelario; ap/ Juan Garcia & Ysavel Romero; am/ Ygnacio Candelario & Concepcion Chaves; gp/ Ramon Lucero & Leocadia Sanches.

GARCIA, Jose Abran
bap 22 Oct 1844, 6 days old; legit s/ Diego Antonio Garcia & Serafina Sanches; ap & am/ not stated; gp/ Julio Archuleta & Reyes Cedillo.

GRIEGO, Maria Francisca
bap 26 Oct 1844, 3 days old; legit d/ Deciderio Griego & Guadalupe Lucero; ap & am/ not stated; gp/ Miguel Perea & Candida Griego.

SANCHES, Maria Simona
bap 27 Oct 1844, 6 days old; legit d/ Jose Miguel Sanches & Paula Garcia; ap & am/ not stated; gp/ Juan Nerio Lovato & Dolores Cedillo.

SABEDRA, Elogia
bap 27 Oct 1844, 5 days old; legit d/ Bibiano Sabedra & Dolores Chaves; ap/ Francisco Sabedra & Maria de la Lus Chaves; am/ Vicente Chaves & Guadalupe Chaves; gp/ Jose Nieves Lusero & Maria Eulogia Sabedra.

Frame 2078, #51
HERRERA, Maria de la Lus
bap 27 Oct 1844, 7 days old; legit d/ Juan Herrera & Barbara Jaramillo; ap/ Vicente Herrera & Maria Antonia Sanches; am/ Miguel Jaramillo & Gertrudes Candelario; gp/ Salbador Herrera & Maria Ygnacia Chaves.

LOPES, Maria Merced
bap 27 Oct 1844, 3 days old; legit d/ Miguel Lopes & Francisca Ginsa; ap & am/ not stated; gp/ Pedro Lopes & Guadalupe Candelario.

NS, Monica
bap 28 Oct 1844; Indian of the Ute tribe, d/ unknown parents & in the household Don Ambrocio Armijo; gp/ Juan Armijo & Placida Armijo.

Frames 2078-2079
GARCIA, Maria Albina Merced
bap 28 Oct 1844, days old; legit d/ Juan Garcia & Juana Maria Archuleta; ap/ Felis Garcia & Ysabel Lopes; am/ Antonio Archuleta & Josefa Lujan; gp/ Ambrocio Garcia & Ludubina Sandobal.

PINEDA, Petra
bap 31 Oct 1844, 3 days old; legit d/ Nepomuseno Pineda & Josefa Truxillo; ap & am/ not stated; gp/ Juan Cristobal Gallego & Petra Padilla.

SANCHES, Jose Santos
bap 3 Nov 1844, 4 days old; legit s/ Diego Sanches & Juana Griego; ap & am/ not stated; gp/ Antonio Martin & Ludubina Martin.

PEÑA, Maria Ylaria
bap 3 Nov 1844, 5 days old; legit d/ Ramon Peña & Rosalia Ginso; ap & am/ not stated; gp/ Cicilio Romero & Rosa Romero.

Frame 2080, #52
SEDILLO, Manuela
bap 3 Nov 1844, 7 days old; legit d/ Pedro Sedillo & Petra Jaramillo; ap/ Pablo Sedillo & Madalegna Candelario; am/ Pablo Jaramillo & Concepcion Gutierres; gp/ Rafael Martin & Rafaela Anaya.

GRIEGO, Jose Maria
bap 3 Nov 1844, 4 days old; legit s/ Pedro Griego & Maria Salasar; ap & am/ not stated; gp/ Pedro Lopes & Guadalupe Candelario.

GARCIA, Ana Maria
bap 3 Nov 1844, 8 days old; legit d/ Juan Garcia & Concepcion Anaya; ap & am/ not stated; gp/ Manuel Gregorio Jaramillo & Maria Josefa Garcia.

MOYA, Maria Rafaela Eulalia
bap 3 Nov 1844; legit d/ Juan Andres Moya & Simona Sanches; ap/ Juan Moya & Manuela Barranca; am/ Mariano Sanches & Francisca Gabaldon; gp/ Gabrel Sanches & Rafaela Ruis.

Frame 2081
LUSERO, Maria Fabiana
bap 7 Nov 1844, 2 days old; legit d/ Gabrel Lusero & Gertrudes Gamboa; ap & am/ not stated; gp/ Jose Miguel Santillanes & Maria Josefa Martin.

NS, Maria Librada Nicolasa
bap 7 Nov 1844, 4 days old; d/ unknown parents; gp/ Juan Gutierres & Gregoria Armijo.

BARELA, Andrea
bap 10 Nov 1844, 4 days old; legit s/ Manuel Barela & Vicenta Gallego; ap/ Santiago Barela & Juana Aranda; am/ Juan Gallego & Manuela Gutierres; gp/ Don Ambrocio Armijo & Doña Candelaria Otero.

Frame 2082, #53
NUANES, Ambrocio
bap 12 Nov 1844, 3 days old; legit s/ Miguel Nuanes & Dolores Griego; ap & am/ not stated; gp/ Domingo Sanches & Maria de la Luz Perea.

GARCIA, Juan Bivian
bap 12 Nov 1844, 5 days old; legit s/ Jose Antonio Garcia & Polinaria Salasar; ap & am/ not stated; gp/ Juan Nuanes & Dolores Gonsales, residents of San Antonio.

BUTIERRES, Jose Consecion
bap 12 Nov 1844, 6 days old; legit s/ Juan Butierres & Francisca Anaya; ap & am/ not stated; gp/ Manuela Garcia & Concepcion Lopes.

Frames 2082-2083
GARCIA, Josefa de los Dolores
bap 12 Nov 1844, 4 days old; legit d/ Bartolo Garcia & Juana M. Padia; ap & am/ not stated; gp/ Felipe Mestas & Marselina Mestas.

LUSERO, Jose Yjinio
bap 12 Nov 1844, 6 days old; legit s/ Pedro Lusero & Encarnacion Griego; ap & am/ not stated; gp/ Pedro Lusero & Monica Lusero, residents of Los Ranchos.

LUSERO, Jose Desiderio
bap 12 Nov 1844, 2 days old; legit s/ Juan Lusero & Juana Duran; ap & am/ not stated; gp/ Bisente Mestas & Petrona Griego, residents of San Antonio.

NS, Maria Guadalupe
bap 12 Nov 1844, 4 days old; d/ unknown parents; gp/ Pomuseno Gabaldon & Maria Gabaldon.

Frame 2084, #54
NS, Maria Ysabel
bap 12 Nov 1844, 8 days old; d/ unknown parents; gp/ Juan Apodaca & Maria Sanches.

ARMIJO, Jose Carlos Trinidad
bap 16 Nov 1844, 6 days old; legit s/ Pedro Armijo & Maria de la Luz Garcia; gp/ Mariano Armijo & Juana Armijo.

LOPES, Dolores Rayos
bap 17 Nov 1844, 3 days old; legit s/ Ambrocio Lopes & Catarina Xaramio; ap & am/ not stated; gp/ Ysidro Garcia & Maria Martin.

NS, Juana Ruperta
bap 17 Nov 1844, 8 days old; child from the Ute tribe, in the household of Doña Rosalia Mestas; gp/ Mariano Mestas & Juana Armijo.

Frame 2085
SANTILLANES, Maria Ujenia
bap 17 Nov 1844, 2 days old; legit d/ Antonio Santillanes & Gertrudis Aragon; ap & am/ not stated; gp/ Juan Andres Moya & Simona Sanches.

GURULE, Maria Antonia
bap 17 Nov 1844, 4 days old; legit d/ Juana Gurule & unknown father; gp/ Juan Candelaria & Maria Antonia Garcia.

GABALDON, Jose Romano
bap 17 Nov 1844, 6 days old; legit s/ Miguel Gabaldon & Juana Lopes; ap & am/ not stated; gp/ Jose Dolores Muñis & Juana Marques.

Frame 2086, #55
GURULE, Maria de Jesus
bap 17 Nov 1844, 6 days old; legit d/ Manuel Gurule & Maria Getrudes Perea; ap & am/ not stated; gp/ Juan Aragon & Maria Rosalia Gonsales.

NS, Jose Aristeo
bap 17 Nov 1844, 4 days old; s/ unknown parents; gp/ Jose Chaves & Monica Lusero.

ABILA, Maria Josefa del Carmen
bap 25 Nov 1844, 8 days old; legit d/ Miguel Abila & Maria Lugarda Montoya; ap & am/ not stated; gp/ Don Fernando Aragon & Doña Encarnacion Baldes.

Frame 2087
CANDELARIA, Maria Catalina
bap 1 Dec 1844, 5 days old; legit d/ Antonio Candelaria & Antonia Sena; ap & am/ not stated; gp/ Domingo Sanches & Maria de la Luz Perea.

SANDOBAL, Cicilia Nestora
bap 1 Dec 1844, 4 days old; legit d/ Francisco Sandobal & Soledad Martines; ap & am/ not stated; gp/ Julian Sanches & Juana Candelaria.

LUSERO, Maria Josefa
bap 1 Dec 1844, 6 days old; legit d/ Francisco Lusero & Visenta Martines; ap & am/ not stated; gp/ Jose Tomas Apodaca & Ysidora Candelaria.

Frame 2088, #56
MONTOYA, Nicolasa
bap 15 Dec 1844, 3 days old; legit d/ Juan Bautista Montoya & Juana Rafaela Aragon; ap & am/ not stated; gp/ Agustin Sisneros & Manuela Sanches.

PADILLA, Maria Guadalupe
bap 15 Dec 1844, 4 days old; legit d/ Jose Manuel Padilla & Ysidora Arias; ap & am/ not stated; gp/ Juan Christoval Arias & Juliana Padilla.

SANDOVAL, Jose Dario
bap 17 Dec 1844, 4 days old; legit s/ Antonio Sandoval & Desideria Candelaria; ap & am/ not stated; gp/ Jose Domingo Romero & Maria Petra Padia.

Frame 2089
TORRES, Maria Juana
bap 26 Dec 1844, 6 days old; legit d/ Francisco Torres & Juliana Montoya; ap & am/ not stated; gp/ Jose Antonio Garcia & Dolores Xaramillo.

GARCIA, Maria Jesus
bap 31 Dec 1844, 7 days old; legit d/ Miguel Garcia & Rosalia Barela; ap & am/ not stated; gp/ Pedro Aranda & Soledad Aranda.

MONTAÑO, Jesus Maria
bap 2 Jan 1845, 2 days old; d/ Jose Montaño & Teresa Miera; ap & am/ not stated; gp/ Jose Antonio Garcia & Tomasa Griego.

Frame 2090, #57
PADILLA, Jose Antonio
bap 15 Jan 1845; legit s/ Baltasar Padilla & Maria Garcia; ap & am/ not stated; gp/ Antonio Trujillo & Gregoria Trujillo.

APODACA, Jose Nicanor
bap 16 Jan 1845, 7 days old; legit s/ Lino Apodaca & Clara Padilla; ap/ Rafael Apodaca & Estefana Salasar; am/ Agustin Padilla & Dolores Gonsales; gp/ Juan Gonsales & Luz Rael.

GURULE, Maria Sevastiana
bap 30 Jan 1845, 2 days old; legit d/ Jose Graviel Gurule & Nicolasa Luna, residents of Alameda; ap/ Domingo Gurule & Antonia Gonsales; am/ Ysidoro Luna & Antonia Candelaria; gp/ Jose Ramon Rael & Margarita Montoya.

Frame 2091
SANCHES, Jose de la Luz
bap 3 Feb 1845, 4 days old; legit s/ Diego Sanches & Juana Maria Gallego; ap & am/ not stated; gp/ Ramon Aragon & Ana Maria Cordoba.

GUTIERRES, Jesus Maria
bap 16 Feb 1845, 2 days old; legit s/ Manuel Gutierres & Teresa Arias; ap/ Miguel Gutierres & Manuela Bernal; am/ Juan Arias & Merced Gomes; gp/ Antonio Sandobal & Dolores Montolla.

ARMIJO, Maria Felicita
Bap 16 Feb 1845, 3 days old; legit d/ Rafael Armijo & Josefa Chabes; ap/ not stated; am/ Juan Antonio Chabes & Gertrudes Torres; gp/ Atanacio Montolla & Maria Mares.

Frame 2092, #58
GARCIA, Ramon
bap 20 Feb 1845, 4 days old; legit s/ Manuel Garcia & Hilaria Lucero; ap/ Tomas Garcia & Bernarda Tafolla; am/ Gregorio Lucero & Marta Lopes; gp/ Manuel (Martin) & Maria Antonia Martin.

CANDELARIA, Maria Santos
bap 23 Feb 1845, 5 days old; legit d/ Juan Candelaria & Juana Sanches; ap/ Salbador Candelaria & Gertrudis Lopes; am/ not stated; gp/ Jose Lopes (who named her) & Maria Josefa Montaño.

MONTAÑO, Jose Polinario
bap 23 Feb 1845, 6 days old; legit s/ Toribio Montaño & Marcelina Baca; ap/ Jose Miguel Montaño & Barbara Garcia; am/ Diego Baca & Francisca Savedra; gp/ Gregorio Armenta & Dolores Martines.

Frames 2092-2093
MARTINES, Jose Damasio
bap 23 Feb 1845, 2 days old; legit s/ Jose Martines & Gertrudis Martines; ap/ Jose Antonio Martines & Maria Ygnacia Griego; am/ not stated; gp/ Julian Gallego & Maria Sista Duran.

JARAMILLO, Juan Nepomuceno
bap 24 Feb 1845, 2 days old; legit s/ Antonio Jaramillo & Maria Garcia; ap & am/ not stated; gp/ Manuel Gonsales & Manuela Gonsales.

NS, Pedro Antonio
bap 28 Feb 1845; Ute Indian in the household of Don Antonio Ruis; gp/ Jose Armijo & Beneranda Sanches.

Frames 2093-2094, #59
NOANES, Francisca Teodora
bap 2 Mar 1845, 3 days old; legit d/ Antonio Noanes & Candelaria Griego; ap & am/ not stated; gp/ Rafael Aragon & Catarina Chabes.

NS, Maria del Carmen Refugio
bap 2 Mar 1845; Ute Indian child; gp/ Gregoria Candelaria.

APODACA, Jose Feliz
bap 2 Mar 1845, 3 days old; legit s/ Roman Apodaca & Manuela Candelaria; ap & am/ not stated; gp/ Juan Apodaca & Maria Sanches.

CANDELARIO, Maria Biatris
bap 2 Mar 1845, 3 days old; legit d/ Tomas Candelario & Maria Armijo; ap/ Pablo Candelario & Andrea Montolla; am/ not given; gp/ Jose Armijo & Beneranda Sanches.

Frame 2095
TAPIA, Domingo de Jesus
bap 6 Mar 1845, 1 day old; legit s/ Manuel Tapia & Antonia Armenta; ap & am/ not stated; gp/ Manuel Antonio Padilla & Maria Ysidora Griego.

GOMES, Albino Sesario
bap 10 Mar 1845, 3 days old; legit s/ Juan Gomes & Juliana Gonsales; ap/ Antonio Gomes & Maria Ygnacia Arias; am/ not given; gp/ Julian Sanches & Juana Candelaria.

GARCIA, Juana Gregoria
bap 10 Mar 1845, 2 days old; legit d/ Hilario Garcia & Marcelina Griego; ap & am/ not stated; gp/ Aban Duran & Gregoria Sanches.

Frame 2096, #60
LOPES, Maria Carlota
bap 10 Mar 1845, 2 days old; legit d/ Pedro Lopes & Guadalupe Candelaria; ap/ Francisco Lopes & Rosalia Duran; am/ not given; gp/ Mariano Armijo & Maria Montolla.

NS, Maria
bap 11 Mar 1845, 3 days old; d/ unknown parents; gp/ Salbador Martines & Dolores Torres.

GRIEGO, Maria Victoria
bap 13 Mar 1845, 3 days old; legit d/ Geronimo Griego & Albina Lucero; ap & am/ not stated; gp/ Baltasar Martines & Dolores Apodaca.

Frames 2096-2097
GRIEGO, Maria Tomasa
bap 13 Mar 1845, 3 days old; legit d/ Geronimo Griego & Gertrudis Garcia; ap & am/ not stated; gp/ Juan Pablo Martines & Maria Cicilia Candelaria.

OLGUIN, Jose Gregorio
bap 14 Mar 1845, 2 days old; legit s/ Jesus Olguin & Maria Antonia Jaramillo; ap & am/ not stated; gp/ Juan Ballejos & Maria Gertrudes Ballejos.

ANALLA, Juan Jose
bap 14 Mar 1845, 2 days old; legit s/ Jesus Analla & Francisca Baca; ap/ Antonio Analla & Tomasa Tafolla; am/ not stated; gp/ Juan Apodaca & Maria Sanches.

Frames 2097-2098, #61
PACHECO, Jose Leandro
bap 15 Mar 1845, 3 days old; legit s/ Juan Pacheco & Juliana Gutierres; ap/ Francisco Pacheco & Juana Rael; am/ not given; gp/ Pedro Martines & Maria Gertrudis Apodaca.

SAMORA, Francisco Roman
bap 16 Mar 1845, 4 days old; legit s/ Christobal Samora & Maria Martines; ap/ not given; am/ Juan Martines & Juliana Montaño; gp/ Jose Miguel Lucero & Catarina Gutierres.

DURAN, Maria Josefa
bap 16 Mar 1845, 1 day old; legit d/ Antonio Duran & Tomasa Gutierres; ap/ Mateo Duran & Maria Antonia Muñiz; am/ not given; gp/ Jose Dolores Samora & Soledad Garcia.

LOPES, Maria del Rosario
bap 3 Apr 1845, 1 day old; legit d/ Bernabe Lopes & Cipriana Perea; ap & am/ not stated; gp/ Seledon Apodaca & Juana Apodaca.

Frame 2099
ROMERO, Jose Octabiano
bap 3 Apr 1845, 2 days old; legit s/ Manuel Romero & Marcelina Armijo; ap & am/ not stated; gp/
Manuel Apodaca & Francisca Aragon.

ANALLA, Jose Bitoriano
bap 5 Apr 1845, 2 days old; legit s/ Feliz Analla & Cicilia Gurule; ap & am/ not stated; gp/ Juan Armenta
& Biatris Garcia.

Frames 2099-2100, #62
SANCHES, Maria de la Piedad
bap 5 Apr 1845, 2 days old; legit d/ Jose Maria Sanches & Maria Antonia Jaramillo; ap & am/ not stated;
gp/ Jesus Maria Gallego & Maria Rosario Garcia.

GALLEGO, Jose Tiofilo
bap 7 Apr 1845, 3 days old; legit s/ Balentino Gallego & Manuela Apodaca; ap & am/ not stated; gp/ Blas
Lucero & Rosalia Tenorio.

ANALLA, Jose de la Luz
bap 7 Apr 1845, 3 days old; legit s/ Juan Analla & Dolores Montaño; gp/ Feliz Ortega & Relles Sanches.

SANDOBAL, Jose Carlos
bap 8 Apr 1845, 1 day old; legit s/ Jose Sandobal & Josefa Garcia; ap & am/ not stated; gp/ Manuel
Sanches & Acension Sanches.

Frame 2101
PADILLA, Jose Epimenio
bap 10 Apr 1845, 6 days old; legit s/ Jose Dolores Padilla & Maria Dolores Sandobal; ap/ Julian Padilla &
Ana Maria Padilla; am/ not stated; gp/ Pablo Armijo.

NOANES, Jose Estanislado
bap 10 Apr 1845, 3 days old; legit s/ Santiago Noanes & Manuela Atencio; ap/ Geronimo Noanes &
Barbara Maes; am/ Gaspar Atencio & Maria Ysabel Candelario; gp/ Anastacio Noanes & Barbara Gurule.

Frames 2101-2102, #63
GARCIA, Manuel Gregorio
bap 10 Apr 1845, 3 days old; legit s/ Jose Garcia & Guadalupe Baca; ap/ Ramon Garcia & Acencion
Lopes; am/ not given; gp/ Jesus Jose Apodaca & Dolores Torres.

GRIEGO, Juan Maximo
bap 4 May 1845, 3 days old; legit s/ Ysidro Griego & Paula Garcia; ap/ Jose Griego & Gertrudis
Valencia; am/ Francisco Garcia & Relles Candelaria; gp/ Miguel Montaño & Clara Candelario.

GALLEGO, Jose Miguel
bap 4 May 1845, 7 days old; legit s/ Jose Atanacio Gallego & Petrona Martines, ap/ Martin Gallego &
Guadalupe Baca; am/ Felipe Martines & Victoria Arias; gp/ Pedro Aranda & Rosalia Jaramillo.

Frames 2102-2103
MESTA, Maria Felicita
bap 4 May 1845, 3 days old; legit s/ Pedro Mesta & Dolores Apodaca; ap/ not given; am/ Juan Apodaca
& Maria Sanches; gp/ Don Manuel Armijo & Doña Rosalia Mestas.

GARCIA, Juan Nepomuceno
bap 4 May 1845, 5 days old; legit s/ Juan Christobal Garcia & Josefa Garcia; ap & am/ not stated; gp/
Juan Pedro Carabajal & Gertrudis Gonsales.

GARCIA, Manuela Antonia
bap 4 May 1845, 3 days old; legit d/ Jose Garcia & Nepomucena Rael; ap/ Andres Garcia & Juana Garcia;
am/ not stated; gp/ Salbador Tafolla & Juana Lucero.

Frames 2103-2104, #64
GARCIA, Maria Rufina
bap 4 May 1845; 3 days old; legit d/ Jose Garcia & Petra Aragon; ap & am/ not stated; gp/ Jose Higinio
Lucero & Ramona Montolla.

NS, Jose Polinario
bap 7 May 1845, 2 days old; s/ unknown parents; gp/ Pedro Lucero & Encarnacion Griego.

NS, Maria Ysidora
bap 7 May 1845, 3 days old; d/ unknown parents; gp/ Jose Maria Ortega & Juana Duran.

Frames 2104-2105
GUTIERRES, Jose Crecencio
bap 7 May 1845, 2 days old; legit s/ Fernando Gutierres & Decideria Arias; ap/ Francisco Gutierres &
Manuela Bernal; am/ not given; gp/ Pablo Barela & Paula Garcia.

CANDELARIA, Jose Jorge
bap 7 May 1845, 4 days old; s/ Jose Rafael Candelaria & Tomaza Garcia; ap & am/ not stated; gp/
Francisco Garcia & Paula Sandoval.

GARCIA, Jose Marcelino
bap 7 May 1845, 6 days old; legit s/ Jose Garcia & Maria Ysidora Gonsales; ap/ Juan Guadalupe Garcia
& Dolores Candelario; am/ Antonio Gonsales & Clara Garcia, gp/ Bicente Lopes & Rafela Duran.

NS, Jose Donaciano
bap 9 May 1845; s/ unknown Indian parents; gp/ Jose Sabedra & Francisca Garcia.

Frame 2106, #65
BARELA, Maria Monica
bap 9 May 1845, 3 days old; legit d/ Anastacio Barela & Maria Rafaela Garcia; ap/ Santiago Barela &
Juana Aranda; am/ Tadeo Garcia & Jacinta Perea; gp/ Francisco Aranda & Barbara Montaño.

CANDELARIA, Jose Solomon
bap 9 May 1845, 2 days old; legit s/ Francisco Candelaria & Ysabel Chabes; ap & am/ not stated; gp/
Felipe Martines & Maria Juana Apodaca.

NS, Esmeregildo
bap 9 May 1845, 1 day old; s/ unknown parents; gp/ Antonio Aragon & Maria Estefana Aragon.

Frame 2107
NS, Jose Gregorio
bap 10 May 1845, 4 days old; s/ unknown parents; gp/ Paulin Aldaz & Tomasa Sena.

ANALLA, Jose de la Cruz
bap 10 May 1845, 1 day old; legit s/ Jose Rosalio Analla & Teresa Candelaria; ap & am/ not stated; gp/ Salbador Garcia & Paula Sandobal.

BARELA, Juan Antonio Aban
bap 11 May 1845, 2 days old; legit s/ Antonio Aban Barela & Maria Catarina Ortiz; ap/ Juan Barela & Josefa Chabes; am/ Lorenso Ortiz & Rafaela Ruiz; gp/ Antonio Aragon & Maria Estefana Aragon.

Frame 2108, #66
SANCHES, Maria Rosalia
bap 11 May 1845, 3 days old; legit d/ Jose Sanches & Maria Dolores Chabes; ap/ Juan Andres Sanches & Maria Josefa Sena; am/ not stated; gp/ Antonio Maria Lucero & Maria Filomena Lucero.

BACA, Maria Teodora
bap 11 May 1845, 2 days old; legit d/ Antonio Baca & Manuela Lucero; ap/ Rafael Baca & Juana Rita Candelaria; am/ Alfonso Lucero & Manuela Chrespin; gp/ Blas Muñiz & Maria Ygnacia Martines.

Frames 2108-2109
MARTINES, Maria Florentina
bap 11 May 1845, 4 days old; legit d/ Miguel Antonio Martines & Francisca Carabajal; ap/ Rafael Martines & Manuela Tafolla; am/ Juan Pedro Carabajal & Gertrudis Gonsales; gp/ Manuel Garcia & Concepcion Lopes.

CHABES, Jose Estanislado
bap 16 May 1845, 3 days old; legit s/ Miguel Chabes & Dicideria Gurule; ap & am/ not stated; gp/ Manuel Sanches & Carmen Sanches.

SANDOBAL, Jose Maria
bap 17 May 1845, 4 days old; legit s/ Juan Sandobal & Justa Garcia; ap/ Jose Sandobal & Petra Sabedra; am/ not stated; gp/ Jose Armijo & Beneranda Sanches.

Frame 2110, #67
LUCERO, Jose Donaciano
bap 21 May 1845, 2 days old; legit s/ Jose Lucero & Maria Gertrudis Gutierres; ap/ Juan Jose Lucero & Petra Lopes; am/ Antonio Gutierres & Francisca Sanches; gp/ Priest, Don Nicolas Valencia & Doña Paula Martines.

NS, Jose
bap 4 May 1845, 3 days old; s/ unknown parents; gp/ Jose Barela & Dolores Barela.

Frames 2110-2111
SANCHES, Juliana
bap 29 May 1845, 4 days old; legit d/ Manuel Sanches & Petra Chaves; gp/ Fernando Xaramio & Petra Sanches.

Note: Priest's annotation.

Frame 2112, #68
TRUJILLO, Felipe Neri
bap 1 Jun 1845, 2 days old; legit s/ Santiago Trujillo & Maria Gutierres; ap/ Jose Trujillo & Soledad Balencia; am/ Miguel Gutierres & Gregoria Armijo; gp/ Manuel Candelaria & Ana Maria Trujillo.

MONTAÑO, Pedro Selestino
bap 1 Jun 1845, 4 days old; legit s/ Jose Manuel Montaño & Guadalupe Garcia; ap/ Juan Jose Montaño & Miquela Santillanes; am/ Julian Garcia & Barbara Serna; gp/ Jose Montaño & Tereza Miera.

Frame 2113
CANDELARIA, Juan Antonio de Jesus
bap 1 Jun 1845, 4 days old; legit s/ Julian Candelaria & Ana Maria Garcia; ap/ Jose Tomas Candelaria & Ana Maria Gayego; am/ Diego Antonio Garcia & Ramona Candelaria; gp/ Domingo Sanchez & Maria de la Luz Perea.

NUANEZ, Juana Gregoria
bap 13 Jun 1845, 6 days old; legit d/ Andres Nuanez & Manuela Armijo; ap/ Miguel Nuanez & Andrea Candelaria; am/ Cristobal Armijo & Matilde Barbero; gp/ Juan Gutierrez & Gregoria Armijo.

Frames 2113-2114, #69
GONSALEZ, Maria Daniel
bap 15 Jun 1845; legit d/ Jose Gonsalez & Francisca Santillanes; ap/ Francisco Gonsalez & Josefa Alire; am/ Nicolas Santillanes & Maria Luiza Garcia; gp/ Domingo Romero & Petra Garcia.

BACA, Jose Epimenio
bap 15 Jun 1845; legit s/ Manuel Baca & Guadalupe Garcia; ap/ Simon Baca & Ysabel Apodaca; am/ Antonio Garcia & Margarita Rael; gp/ Pedro Perea & Maria Jesus Jaramillo, of Alameda.

GRIEGO, Maria del Refugio
bap 4 Jul 1845; legit d/ Dionicio Griego & Maria Manuela Carabajal; ap/ Miguel Griego & Josefa Duran; am/ Domingo Carabajal & Toribia Sanchez; gp/ Francisco Griego & Soledad Sanchez.

Frame 2115
MONTOYA, Maria Clara
bap 8 Jul 1845; legit d/ Atanacio Montoya & Maria Mares; ap/ Juan Montoya & Soledad Ortega; am/ Nicolas Mares & Manuela Garcia; gp/ Miguel Montaño & Clara Candelaria.

GUTIERRES, Maria Santana
bap 9 Jul 1845, 4 days old; legit d/ Felipa Gutierres & unknown father; gp/ Jose Antonio Balencia & Juliana Gutierrez.

MOYA, Maria Nicolasa
bap 13 Jul 1845; legit d/ Jesus Moya & Maria Antonia Romero; ap & am/ not stated; gp/ Jose Gabriel Gurule & Maria Nicolasa Luna.

Frame 2116, #70
CHABEZ, Maria de los Angeles
bap 10 Aug 1845; legit d/ Antonio Chabez & Maria Ygnacia Montoya; ap/ Jeronimo Chabez & Encarnacion Gonsalez; am/ Mariano Montoya & Maria Reyez Mestas, of Alameda; gp/ Santiago Gonsalez & Manuela Aragon.

GARCIA, Jesus Jermenico
bap 10 Aug 1845; legit s/ Dolores Garcia & Ygnacia Sabedra; ap/ Pedro Garcia & Getrudiz Sanchez; am/ Miguel Zamora & Marcelina Chabez; gp/ Juan Garcia & Maria Chabez.

LOPEZ, Maria Leonor del Refugio
bap 10 Aug 1845; legit d/ Mateo Lopez & Josefa Lopez; ap & am/ not stated; gp/ Juan Apodaca & Manuela Gutierrez.

Frame 2117
LUCERO, Jose Ygnacio
bap 13 Aug 1845; legit s/ Jose Lucero & Eulogia Sabedra; ap/ Andres Lucero & Tomasa Garcia; am/ Francisco Sabedra & Maria de la Lus Chabes, of Atrisco; gp/ Pablo Lucero & Gabriela Jaramillo.

SANDOBAL, Maria Guadalupe
bap 15 Aug 1845; legit d/ Jose Sandobal & Maria Gertrudiz Gonsalez; ap/ Miguel Sandobal & Ygnacia Armenta; am/ Jose Gonsalez & Maria Rosa Rael, of Alameda; gp/ Francisco Sandobal & Soledad Muñiz.

Frames 2117-2118, #71
CHABEZ, Juan Bautista
bap 17 Aug 1845; legit s/ Jose Dolores Chabez & Juliana Griego; ap/ Bartolo Chabez & Manuela Duran; am/ Pablo Griego & Ysidora Apodaca, of Albuquerque; gp/ Rumaldo Griego & Nicolasa Griego.

NS, Bitoria
bap 7 Sep 1845; d/ unknown parents; gp/ Sisilio Romero & Rosa Romero.

MARTIN, Jose Trenidad
bap 7 Sep 1845; legit s/ Antonio Martin & Manuela Candelaria; ap/ Manuel Martin & Luz Griego; am/ Miguel Candelaria & Rafaela Garcia, of Albuquerque; gp/ Juan Martin & Difonsa Olgin.

MALDONADO, Rosa
bap 7 Sep 1845; legit d/ Anselmo Maldonado & Maria Bibiana Castio; ap/ Domingo Maldonado & Maria Manuela Aragon; am/ not given; gp/ Jose Manuel Romero & Trenidad Montoya, of Alameda.

Frame 2119
GARCIA, Vitoriano
bap 9 Sep 1845; legit s/ Salbador Garcia & Soledad Garcia; ap & am/ not stated; gp/ Blas Muñis & Maria Ygnacia Martinez.

NS, Maria Agustina
bap 10 Sep 1845; d/ unknown parents; gp/ Mariano Marez & Maria Manuel Serna, of Albuquerque.

NS, Maria Ygnacia
bap 10 Sep 1845; d/ unknown parents; gp/ Lorenzo Sandobal & Maria Ygnacia Sandobal, of Alameda.

Frame 2120, #72
CHABES, Jose Nestor
bap 11 Sep 1845; legit s/ Rafael Chabes & Apolonia Lusero; ap & am/ not stated; gp/ Jose Rafael (Ortiz) & Desideria Ortiz, of Alameda.

APODACA, Jose de Jesus Perfidio
bap 16 Sep 1845; legit s/ Juan Apodaca & Maria de la Luz Padia; ap/ Rafael Apodaca & Ana Maria Romero; am/ Julian Padilla & Ana Maria Padilla; gp/ Pedro Antonio Perea & Maria de la Luz Perea, of Alameda.

NS, Francisco Antonio
bap 18 Sep 1845, 5 days old; s/ unknown parents; gp/ Pedro Candelario & Maria Petra Apodaca.

Frame 2121
ROMERO, Maria Rafaela
bap 22 Sep 1845, 9 days old; legit d/ Lorenso Romero & Merced Muñis; ap/ Diego Romero & Encarnacion Valencia; am/ Francisco Muñis & Teodora Arias; gp/ Anastacio Barela & Rafaela Garcia.

CARRILLO, Jose Maria Benselan
bap 23 Sep 1845, 6 days old; legit s/ Jose Carrillo & Cicilia Ramires; gp/ Felis Sanches & Sebastiana Sena.

Frames 2121-2122, #73
MONTAÑO, Maria Juliana
bap 28 Sep 1845; legit d/ Lorenso Montaño & Petra Candelario; ap/ Antonio Montaño & Manuela Martinez; am/ Vicente Candelaria & Ana Maria Chabez; gp/ Juan Gonsales & Luz Rael.

NS, Jose Dario
bap 28 Sep 1845; s/ unknown parents; gp/ Jose Dario Aragon & Maria Aragon, of Albuquerque.

NS, Maria Agapita
bap 28 Sep 1845; d/ unknown parents; gp/ Francisco Lucero & Bisenta Martines, of Albuquerque.

LOPEZ, Maria Marselina
bap 28 Sep 1845; legit d/ Bicente Lopez & Guadalupe Baca; ap & am/ not stated; gp/ Juan Jose Marquez & Mariana Marquez.

Frame 2123
LUJAN, Maria Juana Dolores
bap 28 Sep 1845; legit d/ Jose M^l Lujan & Dolores Duran; ap & am/ not stated; gp/ Miguel Antonio Martines & Maria Francisca Carabajal, of Albuquerque.

TURRIETA, Jose Manuel
bap 28 Sep 1845; legit s/ Vicente Turrieta & Maria Antonia Jaramio; ap/ Toribi Turrieta & Rafaela Alderete; am/ Miguel Jaramio & Getrudiz Griego; gp/ Jose Antonio Garcia & Sabel Gallego, of Albuquerque.

URTADO, Merced (of Alameda)
bap 29 Sep 1845; legit d/ Mariano Urtado & Getrudis Sanches; ap/ Pedro Urtado & Juana Barela; am/ Mariano Sanches & Carmen Escudero; gp/ Felipe Garcia & Francisca Garcia, of Alameda.

Frames 2123-2124, #74
NS, Maria Sipriana
bap 5 Oct 1845, 3 days old; d/ unknown parents; gp/ Lino Cordoba & Eluteria Garcia.

NS, Juan Antonio
bap 7 Oct 1845, 2 days old; s/ unknown parents; gp/ Felipe Garcia & Maria del Rosario Marques.

PACHECO, Gertrudis
bap 8 Oct 1845, 6 days old; legit d/ Francisco Pacheco & Manuela Truxillo; ap & am/ not stated; gp/ Salbador Sandobal & Juana Truxillo.

LUSERO, Gertrudis (twin)
LUSERO, Maria del Rosario (twin)
bap 12 Oct 1845, 7 days old; legit d/ Juan Antonio Lusero & Maria Dolores Gutierres; ap & am/ not stated; first gp/ Salbador Jaramillo & Maria Gertrudes Baca; second gp/ Jose Armijo & Guadalupe Chaves.

Frame 2125
SALASAR, Jose Francisco
bap 12 Oct 1845, 8 days old; legit s/ Lorenso Salasar & Manuela Baca; ap/ Salbador Salasar & Juana Maria Trebol; am/ Sabino Baca & Tomasa Lopes; gp/ Juan Garcia & Maria Concepcion Anaya.

ROMERO, Jose Teofilo
bap 14 Oct 1845, 3 days old; legit s/ Domingo Romero & Petra Padilla; ap/ Miguel Romero & Juana Garcia; am/ Julian Padilla & Ana Maria Padilla; gp/ Jose Gonsales & Francisca Antonia Santillanes.

LUSERO, Jose Pilar
bap 15 Oct 1845, 4 days old; legit s/ Blas Lusero & Rosalia Tenorio; ap/ Andres Lusero & Tomasa Garcia; am/ Julian Tenorio & Benigna Chaves; gp/ Don Mariano Ysisarri & Doña Juana Otero.

ALFAROS, Jose Florencio
bap 19 Oct 1845, 3 days old; legit s/ Guadalupe Alfaros & Paubla Griego; ap/ Jose Maria Alfaros & Juana Mora; am/ Manuel Garcia & Manuela Perea; gp/ Julian Gallego & Maria Sista Duran.

Frame 2126, #75
[Note: On 20 Nov 1845, Father Ortiz turned over the records to Father Gallegos.]

GRIEGO, Maria Florentina
bap 20 Oct 1845, 15 days old; legit d/ Tomas Griego & Ascencion Contreras, residents of Albuquerque; ap/ Jose Griego & Maria Martin; am/ Tomas Contreras & Paula Chaves; gp/ Andres Moya & Simona Sanches, residents of the same.

SISNEROS, Maria Ursula
bap 21 Oct 1845, 20 days old; legit d/ Agustin Sisneros & Juana Sanches, of Alameda; ap/ Bicente Sisneros & Anna Maria Nevares; am/ Mariano Sanches & Maria del Carmen Escuerdo; gp/ Marcelino Aragon & Rosalia Gonsales, of Alameda.

Frame 2127
SANCHES, Jose Feliciano
bap 22 Oct 1845, 4 days old; legit s/ Jose Sanches & Clara Chaves, of Los Ranchos de Atrisco; ap/ Gabriel Sanches & Juana Sedillo; am/ Antonio Chaves & Gertrudis Valdes; gp/ Jose Lucero & Maria Eulogia Sabedra, of Los Ranchos de Atrisco.

PACHECO, Maria Petra
bap 26 Oct 1845, 5 days old; legit d/ Juan Pacheco & Maria Juana Carabajal, of Albuquerque; ap/ Jose Pacheco & Juana Sedio; am/ Juan Pedro Carbajal & Gertrudes Gonsales; gp/ Juan Pomoceno Carabajal & Maria Dolores Carabajal, of the same place.

Frames 2127-2128, #76
SANCHES, Rafaela
bap 26 Oct 1845, 3 days old; legit d/ Francisco Sanches & Manuela Sanches, of Albuquerque; ap/ Gabriel Sanches & Juana Sedio; am/ Ramon Sanches & Barbara Montoya; gp/ Gregorio Garcia & Juana Maria Vaca.

SANCHES, Nestor
bap 26 Oct 1845, 3 days old; legit s/ Domingo Sanches & Perfeta Montoya, of Alameda; ap/ Diego Antonio Sanches & Maria Ygnacia Anaya; am/ Pedro Montoya & Ana Maria Luna; gp/ Santiago Perea & Maria de la Lus Perea.

MARTIN, Jesus Maria y Jose
bap 4 Nov 1845, 7 days old; s/ Baltasar Martin & Maria Dolores Apodaca, of Alameda; ap/ Jose Martin & Juana Griego; am/ Rafael Apodaca & Juana Maria Romero; gp/ Rafael Apodaca & Juana Maria Romero, of the same place.

Frame 2128-2129
APODACA, Jesus Jose
bap 6 Nov 1845, 3 days old; legit s/ Jose Francisco Apodaca & Nicolasa Burle, of Corrales; ap/ Nicolas Apodaca & Maria de la Luz Garcia; am/ Ygnacio Burle & Maria Polonia Nieta; gp/ Pedro Antonio Perea & Maria Sevastiana Sena.

GALLEGOS, Maria Francisca
bap 14 Nov 1845, 6 days old; legit d/ Francisco Gallegos & Maria Tomas Candelaria; ap/ Alejandro Gallegos & Lus Gonsales; am/ Catarina Candelaria; gp/ Francisco Teodoro Jaramio & Maria Antonia Teresa de Jesus Armijo, residents of the Ranchos de Albuquerque.

CANDELARIO, Jose Manuel
bap 15 Nov 1845, 10 days old; legit s/ Salbador Candelario & Juana Jaramio, residents of los Candelarias; ap/ Catarina Candelaria; am/ Julian Jaramio & Juana Maria Arias; gp/ Rafael Armijo & Josefa Chavez, of the same place.

Frames 2129-2130, #77
BUTIERRES, Jose Miguel
bap 26 Nov 1845, 2 days old; legit s/ Juan Pablo Butierres & Josefa Martin, residents of Albuquerque; ap/ Miguel Butierres & Gregoria Armijo; am/ Jose Antonio Martin & Monica Jaramio, residents of los Candelarias; gp/ Juan Butierres & Maria Butierres, residents of los Candelarias.

ARMIJO, Rafael Gregorio de la Trinidad
bap 23 Nov 1845, 3 days old; legit s/ Jose Armijo & Beneranda Sanches, residents of Albuquerque; ap/ Ambrocio Armijo & Maria Antonia Ortiz; am/ Gabriel Sanches & Rafaela Ruis; gp/ Clara Sarracino.

CARABAJAL, Jose Antonio
bap 24 Nov 1845, 4 days old; legit s/ Meregildo Carabajal & Margarita Duran, residents of los Duranes; ap/ Calletano Carabajal & Romona Perea; am/ Salbador Duran & Valbaneda Garcia; gp/ Francisco Duran & Bernarda Burule, of Albuquerque.

Frames 2130-2131
GARCIA, Felipe
bap 25 Nov 1845, 4 days old; legit s/ Lucas Garcia & Rosalia Garcia, residents of los Candelarias; ap/ Francisco Garcia & Maria Encarnacion Apodaca; am/ Juan Garcia & Juan Vitoria Montaño; gp/ Jesus Gonsales & Juana Apodaca, residents of the same.

BUTIERRES, Maria Feliciana
bap 8 Dec 1845, 2 days old; legit d/ Felipe Butierres & Maria Lorensa Perea, of los Griegos; ap/ Miguel Butierres & Cimona Griego; am/ Juan Perea & Maria Gertrudis Jaramio; gp/ Mariano Mares & Maria Manuela Serna.

ANALLA, Maria Nicolasa
bap 14 Dec 1845, 9 days old; natural d/ Polonia Analla, resident of Alameda; am/ Rafael Analla & Maria de Jesus Gallego; gp/ Roque Chaves & Maria Desideria Candelario.

Frames 2131-2132, #78
MARES, Maria Alvina
bap 17 Dec 1845, 1 day old; legit d/ Jose Manuel Mares & Francisca Candelaria, residents of Atrisco; ap/ Nicolas Mares & Maria Manuela Candelaria; am/ Juan Pablo Candelaria & Francisca Errera; gp/ Manuel Candelaria & Juliana Candelaria.

ESPALIN, Juana Maria
bap 18 Dec 1845, 1 day old; legit d/ Seferino Espalin & Anna Maria Romero; ap/ Florentino Espalin & Francisca Garcia; am/ Miguel Romero & Maria Romero; gp/ Jose Apodaca & Gabriela Apodaca.

JARAMIO, Maria Lasara
bap 18 Dec 1845, 1 day old; legit d/ Manuel Jaramio & Josefa Baca, residents of los Ranchos; ap/ Juan Bautista Jaramio & Encarnacion Garcia; am/ Juan Andres Baca & Guadalupe Tafolla; gp/ Francisco Ortega & Ygnacia Vasan.

MARES, J. Maria
bap 20 Dec 1845, 8 days old; natural s/ Polonia Mares, resident of los Candelarias; am/ Nicolas Mares & Manuela Garcia; gp/ Rafael Lopes & Maria Luisa Chaves.

Frame 2133
BUTIERRES, Maria Gregoria
bap 20 Dec 1845, 2 days old; legit d/ Rafael Butierres & Maria Dolores Trujillo, residents of los Ranchos de Albuquerque; ap/ Miguel Butierres & Maria Gregoria Armijo; am/ Jose Trugillo & Maria Gregoria Trugillo; gp/ Jose Trugillo & Maria Gregoria Trugillo, of the same place.

ANAYA, Maria Demetria
bap 22 Dec 1845, 3 days old; legit d/ Jesus Anaya & Francisca Baca, residents of Albuquerque; ap/ Antonio Anaya & Tomasa Tafolla; am/ Lino Baca & Francisca Samora; gp/ Amador Candelaria & Maria Armijo, residents of the same.

GRIEGO, Julio
bap 24 Dec 1845, 2 days old; legit s/ Loreto Griego & Mariana Sanches, residents of los Ranchos; ap/ Antonio Griego & Guadalupe Gonsales; am/ Feliz Sanches & Anna Maria Padilla; gp/ Bicente Sanches & Octabiana Sanches, of the same place.

SANCHES, Salbador Manuel
bap 24 Dec 1845, 2 days old; natural s/ Trinidad Sanches, residents of Albuquerque; am/ Manuel Sanches & Anna Maria Garcia; gp/ Jose Lucero & Micaela Armijo, residents of the same.

Frame 2134, #79
LOPES, Maria Trinidad
bap 24 Dec 1845, 3 days old; legit d/ Teodoro Lopes & Maria Josefa Chaves, of los Barelas; ap/ Manuel Lopes & Maria de la Crus Romero; am/ Augustin Chaves & Maria Juana Sanches; gp/ Juan Antonio Aragon & Maria Estefana Aragon, of the same place.

GALLEGOS, Manuela Antonia
bap 28 Dec 1845, 3 days old; legit d/ Ramon Gallegos & Rosalia Montaño, residents of Albuquerque; ap/ Antonio Jose Gallegos & Madalena Garcia; am/ Torivio Montaño & Ana Maria Candelaria; gp/ Francisco Butierres & Dolores Ortega, residents of the same.

GARCIA, Beneranda
bap 28 Dec 1845, 2 days old; legit d/ Juan Garcia & Ynes Luna, residents of Albuquerque; ap/ Juan Ygnacio Garcia & Juana Baleranda; am/ Tomas Luna & Rafaela Garcia; gp/ Juan Gonsales & Ysabel Gonsales, residents of the same.

Frames 2134-2135
VIGIL, Jose Tomas
bap 29 Dec 1845, 3 days old; natural s/ Maria Romona Vigil, resident of Los Ranchos; am/ Francisco Vigil & Margarita Salazar; gp/ Francisco Duran & Maria Gregoria Sanches, residents of Albuquerque.

GRIEGO, Maria Nicanora
bap 4 Jan 1846, 5 days old; legit d/ Gregorio Griego & Francisca Apodaca, residents los Griegos; ap/ Jose Maria Griego & Candelaria Armijo; am/ Juan Apodaca & Maria Manuela Gurule; gp/ J. Tomas Apodaca & Ysidora Candelaria.

ARCHIBEQUE, Maria Justa
bap 4 Jan 1846, 3 days old; natural d/ Vitoria Archibeque, residents of Albuquerque; am/ Matias Archibeque & Maria Manuela Sanches; gp/ J. Maria Madrid & Maria Justa Garcia, of the same place.

APODACA, Reyes
bap 5 Jan 1846, 6 days old; legit d/ Juan Jose Apodaca & Concepcion Romero, residents of Alameda; ap/ Dionicio Apodaca & Maria Luteria Garcia; am/ Baltasar Romero & Maria Paula Lucero; gp/ Pedro Martines & Maria Gertrudis Apodaca.

Frame 2136, #80
TRUGILLO, Gregoria
bap 6 Jan 1846, 7 days old; legit d/ Pablo Trugillo & Maria de la Luz Gallegos, residents of los Ranchos of Albuquerque; ap/ Juan Antonio Trugillo & Juana Montoya; am/ J. Miguel Gallegos & Maria Dolores Martines; gp/ Toribio Trugillo & Gregoria Trugillo, residents of the same.

RAEL, Ynocencia Preciliana
bap 6 Jan 1846, 10 days old; legit d/ Santiago Rael & Maria Serafina Martines, residents of Alameda; ap/ Eusebio Rael & Rosa Montoya; am/ Agustin Martines & Candelaria Chaves; gp/ Manuel Garcia & Rafaela Rael, residents of the same.

LUCERO, Manuela Serafina
bap 7 Jan 1846, 3 days old; legit d/ Francisco Lucero & Dolores Baca, residents of San Antonio; ap/ J. Antonio Lucero & Rafaela Archuleta; am/ Reyes Baca & Manuela Archuleta; gp/ Pablo Baca & Anna Maria Noanes, residents of the same.

Frames 2136-2137
GARCIA, Maria Manuela
bap 10 Jan 1846, 10 days old; legit d/ Gregorio Garcia & Juana Maria Baca, residents of Albuquerque; ap/ Ysidro Garcia & Gertrudes Sanches; am/ Juan Jose Baca & Maria Gertrudes Castillo; gp/ Juan Andres Moya & Maria Gertrudis Castillo, of the same place.

MARTINES, Guadalupe
bap 15 Jan 1846, 2 days old; natural d/ Mersed Martines, residents of Albuquerque; am/ Pablo Martines & Nicolasa Ramires; gp/ Antonio Jose Armijo & Guadalupe Sabedra, residents of the same.

MARTIN, Jose Nicanor
bap 15 Jan 1846, 3 days old; legit s/ Felipe Martin & Juana Apodaca, residents of Alameda; ap/ Jose Antonio Martin & Quiteria Griego; am/ Rafael Apodaca & Juana Maria Romero; gp/ Rafael Apodaca & Juana Maria Romero.

Frames 2137-2138, #81
MARTIN, Josefa
bap 15 Jan 1846, 4 days old; legit d/ Felipe Martin & Bitoria Arias, residents of Albuquerque; ap/ Juan Esteban Martin & Maria Luisa Mora; am/ Miguel Arias & Maria Ygnacia Balencia; gp/ Jose Mares & Francisca Mares, residents of the same.

MONTAÑO, Juana Nepomucena
bap 15 Jan 1846, 9 days old; legit d/ Miguel Montaño & Maria Clara Candelaria, residents of los Ranchos; ap/ Antonio Montaño & Manuela Antonia Martines; am/ Vicente Candelaria & Anna Maria Chaves; gp/ Juan Esteban Sanches & Juana Garcia, residents of the same.

GALLEGO, Juan Nepomuceno
bap 16 Jan 1846, 1 day old; legit s/ Rafael Gallego & Ysabel Trujillo, residents of los Ranchos; ap/ Jose Miguel Gallego & Anna Maria Mora; am/ Jose Miguel Trujillo & Bitoria Duran; gp/ Juan Manuel Madrid & Rafaela Madrid, residents of the same.

Frames 2138-2139
CORDOBA, Eligia Lucia
bap 16 Jan 1846, 8 days old; legit d/ Leonicio Cordoba & Juana Sanches, residents of Alameda; ap/ Marcos Cordova & Rafaela Garcia; am/ Jose Sanches & Gregoria Rael; gp/ Julian Sanches & Juana Candelaria, residents of the same.

MONTOYA, Jose Anastacio
bap 21 Jan 1846, 11 days old; legit s/ Jose Montoya & Loreta Arias, of los Ranchos de Albuquerque; ap/ Juan Montoya & Maria Griego; am/ Felipe Arias & Maria Felipa Garcia; gp/ Pedro Garcia & Rafaela Garcia, of the same.

GUTIERRES, Jose Junino
bap 22 Jan 1846, 3 days old; legit s/ Manuel Gutierres & Maria Teresa Arias, of los Ranchos de Albuquerque; ap/ Francisco Gutierres & Manuela Baca; am/ Juan Arias & Merced Gomes; gp/ Juan Mansanares & Maria Estefana Jaramio, of the same place.

Frames 2139-2140, #82
BARELA, Antonia Teresa
bap 24 Jan 1846; legit d/ Pablo Barela & Paula Garcia, of los Ranchos de Albuquerque; ap/ Santiago Barela & Juana Aranda; am/ Juan Antonio Garcia & Gregoria Candelaria; gp/ Juan Esteban Sanches & Juana Garcia, of the same place.

ARAGON, Mariano
bap 24 Jan 1846, 8 days old; legit s/ Jose Maria Aragon & Ygnacia Madrid, of los Ranchos de Albuquerque; ap/ Juan Andres Aragon & Manuela Brito; am/ Bernardo Madrid & Gregoria Griego; gp/ Mariano Barela & Rafaela Garcia, of the same place.

DURAN, Rufina
bap 24 Jan 1846, 3 days old; legit d/ Antonio Duran & Barbara Carabajal, residents of Albuquerque; ap/ Juan Rafael Duran & Manuela Muñis; am/ Miguel Carabajal & Jacinta Lopez; gp/ Antonio Baca & Manuela Lucero, of the same place.

Frame 2141
OTERO, Francisco
bap 1 Feb 1846, 3 days old; natural s/ Josefa Otero, resident of San Antonio; am/ Julian Otero & Manuela Antonia Padiya; gp/ Santiago Otero & Guadalupe Otero, of the same place.

CANDELARIA, Maria Martina
bap 1 Feb 1846, 2 days old; legit d/ Jose Candelaria & Maria Bernarda Sanches, of Atrisco; ap/ Juan Pablo Candelaria & Guadalupe Errera; am/ Ynacio Sanches & Manuela Anaya; gp/ Jose Luis Sanches & Maria Dolores Garcia, of the same place.

AASF, Reel #2
B-10 (Box 7b) 1846–1850

Frame 2143, #1
NIETO, Juan Policarpo
bap 5 Feb 1846, 10 days old; legit s/ Jose Dolores Nieto & Gertrudis Garcia, residents of Alameda; ap/ Juan Nieto & Petra Valdes; am/ Lagos Garcia & Juana Trujillo; gp/ Jose Ramon Rael & Bibiana Chaves, all from the same place.

BACA, Jose Napoleon
bap 8 Feb 1846, 3 days old; legit s/ Juan Baca & Rafaela Cordova, residents of Alameda; ap/ Simon Baca & Pascuala Garcia; am/ Nicolas Cordova & Ygnacia Duran; gp/ Juan Jose Apodaca & Luz Padilla, all from the same place.

CHAVES, Jose Rumaldo
bap 10 Feb 1846, 4 days old; legit s/ Mariano Chaves & Monica Romero, residents of Alameda; ap/ Pedro Chaves & Margarita Montoya; am/ Santiago Romero & Juana Candelaria; gp/ Antonio Garcia & Juana Sais, of the same place.

MARTIN, Maria Eulalia
bap 12 Feb 1846, 6 days old; legit d/ Jose Manuel Martin & Maria Luisa Aragon, residents of Alameda; ap/ Juan Jose Martin & Antonia Garcia; am/ Juan de Jesus Aragon & Rosalia Gonsales; gp/ Jose Tomas Jaramio & Maria Barbara Garcia.

Frame 2144, #2
MONTOYA, Maria Marta de los Dolores
bap 13 Feb 1846, 6 days old; legit d/ Juan Montoya & Maria Martin, residents of Alameda; ap/ Miguel Montoya & Pabla Martin; am/ Pablo Martin & Juana Garcia; gp/ Jose Ygnacio Gonsales & Tomasa Moya, of the same place.

GARCIA, Antonia
bap 13 Feb 1846, 10 days old; d/ Maria Garcia, residents of Albuquerque; am/ Anna Maria Garcia, gp/ Salbador Lopes & Dolores Perea, of the same place.

CANDELARIA, Jose Lorenzo
bap 15 Feb 1846, 2 days old; legit s/ Jesus Maria Candelaria & Isabel Chaves, residents of Barelas; ap/ Jose Candelaria & Tomasa Padilla; am/ Juan Antonio Chaves & Gertrudis Torres; gp/ Manuel Aragon & Maria Gallegos, all of Barelas.

Frames 2144-2145, #3
CANDELARIA, Maria Francisca
bap 15 Feb 1846, 3 days old; legit d/ Jesus Candelaria & Paula Chaves, residents of Barelas; ap/ Antonio Candelaria & Antonia Garcia; am/ Juan Antonio Chaves & Gertrudis Torres; gp/ Salvador Romero & Francisca Chaves, of the same place.

GARCIA, Jose Benito de la Trinidad
bap 15 Feb 1846, 4 days old; legit s/ Juan Rafael Garcia & Encarnacion Lucero, of los Duranes; ap/ Juan Rafael Garcia & Manuela Muñis; am/ Gregorio Lucero & Marta Lopes; gp/ Mariano Armijo & Clara Armijo, residents of Albuquerque.

SANDOBAL, Jose Benino
bap 15 Feb 1846, 3 days old; natural s/ Maria Juana Sandobal, residents of Albuquerque; am/ Jose Sandobal & Petrona Sabedra; gp/ Jose Maria Madrid & Maria Justa Garcia, of the same place.

GARCIA, Maria Juana Rumalda
bap 15 Feb 1846, 3 days old; legit d/ Pablo Garcia & Maria Gertrudis Sanches, residents of Alameda; ap/ Antonio Garcia & Antonia Tafoya; am/ Jose Sanches & Gregoria Rael; gp/ Nereo Sandobal & Encarnacion Garcia, of the same place.

Frame 2146, #4
GARCIA, Seberino
bap 15 Feb 1846, 5 days old; natural s/ Maria Santos Garcia, residents los Griegos; am/ Manuel Garcia & Josefa Molina; gp/ Juan Calletano Martines & Maria Eldifonsa Olguin, of the same place.

CHAVES, Maria Librada de los Dolores
bap 15 Feb 1846, 3 days old; legit d/ Jose Maria Chaves & Isabel Apodaca, residents of Albuquerque; ap/ Jose Chaves & Catalina Baldonado; am/ Tomas Apodaca & Tomasa Varela; gp/ Juan de Jesus Chaves & Beneranda Abreu, residents of Peralta.

CANDELARIA, Jose Maria
bap 16 Feb 1846; adopted s/ Miguel Antonio Candelaria & Barbara Apodaca, residents of Los Barelas; ap/ Jose Candelarias & Tomasa Padilla; am/ Francisco Apodaca & Maria Serafina Chaves; gp/ Miguel Antonio Candelaria & Barbara Apodaca.

SABEDRA, Maria Francisca
bap 20 Feb 1846, 2 days old; legit d/ Francisco Sabedra & Dolores Garcia, residents of Albuquerque; ap/ Juan Cristobal Sabedra & Maria Paula Duran; am/ Jose Antonio Garcia & Ygnacia Candelaria; gp/ Juan Garcia & Maria Chaves, of the same place.

Frame 2147, #5
GARCIA, Jose Matias
bap 25 Feb 1846, 2 days old; legit s/ Manuel Garcia & Miquela Duran, residents of Albuquerque; ap/ Juan Luis Garcia & Leonarda Lopes; am/ Teodoro Duran & Varbara Sedillo; gp/ Francisco Duran & Anna Maria Duran, of the same place.

GARCIA, Maria Seferina
bap 26 Feb 1846, 7 days old; legit d/ Salbador Garcia & Maria Juana Romero; ap/ Jose Antonio Garcia & Soledad Sandobal; am/ Santiago Romero & Dolores Candelaria; gp/ J. Manuel Errera & Maria de la Luz Sandobal, all residents of Alameda.

GARCIA, Juan Bautista
bap 28 Feb 1846, 4 days old; legit s/ Juan Manuel Garcia & Manuela Perea, residents of Corrales; ap/ Vicente Garcia & Maria Manuela Romero; am/ Jose Perea & Juana Griego; gp/ Jose Luis Garcia & Marcelina Trugillo, residents of Alameda.

Frame 2148, #6
ANAYA, Jose Nestor
bap 28 Feb 1846, 3 days old; natural s/ Sesaria Anaya, resident of San Antonio; am/ Martin Anaya & Beatris Garcia; gp/ Jose Antonio Aranda & Paula Aranda, of Ranchos de Albuquerque.

GUTIERRES, Maria Soledad
bap 1 Mar 1846, 6 days old; legit d/ Jose Maria Gutierres & Anna Maria Anaya, residents of San Antonio; ap/ Jose Gutierres & Maria Juana Gonsales; am/ Domingo Anaya & Dolores Griego; gp/ Vicente Maes & Petrona Anaya, of the same place.

MOYA, Pedro Jose
bap 2 Mar 1846, 9 days old; legit s/ Jose Maria Moya & Dolores Sais, residents of Alameda; ap/ Eusebio Moya & Maria Montoya; am/ Salbador Sais & Maria Juana Aragon; gp/ Juan Domingo Tafoya & Anna Maria Martin, of the same place.

ZAMORA, Jose Pablo
bap 3 Mar 1846, 3 days old; legit s/ Pablo Zamora & Pascuala Baca, residents of los Ranchos; ap/ Juan Zamora & Juliana Montaño; am/ Reyes Baca & Manuela Archuleta; gp/ Priest, Don Nicolas Valencia & Doña Ana Maria Aragon.

Frame 2149, #7
CORDOVA, Anna Maria Nestora
bap 4 Mar 1846, 5 days old; legit d/ Jose Cordova & Tomasa Trujillo, residents of Alameda; ap/ Nicolas Cordova & Ygnacia Duran; am/ Juan Antonio Trujillo & Juana Montolla; gp/ Jose Luis Garcia & Marcelina Trujillo, of the same place.

SEDILLO, Maria Rosa
bap 4 Mar 1846, 10 days old; natural d/ Maria Sedillo, residents of los Barelas; am/ Juan Sedillo & Gregoria Candelaria; gp/ Vicente Romero & Rosa Candelaria, of Albuquerque.

GRIEGO, Maria Dolores
bap 6 Mar 1846, 4 days old; legit d/ Juan Griego & Ysabel Gurule, of los Ranchos de Albuquerque; ap/ Jose Griego & Dolores Duran; am/ not stated; gp/ Juan Candelaria & Antonia Garcia, of los Barelas.

ARIAS, Maria Josefa
bap 25 Feb 1846, 5 days old; d/ Atencio Arias & Francisca Jaramillo; gp/ Francisco Abila & Teresa Arias.

Frame 2150, #8
SEDILLO, Juan Jose
bap 11 Mar 1846, 6 days old; legit s/ Salbador Sedillo & Rita Sedillo, residents of los Barelas; ap/ Salbador Sedillo & Juana Maria Sanches; am/ Gregorio Sedillo & Juana Candelaria; gp/ Juan Apodaca & Maria Isabel Sanches, of Albuquerque.

SABEDRA, Nestor
bap 11 Mar 1846, 8 days old; legit s/ Juan Sabedra & Ysabel Lopes, residents of los Duranes; ap/ Pablo Sabedra & Gertrudis Apodaca; am/ Leonicio Lopes & Gertrudis Perea; gp/ Juan Cristobal Lucero & Juana Apodaca, residents of Ranchos de Albuquerque.

MORA, Maria Gregoria
bap 16 Mar 1846, 3 days old; legit d/ Santiago Mora & Maria Josefa Archibeque, residents of Albuquerque; ap/ Francisco Mora & Maria Romona Montaño; am/ Matias Archibeque & Dolores Garcia; gp/ Jose Rafael Mora & Maria Ysidora Candelaria, residents of Los Griegos.

Frames 2150-2151, #9
SEDILLO, Jesus Maria
bap 16 Mar 1846, 15 days old; natural s/ Candelaria Sedillo, residents of Atrisco; am/ Julian Sedillo & Sipriana Garcia; gp/ Jose Armijo & Dolores Sedillo, residents of Albuquerque.

LUCERO, Maria Gregoria
bap 16 Mar 1846, 3 days old; legit d/ Pedro Lucero & Encarnacion Griego, residents of los Poblanos; ap/ Lorenzo Lucero & Crus Griego; am/ Jose Griego & Pablo Ortega; gp/ Simon Griego & Anna Maria Gurule, of the same place.

TORRES, Jose Juan
bap 16 Mar 1846, 2 days old; legit s/ Gregorio Torres & Gregoria Candelaria, residents of los Griegos; ap/ not stated; am/ Juan Vicente Candelaria & Candelaria Lobato; gp/ Salbador Griego & Francisca Griego, of the same place

ARMIJO, Juan Nepomoceno Longino
bap 16 Mar 1846, 3 days old; legit s/ Juan Cristobal Armijo & Juana Chaves, residents of los Ranchos; ap/ Juan Armijo & Rosalia Ortega; am/ Francisco Chaves & Anna Maria Castillo; gp/ Juan Armijo & Josefa Armijo, of the same place.

Frame 2152, #10
GUTIERRES, Maria Josefa
bap 17 Mar 1846, 3 days old; legit d/ Ylario Gutierres & Maria Nicolasa Griego, residents of los Griegos; ap/ Miguel Gutierres & Juana Simona Griego; am/ Mariano Griego & Andrea Martin; gp/ Mariano Mares & Maria Trinidad Serna, residents of los Candelarias.

GARCIA, Maria Josefa Longina
bap 19 Mar 1846, 4 days old; legit d/ Rumaldo Garcia & Anna Maria Arias, residents of los Ranchos; ap/ Juan Cristobal Garcia & Maria Josefa Gonsales; am/ Juan Arias & Merced Gomes; gp/ Agustin Sisneros & Maria Juana Sanches, of the same place.

OTERO, Maria Guadalupe
bap 21 Mar 1846, 3 days old; legit d/ Santiago Otero & Anna Maria Samora, residents of San Antonio; ap/ Julian Otero & Manuela Antonia Padilla; am/ Jose Samora & Rafaela Martin; gp/ Jose Santos Otero & Manuela Antonia Padilla, of the same place.

Frames 2152-2153, #11
BACA, Maria Perfecta
bap 28 Mar 1846, 3 days old; legit d/ J. Manuel Baca & Maria Gertrudis Apodaca, residents of Alameda; ap/ Simon Baca & Ysabel Chavez; am/ Lionisio Apodaca & Maria Luteria Garcia; gp/ Juan Domingo Tafoya & Anna Maria Martin, of the same place.

JARAMILLO, Maria Ruperta Josefa
bap 29 Mar 1846, 2 days old; legit d/ Manuel Jaramillo & Gertrudis Maestas, residents of Albuquerque; ap/ J. Miguel Jaramillo & Anna Maria Ortega; am/ Mariano Mestas & Guadalupe Chavez; gp/ Andres Ortega & Ygnacia Basan, of the same place.

ARMIJO, Jesus Maria
bap 29 Mar 1846, 2 days old; legit s/ Antonio Jose Armijo & Guadalupe Sabedra, residents of Albuquerque; ap/ Ambrocio Armijo & Maria Antonia Ortiz; am/ Pablo Sabedra & Gertrudis Apodaca; gp/ Salbador Jaramillo & Gertrudis Baca, of Atrisco.

GRIEGO, Maria Petra
bap 29 Mar 1846, 3 days old; legit d/ Ylario Griego & Maria de Jesus Garcia, residents of Albuquerque; ap/ Pablo Griego & Ysidora Apodaca; am/ Jose Garcia & Marta Duran; gp/ Jose Garcia & Pascuala Apodaca, residents of Peralta.

Frame 2154, #12
CANDELARIA, Sebastian
bap 4 Apr 1846, 1 day old; legit s/ Rumaldo Candelaria & Maria Josefa Garcia, residents of Los Duranes; ap/ Juan Cristoval Candelaria & Ysidora Garcia; am/ Diego Antonio Garcia & Maria Ramona Candelaria; gp/ Juan Jose Ballejos & Maria Gertrudis Ballejos.

BARELA, Maria Cleofes
bap 7 Apr 1846, 3 days old; legit d/ Manuel Barela & Vicenta Gallegos, of Ranchos of Albuquerque; ap/ Santiago Barela & Juana Aranda; am/ Juana Gallego & Manuela Gurule; gp/ Jose Griego & Manuela Gallego, of the same place.

GONZALES, Maria Exelza
bap 7 Apr 1846, 2 days old; legit d/ Antonio Gonzales & Maria Garcia, residents of los Candelarias; ap/ Jose Antonio Gonzales & Maria Candelaria; am/ Francisco Garcia & Soledad Lopes; gp/ Juan Gutierres & Maria Francisca Anaya.

Frames 2154-2155, #13
ARIAS, Jose Simon
bap 11 Apr 1846, 15 days old; natural s/ Concepcion Arias, of los Ranchos de Albuquerque; am/ Juan Arias & Merced Gomes; gp/ Jose Montoya & Loreta Arias, residents of Ranchos de Albuquerque.

CARABAJAL, Juan Feliz
bap 11 Apr 1846, 12 days old; legit s/ Gregorio Carabajal & Juana Lovato, residents of San Antonio; ap/ Juan de Jesus Carabajal & Maria Luisa Archuleta; am/ Diego Lovato & Matilde Duran; gp/ Vitoriano Martines & Maria Luisa Archuleta of the same place.

APODACA, Selsa de Jesus
bap 11 Apr 1846, 4 days old; legit d/ Gregorio Apodaca & Lugarda Duran, residents of los Duranes; ap/ Ramon Apodaca & Juana Rafaela Lopes; am/ Rafael Duran & Rosa Gurule; gp/ Pedro Contreras & Maria Josefa Contreras, of the same place.

GARBISO, Maria Juana
bap 12 Apr 1846, 10 days old; legit d/ J. Maria Garbiso & Maria Vitoria Duran, residents of Albuquerque; ap/ Juan Garbiso & Maria Muñis; am/ Polonio Duran & Maria Muñisa; gp/ Jose Guadalupe Alfaro & Maria Paula de los Dolores Garcia, residents of Alameda.

Frame 2156, #14
DURAN, Maria Ysidora
bap 12 Apr 1846, 3 days old; legit d/ J. Alvino Duran & Maria Juliana Ruibal, residents of los Duranes; ap/ Juan Duran & Juliana Garcia; am/ Ygnacio Ruibal & Maria de Jesus Lujan; gp/ Ventura Armijo & Sesaria Caravajal, of Albuquerque.

VASAN, Maria Josefa Leona Genoveva
bap 13 Apr 1846, 4 days old; legit d/ Juan de la Crus Vasan & Rafaela Samora, residents of Alameda; ap/ Ygnacio Vasan & Polonia Gutierres; am/ Jose Antonio Samora & Dolores Moya; gp/ Antonio Jose Martin & Maria de la Luz Basan, all residents of Alameda.

ORTEGA, Maria Dolores
bap 13 Apr 1846, 16 years, adult; adopted d/ Andres Ortega; gp/ Ygnacia Basan, residents of the plaza of los Poblanos.

Frames 2156-2157, #15
LUCERO, Juan de Dios
bap 19 Apr 1846, 10 days old; legit s/ Ramon Lucero & Ucaria Sanches, residents of Alameda; ap/ Miguel Lucero & Maria Dimas Martines; am/ Domingo Sanches & Maria de las Lus NS; gp/ Juan de Dios Chaves & Monica Lucero, of Los Ranchos.

DURAN, Manuel Perfecto
bap 19 Apr 1846, 2 days old; legit s/ Abad Duran & Gregoria Sanches, resident of los Ranchos; ap/ Manuel Duran & Maria Matilda Lucero; am/ Antonio Sanches & Juliana Montaño; gp/ Manuel Antonio Garcia & Benigna Garcia of the same place.

CHABES, Jose Leon
bap 19 Apr 1846, 11 days old; legit s/ Pedro Chabes & Maria Ysabel Martines, residents of Los Candelarias; ap/ Calistro Chabes & Maria Garcia; am/ Jose Antonio Garcia & Monica Jaramillo; gp/ Juan Pablo Butieres & Maria Josefa Martines, of the same place.

MARTINES, Jose Mauricio
bap 19 Apr 1846, 7 days old; natural s/ Francisca Martines, resident of Los Ranchos, in the household of Antonia Martines; gp/ Valentin Gallegos & Manuela Apodaca, residents of Los Ranchos.

Frame 2158, #16
GARCIA, Ermogenio Jacobo
bap 20 Apr 1846, 2 days old; legit s/ Antonio Garcia & Carmen Mestas, residents of Albuquerque; ap/ Felis Garcia & Maria Ysabel Lopes; am/ Ana Maria Mestas; gp/ Diego Lopes & Juana Armijo.

ALVARES, Anselmo
bap 22 Apr 1846, 5 days old; legit s/ Agapito Alvares & Juana Garcia, residents of the plaza of Tabalopa; ap/ Vicente Alvares & Victoria Sanches; am/ Pablo Garcia & Antonia Martines; gp/ Esteban Gonsales & Maria Dolores Arias, residents of Los Ranchos.

PEREA, Sotero
bap 24 Apr 1846, 3 days old; legit s/ Francisco Perea & Paula Sandobal, residents of Albuquerque; ap/ Rafael Perea & Carmel Romero; am/ Jose Sandobal & Petrona Sabedra; gp/ Jose Rafael Sanches & Guadalupe Sanches, residents of Albuquerque.

Frame 2159, #17
ANSURES, Pedro
bap 24 Apr 1846, 7 days old; natural s/ Juana Ansures, resident of los Barelas; am/ Juan Ansures & Maria Candelaria; gp/ P. Montolla & Candelaria Montolla, of the same place.

GUTIERES, Jose de Jesus
bap (day torn) Apr 1846, 4 days old; legit s/ Ologio Gutieres & Encarnacion Garcia; ap/ Simon Butieres & Juana Lopes; am/ Martin Garcia & Anamaria Apodaca; gp/ Lucas Garcia & Maria Rocalia Garcia; residents of los Candelarias.

NS, Maria Lorensa
bap 29 Apr 1846, 4 days old; d/ unknown parents; gp/ Jose Antonio Aranda.

Frame 2160, #18
SENA, Maria Justa del Pilar
bap 2 May 1846, 5 days old; legit d/ Miguel Sena & Maria Ysidora Garcia; ap/ Francisco Cena & Maria Manuela Martines; am/ Juan Garcia & Maria Francisca Gallegos; gp/ Luis Garcia & Maria Paula Martines, residents of Alameda.

HERRERA, Maria Gabriela
bap 6 May 1846, 1 day old; legit d/ Salbador Herrera & Maria Ygnacia Chaves, of Atrisco; ap/ Vicente Herrera & Maria Antonia Montaño; am/ Antonio Chaves & Maria Manuela Garcia; gp/ Antonio Jose Chaves & Maria Manuela Garcia, of the same place.

Frames 2160-2161, #19
BACA, Maria Gertrudis
bap 7 May 1846, 3 days old; natural d/ Maria Lorensa Baca, of Atrisco; am/ Jose Maria Baca & Juana Sanches; gp/ Salvador Jaramio & Maria Gertrudis Baca, of the same place.

LUSERO, Jose Tanislado
bap 10 May 1846, 4 days old; legit s/ Jose Yginio Lusero & Maria Ramona Montoya, residents of los Ranchos; ap/ Diego Lucero & Maria Angela Romero; am/ Rafael Montoya & Anna Maria Duran; gp/ Rafael Montoya & Anna Maria Duran, of the same place.

SANTIYANES, Jose Yrineo de Jesus
bap 10 May 1846, 10 days old; legit s/ Miguel Santiyanes & Josefa Martin, residents of Corrales; ap/ Facundo Santiyanes & Anna Maria Lovato; am/ Antonio Martin & Manuela Trujillo, gp/ Ramon Martines & Juliana Gutierres, residents of Corrales.

Frames 2161-2162, #20
MARTIN, Juan Nepomoceno
bap 10 May 1846, 3 days old; legit s/ Gregorio Martin & Gregoria Gurule, residents of the plaza of los Griegos; ap/ Miguel Martin & Dorotea Gallego; am/ Anna Maria Gurule; gp/ Francisco Duran & Bernarda Gurule, residents of Albuquerque.

ARAGON, Maria Miquela
bap 12 May 1846, 5 days old; legit d/ Jose Manuel Aragon & Soledad Cordoba, residents of Corrales; ap/ Usebio Aragon & Maria Miguela Sanches; am/ Diego Cordoba & Maria Juliana Santiyanes; gp/ Juan Jose Gonsales & Encarnacion Perea, of the same place.

MUÑIS, Juan Jose Leon
bap 12 May 1846, 25 days old; legit s/ Juan Cristobal Muñis & Anna Maria Pacheco, residents of the plaza of San Antonio; ap/ not stated; am/ Ventura Pacheco & Paula Sanches; gp/ Jose Santos Gonsales & Maria Guadalupe Otero, of the same place.

Frames 2162-2163, #21
RAEL, Tanislado
bap 15 May 1846, 9 days old; natural s/ Petrona Rael, resident of Alameda; am/ Juan Antonio Rael & Soledad Miera; gp/ Juan Gonsales & Maria de la Luz Real, of the same place.

GARCIA, Maria Filomena
bap 16 May 1846, 4 days old; legit d/ Prudencio Garcia & Barbara Montoya, residents of Alameda; ap/ Lagos Garcia & Juana Trujillo; am/ J. Mariano Montoya & Maria Reyes Mestas; gp/ Pedro Antonio Montoya & Maria de la Luz Lopes, of the same place.

ALIRE, Juan Nepomuceno
bap 16 May 1846, 8 days old; legit s/ J. Venito Alire & Juana Cordoba, residents of Alameda; ap/ Jose Andres Alire & Margarita Apodaca; am/ Marcos Cordoba & Juana Duran; gp/ Jose Martin & Maria Gertrudis Salazar, of the same place.

MARTIN, Juana Nepomocena
bap 17 May 1846, 4 days old; legit d/ Jose Antonio Martin & Maria Luteria Griego, residents of the plaza of los Gallegos; ap/ Jose Martin & Maria Antonia Gallego; am/ Miguel Griego & Maria Gertrudis Garcia; gp/ Rafael Apodaca & Juana Maria Romero, of Alameda.

Frame 2164, #22
SANTILLANES, Juan Jose
bap 21 May 1846, 4 days old; natural s/ Juana Santillanes, residents of the plaza los Duranes; am/ Luciano Santillanes & Maria Gertrudis Duran; gp/ Juan Calletano Garcia & Maria Teresa Andrea Noanes, residents of the plaza of los Griegos.

GALLEGO, Maria Gregoria
bap 23 May 1846, 4 days old; natural d/ Maria Reyes Gallego, of los Ranchos de Albuquerque; am/ Jose Pablo Gallego & Juana Mora; gp/ Jose Dolores Gallego & Gregoria Trujillo, of the same place.

MARTIN, Rita de Jesus
bap 24 May 1846, 4 days old; legit d/ Pablo Martin & Sicilia Candelaria, residents of Alameda; ap/ Jose Martin & Juana Garcia; am/ Estevan Candelaria & Maria de Jesus Luna; gp/ Ramon Candelaria & Maria de Jesus Luna.

Frames 2164-2165, #23
ROMERO, Jose Feliz
bap 24 May 1846, 4 days old; legit s/ Vitorio Romero & Maria Trinidad Montoya; ap/ Luis Jose Romero & Maria Varbara Aragon; am/ Jose Maria Montoya & Maria Tula Garcia; gp/ Diego Antonio Montoya & Maria Barbara Aragon, residents of los Corrales.

GRIEGO, Jose Vicente
bap 24 May 1846, 4 days old; legit s/ Juan Griego & Estefana Garcia, residents of Corrales; ap/ not stated; am/ Diego Antonio Garcia & Estefana Apodaca; gp/ Luis Jose Carrillo & Nicolasa Lucero, of the same place.

LOBATO, Carlota
bap 26 May 1846, 5 days old; legit d/ Agustin Lobato & Quirina Gabaldon, residents of Albuquerque; ap/ Juan Lobato & Maria Casados; am/ Nepomuceno Gabaldon & Barbara Mestas; gp/ Mariano Hinojos & Francisca Hinojos.

ALDAS, Maria de la Luz
bap 27 May 1846, 4 days old; legit d/ Paulin Aldas & Tomasa Sena, residents of los Ranchos; ap/ not stated; am/ Francisco Sena & Manuela Martin; gp/ Andres Pais & Alvina Gurule, residents of Alameda.

Frame 2166, #24
RAMIRES, Maria Fernanda
bap 30 May 1846, 8 days old; legit d/ Simon Ramires & Maria Rosalia Lusero, residents of Albuquerque; ap/ Maria Ramires; am/ Jose Lusero & Francisca Lucero; gp/ Felipe Ruibal & Maria de Jesus Lujan, of the same place.

GARCIA, Juana Maria
bap 31 May 1846, 10 days old; legit d/ Juan Antonio Garcia & Rosa Gallego, residents of Chilili; ap/ Francisco Garcia & Ynes Oslay; am/ Rafael Gallego & Barbara Gonsales; gp/ Juan Cristobal Moya & Rufina Gallego, of the same place.

VALENCIA, Marcelina de los Dolores
bap 8 Jun 1846, 4 days old; legit d/ Julian Valencia & Refugia Rael, residents of Alameda; ap/ Juan Domingo Valencia & Maria Ygnacia Zalazar; am/ Eusibio Rael & Rosa Montoya; gp/ Jose Miera & Marcelina Miera, residents of Algodones.

Frame 2167, #25
PACHECO, Jose Amador
bap 10 Jun 1846, 10 days old; legit s/ Christobal Pacheco & Manuela Anaya, residents of Alameda; ap/ Jose Antonio Pacheco & Juana Torres; am/ Miguel Anaya & Maria Gallego; gp/ Jose Samora & Josefa Montaño, residents of Albuquerque.

ARMENTA, Juan Jose
bap 15 Jun 1846, 1 month old; legit s/ Jose Ynes Armenta & Dolores Sandobal, residents of Chilili; ap/ not stated; am/ Dionicio Sandobal & Juana Martin; gp/ Francisco Sandobal & Soledad Martin, of the same place.

LUCERO, Jose Victor Vacilio de Jesus
bap 15 Jun 1846, 1 day old; legit s/ Miguel Lucero & Maria Rita Salas, of los Ranchos de Albuquerque; ap/ not stated; am/ Manuel Salas & Maria Josefa Carrillo; gp/ Jose Guadalupe Chaves & Maria Leonarda Padilla, of the same place.

ARMIJO, Antonio Jose
bap 20 Jun 1846, 7 days old; legit s/ Teodoro Armijo & Paula Jaramio, residents of Atrisco; ap/ Santiago Armijo & Petra Perea; am/ Miguel Antonio Jaramio & Lorenza Lucero; gp/ Juan Sedillo & Sipriana Garcia, of the same place.

Frame 2168, #26
SANTILLANES, Maria Nicolasa
bap 21 Jun 1846, 8 days old; natural d/ Maria Juliana Santillanes, residents of los Duranes; ap/ Luciano Santillanes & Gertrudis Duran; gp/ Jose Celto Garcia & Maria Nicolasa Duran, of the same place.

LUCERO, Jose Antonio
bap 26 Jun 1846, 2 days old; legit s/ Ygnacio Lucero & Josefa Lopez, residents of Albuquerque; ap/ Gregorio Lucero & Marta Lopez; am/ Francisco Lopez & Rosalia Duran; gp/ Pedro Lopez & Guadalupe Candelaria, of the same place.

GARCIA, Juan Francisco
bap 27 Jun 1846, 1 day old; legit s/ Jose Garcia & Manuela Anaya, residents of Albuquerque; ap/ Juan Garcia & Manuela Mestas; am/ Antonio Anaya & Tomasa Tafolla; gp/ Jose Nestor Anaya & Maria del Rosario Anaya, of the same place.

Frame 2169, #27
TAFOYA, Jose Loreto
bap 12 Jul 1846, 2 days old; natural s/ Maria Francisca Tafoya, residents of Albuquerque; am/ Juan Ygnacio Tafolla & Maria Antonia Baca; gp/ Loreto Carabajal & Maria Dolores Carabajal, of the same place.

ATENCIO, Jose Tranquilino de Jesus
bap 12 Jul 1846, 7 days old; legit s/ Dionicio Atencio & Maria Francisca Sanches, residents of los Ranchos of Albuquerque; ap/ Gaspar Atencio & Ysabel Chaves; am/ Juan Sanches & Manuela Gonsales; gp/ Gregorio Atencio & Maria Juliana de Altagracia Atencio, of the same place.

TAFOYA, Juan de Jesus
bap 12 Jul 1846, 2 days old; natural s/ Maria Francisca Tafoya, residents of Albuquerque; am/ Juan Ygnacio Tafolla & Maria Antonia Baca; gp/ Juan Martines & Maria Martines, of the same place.

Frames 2169-2170, #28
GONSALES, Antonio Maria
bap 12 Jul 1846, 12 days old; legit s/ Francisco Gonsales & Petra Gonsales, residents of Alameda; ap/ Antonio Gonsales & Juana Sandobal; am/ Antonio Gonsales & Gertrudis Gurule; gp/ Tomas Tafoya & Soledad Montoya, of the same place.

ARMIJO, Maria Liborata
bap 20 Jul 1846, 2 years old; Navajo, adopted d/ Jose Armijo & Guadalupe Chaves; gp/ Julian Sedillo & Maria del Rosario Sedillo, all residents of Atrisco.

PEREA, Mariana
bap 26 Jul 1846, 5 days old; legit d/ Manuel Perea & Juana Garcia, of los Ranchos de Albuquerque; ap/ J. Manuel Perea & Juana Duran; am/ Yldefonso Garcia & Juana Martin; gp/ Manuel Varela & Vicenta Gallego, of the same place.

GARCIA, Maria Trinidad de la Cruz
bap 26 Jul 1846, 4 days old; legit d/ Manuel Garcia & Rafaela Rael, of los Ranchos de Albuquerque; ap/ Miguel Garcia & Antonia Maria Vallejos; am/ Juan Antonio Rael & Soledad Miera; gp/ Antonio Sandobal & Marcelina Miera.

Frame 2171, #29
TORRES, Maria Encarnacion
bap 30 Jul 1846, 4 days old; legit d/ Juan Torres & Dolores Gutierres, residents of los Griegos; ap/ Pedro Antonio Torres & Guadalupe Garcia; am/ Miguel Gutierres & Simona Griego; gp/ Jose Torres & Josefa Antonia Garcia, residents of los Duranes.

CAVEZ, Maria Merced
bap 3 Aug 1846, 2 days old; legit d/ Jose Dolores Cavez & Nicanora Garcia; ap/ Jabiel Cavez & Maria del Jesus Armijo; am/ Jose de Jesus Garcia & Rosa Baca; gp/ Mariano Herrera & Ramona Herrera, of the same place.

LUJAN, Anna Maria
bap 6 Aug 1846, 11 days old; natural d/ Rosalia Lujan, de la Hacienda de Fuerta; am/ Juan Antonio Lujan
& Maria Martines; gp/ Jose Maria Chaves & Ysabel Apodaca, residents of Albuquerque.

Frame 2172, #50
GARCIA, Maria Rufina
bap 8 Aug 1846, 6 days old; legit d/ Jose Garcia & Juana Butierres; ap/ not stated; am/ Jose Maria
Butierres & Maria Martin; gp/ Jose Ygnes Chaves & Pina Apodaca, all of Barelas.

GUTIERRES, Juan Domingo
bap 8 Aug 1846, 3 days old; legit s/ Juan Ynes Gutierres & Marcelina Serna, of los Ranchos de
Albuquerque; ap/ Pascual Gutierres & Manuela Garcia; am/ Antonia Serna & Paula Garcia; gp/ Jose
Maria Lucero & Antonia Teresa Gallego, of the same place.

GRIEGO, Macimo
bap 8 Aug 1846, 8 days old; legit s/ Jose Maria Griego & Teresa Gutierres, residents of los Griegos; ap/
Juan Domingo Griego & Gertrudes Candelaria; am/ Jose Poblano Ortega & Dolores Gutierres; gp/ Felipe
Lopes & Juliana Torres, of the same place.

Frame 2173, #51
PADIA, Maria del Refugio
bap 16 Aug 1846, 5 days old; legit s/ Manuel Antonio Padia & Ysidora Griego, residents of los Griegos;
ap/ Bartolo Padilla & Gertrudis Garcia; am/ Jose Maria Griego & Guadalupe Mora; gp/ Juan Apodaca &
Maria Ysabel Sanches, residents of Albuquerque.

ARMIJO, Maria
bap 16 Aug 1846, 16 years old; Navajo adopted d/ Don Juan Armijo; gp/ same.

SANDOBAL, Maria Ygnacia
bap 16 Aug 1846, 15 days old; natural d/ Gertrudis Sandobal, resident of los Barelas; am/ Antonio
Sandobal; gp/ Juan Antonio Chaves & Gertrudis Torres, of the same place.

Frames 2173-2174, #32
GARCIA, Jose Meliton
bap 19 Aug 1846, 4 days old; legit s/ Venancio Garcia & Miquela Garcia, of Alameda; ap/ Diego Garcia
& Paula Salazar; am/ Juan Garcia & Juana Maria Chavez, gp/ Salbador Manuel Garcia & Juana Maria
Romero, of the same place.

MONTOYA, Roque Juan
bap 20 Aug 1846, 5 days old; legit s/ Vicente Montoya & Josefa Martin, residents of los Candelarias; ap/
Pedro Montoya & Maria Luna; am/ Pedro Martin & Dolores Abeita; gp/ Francisco Martin & Encarnacion
Lucero, of the same place.

BENABIDES, Seferina
bap 30 Aug 1846, 4 days old; legit d/ Manuel Benabides & Juana Lopes, residents of Ranchos of
Albuquerque; ap/ Manuel Benabides & Paula Martin; am/ Mateo Lopes & Maria Manuela Candelaria; gp/
Jose Chabes & Maria Chabes, of the same place.

Baptisms – Albuquerque, New Mexico
1829–1850

GARCIA, Maria Carlota Epimenia
bap 3 Sep 1846, 3 days old; legit d/ Francisco Garcia & Ysidora Garcia, residents of Albuquerque; ap/ Braula Garcia; am/ Ysidro Garcia & Maria Altagracia Martines; gp/ Pablo Armijo & Dolores Garcia, of the same place.

Frame 2175, #33
ANAYA, Maria Placida del Rayo
bap 9 Sep 1846, 15 days old; adopted d/ Ramon Anaya & Anna Maria Lopes, residents of Albuquerque; ap/ Manuel Anaya & Maria Antonia Apodaca; am/ Miguel Lopes & Lucia Duran; gp/ (blank).

CASTILLO, Nicolas
bap 13 Sep 1846, 3 days old; legit s/ Juan Miguel Castillo & Rosalia Martin, residents of Alameda; ap/ Antonio Jose Castillo & Quiteria Chaves; am/ not stated; gp/ Marcos Gurule & Vernarda Torres, of the same place.

SAMORA, Maria Rosalia
bap 18 Sep 1846, 3 days old; legit d/ Vicente Samora & Josefa Jaramillo, residents of San Antonio; ap/ Miguel Samora & Manuela Martin; am/ Juan Jose Jaramillo & Trinidad Otero; gp/ Juan Nepomuceno Carabajal & Maria Rosalia Carabajal, of the same place.

Frame 2176, #34
ARAGON, Maria Venigna
bap 21 Sep 1846, 3 days old; natural d/ Juana Rafaela Aragon, resident of los Ranchos de Albuquerque; am/ Juan Andres Aragon & Manuela Brito; gp/ Jose Mansanares & Maria Estafana Jaramillo, of the same place.

GONZALES, Vicente Dolirio
bap 21 Sep 1846, 7 days old; legit s/ Santos Gonzales & Guadalupe Otero, residents of San Antonio; ap/ not stated; am/ Santiago Otero & Manuela Padilla; gp/ Vicente Apodaca & Anna Maria Mestas, of the same place.

GONSALES, Antonio
bap 22 Sep 1846, 8 days old; natural s/ Juana Andrea Gonsales, residents of Albuquerque; gp/ Jose Manuel Gonsales & Antonia Rosa Carrillo; gp/ Antonio Avad Jaramillo & Maria Siselia Jaramillo, of the same place.

Frames 2176-2177, #35
GARCIA, Jose Miguel
bap 27 Sep 1846, 3 days old; legit s/ Alejo Garcia & Gracia Garcia, residents of Albuquerque; ap/ Juan de Jesus Garcia & Rosa Sabedra; am/ Juan Asencio Garcia & Teodora Padilla; gp/ Miguel Sabedra & Nestora Montoya, of the same place.

MONTOYA, Anna Maria de Atocha
bap 29 Sep 1846, 3 days old; legit d/ Jose Rafael Montoya & Maria Gertrudis Chaves, residents of Albuquerque; ap/ Juan Cristobal Montoya & Maria Luisa Padilla; am/ Agustin Chaves & Juana Sanches; gp/ Vicente Montoya & Guadalupe Montoya, residents of los Padillas.

CANDELARIA, Miquela de Altagracia
bap 30 Sep 1846, 1 day old; legit d/ Manuel Candelaria & Manuela Sandobal, residents of Albuquerque; ap/ Pablo Candelaria & Madalena Trujillo; am/ Miguel Sandobal & Francisca Lopes; gp/ Jose Montoya & Rosalia Montoya, of the same place.

Frames 2177-2178, #36
CANDELARIA, Jose Nestor
bap 7 Aug 1846, 4 days old; legit s/ Francisco Candelaria & Trinidad Lopes, residents of the plaza of los Griegos; ap/ Juan Pablo Candelaria & Guadalupe Garcia; am/ Antonio Lopes & Fabiana Garcia; gp/ Juan Calletano Garcia & Andrea Nuanes, of the same place.

MONTOYA, Anna Maria
bap 9 Oct 1846, 3 days old; legit d/ Sicilio Montoya & Juana Sandobal, of the plaza of los Ranchos; ap/ Rafael Montoya & Anna Maria Duran; am/ Jose Dolores Sandobal; gp/ the same as paternal grandparents.

CHAVES, Ysabel
bap 15 Oct 1846, 1 day old; legit d/ Juan Antonio Chaves & Gertrudis Torres, residents of los Barelas; ap & am/ not stated; gp/ Jesus Maria Candelaria & Ysabel Torres, of the same place.

Frame 2179, #37
MUÑIS, Pedro
bap 18 Oct 1846, 5 days old; legit s/ Manuel Muñis & Maria Josefa Candelaria, residents of los Poblanos de San Antonio; ap/ Miguel Muñis & Encarnacion Candelaria; am/ Merijildo Candelaria & Dolores Jaramillo; gp/ Rafael Mirabel & Maria Viviana Noanes, residents of Los Peraltas.

SANTIYANES, Maria Luisa
bap 18 Oct 1846, 6 days old; natural d/ Maria Antonia Santiyanes, resident of los Ranchos; am/ Jose Rafael Santiyanes & Francisca Antonia Garcia; gp/ Jose Rafael Garcia & Maria Luisa Garcia, of the same place.

SANCHES, Maria Veneranda Nepomucena
bap 21 Oct 1846, 7 days old; legit d/ Rafael Sanches & Gertrudes Candelaria, residents of los Barelas; ap & am/ not stated; gp/ Juan Sanches & Manuel Sanches, of the same place.

Frame 2180, #38
GUTIERRES, Maria Rafaela
bap 24 Oct 1846, 8 days old; legit d/ Fernando Gutierres & Josefa Gonsales, residents of Corrales; ap/ Pedro Antonio Gutierres & Francisca Griego; am/ Juan Gonsales & Maria Antonia Armijo; gp/ Juan Gonsales & Maria de la Luz Rael, residents of Alameda.

LUCERO, Pedro Alcantara
bap 25 Oct 1846, 5 days old; legit s/ Tomas Lucero & Dolores Valencia, of los Ranchos de Albuquerque; ap/ Juan Lucero & Antonia Martines; am/ Juan Domingo Valencia & Maria Ygnacia Salazar; gp/ Dolores Gallego & Gregoria Trujillo, of the same place.

SANCHES, Jose Placido
bap 25 Oct 1846, 15 days old; legit s/ Cristobal Sanches & Concepcion Valencia, of los Ranchos de Albuquerque; ap/ Felipe Sanches & Anna Maria Trugillo; am/ Juan Domingo Valencia & Maria Ygnacia Salazar; gp/ Diego Romero & Nepomuceno Muñis, residents of the plaza of los Gallegos.

Frame 2181, #39
LOPES, Francisca
bap 21 Oct 1846, 4 days old; legit d/ Calletano Lopes & Juliana Jaramillo, residents of the plaza of los Candelarias; ap/ Rafael Lopez & Ysidora Chaves; am/ unknown; gp/ Manuel Apodaca & Maria Francisca Aragon, residents of Barelas.

SANCHES, Maria Erinea
bap 3 Nov 1846, 5 days old; legit d/ Juan Estevan Sanches & Juana Garcia, of los Ranchos de Albuquerque; ap/ Domingo Sanches & Maria de la Luz Candelaria; am/ Miguel Garcia & Rosalia Varela; gp/ Juan de Dios Chaves & Monica Lucero, of the same place.

APODACA, Jose Agustin de los Santos
bap 4 Nov 1846, 11 days old; s/ Trinidad Apodaca, of los Ranchos de Albuquerque; am/ Jose Apodaca & Paula Anaya; gp/ Agustin Sisneros & Ruperta Sisneros, of the same place.

Frame 2182, #40
APODACA, Jesus Maria
bap 4 Nov 1846, 3 days old; legit s/ Simon Apodaca & Maria Josefa Sandobal, residents of Alameda; ap/ Rafael Apodaca & Estafana Salazar; am/ Miguel Sandobal & Manuela Gurule; gp/ Jesus Maria Jaramillo & Lorenza Lucero, of the same place.

GURULE, Juan Cristobal
bap 5 Nov 1846, 1 day old; legit s/ Manuel Gurule & Juana Aranda, of los Ranchos de Albuquerque; ap/ Vicente Gurule & Juana Chaves; am/ Juan Cristobal Aranda & Soledad Armijo; gp/ Pedro Armijo & Rosalia Armijo, of the same place.

GUTIERRES, <u>Juan</u> Francisca Ydubigen
bap 6 Nov 1846, 1 day old; legit d/ Antonio Gutierres & Luperta Lopes, residents of los Barelas; ap/ Antonio Gutierres & Francisca Sanches; am/ Mateo Lopez & Maria Manuela <u>Padia</u>; gp/ Jesus Lopes & Lionor Lopes, of the same place.

Frame 2183, #41
SANCHES, Maria Petronila de Refugio
bap 7 Nov 1846, 3 days old; legit d/ Jose Sanches & Martina Sanches, of Ranchos de Atrisco; ap/ Antonio Jose Sanches & Rosalia Martin; am/ Jose Gabriel Sanches & Juana Sedillo; gp/ Gabriel Sanches & Rafaela Ruiz, residents of Albuquerque.

GARCIA, Andres Venito
bap 12 Nov 1846, 3 days old; legit s/ Juan Antonio Garcia & Gregoria Candelaria, of Ranchos de Albuquerque; ap/ Juan Garcia & Ysabel Romero; am/ Ygnacio Candelaria & Concepcion Chaves; gp/ Francisco Montaño & Ygnacia Montaño, residents of the same place.

SANCHES, Filomena
bap 13 Nov 1846, 3 days old; legit s/ Dolores Sanches & Concepcion Candelaria, of Atrisco; ap/ Nicolas Sanches & Juana Carbajal; am/ Jose Candelaria & Dolores Gutierres; gp/ Juan Padilla & Rosalia Chaves, of the same place.

Frame 2184, #42
GRIEGO, Santiago de Jesus
bap 16 Nov 1846, 4 days old; legit s/ Simon Griego & Anna Maria Gurule, residents of los Poblanos; ap/ Juan Griego & Carmen Gomes; am/ Vicente Gurule & Maria Garcia; gp/ Miguel Noanes & Dolores Griego, of the same place.

LUCERO, Felicita
bap 16 Nov 1846, 3 days old; legit d/ Juan Cristobal Lucero & Maria Juana Apodaca, of los Ranchos de Albuquerque; ap/ Juan Lucero & Antonia Martin; am/ Jose Apodaca & Vitorio Garcia; gp/ Jesus de Dios Chaves & Monica Lucero, all residents of Ranchos de Albuquerque.

GARCIA, Diego
bap 16 Nov 1846, 3 days old; legit s/ Juan Garcia & Juana Vitoria Garcia, of los Candelarias; ap/ Juan Garcia & Juana Varbero; am/ Juan Jose Garcia & Francisca Gonsales, gp/ Jose Dolores Samora & Soledad Garcia.

Frame 2185, #43
SABEDRA, Pedro Antonio
bap 18 Nov 1846, 6 days old; legit s/ Miguel Sabedra & Nestora Montoya, of los Ranchos de Albuquerque; ap/ Francisco Sabedra & Maria de la Lus Chaves; am/ Antonio Montoya & Florentina Ortis; gp/ Salbador Armijo & Placida Armijo, residents of Albuquerque.

MARTIN, Nestor
bap 28 Nov 1846, 4 days old; legit s/ Jose Martin & Maria Gertrudes Salazar, residents of Alameda; ap/ Jose Martin & Rosalia Lucero; am/ Dionicio Salazar & Maria Valencia; gp/ Nicolas Gurule & Donaciana Martin, residents of los Ranchos of Albuquerque.

GARCIA, Jose Nestor
bap 28 Nov 1846, 3 days old; legit s/ Dionicio Garcia & Maria Petra Romero, residents of los Griegos; ap/ Juan Luis Garcia & Gertrudes Griego; am/ Valtasar Romero & Paula Lucero, gp/ Miguel Noanes & Maria Tranquilina Noanes, of the same place.

Frame 2186, #44
ANAYA, Juan Nepomuceno Remigio
bap 29 Nov 1846, 10 days old; legit s/ Ambrosio Anaya & Catarina Apodaca, residents of Albuquerque; ap/ Jose Anaya & Ascension Martin; am/ Ramon Apodaca & Juana Rafaela Lopez; gp/ Juan Nepomuceno Carabajal & Gertrudis Gonsales, of the same place.

SANCHES, Trinidad
bap 29 Nov 1846, 6 days old; legit d/ Juan Sanches & Guadalupe Chaves, of San Mateo; ap/ Antonio Jose Sanches & Rosalia Martin; am/ Juan Chaves & Juliana Rael; gp/ Mariana Sarracino, of Albuquerque.

GARCIA, Maria Andrea Nicolasa
bap 6 Dec 1846, 4 days old; legit d/ Jose Dubigen Garcia & Maria Nepomucena Rael, of Alameda; ap/ Andres Garcia & Juana Torres; am/ Antonio Rael & Maria Francisca Padilla; gp/ Jose Dolores Sandobal & Josefa Garcia, of the same place.

Frame 2187, #45
LOPES, Jose Maria
bap 6 Dec 1846, 5 days old; legit s/ Jose Vernave Lopes & Sipriana Perea, of los Griegos; ap/ Rafael Lopes & Maria Antonia Moya; am/ Jose Antonio Perea & Lucia Garcia; gp/ Felipe Lopes & Maria Juana Lopes, of the same place.

BUSTOS, Juana Maria de Atocha
bap 6 Dec 1846, 4 days old; legit d/ Baltasar Bustos & Maria Marques, residents of los Barelas; ap/ Blaz Bustos & Maria Candelaria; am/ Antonio Marques & Maria Dolores Toledo; gp/ Jose Venabides & Maria Candelaria, of the same place.

APODACA, Maria Rosalia
bap 14 Dec 1846, 9 days old; legit d/ Lino Apodaca & Maria Clara Padia, residents of Alameda; ap/ Rafael Apodaca & Maria Estefana Salazar; am/ Agustin Padilla & Maria Dolores Gonsales; gp/ Manuel Jaramillo & Maria Gertrudis Mestas, of the same place.

Frames 2187-2188, #46
ROMERO, Jose Venceslado
bap 16 Dec 1846, 8 days old; legit s/ Manuel Romero & Juliana Sanches, residents of Albuquerque; ap/ Francisco Antonio Romero & Ursula Garcia; am/ Salbador Sanches & Olalla Tafolla; gp/ Salbador Romero & Francisca Chavez, residents of los Barelas.

SEGUNDO, Jose Antonio
bap 16 Dec 1846, 15 days old; legit s/ Manuela Segundo & Monica Candelaria, of los Candelarias; ap/ Manuel Segundo & Vicenta Duran; am/ Maria Catarina Candelaria; gp/ Jose Viteriano Griego & Jesus Candelaria, of the same place.

CANDELARIA, Juan
bap 16 Dec 1846, 6 days old; legit s/ Salbador Candelaria & Maria de Jesus Padilla, residents of Atrisco; ap/ Juan Candelaria & Teresa Sanches; am/ not stated; gp/ Jose Armijo & Guadalupe Chavez, of the same place.

Frames 2188-2189, #47
GARCIA, Juliana
bap 20 Dec 1846, 8 days old; natural d/ Juana Maria Garcia, of los Ranchos de Albuquerque; am/ Felipe Garcia; gp/ Deciderio Garcia & Francisca Luna, of the same place.

GARCIA, Espiridion
bap 20 Dec 1846, 9 days old; legit s/ Jose Antonio Garcia & Polinaria Salazar, residents of Carnue; ap/ Felis Garcia & Ysabel Lopez; am/ Cristobal Salazar & Miquela Montoya, gp/ Francisco Garcia & Maria Rosa Lopez, of the same place.

GURULE, Maria Tomasa
bap 21 Dec 1846, 6 days old; legit d/ Manuel Gurule & Gertrudis Chabes, residents of Alameda; ap/ Antonio Perea & Juliana Chaves; am/ Ana Maria Gonsales & Jose Domingo Gurule; gp/ Jose Manuel Martin & Rosa Montoya, residents of Alameda.

GABALDON, Jose de la Trinidad
bap 29 Dec 1846, 3 days old; legit s/ Miguel Gabaldon & Juana Lopez, from the Rancho de Atrisco; ap/ Ygnacio Gabaldon & Miquela Sanches; am/ Antonio Lopez & Miquela Jaramillo; gp/ Jose Saracino & Mariana Saracino, of the same place.

Frame 2190, #48
LUCERO, Maria Juana de la Trinidad Evangelista
bap 30 Dec 1846, 4 days old; legit d/ Jose Maria Lucero & Antonia Teresa Gallego, residents of los Ranchos de Atrisco; ap/ Francisco Lucero & Maria Manuela Aragon; am/ Cristobal Gallego & Carmen Gutieres; gp/ Joaquin Alejandro Basan & Maria de los Angeles Ortega, of the same place.

BAROS, Varbaro
bap 2 Jan 1847, 15 days old; legit s/ Juan Nepomuceno Baros & Maria Antonia Chaves, residents of San Antonio; ap/ Juan Antonio Baros & Maria Zalazar; am/ Bautista Chaves & Maria Guadalupe Montoya; gp/ Miguel Chaves & Nicolasa Montoya, of the same place.

Frames 2190-2191, #49
HERRERA, Rumaldo Felozoro
bap 8 Jan 1847, 6 days old; legit s/ Manuel Herrera & Vegnina Chaves, residents of Atrisco; ap/ Vicente Herrera & Maria Antonia Sanches; am/ Antonio Chaves & Manuela Garcia; gp/ Salbador Herrera & Maria Ygnacio Chaves, of the same place.

PADILLA, Jose Julian
bap 8 Jan 1847, 4 days old; legit s/ Valtasar Padilla & Juana Garcia, residents of Alameda; ap & am/ not stated; gp/ Antonio Garcia & Juana Sais, of the same place.

CANDELARIA, Maria Carlota de Jesus
bap 15 Jan 1847, 4 days old; legit d/ Francisco Candelaria & Ysabel Garcia, residents of los Candelarias; ap/ Cacimiro Candelaria & Matilde Griego; am/ Blas Garcia & Maria Reyes Apodaca; gp/ Jose Atanacio Montoya & Maria Margarita Mares.

CANDELARIA, Juan Pablo
bap 16 Jan 1847, 3 days old; legit s/ Juan Antonio Candelaria & Maria Antonia Sena, residents of los Ranchos of Albuquerque; ap/ Ramon Candelaria & Maria Manuela Martin; am/ Francisco Sena, deceased, & Maria Manuela Martin; gp/ same as paternal grandparents.

Frame 2192, #50
MARES, Juan Pablo
bap 17 Jan 1847, 4 days old; legit s/ Ramon Mares & Luz Jaramillo, residents of los Candelarias; ap/ Juan Pablo Mares & Juana Noanes; am/ Ramon Jaramillo & Reyes Armijo; gp/ Andres Noanes & Juana Nepomucena Armijo, of the same place.

GURULE, Ylaria
bap 20 Jan 1847, 5 days old; legit d/ Vicente Gurule & Juana Candelaria, residents of San Antonio; ap/ Juan Cristobal Gurule & Ynes Martin; am/ Ermeregilda Candelaria & Dolores Jaramillo; gp/ Felipe Garcia & Paula Chaves, of the same place.

LUCERO, Jose Felipe
bap 23 Jan 1847, 4 days old; legit s/ Cleto Lucero & Gabriela Candelaria, residents of Alameda; ap/ Jose Lucero & Maria Dolores Garcia; am/ Ygnacio Candelaria & Concepcion Chaves; gp/ Felipe Garcia & Paula Chaves, of the same place.

Frame 2193, #51
GURULE, Miguel
bap 25 Jan 1847, 8 days old; legit s/ Jose Gabriel Gurule & Nicolasa Luna, residents of Alameda; ap/ Jose Domingo Gurule & Anna Maria Gurule; am/ Ysidro Luna & Manuela Candelaria; gp/ Miguel Montaño & Clara Candelaria, residents of los Ranchos de Albuquerque.

PAIS, Julian
bap 24 Jan 1847, 15 days old; legit s/ Andres Pais & Albina Gurule, residents of Alameda; ap/ Jose Pais & Juana Arias; am/ Lagos Gurule & Juana Padilla; gp/ Juan Jose Apodaca & Maria de Luz Padilla.

CRESPIN, Maria Veneranda Eulogia de la Luz
bap 29 Jan 1847, 3 days old; legit d/ Salbador Crespin & Reyes Sedillo, residents of San Antonio; ap/ Francisco Crespin & Maria Gonsales; am/ Salbador Lopes & Maria Sedillo; gp/ Juan Cristobal Rael & Gregoria Lopes, of the same place.

Frame 2194, #52
MADRIL, Pedro Nolasco
bap 31 Jan 1847, 8 days old; legit s/ Juan Manuel Madril & Maria Ynes Perea, of los Ranchos de Albuquerque; ap/ Cristobal Madril & Barbara Padilla; am/ Manuel Perea & Gregoria Garcia; gp/ Reyes Garcia & Dolores Griego, of the same place.

GARCIA, Polinaria
bap 31 Jan 1847, 7 days old; legit d/ Ylario Garcia & Marcelina Griego, of los Ranchos de Albuquerque; ap/ Francisco Garcia & Reyes Candelaria; am/ Jose Griego & Gertrudis Valencia; gp/ Dionicio Griego & Maria Ynes Romero, of the same place.

GARCIA, Maria Ygnacia Teodosa
bap 1 Feb 1847, 3 days old; legit d/ Diego Garcia & Serafina Candelaria, residents of San Antonio; ap/ Vicente Garcia & Matilde Lucero; am/ Salbador Candelaria & Rita Sanches; gp/ Blas Muñis & Maria Ygnacia Lucero, of the same place.

Frame 2195, #53
ANAYA, Martin de Jesus
bap 1 Feb 1847, 3 days old; legit s/ Andres Anaya & Anna Maria Candelaria, of los Ranchos de Albuquerque; ap/ Juan Anaya & Francisca Baca; gp/ Francisco Sanches & Maria Manuela Sanches, of the same place.

GARCIA, Francisco Desales
bap 2 Feb 1847; legit s/ Miguel Garcia & Vitalia Apodaca, residents of Corrales; ap/ Francisco Garcia & Anna Maria Montoya; am/ Juan Apodaca & Rosa Garcia; gp/ Jose Domingo Griego & Maria Manuela Lucero, of the same place.

GALLEGO, Jose Nestor
bap 4 Feb 1847, 6 days old; legit s/ Anastacio Gallego & Petrona Martines, of los Ranchos de Albuquerque; ap/ Martin Gallego & Guadalupe Garcia; am/ not stated; gp/ Blas Lucero & Rosalia Tenorio, of the same place.

Frame 2196, #54
ANAYA, Juan Andres
bap 5 Feb 1847, 1 day old; legit s/ Jose Re(cut off) Anaya & Teresa Candelaria, residents of Atrisco; ap/ Manuel Anaya & Maria Ysidora Gonsales; am/ Pablo Candelaria & Guadalupe Herrera; gp/ Francisco Ramon Griego & Maria Soledad Sanches, of the same place.

MARTIN, Jesus Ramon Andres
bap 5 Feb 1847, 3 days old; legit s/ Dolores Martin & Dolores Torres, of Albuquerque; ap/ Rafael Martin & Manuela Anaya; am/ Lorenzo Torres & Juana Ruis; gp/ Jesus Lopes & Juana Armijo.

GARCIA, Pedro Nolasco
bap 6 Feb 1847, 8 days old; legit s/ Diego Garcia & Juliana Zalazar, residents of Alameda; ap/ Andres Garcia & Juana Torres; am/ Luis Zalazar & Ysabel Rael; gp/ Esteban Sandobal & Toribio Garcia, of the same place.

Frame 2197, #55
SANCHES, Emilia
bap 8 Feb 1847, 4 days old; legit d/ Jose Sanches & Clara Chaves, of los Ranchos de Albuquerque; ap/ Gabriel Sanches & Juana Sedillo; am/ not stated; gp/ Andres Anaya & Nestora Montoya, of the same place.

HURTADO, Jose Agustin de Jesus
bap 8 Feb 1847, 6 days old; legit s/ Mariano Hurtado & Gertrudis Sanches, residents of Alameda; ap/ Ysidro Hurtado & Juana Varela; am/ Mariano Sanches & Carmel Escudero; gp/ Agustin Sisneros & Ruperta Sisneros, residents of Ranchos de Albuquerque.

PEREA, Maria Dorotea Gabriela
bap 10 Feb 1847, 4 days old; legit d/ Miguel Perea & Candida Griego, residents of Albuquerque; ap/ Rafael Perea & Carmel Anaya; am/ Rafael Griego & Barbara Apodaca; gp/ Miguel Samora & Manuela Martines, residents of San Antonio.

Frame 2198, #56
BARRERAS, Jose Benigno
bap 10 Feb 1847, 3 days old; legit s/ Francisco Barreras & Vibiana Noanes, residents of San Antonio; ap/ not stated; am/ Anastacio Noanes & Barbara Chaves; gp/ Juan Jose Luna & Rafaela Candelaria, residents of Bosque del Pino.

PADILLA, Antonio
bap 10 Feb 1847, 4 days old; legit s/ Jose Antonio Padilla & Maria Juana Butierres, residents of Alameda; ap/ Joaquin Padilla; am/ Loreto Butierres & Manuela Rael; gp/ Antonio Abad Gallego & Maria Petra Padilla, of the same place.

BUTIERRES, Jose Valentino
bap 10 Feb 1847, 5 days old; legit s/ Mariano Butierres & Juana Romero, residents of los Griegos; ap/ Pedro Antonio Butierres & Guadalupe Griego; am/ Gregorio Romero & Rafaela Baros; gp/ Guadalupe Alfaros & Maria Barela.

Frame 2199, #57
GARCIA, Jose Gabino
bap 20 Jan 1847, 3 days old; legit s/ Julian Garcia & Juana Lorensa Aragon, residents of los Duranes; ap/ Faustin Garcia & Francisca Gonsales, am/ Manuel Aragon & Teresa Varbero; gp/ Antonio Santillanes & Paula Contreras.

ARMENTA, Maria Josefa
bap 10 Feb 1847, 3 days old; legit d/ Nicolas Armenta & Juana Anaya, residents of San Antonio; ap/ not stated; am/ Rafael Anaya & Ynes Garcia; gp/ Juan Anaya & Sesaria Anaya, of the same place.

Frame 2200, #58
PEREA, Jose Vacilio
bap 11 Feb 1847, 9 days old; legit s/ Jose Perea & Albina Gurule, residents of San Antonio; ap/ Ygnacio Perea & Francisca Martines; am/ Jose Gurule & Francisco Gurule; gp/ Antonio Rodrigues & Manuela Rodrigues, residents of the same.

HERRERA, Maria Merced
bap 11 Feb 1847, 2 days old; legit d/ Juan Herrera & Maria Varbara Jaramillo, residents of Atrisco; ap/ Vicente Herrera & Maria Antonia Sanches; am/ Miguel Jaramillo & Gertrudes Griego; ap/ Jose Antonio Garcia & Maria Ysabel Gallego, of the same place

GARCIA, Placida
bap 11 Feb 1847, 3 days old; legit d/ Cleto Garcia & Nicolasa Duran, residents los Duranes; ap/ Juan Maria Garcia & Antonia Anaya; am/ Manuel Duran & Manuela Muñis; gp/ Juan Bautista Garcia & Josefa Lucero, residents of the same.

Frame 2201, #59
PACHECO, Maria Juliana
bap 21 Feb 1847, 5 days old; legit d/ Juan Pacheco & Juliana Gutierres, residents of Alameda; ap/ Francisco Pacheco & Juana Gonsales; am/ Pascual Gutierres & Manuela Gallego; gp/ Lino Apodaca & Maria Clara Padilla.

MARTIN, Maria Margarita Felicita
bap 23 Feb 1847, 1 day old; legit d/ Ambrocio Martin & Trinidad Ruis, residents of Albuquerque; ap/ Rafael Martin & Manuela Tafolla; am/ Ygnacio Ruis & Maria Ysidora Lopez; gp/ Diego Lopez & Juana Lopez, of the same place.

SAMORA, Maria Serafina
bap 23 Feb 1847, 4 days old; legit d/ Ramon Samora & Maria Gregoria Candelaria, of plaza of los Candelarias; ap/ Miguel Samora & Marcelina Gallego; am/ Jose Candelaria & Francisca Gabaldon; gp/ Pedro Contreras & Maria Josefa Contreras, residents of los Duranes.

Frame 2202, #60
TRUJILLO, Matias Romulo
bap 23 Feb 1847, 1 day old; legit s/ Santiago Trujillo & Maria Salome Gutierres, residents of los Candelarias; ap/ Jose Trujillo & Soledad Valencia; am/ Jose Miguel Gutierres & Maria Gregoria Armijo; gp/ Pablo Gutierres & Josefa Martines, of the same place.

LUCERO, Jose Seferino
bap 23 Feb 1847, 5 days old; legit s/ Francisco Lucero & Maria Bisenta Martinez; ap/ Jose Antonio Lusero & Juana Montaño; am/ Felipe Martine & Francisca Mora; gp/ Francisco Sandoval & Juana Apodaca, residents of los Barelas.

GALLEGO, Gregoria
bap 4 Mar 1847, 6 days old; legit s/ Valentin Gallego & Maria Manuela Garcia, from Ranchos of Albuquerque; ap/ Jose Pablo Gallegos & Juana Mora; am/ Juana Garcia; gp/ Antonio Abad Duran & Maria Gracia Sanchez, of the same place.

Frame 2203, #61
LUJANA, Maria Juana
bap 7 Mar 1847, 3 days old; legit d/ Miguel Lujana & Simona Lucero, residents of the plaza of los Gallegos; ap/ Mariano Lujana & Manuela Garcia; am/ Lorenso Lucero & Crus Griego; gp/ Miguel Navarres & Dolores Griego, residents of the plaza of los Poblanos.

APODACA, Jose Eluterio
bap 7 Mar 1847, 6 days old; legit s/ Jose Antonio Apodaca & Juan Samora, residents of San Antonio; ap/ Nicolas Apodaca & Maria de la Luz Garcia; am/ Jose Samora & Rafaela Martin; gp/ Francisco Lucero & Maria Dolores Baca, of the same place.

CHAVES, Maria Clara
bap 7 Mar 1847, 7 days old; natural d/ Maria Juana Chaves, resident of the plaza of los Candelarias; am/ Geronimo Chaves & Encarnacion Gonsales; gp/ Fernando Gonsales & Josefa Gonsales, of the same place.

Frame 2204, #62
BERNAL, Maria Gertrudis Eutemia
bap 7 Mar 1847, 2 days old; legit d/ Jose Maria Bernal & Maria Estefana Jaramillo, residents of Atrisco; ap/ Antonio Bernal & Maria Valencia; am/ Agustin Jaramillo & Francisca Garcia; gp/ Antonio Sabedra & Antonia Sabedra.

ARAGON, Juan Vicente
bap 7 Mar 1847, 15 days old; legit s/ Marcelino Aragon & Nicolasa Gonsales, residents of los Duranes; ap/ Juan de Jesus Aragon & Rosalia Gonsales; am/ Jose Jaramillo & Guadalupe Sanches; gp/ Julian Sanches & Juana Candelaria.

DURAN, Maria Altagracia
bap 7 Mar 1847, 3 days old; legit d/ Francisco Duran & Bernarda Gurule, residents of Albuquerque; ap & am/ not stated; gp/ Ysidro Garcia & Maria Altagracia Martines, of the same place.

Frame 2205, #63
BALENCIA, Maria Vitoriana
bap 8 Mar 1847, 3 days old; legit d/ Bernardo Balencia & Anna Maria Aragon, of Ranchos of Albuquerque; ap/ Juan Domingo Valencia & Paula Martin; am/ Tomas Aragon & Gertrudis Garcia; gp/ Cristobal Sanches & Concepcion Valencia, of the same place.

MOYA, Maria de Jesus
bap 16 Mar 1847, 20 days old; legit d/ Jesus Moya & Maria Antonia Murrieta, residents of Chilili Pueblo; ap/ Gabriel Moya & Maria Antonia Urtado; am/ not stated; gp/ Juan Lucero & Maria de Jesus Lucero, residents of same.

GOMES, Jose Abran
bap 16 Mar 1847, 6 days old; legit s/ Juan Gomes & Juliana Gonsales, residents of the plaza of los Lunas; ap/ Juan Gomes & Ygnacia Arias; am/ NN Gonsales & Victoria Garcia; gp/ Jose Valentin Sandobal & Maria Ygnacia Sandobal, of the same place.

Frame 2206, #64
MONTAÑO, Josefa
bap 16 Mar 1847, 1 month old; Navajo, adopted d/ Jose Montaño & Maria Teresa Miera, of Ranchos of Albuquerque; gp/ Francisco Montaño & Soledad Miera, residents of the same place.

PEREA, Jose Patricio
bap 15 Mar 1847, 4 days old; legit s/ Antonio Perea & Candelaria Vernal, residents of Alameda; ap/ Luis Perea & Guadalupe Garcia; am/ not stated; gp/ Antonio Garcia & Maria Quiterria Garcia, of the same place.

LOPES, Epigmenia
bap 24 Mar 1847, 3 days old; legit s/ Teodoro Lopes & Josefa Chaves, residents of los Barelas; ap/ Manuel Lopes & Cruz Romero; am/ Agustin Chaves & Juana Sanches; gp/ Juan Padilla & Rosalia Chaves, residents of Atrisco.

Frame 2207, #65
ROMERO, Jose Venito Abad
bap 28 Mar 1847, 7 days old; legit s/ Diego Romero & Nepomucena Muñis, residents of los Griegos; ap/ Santiago Romero & Ygnacia Valencia; am/ Lucrecio Muñis & Maria Guadalupe Sanches; gp/ Jose de la Crus Romero & Manuela Muñis, residents of Bernalillo.

ARMIJO, Rosalia
bap 28 Mar 1847, 6 days old; Navajo, adopted d/ Juan Cristobal Armijo & Juana Chaves, residents of Ranchos of Albuquerque; gp/ same adoptive parents.

ARMIJO, Paula
bap 28 Mar 1847, 20 years old, adult; Navajo, adopted d/ Juan Cristobal Armijo & Juana Chaves, residents of Ranchos of Albuquerque; gp/ same adoptive parents.

Frames 2207-2208, #66
LOPES, Jose Macimiano
bap 28 Mar 1847, 15 days old; legit s/ Ygnacio Lopes & Gregoria Garcia, residents of San Antonio; ap/ Salbador Lopes & Marta Sedillo; am/ Diego Garcia & Reyes Candelaria; gp/ Pedro Baca & Juana Lopes, of the same place.

TORRES, Jose Ramon
bap 28 Mar 1847, 4 days old; legit s/ Felipe Torres & Bernardina Garcia, of los Ranchos de Albuquerque; ap/ Jose Torres & Anna Maria Griego; am/ Jose Garcia & Reyes Candelaria; gp/ Pedro Antonio Apodaca & Maria de la Luz Perea, of the same place.

NOANES, Francisco Antonio
bap 28 Mar 1847, 4 days old; legit s/ Santiago Noanes & Manuela Atencio, residents of San Antonio; ap/ Geronimo Noanes & Barbara Maes; am/ Gaspar Atencio & Ysabel Chaves; gp/ Juan Garcia & Juana Maria Mestas, residents of same.

Frames 2208-2209, #69
OTERO, Antonio Abad
bap 29 Mar 1847, 1 month old; legit s/ Juan Otero & Rosalia Jaramillo, residents of San Antonio; ap & am/ unknown; gp/ Pablo Gonsales & Francisca Antonia Santillanes, of los Ranchos de Albuquerque.

MORA, Maria Selentina
bap 6 Apr 1847, 5 days old; legit d/ Estevan Mora & Juana Maria Griego, of los Ranchos de Albuquerque; ap/ Ysidro Mora & Juana Marques; am/ Francisco Griego & Maria Serna; gp/ Luis Mares & Teresa Garcia, of the same place.

ARIAS, Jose Ricardo
bap 6 Apr 1847, 5 days old; legit s/ Salbador Arias & Rosa Padilla, of los Ranchos de Albuquerque; ap/ Juan Cristobal Arias & Tomasa Garcia; am/ Julian Padilla & Anna Maria Padilla; gp/ Pedro Arias & Maria Tomasa Martin, of the same place.

ANAYA, Dionicio
bap 9 Apr 1847, 1 day old; legit s/ Juan Anaya & Dolores Sanches, of the ranchos de Atrisco; ap/ Pablo Anaya & Juana Tafolla; am/ Juan Andres Sanches & Josefa Griego; gp/ Juan Garcia & Concepcion Anaya, of the same place.

Frame 2210, #70
LUCERO, Jose Amado
bap 11 Apr 1847, 22 days old; legit s/ Mariano Lucero & Maria Antonia Duran, of San Antonio; ap/ Gaspar Lucero & Francisca Salas; am/ Tomas Duran & Trinidad Montaño; gp/ Jose Samora & Josefa Montaño, of the plaza of los Griegos.

SANCHES, Jose Leon
bap 11 Apr 1847, 2 days old; legit s/ Jose Sanches & Maria Paula Garcia, of Alameda; ap/ Felipe Sanches & Ramona Gurule; am/ Jose Maria Garcia & Reyes Candelaria; gp/ Pedro Antonio Apodaca & Maria de la Luz Perea, residents of Ranchos of Albuquerque.

TENORIO, Maria Camila Leona
bap 11 Apr 1847, 6 days old; legit d/ Jose Maria Tenorio & Ramona Sisneros, of los Ranchos de Albuquerque; ap/ Manuel Tenorio & Antonia Anaya; am/ Antonio Sisneros & Manuela Antonia Romero; gp/ Jose Ortega & Maria Francisca Ortega, of the same place.

Frame 2211, #71
ABALOS, Maria Francisca
bap 12 Apr 1847, 3 days old; legit d/ Agapito Abalos & Juana Garcia, of los Ranchos de Albuquerque;
ap/ not stated; am/ Pablo Garcia & Antonia Martin; gp/ Manuel Martin & Dolores Martin, of the same
place.

MESTAS, Maria Mersed del Carmel
bap 14 Apr 1847, 1 day old; legit s/ Pedro Mestas & Dolores Apodaca, of the villa; ap/ Mariano Mestas &
Juana Maria Chavez; am/ Juan Apodaca & Maria Ysabel Sanches; gp/ Francisco Ruis & Trinidad
Apodaca, of the same place.

SAMORA, Leonor
bap 16 Apr 1847, 4 days old; legit d/ Felipe Samora & Gertrudis Gallego, of Los Gallegos; ap/ Juan
Francisco Samora & Maria Trinidad Vencia; am/ Antonio Jose Gallegos & Madalena Garcia; gp/ Pedro
Aranda & Rosalia Jaramillo, of the same place.

Frames 2211-2212, #72
PEREA, Maria Trinidad
bap 16 Apr 1847, 3 days old; natural d/ Juana Perea, of los Ranchos de Albuquerque; am/ Salbador Perea
& Juana Garcia; gp/ Jose Antonio Lucero & Natividad Lucero, of the same place.

ARMIJO, Lucas
bap 17 Apr 1847, 3 days old; legit s/ Jose Armijo & Juana Armijo, residents of this plaza; ap/ Lucas
Armijo & Barbara Ortiz; am/ Pedro Armijo & Manuela Garcia; gp/ Barbara Armijo & Cristobal Armijo,
of the same place.

PADILLA, Lorenzo Julio
bap 17 Apr 1847, 4 days old; legit s/ Francisco Padilla & Ysidora Arias; ap/ Julian Padilla & Anna Maria
Padilla; am/ Juan Cristobal Arias & Tomasa Martin; gp/ Lorenzo Montaño & Maria Petra Candelaria.

Frames 2212-2213, #73
LUCERO, Jose Torribio
bap 17 Apr 1847, 3 days old; legit s/ Juan Lucero & Ysabel Garcia, of Albuquerque; ap/ Tomas Lucero &
Bernarda Tafolla; am/ Ramon Garcia & Ascencion Lopes; gp/ Luis Garcia & Luisa Lucero.

HERRERA, Maria Barbara
bap 23 Apr 1847, 7 days old; legit d/ Jose Herrera & Maria de la Luz Sandobal, of Alameda; ap/ Jose
Andres Herrera & Dolores Garcia; am/ Miguel Sandobal & Maria Manuela Gonsales; gp/ Rafael Apodaca
& Juana Romero, of the same place.

MONTOYA, Jose Crecencio
bap 24 Apr 1847, 5 days old; adopted s/ Jose Maria Montoya & Manuela Romero, of Alameda; ap/
Martin Montoya & Manuela Romero; am/ Ramon Gallego & Josefa Benabides; gp/ adoptive parents.

GALLEGO, Maria Polonia
bap 24 Apr 1847, 4 days old; legit d/ Pedro Gallego & Dolores Candelaria, residents of Atrisco; ap/ Juan
Antonio Gallego & Maria Felipa Anaya; am/ Pablo Candelaria & Guadalupe Herrera; gp/ Manuel
Sanchez & Petra Chavez, of the same place.

Frame 2214, #74
GARCIA, Jose Meliton
bap 2 May 1847, 4 days old; legit s/ Salbador Garcia & Juana Romero, residents of Alameda; ap/ Jose Antonio Garcia & Soledad Sandoval; am/ Santiago Romero & Dolores Candelaria, gp/ Juan Jose Apodaca & Maria de la Luz Padilla, of the same place.

MOYA, Jose Amador de Jesus
bap 4 May 1847, 6 days old; s/ Juan Francisco Moya & Paula Anaya, residents of Atrisco; ap/ Vitoriano Moya & Maria de Jesus Martin; am/ Domingo Anaya & Dolores Griego; gp/ Damacio Griego & Manuela Carabajal, residents of same.

PERALTA, Cruz
bap 7 May 1847, 3 days old; legit d/ Jose Peralta & Dolores Montoya, residents of Alameda; ap/ not stated; am/ Pedro Montoya & Anna Maria Luna; gp/ Rumaldo Garcia & Ynes Luna, of the same.

Frames 2214-2215, #75
ORTIZ, Maria Carolina
bap 13 May 1847, 2 days old; natural d/ Monica Ortiz, residents of Albuquerque; gp/ Deciderio Chaves & Concepcion Ortiz.

NUANES, Juan Nepomuceno
bap 20 May 1847, 4 days old; legit s/ Antonio Nuanes & Candelaria Griego, residents of los Griegos; ap/ Jose Manuel Nuanes & Paula Candelaria; am/ Jose Maria Griego & Guadalupe Mora; gp/ Dionicio Garcia & Petra Romero, of the same place.

GARCIA, Juan Nepomuceno
bap 20 May 1847, 4 days old; legit s/ Ambrocio Garcia & Catarina Armijo, residents of los Candelarias; ap/ Martin Garcia & Anna Maria Apodaca; am/ Rafael Armijo & Soledad Peña; gp/ Santiago Trujillo & Anna Maria Gutierrez.

Frames 2215-2216, #76
LUCERO, Juana
bap 20 May 1847, 6 days old; legit d/ Jose Lucero & Eulogia Sabedra, of los Ranchos de Albuquerque; ap/ Andres Lucero & Antonia Garcia; am/ Francisco Sabedra & Maria de la Luz Chaves; gp/ Maximo Varela & Juana Varela, residents of same.

MANSANARES, Juana
bap 20 May 1847, 6 days old; legit d/ Anna Maria Mansanares, of los Ranchos de Albuquerque; am/ Jose Mansanares & Estafana Garcia; gp/ Mariano Varela & Juana Varela, of the same place.

SANDOVAL, Anna Maria Susana
bap 24 May 1847, 12 days old; legit d/ Jose Sandoval & Maria Jocefa Garcia, residents of Alameda; ap/ Miguel Sandobal & Maria Manuela Gonsales; am/ Antonio Garcia & Juana Sais; gp/ Mariano Sandobal & Dubigen Garcia, of the same place.

SAIS, Jose Felipe
bap 25 May 1847, 15 days old; legit s/ Jose Sais & Martina Trujillo, residents of Alameda; ap/ Salbador Sais & Juana Maria Aragon; am/ Mariano Truxillo & Maria Luiza Cordoba; gp/ Juan Trujillo & Lorenza Lucero, of Alameda.

Frame 2217, #77
MONTOYA, Maria Polinaria
bap 25 May 1847, 4 days old; legit d/ Atencio Montoya & Maria Mares; ap/ Bartolo Montoya & Maria Ysabel Garcia; am/ Nicolas Mares & Manuela Garcia; gp/ Juan de Dios Chaves & Maria Lucero, all from los Candelarias.

ARIAS, Bibian
bap 25 May 1847, 5 days old; legit s/ Francisco Arias & Maria Francisca Montoya, of los Ranchos de Albuquerque; ap/ Juan Domingo Arias & Maria Sanches; am/ Rafael Montoya & Manuela Candelaria; gp/ Ynocencio Montaño & Maria Soledad Miera, of los Ranchos de Albuquerque.

GRIEGO, Maria Quirina
bap 25 May 1847, 3 days old; adopted d/ Francisco Griego & Maria Gutierres, of los Ranchos de Albuquerque; ap/ Juan Angel Griego & Anna Maria Gutierres; am/ Jose Gutierres & Francisca Gonsales; gp/ the adoptive parents.

Frame 2218, #78
LUCERO, Altagracia
bap 26 May 1847, 15 days old, illegitimate; adopted d/ Lorensa Lucero, residents of Alameda; am/ Jose Lucero & Cruz Gallego; gp/ Mariano Chaves & Monica Romero, residents of same.

LOPES, Ruperta
bap 27 May 1847, 3 days old; legit d/ Jose Lopes & Dolores Gallego, residents of Barelas; ap/ Mateo Lopes & Maria Manuela Montoya; am/ not stated; gp/ Antonio Gutierres & Ruperta Lopes, of the same place.

ZALAZAR, Maria Juana Beneranda
bap 29 May 1847, 3 days old; legit d/ Juan Zalazar & Maria Barbara Garcia, residents of Alameda; ap/ Juan de Jesus Zalazar & Maria Antonia Perea; am/ Jose Vicente Garcia & Paula Chaves; gp/ Jose Maria Mares & Maria Josefa Garcia, of the same place.

Frames 2218-2219, #79
SANCHES, Teodocio
bap 31 May 1847, 2 days old; legit s/ Manuel Sanches & Petra Chaves, residents of Atrisco; ap/ Ygnacio Sanches & Manuela Anaya; am/ Jose Dolores Chaves & Nicanora Garcia; gp/ Jose Maria Sanches & Manuela Anaya, residents of same.

OLGIN, Maria Teodora
bap 31 May 1847, 3 days old; legit s/ Juan Pablo Olgin & Teresa Gutierres, residents of los Candelarias; ap/ Ventura Olgin & Juana Gutierres; am/ Juan Gutierres & Luz Chaves; gp/ Juan Apodaca & Juana Gutierres, of los Barelas.

SANCHES, Beneranda
bap 31 May 1847, 2 days old; legit d/ Francisco Sanches & Juana Martines, residents of los Gallegos; ap/ Cristobal Sanches & Maria Candelaria; am/ Pedro Martines & Dolores Gallego; gp/ Juan de Jesus Armenta & & Concepcion Griego, of the same place.

Frames 2219-2220, #80
GUTIERRES, Macimiano
bap 7 Jun 1847, 3 days old; natural s/ Paula Gutierres, residents los Candelarias; am/ Simon Gutierres & Dolores Candelaria; gp/Juan Jose Gutierres & Maria Marcelina Garcia, of the same place.

TRUJILLO, Maria Nestora
bap 8 Jun 1847, 4 days old; legit d/ Pedro Trujillo & Anna Maria Gonsales, residents of Alameda; ap/ Juan Antonio Trujillo & Susana Montolla; am/ Jose Antonio Gonsales & Maria Getrudis Garcia; gp/ Juan Chaves & Maria de Jesus Garcia, of the same place.

MOYA, Fernando
bap 18 Jun 1847, 2 days old; legit s/ Juan Cristobal Moya & Antonia Urtado; ap/ Gabriel Moya & Antonia Urtado; am/ Rafael Gallego & Barbara Gonsales; gp/ Jose Maria Lucero & Maria Juliana Gallego, of Chilili.

Frames 2220-2221, #81
SANDOBAL, Jose Quirino
bap 20 Jun 1847, 15 days old; legit s/ Francisco Sandobal & Soledad Martin, residents of Chilili; ap/ Dionicio Sandobal & Juana Martin; am/ Jose Martin & Juana Griego; gp/ Pablo Martin & Maria Sisilia Candelaria, of Alameda.

GUTIERRES, Antonio Jose
bap 20 Jun 1847, 9 days old; illegitimate, adopted s/ Antonio Gutierres & Juana Sandobal, residents of the plaza of Alameda; ap/ Santiago Gutierres & Josefa Martin; am/ Pablo Sandoval & Leonarda Lopes; gp/ the same adoptive parents.

CHAVES, Maria Filomena
bap 10 Jul 1847, 5 days old; legit d/ Miguel Chaves & Decideria Gonsales; ap/ Juan Nepomoceno Chaves & Clara Sanches; am/ Jose Domingo Gonsales & Anna Maria Gurule; gp/ Manuel Garcia & Concepcion Lopes, all residents of Albuquerque.

Frames 2221-2222, #82
GARCIA, Jose Sisilio
bap 10 Jul 1847, 2 days old; legit s/ Juan Rafael Garcia & Josefa Lucero, of los Duranes ap/ Juan Rafael Garcia & Manuela Muñis; am/Gregorio Lucero & Marta Lopes; gp/ Jose Antonio Tafolla & Petra Garcia, residents of same.

LOPEZ, Maria Guadalupe
bap 11 Jul 1847, 6 days old; legit d/ Cleto Lopez & Dolores Candelaria, residents of Barelas; ap & am/ not stated; gp/ Jose Marquis & Marcelina Marques, residents of the same.

SISNEROS, Silvano de Jesus
bap 12 Jul, 2 days old; legit s/ Pablo Sisneros & Francisca Ruis, residents of Candelarias; ap/ Francisco Sisneros & Juana Candelaria; am/ Antonio Ruis & Ysabel Armijo; gp/ Salbador Martin & Dolores Torres, residents of Albuquerque.

Frames 2222-2223, #83
ARMENTA, Carlota
bap 18 Jul 1847, 5 days old; legit d/ Juan Armenta & Encarnasion Griego, residents of los Griegos; ap/ Jose Maria Armenta & Ygnacia Martines; am/ Jose Maria Griego & Guadalupe Mora; gp/ Gregorio Griego & Francisca Apodaca, residents of the same place.

GONSALES, Pedro Antonio
bap 18 Jul 1847, 9 days old; legit s/ Jose de la Cruz (Gonsales) & Maria de Jesus Moya, residents of Alameda; ap/ Juan Gonsales & Maria Gertrudis Moya; am/ Jose Antonio Moya & Maria de Jesus Tafolla; gp/ Pedro Garcia & Gertrudis Gonsales, residents of Corrales.

RAEL, Sinforon
bap 23 Jul 1847, 6 days old; legit d/ Francisco Rael & Gregoria Romero, residents of Alameda; ap/ Antonio Rael & Francisca Padilla; am/ Jose Miguel Romero & Maria Ygnacia Montaño; gp/ Jose Romero & Ygnacia Montaño, of los Ranchos de Albuquerque.

Frames 2223-2224, #84
GUTIERRES, Juana Maria
bap 23 Jul 1847, 5 days old; legit d/ Juan Gutierres & Dolores Lueras, residents of San Antonio; ap & am/ not stated; gp/ Juan Cristobal Trujillo & Maria Trujillo, of the same place.

MARTIN, Maria Nestora
bap 24 Jul 1847, 3 days old; legit d/ Pedro Martin & Gertrudes Apodaca, residents of Alameda; ap/ Antonio Martin & Luciana Lucero; am/ Dionicio Apodaca & Luteria Garcia; gp/ Santos Martines & Maria Luciana Lucero, of the same place.

DURAN, Jose Pantalion
bap 24 Jul 1847, 3 days old; natural s/ Luteria Duran, residents of the plaza of los Duranes; am/ Rafael Duran & Rosa Gurule; gp/ Luciano Santillanes & Juliana Santillanes, of the same place.

ARANDA, Josefa
bap 1 Aug 1847, 8 days old; legit d/ Jose Antonio Aranda & Soledad Armijo, of Ranchos de Atrisco; ap/ not stated; am/ Santiago Armijo & Maria Perea; gp/ Antonio Sandobal & Josefa Aranda, of the same place.

Frame 2225, #87
CARRIO, Manuela
bap 22 Aug 1847, 3 days old; legit d/ Salbador Carrio & Juana Griego, residents of Alameda; ap/ Vicente Carrio & Juana Montoya; am/ Jose Griego & Paula Anaya; gp/ Antonio Trujillo, resident of Alameda.

GRIEGO, Juan Bernardo
bap 22 Aug 1847, 3 days old; legit s/ Dionicio Griego & Maria Ygnes Romero, of los Ranchos de Albuquerque; ap/ Francisco Griego & Maria Antonia Serna; am/ Juan Dionicio Romero & Maria de Jesus Nieto; gp/ Guadalupe Chaves & Leonarda Padilla, of the same place.

VARELA, Jesus Maria
bap 30 Aug 1847, 4 days old; natural s/ Dolores Varela, resident of Barelas; am/ Juan Varela & Josefa Chavez; gp/ Jesus Maria Candelaria & Maria Candelaria, of the same place.

Frame 2226, #88
SANDOBAL, Maria Trinidad
bap 4 Sep 1847, 3 days old; legit d/ Antonio Sandobal & Decideria Candelaria, residents of Albuquerque;
ap/ Miguel Sandobal & Manuela Gonsales; am/ Esteban Candelaria & Maria de Jesus Luna; gp/ Francisco
Lopes & Dolores Chaves, of the same place.

GALLEGO, Jose Francisco
bap 19 Sep 1847, 2 days old; legit s/ Jesus Gallego & Maria del Rosario Garcia, of Atrisco; ap/ Joaquin
Gallego & Mariana Sabedra; am/ Jose Manuel Garcia & Maria Garcia; gp/ Juan Gabaldon & Juana
Lopez, residents of Atrisco.

SANDOBAL, Maria de los Angeles
bap 21 Sep 1847, 2 days old; legit d/ Mariano Sandobal & Maria Garcia, residents of Alameda; ap/
Miguel Sandobal & Manuela Gonsales; am/ Blas Garcia & Francisca Aragon; gp/ Feliz Sanches &
Sebastiana Sena, of the same place.

Frame 2227, #89
SANDOBAL, Mateo
bap 22 Sep 1847, 5 days old; legit s/ Diego Sandobal & Juana Maria Gallego, residents of Alameda; ap/
Antonio Jose Sanches & Rosalia Martines; am/ Juan Gallego & Manuela Gurule; gp/ Dolores Gallego &
Manuela Gurule, residents of los Ranchos.

LOBATO, Manuel de Atocha
bap 22 Sep 1847, 3 days old; legit s/ Jose Lobato & Manuela Rael, residents of Alameda; ap/ Juan Lobato
& Anna Maria Casados; am/ Antonio Rael & Francisca Padilla; gp/ Juan de la Cruz Basan & Maria
Garcia Basan.

SANCHES, Tomasa
bap 22 Sep 1847, 3 days old; legit d/ Diego Sanches & Juana Maria Gallego, residents of Alameda; ap/
Antonio Jose Sanches & Rosalia Martines; am/ Juan Gallego & Manuela Gurule; gp/ Juan de la Crus
Basan & Rafaela Mora.

Frame 2228, #90
ORTEGA, Jesus Maria Joaquin
bap 26 Sep 1847, 3 days old; legit s/ Juan Cristobal Ortega & Maria de la Luz Basan, residents of
Alameda; ap/ Andres Ortega & Juana Olgin; am/ Ygnacio Basan & Polonia Gutierres; gp/ Juan de la Cruz
Basan & Maria de los Angeles Ortega.

SANDOBAL, Petrona
bap 3 Oct 1847, 3 days old; legit d/ Juan Sandobal & Justa Sanches, residents of Albuquerque; ap/ Jose
Sandobal & Petrona Sabedra; am/ Juan Guadalupe Sanches & Dolores Garcia; gp/ Jose Garcia & Dolores
Garcia, residents of same.

MARES, Donaciano Geronimo
bap 4 Oct 1847, 12 days old; legit s/ J. Mares & Josefa Garcia, residents of Alameda; ap/ Nicolas Mares
& Manuela Garcia; am/ Vicente Garcia & Paula Chaves; gp/ Felipe Garcia & Paula Chaves, residents of
same.

Frame 2229, #91
LUCERO, Maria Altagracia de los Dolores
bap 6 Oct 1847, 4 days old; legit d/ Francisco Lucero & Dolores Gallego, residents of San Antonio; ap/ Antonio Jose Lucero & Rafaela Archuleta; am/ Pablo Baca & Veguina Otero; gp/ Santos Gonsales & Guadalupe Otero, residents of same.

CANDELARIA, Francisca de Borga
bap 10 Oct 1847, 4 days old; legit d/ Manuel Candelaria & Anna Maria Trujillo, residents of Alameda; ap/ Esteban Candelaria & Maria de Jesus Luna; am/ Jose Trujillo & Soledad Valencia; gp/ Manuel Jaramillo & Maria Gertrudis Mestas, of the same place.

GALLEGOS, Maria Francisca de Borja
bap 10 Oct 1847, 2 days old; legit d/ Jose Dolores Gallegos & Gregoria Trujillo, of los Ranchos de Albuquerque; ap/ Juan Gallegos & Manuela Gurule; am/ Jose Trugillo & Soledad Balencia; gp/ Anastasio Barela & Rafael Garcia, of the same place.

Frame 2230, #92
GONSALES, Maria Josefa
bap 10 Oct 1847, 5 days old; legit d/ Jose de la Cruz Gonsales & Rosalia Noanes, residents of San Antonio; ap/ not stated; am/ Anastacio Nuanes & Barbara Lucero; gp/ Victoriano Zamora & Josefa Ortega, of the same place.

MONTOYA, Jose
bap 10 Oct 1847, 2 days old; legit s/ Juan Cristobal Montoya & Gregoria Perea, residents of San Antonio; ap/ Juan Rafael Montoya & Maria Gurule; am/ Jose Miguel Perea & Manuela Sanches; gp/ Jose Perea & Maria Perea, residents of same.

LUCERO, Maria Rita
bap 17 Oct 1847, 6 years old; adopted d/ Jose de las Niebes Lucero & Eulogia Sabedra; gp/ Blas Lucero & Rosalia Tenorio, residents of los Ranchos of Albuquerque.

Frame 2231, #93
GALLEGOS, Lucas
bap 20 Oct 1847, 3 days old; s/ Francisco Gallegos & Tomasa Griego, of the plaza of los Candelarias, ap/ Juan de la Cruz Gallegos & Luz Aragon; am/ not stated; gp/ Juan Bautista Jaramillo & Juana Maria Garcia of Ranchos de Albuquerque.

OCAÑO, Salbador
bap 24 Oct 1847, 3 days old; s/ Jose Ocaño & Juana Rafaela Aragon, residents of los Ranchos; ap/ not stated; am/ Juan Andres Aragon & Maria Antonia Brito; gp/ Miguel Duran & Victoria Garcia, of the same place.

Frames 2231-2232, #94
TRUJILLO, Maria Margarita
bap 24 Oct 1847, 10 days old; legit d/ Nepomuceno Trujillo & Josefa Rodriguez, residents of Alameda; ap/ Miguel Trujillo & Maria Antonia Rueda; am/ Manuel Rodriguez & Maria Antonia Griego; gp/ Nepomuceno Espinosa & Juana Maria Espinosa, residents of the pueblo of San Antonio.

Baptisms – Albuquerque, New Mexico
1829–1850

ARMIJO, Antonio Jose
bap 28 Oct 1847, 2 days old; legit s/ Teodoro Armijo & Paula Jaramio, of los Ranchos de Albuquerque; ap/ Santiago Armijo & Petra Chaves; am/ Miguel Antonio Jaramio & Maria Altagracia Lucero; gp/ Antonio Sabedra & Josefa Sabedra, residents of Atrisco.

ANAYA, Rafael
bap 28 Oct 1847, 3 days old, illegitimate; adopted s/ Ramon Anaya & Ana Maria Lopes, of this plaza; gp/ Lucas Anaya & Francisca Anaya, of the same place.

Frames 2232-2233, #95
ARMIJO, Manuel de Atocha
bap 31 Oct 1847, 5 days old; legit s/ Rafael Armijo & Josefa Chaves, residents of los Barelas; ap/ Pablo Armijo & Josefa Chaves; am/ Juan Antonio Chaves & Gertrudis Torres; gp/ Juan Chabes & Gertrudis Torres, of the same place.

ROMERO, Maria Rafaela de los Dolores
bap 31 Oct 1847, 8 days old; legit d/ Manuel Romero & Marcelina Armijo, residents of Barelas; ap/ Francisco Romero & Maria Dolores Montoya; am/ Rafael Armijo & Soledad Peña; gp/ Jose Luera & Gertrudis Apodaca, residents of same.

GARCIA, Jose Santos
bap 31 Oct 1847, 4 days old; legit s/ Juan Garcia & Juana Andrea Nuanes, residents of los Griegos; ap/ Juan Luis Garcia & Maria Gertrudis Griego; am/ Guadalupe Nuanes & Antonia Garcia; gp/ Julian Apodaca & Maria Antonia Griego of the same place.

Frames 2233-2234, #96
CANDELARIA, Maria Dolores
bap 31 Oct 1847, 4 days old, illegitimate; adopted d/ Ramon Candelaria & Teodora Peña; gp/ Ramon Candelaria & Teodora Peña, of los Ranchos.

GARCIA, Jose Gregorio
bap 31 Oct 1847, 2 days old; legit s/ Ambrocio Garcia & Ludobina Sandobal, residents of Albuquerque; ap/ Felis Garcia & Ysabel Lopes, am/ Miguel Sandobal & Manuela Gonsales; gp/ Gregorio Garcia & Juana Maria Baca, residents of Albuquerque.

ANSURIS, Maria Josefa
bap 4 Nov 1847, 15 days old; legit d/ Agustin Ansuris & Antonia Abalos; ap/ Rafael Ansuris & Catarina Lucero; am/ Basilio Abalos & Rosalia Ansuris, from San Antonio; gp/ Basilio Abalos & Rosalia Ansuris.

Frames 2234-2235, #97
GARCIA, Jose Leonardo
bap 7 Nov 1847, 3 days old; legit s/ Candido Garcia & Ana Maria Lopes, residents los Ranchos; ap/ Jose Garcia & Juana Maria Lopes, am/ Jose Lopes & Ana Maria Garcia; gp/ Juan Ysidoro Griego & Maria Ventura Lucero, of the same place.

GRIEGO, Maria Altagracia
bap 7 Nov 1847, 3 days old; legit d/ Fernando Griego & Francisca Carbajal, residents of Atrisco; ap/ Miguel Griego & Josefa Duran; am/ Domingo Carvajal & Toribia Sanches; gp/ Jose Carvajal & Manuela Carbajal, of the same place.

CANDELARIA, Manuela
bap 9 Nov 1847, 2 days old; legit d/ Juan Candelaria & Juana Martina, residents of los Griegos; ap/ Salvador Candelaria & Gertrudis Lopes; am/ not stated; gp/ Felipe Gutieres & Lorensa Jaramio, of the same place.

Frames 2235-2236, #98
ARMIJO, Ygnacia
bap 10 Nov 1847, 3 days old; legit s/ Francisco Armijo & Carmen Sanches, residents of los Candelarias; ap/ Ygnacio Armijo & Francisca Cisneros; am/ Juan Jose Sanches & Rita Luna, of the same place; gp/ Juan Gonsales & Luz Rael, of Alameda.

GONSALES, Yrineo
bap 11 Nov 1847, 11 days old; legit s/ Jose Gonsales & Francisca Santillanes, residents of Albuquerque; ap/ Francisco Gonsales & Tomasa Aliri; am/ Nicolas Santillanes & Maria Luisa Garcia, of the same place; gp/ Jose Maria Sandoval & Maria Teresa Luna.

GARCIA, Jose Nasario
bap 11 Nov 1847, 3 days old; legit s/ Francisco Garcia & Soledad Lopez, residents of los Corrales; ap/ Francisco Garcia & Manuela Garcia; am/ Lasaro Lopes & Gertrudis Santillanes; gp/ Salvador Sandoval & Juana Trujillo, of the same place.

Frames 2236-2237, #99
CANDELARIA, Diego Alcala
bap 15 Nov 1847, 3 days old; legit s/ Jose Candelaria & Marcelina Marques, residents of Barelas; ap/ Antonio Candelaria & Antonia Garcia; am/ Juan Marques & Maria Niebes Molina; gp/ Jesus Baca & Nestoria Baca, of los Barelas.

ABILA, Jose Manuel de Atocha
bap 15 Nov 1847, 6 days old; legit s/ Francisco Abila & Concepcion Arias, residents of los Ranchos; ap/ Tomas Abila & Guadalupe Gonsales; am/ Juan Arias & Merced Gomes; gp/ Juan Basan & Maria de los Angeles Ortega, of the same place.

GARCIA, Teodoro
bap 15 Nov 1847, 3 days old; legit s/ Juan Garcia & Concepcion Anaya, residents Ranchos de Atrisco; ap/ Juan de Jesus Garcia & Rosalia Sabedra; am/ Miguel Anaya & Miquela Ruis; gp/ Teodoro Armijo & Guadalupe Chaves, of the same place.

Frames 2237-2238, #100
CHAVES, Jose Mariano
bap 16 Nov 1847, 4 days old; legit s/ Don Jose Chaves & Doña Manuela Armijo, residents of los Padillas; ap/ Don Francisco Chaves & Anna Maria Castillo; am/ Don Juan Armijo & Rosalie Ortega; gp/ Jose Felipe (Chaves) & Dolores Chaves, of the same place.

GUTIERRES, Juan Andres
bap 19 Nov 1847, 2 days old; legit s/ Ygnacio Gutierres & Ana Maria Valencia, residents of the plaza of los Ranchos; ap/ not stated; am/ Roman Valencia & Juliana Montoya; gp/ Juan Griego & Ysabel Gurule, of the same place.

APODACA, Jesus Maria
bap 21 Nov 1847, 4 days old; legit s/ Pedro Apodaca & Maria de la Luz Perea, residents of Alameda; ap/ Francisco Apodaca & Antonia Garcia; am/ Bartolo Perea & Josefa Garcia; gp/ Felis Sanchis & Sebastiana Sena, of the same place.

Frame 2239, #101
CORDOVA, Maria Gertrudis
bap 21 Nov 1847, 3 days old; legit d/ Jose Cordova & Tomasa Trujillo, residents of los Ranchos; ap/ Nicolas Cordova & Maria Duran; am/ Antonio Trujillo & Juana Montoya; gp/ Antonio J. Luna & Rafaela Luna, of the same place.

GARCIA, Maria Dolores
bap 25 Nov 1847, 2 days old; adopted s/ Juan Jose Garcia & Maria Petra Telles, residents of los Duranes; gp/ adoptive parents.

RAEL, Maria Catarina
bap 25 Nov 1847, 5 days old; d/ Bitoria Rael, of los Ranchos; am/ not stated; gp/ Jose Salasar & Polonia Padilla, residents of same.

Frames 2239-2240, #102
MARTIN, Jose Aniseto
bap 25 Nov 1847, 4 days old; legit s/ Felipe Martin & Juana Apodaca, residents of Alameda; ap/ Jose Antonio Martin & Quiteria Griego; am/ Rafael Apodaca & Juana Maria Romero; gp/ same as above, residents of los Gallegos.

GALLEGO, Jose Ylario
bap 26 Nov 1847, 5 days old; legit s/ Ylario Gallego & Josefa Garcia, residents of Albuquerque; ap/ Pablo Griego & Ysidora Apodaca; am/ Jose Garcia & Marta Lucero; gp/ Cristoval Armijo & Barbara Ortiz, of the same place.

TORRES, Maria Concepcion
bap 28 Nov 1847, 5 days old; legit d/ Francisco Torres & Juliana Salasar, residents of Chilili; ap/ Salvador Torres; am/ not stated; gp/ Jose Maria Lucero & Juliana Gallego, of the same place.

SANDOVAL, Maria
bap 1 Dec 1847, 5 days old; adopted d/ Maria Rita Sandoval, resident of los Barelas; gp/ Jose Antonio Lopes & Dolores Griego, residents of same.

Frame 2241, #103
APODACA, Juan Rafael
bap 2 Dec 1847, 1 day old; legit s/ Juan Apodaca & Juana Gutierres, residents of los Barelas; ap/ Rafael Apodaca & Maria Barbara Molina; am/ Miguel Gutierres & Gregoria Armijo; gp/ the paternal grandparents, of the same place.

GARCIA, Maria Dolores
bap 4 Dec 1847, 2 days old; legit d/ Jose Mariano Garcia & Quirina Apodaca, residents los Griegos; ap & am/ not stated; gp/ Jose Gutierres & Matilda Gutierres, from los Gallegos.

GUTIERRES, Maria Bibiana
bap 5 Dec 1847, 3 days old; legit d/ Jose Rafael Gutierres & Dolores Trujillo, residents of los Candelarias; ap/ Miguel Gutierres & Gregoria Armijo; am/ Jose Trujillo & Soledad Valencia; gp/ Manuel Candelaria & Ana Maria Trujillo, residents of los Ranchos.

Frame 2242, #104
GURULE, Maria Guadalupe
bap 12 Dec 1847, 2 days old; legit s/ Salvador Gurule & Juana Moya, residents of Alameda; ap/ Jose Domingo Gurule & Juana Maria Moya; am/ Usebio Moya & Ana Maria Montoya; gp/ Juan Sais & Maria Ysidora Sais, of the same place.

APODACA, Jose Mariano
bap 12 Dec 1847, 2 days old; legit s/ Juan Apodaca & Maria Garcia, residents of Alameda; ap/ Dionicio Apodaca & Leuteria Garcia; am/ Juan Cristobal Garcia & Leonarda Sandobal; gp/ Mariano Apodaca & Rafaela Apodaca, residents of San Mateo.

NUANES, Guadalupe Melquiades
bap 12 Dec 1847, 1 day old; legit s/ Andres Nuanes & Juana Armijo, residents of los Candelarias; ap/ Jose Miguel Nuanes & Andrea Candelaria; am/ Cristobal Armijo & Matilde Duran; gp/ Marcelino Gallego & Juana Salasar, residents of same.

Frame 2243, #105
LOPES, Jose Guadalupe
bap 12 Dec 1847, 2 days old; legit s/ Salvador Lopes & Relles Candelaria, residents of Barelas; ap/ Jose Dolores Lopes & Maria Barbara Molina; am/ Anrriques Candelaria & Ysabel Garcia; gp/ Juan Francisco Apodaca & Maria del Rallo Apodaca, of the same place.

GRIEGO, Guadalupe
bap 14 Dec 1847, 5 days old; legit d/ Jose Tomas Griego & Monica Contreras, residents of los Duranes; ap/ Miguel Griego & Petra Griego; am/ Tomas Contreras & Paula Chaves; gp/ Pedro Contreras & Guadalupe Contreras, of the same place.

APODACA, Maria Guadalupe
bap 14 Dec 1847, 2 days old; legit d/ Jose Apodaca & Consepcion Romero, residents of Alameda; ap/ Dionisio Apodaca & Leuteria Garcia; am/ Baltasar Romero & Paula Lucero; gp/ Dionicio Garcia & Petra Romero, residents of los Griegos.

Frame 2244, #106
GRIEGO, Santiago
bap 14 Dec 1847, 4 days old; legit s/ Juan Griego & Estefana Garcia, residents of Corrales; gp/ Francisco Griego & Josefa Sandobal; am/ not stated; gp/ Jose Lobato & Manuela Rael, of the same place.

BACA, Jose Guadalupe
bap 15 Dec 1847, 3 days old; legit s/ Juan Baca & Antonia Chaves, residents of Atrisco; ap/ Juan Baca & Antonia Garcia; am/ Juan Chaves & Miquela Sanchis; gp/ Rafael Sanchis & Maria Guadalupe Sanchis, residents of Albuquerque.

TAFOYA, Maria Concepcion
bap 15 Dec 1847, 3 days old; legit d/ Domingo Tafoya & Anna Maria Martin, residents of Alameda; ap/ Ygnacio Tafoya & Maria Antonia Baca; am/ Antonio Jose Martin & Luciana Lucero; gp/ Jose Grabiel Gurule & Maria Nicolasa Luna, of the same place.

Frame 2245, #107
SABEDRA, Maria Esperidion
bap 15 Dec 1847, 1 day old; legit d/ Bibian Sabedra & Maria Dolores Chaves, of Atrisco; ap/ Francisco Sabedra & Maria de la Luz Chaves; am/ Vicente Chaves & Guadalupe Chaves; gp/ Marcos Lovato & Maria Josefa Sabedra, residents of same.

BACA, Jose Francisco
bap 15 Dec 1847, 2 days old; natural s/ Rufina Baca, of this plaza; am/ Diego Baca & Francisca Muñis; gp/ Jose Montoya & Dolores Garcia, of the same place.

GARCIA, Maria Guadalupe de Altagracia
bap 15 Dec 1847, 2 days old; legit d/ Juan Cristobal Garcia & Juana Mestas, residents of San Antonio; ap/ Felis Garcia & Ysabel Lopes; am/ Antonio Archuleta & Nicanora Anaya; gp/ Santiago (Atencio) & Manuela Atencio, of the same place.

Frame 2246, #108
LUCERO, Bibiana
bap 17 Dec 1847, 3 days old; legit d/ Pedro Lucero & Encarnacion Griego, residents of los Gallegos; ap/ Lorenso Lucero & Cruz Griego; am/ Jose Griego & Paula Anaya; gp/ Miguel Bujanda & Cimona Lucero, of the same place.

RAEL, Maria Preciliana
bap 18 Dec 1847, 3 days old; legit d/ Santiago Rael & Seferina Martin, residents of Alameda; ap/ Eusebio Rael & Rosa Martin; am/ Alejandro Martin & Candelaria Chaves; gp/ Mariano Sandobal & Edubigen Garcia.

ARANDA, Maria Manuela
bap 19 Dec 1847, 6 years old; Navajo, adopted d/ Pedro Aranda & Rosalia Jaramio; gp/ Tomas Gonsales & Soledad Aranda, all of los Ranchos.

Frames 2246-2247, #109
ZALAZAR, Maria Tomasa
bap 22 Dec 1847, 2 days old; legit d/ Alonzo Zalazar & Catarina Lucero, residents of Alameda; ap/ Luis Salasar & Maria Ysabel Rael; am/ Diego Lucero & Maria Juliana Gurule; gp/ Baltasar Romero & Maria Paula Lucero, of Alameda.

RUIS, Maria Juana
bap 28 Dec 1847, 1 day old; legit d/ Francisco Ruis & Trinidad Apodaca, residents of Albuquerque; ap/ Juan Apodaca & Ysabel Sanches; am/ not stated; gp/ Juan Apodaca & Ysabel Sanches, of the same place.

GUTIERRES, Maria Ygnocencia de los Angeles
bap 29 Dec 1847, 1 day old; legit d/ Fernando Gutierres & Josefa Gonzales, residents of Corrales; ap/ Pedro Gutierres & wife, NN; am/ Juan Gonsales & Antonia Armijo; gp/ Jose Gonsales & Altagracia Gonzales, of the same place.

SANCHIS, Jose Manuel Vicente
bap 1 Jan 1848, 8 days old; legit s/ Juan Sanchis & Gregoria Candelaria, of Alameda; ap/ Jose Sanchis & Gregoria Rael; am/ Francisco Antonio Candelaria & Lorenza Aguirre; gp/ Jesus Montoya & Ana Maria Montoya, of the same place.

Frame 2248, #110
ESPALIN, Maria Manuela de Altagracia
bap 3 Jan 1848, 3 days old; legit d/ Seferino Espalin & Ana Maria Romero, of los Ranchos de Albuquerque; ap/ unknown; am/ Jose Miguel Romero & Maria Ygnacia Montaño; gp/ Manuel Garcia & Altagracia NS, of this place.

MOYA, Jose de los Reyes
bap 13 Jan 1848, 6 days old; natural s/ Manuela Moya, residents of this plaza; am/ Josefa Moya; gp/ Salvador Martin & Dolores Torres, of the same place.

SANCHIS, Jose Antonio
bap 13 Jan 1848, 4 days old; legit s/ Domingo Sanchis & Perfecta Montoya, residents of Alameda; ap/ Diego Antonio Sanchis & Maria Ygnacia Anaya; am/ Pedro Montoya & Maria Luna; gp/ Antonio Sandoval & Josefa Aranda, of the same place.

Frame 2249, #111
OTERO, Jose Luciano
bap 13 Jan 1848, 5 days old; natural s/ Maria Otero, of San Antonio; am/ Julian Otero & Manuela Antonia Padilla; gp/ Dolores Garcia & Ygnacia Zamora, residents of same.

SANCHIS, Maria Josefa
bap 13 Jan 1848, 2 days old; natural d/ Francisca Sanchis, resident of Albuquerque; ap/ Jose Manuel Sanchis & Dolores Chaves; am/ not stated; gp/ Salvador Martin & Miquela Romero, of the same place.

SAIS, Maria Nicanora
bap 14 Jan 1848, 1 day old; legit d/ Ramon Sais & Margarita Pacheco, residents of Alameda; ap/ Salvador Sais & Ana Maria Alarcon; am/ Francisco Pacheco & Marta Sandobal; gp/ Nepomoceno Aragon & Antonia Herrera, of the same place.

Frames 2249-2250, #112
PADILLA, Julian
bap 18 Jan 1844, 1 day old; natural s/ Dimas Padilla, of this villa; gp/ Juan Padilla & Maria Marques; gp/ Jesus Sanches & Maria Asencion Armijo, of the same place.

SAENS, Maria Canuta
bap 24 Jan 1848, 5 days old; legit d/ Patricio Saens & Monica Gallego, of los Ranchos de Albuquerque; ap/ unknown; am/ Basilio Gallegos & Clara Peña; gp/ Felipe Samora & Gertrudis Gallegos, of the same place.

CANDELARIA, Melquiades
bap 24 Jan 1848, 3 days old; legit s/ Juan Candelaria & Catarina Chaves, of los Barelas; ap/ Antonio Candelaria & Antonia Garcia; am/ Jose Antonio Chaves & Dolores Candelaria; gp/ Jose Chaves & Josefa Chaves, of the same place.

Baptisms – Albuquerque, New Mexico
1829–1850

Frames 2250-2251, #113
APODACA, Maria Trinidad
bap 24 Jan 1848, 6 days old; legit d/ Juan de Dios Apodaca & Tomasa Griego, of los Ranchos; ap/ Jose Apodaca & Paula Anaya; am/ Jose Griego & Dolores Rubi; gp/ Francisco Ortiz & Trinidad Apodaca, of the same place.

APODACA, Jose Meliton
bap 24 Jan 1848, 3 days old; legit s/ Juan Apodaca & Luz Padilla, residents of Alameda; ap/ Rafael Apodaca & Juana Maria Romero; am/ Julian Padilla & Ana Maria Padia; gp/ Baltasar Martines & Dolores Apodaca, of Alameda.

MONTOYA, Jose Francisco
bap 25 Jan 1848, 4 days old; legit s/ Francisco Montoya & Felipa Gutierres; ap/ Manuel Montoya & Ana Maria Gutierres; am/ Ygnacio Gutierres & Maria Francisca Sanchis; gp/ Francisco Arrutia & Maria Dolores Armijo, residents of los Ranchos.

BACA, Gertrudis
bap 30 Jan 1848, 2 days old; legit d/ Jose Antonio Baca & Lorensa Baca, of Atrisco; ap/ Juan Baca & Dolores Benavides; am/ Miguel Baca & unknown; gp/ Juan Sedillo & Maria Sedillo, of the same place.

Frame 2252, #114
LUCERO, Francisco Antonio
bap 30 Jan 1848, 1 day old; legit s/ Juan Cristobal Lucero & Juana Apodaca, of los Gallegos; ap/ Tomas Lucero & Dolores Valencia; am/ Gregorio Apodaca & Barbara Mora; gp/ J. Antonio Martin & Quirina Griego, of the same place.

GONZALES, Maria Francisca
bap 2 Feb 1848, 2 days old; legit d/ Rafael Gonzales & Maria de Jesus Aragon, of Alameda; ap/ unknown; am/ Tadeo Aragon & Maria Luisa Valencia; gp/ Jose Maria Gonsales & Rosalia Gonsales, of the same place.

Frames 2252-2253, #115
BARELA, Maria Candelaria
bap 2 Feb 1848, 2 days old; legit d/ Pablo Barela & Maria Paula Garcia, of Atrisco; ap/ Santiago Varela & Juana Aranda; am/ Juan Antonio Garcia & Maria Gregoria Candelaria; gp/ the same grandparents.

GRIEGO, Sabero de Atocha
bap 6 Feb 1848, 2 days old; legit s/ Jose Gorgonio Griego & Martina Cordova, of Corrales; ap/ Francisco Griego & Maria Antonia Montoya; am/ Jose Antonio Cordova & Quiteria Chaves; gp/ Santiago Gonsales & Manuela Aragon, of the same place.

ORTEGA, Maria de la Cruz
bap 6 Feb 1848, 4 days old; natural d/ Maria Luiza Ortega, of los Ranchos; am/ unknown; gp/ Jose Santos Herrera & Maria Juliana Gutierres, of the same place.

SANCHIS, Jose Andres
bap 6 Feb 1848, 3 days old; legit s/ Jose Maria Sanchis & Martina Sanches, of Atrisco; ap/ Jose Sanches & Rosalia Martines; am/ Gabriel Sanches & Juana Sedillo; gp/ Jose Sanches & Clara Chaves, residents of same.

Frame 2254, #116
ATENCIO, Jose de Jesus
bap 8 Feb 1848, 8 days old; natural s/ Juliana Atencio, residents of los Candelarias; am/ Gaspar Atencio
& Ysabel Mares; gp/ Jose Garcia & Luciana Garcia, of the same place.

ARMIJO, Maria Candelaria
bap 11 Feb 1848, 6 days old; legit s/ Cristobal Armijo & Juan Chaves, of los Ranchos de Albuquerque;
ap/ Juan Armijo & Rosalia Ortega; am/ Francisco Chaves & Ana Maria Castillo; gp/ Nestor Armijo &
Manuela Armijo, of the same place.

GOMES, Juan
bap 11 Feb 1848, 6 days old; natural s/ Luz Gomes, of los Ranchos; am/ Antonio Gomes & Ygnacia
Arias; gp/ Juan Montoya & Gertrudis Sanchis, of Alameda.

Frame 2255, #117
MUÑIS, Juana Nepomucena
bap 11 Feb 1848, 1 day old; legit d/ Juan Cristobal Muñis & Anna Maria Pacheco, residents of
Albuquerque; ap/ Jose Maria Muñis & Barbara Samora; am/ Geronimo Pacheco & Pascuala Sanchis; gp/
Ygnacio Ruis & Pascuala Sanchis, residents of Albuquerque.

JARAMILLO, Juana Maria
bap 11 Feb 1848, 2 days old; legit d/ Manuel Jaramillo & Josefa Baca, of los Ranchos; ap/ Juan Jaramillo
& Juana Maria Encarnacion Garcia; am/ Juan Andres Baca & Maria Guadalupe Garcia; gp/ Francisco
Jaramio & Juana Maria de la Encarnacion Garcia, of the same place.

JARAMIO, Maria Benigna Librado
bap 21 Feb 1848, 3 days old; legit d/ Julian Jaramio & Mariana Lopes, of los Ranchos de Atrisco; ap/
Manuel Jaramio & Gertrudis Lucero; am/ Pascual Lopes & Rosa Garcia; gp/ Tomas Pacheco & Maria
Jaramio, of Pajarito.

Frame 2256, #118
CORDOVA, Maria Gregoria
bap 22 Feb 1848, 1 day old; legit d/ Dionicio Cordova & Juana Sanches, of Alameda; ap/ Marcos
Cordova & Rafaela Aragon; am/ Jose Sanches & Gregoria Rael; gp/ Juan Sanches & Gregoria Candelaria,
of the same place.

GARCIA, Maria Francisca
bap 24 Feb 1848, 1 day old; legit d/ Dionicio Garcia & Petra Romero, of Alameda; ap/ Juan Lino Garcia
& unknown; am/ Baltasar Romero & Paula Lucero; gp/ Francisco Lucero & Catarina Lucero.

PACHECO, Jose Emiterio
bap 24 Feb 1848, 3 days old; legit s/ Juan Pacheco & Juana Carvajal, residents of this plaza; ap/ Jose
Pacheco & Juana Carbajal; am/ Pedro Carvajal & Gertrudis Gonzales; gp/ Francisco Samora & Lugarda
Samora, of los Duranes.

Frame 2257, #119
BALDONADO, Jose Seberiano
bap 28 Feb 1848, 3 days old; legit s/ Ancelmo Baldonado & Viviana Gonzales, of Alameda; ap/ Antonio
Jose Baldonado & Manuela Aragon; am/ Juan Gonsales & Barbara Castillo; gp/ Lino Garcia & Dolores
Garcia, residents of Alameda.

TAPIA, Jose Roman
bap 3 Mar 1848, 3 days old; legit s/ Juan Domingo Tapia & Manuela Garcia, residents of los Griegos; ap/ Ygnacio Tapia & Juana Montaño; am/ Jose Garcia & Juana Flores; gp/ Jose Antonio Montaño & Maria de la Lus Montaño, of the same place.

SANCHES, Maria Borga
bap 3 Mar 1848, 5 days old; legit d/ Domingo Sanches & Quiteria Castillo, of Alameda; ap/ Juan Jose Sanches & Gregoria NS (cut off); am/ Juan Gonsales & Varbara Castillo; gp/ Pablo Varela & Maria Ygnacia Montaño, of Ranchos de Albuquerque.

Frame 2258, #120
DURAN, Jose Habran
bap 7 Mar 1848, 2 days old; legit s/ Antonio Duran & Tomasa Gutierres, of los Duranes; ap/ Mateo Duran & Antonia Muñis; am/ unknown; gp/ Miguel Duran & Juana Duran, of the same place.

MONTAÑO, Maria Quirina
bap 8 Mar 1848, 3 days old; natural d/ Petra Montaño, of Atrisco; am/ Juan Andres Montaño & Josefa Sabedra; gp/ Antonio Jose Armijo & Guadalupe Sabedra, of the same place.

Note: one entry was crossed out.

Frame 2259, #121
BACA, Barbara
bap 8 Mar 1848, 5 days old; legit d/ Manuel Baca & Guadalupe Garcia, of Alameda; ap/ Simon Baca & Lorenza Martin; am/ Antonio Garcia & Margarita Rael; gp/ Julian Martin & Dolores Martin, of the same place.

TAFOLLA, Juana
bap 8 Mar 1848, 5 days old; legit d/ Tomas Tafolla & Soledad Montoya, residents of Alameda; ap/ Juan Ygnacio Tafolla & Antonia Baca; am/ Juan Montoya & Gertrudis Moya; gp/ Diego Armigo & Luz Lopes, of the same place.

ARMENTA, Jose Tomas
bap 9 Mar 1848, 3 days old; legit s/ Gregorio Armenta & Olalla Griego, of los Griegos; ap/ Jose Maria Armenta & Maria Ygnacia Martines; am/ Pedro Griego & Anna Maria Salazar; gp/ Ventura Armijo & Sesaria Carabajal, of the same place.

Frame 2260, #122
GARCIA, Eulogio
bap 11 Mar 1848, 1 day old, illegitimate; adopted s/ Cleto Garcia & Nicolasa Duran, of los Duranes; gp/ Francisco Duran & Vernarda Gurule, of this plaza.

ANAYA, Maria Francisca
bap 12 Mar 1848, 3 days old; natural d/ Polonia Anaya, of Alameda; am/ Rafael Anaya & Maria de Jesus Gallego; gp/ Cristobal Pacheco & Manuela Anaya, of los Griegos.

Frames 2260-2261, #123
CANDELARIA, Maria Leocadia
bap 12 Mar 1848, 3 days old; legit d/ Jesus Candelaria & Maria Paula Chavez, of los Barelas; ap/ Antonio Candelaria & Antonia Garcia; am/ Antonio Chavez & Gertrudis Torres; gp/ Teodoro Lopez & Josefa Chavez, of the same place.

GARCIA, Maria de Borja de Altagracia
bap 12 Mar 1848, 3 days old; natural d/ Trinidad Garcia, of Alameda; am/ Juan Manuel Garcia & Manuela Perea; gp/ Baltasar Martines & Dolores Apodaca, of the same place.

CORIZ, Juliana
bap 14 Mar 1848, 3 days old; legit d/ Juan Felipe Coriz & Santos Molina, of los Barelas; ap & am/ not stated; gp/ Jose Montoya & Antonia Torres, of the same place.

Frames 2261-2262, #124
GARCIA, Jose Macario
bap 14 Mar 1848, 4 days old; legit s/ Jose Dolores Garcia & Ygnacia Samora, residents of San Antonio; ap/ Ysidro Garcia & Gertrudis Sanchez; am/ Miguel Samora & Marcelina Gallego; gp/ Jose Maria Gutierres & Tiburcia Apodaca, of the same place.

GARCIA, Maria Gregoria
bap 15 Mar 1848, 3 days old; legit d/ Salbador Garcia & Maria Soledad Garcia, of Carnue; ap/ Juan Guadalupe Garcia & Dolores Candelaria; am/ Antonio Garcia & Maria Candelaria; gp/ Jose Armijo & Juana Armijo, of this place.

JARAMILLO, Jose Longinos
bap 16 Mar 1848, 1 day old; s/ Dolores Jaramillo, of Ranchos of Atrisco; am/ Agustin Jaramillo & Francisca Garcia; gp/ Miguel Gabaldon & Juana Lopes, resident of same.

Frame 2263, #125
GRIEGO, Nicolas
bap 17 Mar 1848, 3 days old; legit s/ Jose Griego & Manuela Gallegos, of los Ranchos de Albuquerque; ap/ Miguel Griego & Gertrudis Olguin; am/ Martin Gallego & Guadalupe Garcia; gp/ Juan de Dios Chaves & Maria Lucero of the same place.

SANCHES, Jose Patricio de Jesus
bap 18 Mar 1848, 1 day old; legit s/ Francisco Sanches & Ana Maria Sanches, residents of Atrisco; ap/ Gabriel Sanches & Juana Sedillo; am/ Ramos Sanches & Juana Barbara Lucero; gp/ Francisco Baca & Juana Baca, residents of same.

ANALLA, Salvador Antonio (twin)
bap 18 Mar 1848, 1 day old; legit s/ Jose Analla & Josefa Molla, of this plaza; ap/ Antonio Analla & Tomasa Tafolla; am/ Acencio Molla & Juana Sandobal; gp/ Francisco Antonio Romero & Maria Quiteria Molla. [Note: See also entry below.]

Frame 2264, #126
ANALLA, Manuel Antonio (twin)
bap 18 Mar 1848, 1 day old; legit s/ Jose Analla & Josefa Molla, of this plaza; ap/ Antonio Analla & Tomasa Tafolla; am/ Acensio Molla & Juana Sandobal; gp/ Manuel Garcia & Concepcion Lopes, of the same place. [Note: See also entry above.]

ZALASAR, Gabriel Labrado
bap 18 Mar 1848, 1 day old; legit s/ Lorenzo Zalazar & Manuela Baca, residents of Atrisco; ap/ Salbador Zalazar & Juana Sarracino; am/ Sabino Baca & Tomasa Lopes; gp/ Jose Candelaria & Venita Candelaria, resident of same.

GUTIERRES, Maria Juana Librada
bap 20 Mar 1848; legit s/ Antonio Gutierres & Ruperta Lopes, residents of los Barelas; ap/ Antonio Gutierres & Francisca Sanches; am/ Mateo Lopes & Manuela Padilla; gp/ Manuel Benabides & Pascuala Gutierres, of the same place.

Frame 2265
RONQUILLO, Maria Patricia de la Soledad
bap 20 Mar 1848, 4 days old; legit d/ Pedro Ronquillo & Juana Lopes, residents of los Barelas; ap/ Gregorio Ronquillo & Maria Antonia Herrera; am/ Mateo Lopez & Manuela Padilla; gp/ Lucario Ruibal & Juana Ortega, residents of same.

CHAVEZ, Maria Merced
bap 20 Mar 1848, 2 days old; legit d/ Antonio Jose Chavez & Maria Josefa Padilla, of Atrisco; ap/ Antonio NS & Manuela Garcia; am/ Manuel Padilla & Guadalupe Marina; gp/ Jesus Chaves & Dolores Chaves, of the same place.

ALDAS, Mariano de Jesus
bap 21 Mar 1848, 3 days old; legit s/ Paulin Aldas & Tomasa Sena, of Ranchos of Albuquerque; ap/ unknown; am/ Matias Sena & Manuela Martin; gp/ Ramon Candelaria & Mariana Griego, of the same place.

Frame 2266, #128
NIETO, Rumaldo de Jesus
bap 23 Mar 1848, 6 days old; legit s/ Jose Dolores Nieto & Gertrudis Garcia, residents of Alameda; ap/ Juan Nieto & Petra Valdes; am/ Lago Garcia & Juana Trujillo; gp/ Rumaldo Martin & Rosa Montoya.

ARMIJO, Jose Octabiano
bap 23 Mar 1848, 3 days old; legit s/ Juan Armijo & Bentura Montoya, of this town; ap/ Ambrocio Armijo & Maria Antonia Ortiz; am/ Jose Montoya & Maria Antonia Baca; gp/ Jose Armijo & Juana Armijo, of the same place.

SABEDRA, Benito
bap 26 Mar 1848, 3 days old; legit s/ Miguel Sabedra & Nestora Montoya, residents of Atrisco; ap/ Francisco Sabedra & Maria de la Luz Chaves; am/ Antonio Montoya & Florentina Ortiz; gp/ Bibian Sabedra & Dolores Chaves, of the same place.

Frame 2267, #129
PEREA, Miguel Antonio
bap 26 Mar 1848, 4 days old; Navajo, adopted s/ Miguel Perea & Candida Griego, of this plaza; gp/ Miguel Antonio Martin & Francisca Carabajal.

SEDILLO, Maria Trinidad
bap 5 Apr 1848, 3 days old; natural d/ Maria Sedillo, from los Barelas; am/ Gregorio Sedillo & Juana Candelaria; gp/ Antonio Jose Mestas & Rosa Mestas, of the same place.

Frames 2267-2268, #130
APODACA, Juan Jose
bap 8 Apr 1848, 5 days old; legit s/ Dionicio Apodaca & Leuteria Apodaca, from Alameda; ap/ Jose Manuel Apodaca & Rozalia Gonsales; am/ Antonio Garcia & Margarita Rael; gp/ Juan Jose Apodaca & Concepcion Apodaca, of the same place.

GONSALES, Pedro Jose
bap 6 Apr 1848, 3 days old; legit s/ Ramon Gonsales & Francisca Padilla, of Alameda; ap/ Juan Gonsales & Ana Maria Sandobal; am/ Santiago Padilla & Antonia Otero; gp/ Adamacio Gurule & Biscenta Gurule, residents of los Ranchos.

LUCERO, Maria Manuela
bap 30 Mar 1848, 3 days old; legit d/ Jose Maria Lucero & Teresa Gallego, of los Ranchos de Albuquerque; ap/ Francisco Lucero & Manuela Aragon; am/ Cristobal Gallego & Carmel Gutierres; gp/ Francisco Lucero & Manuela Aragon, residents of Alameda.

Frame 2269, #131
GARCIA, Ruperta de Altagracia
bap 30 Mar 1848, 3 days old; legit d/ Feliz Garcia & Carmel Sanches, of this villa; ap/ Feliz Garcia & Ysabel Lopes; am/ Visente Sanches & Anna Maria Mestas; gp/ Juan Francisco Armijo & Ana Maria Ruiz, of the same place.

MOYA, Maria Margarita
bap 30 Mar 1848, 4 days old; legit d/ Andres Moya & Simona Sanches, of this villa; ap/ Juan Moya & Manuela Barela; am/ Mariano Sanches & Francisca Gabaldon; gp/ Gregorio Garcia & Juana Maria Baca, residents of same.

CHAVES, Jose Modesto
bap 1 Apr 1848, 1 day old; legit s/ Jose Maria Chaves & Ysabel Apodaca; ap/ Jose Chavez & Catarina Maldonado; am/ Francisco Apodaca & Tomasa Varela; gp/ Teofilo Chavez & Olimpia Chavez, of this plaza.

Frame 2270, #132
ARMIJO, Juana
bap 2 Apr 1848, 5 days old; legit d/ Martin Armijo & Maria de Jesus Armijo, residents of San Antonio; ap/ Miguel Armijo & Bacilia Gonsales; am/ Pablo Armijo & Josefa Sandobal; gp/ Jose Vicente Gonzales & Juana Gonzales, of San Antonio.

GRIEGO, Felicita
bap 2 Apr 1848, 3 days old; legit d/ Juan Ysidoro Griego & Buenabentura Lucero; ap/ Francisco Griego & Antonia Serna; am/ Juan Lucero & Francisca Martin; gp/ Blaz Lucero & Rosalia Tenorio, of Ranchos of Albuquerque.

GALLEGO, Francisco
bap 2 Apr 1848, 3 days old; natural s/ Rosalia Gallego, of los Ranchos; am/ Jose Pablo Gallego & Juana Mora; gp/ Miguel Montaño & Concepcion Candelaria.

Frame 2271, #135
MARQUES, Juan Meliton
bap 2 Apr 1848, 3 days old; legit s/ Juan Marques & Rosa Candelaria, residents of los Barelas; ap/ Juan Marques & Nievez Molino; am/ Antonio Candelaria & Antonia Garcia; gp/ Felipe Baca & Maria del Socorro Baca, of Barelas.

GUTIERRES, Maria Ysidora
bap 4 Apr 1848, 2 days old; legit d/ Felipe Gutierres & Lorenza Perea, residents of los Griegos; ap/ Miguel Gutierres & Simona Griego; am/ Juan Perea & Gertrudis Jaramillo; gp/ Juan Perea & Andrea Perea, of the same place.

GARCIA, Desiderio
bap 3 Apr 1848, 1 day old; legit s/ Juan Rafael Garcia & Encarnacion Lucero, residents of los Duranes; ap/ Juan Rafael Garcia & Manuela Martin; am/ Gregorio Lucero & Marta Lopez; gp/ Jose Maria Torres & Josefa Lucero.

Frame 2272, #154
ANAYA, Maria Dolores
bap 13 Apr 1848, 2 days old; legit d/ Feliz Anaya & Sisilia Yarbera, of los Ranchos de Albuquerque; ap/ Martin Anaya & Viatris Jaramillo; am/ Anna Maria Yarbera; gp/ Jose Antonio Valencia & Juana Duran, of the same place.

MARINO, Jose Dolores
bap 13 Apr 1848, 3 days old; legit s/ Juan Marino & Anna Maria Gurule, residents of Alameda; ap/ Luis Marino & Ysabel Chaves; am/ Juan Gurule & Bernarda Torres; gp/ Ramon Lucero & Leocaria Sanches, of the same place.

GALLEGO, Juan Domingo
bap 21 Apr 1848, 5 days old; natural s/ Dolores Gallego, resident of los Gallegos; ap/ Ramon Gallego & Rozalia Candelaria; gp/ Juan Ysidoro (Gallego) & Juana Maria Gallego.

Frame 2273, #135
SABEDRA, Maria Petrona
bap 30 Apr 1848, 2 days old; legit d/ Francisco Sabedra & Dolores Garcia, of this villa; ap/ Juan Cristobal Sabedra & Maria Paula Duran; am/ Jose Antonio Garcia & Ygnacia Candelaria; gp/ Francisco Sandoval & Maria Lucero, residents of same, of the same place.

GARCIA, Maria Dolores
bap 1 May 1848, 1 day old; legit d/ Marcial Garcia & Miquela Duran, of this villa; ap/ Juan Luis Garcia & Leonarda Lopez; am/ Teodoro Duran & Maria Lucero; gp/ Loreto Carbajal & Dolores Carbajal, of the same place.

JARAMILLO, Adolfo
bap 1 May 1848, 3 days old; legit s/ Mariano Jaramillo & Manuela Anaya, residents of this plaza; ap/ unknown; am/ Antonio Anaya & Tomasa Tafolla; gp/ Rafael Trujillo & Jesus Montoya, of the same place.

Frame 2274, #136
CANDELARIA, Pedro Jose
bap 1 May 1848, 1 day old; legit s/ Rumaldo Candelaria & Josefa Garcia, residents of los Duranes; ap/
Juan Candelaria & Ysidora Garcia; am/ Diego Garcia & Ramona Candelaria; gp/ Ramon Mares & Luz
Jaramillo, of los Candelarias.

ZALASAR, Benita del Rayo
bap 2 May 1848, 4 days old; legit d/ Juan Zalazar & Manuela Gurule, of los Ranchos de Albuquerque; ap/
Julian Zalazar & Guadalupe Rael; am/ Felipe Gurule & Juana Gutierres; gp/ Adamacio Gurule & Rufina
Gurule, residents of same.

Frames 2274- 2275, #137
MARTINES, Maria Cruz
bap 3 May 1848, 6 days old; legit d/ Pablo Martines & Francisca Moya, residents of los Griegos; ap/
Miguel Martines & Dorotea Gutierres; am/ Jose Moya & Maria Ortiz; gp/ Juan Torres & Dolores Torres,
of the same place.

MONTAÑO, Pedro Jose Solomon
bap 3 May 1848, 4 days old; legit s/ Lorenzo Montaño & Petra Candelaria, of los Ranchos de
Albuquerque; ap/ Antonio Montaño & Manuela Antonia Martin; am/ Vicente Candelaria & Anna Maria
Chaves; gp/ Miguel Montaño & Clara Candelaria, residents of same.

PADILLA, Jose Camilo
bap 8 May 1848, 8 days old; legit s/ Jose Antonio Padilla & Josefa Garcia, residents of Ranchos de
Atrisco; ap/ Antonio Padilla & Guadalupe Chaves; am/ Antonio Garcia & Barbara Zalazar; gp/ Pablo
Jaramillo & Refugia Jaramillo, residents of Ranchos de Atrisco.

Frame 2276, #138
ARMIJO, Maria Francisca
bap 8 May 1848, adult, 16 years old; Navajo adopted d/ Juan Armijo & Anna Maria Gabaldon; gp/ Nestor
Montoya & Placida Armijo, of this plaza.

ARMIJO, Maria Librada
bap 8 May 1848, adult, 12 years old; Navajo adopted d/ Teodoro Armijo & Paula Jaramillo, of Atrisco;
gp/ Mariano Armijo & Gabriela Jaramillo, of this plaza.

BACA, Miguel de Altagracia
bap 9 May 1848, 4 days old; legit s/ Juan Baca & Rafaela Cordova, of Alameda; ap/ Simon Baca & Maria
Lorenza Candelaria; am/ Nicolas Cordova & Ygnacia Duran; gp/ Baltazar Martines & Dolores Apodaca.

Frame 2277, #139
OTERO, Carlota
bap 13 May 1848, 4 days old; legit d/ Manuel Antonio Otero & Josefa Armijo, of Peralta; ap/ Vicente
Otero & Gertrudis Chaves; am/ Juan Cristobal Armijo & Juana Chaves; gp/ Juan Otero & Gertrudis
Chaves, residents of Peralta.

GUTIERRES, Jose Rafael
bap 14 May 1848, 3 days old; s/ Juana Gutierres, resident of los Barelas; am/ Jose Maria Gutierres &
unknown wife; gp/ Juan Perea & Rosalia Perea, of the same place.

SANCHES, Jose Antonio
bap 14 May 1848, 4 days old; legit s/ Jose Antonio Sanches & Francisca Mares, of los Ranchos de Albuquerque; ap/ Domingo Sanches & Maria de la Luz Perea; am/ Luis Mares & Teresa Garcia; gp/ Jesus Abran Mora & Pilar Mora, of the same place.

Frame 2278, #140
CANDELARIA, Maria Antonio
bap 14 May 1848, 2 years old; Navajo, adopted d/ Pedro Candelaria & Petra Apodaca; gp/ Miguel Montaño & Clara Candelaria, all of Ranchos de Albuquerque.

ANAYA, Maria Domingo
bap 14 May 1848, 3 days old; legit d/ Felipe Anaya & Perfecta Ansures, of Ranchos of Atrisco; ap/ Juan Anaya & Francisca Baca; am/ Rafael Ansures & Mariana Sandoval; gp/ Marcos Lovato & Josefa Sabedra, of the same place.

GARCIA, Jose Domingo Serafin
bap 14 May 1848, 4 days old; legit s/ Jose Antonio Garcia & Polinaria Salazar, residents of Carnue; ap/ Feliz Garcia & Ysabel Lopez; am/ Juan Cristobal Salazar & Miquela Sanches; gp/ Antonio Feliz Garcia & Anna Maria Mestas, of this plaza.

Frame 2279, #141
CHABES, Maria Altagracia
bap 15 May 1848, 5 years old; Navajo, adopted d/ Antonio Jose Chabes & Josefa Padilla, of Ranchos de Atrisco; gp/ Jose de las Nieves Lucero & Maria Eulogia Sabedra.

GARCIA, Moises de los Dolores
bap 16 May 1848, 4 days old; legit s/ Salbador Garcia & Rosa Gutierres, of this plaza; ap/ Felix Garcia & Ysabel Lopes; am/ Jose Gutierres & Madalena Montolla; gp/ Antonio Maria Garcia & Juana Montaño, of this plaza.

PADILLA, Maria de la Lus
bap 17 May 1848, 6 days old; legit d/ Juan Padilla & Rosalia Sanches; ap/ Pablo Padilla & Felipa N. NS; am/ Agustin Sanches & Juana Sanches; gp/ Jose Antonio Chavez & Dolores Chavez.

Frame 2280, #142
BACA, Marcial Librado
bap 20 May 1848, 4 days old; legit s/ Juan Baca & Felipa Candelaria, of Ranchos de Atrisco; ap/ Sabino Baca & Tomasa Lopez; am/ Bautista Candelaria & Ascencion Garcia; gp/ Juan Garcia & Concepcion Anaya, of the same place.

ANAYA, Clara
bap 28 May 1848, 3 days old; d/ Andres Anaya & Anna Maria Candelaria, of Atrisco; ap/ Juan Anaya & Francisca Baca; am/ Bautista Candelaria & Acencion Garcia; gp/ Jose Maria Jaramillo & Guadalupe Aragon.

Frames 2280-2281, #143
ROMERO, Jose Bonicio (of Ranchos de Albuquerque)
bap 21 May 1848, 4 days old; natural s/ Rosa Romero; am/ Salbador Romero & Guadalupe Romero; gp/ Antonio Jose Sandobal & Rita Lucero, residents of same.

LOBATO, Jose Epitacio
bap 21 May 1848, 1 day old; legit s/ Agustin Lobato & Quirina Gabaldon, of Albuquerque; ap/ unknown; am/ Nepomoceno Gabaldon & Varbara Mestas; gp/ Nepomuceno Gabaldon & Anna Maria Gabaldon, of the same place.

MARTIN, Maria Ysidora
bap 22 May 1848, 8 days old; legit d/ Juan Pablo Martin & Sisilia Candelaria, residents of Alameda; ap/ Jose Martin & Juana Griego; am/ Esteban Candelaria & Maria de Jesus Luna; gp/ Roman Candelaria & Mariana Griego, residents of same.

Frame 2282, #144
MARTINES, Jose Guadalupe
bap 23 May 1848, 2 days old; legit s/ Antonio Jose Martines & Rosalia Garcia, of los Ranchos; ap/ unknown; am/ Manuel Garcia & Matilda Lucero; gp/ Santiago Martin & Andrea Martin.

GRIEGO, Maria Susana
bap 26 May 1848, 6 days old; natural d/ Petra Griego, from los Griegos; am/ Pedro Griego & Anna Maria Zalazar; gp/ Antonio Nuanes & Cadelaria Griego, of the same place.

ALIRI, Maria Epitacia
bap 28 May 1848, 3 days old; legit d/ Benito Alire & Juana Garcia, of Alameda; ap/ Antonio Alire & Josefa Garcia; am/ Antonio Garcia & Rosa Gutierres; gp/ Gregorio Martines & Gertrudes Salazar.

Frame 2283, #145
ARMIJO, Juan de Dios
bap 28 May 1848, 3 days old; legit s/ Jose Armijo & Maria Guadalupe Chaves, residents of Atrisco; ap/ Santiago Armijo & Petra Perea; am/ Miguel Chaves & Josefa Peralta; gp/ Juan Garcia & Josefa Peralta, of Seboyeta.

LOPEZ, Juan de Jesus
bap 28 May 1848, 8 days old; legit s/ Bernabe Lopez & Sipriana Perea, of los Griegos; ap & am/ not stated; gp/ Juan Griego & Anna Maria Griego, of the same place.

DURAN, Maria de Atocha
bap 1 Jun 1848, 2 days old; legit d/ Domingo Duran & Manuela Sanches, residents of Atrisco; ap/ Josefa Duran; am/ Domingo Sanches & Maria Toribia NS; gp/ Jose Maria Sanches & Tomasa Lucero; all of Atrisco.

Frame 2284, #146
ARMIJO, Maria Albina
bap 7 Jun 1848, 1 day old; natural d/ Manuela Armijo; am/ Carmel Armijo; gp/ Nestor Montoya & Placida Armijo, all of Albuquerque.

SENA, Maria
bap 8 Jun 1848, 6 days old; legit d/ Rafaela Sena & Dolores Candelaria, of Ranchos de Albuquerque; ap/ Francisco Sena & Manuela Martin; am/ Ramon Candelaria & Rafaela Peña; gp/ Vicente Sena & Biviana Chaves, of the same place.

Baptisms – Albuquerque, New Mexico
1829–1850

CORDOBA, Jose Meliton
bap 10 Jun 1848, 8 days old; legit s/ Felis Cordoba & Rosa Garcia, of Alameda; ap & am/ not stated; gp/ Juan Garcia & Juliana Garcia, of los Candelarias.

Frame 2285, #147
LOPEZ, Jose Antonio
bap 17 Jun 1848, 4 days old; legit s/ Jose Lopez & Rosalia Serna, of los Ranchos de Albuquerque; ap/ Gaspar Lopez & Rosalia Duran; am/ Tomas Serna & Rafaela Garcia; gp/ Bartolo Gutierres & Maria Josefa Romero, of the same place.

GARCIA, Ana Maria
bap 25 Jun 1848, 3 days old; legit d/ Juan Garcia & Ynes Cerna, of los Ranchos de Albuquerque; ap/ Juan Ygnacio Garcia & Juana Mirabal; am/ Tomas Cerna & Rafaela Garcia; gp/ Manuel Romero & Ana Maria Romero, of the same place.

ANALLA, Maria Fregonia
bap 25 Jun 1848, 1 day old; natural d/ Marcelina Analla, of Atrisco; am/ Miguel Anaya & Maria Lopes; gp/ Jose Luis Sanchis & Dolores Garcia, of the same place.

Frame 2286, #148
APODACA, Beneranda de Laida
bap 9 Jul 1848, 2 days old; legit d/ Bartolo Apodaca & Soledad Telles, residents of los Barelas; ap/ Jose Apodaca & Gertrudis Lucero; am/ Julio Telles & Cacilda Chaves; gp/ Salbador Romero & Francisca Chaves, of the same place.

GARCIA, Ligorio
bap 10 Jul 1848, 4 days old; legit s/ Jose Dubijen Garcia & Nepomucena Rael, of Alameda; ap/ Andres Garcia & Juana Torres; am/ Antonio Rael & Francisca Padilla; gp/ Jose Lovato & Manuela Rael, of the same place.

JARAMILLO, Juan Nepomoceno
bap 11 Jul 1848, 2 days old; legit s/ Jose Maria Jaramillo & Guadalupe Chaves, of Rancho de Atrisco; ap/ Agustin Jaramillo & Francisca Garcia; am/ Agustin Chaves & Ana Maria Sena; gp/ Juan Baca & Maria Antonia Chaves, of the same place.

Frame 2287, #149
JARAMILLO, Soledad Felicitas
bap 13 Jul 1848, 6 days old; legit d/ Manuel Jaramillo & Maria Mestas, of Alameda; ap/ Miguel Jaramillo & Anna Maria Ortega; am/ Mariano Mestas & Guadalupe Chaves; gp/ Tomas Gonsales & Soledad Aranda, of Barelas de Albuquerque.

ROMERO, Jose Melquiades
bap 23 Jul 1848, 8 days old; natural s/ Dolores Romero, of los Poblanos; am/ Vicente Romero & Maria Antonia Ortega; gp/ Maria Rosa Gutierres.

Frames 2287-2288, #150
GUTIERRES, Mariana de la Virgen
bap 23 Jul 1848, 4 days old; legit d/ Facundo Gutierres & Decideria Arias, from el Rancho; ap/ Francisco Gutierres & Manuela Bernal; am/ Juan Domingo Arias & Juliana Lucero; gp/ Manuel Garcia & Concepcion Garcia, of the same place.

MONTOYA, Maria Benita
bap 18 Jul 1848, 3 days old; natural d/ Guadalupe Montoya, of los Ranchos de Albuquerque; am/ Rafael Montoya & Anna Maria Duran; gp/ Abran de Jesus Abila & Josefa Abila, residents of the same place.

SUARES, Maria Francisca
bap 19 Jul 1848, 4 days old; legit d/ Mateo Suares & Guadalupe Griego, of this plaza; ap/ Calletano Suares & Maria Antonia Belasques; am/ Pablo Griego & Ysidora Apodaca; gp/ Miguel Antonio Martin & Francisca Carabajal, of the same place.

Frame 2289, #151
MONTOYA, Jose Amado
bap 20 Jul 1848, 6 days old; legit s/ Manuel Montoya & Rosa Santillanes, of Corrales; ap/ Miguel Montoya & Catarina Lucero; am/ Miguel Santillanes & Josefa Martin; gp/ Juan Jose Gutierres & Rita Cordova, all of Corrales.

BACHICHA, Maria Macedonia
bap 20 Jul 1848, 8 days old; legit d/ Ramon Bachicha & Rita Tapia, of Pajarito; ap/ unknown; am/ Blas Tapia & Dolores Chaves; gp/ Rafael Griego & Martina Jaramillo, of Pajarito.

Frames 2289-2290, #152
CARABAJAL, Maria de la Luz
bap 20 Jul 1848, 23 days old; legit d/ Hermegildo Carabajal & Margarita Duran, of this plaza; ap/ Calletano Carabajal & Maria Baca; am/ Jose Salbador Duran & Balbaneda Garcia; gp/ Francisco Gutierres & Manuela Bernal. [Note: The record had additional information which probably belongs to another record, but was entered at the end of this entry (am/ Juan Domingo Arias & Maria Juliana Lucero; gp/ Manuel Garcia & Concepcion Garcia, of the same.).]

BACA, Clara Guadalupe
bap 21 Jul 1848, 6 days old; legit d/ Mariano Baca & Dolores Lopes, of this plaza; ap/ Juan Domingo Baca & Margarita Guerra; am/ Roman Lopes & Maria Garcia; gp/ Juan Sanches & Francisca Sanches, of the same place.

LOPES, Jose Noberto
bap 21 Jul 1848, 4 days old; legit s/ Nepomoceno Lopes & Merced Gomes, of this plaza; ap/ Jose Lopes & Maria N. NS; am/ Pablo Martines & Gertrudes Garcia; gp/ Baltazar Sabedra & Juana Sanches, of the same place.

Frame 2291, #153
MARQUES, Carmel
bap 1 Aug 1848, 2 days old; legit d/ Jose Marques & Francisca Torres, residents of los Barelas; ap/ Juan Marques & Maria N. NS; am/ Vicente Torres & Francisca Teresa Trujillo; gp/ Jose Teodoro Chavez & Maria Chavez, of the same place.

GONSALES, Jose Manuel
bap 6 Aug 1848, 3 days old; s/ Sabino Gonsales & Encarnacion Valencia, of Alameda; ap & am/ not stated; gp/ Jose del Balle & Marcelina Valencia, of Ranchos de Albuquerque.

SANCHES, Maria de Rayo
bap 6 Aug 1848, 8 days old; legit d/ Manuel Sanches & Guadalupe Jaramillo; ap/ Andres Sanches & Josefa Martines; am/ Miguel Jaramillo & Gertrudis Griego; gp/ Abran Jaramillo & Paula Jaramillo, residents of Atrisco.

Frame 2292, #154
GARCIA, Juan Cristobal
bap 15 Aug 1848, 5 days old; legit s/ Pablo Garcia & Gertrudis Sanches, of Alameda; ap/ Antonio Garcia & Antonia Tafolla; am/ Jose Sanches & Gregoria Rael; gp/ Rumaldo Garcia & Antonia Lucero, of the same place.

GARCIA, Juliana
bap 18 Aug 1848, 8 days old; legit d/ Gregorio Garcia & Juana Maria Baca, of los Duranes; ap/ Ysidro Garcia & Gertrudes Sanches; am/ Jose Baca & Maria N. NS; gp/ Ysidro Garcia & Edubijen Baca, of the same place.

GARCIA, Maria Seberina
bap 1 Sep 1848, 4 days old; legit d/ Reyes Garcia & Manuela Griego, of los Ranchos de Albuquerque; ap/ Ygnacio Garcia & Juana Cordoba; am/ Antonio Griego & Candelaria Luna; gp/ Juan Cristobal Gurule & Merced Gurule, of Alameda.

Frame 2293, #155
APODACA, Jose Caralampio
bap 4 Sep 1848, 1 day old; legit s/ Juan Apodaca & Maria de Jesus Garcia, residents of los Barelas; ap/ Rafael Apodaca & Josefa Molino; am/ unknown; gp/ Julian Lopes & Cruz Romero, of the same place.

GARCIA, Juan Jose
bap 4 Sep 1848, 3 days old; natural s/ Guadalupe Garcia; am/ Juan Luis Garcia & Leonarda Lopez; gp/ Juan Apodaca & Ysabel Lopez, residents of Albuquerque.

NOANES, Jose Manuel
bap 4 Sep 1848, 9 days old; s/ Santiago Noanes, of San Antonio & Manuela Atencio, of San Antonio; ap/ Geronimo Nuanes & Barbara Maes; am/ Gaspar Atencio & Ysabel Chaves; gp/ Jose Manuel Trujillo & Juliana Martin, of the same place.

Frame 2294, #156
YLISARRI, Maria Donaciana
bap 6 Sep 1848, 15 days old; natural d/ Dolores Ylisarri; gp/ Francisco Mora & Josefa Mora, all of los Ranchos.

GABALDON, Maria Barbara de la Concepcion
bap 9 Sep 1848, 6 days old; legit d/ Juan Gabaldon & Juana Maria Griego, of this plaza, ap/ not stated; am/ Rafael Griego & Barbara Apodaca; gp/ Julian Griego & Barbara Apodaca, of the same place.

SANCHES, Nicolas
bap 10 Sep 1848, 4 days old; legit s/ Diego Sanches & Juana Griego; ap/ Antonio Sanches & Madelena Garcia; am/ Jose Griego & Carmen Martin; gp/ Antonio Montaño & Begnina Griego, of Ranchos of Albuquerque.

Frame 2295, #157
CANDELARIA, Jose Gregorio
bap 11 Sep 1848, 3 days old; legit s/ Salbador Candelaria & Maria de Jesus Padilla, residents of Atrisco;
ap/ Juan Candelaria & Teresa Chaves; am/ Diego Antonio Padilla & Manuela Aguirre; gp/ Teodoro
Armijo & Paula Jaramillo, of the same place.

GUTIERRES, Trenceslao
bap 12 Sep 1848, 5 days old; legit s/ Juan Gutierres & Marcelina Candelaria, of the plaza of los
Candelarias; ap/ Miguel Gutierres & Gregoria Armijo; am/ Jose Candelaria & Francisca Apodaca; gp/
Juan Apodaca & Maria Gutierres, of los Barelas.

SANCHES, Martiana
bap 12 Sep 1848, 6 days old; natural d/ Dolores Sanches, of San Antonio; am/ Vicente Sanches &
Anamaria Mestas; gp/ Antonio Felis Garcia & Jesusita Garcia, of Albuquerque.

Frame 2296, #158
SISNEROS, Jose Francisco
bap 3 Oct 1848, 6 days old; legit s/ Manuel Sisneros & Gertrudis Candelaria; ap/ Francisco Sisneros &
Maria Martin; am/ Manuel Candelaria & Tomasa Gutierres; gp/ Jose Perea & Candelaria Gutierres,
residents of los Barelas.

LOPES, Maria Barbara
bap 4 Oct 1848, 8 days old; legit d/ Pedro Lopes & Guadalupe Candelaria, residents of Atrisco; ap/
Francisco Lopes & Maria Francisca Armijo; am/ Francisco Antonio Candelaria & Lorensa Padilla; gp/
Manuel Candelaria & Barbara Padilla, of the same place.

MARTIN, Brigido
bap 9 Oct 1848, 4 days old; legit d/ Jesus Martin & Bitoriana Moya, of this plaza; ap & am/ not stated;
gp/ Jose Polinario Perea & Francisca Tafolla, of the same place.

Frame 2297, #159
LUCERO, Anna Maria del Pilar
bap 14 Oct 1848, 5 days old; legit d/ Cristobal Lucero & Soledad Garcia, of Alameda; ap/ Francisco
Lucero & Manuela Aragon; am/ Antonio Garcia & Antonia Tafolla; gp/ Juan Sanches & Gregoria
Candelaria, of the same place.

ARIAS, Jesus Marcos
bap 16 Oct 1848, 6 days old; legit s/ Manuel Arias & Ynes Arias, of los Ranchos de Albuquerque; ap/
Pablo Arias & Encarnacion Valencia; am/ Yldifonso Arias & Juana Gutierres; gp/ Albino Garcia &
Manuela Garcia, of the same place.

Frames 2297-2298, #160
ABALOS, Florentino
bap 19 Oct 1848, 3 days old; legit s/ Bacilio Abalos & Rosalia Tafolla, of Alameda; ap/ Vicente Abalos &
Maria Lucero; am/ Rafael Tafolla & Catarina Lujan; gp/ Jose Meliton Trujillo & Agustina Tafolla, of the
same place.

GARCIA, Juan Nepomuceno
bap 28 Oct 1848, 6 days old; legit s/ Cristobal Garcia & Maria Martines, of los Ranchos de Albuquerque; ap/ Juan Garcia & Juliana Montaño; am/ Felipe Martines & Francisca Mora; gp/ Domingo Sanches & Maria de la Luz Perea, of the same place.

ARMIJO, Cristobal
bap 28 Oct 1848, 3 days old; legit s/ Matias Armijo & Catarina Sabedra, of San Antonio; ap/ Santiago Armijo & Petra Perea; am/ Jose Sabedra & Manuela Montoya; gp/ Pedro Armijo & Paula Aranda, of the same place.

Frame 2299, #161
LOPES, Ramona
bap 28 Oct 1848, 3 days old; legit d/ Felipe Lopes & Juana Torres, of Los Griegos; ap/ Antonio Lopez & Rosa NS; am/ Jose Torres & Maria Barbara NS; gp/ Andres Lucero & Tomasa Garcia, of the same place.

CHAVES, Emilea
bap 4 Nov 1848, 6 days old; d/ Juan de Dios Chaves & Monica Lucero, of los Ranchos; ap/ Estanislado Chaves & Soledad Ortega; am/ Mariano Lucero & Marcelina Valencia; gp/ Jose Dolores Chavez & Marcelina Valencia, of the same place.

Frames 2299-2300, #162
LUCERO, Jose Antonio
bap 4 Nov 1848, 6 days old; legit s/ Pedro Lucero & Juana Martin, of los Ranchos; ap/ Francisco Lucero & Maria Ynes Montoya; am/ Joaquin Montaño & Maria Duran; gp/ Cristobal Sanches & Concepcion Valencia, of the same place.

GONSALES, Jose Ylario
bap 6 Oct 1848, 3 days old; legit s/ Ygnacio Gonsales & Concepcion Apodaca, of Alameda; ap/ Jose de la Cruz Gonsales & Maria de Jesus Moya; am/ Dionicio Apodaca & Vitoria Garcia; gp/ Jose Anastacio Cordoba & Maria Tomasa Trujillo, of the same place.

TAPIA, Maria del Raya
bap 8 Oct 1848, 3 days old; legit d/ Francisco Tapia & Trinquilina Nuanes, from los Griegos; ap/ Ygnacio Tapia & Juana Montaño; am/ J. Guadalupe Nuanes & Antonia Garcia; gp/ Pablo Griego & Gertr(cut off) Griego, of the same place.

Frame 2301, #163
ABALOS, Florentino
bap 19 Oct 1848, 6 days old; legit s/ Bacilio Abalos & Rosalia Tafolla, from Alameda; ap/ Vicente Abalos & Maria Lucero; am/ Rafael Tafolla & Catarina Lujan; gp/ Meliton Trujillo & Agustina Tafolla; of the same place.

SAMORA, Juan Cristobal
bap 19 Oct 1848, 8 days old; legit s/ Diego Antonio Samora & Anna Maria Montoya, of Alameda; ap/ Francisco Samora & Maria Ygnacia Tafolla; am/ Cristobal Montoya & Monica Gonsales; gp/ Juan Gonsales & Maria de la Lus Miera, of the same place.

CARABAJAL, Miguel Antonio
bap 25 Oct 1848, 3 days old; natural d/ Rosalia Carabajal; am/ Juan Pedro Carabajal & Gertrudis Gonsales; gp/ Miguel Antonio Martin & Francisca Carabajal, all from this plaza.

Frame 2302, #164
GARCIA, Marcelino
bap 1 Nov 1848, 1 days old; legit s/ Marcelino Garcia & Andrea Martin; ap/ Julian Garcia & Paula Montaño; am/ Antonio Jose Martin & Rosalia Garcia; gp/ Geronimo Griego & Albina Lucero, all of los Ranchos de Albuquerque.

LOPEZ, Maria Ygnes
bap 5 Nov 1848, 3 days old; natural d/ Ysidora Lopez; am/ Luis Lopez & Leonarda Martin; gp/ Antonio Garcia & Andres Carabajal, of Albuquerque.

GARCIA, Manuela de Atocha
bap 5 Nov 1848, 2 days old; legit d/ Luis Garcia & Ygnacia Montoya; ap/ Pablo Garcia & Antonia Martin; am/ Jose Montoya & Luz Candelaria; gp/ Juan Antonio Rodarte & Francisca Candelaria, all of Ranchos.

Frame 2303, #165
GUTIERRES, Juana Merenciana
bap 5 Nov 1848, 8 days old; legit d/ Manuel Gutierres & Teresa Arias, of los Ranchos de Albuquerque; ap/ Francisco Gutierres & Manuela Martin; am/ Juan Arias & Merced Gomes; gp/ Francisco Abila & Concepcion Arias, of the same place.

GARCIA, Maria
bap 5 Nov 1848, 2 days old; legit d/ Juan Garcia & Juana Santillanes, of los Griegos; ap/ Juan Garcia & Antonio Martines; am/ Luciano Santillanes & Gertrudis Duran; gp/ Antonio Santillanes & Carmel Santillanes, of Duranes.

Frames 2303-2304, #166
APODACA, Maria Beneranda
bap 7 Nov 1848, 3 days old; legit s/ Simon Apodaca & Josefa Sandobal; ap/ Rafael Apodaca & Estefana Salazar; am/ Miguel Sandobal & Manuela Gonsales; gp/ Ygnacio Romero & Sisilia Ballegos, residents of Alameda.

GONSALES, Antonio Maria
bap 12 Nov 1848, 3 days old; legit s/ Francisco Gonsales & Petra Gonsales, of Alameda; ap/ Antonio Gonsales & Gertrudis Gurule; am/ Antonio Gonsales & Juana Sandobal; gp/ Mariano Sandobal & Eduvis Garcia, of the same place.

PROVENCIO, Andres
bap 12 Nov 1848 at 8 days old; legit s/ Lucas Provencio & Rita Lucero, of los Ranchos de Albuquerque; ap/ Juan Antonio Provencio & Mariana Lucero; am/ Miguel Lucero & Manuela Apodaca; gp/ Gregorio Estrada & Dimas Serna; all residents of Ranchos de Albuquerque.

Frames 2304-2305, #167
NUANES, Teodora
bap 12 Nov 1848, 4 days old; natural d/ Juana Nuanes, de los Ranchos; am/ Jose Manuel Nuanes & Maria Martin; gp/ Diego Sanches & Juana Griego, of the same place.

MONTOYA, Maria Nestora
bap 13 Nov 1848, 4 days old; legit d/ Crus Montoya; am/ Jose Montoya & Maria Abila; gp/ Nestor Montoya & Marcelina Montoya, of the same place.

MARTIN, Manuel Antonio
bap 13 Nov 1848, 6 days old; legit s/ Ambrocio Martin & Trinidad Ruis, of this plaza; ap/ Rafael Martin & Manuela Anaya; am/ Ygnacio Ruis & Ysidora Lopes; gp/ Diego Lopes & Lus Lopez, of the same place.

Frames 2305-2306, #168
ANAYA, Jose Andres
bap 2 Dec 1848, 8 days old; legit s/ Vitoriano Anaya & Dolores Tapia, residents of Atrisco; ap/ Juan Anaya & Francisca Baca; am/ Lorenso Tapia & Vitoriana Garcia; gp/ Felipe Anaya & Perfecta Ansures, of the same place.

ARMIJO, Jose Gabriel
bap 3 Dec 1848, 5 days old; legit s/ Antonio Jose Armijo & Barbara Sabedra, residents of Albuquerque; ap/ Ambrocio Armijo & Maria Antonia Ortiz; am/ Juan Cristobal Sabedra & Gertrudis Garcia; gp/ Juan Sanches & Rafaela Ruis.

GARCIA, Manuel Catarino (of Alameda)
bap 3 Dec 1848, 6 days old; legit s/ Manuel Garcia & Rafael Rael, of Alameda; ap/ Miguel Garcia & Maria Ballejas; am/ Juan Antonio Rael & Soledad Miera; gp/ Manuel Miera & Soledad Miera, of the same place.

Frame 2307, #169
LUCERO, Maria Gertrudis
bap 4 Dec 1848; legit d/ Francisco Lucero & Dolores Baca, of San Antonio; ap/ unknown; am/ Pablo Baca & Benigna Gutierres; gp/ Rafael Lucero & Altagracia Baca, of the same place.

ARMENTA, Jose Militon
bap 5 Dec 1848, 6 days old; legit s/ Juan de Jesus Armenta & Encarnacion Griego; ap/ Jose Maria Armenta & Ygnacia Martin; am/ Pedro Griego & Anna Maria Zalazar; gp/ Francisco Candelaria & Trinidad Lopez, all of los Griegos.

LUJAN, Maria Benigna de Jesus
bap 12 Dec 1848, 5 days old; legit d/ Juan Lujan & Vibiana Sandobal; ap/ not stated; am/ Bartolo Sandobal & Margarita Lucero; gp/ Jose Silberio Montoya & Francisca Montoya, all from Alameda.

Frame 2308, #170
LOPEZ, Manuel
bap 12 Dec 1848, 3 days old; legit s/ Vicente Lopez & Guadalupe Baca; ap/ Vicente Lopez & Loreta N. NS; am/ Ramon Baca & Rosaria Baca; gp/ Antonio Aragon & Rosaria Martines, of Barelas.

LUCERO, Francisca
bap 13 Dec 1848, 2 days old; legit d/ Vicente Lucero & Rosalia Garcia; ap/ Alfonso Lucero & Manuela Crestina NS; am/ Maria Lucero; gp/ Juan Duran & Juliana Garcia, of los Duranes.

Frames 2308-2309, #171
CANDELARIA, Jose Manuel
bap 15 Dec 1848, 3 days old; legit s/ Manuel Candelaria & Juana Carrio, residents of los Barelas; ap/ Manuel Candelaria & Margarita Chaves; am/ Crus Carrio & Margarita Chaves; gp/ Agustin Candelaria & Dolores Sanches, of the same place.

SANDOBAL, Estefana
bap 18 Dec 1848, 2 days old; natural d/ Rita Sandobal; am/ Antonio Sandobal; gp/ Juan Ortega & Estefana Ortega, all residents of los Barelas.

GARCIA, Maria
bap 18 Dec 1848; natural d/ Juana Garcia, resident of Ferranate; am/ Jose Garcia & Nicanora Sinson; gp/ Manuel Gallegos & Francisquita Hinojos.

Frames 2309-2310, #172
BARREDAS, Damacia Daria
bap 19 Dec 1848, 2 days old; legit d/ Francisco Barredas & Bibiana Nuanes, from San Antonio; ap/ unknown; am/ Anastacio Nuanes & Barbara Garcia; gp/ Vicente Garcia & Simona Nuanes, of this plaza.

GARCIA, Juana
bap 20 Dec 1848, 4 days old; legit s/ Jose Garcia & Ysidora Gonsales, of this plaza, ap/ Juan Garcia & Dolores Candelaria; am/ Antonio Garcia & Dolores Candelaria; gp/ Anastacio Garcia & Clara Garcia, of the same place.

CHAVEZ, Juana
bap 23 Dec 1848, 6 days old; legit d/ Blaz Chavez & Ysabel Gonsales; ap/ not stated; am/ Juan Gonsales & Vitoria Garcia; gp/ Rafael Sena & Dolores Candelaria, of los Ranchos.

Frame 2311, #173
PACHECO, Maria del Rosario
bap 24 Dec 1848, 4 days old; legit d/ Cristobal Pacheco & Manuela Garcia, of los Griegos; ap/ Salbador Pacheco & Juana Torres; am/ Josefa Garcia & Maria N. NS; gp/ Jose Griego & Juana Gutierres, of the same place.

LOPES, Maria Eutimia de Atocha
bap 25 Dec 1848, 7 days old; legit d/ Teodoro Lopes & Josefa Chaves, residents of los Barelas; ap/ Manuel Lopes & Crus Romero; am/ Agustin Chaves & Juana Sanches; gp/ Leonardo Marques & Catalina Sandobal, of the same place.

Frames 2311-2312, #174
MARTIN, Maria Ginobeba
bap 3 Jan 1849, 4 days old; legit d/ Jose Antonio Martin & Quiteria Griego, of los Gallegos; ap/ Jose Martin & Antonia Candelaria; am/ Miguel Griego & Gertrudis Olguin; gp/ Jose Antonio Garcia & Juana Griego, of the same place.

SEDILLO, Maria Juana
bap 8 Jan 1849, 9 days old; legit d/ Jose Dolores Sedillo & Soledad Vernal; ap/ Salbador Sedillo & Juana Sanches; am/ Jose Vernal & Manuela Martin; gp/ Jose de Jesus Santillanes & Maria Rita Lucero, of la Angostura.

PADILLA, Maria Dolores
bap 8 Jan 1849, 3 days old; legit d/ Manuel Padilla & Ysidora Griego, of los Griegos; ap/ Bartolo Padilla & Gertrudis Garcia; am/ Jose Maria Griego & Guadalupe Mora; gp/ Buenabentura Armijo & Sesaria Seberino, of Albuquerque.

Frame 2313, #175
SABEDRA, Manuel Antonio
bap 15 Jan 1849, 4 days old; legit s/ Juan Sabedra & Ysabel Lopes, resident of Duranes; ap/ Pablo Sabedra & Gertrudis Apodaca; am/ Dionicio Lopes & Gertrudis Perea; gp/ Julian Garcia & Teresa Candelaria, of the same place.

GALLEGOS, Marcelina
bap 16 Jan 1849, 5 days old; legit d/ Antonio Gallegos & Juliana Chaves, of Bernalillo; ap/ Ramon Gallego & Josefa Benabides; am/ Diego Chaves & Juliana Montoya; gp/ Rumaldo Garcia & Antonio Lucero, of the same place.

PEREA, Jesus Maria
bap 16 Jan 1849, 6 days old; legit s/ Jose Angel Perea & Manuela Garcia, of los Duranes; ap/ Luis Perea & Guadalupe Garcia; am/ Diego Garcia & Ramona Candelaria; gp/ Julian Candelaria & Anna Maria Garcia, of los Griegos.

Frame 2314, #176
APODACA, Maria del Rosario
bap 16 Jan 1849, 2 days old; legit d/ Jose Apodaca & Concepcion Romero, of Alameda; ap/ Dionicio Apodaca & Luteria Garcia; am/ Baltazar Romero & Paula Lucero; gp/ Alonso Zalazar & Dolores Zalazar, of the same place.

LUCERO, Trinidad
bap 17 Jan 1849, 3 days old; legit d/ Jose de las Nieves Lucero & Eulogia Sabedra, residents Ranchos of Atrisco; ap/ Andres Lucero & Tomasa Garcia; am/ Francisco Sabedra & Maria de la Lus Chaves; gp/ Rafael Candelaria & Ysidora Candelaria, residents of los Barelas.

GARCIA, Pedro Antonio
bap 17 Jan 1849, 1 day old; legit s/ Julian Garcia & Lorenza Aragon, of los Duranes; ap/ Juan Jose Garcia & Francisca Gonsales; am/ J. Manuel Aragon & Tereza Candelaria; gp/ Jose Torres & Josefa Garcia, of the same place.

Frame 2315, #177
SANCHES, Jose Pablo
bap 19 Jan 1849, 3 days old; natural s/ Maria Lorenza Sanches, of Alameda; am/ Salbador Sanches & Encarnacion Gurule; gp/ Juan Jose Apodaca & Maria de Luz Padilla, of the same place.

HERERA, Manuel de Atocha
bap 19 Jan 1849, 2 days old; s/ Salbador Herera & Ygnacia Chaves, residents of Atrisco; ap/ Vicente Herera & Antonia Montaño; am/ Antonio Chaves & Margarita Garcia; gp/ Jose Maria Sanches & Ysidora Herera, of the same place.

Frames 2315-2316, #178
PEREA, Jose Nicanor Camilo
bap 20 Jan 1849, 11 days old, illegitimate; adopted s/ Paula Perea, from San Antonio; am/ Jose Miguel Perea & Manuela Sanches; gp/ Militon Ginso & Paula Perea, resident of San Antonio.

ORTIZ, Jose Trinidad
bap 24 Jan 1849, 3 days old; legit s/ Jose Ortiz & Trinidad Griego, of los Ranchos de Albuquerque; ap/ Matias Ortiz & Anna Maria Martines; am/ Jose Griego & Paula Tafolla; gp/ Abran Garcia & Nestora Garcia, of the same place.

MESTAS, Jose de Jesus de la Paz
bap 25 Jan 1849, 1 day old; legit s/ Pedro Mestas & Petra Lopez, residents of los Barelas; ap/ Ygnacio Mestas & Gertrudis Lopez; am/ Jose Miguel Lopez & Maria Juana Garcia; gp/ Ambrocio Garcia & Maria Delibina Sandobal.

Frame 2317, #181
GARBISO, Jose Pedro de Jesus
bap (date missing), 3 days old; legit s/ J. Maria Garbiso & Bitoria Duran; ap/ Cristobal Garbiso & Anna Maria Muñis; am/ Manuel Duran & Manuela Muñis, gp/ Juan Duran & Guadalupe Duran, of the same place.

MONTAÑO, Candelaria
bap 2 Feb 1849, 3 days old; legit d/ Miguel Montaño & Clara Candelaria, of los Ranchos; ap/ Antonio Montaño & Manuela Antonia Martines; am/ Vicente Candelaria & Anna Maria Chavez; gp/ Jose Montaño & Tereza Miera, residents of same.

CANDELARIA, Donaciano Justiniano
bap 3 Feb 1849, 3 days old; legit s/ Roman Candelaria & Mariana Varela, of los Ranchos de Albuquerque; ap/ Esteban Candelaria & Maria de Jesus Luna; am/ Jose Griego & Manuela Varela; gp/ Miguel Garcia & Rosalia Varela, of the same place.

Frame 2318, #182
TORRES, Maria Placida del Refugio
bap 4 Feb 1849, 3 days old; natural d/ Francisca Torres, resident of los Barelas; ap/ Francisca Torres; gp/ Julian Lopes & Trinidad Lopes, of the same place.

GRIEGO, Jose Andalecio
bap 6 Feb 1849, 5 days old; legit s/ Juan Griego & Maria Griego, of los Griegos; ap/ Lorenzo Griego & Guadalupe Candelaria; am/ Jose Griego & Tomasa Samora; gp/ Jose Maria Baca & Josefa Baca, of Albuquerque.

Frames 2318-2319, #183
ARAGON, Maria Francisca
bap 6 Feb 1849, 3 days old; legit d/ Marcelino Aragon & Nicolasa Jaramio, of Alameda; ap/ Juan de Jesus Aragon & Rosalia Gonsales; am/ unknown; gp/ Luis Tafolla & Maria Antonia Gonsales, of los Corrales.

VALENCIA, Pedro Jose
bap 7 Feb 1849, 8 days old; legit s/ Bernardo Valencia & Anna Maria Aragon, of Ranchos de Albuquerque; ap/ Juan Domingo Valencia & Paula Martines; am/ Juan Tomas Aragon & Gertrudis Garcia; gp/ same as the paternal grandparents.

APODACA, Maria Petra
bap 8 Feb 1849, 18 days old; natural d/ Juana Apodaca, of los Ranchos; am/ Francisco Apodaca & Juana Espinosa; gp/ Ysidro Griego & Placida Valencia, of the same place.

Frame 2320, #184
GRIEGO, Maria Juliana
bap 8 Feb 1849, 2 days old; legit d/ Rumaldo Griego & Candelaria Montoya, residents of los Barelas; ap/ Pablo Griego & Ysidora Apodaca; am/ Rafael Montoya & Maria Gertrudis Chavez; gp/ J. Dolores Chavez & Juliana Griego, of Albuquerque.

GONSALES, Maria Carlota
bap 8 Feb 1849, 5 days old; legit d/ Tomas Gonsales & Soledad Aranda, of los Ranchos de Albuquerque; ap/ Antonio Gonsales & Lugarda Garcia; am/ Pedro Aranda & Rosalia Jaramillo; gp/ the maternal grandparents.

GARCIA, Maria Ygnacia Dorotea
bap 9 Feb 1849, 9 days old; legit d/ Diego Garcia & Serafina Lopes, of San Antonio; ap/ unknown; am/ Salbador Candelaria & Rita Sanchez; gp/ Jose Perea & Maria Perea, of the same place.

Frame 2321, #185
LUJAN, Candelaria
bap 15 Feb 1849, 6 days old; legit d/ Juan Lujan & Sesaria Anaya; ap/ Francisco Lujan & Bitoria Garcia; am/ Martin Anaya & Beatris Romero; gp/ Antonio Sandobal & Josefa Aranda, all of los Ranchos de Albuquerque.

SANCHES, Jose de la Luz
bap 16 Feb 1849, 3 days old; legit s/ Manuel Sanches & Petra Chaves, residents of Atrisco; ap/ Ygnacio Sanches & Manuela Anaya; am/ Jose Dolores Chaves & Nicanora Garcia; gp/ Luiz Sanches & Dolores Garcia, of the same place.

Frame 2321-2322, #186
CORDOBA, Jose Agapito
bap 18 Feb 1849, 3 days old; legit s/ Lino Cordoba & Dolores Sanches; ap/ Jose Cordoba & Maria Gonsales; am/ Domingo Sanches & Quiteria Gonsales; gp/ Manuel Jaramillo & Gertrudis Mestas.

GARCIA, Jose Gregorio
bap 19 Feb 1849, 3 days old; legit s/ Cleto Garcia & Nicolasa Duran, of los Duranes; ap/ Jesus Maria Garcia & Antonia Anaya; am/ Manuel Duran & Manuela Garcia, gp/ Gregorio Lucero & Margarita Lucero, of the same place.

TORRES, Maria Ruperta
bap 21 Feb 1849, 8 days old; legit d/ Benito Torres & Trinidad Gutierres; ap/ Pedro Torres & Guadalupe Garcia; am/ Juan Gutierres & Manuela Lopez; gp/ Juan Candelaria & Trinidad Lopes, of the plaza.

Frame 2323, #187
ARCHULETA, Juliana
bap 21 Feb 1849, 4 days old; legit d/ Vicente Archuleta & Antonia Jaramillo; ap/ Jose Archuleta; am/ Miguel Jaramillo & Gertrudis Griego; gp/ Manuel Sanches & Guadalupe Jaramillo, all residents of los Atrisco.

TRUJILLO, Jose Domingo
bap 4 Mar 1849, 5 days old; legit s/ Nicanor Trujillo & Gregoria Garcia; ap/ unknown; am/ Simon Garcia & Josefa Padilla; gp/ Jose Domingo Padilla & Juana Lucero, all residents of San Antonio.

SANDOBAL, Jose Melquides
bap 4 Mar 1849, 3 days old; legit s/ Francisco Sandobal & Soledad Martines, of Chilili; ap/ Dionicio Sandoval & Juana Martin; am/ Jose Martines & Juana Maria Griego; gp/ Baltasar Martines & Dolores Apodaca; residents of Albuquerque.

Frame 2324, #188
HERRERA, Maria Paula Bernarda
bap 7 Mar 1849, 3 days old; legit d/ Antonio Herrera & Clara Gonsales, of Alameda; ap/ unknown; am/ Juan Gonsales & Anna Maria Sandoval; gp/ Baltasar Martines & Dolores Apodaca, of the same place.

GARCIA, Jose Nestor
bap 7 Mar 1849, 2 days old; legit s/ Antonio Garcia & Juana Gutierres, of Alameda; ap/ not stated; am/ Loreto Gutierres & Maria Manuela Rael; gp/ Baltasar Martines & Dolores Apodaca, of the same place.

Frames 2324-2325, #189
MARTIN, Miguel Antonio
bap 8 Mar 1849, 3 days old; legit s/ Manuel Martin & Anna Maria Duran; ap/ Rafael Martin & Manuela Anaya; am/ Francisco Duran & Bernarda Aragon; gp/ Miguel Antonio Martin & Francisca Carabajal, residents of Albuquerque.

APODACA, Maria Juana
bap 8 Mar 1849, 3 days old; legit d/ Jose Maria Apodaca & Tomasa Sabedra, of Albuquerque; ap/ Roman Apodaca & Manuela Candelaria; am/ Manuel Sabedra & Elena Duran; gp/ Seledon Apodaca & Juana Apodaca, of the same place.

MOYA, Francisca
bap 9 Mar 1849, 5 days old; legit d/ Vitorino Moya & Maria de Jesus Martines, of los Griegos; ap/ Manuel Moya & Juliana Garcia; am/ Pedro Martines & Juana Garcia; gp/ Juan de Jesus Armenta & Encarnacion Griego, of the same place.

Frames 2325-2326, #190
RUIBAL, Jose Albino
bap 11 Mar 1849, 5 days old; legit s/ Jose Ruibal & Maria Martin; gp/ Jose Gutierres & Manuela Antonia Chaves, all of Bernalillo.

SALAZAR, Josefa
bap 11 Mar 1849, 2 days old; legit d/ Jerbasio Salazar & Rosaria Jaramillo; gp/ Ygnacio Gallegos & Refugia Gallegos, residents of Bernalillo.

TORRES, Maria
bap 11 Mar 1849; 6 days old; legit d/ Juan Torres & Juana Chaves; gp/ Felipe Martines & Dolores Gutierres, residents of Bernalillo. [Note: parish of Sandia].

Frames 2326-2327, #191
GARCIA, Ysidro Longino
bap 21 Mar 1849, 5 days old; natural s/ Maria Antonia Garcia, residents of Albuquerque; am/ Felis Garcia & Ysabel Lopes, gp/ Juan Cristobal Garcia & Juana Maria Mestas, of the same place.

TRUJILLO, Josefa de Altagracia
bap 21 Mar 1849, 7 days old; natural d/ Guadalupe Trujillo, from San Antonio; am/ Antonio Trujillo & Marta Crespin; gp/ J. Dolores Garcia & Ygnacia Samora, of the same place.

HERRERA, Maria Albina
bap 27 Mar 1849, 7 days old; legit d/ Vibiano Herrera & Juana Gurule, residents of Chilili; ap/ Francisco Herrera & Francisca Gonzales; am/ Marcelo Gurule & Petra Gutierres; gp/ Facundo Gutierres & Decideria Arias, of Ranchos de Albuquerque.

Frame 2328, #192
ARAGON, Josefa
bap 27 Mar 1849, 2 days old; natural d/ Manuela Aragon, resident of this plaza; am/ Ylario Aragon & Juliana Gallegos; gp/ Jose Sabedra & Maria de la Luz Sabedra, of the same place.

CARRIO, Jesus
bap 1 Apr 1849, 3 days old; natural s/ Gertrudis Carrio, of los Corrales; am/ Santiago Carrio & Lugarda Gutierres; gp/ Tomas Montoya & Juana Gutierres.

GALLEGO, Jose Sisto
bap 1 Apr 1849, 4 days old; legit s/ Pedro Gallego & Dolores Candelaria, of Atrisco; ap/ not stated; am/ Pablo Candelaria & Guadalupe Herrera; gp/ Salvador Herrera & Maria Ygnacia Chaves, of the same place.

Frame 2329, #193
DURAN, Francisca
bap 2 Apr 1849, 2 days old; legit d/ Abad Duran & Andrea Martin, of los Ranchos; ap/ Manuel Duran & Matilde Lucero; am/ Felipe Martin & Vitoria Carrio; gp/ Pablo Garcia & Placida Garcia, of the same place.

ARELLANES, Maria Francisca
bap 2 Apr 1849, 8 days old; legit d/ Teodoro Arellanes & Rosalia Montoya, of Alameda; ap/ Jose Arellanes & Manuela Perea; am/ Cristobal Montoya & Monica Gonsales; gp/ Felipe Garcia & Rafaela Miera, of the same place.

MORA, Jose Felis
bap 3 Apr 1849, 2 days old; legit s/ Esteban Mora & Juana Maria Griego, of los Ranchos; ap/ Ysidro Mora & Juana Marques; am/ Francisco Griego & Antonia Serna; gp/ Jose Felis (Lucero) & Maria Bentura Lucero, of the same place.

Frame 2330, #194
GUTIERRES, Juana
bap 8 Apr 1849, 8 days old; legit d/ Juan Gutierres & Juana Mora; ap/ Rafael Gutierres & Josefa Mares; am/ Ysidro Mora & Dolores Baca, gp/ Francisco Lucero & Juana Marques, all from San Antonio.

CHAVES, Maria Francisca
bap 10 Apr 1849, 3 days old; legit d/ Miguel Chaves & Decideria Gurule, from Alameda; ap/ not stated; am/ Jose Gurule & Maria Gonsales; gp/ Miguel Antonio Martin & Francisco Carabajal, of this plaza.

Frames 2330-2331, #195
GOMES, Josefa
bap 14 Apr 1849; legit d/ Juan Gomes & Juliana Gonsales, of los Ranchos de Albuquerque; ap/ Antonio Gomes & Maria Ygnacia Arias; am/ Francisco Gonsales & Victoria Garcia; gp/ Antonio Sanches & Josefa Aranda, of the same place.

GARCIA, Juan Ysidro
bap 16 Apr 1849, 4 days old; legit s/ Antonio Jose Garcia & Josefa Garcia; ap/ Manuel Garcia & Manuela Perea; am/ Blas Garcia & Francisca Aragon; gp/ Francisco Antonio Garcia & Manuela Perea, all residents from Alameda.

RAEL, Ruperta
bap 20 Apr 1849, 17 days old; legit d/ Francisco Rael & Miquela Archuleta; ap/ Juan Rael & Maria Encarnacion Gurule; am/ Antonio Archuleta & Nicanora Cedio; gp/ Francisco Gurule & Gregoria Perea, all residents of San Antonio.

Frames 2331-2332, #196
SABEDRA, Manuel Trinidad (of Albuquerque)
bap 20 Apr 1849, 6 days old; legit s/ Juan Sabedra & Luiza Duran; ap/ Manuel Sabedra & Elena Duran; am/ Francisco Duran & Lorensa Ramires; gp/ Jose Armijo & Concepcion Lopes, all residents of Albuquerque.

OTERO, Julian
bap 21 Apr 1849, 4 days old; legit s/ Juan Otero & Rozalia Jaramillo; ap/ unknown; am/ Pablo Jaramillo & Loreta Garcia; gp/ Ramon Anaya & Juana Garcia, all residents of Albuquerque.

GALLEGOS, Jose
bap 21 Apr 1849, 4 days old; legit s/ Valentino Gallegos & Manuela Apodaca; ap/ Jose Pablo Gallegos & Juana Mora; am/ Jose Apodaca & Juana Gurule; gp/ Pedro Garcia & Rumalda Martines, all residents from Ranchos de Albuquerque.

Frame 2333, #197
LOPES, Jose Manuel
bap 23 Apr 1849, 3 days old; natural s/ Brigida Lopes; am/ unknown; gp/ Diego Lopes & Manuela Duran, all residents of Albuquerque.

DURAN, Maria Manuela
bap 23 Apr 1849, 3 days old; legit d/ Juan Duran & Ysabel Gurule; ap/ Josefa Duran; am/ Marcelino Gurule & Dolores Garcia; gp/ Manuel Gurule & Rosa Garcia, of los Ranchos de Albuquerque.

GARCIA, Catarina
bap 6 May 1849, 6 days old; legit d/ Bartolo Garcia & Juana Maria Padilla, residents of Atrisco; ap/ Juan Garcia & Barbara Chaves; am/ Diego Antonio Padilla & Manuela Guirre; gp/ Felipe Herrera & Juana Garcia, residents of the same.

Frame 2334, #198
GONSALES, Miguel Antonio
bap 7 May 1849, 6 days old; legit s/ Santos Gonsales & Guadalupe Otero, of San Antonio; ap/ Jose Gonsales & Maria Nicolasa NS; am/ Julian Otero & Maria Antonia Padilla; gp/ Manuel Antonio Martin & Francisca Carbajal, of this plaza.

ARMIJO, Maria Juana
bap 7 May 1849, 7 days old; natural d/ Guadalupe Armijo; am/ Juan Armijo; gp/ Manuel Candelaria & Polonia Gonsales, residents of los Candelarias.

MARTIN, Maria Teodora
bap 7 May 1849, 10 days old; legit d/ Jose Gregorio Martin & Maria Gertrudis Brito, of Alameda; ap/ Jose Manuel Martin & Rosalia Lucero; am/ Antonio Brito & Maria Zalazar, of the same place.

Frame 2335, #199
BACA, Francisco Antonio
bap 8 May 1849, 4 days old; s/ Jose Manuel Baca & Tomasa Apodaca; ap/ Simon Baca & Lorenza Sanches; am/ Dionicio Apodaca & Luteria Garcia; gp/ Pedro Martin & Maria Romula Apodaca, all residents of Alameda.

MONTOLLA, Maria Gertrudis
bap 9 May 1849, 4 days old; natural d/ Maria Antonia Montolla, residents of Albuquerque; am/ Guadalupe Martin; gp/ Pablo Martin & Estefana Martin, of the same place.

Frames 2335-2336, #200
MARES, Maria Estanislada Presiliana
bap 9 May 1849, 3 days old; legit d/ Jose Miguel Mares & Manuela Garcia, of los Candelarias; ap/ Pablo Mares & Anna Maria Nuanes; am/ Diego Antonio Garcia & Maria Ramona Candelaria; gp/ Juan Andres Moya & Manuela Moya, residents of Albuquerque.

BACA, Josefa
bap 10 May 1849, 4 days old; natural d/ Maria Baca; am/ Diego Baca & Mariquita Samora; gp/ Nestor Anaya & Maria Anaya, all residents of Albuquerque.

MARTINES, Maximo
bap 12 May 1849, 5 days old; legit s/ Tiburcio Martines & Teresa Jaramillo, residents Ranchos of Atrisco; ap/ Jose Maria Martines & Barbara Candelaria; am/ Bautista Jaramillo & Encarnacion Garcia; gp/ Manuel Vicente Jaramillo & Maria Josefa Baca, of the same place.

Frame 2337, #201
GARCIA, Manuela Antonia
bap 15 May 1849, 2 days old; d/ Romualdo Garcia & Ana Maria Arias, of los Ranchos de Albuquerque; ap/ Juan Cristobal Garcia & Josefa Martin; am/ Juan Arias & Merced Gomes; gp/ Esteban Mora & Juana Maria Griego, of the same place.

CRESPIN, Trinidad
bap 15 May 1849, 3 days old; legit d/ Salbador Crespin & Ana Maria de los Relles Lopes, of San Antonio; ap/ Francisco Crespin & Maria N. NS; am/ Salbador Lopes & Marta Sedillo; gp/ Mariano Antonio Muñis & Maria Josefa Candelaria, of the same place.

CANDELARIA, Bonifacio
bap 16 May 1849, 1 day old; legit s/ Miguel Candelaria & Francisca Garcia, of los Ranchos; ap/ Ramon Candelaria & Manuela Sena; am/ Jose Garcia & Josefa Rael; gp/ Pablo Varela & Paula Garcia, of the same place.

Baptisms – Albuquerque, New Mexico
1829–1850

Frame 2338, #202
ARIAS, Maria Antonia
bap 20 May 1849, 5 days old; legit d/ Florencio Arias & Francisca Montoya; ap/ Domingo Arias & Juliana Lucero; am/ Rafael Montoya & Anna Maria Duran; gp/ Antonio Arias & Trinidad Arias, residents of los Ranchos de Albuquerque.

SALAZAR, Felis
bap 21 May 1849, 4 days old; legit s/ Juana Salazar & Manuela Gurule; ap/ Luis Salazar & Antonia Gurule; am/ Felipe Gurule & Juana Gutierres; gp/ Anastacio Varela & Rafaela Garcia, all residents of Ranchos de Albuquerque.

LUCERO, Francisco
bap 19 May 1849, 3 days old; natural s/ Patrona Lucero, from los Ranchos; am/ Ysidro Gutierres & Dolores Martin; gp/ Jose Dario Aragon & Rafaela Luna, residents of same.

Frame 2339, #203
SANCHES, Juana
bap 26 May 1849, 3 days old; legit d/ Vicente Sanches & Francisca Mares, from los Ranchos; ap/ Domingo Sanches & Maria de la Lus Perea; am/ Luz Mares & Maria Petra Peña; gp/ Joachin Sanches & Maria de los Lus Perea, residents of same.

SAMORA, Juan Maria
bap 27 May 1849, 6 days old; legit d/ Ramon Samora & Gregoria Candelaria; ap/ Miguel Samora & Marcelina Gallegos; am/ Jose Candelaria & Francisca Gonsales; gp/ Juan Jose Garcia & Anna Maria Garcia, all residents of los Candelarias.

RUIS, Jose Manuel Esquipulo
bap 30 May 1849, 3 days old; legit s/ Ramon Ruis & Josefa Lopez; ap/ Javier Ruis & Viviana Madrid; am/ Jose Lopes & Maria Martin; gp/ Manuel Apodaca & Francisca Aragon, all of los Barelas.

Frame 2340, #204
GARCIA, Maria Josefa de Jesus
bap 3 Jun 1849, 6 days old; legit d/ Miguel Garcia & Rosalia Varela; ap/ Luis Garcia & Tomasa Montaño; am/ Santiago Varela & Juana Aranda; gp/ Manuel Ylisarri & Josefa Ylisarri, all residents of Ranchos de Albuquerque.

APODACA, Maria Beneranda
bap 3 Jun 1849, 4 days old; legit d/ Juan Apodaca & Luz Padilla, from Alameda; ap/ Rafael Apodaca & Juana Maria Romero; am/ Julian Padilla & Anna Maria Padilla; gp/ Juan Apodaca & Ysabel Sanches, of Albuquerque.

CANDELARIA, Maria Josefa
bap 3 Jun 1849, 8 days old; legit d/ Jose Candelaria & Rosalia Armijo; ap/ Jose Candelaria & Francisca Gonsales; am/ Ygnacio Armijo & Francisca Sisneros; gp/ Pablo Gutierres & Josefa Martines, all residents of los Candelaria.

Baptisms – Albuquerque, New Mexico
1829–1850

Frame 2341, #205
GUTIERRES, Maria Soledad de Altagracia
bap 3 Jun 1849, 10 days old; legit d/ Eulogio Gutierres & Encarnacion Garcia; ap/ Simon Gutierres & Maria Antonia Jaramillo; am/ Martin Garcia & Anna Maria Apodaca; gp/ Ambrosio Garcia & Catarina Armijo, residents of los Candelarias.

CANDELARIA, Yrinea de Jesus
bap 3 Jun 1849, 6 days old; natural d/ Concepcion Candelaria, resident of Atrisco; am/ Jose Candelaria & Dolores Gutierres; gp/ Juan Garcia & Gertrudis Garcia, residents of Ranchos de Atrisco.

GABALDON, Maria Trinidad del Refugio
bap 3 Jun 1849, 7 days old; legit d/ Miguel Gabaldon & Juana Lopes; ap/ Ygnacio Gabaldon & Miquela Sanches; am/ Antonio Lopez & Miquela Jaramillo; gp/ Francisco Garcia & Gregoria Garcia, all of Ranchos de Atrisco.

Frame 2342, #206
MONTOYA, Maria Sicilia
bap 3 Jun 1849, 5 days old; natural d/ Francisca Montoya, of Alameda; am/ Jose Maria Montoya & Dolores Montoya; gp/ Felipe Mesta & Anna Josefa Mestas, of Albuquerque.

GARCIA, Mariana de Jesus
bap 11 Jun 1849, 2 days old; legit d/ Marcos Garcia & Polonia Mares; ap/ Juan Pablo Garcia & Gregoria Garcia; am/ Nicolas Mares & Manuela Garcia; gp/ Atanacio Montoya & Maria Mares, all of los Candelarias.

CHAVES, Manuel Antonio
bap 12 Jun 1849, 3 days old; legit s/ Blas Chaves & Paula Chaves, residents of Atrisco; ap/ Juan Jose Chaves & Josefa Trujillo; am/ Antonio Jose Chaves & Manuela Garcia; gp/ Jose Antonio Chaves & Josefa Padilla, residents of the same place.

Frame 2343, #207
CHAVES, Maria Antonio
bap 15 Jun 1849, 7 days old; legit d/ Mariano Chaves & Monica Romero; ap/ Pedro Chaves & Margarita Montoya; am/ Santiago Romero & Dolores Candelaria; gp/ Mariano Sandobal & Dubigen Garcia, all from Alameda.

PADILLA, Jose Ramon
bap 16 Jun 1849, 4 days old; legit s/ Julian Padilla & Maria de la Luz Lucero, from Alameda; ap/ Santiago Padilla & Manuela Sanches; am/ Julian Lucero & Anna Maria Martin; gp/ Ramon Garcia & Gertrudis Sanches, of the same place.

Frames 2343-2344, #208
APODACA, Jose Mariano
bap 17 Jun 1849, 6 days old; legit s/ Francisco Apodaca & Beneranda Sedillo, residents of los Barelas; ap/ Francisco Apodaca & Juana Varela; am/ Pedro Sedillo & Francisca Chaves; gp/ Salbador Romero & Francisca Chaves, of the same place.

SALAZAR, Francisca Antonia
bap 19 Jun 1849, 2 days old; legit d/ Jose Salazar & Maria Archibeque, of Corrales; ap/ Diego Salazar & Josefa Baca; am/ Marcelino Archibeque & Juana Salazar; gp/ Juan Nepomuceno Martin & Tomasa Jaramillo, all of Corrales.

BACA, Maria Leonore
bap 20 Jun 1849, 8 days old; legit d/ Jose Baca & Juana Gutierres; ap/ Simon Baca & Lorenza Candelaria; am/ Antonio Gutierres & Manuela Garcia; gp/ Juan Baca & Juana Baca, all of Barelas.

Frames 2344-2345, #209
GONSALES, Maria Placida
bap 25 Jun 1849, 3 days old; natural d/ Manuela Gonsales, from San Antonio; am/ Manuel Gonsales & Antonia Rosa Lovato; gp/ Juan Miguel Lovato & Matilde Duran, of the same place.

TENORIO, Juana Trinidad
bap 5 Jul 1849, 6 days old; legit d/ Antonio Tenorio & Candelaria Lujan, from Corrales; ap & am/ not stated; gp/ Antonio Sangre & Maria de la Luz Ansara, residents of the pueblo of Sandia.

GARCIA, Maria Camila de los Dolores
bap 11 Jul 1849, 6 days old; legit d/ Salbador Garcia & Juana Romero; ap/ Jose Antonio Garcia & Soledad Sandobal; am/ Santiago Romero & Dolores Candelaria; gp/ Baltasar Martin & Dolores Apodaca, all from Alameda.

Frame 2346, #210
CANDELARIA, Maria de los Dolores
bap 15 Jul 1849, 5 days old; legit d/ Antonio Jose Candelaria & Altagracia Garcia; ap/ Juan Candelaria & Maria Ysidora Garcia; am/ Antonio Maria Garcia & Juana Montaño; gp/ Manuel Romero & Ygnacia Montaño, of los Ranchos.

CANDELARIA, Maria Josefa
bap 18 Jul 1849, 3 days old; legit d/ Manuel Candelaria & Barbara Padilla; ap/ Pablo Candelaria & Maria de Jesus Guerra; am/ Juan Padilla & Rozalia Chaves; gp/ Jesus Candelaria & Josefa Candelaria, residents of Atrisco.

TRUJILLO, Bisenta Felisitas
bap 22 Jul 1849; legit d/ Jose Trujillo & Maria Lusera Otero; ap/ Pedro Trujillo & Maria Francisca Gurule; am/ Julian Otero & Manuela Antonia Padilla; gp/ Juan Gutierres & Juana Gutierres, all from San Antonio.

Frame 2347, #211
GONSALES, Juan de Dios
bap 29 Jul 1849, 2 days old; natural s/ Josefa Gonsales; am/ Manuel Gonsales & Anna Maria N. NS; gp/ Juan de Dios Griego & Maria Ysidora Garcia, all of Corrales.

NUANES, Jose de Jesus
bap 30 Jul 1849, 2 days old; adopted s/ Miguel Nuanes & Dolores Griego; gp/ Francisco Serna & Juana Maria Gallegos, all residents of los Poblanos.

DURAN, Maria del Carmel
bap 6 Aug 1849, 3 days old; natural d/ Luteria Duran, from los Duranes; am/ Rafael Duran & Rosa
Gurule; gp/ Antonio Santillanes & Gertrudis Aragon, of the same place.

Frame 2348, #212
PEREA, Maria Daniela
bap 7 Aug 1849, 3 days old; legit d/ Miguel Perea & Maria Candida Herrera; ap/ Rafael Perea & <u>Manuel</u>
Romero; am/ Rafael Griego & Barbara Apodaca; gp/ Domingo Romero & Petra Padilla, residents of
Alameda.

ARMIJO, Maria Belen Trinidad
bap 19 Aug 1849, 1 day old; legit d/ Jose Armijo y Ortis & Juana Armijo; ap/ Lucas Armijo & Barbara
Ortis; am/ Pedro Armijo & Manuela Ortis; gp/ Tomas Montoya & Miquela Montoya. [Note: Father's
name as shown on film.]

Frames 2348-2349, #215
GALLEGO, Maria Rafaela
bap 4 Sep 1849, 2 days old; natural d/ Albina Gallego, from los Candelarias; am/ Alejandro Gallego &
Lus Aragon, gp/ Rafael Lopes & Luisa Chaves, of the same place.

GARCIA, Maria Antonia
bap 4 Sep 1849, 3 days old; natural d/ Gregoria Garcia, of Corrales; am/ Seledon Garcia & Maria Ysidora
Lopes; gp/ Ynacio Lucero & Gregoria Montoya, of the same place.

SANCHES, Juan Antonio
bap 7 Sep 1849, 3 days old; legit d/ Domingo Sanches & Perfecta Luna, from los Lunitas; ap/ Jose
Sanches & Paula Anaya; am/ Pedro Montoya & Maria Luna; gp/ Juan Antonio Garcia & Francisca
Candelaria, of the same place.

Frame 2350, #214
ORTIZ, Jose Tomas de la Luz
bap 7 Sep 1849, 3 days old; natural s/ Monica Ortiz, residents of Albuquerque; am/ Lorenza Ortiz; gp/
Jesus Jose Chaves & Tomasa Jaramillo, of the same place.

GALLEGO, Juan Bartolome
bap 16 Sep 1849, 8 days old; natural s/ Maria Francisca Gallego; am/ Maria Guadalupe Fresques; gp/ Jose
Dionisio Gallego & Maria Guadalupe Gutieres.

GUIT, Maria Sedat
bap 17 Sep 1849, 1 month old; d/ Julian Guit (resident of this plaza and Methodist, he is Protestant) &
Rosa Anna NS (Catholic); ap/ Tomas Guit & Lus Erled; am/ unknown; gp/ Salbador Armijo & Maria de
las Nieves Armijo, Catholic & residents of this plaza.

Frame 2351, #215
TRUGIO, Maria Francisca
bap 24 Sep 1849, 10 days old; legit d/ Antonio Trugio & Concepcion Garcia; ap/ Jose Trugio & Soledad
Balencia; am/ Juan Antonio Garcia & Maria Gregoria Candelaria; gp/ Juan Antonio Garcia & Gregoria
Candelaria, residents of the plaza de los Ranchos de Albuquerque.

GRIEGO, Jose Agapito
bap 26 Sep 1849, 4 days old; legit s/ Jose Maria Griego & Juana Ortega; ap/ Juan Domingo Griego & Maria Juana Candelaria; am/ Bernardo Ortega & Rosa Ortega; gp/ Jose Gregorio Griego & Maria Candelaria Griego, of los Griegos.

PACHECO, Catarina
bap 27 Sep 1849, 5 days old; natural d/ Juana Pacheco, from this plaza; am/ Antonio Pacheco & Juana Martin; gp/ Lucas Analla in place of Eduent Balinet & Catarina Ennriques, residents of this plaza.

Frame 2352, #216
CANDELARIA, Maria Lina de la Merced
bap 27 Sep 1849, 2 days old; legit d/ Antonio Jose Candelaria & Altagracia Lopes, residents of los Barelas; ap/ Enriques Candelaria & Ysabel Lopes; am/ Cleto Lopes & Dolores Chaves; gp/ Manuel Garcia & Maria del Refugio Mestas, of Albuquerque.

MONTOLLA, Jose Miguel
bap 29 Sep 1849, 6 days old; legit s/ Francisco Montolla & Cencion Garcia, from Corrales; ap/ Jose Manuel Montolla & Catarina Lucero; am/ Jose Miguel Garcia & Josefa Chacona; gp/ Pablo Lucero & Catarina Lucero, of Corrales.

BUSTAMANTE, Filomeno de la Merced
bap 30 Sep 1849, 9 days old; legit s/ Carpio Bustamante & Guadalupe Larrañaga; ap/ Bernardo Bustamante & Anastacia Griego; am/ Mariano Larrañga & Jesusa Ortis; gp/ Felipe Gurule & Ana Maria Chabes, all of Alameda.

Frame 2353, #217
CARABAJAL, Maria de los Angeles
bap 5 Oct 1849, 4 days old; legit d/ Francisco Carabajal & Catarina Lucero, from Alameda; ap/ not stated; am/ Pablo Lucero & Antonio Luna; gp/ Jose Peralta & Dolores Montolla, from los Ranchos.

TRUGILLO, Jose Atilano
bap 10 Oct 1849, 8 days old; natural s/ Juana Trugillo, from San Antonio; am/ Jose Manuel Trugillo & Juliana Martin; gp/ Pedro Jose Nuanes & Juana Ygnacia Nuanes, of the same place.

TAPIA, Manuel Antonio
bap 10 Oct 1849, 4 days old; natural s/ Juana Tapia, from this plaza; am/ Jose Tapia & Manuela Lusero; gp/ Jose Rafael Sanches & Guadalupe Sanches, of the same place.

Frames 2353-2354, #218
CORDOBA, Maria Encarnacion Susana
bap 13 Oct 1849, 4 days old; legit d/ Juan Miguel Cordoba & Barbara Martin, from Corrales; ap/ Jose Antonio Cordoba & Quiteria Chabes; am/ Francisco Martin & Encarnacion Chabes; gp/ Pablo Griego & Juana Montoya, residents of Corrales.

MARQUEZ, Jose Francisco Leon
bap 15 Oct 1849, 4 days old; legit s/ Gaspar Marquez & Bibiana Baca, of Alameda; ap/ Simon Baca & Lorensa Duran; am/ Felipe Trujillo & Dionicio Gonsales; gp/ Pomuceno Leon & Josefa Elena NS, natives of Sandia Pueblo.

MORA, Jose del Pilar
bap 14 Oct 1849, 3 days old; legit s/ Luciano Mora & Manuela Antonia Trujillo; am/ Juan Trugillo & Manuela Apodaca; ap/ not stated; gp/ Francisco Rael & Dolores Otero.

MONTAÑO, Maria Celis
bap 14 Oct 1849, 6 days old; d/ Toribio Montaño & Marcelina Baca, from los Griegos; ap/ Jose Miguel Montaño & Rosalia Griego; am/ Diego Baca & Francisca Samora; gp/ Jose Tomas Apodaca & Ysidora Candelaria.

Frame 2355, #219
DURAN, Maria Placida
bap 14 Oct 1849, 2 days old; legit d/ Antonio Duran & Tomasa Gutierres, of los Duranes; ap/ not stated; am/ Miguel Muñis & Ysabel Jaramio; gp/ Jose Cleto Garcia & Nicolasa Duran, all of the same place.

GARCIA, Manuel Antonio
bap 14 Oct 1849, 3 days old; legit s/ Juan Garcia & Ysabel Lopes, of this villa; ap/ Tomas Tafoya & Bernarda Garcia, am/ Ramon Garcia & Cencion Lopes, gp/ Ambrocio Garcia & Concepcion Lopes, of the same place.

ARMIJO, Jose Rafael (of Albuquerque)
bap 25 Oct 1849, 3 days old; legit s/ Juan Armijo & Nicolasa Griego; ap/ Francisco Armijo & Catalina Aragon; am/ Pablo Griego & Ysidora Apodaca; gp/ Mateo Suares & Guadalupe Griego, all of Albuquerque.

Frame 2356, #220
GERNENTO, Manuel Antonio
bap 25 Oct 1849, 6 days old; legit s/ Jose Agapito Gernento & Maria Josefa Tapia; ap/ Juan Gernento & Bitoria Jaramillo; am/ Lorenso Tapia & Maria Antonia Chabes; residents of los Padillas; gp/ Dolores Lusero & Petra Lusero of Albuquerque.

SANDOBAL, Maria Angela
bap 25 Oct 1849, 6 days old; legit d/ Esteban Sandobal & Torribia Garcia, from Alameda; ap/ Agustin Sandobal & Francisca Romero; am/ Andres Garcia & Juana Torres; gp/ Francisco Mata & Luisa Lucero, all of Alameda.

Frames 2356-2357, #221
GRIEGO, Maria Trinidad
bap 28 Oct 1849, 3 days old; legit d/ Pablo Griego & Gregoria Apodaca, from los Griegos; ap/ Jose Miguel Griego & Dolores Garcia; am/ Julian Apodaca & Antonia Candelaria; gp/ Atanacio Apodaca & Geralda Griego, of los Griegos.

ARMIJO, Jose Santos
bap 4 Nov 1849, 3 days old; legit s/ Teodoro Armijo & Paubla Jaramio; ap/ Santiago Armijo & Petra Perea; am/ Miguel Jaramio & Lorensa Lucero; gp/ Pedro Armijo & Lupe Sabedra, all of San Antonio.

CANDELARIA, Jose Damacio
bap 4 Nov 1849, 4 days old; natural s/ Gregoria Candelaria; am/ Pablo Candelaria & Madalena Garcia; gp/ Salbador Garcia & Soledad Garcia, all residents of Carnue.

Frames 2357-2358, #222
SANCHEZ, Manuel Antonio
bap 9 Nov 1849, 3 days old; legit s/ Pedro Sanchez & Maria Molina; ap/ Andres Sanchez & Josefa Serna; am/ Dolores Molina & Maria Duran; gp/ Manuel Jaramillo & Dolores Jaramillo, residents of Atrisco.

LUCERO, Severiano de Jesus
bap 10 Nov 1849, 3 days old; legit s/ Vicente Lucero & Rosalia Lopes, residents of Albuquerque; ap/ Alfonso Lucero & Manuela Carabajal; am/ Ygnacio Lucero & Madalena Jaramillo; gp/ Gorge Armijo & Alta Gracia Armijo, of Albuquerque.

GONSALES, Maria Antonia
bap 12 Nov 1849, 5 days old; legit d/ Jose de la Cruz Gonsales & Rosalia Nuanes; ap/ Miguel Gonsales & Maria de la Luz Jaramillo; am/ Anastacio Nuanes & Varbara Gurule; gp/ Antonio Jose Garcia & Maria Simona Garcia, of Albuquerque.

ARANDA, Josefa
bap 15 Nov 1849, 2 days old; adopted d/ Jose Antonio Aranda & Paula Aranda, of los Ranchos; gp/ same as above.

Frame 2359, #223
LOBATO, Maria Plasida
bap 19 Nov 1849, 5 days old; adopted d/ Maria Lobato; am/ not stated; gp/ Salbador Arias & Rosa Padia, residents of los Ranchos.

SAMORA, Andrea Amada
bap 4 Dec 1849, 4 days old; legit d/ Juan Samora & Manuela Gutierres; ap/ Miguel Samora & Marselina Gallego; am/ Felipe Gutierres & Juana Gurule; gp/ Lusiano Mora & Francisca Mora, of San Antonio.

ANAYA, Maria Piedad de Altagracia
bap 4 Dec 1849, 14 days old; legit d/ Ambrocio Anaya & Catarina Apodaca; ap/ Jose Anaya & Sencion Martin; am/ Ramon Apodaca & Juana Lopes; gp/ Ambrocio Armijo & Alta-gracia Armijo, residents of Albuquerque.

Frame 2360, #224
GARCIA, Maria Trinidad
bap 4 Dec 1849, 6 days old; legit d/ Dionicio Garcia & Josefa Gutieres; ap/ Juan Luis Garcia & Juliana Griego; am/ Juana Gutieres & Francisca Sandobal, of los Griegos; gp/ Juan Sandobal & Justa Garcia.

MARTIN, Jose Francisco
bap 5 Dec 1849, 20 days old; legit s/ Jose Martin & Maria Diluvina Martin; ap/ Antonio Jose Martin & Maria Josefa Vigil; am/ Felipe Martin & Francisca Mora; gp/ Aban Duran & Andrea Martin, all residents of los Ranchos.

MORA, Jose Francisco
bap 5 Dec 1849, 10 days old; legit s/ Jose Mora & Anna Maria Gonsales, from Alameda; ap/ Andres Mora & Josefa Montaño; am/ Cristobal Montolla & Monica Gonsales; gp/ Juan Sanches & Gregoria Candelaria, of Alameda.

Frame 2361, #225
SANCHES, Maria Ysabel del Carmen
bap 7 Dec 1849, 8 days old; legit d/ Juan Sanches & Gregoria Candelaria, of Alameda; ap/ Jose Sanches
& Gregoria Rael; am/ Francisco Antonio Candelaria & Lorenza Padilla; gp/ Juan Jose Sanches & Rita
Luna, of Alameda.

APODACA, Maria Gabriela
bap 9 Dec 1849, 5 days old; legit d/ Juan Cristobal Apodaca & Rosalia Candelaria of los Griegos; ap/
Juan Apodaca & Manuela Griego; am/ Vicente Candelaria & Maria Relles Griego; gp/ Marcos Garcia &
Maria Monica Candelaria, of the same place.

Frames 2361-2362, #226
GARCIA, Nicolasa
bap 9 Dec 1849, 4 days old; legit d/ Ambrocio Garcia & Deluvina Apodaca, residents of Albuquerque;
ap/ Felis Garcia & Ysabel Lopes; am/ not stated; gp/ Manuel Antonio Romero & Juliana Sanches, of the
same place.

APODACA, Jose Nicolas Ambrocio
bap 9 Dec 1849, 5 days old; legit s/ Juan Apodaca & Juana Gutierres, residents of los Barelas; ap/ Rafael
Apodaca & Barbara Molina; am/ Miguel Gutierres & Gregoria Armijo, of the same place.

MARES, Maria Toribia
bap 9 Dec 1849, 5 days old; legit d/ Jose Mares & Relles Romero, from los Ranchos; ap/ Luis Mares &
Teresa Garcia; am/ Juan Antonio Romero & Maria Martin; gp/ Antonio Montaño & Maria Antonia
Montaño, of the same place.

Frames 2362-2363, #227
GUTIERRES, Jose Labal
bap 9 Dec 1849, 5 days old; legit s/ Juan Gutierres & Josefa Molla, residents of Atrisco; ap/ unknown;
am/ Manuel Analla & Maria Ysidora Jaramillo; gp/ Antonio Sabedra & Maria Chaves, of the same place.

ARCHULETA, Jose Melquiades
bap 12 Dec 1849, 8 days old; legit s/ Ramon Archuleta & Antonia Gutierres; ap/ Mateo Archuleta &
Relles Sedillo; am/ Jose Gutierres & Gertrudes Gomes; gp/ Salbador Crespin & Relles Lopes, all of San
Antonio.

CANDELARIA, Jose Dolores
bap 12 Dec 1849, 10 days old; legit s/ Julian Candelaria & Annamaria Garcia; ap/ Juan Candelaria &
Annamaria Duran; am/ Manuel Garcia & Ramona Candelaria; gp/ Soledad Garcia.

SAMORA, Ambrocio Albino
bap 12 Dec 1849, 6 days old; legit s/ Felipe Samora & Gertrudis Gallego, of Los Gallegos; ap/ Jose
Samora & Ygnacia Valencia; am/ Antonio Jose Gallego & Madalena Garcia; gp/ Don Ambrosio Armijo
& Doña Candelaria Otero, residents of los Poblanos.

Frame 2364, #228
LOVATO, Maria Guadalupe
bap 12 Dec 1849, 12 days old; legit s/ Agustin Lovato & Quirina Gabaldon; ap/ Juan Lovato & Maria
Casados; am/ Nepomoceno Gabaldon & Barbara Mestas; gp/ Juan Felipe Lovato & Barbara Mestas, all of
this plaza.

MARTIN, Maria Guadalupe
bap 13 Dec 1849, 2 days old; legit d/ Manuel Martin & Juliana Candelaria; ap/ Jose Martin & Victoria Griego; am/ Ylario Candelaria & Valentina Gutierres; gp/ Jose Martin & Leonarda Perea, all of los Griego.

DURAN, Juan Rafael
bap 13 Dec 1849, 8 days old; legit s/ Luciano Duran & Rosalia Montolla; ap/ Juan Rafael Duran & Josefa Apodaca; am/ Jose Montolla & Dolores Garcia; gp/ the paternal grandparents.

Frame 2365, #229
TORRES, Miguel Antonio
bap 14 Dec 1849, 3 days old; natural s/ Dolores Torres, from los Griegos; am/ Juan Torres & Dolores Gutierres; gp/ Anisteo Gutierres & Simona Griego, of the same place.

TENORIO, Maria Damasa
bap 14 Dec 1849, 4 days old/ legit d/ Jose Maria Tenorio & Ramona Sisneros, from los Poblanos; ap/ Jose Tenorio & Maria Garatusa; am/ not stated; gp/ Guadalupe Gutierres & Maria de los Angeles Ortega, of the same place.

CANDELARIA, Jose
bap 23 Dec 1849, 7 years old; Ute, adopted s/ Francisco Antonio Candelaria & Lorensa Padilla; gp/ Pedro Lopes & Guadalupe Candelaria, all residents of Atrisco.

Frame 2366, #230
ROMERO, Maria Luisa
bap 29 Dec 1849, 8 days old; natural d/ Josefa Romero, of los Griegos; am/ Francisco Romero & Barbara Lucero; gp/ Jose Antonio Lucero & Rita Lucero, of the same place.

CANDELARIA, Tomasa
bap 29 Dec 1849, 5 days old; legit d/ Deciderio Candelaria & Petra Lucero, of los Candelarias; ap/ Julian Candelaria & Annamaria Garcia; am/ Diego Lucero & Angela Romero; gp/ Francisco Salazar & Dolores Romero, of the same place.

SANCHES, Jose Dolores
bap 29 Dec 1849, 6 days old; natural s/ Maria Sanches, of this plaza; am/ Manuel Sanches & Annamaria Jaramillo; gp/ Dolores Lucero & Petra Lucero, of the same place.

Frames 2366-2367, #231
CHAVES, Venceslado
bap 30 Dec 1849, 8 days old; legit s/ Antonio Chaves & Josefa Padilla, residents of Atrisco; ap/ Antonio Chaves & Manuela Garcia; am/ Jose Manuel Padilla & Guadalupe Marina; gp/ Salbador Herrera & Maria Ygnacia Chaves, of the same place.

SERNA, Jesus Maria
bap 1 Jan 1850, 4 days old; natural s/ Rosalia Serna, of this plaza; am/ Tomas Serna & Rafaela Garcia; gp/ Juan Antonio Lucero & Natividad Lucero, of this plaza.

ARMIJO, Pedro Prisiliano
bap 1 Jan 1850, 8 days old; legit s/ Don Juan Cristobal Armijo & Doña Juana Chaves, of the plaza of
Gallegos; ap/ Don Juan Armijo & Doña Rosalia Ortega; am/ Don Francisco Chaves & Doña Annamaria
Castillo; gp/ Juan Armijo & Rafaela Armijo, residents of the same.

Frames 2367-2368, #232
GRIEGO, Pedro Prisiliano
bap 1 Jan 1850, 7 days old; s/ Desiderio Griego & Guadalupe Apodaca, from los Griegos; ap/ Jose
Miguel Griego & Dolores Garcia; am/ Juan Apodaca & Manuela Candelaria; gp/ Leonicio Garcia & Petra
Romero, of los Griegos.

TAPIA, Luciano
bap 7 Jan 1850, 10 days old; legit s/ Juan Domingo Tapia & Manuela Pacheco, of los Griegos; ap/ Ynacio
Tapia & Francisca Montaño; am/ Salbador Pacheco & Juana Torres; gp/ Calletano Garcia & Andrea
Nuanes, of los Candelarias.

MARTIN, Maria Gertrudis
bap 10 Jan 1850, 5 days old; natural d/ Marta Martin; am/ Jose Martin & Guadalupe Barela; gp/ Jesus
Maria Martin & Gertrudis Martin, of this plaza.

GARCIA, Maria Arcadia
bap 12 Jan 1850, 3 days old; legit d/ Bautista Garcia & Josefa Lucero, los Duranes; ap/ Juan Rafael
Garcia & Manuela Muñis; am/ Jose Lucero & Maria Garcia; gp/ Julian Garcia & Lorenza Aragon.

Frame 2369 #233
MONTOYA, Maria Soledad
bap 13 Jan 1850, 4 days old; legit d/ Francisco Montoya & Francisca Romero, from el Rancho; ap/ Juan
Montoya & Soledad Ortega; am/ Diego Romero & Encarnacion Valencia; gp/ Juan de Dios Chaves &
Monica Lucero, of los Ranchos.

GARCIA, Maria Marcelina
bap 16 Jan 1850, 3 days old; legit d/ Juan Antonio Garcia & Maria Gregoria Candelaria, from Ranchos;
ap/ Juan Garcia & Ysabel Romero; am/ Ygnacio Candelaria & Maria Concepsion Chabes, of los Corrales;
gp/ Jose Cleto Lusero & Maria Gavriela Candelaria, from Alameda.

CRESPIN, Jose Antonio
bap 17 Jan 1850, 5 days old; legit s/ Patricio Crespin & Maria Peña, from Ranchos; ap/ Diego Crespin &
Rosa Sandobal; am/ Bacilio Peña & Clara Gallegos; gp/ Mariano Varela & Rafaela Garcia, residents of
the same place.

Frame 2370, #234
JARAMILLO, Maria Eulogia
bap 18 Jan 1850, 3 days old; legit d/ Jose Maria Jaramillo & Josefa Sena; ap/ Agustin Jaramillo &
Francisca Sabedra; am/ unknown; gp/ Jose Lucero & Maria Ologia Sabedra, of Ranchos de Atrisco.

OLGIN, Jose Teofilo
bap 18 Jan 1850, 3 days old; legit s/ Juan Pablo Olgin & Teresa Gutierres; ap/ Buenabentura Olgin &
Juana Gutierres; am/ Juan Gutierres & Lupe Garcia; gp/ Jose Maria Jaramiyo & Maria Petra Gallego, of
los Candelarias.

ANAYA, Gertrudis
bap 18 Jan 1850, 5 days old; legit d/ Juan Anaya & Lupe Sanches; ap/ Manuel Anaya & Manuela Lopes; am/ Ololla Tafolla & Salbador Sanches; gp/ Manuel Antonio Romero & Juliana Sanches, all from Albuquerque.

Frame 2371, #235
RUIBAL, Jose Ynes
bap 24 Jan 1850, 6 days old; legit s/ Miguel Ruibal & Juana Tafolla, of Corrales; ap/ Francisco Ruibal & Gertrudis Garcia; am/ Jesus Tafolla & Gertrudis Tafolla; gp/ Domingo Griego & Maria Ynes Ruiz.

KING, Jose
bap 24 Jan 1850, 8 days old; s/ Santiago King & Maria Mais, American protestants living in this town; gp/ Julian Griego & Annamaria Griego, of this plaza.

CHABES, Maria Antonia
bap 24 Jan 1850, 8 days old; natural d/ Maria Dolores Chabes; am/ Bicente Chaves & Guadalupe Carrillo, residents of Albuquerque; gp/ Francisco Senon & Maria Aragon, of Albuquerque.

Frame 2372, #236
VARELA, Escolastica de la Paz
bap 26 Jan 1850, 3 days old; legit d/ Manuel Varela & Maria Vicenta Gallegos; ap/ Santiago Varela & Juana Aranda; am/ Juan Gallegos & Manuela Antonia Gurule, of los Ranchos; gp/ Dolores Gallegos & Maria Gregoria Trujillo, of the same place.

GRIEGO, Jose Dabid
bap 27 Jan 1850, 4 days old; legit s/ Jose Griego & Manuela Gallego, of los Ranchos de Albuquerque; ap/ Miguel Griego & Gertrudis Olguin; am/ Martin Gallego & Guadalupe Garcia; gp/ Rosalia Barela & Felipe Garcia, of los Ranchos.

SABEDRA, Jose Anastacio
bap 27 Jan 1850, 5 days old; s/ Francisco Sabedra & Maria de la Luz Chaves, residents of Atrisco; ap/ Nestor Montoya & Florentina Ortis; am/ not stated; gp/ Salvador Errera & Maria Ygnacia Chaves, of the same place.

Frames 2372-2373, #237
GUTIERRES, Ambrosio de Jesus
bap 27 Jan 1850, 3 days old; legit s/ Juan Ygnes Gutierres & Marcelina Gurule, of los Poblanos; ap/ Pascual Gutierres & Manuelita Gallegos; am/ unknown; gp/ Aban Aragon & Juana Nuanes, of los Poblanos.

CHABES, Maria Ramona
bap 28 Jan 1850, 20 days old; legit d/ Jose Dolores Chabes & Nicanora Garcia; ap/ Jabiel Chabes & Maria Jesus Armijo; am/ Juan de Jesus Garcia & Rosa Sabedra; gp/ Juan Errera & Barbara Jaramillo, all residents of Atrisco

LUCERO, Donaciano de Jesus
bap 31 Jan 1850, 3 days old; legit s/ Juan Lucero & Jesusa Contreras; ap/ Gregorio Lucero & Marta Lopes; am/ Jose Tomas Contreras & Paula Chabes, of los Duranes; gp/ Felipe Nerio Garcia & Maria Barbara Garcia, of Alameda.

Frame 2374, #238
MARTINES, Maria Antonia
bap 1 Feb 1850, 8 days old; legit d/ Gabriel Martines & Casilda Chabes; ap/ Juan Manuel Martines & Maria Antonia Lucero; am/ Jose Maria Chabes & Anna Maria Trujillo, of San Antonio; gp/ Jose Antonio Muñiz & Maria Bicenta Muñiz, of San Antonio.

GARCIA, Maria Petra
bap 3 Feb 1850, 3 days old; legit d/ Gregorio Garcia & Juana Maria Baca; ap/ Ysidro Garcia & Gertrudis Sanches; am/ Juan Jose Baca & Maria Gertrudis Castillo; gp/ Ysidro Garcia & Gertrudis Sanches, of Albuquerque.

BACA, Martin de Jesus
bap 3 Feb 1850, 4 days old; legit s/ Juan Baca & Felipa Candelaria; ap/ Sabino Baca & Tomasa Lopes; am/ Bautista Candelaria & Asencion Garcia, residents of Ranchos de Atrisco; gp/ Pablo Jaramillo & Benita Candelaria, residents of same.

Frame 2375, #239
LUCERO, Candelaria
bap 4 Feb 1850, 3 days old; legit d/ Pedro Lucero & Encarnacion Griego; ap/ Lorenzo Lucero & Cruz Griego; am/ Jose Griego & Paula Garcia, of los Ranchos; gp/ Antonio Maria Sanches & Maria Nestora Sanches, of los Poblanos. [Note: Probable twin; see also LUCERO, Maria Gregoria.]

CANDELARIA, Maria Candelaria de la Trinidad
bap 4 Feb 1850, 3 days old; natural d/ Rallas Candelaria; am/ Rafael Candelaria & Maria Antonia Garcia, of Albuquerque; gp/ Manuel Garcia & Francisca Lopes.

LUCERO, Candelaria (twin)
bap 5 Feb 1850, 4 days old; legit d/ Blas Lucero & Rosalia Tenorio; ap/ Andres Lucero & Tomasa Garcia; am/ Julian Tenorio & Benigna Chabes, of los Ranchos; gp/ Jose de los Nieves Lucero & Maria Eulogia Sabedra, of Ranchos de Atrisco. [Note: See also entry below.]

Frame 2376, #240
LUCERO, Blas (twin)
bap 5 Feb 1850, 4 days old; legit s/ Blas Lucero & Rosalia Tenorio; ap/ Andres Lusero & Tomasa Garcia; am/ Julian Tenorio & Benigna Chabes, of Ranchos de Albuquerque; gp/ Pedro Armijo & Rosalia Armijo, of the same place. [Note: See also entry above.]

LUCERO, Maria Gregoria
bap 6 Feb 1850, 5 days old; legit d/ Pedro Lucero & Maria Encarnacion Griego; ap/ Lorenzo Lucero & Cruz Griego; am/ Jose Griego & Paula Garcia, of los Gallegos; gp/ Miguel Nuanes & Juana Nuanes, of los Poblanos.[Note: Probable twin; see also LUCERO, Candelaria.]

GRIEGO, Maria Juliana
bap 16 Feb 1850, 7 days old; legit d/ Florentino Griego & Albina Romero; ap/ Jose Miguel Griego & Dolores Garcia; am/ Diego Romero & Juliana Montaño, of los Griegos; gp/ Bitoriano Garcia & Barbara Griego.

Frame 2377, #241
GARCIA, Grabiela de Jesus
bap 17 Feb 1850, 9 days old; legit d/ Juan Garcia & Concepcion Anaya; ap/ Miguel Anaya & Miquela Ruis; am/ Lorenso Ruis, of Ranchos de Atrisco, gp/ Teodor Armijo & Paula Jaramio of the same place.

GUTIERRES, Maria Barbara
bap 17 Feb 1850, 3 days old; legit d/ Pedro Gutierres & Maria Martina Gomes; ap/ Francisco Gutierres & Manuela Bernal; am/ Jose Gomes & Gregoria Griego; gp/ Jesus Garcia & Antonia Rosa Armijo, from los Poblanos.

ARMIJO, Maria Guadalupe
bap 17 Feb 1850, 9 years old; Navajo, natural d/ Jose Armijo, of los Poblanos; gp/ Antonio Garcia & Tomasa Tafolla, of Albuquerque.

Frame 2378, #242
GRIEGO, Maria Beneranda
bap 18 Feb 1850, 8 days old; legit s/ Juan Griego & Candelaria Perea; ap/ Juan Antonio Griego & Manuela Carrillo; am/ Jose Maria Perea & Polonia Chabes, from Corrales; gp/ Juan Cristobal Candelaria & Maria Luarda Perea, from Corrales.

SANDOBAL, Jose Maria
bap 18 Feb 1850, 7 days old; legit s/ Juan Sandobal & Encarnacion Apodaca; ap/ Juan Francisco Sandobal & Juana Archibeque; am/ Mariano Apodaca & Josefa Montoya, of los Corrales; gp/ Pedro Jose Martin & Rita Montoya, of Corrales.

RAEL, Manuel Antonio
bap 19 Feb 1850, 7 days old; natural s/ Estefana Rael; am/ Juan Rael & Ygnacia Marques; gp/ Juan Antonio Lucero & Maria Lucero, of Rancho de Albuquerque.

Frame 2379, #243
SISNEROS, Maria Benigna Beneranda
bap 20 Feb 1850, 7 days old; legit d/ Manuel Sisneros & Maria Gertrudis Candelaria; ap/ Transito Sisneros & Juana Maria Candelaria; am/ Jose Candelaria & Tomasa Padilla, of los Candelarias; gp/ Pablo Sisneros & Francisca Ruis, of the same place.

MARES, Maria Margarita
bap 23 Feb 1850, 2 days old; legit d/ Jose Manuel Mares & Francisca Candelaria; ap/ Nicolas Mares & Manuela Sanches; am/ Juan Pablo Candelaria & Maria Gerrera, of Atrisco; gp/ Pedro Lorenzo Gallego & Maria Dolores Candelaria, of Atrisco.

GINZO, Jesus Jose
bap 23 Feb 1850, 16 days old; legit s/ Meliton Ginzo & Refujio Gurule; ap/ Santiago Ginzo & Manuela Anaya; am/ Juan de Dios Gurule & Lus Lujan, of San Antonio; gp/ Salbador Crespin & Relles Lopes, of the same place.

Frame 2380, #244
TRUJILLO, Jose Felis
bap 23 Feb 1850, 7 days old; natural s/ Juana Trujillo; am/ Juan Trujillo & Manuela Apodaca, from San Antonio; gp/ Jose Dario Lopes & Marta Lopes, of San Antonio.

GUTIERRES, Maria Nestora
bap 28 Feb 1850, 4 days old; natural d/ Felipa Gutierres; am/ Pascual Gutierres & Manuela Gallego of los Poblanos; gp/ Francisco Muñis & Barbara Gutieres of los Poblanos.

PEREA, Maria Ascencion
bap 1 Mar 1850, 3 days old; legit d/ Santiago Perea & Jesusita Jaramillo; ap/ Bartolo Perea & Josepa Griego; am/ Juan Jaramillo & Margarita Sena, of Alameda; gp/ Felis Sanches & Sebastiana Sena, of Alameda.

Frame 2381, #245
PINEDA, Jose Manuel Miterio
bap 3 Mar 1850, 3 days old; legit s/ Nepomenceno Pineda & Jusepa Trujillo; ap/ Pedro Pineda & Ana Maria Martin; am/ Juan Jose Trujillo & Ana Maria Tapia, of Alameda; gp/ Jose Manuel Padia & Maria Rosa Padia, of Alameda.

GALLEGO, Maria Manuela
bap 3 Mar 1850, 4 days old; legit d/ Francisco Gallego & Ramona Vijil; ap/ Juan Gallegos & Manuela Gurule; am/ Juan Vijil & Maria Manuela Salazar, of los Ranches; gp/ Juan Cristobal Lucero & Juana Apodaca, from los Gallegos.

ANALLA, Jose Emiterio
bap 6 Mar 1850, 3 days old; legit s/ Andres Analla & Ana Maria Garcia; ap/ Juan Analla & Francisca Baca; am/ Cencion Garcia, of los Rancho de Atrisco; gp/ Salbador Garamio & Maria Gertrudes Baca, of Atrisco.

Frame 2382, #246
NUANES, Jose Emiterio
bap 6 Mar 1850, 3 days old; legit s/ Antonio Nuanes & Candelaria Griego; ap/ not stated; am/ Jose Maria Griego & Lupe Mora; gp/ Deciderio Griego & Maria Lupe Apodaca, residents of los Griegos.

ARAGON, Maria Tomasa
bap 7 Mar 1850, 3 days old; legit d/ Dario Aragon & Rafaela de Serna; ap/ Rafael Aragon & Catalina Sabedra, of Albuquerque; am/ Diego de Serna & Maria Paula Perea; gp/ Diego de Serna & Paula Perea, all of Albuquerque.

DURAN, Jose Miterio
bap 7 Mar 1850, 3 days old; legit s/ Manuel Duran & Ysabel Garcia; am/ Mateo Duran & Tomasa Muñis; ap/ Ysidro Garcia & Getrudes Sanches, of los Duranes; gp/ Jose Dolores Sabedra & Miguela Garcia.

Frame 2383, #247
MARTIN, Juana Casimira
bap 8 Mar 1850, 4 days old; legit d/ Antonio Jose Martin & Rosalia Garcia; ap/ Merejildo Martin & Ysabel Romero; am/ Manuel Garcia & Matilda Lusero, of los Ranchos; gp/ Jose Tiburcio Martin & Antonia Teraza Jaramillo.

ROMERO, Maria Tomasa
bap 8 Mar 1850, 2 days old; legit d/ Manuel Romero & Marselina Armijo; ap/ Francisco Romero & Dolores Romero; am/ Rafael Armijo & Soledad Peña, of los Barelas; gp/ Juan Francisco Apodaca & Maria Soledad Apodaca, from los Barelas.

GRIEGO, Maria Tomasa
bap 9 Mar 1850, 3 days old; legit d/ Juan Griego & Maria Lus Muñis; ap/ Jose Griego & Andrea Martin; am/ Pedro Muñis & Neposena Maria Montaño, of los Griegos; gp/ Manuel Tapia & Toña Martin, of los Griegos.

Frame 2384, #248
HURTADO, Maria Antonia
bap 9 Mar 1850, 3 days old; legit d/ Mariano Hurtado & Maria Jertrudis Sanches; ap/ Ysidro Hurtado & Juana Varela; am/ Mariano Sanches & Carmel Escudero, of Alameda; gp/ Nestor Jaramillo & Maria Jaramillo, of Alameda.

ARMIJO, Maria Juana
bap 11 Mar 1850, 4 days old; natural d/ Manuela Armijo; am/ Carmel Armijo, of Albuquerque; gp/ Rumaldo Ruiz & Ascencion Armijo, residents of Albuquerque.

GARCIA, Juan de Dios
bap 11 Mar 1850, 3 days old; legit s/ Antonio Garcia & Carmel Sanches, ap/ Felis Garcia & Ysabel Lopes, am/ Bicente Sanches & Ana Maria Mestas, of Albuquerque, gp/ Ambrocio Garcia & Maria Sandobal, of the same place.

Frame 2385, #249
VARELA, Anastacio
bap 13 Mar 1850, 11 days old; legit s/ Pablo Varela & Paula Garcia; ap/ Santiago Varela & Juana Aranda; am/ Juan Antonio Garcia & Gregoria Candelaria, of Ranchos de Albuquerque; gp/ Antonio Varela & Rafaela Garcia, of los Ranchos.

CANDELARIA, Francisca Euloguia
bap 14 Mar 1850, 5 days old; legit d/ Lorenso Candelaria & Madalena Duran; ap/ Antonio Candelaria & Manuel Garcia; am/ Salbador Duran & Maria Garcia, of los Ranchos; gp/ Jesus Varela & Juana Lorenza Varela, of los Ranchos.

GUTIERRES, Maria Erinea
bap 14 Mar 1850, 3 days old; legit d/ Juan Pablo Gutierres & Maria Josefa Martin; ap/ Miguel Gutierres & Gregoria Armijo; am/ Jose Antonio Martin & Monica Jaramillo, of los Candelarias; gp/ Andres Nuanes & Juana Nepomucena Armijo, of los Candelarias.

Frame 2386, #250
SABEDRA, Manuel Antonio
bap 14 Mar 1850, 8 days old; legit s/ Mariano Sabedra & Nicanora Jaramillo; ap/ Pablo Sabedra & Gertrudis Apodaca; am/ Jose Dolores Jaramillo & Josefa Gerrera, of Atrisco; gp/ Jose Dolores Lucero & Petra Lucero.

APODACA, Maria Ferminia
bap 14 Mar 1850, 7 days old; legit d/ Pablo Apodaca & Maria (written over); ap/ Miguel Apodaca & Catarina Garcia; am/ Francisco (written over) & Candelaria Garcia, of los Ranchos; gp/ Tomas Pacheco & Ana Maria Jaramillo, from los Ranchos.

PADILLA, Rumaldo
bap 18 Mar 1850, 2 days old; legit s/ Bicente Padilla & Juana Chabes; ap/ Jose Manuel Padilla & Guadalupe Moreña; am/ Antonio Chabes & Manuela Garcia; gp/ Antonio Jose Chabes & Josefa Padia, of Atrisco.

Frame 2387, #251
MARTINES, Maria Josefa
bap 20 Mar 1850, 2 days old; legit d/ Juan Pablo Martines & Cecilia Candelaria; ap/ Jose Martines & Juana Griego; am/ Esteban Candelaria & Maria Jesus Luna, of Alameda; gp/ Pedro Martines & Maria de Jesus Martines, of los Ranchos.

JARAMILLO, Maria Victoriana
bap 23 Mar 1850, 6 days old; legit d/ Manuel Jaramillo & Gertrudis Mestas, of Alameda; ap/ Jose Miguel Jaramillo & Annamaria Poblano; am/ Mariano Mestas & Guadalupe Chaves; gp/ Don Pedro Aranda & Rosalia Jaramillo, of los Ranchos.

MOYA, Maria Dolores
bap 23 Mar 1850, 2 days old; legit s/ Juan Andres Moya & Simona Sanchis, of this plaza; ap/ Juan Moya & Manuela Barela; am/ Mariano Sanchis & Francisca Gabaldon, from Albuquerque; gp/ Salbador Armijo & Plasida Armijo, of Albuquerque.

Frame 2388, #252
RUIS, Maria Soledad de los Dolores
bap 23 Mar 1850, 1 day old; legit d/ Francisco Ruis & Trinidad Apodaca, of this plaza; ap/ Atanacia Dominguez; am/ Juan Apodaca & Maria Ysabel Sanchis; gp/ Agustin Lobato & Quitira Gabaldon, all of the same place.

GUTIERRES, Jose Abraan
bap 24 Mar 1850, 5 days old; legit s/ Fernando Gutierres & Josefa Gonsales; ap/ not stated; am/ Juan Gonsales & Maria Antonia Armijo, of los Corrales; gp/ Felipe Garcia & Soledad Miera of Alameda.

DURAN, Maria de Jesus
bap 24 Mar 1850, 3 days old; legit d/ Jose Albino Duran & Juliana Roibal; ap/ Juan Duran & Juliana Garcia; am/ Ygnacio Roibal & Maria de Jesus Lujan, of Albuquerque; gp/ Jose Dolores Lucero & Petra Lucero, of the same place.

Frame 2389, #253
PEREA, Jose Maria de la Encarnacion
bap 28 Mar 1850, 2 days old; legit s/ Francisco Perea & Paula Sandobal; ap/ Rafael Perea & Carmel Romero; am/ Jose Sandobal & Petrona Sabedra, of Albuquerque; gp/ Salbador Martin & Dolores Torres, of the same place.

GARCIA, Maria Encarnacion
bap 28 Mar 1850, 4 days old; legit d/ Antonio Garcia & Polonia Salasar; ap/ Felix Garcia & Asencion Candelaria; am/ Jose Salazar & Miquela Garcia; gp/ Juan Carbajal & Anastacia Pacheco, of this plaza.

GUTIERRES, Juan
bap 29 Mar 1850, 8 days old; legit s/ Bicente Gutierres & Quiteria Sedillo, from San Antonio; ap/ Juan Gutierres & Manuela Mora; am/ Antonio Sedillo & Gregoria Otero; gp/ Juan Apodaca & Maria Antonia Gutierres, of this plaza.

Frame 2390, #254
MUÑIS, Maria Encarnacion
bap 30 Mar 1850, 6 days old; legit d/ Cristobal Muñis & Ana Maria Pacheco, of this plaza; ap/ Jose Maria Muñis & Barbara Samora; am/ Geronimo Pacheco & Pascuala Sanches; gp/ Francisco Gutierres & Candelaria Martin, of this plaza.

GURULE, Jose
bap 31 Mar 1850, 5 days old; legit s/ Jose Gurule & Dimas Serna; ap/ Maria Gurule; am/ Tomas Serna & Rafaela Garcia; gp/ Juan Gomes & Juliana Gonsales, of los Ranchos.

ALFAROS, Encarnacion
bap 2 Apr 1850, 3 days old; legit d/ Guadalupe Alfaros & Paula Garcia, of Alameda; ap/ Joaquin Alfaros & Juana Mata; am/ Juan Garcia & Manuela Perea; gp/ Jose Garcia & Marcelina Trujillo, of Alameda.

Frame 2391, #255
BACA, Juan Estanislado
bap 2 Apr 1850, 8 days old; legit s/ Manuel Baca & Guadalupe Garcia; ap/ Simon Baca & Lorensa Martin; am/ Antonio Garcia & Margarita Rael; gp/ Bartolo Martin & Maria Martin of Alameda.

ANALLA, Maria Ysidora
bap 5 Apr 1850, 4 days old; legit d/ Jose Analla & Teresa Herrera, residents of Atrisco; ap/ Manuel Analla & Ysidora Gonsales; am/ Juan Pablo Herrera & Guadalupe Candelaria; gp/ Pedro Lopes & Guadalupe Candelaria, of Atrisco.

NUANES, Donaciano
bap 5 Apr 1850, 6 days old; legit s/ Santiago Nuanes & Manuela Atencio, of los Candelarias; ap/ Ermenegildo Nuanes & Barbara Lopes; am/ Gaspar Atencio & Ysabel Candelaria; gp/ Manuel Candelaria & Francisca Candelaria, of San Antonio.

Frame 2392, #256
APODACA, Vicente Ferrer
bap 8 Apr 1850, 8 days old; legit s/ Pedro Apodaca & Maria de la Crus Perea of la Alameda; ap/ Jose Francisco Apodaca & Maria Antonia Garcia; am/ Bartolo Perea & Maria Josefa Candelaria; gp/ Pedro Antonio Perea, residents of la Alameda.

SAIS, Jesus Maria
bap 9 Apr 1850, 6 days old; legit s/ Jose Sais & Martina Trujillo, of Alameda; ap/ Salvador Sais & Juana Aragon; am/ Mariano Trujillo & Luisa Cordova; gp/ Antonio Gutierres & Juana Sandoval, of Alameda.

GRIEGO, Maria Francisca
bap 9 Apr 1850, 2 days old; legit d/ Andres Griego & Barbara Candelaria; ap/ Santiago Griego & Maria Valencia; am/ Juan Jose Candelaria & Andrea Gurule; gp/ Mariano Mercado & Gregoria Martin, residents of San Antonio.

Frame 2393, #257
SEDILLO, Maria
bap 9 Apr 1850, 5 days old; legit s/ Pedro Sedillo & Petra Jaramillo, of this plaza; ap/ Salbador Sedillo & Juana Nuanes; am/ Jose Jaramillo & Dolores Candelaria; gp/ Jose Gonsales & Maria Rosalia Nuanes, of San Antonio.

CORDOBA, Juan Bautista
bap 14 Apr 1850, 4 days old; natural s/ Juana Maria Cordoba, of Alameda; am/ Nicolas Cordova & Maria Ygnacia Duran; gp/ Jose Cordova & Tomasa Trugillo, of the same place.

MONTOLLA, Maria Polonia
bap 14 Apr 1850, 6 days old; legit d/ Juan Montolla & Gertrudis Sanchis, of Alameda; ap/ Dolores Sanchis & Encarnacion Gurule; am/ Pedro Montolla & Maria Luna; gp/ Bicente Montolla & Josefa Martin, of Corrales.

Frames 2393-2394, #258
CARABAJAL, Maria Petra
bap 18 Apr 1850, 5 days old; natural d/ Rosalia Carabajal, residents of this plaza; am/ Juan Pedro Carabajal & Gertrudis Gonsales; gp/ Juan Cedillo & Juana Carabajal, of the same place.

DURAN, Maria Monica
bap 4 May 1850, 2 days old; legit d/ Jesus Duran & Lugarda Samora, of this plaza; ap/ Francisco Duran & Lorensa Ramires; am/ Dolores Samora & Ana Maria Perea; gp/ Antonio Santillanes & Maria Santillanes, of the same place.

MOLLA, Jose Julian
bap 6 May 1850, 4 days old; legit s/ Jesus Molla & Maria Antonia Muriela, from Chilili; ap/ Grabiel Molla & Maria Urtada; am/ unknown; gp/ Jose Lucero & Maria Juliana Gallego, from the same place.

Frame 2395, #259
SANCHES, Maria Josefa de los Dolores
bap 7 May 1850, 4 days old; legit d/ Jose Sanches & Clara Chabes, residents of Atrisco; ap/ Gabriel Sanches & Juana Sedillo; am/ Antonio Chaves & Francisca Baldes; gp/ Eutimio Chaves & Josefa Chaves, of the same place.

SABEDRA, Maria Benina Librada
bap 7 May 1850, 6 days old; natural d/ Maria Dolores Sabedra, residents of Atrisco; am/ Maria de Luz Sabedra; gp/ Jose Luciano Ansures & Mariana Sandobal, of the same place.

LOPES, Jose
bap 8 May 1850, 6 days old; legit s/ Felipe Lopes & Juliana Torres, of los Griegos; ap/ Juan Lopes & Guadalupe Garcia; am/ unknown; gp/ Matias Armijo & Catarina Sabedra, of San Antonio.

APODACA, Meliton
bap 9 May 1850, 5 days old; legit s/ Juan Apodaca & Maria Garcia, of Alameda; ap/ Dionicio Apodaca & Luteria Garcia; am/ Juan Garcia & Leonarda Lopes; gp/ Jose Manuel Baca & Maria Apodaca, residents of the same.

Frame 2396, #260
GRIEGO, Jose Gregorio
bap 9 May 1850, 2 days old; legit s/ Miguel Griego & Jesus (cut off) Garcia; ap/ Jose Maria Griego & Guadalupe Mora; am/ Francisco Garcia & Manuela Gabaldon, of Balencia; gp/ Jesus Lucero & Barbara Torres, of los Griegos.

MARTIN, Jose Eliseo
bap 9 May 1850, 4 days old; legit s/ Felipe Martin & Juana Apodaca; ap/ Jose Antonio Martin & Quiteria Griego; am/ Rafael Apodaca & Juana Hilaria Romero, of Alameda; gp/ Felis Sanchis & Sabastiana Sena.

MONTAÑO, Manuel
bap 19 May 1850, 8 days old; legit s/ Lorenso Montaño & Maria Petra Candelaria, from los Ranchos; ap/ Antonio Montaño & Manuela Antonia Martines; am/ Vicente Candelaria & Anna Maria Chaves; gp/ Jesus Apodaca & Maria Consepcion Candelaria.

Frame 2397, #261
CANDELARIA, Maria Petra
bap 19 May 1850, 4 days old; legit d/ Rumualdo Candelaria & Maria Josefa Garcia, of los Duranes; ap/ Juan Cristobal Candelaria & Ysidora Garcia; am/ Diego Garcia & Ramona Candelaria; gp/ Andres Nuanes & Juana Nepumocena Armijo, all residents of los Duranes.

JARAMIO, Ysidora de la Luz
bap 19 May 1850, 4 days old; legit d/ Manuel Jaramio & Josefa Baca of los Poblanos; ap/ Bautista Jaramio & Encarnacion Garcia; am/ Juan Andres Baca & (not stated); gp/ Guadalupe Gutierres & Maria de los Angeles Ortega, of the same place.

SANCHES, Antonio Jose
bap 27 May 1850, 3 days old; legit s/ Jose Sanches & Ramona Castillo of los Corrales; ap/ Jose Sanches & Manuela Gallego; am/ Juan Castillo & Catarina Garcia; gp/ Pablo Griego & Maria Juana Montolla, of same place.

Frames 2397-2398, #262
SANDOVAL, Maria Alta Gracia
bap 27 May 1850, 4 days old; legit d/ Juan Sandoval & Maria Justa Garcia, of Albuquerque; ap/ Jose Sandoval & Petrona Sabedra; am/ Juan Guadalupe Garcia & Dolores Candelaria; gp/ Felipe Albarado & Alta Gracia Perea, of the same place.

SANDOBAL, Felipe Trinidad
bap 28 May 1850, 8 days old; natural s/ Manuela Sandobal, of Albuquerque; am/ Jose Sandobal & Francisca Lopes; gp/ Francisco Sabedra & Dolores Garcia, all of Albuquerque.

ANALLA, Manuel Antonio
bap 1 Jun 1850, 3 days old; legit s/ Felis Analla & Sisilia Barbero, of los Griegos; ap/ Martin Analla & Beatris Garcia; am/ Jesus Barbero & Ann Maria Gurule; gp/ Juan Lujan & Sesaria Analla, of San Antonio.

Frames 2398-2399, #263
BARELA, Manuel Antonio
bap 2 Jun 1850, 4 days old; legit s/ Anastacio Barela & Rafaela Garcia, of los Ranchos; ap/ Santiago Barela & Juana Aranda; am/ Tadeo Garcia & Jacinta Perea; gp/ Manuel Barela & Bicenta Gallego, of the same place.

GRIEGO, Maria de los Lagos
bap 16 Jun 1850, 4 days old; legit d/ Damacio Griego & Maria Manuela Carbajal, residents of Atrisco; ap/ Miguel Griego & Josefa Duran; am/ Domingo Carbajal & Toribia Sanches; gp/ Jose Maria Chabes & Dolores Chabes, residents of Atrisco.

GONSALES, Maria Antonia
bap 16 Jun 1850, 3 days old; legit d/ Ramon Gonsales & Francisca Padia, of Alameda; ap/ Juan Gonsales & Ana Maria Sandobal; am/ Santiago Padia & Maria Antonia Otero; gp/ Agustin Padia & Maria Dolores Gonsales, of Alameda.

Frames 2399-2400, #264
TAPIA, Maria Francisca
bap 16 Jun 1850, 6 days old; legit d/ Manuel Tapia & Antonia Armenta; ap/ Ygnacio Tapia & Juana Montaño; am/ Jose Maria Armenta & Ygnacia Martin; gp/ Jesus Lucero & Alfonsa Samora.

SAMORA, Maria Castola
bap 19 Jun 1850, 4 days old; d/ Jose Samora & Josefa Montaño, of Los Ranchos; ap/ Francisco Samora & Ygnacia Balencia; am/ Pedro Montaño & Nepomuceno Muñis; gp/ Jose Dolores Samora & Soledad Garcia.

GONSALES, Antonio
bap 21 Jun 1850, 5 days old; legit s/ Antonio Jose Gonsales & Juliana Gutierres, of Corrales; ap/ Jose Gonsales & Gertrudis Chabes; am/ Juan Gutierres & Rita Cordoba; gp/ Pablo Lucero & Catarino Lucero, of Corrales.

Frames 2400-2401, #265
GARCIA, Pablo Gregorio de la Trinidad
bap 28 Jun 1850, 3 days old; legit s/ Juan Garcia & Juana Maria Mestas, residents of Albuquerque; ap/ Felis Garcia & Ysabel Lopes; am/ Pedro Mestas & Maria Antonia Duran; gp/ Antonio Maria Garcia & Gregoria Garcia.

NS, Pedro Antonio
bap 4 Jul 1850, 2 days old; s/ unknown parents, left at the home of Agustin Lobato; gp/ Agustin Lobato & Quiteria Gabaldon.

GARCIA, Teofilo
bap 6 Jul 1850, 2 days old; legit s/ Luis Garcia & Paula Martin; ap/ Juan Jose Garcia & Maria Francisca Gallegos; am/ Jose Martin & Luciana Lucero, of Alameda; gp/ Rumaldo Montoya & Rosa Montoya.

ARIAS, Luciano
bap 7 Jul 1850, 6 days old; legit s/ Atanacio Arias & Ynes Sais; ap/ Pablo Arias & Encarnacion Balencia; am/ Alfonso Sais & Juana Mora, of Chilili; gp/ Miguel Espinosa & Peregrina Estrada, of Chilili.

Frame 2402, #266
GARCIA, Mariano
bap 7 Jul 1850, 3 days old; legit s/ Jose Garcia & Josefa Candelaria, residents of Atrisco; ap/ not stated; am/ Francisco Antonio Candelaria & Lorensa Padilla; gp/ Mariano Herrera & Maria de la Luz Herrera.

ALIRI, Maria
bap 8 Jul 1850, 2 days old; natural d/ Josefa Aliri, of San Antonio; am/ Jose Aliri & Teodora Sandoval; gp/ Jose Martin & Anastacia Bueno.

Frames 2402-2403, #267
CARABAJAL, Francisco Antonio de Padua
bap 20 Jul 1850, 5 days old; legit s/ Jose Carabajal & Maria del Rosario Zedillo, residents of Atrisco; ap/ Domingo Carabajal & Toribia Sanches; am/ Julian Sedillo & Sipriana Garcia, of the same; gp/ Jose Armijo & Beneranda Sanches, of Albuquerque.

GALLEGOS, Maria Josefa
bap 28 Jul 1850, 3 days old; legit d/ Antonio Gallegos & Maria Sanches, ap/ Rafael Gallegos & Barbara Gonsales; am/ Domingo Sanches & Maria de la Lus Candelaria, gp/ Juan Castillo & Rosalia Martin, residents of Alameda.

LUCERO, Feliciano
bap 3 Aug 1850, 2 days old; legit s/ Juan Lucero & Juana Apodaca; ap/ Tomas Lucero & Dolores Valencia; am/ Gregorio Apodaca & Barbara Samora; gp/ Dolores Samora & Soledad Garcia, of los Gallegos.

Frames 2403-2404, #268
GONSALES, Jose
bap 7 Aug 1850, 3 days old; legit s/ Jose Gonsales & Maria Francisca Santillanes; ap & am/ not stated; gp/ Paulina Aldas & Juana Maria Baca, of los Ranchos.

APODACA, Maria Rosalia
bap 11 Aug 1850, 3 days old; legit d/ Mariano Apodaca & Manuela Gonsalez, of San Mateo; ap/ Francisco Apodaca & Maria Antonia Garcia; am/ Juan Cristobal Gonsales & Petra Martines; gp/ Jose Maria Sanches & Maria Martina Sanches, of the same place.

LOPES, Maria Trinidad
bap 11 Aug 1850, 4 days old; legit d/ Julio Lopes & Rita Gutierres, residents of this parish; ap/ Mateo Lopes & Manuela Chaves; am/ Antonio Gutierres & Ruperta Lopes; gp/ Teodoro Lopes & Josefa Chabes, of the same place.

Frames 2404-2405, #269
TRUGILLO, Maria del Pilar
bap 11 Aug 1850, 3 days old; legit d/ Mariano Trugillo & Maria Claudia Sandobal, of Alameda; ap/ Mariano Trugillo & Maria Luisa Cordoba; am/ Pedro Sandobal & Juana Chaves; gp/ Jesus Maria Trugillo & Lorensa Lucero, of the same place.

GARCIA, Maria Manuela
bap 8 Aug 1850, 2 days old; legit d/ Juan Garcia & Andrea Noanes, residents of this parish; ap/ Juan Luis Garcia & Maria Gertrudis Griego; am/ Guadalupe Noanes & Maria Antonia Garcia; gp/ Francisco Lucero & Manuela Aragon.

CARABAJAL, Jose Bibian
bap 18 Aug 1850, 3 days old; legit s/ Juan Pedro Carabajal & Gertrudis Gonsales, of this plaza; ap/ Lorenzo Carabajal & Quiterna Sandobal; am/ Manuel Gonsales & Toribia Garcia; gp/ Nepomuceno Caravajal & Anastacia Pacheco, of the same place.

Frames 2405-2406, #270
TAFOYA, Antonio Jose
bap 20 Aug 1850, 2 days old; legit s/ Domingo Tafoya & Ana Maria Martin, of Alameda; ap/ Juan Ygnacio Tafoya & Antonia (smeared); ap/ Antonio Jose Martin & Maria Luciana Lu(cut off); gp/ Antonio Jose Martin & Luciana Luc(cut off), residents of Alameda.

MARTIN, Jose Anastacio
bap 25 Aug 1850, 3 days old; legit s/ Jose Martin & Gertrudis Nieto, of los Ranchos; ap/ Jose Martin & Rosalia Lucero; am/ Maria Nieto; gp/ Jesus Barela & Vicenta Gallegos, of los Ranchos.

MARTIN, Juana Maria Nepomocena
bap 26 Aug 1850, 6 days old; legit d/ Mariano Martin & Bictoria Duran, of los Ranchos of Albuquerque; ap/ Felipe Martin & Francisca Mora; am/ Salvador Duran & Gertrudis Garcia, of the same place; gp/ Bonifacio Garcia & Maria Garcia, of the same place.

Frames 2406-2407, #271
SALASAR, Maria Ecelsa
bap 26 Aug, 3 days old; legit d/ Juan Salasar & Maria Paula Garcia; ap/ Ygnacio Salasar & Encarnacion Guerrero; am/ Francisco Garcia & Maria Relles Candelaria; gp/ Santiago Perea & Maria Jesus Jaramillo, all residents of Alameda.

ARAGON, Maria Luisa
bap 28 Aug 1850, 3 days old; legit d/ Juan Aragon & Maria de Jesus Lujan, residents of Albuquerque; ap/ Jose Aragon & no knowledge of grandmother; am/ Jose Maria Lujan & Dolores Duran; gp/ Tomas Lopes & Maria Lujan, residents of Albuquerque.

APODACA, Antonio Jose
bap 31 Aug 1850, 4 days old; legit s/ Seledon Apodaca & Luz Saabedra, residents of Albuquerque; ap/ Roman Apodaca & Manuela Candelaria; am/ Pablo Saabedra & Gertrudis Lopes; gp/ Antonio Garcia & Teresa Garcia, of the same place.

Frames 2407-2408, #272
ARAGON, Maria Dolores
bap 31 Aug 1850, 6 days old; natural d/ Juana Rafela Aragon; am/ Juan Andres Aragon & Manuela Brito, residents of Ranchos de Albuquerque; gp/ Juan Griego & Ysabel Gurule, residents of same.

LUCERO, Trinidad
bap 2 Sep 1850, 6 days old; legit s/ Jose de las Nieves Lucero & Eulogia Sabedra, of this plaza; ap/ Andres Lucero & Maria de la Lus Chaves; am/ Francisco Sabedra & Tomasa Garcia; gp/ Bibian Sabedra & Manuela Romero, of Atrisco.

GONZALES, Maria Antonina
bap 2 Sep 1850, 5 days old; legit d/ Jose Ygnacio Gonzales & Concepcion Apodaca, of Alameda; ap/ Crus Gonzales & Maria de Jesus Molla; am/ Dionicio Apodaca & Luteria Garcia; gp/ Pedro Martin & Gertrudis Apodaca, of Alameda.

Frame 2409, #273
ROMERO, Diego Antonio
bap 4 Sep 1850, 3 days old; legit s/ Lorenso Romero & Maria Sandobal, of Alameda; ap/ Diego Romero
& Encarnacion Valencia; am/ Juan Domingo Sandobal & Concepcion Montolla; gp/ Jose Maria Sandobal
& Teresa Luna, of Alameda.

LUCERO, Jose
bap 4 Sep 1850, 5 days old; legit s/ Atanacio Lucero & Geralda Griego; ap/ Juan Lucero & Manuela
Griego; am/ Jose Miguel Griego & Dolores Garcia; gp/ Juan Pablo Gutierres & Josefa Martin, of
Candelaria.

Frames 2409-2410, #274
GALLEGO, Luisa
bap 5 Sep 1850, 8 days old; legit d/ Andres Gallego & Maria Ysabel Jaramillo; ap/ Antonio Gallego &
Maria Antonia Chaves; am/ Ygnacio Jaramillo & Paula Armijo; gp/ Antonio Jose Sanches & Maria
Miquela Gallegos, of Bernalillo.

MONTOLLA, Maria Trinidad
bap 8 Sep 1850, 6 days old; legit d/ Anastacio Montolla & Juana Baca; ap & am/ not stated; gp/ Pablo
Montaño & Josefa Montolla.

CANDELARIA, Donaciana
bap 25 Sep 1850, 8 days old; legit d/ Manuel Candelaria & Juana Garcia, of los Griegos; ap/ Vicente
Candelaria & Relles Griego; am/ Juan Pablo Garcia & Gregoria Garcia; gp/ Tomas Griego & Monica
Contreras, of the same place.

Frames 2410-2411, #275
PACHECO, Jose Miguel
bap 29 Sep 1850, 5 days old; s/ Juan Pacheco & Juliana Gutierres, of Alameda; ap/ Francisco Pacheco &
Juana Gonsales; am/ Salbador Gutierres & Manuela Gallegos; gp/ Francisco Mata & Luisa Lucero, of
Alameda.

TRUGILLO, Maria Mauricia
bap 29 Sep 1850, 8 days old; legit d/ Nicanor Trugillo & Gregoria Garcia, from Carnue; ap/ Antonio
Trugillo & Manuela Samora; am/ Simon Garcia & Gregoria Padilla; gp/ Jose Garcia & Damacia Garcia,
from Albuquerque.

PADILLA, Perfiliana de los Dolores
bap 29 Sep 1850, 6 days old; legit d/ Juan Jose Padilla & Manuela Aguirre, of this plaza; ap/ Diego
Antonio Padia & Barvara Aguirre; am/ Juan Gallegos & Manuela Gurule, of the same place; gp/ Jesus
Gallegos & Manuela Gurule.

Frames 2411-2412, #276
RAEL, Miguel Antonio
bap 29 Sep 1850, 10 days old; natural s/ Victoria Rael, of Corrales; am/ Juan Rael & Maria Gurule of
Ranchos de Albuquerque; gp/ Jose Maria Lusero & Tomasa Lucero, of the same place.

NOANES, Jose Ygnacio
bap 29 Sep 1850, 6 days old; s/ Andres Noanes & Juana Armijo, of los Candelarias; ap/ Jose Miguel Noanes & Andrea Candelaria; am/ Cristobal Armijo & Marilda Barrera, of the same place; gp/ Lino Samora & Soledad Garcia.

GONSALES, Maria Tomasa
bap 29 Sep 1850, 11 days old; natural d/ Maria Rosa Gonsales; am/ Juan de Jesus Gonsales & Tomasa Aragon, from Alameda; gp/ Jose Dolores Padia & Ana Maria Gurule.

Frames 2412-2413, #277
MONTOLLA, Juan
bap 2 Oct 1850, 6 days old; legit s/ Atanacio Montolla & Margarita Mares, of Candelaria; ap/ Juan Montolla & Soledad Ortega; am/ Nicolas Mares & Manuela Garcia; gp/ Nicolas Mares & Clara Montolla, of the same place.

GRIEGO, Francisco
bap 6 Oct 1850, 8 days old; legit s/ Rumaldo Griego & Candelaria Montolla, residents of los Barelas; ap/ Pablo Griego & Ysidora Apodaca; am/ Rafael Montolla & Gertrudis Chaves; gp/ Cristobal Armijo & Cornelia Montoya, of this plaza.

GONSALES, Santos Cornelio
bap 7 Oct 1850, 4 days old; legit s/ Luis Gonsales & Maria de Jesus Lucero; ap/ Vicente Gonsales & Bibiana Chaves; am/ Manuel Lucero & Francisca Garcia; gp/ Miguel Gurule & Concepcion Chaves, residents of Chilili.

Frames 2413-2414, #278
ARAGON, Maria Ygnacia
bap 10 Oct 1850, 8 days old; legit d/ Nepomuceno Aragon & Maria Antonia Guerra; ap/ Juan de Jesus Aragon & Rosalia Gonsales; am/ Manuel Guerra & Barbara Santillanes; gp/ Juan Gonsales & Polonia Guerra, residents of Alameda.

BACA, Jose Bonifacio
bap 16 Oct 1850, 10 days old; legit s/ Jose Baca & Trinidad Garcia, residents of Atrisco; ap/ Juan Baca & Rafaela Trujillo; am/ Juan Manuel Garcia & Manuela Perea; gp/ Jose Apodaca & Manuela Apodaca, residents of Alameda.

GARCIA, Polinario
bap 16 Oct 1850, 6 days old; natural s/ Tomasa Garcia, of this plaza; am/ Jose Garcia & Bibiana Candelaria; gp/ Polinario Perea & Francisca Tafolla, of this town.

Frame 2415, #279
GARCIA, Maria Brigida
bap 17 Oct 1850, 8 days old; legit d/ Juan Garcia & Dolores Chaves, residents of Atrisco; ap/ Juan de Jesus Garcia & Rosa Folanca; am/ Antonio Chaves & Manuela Garcia; gp/ Jose Maria Sanches & Ysidora Herrera, of the same place.

MARTIN, Maria Guadalupe
bap 17 Oct 1850, 8 days old; natural d/ Estefana Martin; adopted by Gertrudis Sanches; am/ Pablo Martin & Gertrudis Sanches; gp/ Juan Jose Garcia & Manuela Sandobal, of this plaza.

SANCHES, Jose Solomon
bap 19 Oct 1850, 5 days old; legit s/ Cristobal Sanches & Concepcion Valencia, of los Ranchos de Albuquerque; ap/ Felipe Sanches & Annamaria Trujillo; am/ Juan Domingo Valencia & Maria Ygnacia Salazar; gp/ Torribio Trujillo & Petra Trujillo, of los Ranchos.

Frame 2416, #280
Notation, "end of book."

NS, Pedro Antonio
bap 4 Jul 1850, 2 days old; s/ unknown parents, left at the home of Agustin Lobato; gp/ Agustin Lobato & Quiteria Gabaldon.

INDEX OF BAPTISMS – CHILDREN/ADULTS

NOTE: Same names on a page, but with different familial information, are indicated by (1) or (2) following the name.

Maria Vitoriana, 170
Maria Ygnacia, 41
Meliton, 341
Nestor, 237
Pedro Antonio, 50
Reyes, 260
Rumaldo, 152
Selsa de Jesus, 267
Vicente Ferrer, 340
Ysidora, 89
Ysidro Antonio, 22
ARAGON
Ana Maria Agapita, 140
Antonio, 139
Antonio Jose, 225
Jesus Maria, 230
Jose Dario, 14
Jose de Jesus, 182
Jose de los Relles, 66
Jose Norberto, 134
Josefa, 321
Juan de Jesus, 84
Juan Vicente, 283
Lorenzo, 215
Maria Barbara, 181
Maria Barbara de los Dolores, 12
Maria del Rallo Gertrudis, 94
Maria Dolores, 345
Maria Felipe Valeria, 43
Maria Francisca, 318
Maria Luisa, 345
Maria Miquela, 269
Maria Monica, 224
Maria Teresa de Jesus, 12
Maria Tomasa, 337
Maria Venigna, 274
Maria Ygnacia, 347
Mariano, 262
Miguel Antonio, 85
ARANDA
Antonio Jose Bernabe, 57
Jose, 204
Jose Antonio, 6
Josefa, 290, 330
Josefa Ygnacia de la Cruz, 77
Maria Antonia Fabiana, 164
Maria Josefa, 34
Maria Manuela, 297
Maria Teresa de Jesus, 122
Maria Vicenta del Rayo, 155
Soledad Bartola, 45

ARCHIBEQUE. *See also* ARCHIVEQUE;
ARCHIVIQUE
Jose Clemente, 100
Jose Francisco Carso, 133
Maria del Rallo, 105
Maria Justa, 260
Pablo Antonio, 180
ARCHIVEQUE. *See also* ARCHIBEQUE
Maria Begnina, 137
ARCHIVIQUE. *See also* ARCHIBEQUE
Ana Maria, 42
ARCHULETA
Jose Melquiades, 331
Juliana, 319
Maria Monica, 44
Maria Ramona de los Dolores, 46
Pedro, 152
Salbador Manuel, 116
ARELLANES
Maria Francisca, 321
ARIAS
Bibian, 288
Jesus Marcos, 312
Jose Antonio, 145
Jose Antonio de Jesus, 123
Jose Ricardo, 285
Jose Simon, 18, 267
Juan Andres, 48
Juan Antonio, 49
Juana Catarina, 150
Luciano, 343
Maria Antonia, 324
Maria Jesus, 204
Maria Josefa, 166, 265
Maria Rosalia, 105
Maria Rufina, 80
Maria Rufina Cesaria, 167
Maria Trinidad, 19
Maria Ygnacia, 179
Pedro Jose, 31, 202
ARMENTA
Carlota, 290
Jose Bentura, 192
Jose Militon, 315
Jose Tomas, 301
Juan Jose, 271
Maria Josefa, 282
Maria Petra, 231
ARMIJO
Ambrocio de Jesus, 114
Ana Maria, 214

Marcial Librado, 307
Maria Albina, 162
Maria Aniceta, 108
Maria del Rallo, 78
Maria del Rallo de Jesus, 84
Maria Dolores, 33
Maria Eluteria, 55
Maria Francisca, 62
Maria Geronima, 114
Maria Gertrudis, 269
Maria Josefa, 227
Maria Juana, 92, 172
Maria Juliana, 99
Maria Leonore, 326
Maria Manuela, 202
Maria Perfecta, 266
Maria Petra, 165
Maria Quirina, 127
Maria Rafaela, 60
Maria Rosa, 176
Maria Soledad, 198
Maria Soledad Natividad, 177
Maria Teodora, 253
Maria Teresa de Jesus, 12
Martin de Jesus, 335
Maximo, 196
Miguel de Altagracia, 306
Rumaldo, 137
Salbador Antonio, 3, 129
Teresa, 230
BACHICHA
Maria Lina Alta Gracia, 194
Maria Macedonia, 310
Salvador Antonio, 232
BALDES. *See also* VALDES
Miguel Antonio, 114
BALDONADO. *See also* MALDONADO
Antonio Jose, 194
Jose Seberiano, 300
Juan Pablo, 154
Juan Ygnacio, 223
BALENCIA. *See also* VALENCIA
Jose Miguel, 172
Juan Esteban, 60
Juan Pablo, 183
Juana de los Reyes, 221
Maria Placida, 206
Maria Vitoriana, 284
BALLEJOS. *See also* VAYEJOS
Jose de la Luz, 238

BARELA. *See also* VARELA
Ana Maria Magdalena, 10
Andrea, 149, 246
Antonia Teresa, 262
Barbara, 186
Filomena, 220
Jose Desiderio Romulo, 201
Jose Francisco, 226
Jose Rafael, 98
Juan Antonio, 156
Juan Antonio Aban, 253
Juan Esteban, 217
Juana, 188
Manuel Antonio, 342
Manuel Gregorio, 13
Maria Candelaria, 299
Maria Cleofes, 267
Maria Gabriela, 168
Maria Josefa, 168
Maria Monica, 252
Maria Petronila de los Dolores, 56
Mariano Luis, 186
Pedro Nolasco, 152
BAROS. *See also* VAROS
Juan Nepomuseno, 214
Varbaro, 279
BARRANCA
Jose Nicanor, 196
BARREDAS
Damacia Daria, 316
BARRERAS
Jose Antonio, 114
Jose Benigno, 281
Juan Nepomuceno Crisostano, 227
BARRIO. *See also* BARRIOS
Visente Perfecto, 21
BARRIOS. *See also* BARRIO
Maria Antonia, 49
BENABIDES. *See also* BENAVIDES;
BENEBIDES
Maria del Rallo Clara, 116
Rosa, 193
Seferina, 273
BENAVIDES. *See also* BENABIDES
Benigna, 242
BENEBIDES. *See also* BENABIDES
Jesus Maria, 154
BERNAL
Manuel Antonio, 190
Maria Gertrudis Eutemia, 283

Jose Justo, 219
Jose Luciano, 240
Jose Mariano, 294
Jose Modesto, 304
Jose Ramon, 184
Jose Rumaldo, 263
Jose Sacramento, 232
Jose Vicente, 6
Juan Cristobal, 35
Juan de Dios, 200
Juan Jose de los Dolores, 180
Juan Pedro, 8
Juana, 176
Juana Maria, 7
Juana Rufina, 197
Manuel Antonio, 325
Marcos, 221
Maria Antonio, 325
Maria Barbara, 236
Maria Benina, 169
Maria Candelaria, 239
Maria Catarina, 8
Maria Clara, 283
Maria de la Luz, 176
Maria Estefana, 242
Maria Faustina, 201
Maria Filomena, 289
Maria Francisca, 167, 321
Maria Librada de los Dolores, 264
Maria Rosalia, 150
Maria Trinidad, 16
Pablo, 174
Polidoro Romulo, 201
Tomasa, 203
Venceslado, 332
Vitor Bensenlao, 167
Yldefonso Desiderio, 136
Ysabel, 275
CHAVEZ. *See also* CAVEZ; CHAVES
    Eulogio, 41
    Jesus Maria Jose, 40
    Jose Eleuterio, 33
    Jose Gabriel Eleuterio, 50
    Jose Rafael, 27
    Juan Crisanto, 27
    Juana, 316
    Juana Maria, 5
    Maria Benigna, 51
    Maria Francisca, 51
    Maria Gertrudis, 45
    Maria Merced, 303

Visente Perfecto, 16
CHRESPIN. *See also* CRESPIN
    Jose Francisco Cornelio, 130
    Maria Paula, 87
CISNERO. *See also* SISNERO
    Jose Tomas Anisteo, 101
CONTRERAS
    Juan Christobal, 128
    Maria Guadalupe, 28, 162
    Maria Ysidora, 56
CORDOBA. *See also* CORDOVA
    Ana Maria de Jesus, 62
    Antonio Jose Quirino, 173
    Eligia Lucia, 262
    Francisco de la Encarnacion, 89
    Jesus Maria, 79
    Jose Agapito, 319
    Jose Meliton, 309
    Juan Bautista, 341
    Juan de Dios, 122
    Maria Benina de los Dolores, 154
    Maria Encarnacion Susana, 328
    Maria Francisca, 96, 194
    Maria Leonor, 207
    Maria Micaela, 73
    Maria Nicolasa, 114
    Maria Polonia, 85
    Maria Rufina, 167, 171
    Pedro, 145
CORDOVA. *See also* CORDOBA
    Anna Maria Nestora, 265
    Apolonio, 237
    Jose Eliseo, 201
    Jose Maria, 8
    Jose Maria Nabonor, 45
    Jose Ygnacio, 46
    Maria Edubigen, 209
    Maria Exselsa, 238
    Maria Gertrudis, 295
    Maria Gregoria, 300
    Maria Juana, 136
    Maria Marcelina, 227
    Maria Merced, 223
    Simon, 34
CORIZ
    Juliana, 302
CRESPIN. *See also* CHRESPIN
    Jose Antonio, 333
    Jose Pablo Estanislao, 240
    Maria Petra, 159
    Maria Veneranda Eulogia de la Luz, 280

Antonio Abad, 181
Antonio Maria, 126
Cipriano, 39
Diego Antonio, 346
Francisca, 35
Francisco de Paula, 35
Jesus Maria y Jose, 60
Jose Amador, 90
Jose Anastacio, 2, 52
Jose Bonicio, 307
Jose de Jesus, 222
Jose Estanislao, 10
Jose Feliz, 270
Jose Francisco, 206
Jose Maria, 81
Jose Mateo, 51
Jose Melquiades, 309
Jose Nestor, 192
Jose Octabiano, 251
Jose Teodoro, 107
Jose Teofilo, 257
Jose Venceslado, 278
Jose Venito Abad, 284
Juan Antonio, 14
Juan Christobal Eulogio, 157
Julian Antonio, 115
Julian de Jesus, 80
Manuel, 185
Maria Albina, 105
Maria Barbara, 110
Maria del Rallo, 81, 90
Maria Encarnacion, 71
Maria Gregoria, 153
Maria Josefa Ygnacia, 1
Maria Luisa, 332
Maria Polonia, 83
Maria Rafaela, 256
Maria Rafaela de los Dolores, 293
Maria Ramona, 121
Maria Rosalia, 14
Maria Tomasa, 337
Maria Valvina, 34
Maria Ygnacia, 151
Maria Ysidora, 9
Miguel, 198
Nicolas, 243
RONQUILLO
Maria Patricia de la Soledad, 303
RUBI
Jose, 202

RUIBAL
Jose Albino, 320
Jose Ynes, 334
RUIS. *See also* RUIZ
Jesus Maria Trinidad, 186
Jose Manuel Esquipulo, 324
Leocardo Melquiades Nepomuceno, 29
Loecadio, 29
Maria Juana, 297
Maria Soledad de los Dolores, 339
Romualdo, 4
RUIZ. *See also* RUIS
Manuel Melquides, 70

SABEDRA. *See also* SAVEDRA
Ambrocio, 205
Ana Maria, 10
Benito, 303
Elogia, 245
Jose Anastacio, 334
Jose Miguel, 154
Jose Nabor, 10
Jose Nestor, 141
Juan Jesus, 149
Manuel Antonio, 317, 338
Manuel Trinidad, 322
Maria Antonia, 141
Maria Barbara Candelaria, 100
Maria Benina Librada, 341
Maria de la Luz de los Dolores, 202
Maria Esperidion, 297
Maria Francisca, 264
Maria Grabiela, 82
Maria Josefa de los Dolores, 341
Maria Miquela de los Dolores, 177
Maria Petrona, 305
Maria Rosa, 55
Maria Tomasa, 92, 215
Nestor, 265
Paubla, 202
Pedro Antonio, 277
Placida, 164
Teodocio, 212
SAENS. *See also* SAISN; SANIS
Juan Jose, 238
Juana Maria, 242
Maria Canuta, 298
SAES. *See also* SAEZ; SAIS
Lazaro, 14
SAEZ. *See also* SAIS
Juan Andres, 33

Jose Francisco Antonio, 69
Jose Gabriel, 153
Jose Geronimo, 115
Jose Guadalupe, 161
Jose Leon, 285
Jose Maria, 80
Jose Mariano Ruperto, 204
Jose Mauricio, 194
Jose Melquiades, 108
Jose Pablo, 32, 317
Jose Patricio de Jesus, 302
Jose Placido, 275
Jose Refugio, 191
Jose Santos, 245
Jose Solomon, 348
Jose Tomas, 14, 105
Jose Toribio, 125
Jose Victorino, 4
Jose Ynocencio Mellisos, 233
Juan Antonio, 327
Juan Felipe, 32
Juan Jose, 147, 228
Juan Nepomenceno, 172
Juan Nepomuceno Francisco Trinidad, 43
Juan Ynocencio, 233
Juana, 324
Juana Josefa Ygnacia, 36
Juana Maria, 82, 97
Juana Maria de Rallo, 134
Juliana, 254
Lorensa, 185
Luz, 26
Manuel, 150
Manuel Antonio, 130, 155, 203
Maria, 153
Maria Antonia, 3
Maria Borga, 301
Maria Catarina, 111
Maria Clara, 124, 145
Maria de Altagracia, 84
Maria de la Paz, 175
Maria de la Piedad, 251
Maria de los Angeles, 173
Maria de los Dolores, 79
Maria de los Dolores Paulina, 9
Maria de Rayo, 311
Maria del Refugio, 118
Maria Erinea, 276
Maria Francisca, 11, 232
Maria Gertrudes de los Dolores, 87
Maria Guadalupe, 153

Maria Jacoba, 70
Maria Josefa, 149
Maria Josefa de Jesus, 228
Maria Josefa de los Dolores, 341
Maria Juana, 76, 217
Maria Leonor, 205
Maria Luisa del Rosaria Celestina, 143
Maria Manuela de Jesus, 29
Maria Marcelina de Jesus, 17
Maria Petra Francisca, 92
Maria Petronila de Refugio, 276
Maria Quirina, 173
Maria Regina, 26
Maria Rosalia, 253
Maria Rufina, 50
Maria Simona, 244
Maria Soledad del Rayo, 193
Maria Teodoria Marcelina, 56
Maria Teresa de Jesus, 110
Maria Tomasa, 87
Maria Veneranda Nepomucena, 275
Maria Victoria Dolores, 239
Maria Ysabel, 65
Maria Ysabel del Carmen, 331
Martiana, 312
Miguel Antonio, 184
Nestor, 258
Nicolas, 311
Pedro, 171
Pedro Antonio, 86
Rafaela, 258
Salbador Antonio, 84
Salbador Manuel, 260
Santiago, 59
Teodocio, 288
Teodoro Caciano, 170
Teresa de Jesus, 219
Tomasa, 291
Trinidad, 277
Ysidro de la Trinidad, 55
SANCHEZ. *See also* SANCHES
   Jose Nestor, 50
   Luis Jose, 211
   Manuel Antonio, 330
   Maria Marcelina, 1
SANCHIS. *See also* SANCHES
   Jose Andres, 299
   Jose Antonio, 298
   Jose Manuel Vicente, 298
   Maria Josefa, 298

NOTE: Same names of a page but with different familial information, are indicated by (1) or (2) following the name.

Salvador, 132
Sesaria, 264, 319
Sipriana, 208
Soledad, 135
Tomas, 20
Victoria, 22
Vitoriano, 315
Ysidro, 14
ANSURES. *See also* ANSURIS; ANZURES
Juana, 268
Juana Catarina, 9
Luciano, 56
Perfecta, 307
Rafael, 105, 140
Rafaela, 31
Teodora, 180
ANSURIS. *See also* ANSURES
Agustin, 293
ANZURES. *See also* ANSURES
Rafael, 52
APODACA
Antonio, 85, 89
Barbara, 1, 20, 36, 69, 130, 194, 264
Bartolo, 309
Barvara, 242
Bicente, 93
Catalina, 155
Catarina, 277, 330
Christoval, 56
Concepcion, 313, 345
Cristobal, 45
Deluvina, 331
Dionicio, 304
Dolores, 225, 232, 252, 286
Encarnacion, 4, 74, 336
Francisca, 153, 232, 260
Francisco, 8, 33, 58, 96, 154, 194, 197, 325
Gertrudes, 290
Gertrudis, 10, 39, 232
Gregoria, 329
Gregorio, 4, 170, 199, 218, 267
Guadalupe, 333
Isabel, 264
Jesus, 208
Jose, 296, 317
Jose Antonio, 57, 159, 283
Jose Bentura, 153
Jose Francisco, 64, 182, 258
Jose Manuel, 148
Jose Maria, 320
Jose Miguel, 70

Josefa, 10, 40, 66, 118, 158
Juan, 20, 43, 71, 76, 131, 132, 142, 164, 174, 203, 241, 256, 295, 296, 299, 311, 324, 331, 341
Juan Antonio, 30, 50
Juan Antonio (1), 148
Juan Antonio (2), 148
Juan Cristobal, 331
Juan de Dios, 299
Juan Jose, 36, 260
Juana, 261, 295, 299, 318, 342, 344
Juana Nepomucena, 51
Julian, 22, 54, 129, 168, 215
Leonicio, 71
Leuteria, 304
Lino, 248, 278
Lionicio, 204
Manuela, 56, 251, 322
Maria Bernardina, 51
Maria Dolores, 258
Maria Francisca, 185
Maria Gertrudis, 266
Maria Juana, 277
Maria Petra, 151
Maria Ygnes, 198
Maria Ysabel, 167, 201
Maria Ysidora, 29
Mariano, 344
Pablo, 53, 102, 145, 338
Pedro, 295, 340
Petra, 39, 90, 307
Quirina, 295
Rafael, 18, 32, 34, 70, 80, 84, 111, 141, 152, 230
Ramon, 22, 178
Roman, 249
Salbador, 107, 152, 189
Salvador, 41
Santos, 155, 237
Seledon, 345
Simon, 240, 276, 314
Simona, 218
Tomasa, 196, 230, 323
Trinidad, 276, 297, 339
Vitalia, 280
Ynes, 101
Ysabel, 58, 103, 146, 304
ARAGON
Aban, 215
Ana Maria, 206
Anna Maria, 284, 318

Antonio, 43
Catarina, 196
Concepcion, 237
Consepcion, 207
Dario, 337
Eusebio, 84, 134
Francisca, 38, 63
Gertrudis, 247
Jesus, 110
Jose Manuel, 224, 230, 269
Jose Maria, 262
Jose Miguel, 12
Josefa, 213
Juan, 345
Juan Andres, 12, 85
Juan de Jesus, 66
Juan Rafael, 14, 140, 182, 225
Juana, 140, 183, 197
Juana Lorensa, 115, 158, 282
Juana Rafaela, 126, 163, 212, 248, 274, 292
Juana Rafela, 345
Lorenza, 317
Luisa, 187
Manuela, 7, 89, 127, 166, 204, 321
Marcelino, 283, 318
Maria, 78
Maria Angela, 65
Maria de Jesus, 31, 299
Maria Gertrudis, 181
Maria Jesus, 190
Maria Juana, 144
Maria Luisa, 148, 263
Maria Manuela, 167
Maria Petra, 216
Maria Ysabel, 207
Martin, 139
Nepomuceno, 347
Petra, 252
Rafael, 94
Rafaela, 83
Rosalia, 66
ARANDA
Francisco, 164, 204
Jose Antonio, 290, 330
Juan Christobal, 57
Juan Cristobal, 34
Juan Cristoval, 6
Juana, 10, 276
Paula, 330
Pedro, 45, 77, 122, 155, 297
Soledad, 319

ARCHIBEQUE. *See also* ARCHIVEQUE;
    ARCHIVIQUE
Josefa, 180
Marcelino, 100
Maria, 326
Maria Josefa, 265
Marselino, 133
Matias, 105
Vitoria, 260
ARCHIVEQUE. *See also* ARCHIBEQUE
Juan, 137
ARCHIVIQUE. *See also* ARCHIBEQUE
Matias, 42
ARCHULETA
Agustin, 46
Juana Maria, 83, 245
Manuela, 30
Mateo, 44, 116
Miquela, 322
Pedro, 152
Ramon, 331
Silberia, 12
Vicente, 319
ARELLANES
Teodoro, 321
ARIAS
Ana Maria, 46, 72, 128, 169, 210, 238, 323
Anna Maria, 266
Atanacio, 166, 202, 343
Atencio, 265
Bitoria, 261
Christobal, 80
Concepcion, 179, 267, 294
Decideria, 252, 309
Dolores, 150, 195, 242
Florencio, 324
Francisco, 288
Juan, 18
Juan Christoval, 123
Juan Cristobal, 31, 48, 167, 204
Juan Domingo, 19, 49, 105, 150
Juana, 156, 189, 208
Juana Maria, 152, 185
Loreta, 74, 199, 235, 262
Manuel, 312
Maria Loreta, 120
Maria Teresa, 262
Maria Ysidora, 220
Petrona, 229
Salbador, 285
Teodora, 104

Maria, 323
Maria Dolores, 10
Maria Francisca, 24
Maria Lorensa, 269
Mariano, 224, 310
Marselina, 164, 184
Miguel, 36
Pablo, 33, 55, 92
Pascuala, 205, 236, 265
Rafaela, 5
Ramon, 59, 177, 198, 229
Refugio, 144, 176
Reyes, 30
Rosalia, 141, 227
Rufina, 297
Sabino, 78, 192
Simon, 34, 60, 162, 202
BACHICHA
Manuel, 194, 232
Ramon, 310
BALDES. *See also* VALDES
Antonio, 114
BALDONADO. *See also* MALDONADO
Ancelmo, 300
Anselmo, 223
Antonio Jose, 154
Juan Antonio, 194
Rosalia, 178, 206
BALENCIA. *See also* VALENCIA
Bernardo, 183, 206, 284
Dolores, 190
Encarnacion, 157
Juan, 60, 172, 221
Maria Concepcion, 153
BALLEJO. *See also* BALLEJOS
Petrona, 148
BALLEJOS. *See also* BALLEJO; VAYEJOS
Ana Maria, 111
Guadalupe, 72, 108
Josefa, 20
Petra, 148
Santos, 238
BARBERA
Rosa, 30
BARBERO
Sisilia, 342
BARELA. *See also* BARRELA; VARELA
Anastacio, 156, 188, 252, 342
Antonio, 13, 98, 152, 186, 226
Antonio Abad, 56
Antonio Aban, 253

Jesus, 201
Manuel, 149, 168, 186, 220, 246, 267
Maria Manuela, 64
Maria Tomasa, 33
Pablo, 262, 299
Paublo, 217
Rosalia, 18, 149, 183, 218, 248
Santiago, 10
Tomasa, 8, 96, 154, 194
BAROS. *See also* VAROS
Juan Nepomuceno, 279
Juana, 19
Ramon, 214
BARRANCA
Felipe, 196
BARREDAS
Francisco, 316
BARRELA. *See also* BARELA
Rosalia, 104
Tomaza, 58
BARRERAS
Francisco, 227, 281
Guadalupe, 44, 69, 106, 192, 237
Ysidro, 114
BARRIO. *See also* BARRIOS
Jose, 21
BARRIOS. *See also* BARRIO
Jose, 49
BASAN. *See also* VASAN
Maria de la Lus, 210
Maria de la Luz, 239, 291
Maria Ygnacia, 95
BELARDE
Josefa, 203
BELASQUES
Maria Antonia, 171
BENABIDES. *See also* BENAVIDES
Barbara, 57
Juan Manuel, 116, 154, 193
Manuel, 273
Maria Barbara, 159
BENAVIDES. *See also* BENABIDES
Juan Manuel, 242
BERNAL
Jose Maria, 190, 283
BRITO
Antonio, 91
Francisca, 21
Maria Gertrudis, 323
BUGANDA
Miguel, 210

Beginia, 101
Begnina, 68
Blas, 66, 140
Casilda, 335
Clara, 341
Dolores, 84, 86
Felipe, 112
Fernando, 75
Gabriel, 143
Gertrudis, 58, 136, 278
Guadalupe, 92, 142
Jose, 89, 139
Jose Antonio, 106
Jose Dolores, 59, 103, 144, 334
Jose Maria, 81, 146
Jose Miguel, 110
Josefa, 249
Juan, 142
Juan Antonio, 70
Juan de Dios, 85, 139
Juana, 99, 103, 138, 339
Juana Maria, 65, 87
Juliana, 96
Manuela Antonia, 115
Maria Dolores, 130, 253, 334
Maria Gertrudis, 77, 86, 166
Maria Guadalupe, 125
Maria Paula, 61
Maria Serafina, 98
Mariano, 76
Miguel, 78, 143, 253
Nicolas, 82
Paubla, 146
Paula, 66
Pedro, 129, 268
Polonia, 73
Quirina, 114
Rafael, 256
Rita, 143
Romualdo, 136
Rumaldo, 106
Tomas, 67
Toribio, 100, 143
Xabier, 75
Ysabel, 252

CHABEZ. *See also* CHAVES; CHAVEZ
Antonio, 255
Francisca, 97
Jose Dolores, 255

CHAMA
Pomuzena, 67

CHAVES. *See also* CHABES; CHABEZ; CHAVEZ
Ana Maria, 11, 52, 181, 223
Antonia, 296
Antonio, 8, 184, 332
Apolonia, 237
Benina, 200
Blas, 19, 325
Catarina, 298
Clara, 258, 281
Deciderio, 185
Diego, 195
Dolores, 14, 229, 245, 347
Felipe, 136
Francisco, 201, 209
Gertrudes, 209
Getrudes, 223
Gregoria, 134
Guadalupe, 30, 201, 272, 277, 309
Isabel, 263
Jesus, 45, 240
Jose, 6, 171, 200, 242, 294
Jose Antonio, 150, 219
Jose Dolores, 188, 232
Jose Maria, 167, 201, 264, 304
Josefa, 191, 224, 228, 233, 284, 293, 316
Juan, 16, 176, 193, 237, 300
Juan Antonio, 8, 275
Juan de Dios, 180, 239, 313
Juana, 7, 174, 196, 220, 243, 266, 284, 320, 333
Juana Maria, 2, 19, 159, 191
Juliana, 317
Leocadia, 11
Maria Antonia, 279
Maria Benigna, 156
Maria de la Luz, 334
Maria Dolores, 195, 297
Maria Gertrudes, 176
Maria Gertrudis, 274
Maria Guadalupe, 308
Maria Josefa, 260
Maria Juana, 137, 283
Maria Juliana, 218
Maria Manuela, 22
Maria Ygnacia, 115, 151, 188, 269
Maria Ysabel, 185
Maria Ysavel, 235
Mariano, 263, 325
Miguel, 179, 221, 289, 321
Patricio, 169

Paula, 2, 28, 56, 162, 240, 263, 325
Pedro, 7, 35, 178, 236
Petra, 232, 254, 288, 319
Romualdo, 46
Rosalia, 205
Rufina, 3
Rumaldo, 167, 197
Salvador, 203
Teresa, 152
Tomasa, 73
Vegnina, 279
Ygnacia, 317
Ysabel, 133, 166, 207
CHAVEZ. *See also* CAVEZ; CHAVES
    Antonio Jose, 303
    Benigna, 25
    Blas, 5, 50
    Blaz, 316
    Jose, 33
    Jose Dolores, 27
    Juan, 45, 51
    Juan de Dios, 40
    Juana, 22
    Maria Paula, 302
    Maria Ysabel, 5
    Nicolas, 16, 41
    Rafael, 51
    Romualdo, 27
    Ysidora, 51
CHRESPIN. *See also* CRESPIN
    Juan Andres, 87, 130
    Marta, 71
CHRISPIN. *See also* CRESPIN
    Antonbia, 119
CISNERO. *See also* CISNEROS; SISNERO
    Pablo, 101
CISNEROS. *See also* CISNERO; SISNEROS
    Francisca, 131
CONTRERAS
    Ascencion, 257
    Barbara, 21, 60, 113
    Jesusa, 334
    Jose Tomas, 56
    Juan Francisco, 128
    Monica, 198, 228, 296
    Tomas, 28, 162
CORDOBA. *See also* CORDOVA
    Barbara Antonia, 72
    Bautista, 122
    Diego, 62
    Dionicio, 173

Dolores, 242
Domingo, 207
Felis, 85, 309
Jose Anastacio, 114
Juan, 154, 194
Juan Bautista, 73
Juan Miguel, 328
Juana, 167, 270
Juana Maria, 341
Leonicio, 145, 262
Lino, 319
Luiza, 76
Manuela, 61
Marcos, 89, 171
Maria Lina, 158
Maria Luisa, 137
Maria Rafaela, 176
Mariana, 128
Mariano, 96
Natibidad, 68
Nicolasa, 150, 196
Rafaela, 62, 108
Rita, 118
Soledad, 269
Vicente, 79
CORDOVA. *See also* CORDOBA
    Barbara, 16
    Bautista, 8, 34
    Dionicio, 238, 300
    Domingo, 237
    Gregoria, 162
    Jose, 136, 227, 265, 295
    Juan Bautista, 46
    Juan Jose, 223
    Juana, 134, 201
    Marcos, 45
    Maria Natividad, 21
    Martina, 299
    Rafaela, 221, 263, 306
    Ramon, 209
CORIZ. *See also* CORRIS
    Juan Felipe, 302
CORRIS. *See also* CORIZ
    Ysidora, 133
CRESPIN. *See also* CHRESPIN; CHRISPIN
    Juan Andres, 43, 159
    Marta, 132
    Marta Ricarda, 38
    Patricio, 333
    Salbador, 280, 323
    Salvador, 226, 240

Soledad, 54, 61, 85, 117, 126, 158, 173, 226, 255, 312
Teresa, 52
Tomasa, 53, 347
Tomaza, 252
Torribia, 329
Trinidad, 302, 347
Valentin, 21
Venancio, 273
Viatris, 68
Vicente, 146
Victoria, 10, 57, 113
Ygnacia, 162
Ylario, 211, 280
Ysabel, 1, 29, 53, 138, 157, 180, 206, 223, 279, 286, 337
Ysidora, 24, 138, 235, 274
Ysidro, 27, 83
Yzabel, 91

GARVISO. *See also* GARBISO; GARVISU; GARVIZO
Felix, 4
Maria Antonia, 8

GARVISU. *See also* GARVISO
Antonia, 38

GARVIZO. *See also* GARVISO
Maria Antonia, 54

GARZIA. *See also* GARCIA
Juana, 55

GAUNA. *See also* GUANA
Juan, 119, 136

GAVALDON
Vitoria, 208

GAYEGO. *See also* GALLEGO
Christoval, 54

GERNENTO
Jose Agapito, 329

GINNSA. *See also* GINSA
Juana, 210

GINSA. *See also* GINNSA; GINSO
Francisca, 245

GINSO. *See also* GINSA; GINZO; JINSO
Manuela, 218
Rita, 69, 121
Rosalia, 212, 245
Santiago, 68, 112

GINZO. *See also* GINSO
Maria Rosalia, 61
Meliton, 336
Rosalia, 102

GOMES. *See also* GOMEZ
Brigida, 77
Gertrudes, 181
Gertrudis, 17, 65, 123
Jose, 21
Juan, 220, 250, 284, 322
Luz, 300
Maria, 158, 195
Maria Martina, 336
Merced, 310

GOMEZ. *See also* GOMES
Euduvige, 43

GONSALES. *See also* GONSALEZ; GONZALES; GONZALEZ
Ana Maria, 168
Anna Maria, 289, 330
Antonio, 28, 59, 138, 192
Antonio Jose, 343
Antonio Maria, 139
Apolonia, 145, 229
Baltasar, 189, 234
Bibiana, 113, 223
Christobal, 91
Clara, 320
Crus, 186, 231
Cruz, 87
Decideria, 289
Dolores, 191
Encarnacion, 129
Esteban, 150, 195
Estefana, 156
Estevan, 242
Francisca, 9
Francisco, 8, 94, 117, 125, 171, 190, 193, 221, 243, 272, 314
Gertrudes, 102, 183
Gertrudis, 72, 146, 344
Getrudes, 221
Hilario, 5, 111
Jose, 1, 20, 27, 80, 120, 161, 294, 344
Jose Agaton, 204
Jose Antonio, 235
Jose de la Cruz, 290, 292, 330
Josefa, 233, 275, 326, 339
Juan, 10, 49, 83, 94, 117, 145, 184, 241
Juan Albino, 124
Juan Bautista, 140
Juan Crisostomo, 10
Juan de la Crus, 132
Juan Maria, 44
Juan Miguel, 111

Guadalupe, 131, 168, 213, 310
Hilario, 129
Jose, 47, 62, 64, 102, 117, 137, 169, 171, 180,
    210, 302, 334
Jose Eusevio, 52
Jose Gabriel, 136
Jose Gorgonio, 299
Jose Maria, 40, 273, 328
Jose Miguel, 9, 39
Jose Ramos, 69
Jose Tomas, 124, 198, 228, 296
Jose Vitoriano, 45
Josefa, 97, 141
Juan, 64, 113, 114, 156, 208, 242, 265, 270,
    296, 318, 336, 338
Juan Antonio, 82, 139, 206, 244
Juan Domingo, 6
Juan Isidoro, 99
Juan Ysidor, 135
Juan Ysidoro, 165, 241, 304
Juan Ysidro, 62, 188
Juan Ysidror, 216
Juana, 152, 154, 194, 220, 244, 245, 290, 311
Juana Gregoria, 187
Juana Maria, 112, 139, 164, 208, 285, 311, 321
Juliana, 255
Lorensa, 162
Loreto, 260
Luis, 3
Madalena, 90, 204
Magdalena, 6, 36, 173
Manuel, 18, 39, 54, 83, 104, 135, 166
Manuela, 311
Marcelina, 156, 198, 250, 280
Maria, 226, 318
Maria Antonia, 168
Maria Candelaria, 183, 214
Maria del Rosario, 170
Maria Dimas, 140
Maria Encarnacion, 335
Maria Lorensa, 114
Maria Luteria, 270
Maria Nicolasa, 266
Maria Petrona, 178
Maria Relles, 112
Maria Reyes, 147
Martina, 211
Matilde, 146
Micaela, 165
Miguel, 223, 341
Nicolasa, 329

Olalla, 301
Pablo, 29, 95, 121, 329
Paubla, 257
Pedro, 5, 92, 210, 245
Pedro Asencio, 173
Petra, 40, 308
Petrona, 217
Quiteria, 40, 105, 142, 169, 202, 236, 316
Rafael, 1, 36, 69, 130, 194
Roque, 18
Rumaldo, 319, 347
Simon, 175, 205, 277
Simona, 133
Tomas, 94, 257
Tomasa, 45, 74, 115, 150, 184, 224, 292, 299
Trinidad, 318
Vicente, 23, 170
Vitoria, 19
Ylario, 151, 177, 266
Ysabel, 130, 161, 189, 193
Ysidora, 273, 316
Ysidro, 251
Yzabel, 61
GRIGO. *See also* GRIEGO
    Maria Magdalena, 137
GUANA. *See also* GAUNA
    Candelaria, 83
GUERRA
    Ambrosio, 239
    Maria Antonia, 347
GUIT
    Julian, 327
GURULE. *See also* BURLE
    Albina, 167, 211, 244, 280, 282
    Ana Maria, 134
    Anna Maria, 277, 305
    Antonio, 15, 22, 138
    Barbara, 20
    Bernarda, 38, 123, 174, 283
    Cesilia, 189
    Cicilia, 251
    Decideria, 78, 110, 143, 179, 321
    Dicideria, 253
    Diego, 25, 43, 92, 141
    Domingo, 7
    Encarnacion, 26, 69
    Felipe, 17, 69, 90
    Francisca, 128
    Gabriel, 26
    Gertrudis, 52, 109, 140
    Grabiel, 67, 84, 227

Maria Antonia, 155, 205, 250, 251
Maria de la Lus, 128
Maria Estefana, 283
Maria Lorensa, 172
Maria Lus, 237
Maria Paula, 79
Maria Rosalia, 210
Maria Varbara, 282
Maria Ysabel, 346
Mariano, 305
Miguel, 33
Miguel Antonio, 34
Nicanora, 338
Paubla, 199
Paula, 119, 306
Petra, 158, 245, 340
Relles, 92
Reyes, 35, 229
Roman, 11
Rosalia, 38, 45, 77, 97, 122, 145, 155, 175, 285
Rosaria, 320
Rozalia, 322
Salbador, 92
Salvador, 198
Sidro, 65
Soledad, 122
Teresa, 323
Tomasa, 95
Ylario, 175
Ysabel, 107
Ysidro, 90, 117
JARAMIO. *See also* JARAMILLO
Juana, 258
Julian, 300
Manuel, 259, 342
Maria Antonia, 256
Nicolasa, 318
Paubla, 329
Paula, 271, 293
Rosalia, 297
JARAMIYO. *See also* JARAMILLO
Agustin, 54
Manuel, 57
Miguel, 57
JINSO. *See also* GINSO
Rosalia, 127
Santiago, 33, 133
JOYANCA
Manuela, 33

KING
Santiago, 334

LALANDA
Dolores, 193
LARRAÑAGA
Guadalupe, 66, 175, 224, 328
LAURIANO. *See also* LOURIANO
Jose, 141
Juan, 127
Juan Cristobal, 148
Teodoro, 191
LEAL
Agustin, 234
LOBATO. *See also* LOVATO
Agustin, 197, 270, 308
Candelaria, 21, 125
Diego, 17
Dolores, 108
Jose, 291
Juan, 53
Juan Felipe, 27, 82, 110
Marcelino, 23
Maria, 330
Maria Manuela, 5
Maria Nepomucena, 108
LOPES. *See also* LOPEZ
Altagracia, 328
Ambrocio, 247
Ana Maria, 7, 69, 97
Ana Maria (1), 293
Ana Maria (2), 293
Ana Maria de los Relles, 323
Anna Maria, 274
Antonia, 112
Antonio, 1, 6
Balbina, 83, 124
Barbara, 101, 144
Bernabe, 18, 250
Bernabel, 165
Bisente, 68
Brigida, 322
Calletano, 220, 276
Carlos, 21, 60, 113
Catalina, 179
Cleto, 239
Concepcion, 105
Dolores, 16, 62, 114, 125, 208, 219, 241, 310
Felipe, 70, 115, 166, 195, 313, 341
Francisco, 35, 58, 77, 116, 189, 215, 241
Gaspar, 70

Blas, 225, 335
Buenabentura, 304
Catarina, 297, 328
Cleto, 231, 280
Cristerna, 236
Cristobal, 312
Dario, 231
Diego, 108, 229
Dolores, 97
Encarnacion, 63, 99, 125, 263, 305
Francisco, 7, 127, 243, 261, 283, 292, 315
Gabrel, 246
Guadalupe, 244
Hermenegildo, 4, 231
Hilaria, 249
Jose, 155, 253, 255, 287
Jose de las Niebes, 292
Jose de las Nieves, 317, 345
Jose Maria, 224, 279, 304
Jose Miguel, 239
Jose Ygnacio, 174
Josefa, 239, 289, 333
Juan, 124, 132, 286, 334, 344
Juan Andres, 238
Juan Cristobal, 277, 299
Juan Cristoval, 239
Juan Jose, 136
Juan Pedro, 101
Juana, 238
Juliana, 19, 49, 105
Lorensa, 288
Lorenso, 116
Luciana, 156
Manuela, 110, 129, 235, 237, 253
Maria, 97
Maria Bentura, 135
Maria de Jesus, 347
Maria de la Luz, 325
Maria Dolores, 3
Maria Luciana, 11, 106
Maria Rosa, 230
Maria Simona, 210
Mariano, 285
Miguel, 243, 271
Monica, 40, 239, 313
Pablo, 6
Patrona, 324
Paula, 10, 121
Pedro, 265, 297, 313, 335
Petra, 332
Ramon, 231, 268

Rita, 314
Rosalia, 12, 130, 159
Rubi, 236
Sebastian, 132
Simona, 283
Tomas, 24, 275
Vicente, 315, 330
Ygnacio, 46, 241, 271
Ylaria, 151
LUERAS
Dolores, 290
LUJAN. *See also* LUJANA
Candelaria, 326
Catalina, 140
Eulogio, 117
Jose Maria, 40, 68, 102, 127, 169
Jose M^l, 256
Juan, 315, 319
Juan Antonio, 38, 208
Maria de Jesus, 345
Maria de la Lus, 77
Maria de la Luz, 41
Maria Rita, 143
Miguel, 31, 53, 88, 142
Pablo, 3, 33, 65, 102, 146
Petra, 77
Rita, 101
Rosalia, 273
LUJANA. *See also* LUJAN
Miguel, 283
LUNA
Candelaria, 82, 206, 244
Diego, 22, 51
Francisca, 58, 116, 189, 241
Francisco, 28, 88, 128
Francisco de Jesus, 64
Maria Antonia, 6
Maria Candelaria, 139
Maria de Jesus, 96
Maria Jesus, 26
Maria Nicolasa, 130, 164, 227
Maria Rita, 85, 185
Micaela, 67
Nicolasa, 26, 84, 248, 280
Perfecta, 327
Rita, 145
Teresa, 19
Ynes, 260
LUSERO. *See also* LUCERO; LUZERO
Albina, 25
Andres, 179

Luis, 52
Manuela Antonia, 180
Margarita, 347
Maria, 254, 288
Nicolas, 20, 214
Polonia, 259, 325
Ramon, 128, 159, 196, 237, 279
MAREZ. *See also* MARES
Manuel, 233
MARGIL
Maria Ygnacia, 224
MARINO. *See also* MARIÑO
Juan, 305
MARIÑO. *See also* MARINO
Juan, 165
Rosalia, 85
MARQUES. *See also* MARQUEZ
Ana Maria, 201
Antonio, 170
Jose, 111, 197, 219, 310
Jose Dolores, 95
Juan, 305
Juana, 170
Marcelina, 294
Maria, 83, 163, 189, 198, 234, 278
Maria de la Lus, 111
Maria del Rosario, 177
Ramon, 223
MARQUEZ. *See also* MARQUES
Ana Maria, 47
Gaspar, 328
Luz, 44
MARTIN
Ambrocio, 282, 315
Ana, 209
Ana Maria, 143, 164, 175, 217, 242, 345
Andrea, 314, 321
Anna Maria, 297
Antonia, 30, 189
Antonio, 199, 255
Antonio Jose, 11, 156, 190, 337
Baltasar, 232, 258
Barbara, 328
Dolores, 6, 151, 171, 281
Estefana, 347
Felipe, 16, 140, 181, 229, 295, 342
Felipe (1), 261
Felipe (2), 261
Francisco, 4, 209
Gertrudis, 11
Gregorio, 199, 269

Guadalupe, 30
Jesus, 312
Jesus de la Crus, 1
Jose, 12, 140, 161, 205, 207, 229, 277, 330, 345
Jose Antonio, 19, 169, 202, 270, 316
Jose de la Crus, 152
Jose Gregorio, 192, 323
Jose Manuel, 263
Jose Maria, 239
Josefa, 2, 34, 160, 165, 258, 269, 273
Juan, 5, 31, 67, 135
Juan Jose, 244
Juan Pablo, 196, 308
Juana, 313
Luduvina, 188
Manuel, 320, 332
Manuela, 32, 62, 210
Maria, 72, 160, 263, 320
Maria Antonia, 11, 81, 164
Maria Diluvina, 330
Maria Dolores, 156
Maria Jesus, 168
Maria Josefa, 338
Maria Ygnacia, 155
Mariano, 345
Marta, 333
Miguel Antonio, 197, 228
Pablo, 1, 16, 73, 158, 161, 237, 270
Paublo, 182
Paula, 343
Pedro, 290
Rafael, 23, 72
Rafaela, 9, 42, 142
Rosalia, 157, 159, 231, 274
Rozalia, 57
Seferina, 297
Serafina, 218
Soledad, 289
Tomasa, 31, 48
Vicenta, 200
Vicente, 240
MARTINA
Juana, 10, 294
MARTINES. *See also* MARTINEZ
Altagracia, 238
Ana Maria, 83, 118
Anamaria, 135
Antonia, 50, 119
Antonio Jose, 73, 106, 308
Donasiana, 93

Lorenza, 305
Luz, 17
Manuel, 8, 49, 52, 140, 157, 191, 222, 272
Manuel (1), 109
Manuel (2), 109
Manuela, 264
Manuela Antonia, 67, 134
Marcos, 242
Maria de la Crus, 340
Maria de la Lus, 108, 191
Maria de la Luz, 59, 295
Maria Dolores, 150
Maria Getrudes, 216, 247
Maria Leonarda, 74
Maria Lorensa, 259
Maria Ygnacia, 191
Maria Ynes, 280
Miguel, 234, 281, 303, 327
Paula, 22, 51, 56, 57, 317
Pedro Antonio, 148
Ramona, 24
Salbador, 64, 119
Santiago, 337
Sipriana, 69, 278, 308
Soledad, 60
PINEDA
Antonio, 48
Miguel Antonio, 168
Nepomenceno, 337
Nepomuseno, 172, 188, 245
PINO
Juan Antonio, 78
Maria Gertrudis, 9
PRIMO
Nicanora, 134
PROBENCIO. *See also* PROVENCIO
Jose, 127
PROVENCIO. *See also* PROBENCIO
Lucas, 314

RAEL
Andrea, 79
Antonia, 213
Antonio, 11
Bitoria, 295
Cristobal, 202
Dolores, 189, 219
Estefana, 13, 161, 199, 336
Francisco, 231, 290, 322
Gertrudes, 143
Jose, 207

Juan, 26, 104, 194
Julian, 81
Juliana, 48, 203
Lorensa, 188
Loreta, 129
Manuela, 183, 202, 230, 291
Maria, 73
Maria Bitoria, 173
Maria Juana, 209
Maria Lus, 154
Maria Manuela, 3
Maria Nepomucena, 277
Maria Rafaela, 182
Maria Rita, 5, 141, 168, 216
Nepomucena, 252, 309
Nepomusena, 187
Petrona, 269
Rafael, 315
Rafaela, 29, 114, 155, 230, 272
Refugia, 271
Refugio, 4
Rita, 111
Rosalia, 44
Santiago, 98, 218, 261, 297
Victoria, 346
RAMIRES. *See also* RAMIREZ
Antonio, 137
Cicilia, 256
Maria Nicolasa, 132
Simon, 271
RAMIREZ. *See also* RAMIRES
Ana Maria, 46
RIBERA
Viviana, 4
RIOS
Micaela, 14
RODARTE
Juan, 2
Pablo, 81
RODRIGUES. *See also* RODRIGUEZ
Maria, 215
RODRIGUEZ. *See also* RODRIGUES
Josefa, 292
Maria Dolores, 181
ROIBAL. *See also* RUIBAL
Juliana, 339
ROMAN
Pablo, 41
ROMERO
Albina, 335
Ana Maria, 298

Andres, 107
Anna Maria, 259
Antonio, 52, 80, 83, 110, 115, 157
Antonio Jose, 153
Baltasar, 10
Baltazar, 60, 121
Bicente, 94
Concepcion, 260, 317
Consepcion, 296
Cruz, 60
Diego, 34, 71, 90, 284
Diego Antonio, 1, 2, 14, 35
Dolores, 149, 174, 309
Domingo, 105, 192, 257
Eulogia, 105
Francisca, 333
Francisco, 198
Gabriela, 229
Gregoria, 231, 290
Jose Manuel, 222
Jose Miguel, 14, 81, 126
Josefa, 332
Juan, 243
Juana, 6, 39, 80, 168, 188, 197, 211, 213, 234,
    282, 287, 326
Justa, 39
Lino, 51, 181, 206
Lorenso, 256, 346
Luis, 9
Lus, 31
Manuel, 39, 90, 151, 251, 278, 293, 337
Manuela, 286
Maria Antonia, 255
Maria del Carmen, 121
Maria Dolores, 55
Maria Elogia, 136
Maria Juana, 79, 264
Maria Petra, 277
Maria Sista, 240
Maria Ygnes, 290
Monica, 263, 325
Petra, 300
Ramon, 229
Ramona, 134
Relles, 331
Rosa, 307
Sista, 185
Vitorio, 270
RONQUILLO
Pedro, 303

RUBI
Guadalupe, 23
Rafael, 202
RUBIN
Guadalupe, 170
Juana, 201
RUIBAL. *See also* ROIBAL
Jose, 320
Maria Juliana, 267
Miguel, 334
RUIS. *See also* RUIZ
Ana Maria, 186
Francisca, 101, 201, 289
Francisco, 297, 339
Marcos, 29
Martia Francisca, 169
Rafaela, 70, 92, 143
Ramon, 324
Trinidad, 282, 315
Ygnacio, 4
Ygnes, 147
Ynes, 116
RUIZ. *See also* RUIS
Francisca, 41, 66
Marcos, 70

SAABEDRA. *See also* SABEDRA
Luz, 345
SABEDRA. *See also* SAABEDRA; SAVEDRA
Barbara, 315
Bibian, 297
Bibiano, 245
Catarena, 94
Catarina, 140, 182, 313
Eulogia, 87, 178, 255, 287, 292, 317, 345
Francisco, 164, 202, 264, 305, 334
Guadalupe, 149, 177, 205, 266
Jose, 100
Juan, 10, 215, 265, 317, 322
Juan Christobal, 55
Juan Cristobal, 92, 141
Lucas, 202
Manuel, 82, 141
Maria Antonia, 154
Maria Dolores, 341
Maria Eulogia, 138
Mariano, 338
Miguel, 212, 277, 303
Pablo, 10
Tomasa, 320
Ygnacia, 255

SANTILLAN. *See also* SANTILLANES
  Catarina, 1
SANTILLANES. *See also* SANTILLAN;
    SANTILLAÑES; SANTIYANES
  Antonio, 11, 157, 247
  Barbara, 32, 105
  Diego, 139, 179
  Francisca, 130, 254, 294
  Gertrudis, 20, 51, 106, 157
  Jose, 39
  Jose Miguel, 34, 68, 154
  Juana, 270, 314
  Juliana, 62, 147
  Maria Albina, 98
  Maria Barbara, 62
  Maria Francisca, 344
  Maria Francisca Antonia, 161
  Maria Juana, 102
  Maria Juliana, 271
  Maria Micaela, 84
  Miguel, 165
  Miguela, 134
  Monica, 94, 124
  Rosa, 218, 310
SANTILLAÑES. *See also* SANTILLANES
  Miguel, 2
SANTISTEBAN. *See* SANTIESEBAN
SANTIYANES. *See also* SANTILLANES
  Maria Antonia, 275
  Miguel, 269
  Monica, 62
SARRACINO
  Apolonia, 145
  Francisco, 55
  Mariana, 76
  Teodora, 102
  Ysabel, 53
SAVEDRA. *See also* SABEDRA
  Catalina, 14, 225
  Cristobal, 98
  Francisco, 235
  Jose, 8
  Juan Cristoval, 39
  Luis, 224
  Manuel, 38
  Marcelina, 49
  Maria Eulogia, 214
  Pablo, 39
SEDILLO. *See also* CEDILLO; SEDIYO;
    ZEDILLO
  Barbara, 5, 68

  Beneranda, 325
  Blas, 201
  Candelaria, 149, 265
  Jose Dolores, 316
  Juana, 23, 29
  Julian, 24, 61, 170
  Maria, 265, 303
  Pedro, 97, 205, 245, 340
  Perfecto, 95
  Quiteria, 339
  Relles, 116
  Reyes, 21, 44, 280
  Rita, 95, 265
  Salbador, 265
  Toribio, 45, 142, 179
  Yldefonsa, 41
SEDIYO. *See also* SEDILLO
  Maria Juana, 52
SEGUNDO
  Manuela, 278
SENA. *See also* CENA
  Alfonsa, 75
  Antonia, 247
  Concepcion, 28, 128
  Consaupcion, 64
  Francisca, 148
  Josefa, 333
  Juana, 118
  Maria Antonia, 279
  Maria Tomasa, 79
  Miguel, 85, 138, 235, 269
  Rafaela, 308
  Tomasa, 137, 270, 303
  Yldefonsa, 143
SERNA. *See also* CERNA
  Antonio, 44
  Antonio Maria, 165, 203
  Blas, 20
  Cacildo, 12
  Dimas, 340
  Francisco, 175
  Jose Patricio, 10
  Manuela, 34, 46
  Marcelina, 273
  Maria Manuela, 8, 73
  Maria Paula, 22
  Maria Rosalia, 194
  Maria Ynes, 235
  Matias, 19
  Rafaela de, 337
  Rosalia, 309, 332

ABALOS
  Basilio, 293
  Vicente, 312, 313
ABEITA. *See also* ABEITIA
  Dolores, 238, 273
ABEITIA. *See also* ABEITA; ABEYTA;
      BEITIA
  Dolores, 4
ABEYTA. *See also* ABEITIA
  Dolores, 10
  Hermenegildo, 186
  Juan Crus, 165
ABILA. *See also* AVILA
  Abran de Jesus, 310
  Francisco, 166, 265, 314
  Josefa, 310
  Maria, 314
  Miguel, 175
  Rita, 174
  Tomas, 294
ABREU
  Beneranda, 264
  Santiago, 28
AGUILAR
  Maria Josefa, 186
AGUIRRE
  Ana Maria, 130, 176
  Anna Maria, 45
  Barvara, 346
  Francisco, 170
  Lorenza, 298
  Manuela, 51, 83, 94, 139, 142, 180, 203,
      220, 312
  Maria, 84, 89
ALARCON
  Ana Maria, 298
ALARI. *See also* ALIRI
  Santiago, 201
ALBARADO
  Felipe, 342
ALBARES. *See also* ALVARES
  Maria, 110
ALDAS. *See also* ALDAZ
  Paulina, 344
  Paulino, 234
ALDAZ. *See also* ALDAS
  Paulin, 253
ALDERETE
  Rafaela, 256

ALEJA. *See also* ALEJO
  Ysabel, 17
ALEJO. *See also* ALEJA; ALEXA; ALEXO
  Maria Ysabel, 74
ALEXA. *See also* ALEJO
  Ascencion, 17
ALEXO. *See also* ALEJO
  Pasquala, 15
ALFARO. *See also* ALFAROS
  Guadalupe, 186, 190
  Jose Guadalupe, 267
  Juan, 240
ALFAROS. *See also* ALFARO
  Guadalupe, 282
  Joaquin, 340
  Jose Maria, 184, 257
  Juan, 132
  Miguel, 211
ALIRE. *See also* ALIRI
  Antonio, 308
  Benito, 162
  Jose Andres, 270
  Jose Benito, 117, 230
  Josefa, 254
  Manuel, 227
ALIRI. *See also* ALARI; ALIRE
  Jose, 343
  Tomasa, 294
ALVARES. *See also* ALBARES
  Vicente, 268
ANALLA. *See also* ANAYA
  Ana Maria, 13
  Antonia, 134
  Antonio, 67, 74, 123, 250, 302
  Felipe, 10, 68, 135
  Jose, 63
  Juan, 337
  Juana, 79
  Lucas, 328
  Manuel, 77, 81, 85, 97, 102, 108, 125, 132,
      331, 340
  Manuela, 70
  Marcos, 74
  Maria, 77, 105, 121
  Maria Ygnacia, 59, 69, 76, 96
  Mariano, 65
  Martin, 342
  Pablo, 65
  Pedro, 88, 96
  Rafael, 259
  Rosalia, 97, 106, 111

Juana, 15, 18, 25, 44, 64, 83, 104, 122, 149,
168, 186, 188, 217, 218, 219, 220,
244, 246, 252, 262, 267, 299, 324,
334, 338, 342
Maria Dolores, 73
Paula, 264, 313, 330
Pedro, 15, 25, 91, 105, 106, 117, 138, 164,
176, 188, 200, 205, 208, 228, 240,
248, 251, 286, 319, 339
Rosalia, 225
Soledad, 248, 297, 309
ARBIZU
Manuela, 15
ARCHIBECCO. *See also* ARCHIBEQUE
Juana, 136
ARCHIBEQUE. *See also* ARCHIBECCO;
ARCHIVEQUE
Agustin, 100, 133
Juana, 230, 243, 336
Marcelino, 114, 326
Matias, 260, 265
ARCHIVEQUE. *See also* ARCHIBEQUE
Agustin, 137
ARCHULETA
Antonio, 83, 245, 297, 322
Jose, 319
Julio, 244
Manuela, 55, 92, 261, 265
Maria, 33, 83, 96, 124, 128
Maria de Jesus, 26
Maria Jesus, 26
Maria Luis, 227
Maria Luisa, 9, 267
Maria Nasarena, 12
Mateo, 5, 331
Rafaela, 261, 292
ARELLANES
Jose, 321
ARIAS
Antonio, 211, 324
Concepcion, 155, 314
Decideria, 321
Desideria, 242
Domingo, 324
Felipe, 105, 120, 262
Gregoria, 120, 191
Josefa, 57
Juan, 46, 72, 238, 248, 262, 266, 267, 294,
314, 323
Juan Christobal, 152
Juan Christoval, 248

Juan Cristobal, 153, 220, 285, 286
Juan Domingo, 242, 288, 309, 310
Juana, 94, 140, 244, 280
Juana Maria, 258
Juana Micaela, 158
Loreta, 163, 267
Manuela, 72
Maria Dolores, 185, 268
Maria Ycidora, 129
Maria Ygnacia, 250, 322
Maria Ysidora, 146, 153
Micaela, 93, 111, 120
Miguel, 18, 89, 104, 140, 150, 229, 261
Pablo, 80, 123, 167, 312, 343
Paublo, 202, 204
Pedro, 285
Salbador, 146, 330
Teodora, 256
Teresa, 151, 166, 265
Trinidad, 324
Victoria, 251
Ygnacia, 220, 284, 300
Yldifonso, 312
ARMENTA
Gregorio, 249
Jose Maria, 212, 290, 301, 315, 343
Juan, 251
Juan de Jesus, 158, 288, 320
Juan de Luis, 131
Maria Ygnacia, 3, 62
Matias, 192
Tomasa, 92
Ygnacia, 19, 22, 50, 59, 255
ARMIJO
Alta Gracia, 330
Alta-gracia, 330
Amador, 150
Ambrocio, 2, 4, 100, 114, 164, 193, 239,
243, 245, 246, 259, 266, 303, 315,
330
Ambrosio, 15, 27, 35, 42, 45, 331
Ana Maria, 236
Antonia, 217, 297
Antonia Rosa, 336
Antonio Jose, 49, 100, 160, 164, 185, 261,
301
Ascencion, 338
Barbara, 6, 11, 33, 61, 87, 99, 103, 137, 154,
191, 286
Bicente, 101
Bisente, 65, 76

Manuela, 25, 57, 304, 339
Margarita, 187
Maria, 282
Mariano, 262
Pablo, 252
Rosalia, 45, 82, 334
Santiago, 18, 64, 149, 168, 186, 188, 217,
      218, 220, 246, 252, 262, 267, 342
Tomasa, 38, 167, 201, 241
BAROS
   Juan Antonio, 214, 279
   Rafaela, 282
BARRANCA
   Manuela, 246
BARRELA. *See also* BARELA
   Bisente, 68
   Casilda, 68
   Juan, 58
   Manuela, 70, 123
   Maria Rosalia, 66
   Pablo, 83
   Rosalia, 126
   Rozalia, 62
   Santiago, 104
   Tomasa, 72
BARRERA
   Marilda, 347
BARRERAS
   Gertrudis, 180
   Guadalupe, 198
   Jose, 114
   Jose Antonio, 227
   Juan, 148
BASAN. *See also* BAZAN; VASAN
   Joaquin Alejandro, 279
   Juan, 294
   Juan de la Crus, 291
   Juan de la Cruz, 199, 291
   Juaquin Alejandro, 179
   Maria de la Luz, 199, 243, 267
   Maria Garcia, 291
   Maria Tomasa, 142
   Maria Ygnacia, 17, 26, 162, 167, 193
   Ygnacia, 1, 7, 9, 40, 43, 57, 67, 77, 118, 150,
      155, 156, 195, 210, 239, 266, 267
   Ygnacio, 210, 239, 291
BASQUES
   Barbara, 87, 132, 186, 227, 231
BAUTISTA
   Juan, 56

BAYEJOS. *See also* BALLEJOS
   Patricio, 56
BAZAN. *See also* BASAN
   Maria de la Luz, 54
   Maria Ygnacia, 36
   Ygnacia, 65, 90
BEITIA. *See also* ABEITIA
   Dolores, 119
BELARDE
   Ana Maria, 201
   Juan Cruz, 203
   Reyes, 192
BELASQUES. *See also* VELASQUES
   Maria Ana, 21
   Maria Antonia, 54, 168, 310
   Maria Micaela, 187, 217
   Micaela, 71
BELENCIA. *See also* BALENCIA
   Julian, 18
   Maria Ygnacia, 141
BELLEJOS. *See also* BALLEJOS
   Maria de los Angeles, 183
BENABIDES. *See also* BENAVIDES;
      BENEBIDES
   Barbara, 109
   Jose, 90, 148
   Josefa, 286, 317
   Juan Manuel, 179
   Manuel, 4, 57, 193, 273, 303
   Maria Antonia, 148
BENAVIDES. *See also* BENABIDES;
      VENAVIDES
   Dolores, 299
   Jose, 241, 242
   Juan Manuel, 93
   Manuel, 185
BENEBIDES. *See also* BENABIDES
   Juan Manuel, 106
BERNAL. *See also* BERNALA; VERNAL
   Antonio, 283
   Barbara, 4, 136, 229
   Carlota, 234
   Manuela, 150, 248, 252, 309, 310, 336
   Simona, 170, 171, 201, 203
BERNALA. *See also* BERNAL
   Manuela, 207
BLEA
   Maria Rafaela, 143
BRITO
   Antonio, 323
   Bernarda, 51, 82

Felipe, 21
Manuela, 25, 262, 274, 345
Maria Antonia, 292
Maria Manuela, 75, 212
BUENO
Anastacia, 343
BUJANDA
Miguel, 297
BURLE. *See also* GURULE
Ygnacio, 258
BURTIERES. *See also* BURTIERRES
Domingo, 80
Josefa, 80
Juan, 80
Manuel, 97
Maria Rosa, 80
Polonia, 80
BURTIERRES. *See also* BURTIERES;
    BUTIERRES; BUTTIERREZ
Ana Maria, 118
Antonio, 59, 63, 90, 116, 126
Barbara, 123
Beginia, 119
Begnina, 116
Bernarda, 65
Bernardo, 84
Carmen, 102
Cidro, 109
Consancion, 64
Dolores, 95, 96
Francisco, 61, 75
Guadalupe, 70
Jose, 95
Jose Maria, 114
Juan, 56, 63, 82, 113
Juan Jose, 115
Juan Manuel, 51
Juan Pablo, 107
Juliana, 124
Luiza, 55, 69
Manuel, 82, 106, 111
Maria Antonia, 94, 113
Maria Brigida, 72
Maria Clara, 89
Maria Gertrudis, 66, 87, 116
Maria Gregoria, 86
Maria Lubina, 85
Maria Luisa, 76, 91
Maria Rita, 72
Maria Salome, 68, 97, 110, 128, 131
Mariano, 86

Miguel, 67, 70, 85, 98, 106, 118, 124, 125
Nicolasa, 121
Pablo, 95
Pedro, 124
Polonia, 83, 92
Rafael, 55, 63, 68, 92
Relles, 75
Rita, 95
Santiago, 67, 69, 85, 126
Simon, 68
Teresa, 115, 122
Tereza, 64
Ygnacio, 74
Ysidro, 87
BURTIERREZ. *See also* BURTIERRES
Maria Gertrudis, 109
BURULE. *See also* GURULE
Bernarda, 259
Biscenta, 304
BUSTAMANTE
Bernado, 66
Bernardo, 175, 224, 328
Dolores, 238
Jose Antonio, 238
BUSTOS
Blaz, 278
Francisca, 197
BUTIERES. *See also* BUTIERRES
Juan Pablo, 268
Simon, 268
BUTIERRES. *See also* BURTIERRES;
    BUTIERES; BUTTIERREZ;
    GUTIERRES
Bernardo, 17
Francisco, 260
Jose Maria, 273
Juan, 96, 258
Loreto, 281
Maria, 258
Miguel, 258, 259
Pedro, 69, 78
Pedro Antonio, 282
Rosa, 54
BUTTIERREZ. *See also* BURTIERRES;
    BUTIERRES
Maria Gertrudis, 105

CANDELARIA. *See also* CANDELARIA Y
    MIRABEL; CANDELARIAS;
    CANDELARIO; CANDELERIA
Agustin, 315

Maria Barbara, 9, 15, 60, 192
Maria Catarina, 278
Maria Cecilia, 153
Maria Cicilia, 250
Maria Consepcion, 342
Maria de la Lus, 135, 344
Maria de la Luz, 68, 276
Maria Decideria, 10
Maria Dolores, 125, 132, 336
Maria Gabriela, 141
Maria Gavriela, 333
Maria Gregoria, 27, 129, 142, 147, 299, 327
Maria Josefa, 169, 323, 340
Maria Juana, 101, 328
Maria Juliana, 122
Maria Lorenza, 306
Maria Manuela, 155, 160, 185, 259, 273
Maria Monica, 331
Maria Paubla, 142
Maria Paula, 6, 35
Maria Petra, 286
Maria Ramona, 1, 11, 98, 267, 323
Maria Relles, 345
Maria Reyes, 147, 180
Maria Sisilia, 289
Maria Soledad, 77
Maria Teresa, 115
Maria Ygnacia, 53
Maria Ysabel, 91
Maria Ysidora, 265
Merijildo, 275
Micaela, 65
Miguel, 255
Miguel Antonio, 78, 84, 264
Nepomucena, 138
Pablo, 32, 43, 65, 75, 79, 102, 239, 275, 281, 286, 321, 326, 329
Pasquala, 17
Paubla, 183
Paublo, 178
Paula, 79, 109, 287
Pedro, 28, 60, 162
Petra, 62, 124, 162
Petrona, 54
Rafael, 91, 317, 335
Rafaela, 281
Ramon, 31, 150, 186, 196, 270, 279, 293, 303, 308, 323
Ramona, 47, 62, 101, 126, 235, 254, 306, 317, 331, 342
Relles, 251

Reyes, 280, 284, 285
Roman, 308
Rosa, 265
Rozalia, 305
Rumaldo, 85
Salbador, 79, 95, 249, 280, 319
Salvador, 294
Teresa, 32, 108, 317
Tereza, 63, 317
Tomas, 4, 19, 56, 58
Venita, 303
Vicente, 238, 256, 261, 306, 318, 331, 342, 346
Victoria, 27
Visente, 39
Ygnacia, 17, 40, 111, 235, 264, 305
Ygnacio, 11, 15, 45, 52, 64, 109, 119, 122, 163, 231, 276, 280, 333
Ylario, 332
Ysabel, 37, 101, 340
Ysidora, 247, 260, 317, 329
CANDELARIA Y MIRABEL. *See also* CANDELARIA; MIRABEL
Jose Tomas, 68
CANDELARIAS. *See also* CANDELARIA
Jose, 264
CANDELARIO. *See also* CANDELARIA
Amador, 204, 236
Ana Maria, 197, 204, 237
Antonia Teresa de Jesus, 203
Antonio, 53, 200
Apolonia, 217
Balbina, 214
Barbara, 178
Casimiro, 223
Clara, 251
Dolores, 211, 222, 226, 229, 234, 236, 252
Esteban, 196, 217, 220, 237, 244
Estevan, 217
Florencio, 112
Francisca, 216
Francisco, 194, 210, 235
Francisco Antonio, 219
Gabriela, 236, 244
Gertrudes, 204, 223, 245
Gregoria, 217, 244
Guadalupe, 201, 202, 245
Jacinta, 188
Jose, 166, 214, 219
Jose Francisco, 203
Jose Leonardo, 217

Dolores, 80, 106, 209, 275, 288, 291, 334
Dorotea, 135, 269
Doroteo, 126
Felipe, 46, 47, 134, 243
Francisca, 138, 235
Francisco, 77
Gertrudes, 168
Gertrudis, 47, 49, 124, 131, 136, 158, 298
Getrudes, 223
J. Miguel, 261
Jesus, 86, 88, 180, 346
Jesus Maria, 227, 251
Joaquin, 80, 88, 228, 291
Jose, 54, 82, 142, 154, 231
Jose Anastacio, 188
Jose Dionisio, 327
Jose Dolores, 270
Jose Mariano, 132
Jose Miguel, 205, 242, 261
Jose Pablo, 270, 283, 304, 322
Jose Ygnacio, 13, 18, 51
Juan, 7, 47, 49, 80, 124, 158, 168, 173, 186,
       187, 203, 220, 234, 246, 291, 292,
       334, 337, 346
Juan Antonio, 286
Juan Cristobal, 245
Juan de la Cruz, 292
Juan Ysidoro, 305
Juana, 267
Juana Maria, 121, 305, 326
Julian, 236, 249, 257
Juliana, 295, 321
Manuel, 316
Manuela, 65, 267, 282, 337, 342, 346
Manuelita, 334
Marcelina, 27, 214, 218, 234, 282, 302, 324
Marcelino, 296
Maria, 78, 159, 240, 263, 271
Maria Andrea, 178
Maria Antonia, 177, 202, 270
Maria Bicenta, 133
Maria Cimona, 125
Maria de Jesus, 259, 301
Maria Francisca, 85, 269, 343
Maria Josefa, 137
Maria Juliana, 289, 341
Maria Luiza, 76
Maria Manuela, 165, 169, 202
Maria Miquela, 346
Maria Pascuala, 114
Maria Petra, 333

Maria Vicenta, 136
Maria Ysabel, 111, 185, 282
Maria Ysavel, 185
Marselina, 330
Martin, 122, 169, 206, 251, 281, 302, 334
Nepomucena, 89
Nepomusena, 107
Pascuala, 90
Pasquala, 57
Paublo, 205, 216
Pedro Lorenzo, 336
Rafael, 75, 94, 142, 192, 220, 271, 289, 344
Ramon, 49, 105, 107, 149, 204, 228, 286,
       305, 317
Refugia, 320
Rosa, 24
Rosalia, 26, 75, 142, 216
Rufina, 271
Sabel, 256
Salbador, 106
Salvador, 19
Santiago, 39
Soledad, 58
Teresa, 71, 93, 120
Valentin, 268
Vicenta, 134, 198, 272, 345
Vicente, 214
Ygnacio, 320
GALLEGOS. *See also* GALLEGO
    Alejandro, 258
GARAMIO. *See also* JARAMILLO
    Salbador, 337
GARATUSA
    Maria, 332
GARBISO
    Antonio, 190
    Cristobal, 318
    Guadalupe, 106, 110
    Juan, 267
    Maria Barbara, 210
GARCIA. *See also* GARCIA DE NORIEGA;
       GARCIA DEL VALLE; GARCIA
       JURADO; GARZIA; LUCERO Y
       GARCIA
    Abran, 318
    Acencio, 104
    Acencion, 307
    Agustin, 134
    Albino, 312
    Alejo, 144, 221
    Alfonsa, 94

Maria Paula, 50, 269
Maria Petrona, 171
Maria Rosalia, 173
Maria Ygnacia, 92, 131, 253, 301
Maria Ynes, 89
Marta, 21, 239
Melchor, 67
Miguel, 126, 135, 226, 306
Miguel Antonio, 256
Pablo, 93, 94, 122, 261, 310
Paubla, 183, 202, 204, 222
Paula, 9, 37, 80, 83, 90, 91, 93, 110, 253, 318
Pedro, 22, 77, 98, 99, 119, 135, 194, 250, 260, 288, 320, 339
Petra, 344
Rafael, 238, 253
Rafaela, 89, 122
Ramon, 269
Rosalia, 70, 80, 87, 92, 291, 299
Rosaria, 315
Rozalia, 80
Rumalda, 322
Salbador, 95, 123, 129, 250
Salbador Antonio, 79
Santos, 290
Tomas, 201
Tomasa, 177
Vitoriano, 267
Ygnacia, 238, 241, 290
Ynes, 92
Ysabel, 53
Ysidro, 89, 91, 119, 188
MARTINEZ. *See also* MARTINES
Antonia, 17
Candelaria, 100
Felipe, 98
Francisco, 48
Gregoria, 89
Jose, 100
Madelina, 87
Manuela, 256
Marcos, 27
Maria Mª, 66
Maria Paula, 105
Maria Ygnacia, 255
Maria Ynes, 24
Pablo, 19
Paula, 6
Rosalia, 50

MARTINO
Luis, 11
MASCARENAS. *See also* MASCAREÑAS
Maria Manuela, 225
MASCAREÑAS. *See also* MASCARENAS
Maria Natividad, 133
MASTAS. *See also* MAESTAS
Rosalia, 183
MATA
Francisco, 179, 212, 329, 346
Juana, 211, 340
Maria, 184
Maria Lus, 240
MEDINA
Barbara, 20
Maria Catarina, 53
MERCADO
Mariano, 340
MESTA. *See also* MAESTAS
Felipe, 325
MESTAS. *See also* MAESTAS; MESTES
Ambrocio, 91
Ana Josefa, 91
Ana Maria, 16, 27, 68, 77, 112, 121, 144, 268, 338
Anamaria, 312
Anna Josefa, 325
Anna Maria, 274, 304, 307
Antonia, 24, 65
Antonio Jose, 303
Barbara, 270, 331
Bautista, 82
Bisente, 246
Carmen, 230
Catalina, 22
Catarina, 3
Felipe, 240, 246
Francisco, 65, 90
Gertrudis, 224, 319
Ignacio, 117
Jose, 109
Josefa, 17, 41, 228
Juan de Dios, 141
Juan Felipe, 207
Juana, 204
Juana Maria, 214, 285, 320
Lorenzo, 91
Manuel, 225
Manuela, 22, 32, 41, 46, 192, 230, 272
Maria Antonia, 10, 101
Maria del Refugio, 328

MONTOYA. *See also* MONTOLLA
Alta Gracia, 29
Altagracia, 24
Ana Maria, 154, 209, 296, 298
Anastacio, 223
Andrea, 217, 239
Anna Maria, 280
Antonia, 18, 52
Antonio, 140, 212, 277, 303
Apolonia, 227, 229
Asencion, 63
Atanacio, 325
Barbara, 20, 229, 258
Bartolo, 205, 288
Bentura, 218
Blas, 58
Candelaria, 191
Cecilio, 216
Christobal, 70, 89
Concepcion, 6
Cornelia, 347
Cristobal, 6, 313, 321
Diego, 240
Diego Antonio, 243, 270
Dolores, 4, 31, 35, 43, 180, 194, 325
Felipe, 4, 5, 7, 8, 35, 46, 86
Francisca, 28, 162, 315
Francisco, 69
Gregoria, 327
Guadalupe, 274
J. Mariano, 270
Jesus, 298, 305
Jose, 13, 153, 163, 171, 177, 230, 267, 275, 297, 302, 303, 314
Jose Alexandro, 13
Jose Antonio, 5, 51, 205, 224
Jose Atanacio, 279
Jose Cicilio, 221, 237
Jose Cristobal, 187
Jose Maria, 61, 223, 270, 286, 325
Jose Mariano, 184
Jose Miguel, 213, 235
Jose Nestor, 212
Jose Rafael, 191
Jose Silberio, 315
Jose Tomas, 241
Josefa, 30, 336
Juan, 7, 33, 47, 57, 63, 67, 136, 148, 156, 194, 200, 207, 214, 216, 223, 225, 240, 243, 254, 262, 300, 301, 333
Juan Cristobal, 7, 274

Juan Cristoval, 5
Juan de los Reyes, 46
Juan Maria, 220, 237, 239
Juan Rafael, 292
Juan Reyes, 192
Juana, 16, 28, 132, 205, 237, 242, 243, 261, 290, 295, 328
Juana Barbara, 179, 205, 209, 233
Juana Maria, 58
Juana Paula, 229
Juliana, 294, 317
Lorenso, 16
Lugarda, 6
Luis, 62
Luisa, 232
Manuel, 200, 299
Manuela, 313
Marcelina, 238, 314
Margarita, 229, 248, 263, 325
Maria, 264
Maria Anastacia, 223
Maria Antonia, 194, 299
Maria Concepcion, 173
Maria de la Lus, 87
Maria de la Luz, 27
Maria Dolores, 207, 243, 293
Maria Francisca, 237
Maria Guadalupe, 279
Maria Josefa, 5
Maria Juana, 132, 139, 155, 194, 235
Maria Lugarda, 55, 175
Maria Manuela, 288
Maria Miguela, 187
Maria Paula, 10, 45
Maria Ramona, 142, 143, 190, 221
Maria Rita, 136
Maria Rosa, 86
Maria Santos, 239
Maria Ygnacia, 50, 153, 171
Maria Ynes, 313
Maria Ysabel, 69
Mariano, 8, 20, 255
Martin, 286
Micaela, 170, 227
Miguel, 263, 310
Miquela, 278, 327
Nerio, 144
Nestor, 306, 308, 314, 334
Nestora, 214, 274, 281
Nicolasa, 279
Pablo, 4, 7, 58, 191

Lorenso, 315, 329
Manuel, 338
Manuela, 180
Maria, 6
Prudencio, 110, 115
Ygnacio, 69, 212, 301, 313, 343
Ynacio, 333
TELLES. *See also* TEYES
Jose Maria, 214
Josefa, 68
Julio, 5, 68, 309
Maria Petra, 109, 170, 295
Maria Soledad, 76
Soledad, 118, 125, 141, 147, 166, 213, 218
Tomas, 111
TENORIO
Ana Maria, 201, 234
Dolores, 106
Grabiela, 117
Jose, 17, 33, 38, 41, 201, 332
Jose Francisco, 238
Jose Maria, 146
Jose Ramon, 161
Josefa, 125
Juana, 185
Julian, 4, 18, 26, 40, 42, 46, 74, 96, 108, 122,
    201, 210, 225, 257, 335
Manuel, 134, 214, 216, 285
Maria Antonia, 201
Maria Jesus, 137
Maria Josefa, 161
Maria Manuela, 238
Rafaela, 90
Rosalia, 122, 146, 193, 195, 209, 251, 281,
    292, 304
Salbador, 169, 203
Salvador, 230
TEYES. *See also* TELLES
Julio, 55
Maria Petra, 146
TOLEDO
Maria Dolores, 115, 278
TORRES
Antonia, 302
Barbara, 341
Barbara Antonia, 171
Benito, 216
Bernarda, 305
Dolores, 2, 9, 10, 29, 33, 42, 43, 53, 60, 68,
    70, 72, 74, 77, 83, 102, 104, 107,

116, 122, 131, 135, 182, 194, 211,
    250, 251, 289, 298, 306, 339
Felipe, 193, 213, 220
Francisca, 318
Francisco, 122
Gertrudes, 166, 249
Gertrudis, 73, 133, 263, 273, 293, 302
Jose, 7, 14, 18, 63, 64, 180, 243, 272, 285,
    313, 317
Jose Maria, 30, 70, 235, 305
Juan, 11, 172, 199, 306, 332
Juana, 147, 162, 187, 207, 271, 277, 281,
    309, 316, 329, 333
Juliana, 273
Lasaro, 72, 93, 111, 120, 158
Lorenso, 153
Lorenzo, 281
Manuel Antonio, 24
Maria, 86
Maria Dolores, 99, 203
Maria Gertrudis, 5
Maria Josefa, 99
Maria Juliana, 182
Maria Manuela, 3
Maria Soledad, 76
Pedro, 195, 319
Pedro Antonio, 70, 272
Reyes, 204
Salbador, 86, 90, 147
Salvador, 295
Santiago, 6, 70
Teodora, 220
Vernarda, 274
Vicente, 310
Ysabel, 154, 275
TREBOL
Antonia, 6
Juana Maria, 257
TRIGIYO. *See also* TRUGILLO
Maria Micaela, 55
Pablo, 55
TRUGILLO. *See also* TRUJILLO
Ana Maria, 110, 122
Anna Maria, 275
Antonio, 79, 96, 117, 346
Baltasar, 93, 120
Baltazar, 71
Dolores, 117
Gregoria, 261
Guadalupe, 100
Jesus Maria, 344

www.ingramcontent.com/pod-product-compliance
Lightning Source LLC
Chambersburg PA
CBHW080353030426
42334CB00024B/2853